# Games of the North American Indians

# Games of the North American Indians

## Volume 2: Games of Skill

BY

STEWART CULIN

University of Nebraska Press
Lincoln and London

First Bison Book printing: 1992
Most recent printing indicated by the last digit below:
10   9   8   7   6   5   4   3   2   1

Library of Congress Cataloging-in-Publication Data
Culin, Stewart, 1858–1929.
Games of the North American Indians / by Stewart Culin;
introduction to the Bison book edition by Dennis Tedlock.
v. <   >
Reprint of the 1907 ed., issued (in 1 v.) as the: Twenty-fourth annual report of
the Bureau of American Ethnology, 1902–1903.
Contents: v. 1. Games of chance—v. 2. Games of skill.
ISBN 0-8032-6355-4 (v. 1).—ISBN 0-8032-6356-2 (v. 2).—ISBN 0-8032-6357-0
(set)
1. Indians of North America—Games. 2. Indians of North America—Gambling. I. Smithsonian Institution. Bureau of American Ethnology. Annual report. II. Title.
E98.G2C9   1992
790—dc20   92-15261
CIP

Reprinted from the original 1907 edition published as the Twenty-fourth Annual Report of the Bureau of American Ethnology, 1902–1903, Smithsonian
Institution. This Bison Book edition has been divided into two volumes and
subtitles have been added. Volume 1, dealing with games of chance, ended on
p. 382.

♾

# CONTENTS

## Volume 2

# ILLUSTRATIONS

## Volume 2

Volume 2: Games of Skill

# GAMES OF DEXTERITY

The various games of dexterity have been briefly reviewed in the introduction in Volume 1. In one of them—the game of hoop and pole—there are forms in which chance enters, but this is exceptional, and in general the class may be regarded as homogeneous with respect to the skill required in playing the game.

## ARCHERY

I have classified under archery games played with arrows, darts, or analogous objects which are shot or tossed at a mark, excepting the hoop-and-pole or ring-and-dart game, to which the majority of other archery games appear to be related. Simple archery, or shooting at a mark, does not hold a very conspicuous place among the Indian games with the bow and arrow, and but three examples (Montagnais, Hopi, Omaha) are found among the following descriptions. The target is usually an important feature and among several tribes is allied to the ring of the ring-and-dart game. This is especially true of the grass targets used by the Grosventres, Crows, and Tetons, and probably also of that used by the Zuñi. The Potawatomi game in which a bark target is buried is similar to the Zuñi game. The yucca ball of the Navaho, the bundle of hay or bark of the Shuswap, and the kelp of the Makah apparently belong to the same category. The Eskimo game in which darts are thrown at a hole in a wooden target is probably a related form. Another common target is an arrow (Tarahumare, Assiniboin, Teton) or a stick set upright (Western Eskimo). In other games a shot arrow is the target (Shuswap, Thompson, Oglala), or arrows are shot out of a ring. The Omaha shoot to dislodge arrows shot into a tree. Cacti, buffalo lights, and moccasins furnish other targets (Omaha). In another type of arrow game, arrows or darts are tossed (Apache, Eskimo, Hopi, Tewa, Zuñi) or shot (Pawnee, Ponca) at an arrow tossed or shot to the ground so that they fall one across the other, usually so that the feathered ends cross. This game may be regarded as the antetype of the Zuñi sholiwe, and possibly of all the Indian dice games.

ALGONQUIAN STOCK

ARAPAHO.  Oklahoma.

In the story entitled " Found-in-Grass," related by Dr George A. Dorsey,[a] the twins, Spring-Boy and By-the-Door, corresponding with the War Gods, are discovered playing a game of arrows. Winning appears to be determined by one arrow touching another.

CHEYENNE.  Cheyenne reservation, Montana.  (Cat. no. 69981, Field Columbian Museum.)

Six arrows, 29 inches in length, with bulging ends weighted by being wound with wire.  Two are blunt and four have wire-nail points.  These arrows are in pairs, distinguished by bands of blue paint, differently arranged on shafts.  Collected by Mr S. C. Simms in 1901.

GROSVENTRES.  Montana.  (Cat. no. $\frac{50}{1859}$, American Museum of Natural History.)

Wisp of grass (figure 501), wound with sinew, 9 inches in length. Collected in 1901 by Dr A. L. Kroeber, who describes it as an arrow target.

FIG. 501.  Arrow target; length, 9 inches; Grosventre Indians, Montana: cat. no. $\frac{50}{1859}$, American Museum of Natural History.

MONTAGNAIS.  Camp Chateau, Labrador.

George Cartwright [b] says:

The Indians were diverting themselves with shooting at a mark with their arrows; but I can not say, that I think them good archers, although their bows are constructed on an excellent principle; for by the assistance of a back-string the bow preserves its elastic power, and by slackening or tightening this string it is rendered weak enough for a child of 5 years old, or strong enough for the most powerful man amongst them.  As there is something particular in their sport of to-day, I shall endeavor to describe it.  They provide two targets of 4 feet square, made of sticks and covered with deerskins.  These they fix on poles about 8 feet high, and at 50 yards distance from each other.  The men dividing themselves into two parties, each party shoots twenty-one arrows at one of the targets, standing by the other.  That party which puts the most arrows into the target, gains the honor, for they have not the least idea of gaming.  The victors immediately set up shouts of mockery and derision at the conquered party; these they continue for some time, when the wives and daughters of the conquerors join in the triumph and walking in procession round the targets, sing

---

[a] Traditions of the Arapaho, p. 364, Chicago, 1903.
[b] A Journal of Transactions and Events during a Residence of Nearly Sixteen Years on the Coast of Labrador, v. 1, p. 238, Newark, 1792.

a song upon the occasion, priding themselves not a little with the defeat of their opponents, who at length join in the laugh against themselves, and all are friends again, without any offense (seemingly) being either given or taken.

POTAWATOMI.  Kansas.

Mr Wells M. Sawyer communicated to me the following account secured by him from an Indian interpreter:

Ta-te-wan (gambling).  Four players, A, B and C, D, each with a bow and two arrows, play partners.  Two strips of bark about 4 inches wide are placed in piles of earth shaped up like a little grave, the mounds being about 200 feet apart.  One player of each side takes his place near each mound, A, C and B, D.  The arrows of A, C are shot toward the target B, D.  If A strikes near the target, but misses with both arrows, and C fails to strike nearer than A, the latter counts 1.  If either of C's arrows come nearer than A's, C scores 1.  If either hits the target, he scores 5, and if both arrows of A or C hit, the game is won (10 being out).  If both A and C hit the target, neither counts.  The arrows are returned by B, D.

### ATHAPASCAN STOCK

APACHE (CHIRICAHUA).  Arizona.

Mr E. W. Davis communicated to the writer the following account of a game played by Geronimo's band at St Augustine, Florida, in 1889:

The game which interested me most, and one which required considerable skill, consisted in tossing arrows, point first, at a mark about 10 feet away.  As I recollect, the first man to throw his arrow was required to land on the mark.  If he did so, he got his arrow back.  His first throw was his misfortune, and the best he could do was to lose.  He had no chance to win.  Once an arrow in the field, however, the object of the next player was to toss his arrow so that it should cross the first thrown, and so on through the crowd.  I have seen as many as six play, and often all would toss around without any one winning.  In this case the arrows on the ground remained in the pot, so to speak.  The play went on, each player winning as many arrows as he could succeed in crossing with his own, until the whole number were removed.

CHIPEWYAN.  Fort Prince of Wales, Keewatin.

Samuel Hearne [a] says:

They have but few diversions; the chief is shooting at a mark with bow and arrows; and another outdoor game called Holl, which in some measure resembles playing with quoits; only it is done with short clubs, sharp at one end.

NAVAHO.  St Michael, Arizona.

Rev. Berard Haile describes the following game in a letter of June 27, 1902:

Sā-si" oldó (he shoots the yucca).  Bayonet-shaped yucca leaves are placed in hot ashes to make them flexible and moist.  Strings of them are then made and wound around bark or something similarly soft.  A string of buckskin is

---

[a] A Journey from Prince of Wales's Fort in Hudson's Bay to the Northern Ocean, p. 333, London, 1795.

wound in with the ball when it has nearly the required size. A small piece of an oak twig is fastened to the end of the string, and the "yucca" is finished. The shape, I think, would be shown in the accompanying sketch [figure 502].

The stick and ball are thrown into the air, and the stick, being heavier, has a tendency to steady the ball as it falls to the ground. While it is thus falling, the player shoots at it with bow and arrows, scoring if he is successful.

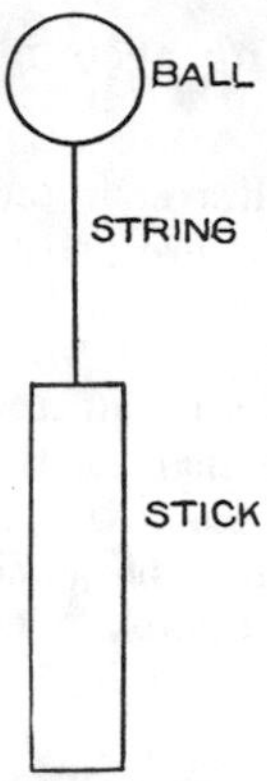

FIG. 502. Arrow target; Navaho Indians, St Michael, Arizona; from sketch by Rev. Berard Haile.

### CADDOAN STOCK

PAWNEE. Nebraska.

John B. Dunbar [a] says:

There were also frequent games played with arrows. One person shot an arrow so that it should fall upon the ground at a distance of from 40 to 60 paces. The players then in succession endeavored to shoot so that their arrows should fall immediately across this arrow. Whoever succeeded took all the arrows discharged. If no one lodged an arrow upon it the player whose arrow lay nearest took all. Another game was for several players to take an arrow between the thumb and forefinger of the right hand and throw it so that it should strike in the ground 20 or 30 paces in advance, the feather end of the shaft sloping back toward the thrower. Then stepping forward another was thrown by each, so as to strike 4 or 5 feet beyond the first. Each arrow that failed to strike fast in the ground entailed a forfeit.

WICHITA. Oklahoma.

In the story of "The Deeds of After-birth Boy," as related by Dr George A. Dorsey,[b] reference is made to the two brothers playing an arrow game called "shooting-ə-small-plaited-sinew-on-the-fly," lia-kukcs. The game was played for arrows.

### ESKIMAUAN STOCK

ESKIMO (WESTERN). Point Barrow, Alaska.

Mr John Murdoch [c] says:

These people have only one game which appears to be of the nature of gambling. It is played with the twisters and marline spikes used for backing the bow, and already described, though Lieut. Ray says he has seen it played with any bits of stick or bone. I never had an opportunity of watching a game of this sort played, as it is not often played at the village. It is a very popular amusement at the deer-hunting camps, where Lieut. Ray often saw it played. According to him the players are divided into sides, who sit on the ground about 3 yards apart, each side sticking up one of the marline spikes for a mark to throw the twisters at. Six of the latter, he believes, make a complete set. One side tosses the whole set one at a time at the opposite stake, and the points which they make are counted up by their opponents from the position of the twisters as they fall. He did not learn how the points were reckoned, except that twisters

[a] The Pawnee Indians. Magazine of American History, v. 8, p. 750, New York, Nov., 1882.

[b] The Mythology of the Wichita, p. 92, Washington, 1904.

[c] Ethnological Results of the Point Barrow Expedition. Ninth Annual Report of the Bureau of Ethnology, p. 364, 1892.

with a mark on them counted differently from the plain ones, or how long the game lasted, each side taking its turn of casting at the opposite stake. He, however, got the impression that the winning side kept the twisters belonging to their opponents. Mr. Nelson informs me in a letter that a similar game is played with the same implements at Norton sound.

## Eskimo (Western).   St Michael, Alaska.

Mr E. W. Nelson [a] describes the following games:

A round block about 6 inches long is cut into the form of a large spool, but with the flaring rim of one end replaced by a sharpened point. The top is from 2½ to 3 inches across and has a deep hole in the center. This spool-like object is planted in the floor of the kashim with the large end upward, and an indefinite number of players gather around it seated crosslegged on the floor. Near the spool is a small pile of short sticks, of uniform size, used as counters. These, with a small, pointed wooden dart, in size and shape almost exactly like a sharpened lead pencil, compose the implements of the game. The first player takes the butt of the dart between the thumb and forefinger, with its point upward and his hand nearly on a level with the spool. Then he gives the dart a deft upward toss, trying to cause it to take a curved course, so that it will fall with the point downward and remain fast in the hole at the top of the spool. If he succeeds he takes one of the counting sticks from the pile and tries again ; when he misses, the dart is passed to the next player, and so on, until the counters are all gone, when the players count up and the one having the most counters is the winner. Ordinarily this game is played by men, women, or children merely for pastime, but sometimes small articles are staked upon the outcome. It is a source of much sport to the players, who banter and laugh like school children at each other's bad play.

Dart-throwing (yokh'-whûk) . . . This is played in the kashim by two or more persons, usually for a prize or stake. The darts are small, short, and made of wood, largest at the point and tapering backward toward the butt, in which is fastened a bird quill for guiding the dart in its flight. In the large end of the dart is fastened a sharp spike of bone, horn, or sometimes of ivory. The target is a small, upright stick of some soft wood planted in the floor. This may be placed in the middle of the room and the players divided into two parties, seated on opposite sides of the target, or it may be placed on one side of the room and the players seated together on the other. In the former case a man is appointed from each side to return the darts to the throwers and to give each player a counter when a point is made. Each player has two darts, which he throws one after the other, and a score is made when a dart remains sticking into the target. Ten small wooden counting sticks are placed on the floor by the target, and one of these is given for each score ; the side gaining the most of these counters takes the prize, and the game begins again.

At Cape Nome, south of Bering strait, a similar dart game was seen, but there the target was a square board-like piece of wood with a dark-colored bull's-eye painted in the center. This was set up in the kashim and the men and boys threw their darts at it, scoring when they hit the bull's-eye. The wooden portion of the darts used in this game,

FIG. 503. Game dart; length, 22¾ inches; Western Eskimo, Cape Nome, Alaska; United States National Museum.

[a] The Eskimo about Bering Strait.   Eighteenth Annual Report of the Bureau of American Ethnology, p. 332, 1899.

both at Cape Nome and St Michael, was from 5 to 6 inches in length and from three-fourths of an inch to an inch in diameter at the larger end. Figure [503] represents a dart from Cape Nome, used for throwing at a square board target with a round black bull's-eye painted on its center. The players place the target on one side of the kashim and stand upon the other side to throw, scoring 1 for each dart that sticks in the bull's-eye. These darts are nearly 2 feet in length and have a tapering wooden handle, largest at the front, with an ivory point fastened in the lower end by a tapering, wedge-shape point, which is inserted in the split end and lashed firmly. The upper end of the shaft tapers to a small, round point, on which is fastened the end of a feather from a cormorant's tail, which serves to guide the dart in its flight.

### KERESAN STOCK

KERES. Acoma, New Mexico.

An Acoma Indian at Zuñi, named James H. Miller, informed the writer that the Acoma Indians have an arrow game in which they shoot at grass tied up.

### KIOWAN STOCK

KIOWA. Oklahoma. (Cat. no. 159913, United States National Museum.)

Six arrows made of a single piece of maple wood, 29¼ inches in length (plate IX).

The heads are carved and painted. According to the collector, Mr James Mooney, the arrows are thrown with the hand, like a javelin, and the player who throws farthest, wins. It is a man's game.

The incised designs, painted red, yellow, green, and blue, are in part easily recognizable as the calumet with primer, bow, and arrow, the lightning, and the symbols of the four directions on the uppermost arrow, which are painted from left to right with the colors red, green, blue, and yellow. Mr Cushing identified others as the war staff, or standard, and shield—day or dawn signs with turkey tracks; day signs with stars; horse tracks and the man sign. Mr Mooney, in reply to my inquiry, informed me that the Kiowa attach no special significance to these carved arrows, and were unable to explain the designs.

### MOQUELUMNAN STOCK

TOPINAGUGIM. Big creek, 2 miles north of Groveland, Tuolumne county, California.

Dr Hudson describes these Indians as playing also a game of shooting at an arrow set up, under the name of thuyamship.

The two contestants, armed with bows and blunt arrows, stand beside an arrow stuck in the ground and shoot alternately from a distance of about 170 feet. Two other players stand near the arrow targets and mark the shots. The players shoot back and forth until one of the two arrow targets is struck and broken.

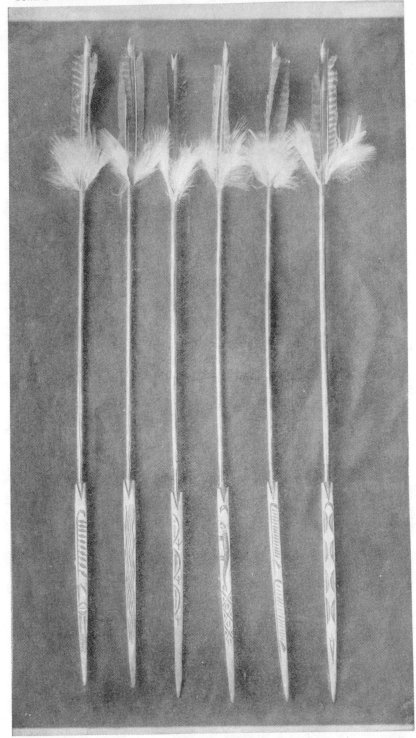

GAMING ARROWS; KIOWA INDIANS, OKLAHOMA; CAT. NO. 159913,
UNITED STATES NATIONAL MUSEUM

PIMAN STOCK

PIMA.  Arizona.

The late Dr Frank Russell [a] described the following boys' games:

Vatâmumulītc hukoyoliwia.—The players stand in a circle while a boy runs around the outside, dragging at the end of a string a bundle of rags. When the play begins each boy deposits an arrow in a heap, and the one who transfixes the bundle as it flies past is entitled to the pile of arrows. At the end the best marksman may have nearly all the arrows. The same runner continues throughout the game, and receives a few arrows as compensation for his services.

Okmaitcĕkĕ.—A bundle of grass, called woliwikke, is tied with willow bark so that it is about 125 mm. long and 50 mm. in diameter. The player tosses the bundle upward with his left hand while holding the bow in his right, ready to shoot the bundle before it can strike the earth. When the bundle is thrown forward instead of upward, it is called tcomält maitcĕkĕ, "to shoot the bundle low."

Naof towe kukrsa, "prickly-pear standing opposite."—There are usually four players, though sometimes two engage in this shooting game. Prickly-pear leaves are set up opposite each other at a distance of about 30 yards. The game is to pierce the leaf with an arrow, and when four are playing the two partners share equally the winnings or losses. Arrows, bows, and such similar property as these ragged urchins possess are wagered. A bow is considered worth from ten to twenty arrows, according to quality.

Kuorsa.—Either two or four may play. The game consists in shooting an arrow so that it will lie on the ground at a distance of about 100 feet and then shooting two more arrows with the intention of casting them across the first.

TARAHUMARE.  Chihuahua, Mexico.

Dr Carl Lumholtz [b] says:

Very common is it to see two young men amusing themselves with shooting-matches, shooting arrows at an arrow which has been shot out into the ground some 50 yards off as a mark. This arrow, as well as the game itself, is called in Mexican Spanish lechuguilla. In Tarahumare the game is called chog'irali, and the target arrow chogira. The arrow coming nearest the chogira counts 1 point; and if it comes within four fingers' width of the aim, it counts 4. The game is for 12 points. The distance is not measured from the points of the arrows, but from the winged parts, one man measuring for all. If a shot strikes so as to form a cross with the chogira, it counts 4. If it only touches the point of the latter in the ground, it counts 2. If two arrows happen to form crosses, neither counts.

Instead of arrows, three sticks may be employed. One is thrown out at a distance and is the chogira, and the other two sticks are thrown toward it and count in a similar way as the arrows. Often while traveling, the Tarahumare play this game, in either form, as they go along the road, perhaps for the entire distance. Two or three pairs may play together.

---

[a] In a memoir to be published by the Bureau of American Ethnology.
[b] Unknown Mexico, v. 1, p. 276, New York, 1902.

SHUSWAP.   Kamloops, British Columbia.
Dr Franz Boas [a] says:

Shooting matches are frequently arranged. An arrow is shot, and then the archers try to hit the arrow which has been shot first. Or a bundle of hay or a piece of bark is thrown as far as possible, and the men shoot at it.

THOMPSON INDIANS (NTLAKYAPAMUK).   British Columbia.
Mr James Teit [b] says:

A shooting game was played as follows: A steep sandy bank was generally chosen. Each player had two arrows. An extra arrow was fired at the bank by one of the party, to remain there as a target. Each player in turn fired his arrows at this target. The person who struck the notched end of the arrow-shaft or target, thereby splitting it in two, won the greatest number of points. The man who shot his arrow so that it stuck into the bank alongside of the arrow target, touching the latter all along the shaft, won the next highest number. A man was stationed near the target to call out the name of the shooter and the place where the arrows struck. The distance chosen to shoot from was according to the wishes of the archers, generally from 40 to 100 yards. In another game one man shot his arrow as far as he could, the others trying to shoot as near to it as possible, and the game was repeated. The man that could shoot the farthest and truest generally won. A large open space with rather soft ground was best suited for this game.

The Indians used to gather at a bluff close to Nicola river, and about 10 or 12 miles from Spences Bridge. Here they tried to shoot their arrows over the top of the bluff and passers-by did the same. Only the strongest shooters could shoot easily over the bluff.

HOPI.   Mishongnovi, Arizona.
Mr Charles L. Owen describes the following game:

The players throw up two sloping embankments at a distance of 200 feet apart. These are 4 feet long and 16 to 18 inches high. In the center of each is placed a conspicuous mark, such as a piece of cotton cloth or a piece of bright tin, at which boys and girls shoot their arrows. The closest shot secures the shooter the first shot at the other target.

Mr A. M. Stephen, in his unpublished manuscript, gives soya nanuveya as the Hopi, and ihŭtiñ as the Tewa name for casting throwing-sticks on the ground in imitation of a game where they cast arrows on the ground, the player trying to cause the fletching of his arrow to lie upon his opponent's in a certain place. The following are terms of the game:

Na-na'-vü-ya, to bet; na-na'-vü-lau-wû, betting, gambling; ho-hüh ak na-na'-vü-ya, to bet arrows; ho'-hü, arrow; pa-vaf-nai-ya, throwing sticks from a short distance to make them lodge in a rock crevice.

[a] Second General Report on the Indians of British Columbia. Report of the Sixtieth Meeting of the British Association for the Advancement of Science, p. 641, London, 1891.
[b] The Thompson Indians of British Columbia. Memoirs of the American Museum of Natural History, v. 2, p. 279, New York, 1900.

SIOUAN STOCK

ASSINIBOIN.   Fort Union, Montana.

Edwin T. Denig [a] says:

Another game is played by the boys and young men which consists of planting an arrow in the snow or ground and each throwing other arrows at it until
struck, and he who strikes the planted arrow is winner of all the arrows then
on the ground.

CROWS.   Crow reservation, Montana.   (Cat. no. 69649, Field Columbian Museum.)

FIG. 504.   Arrow target; length, 12 inches; Crow Indians, Montana; cat. no. 69649, Field Columbian Museum.

Archery target (figure 504), a wisp of sweet grass bent over in the
middle and wound with sinew; length, 12 inches.

This specimen was collected in 1901 by Mr S. C. Simms, who describes the game as follows:

The target is placed 40 feet away from the archer and shot at with an arrow
from an ordinary bow.   If he hits it, he takes up the target, and placing it between the index and second finger of his left hand, cross-
ing and resting on the arrow which is made ready to
shoot, but pointed toward the ground.   [Figure 505.]
Raising the bow and arrow, with the wisp still resting
on it, the wisp is released and the arrow discharged at
it.   If he hits it in the air, he scores an arrow.   It is
thus used in gambling, and is played in the spring by
boys and men.   The game is called bah-but-te'-de-o.

DAKOTA (OGLALA).   Pine Ridge reservation,
South Dakota.   (Cat. no. 22130, Free
Museum of Science and Art, University
of Pennsylvania.)

Toy bow and arrow (figure 506), the bow rudely
cut from hardwood, with a single curve and
a sinew string, 30 inches in length, and the
arrow made of a sapling, with a blunt head,
18 inches in length.

Collected by Mr Louis L. Meeker, who de-

FIG. 505.   Crow Indian
playing grass - target
game, Montana; from
photograph by Mr S. C.
Simms.

[a] Report to Hon. Isaac I. Stevens on the Indian Tribes of the Upper Missouri.   Unpublished manuscript in the library of the Bureau of American Ethnology.

scribes them under the name of hoksila itazipa.  Speaking of the boys,[a] he says:

They play at duels, and the targets for archery are arrows, cactus plants, or the dead body of a small animal.

FIG. 506.  Toy bow and arrow; length of bow, 30 inches; length of arrow, 18 inches; Oglala Dakota Indians, Pine Ridge reservation, South Dakota; cat. no. 22130, Free Museum of Science and Art, University of Pennsylvania.

DAKOTA (TETON).  Pine Ridge reservation, South Dakota.  (Cat. no. $\frac{50}{4236}$, American Museum of Natural History.) Bow and five arrows with wooden points, collected by Dr J. R. Walker.

One arrow is painted black, and is shot upward so that it falls point down. The player then shoots at it with his other arrows, having four trials.

Doctor Walker [b] describes the game of coat shooting, waskate ogle cekutepi, as played by men in which an arrow painted black or wrapped with a black strip of buckskin, or having a tag attached to it, called ogle, coat, is shot high into the air so that it will fall from 50 to 75 yards away.  Then the players stand and shoot at it with bow and arrow.

———— South Dakota.

Rev. J. Owen Dorsey [c] describes the following archery games:

Chun'kshila wanhin'kpe un'pi, Game with bows and small arrows.—These arrows are made of green switches, before the leaves fall in the autumn.  The end of each switch-arrow is charred to a point, and when it hits the bare skin it gives pain.  The boys used to shoot these arrows at the dogs when they went for water.  Played by boys in autumn.

Tachághu yuhá shkátapi, Game with buffalo lights.—The boys used to assemble at the place where they killed the buffalo, and one of them would take a strip of green hide, to which the lights were attached, and drag the latter along the ground to serve as a mark for the rest.  As he went along, the others shot at the lights.  Sometimes the boy stood still, grasping a long withe fastened to the lights, which he swung round and around his head as he passed around the circle of players, who shot at the lights.  Now and then, when a boy sought to recover his arrow, the other boy would strike him on the head with the lights, covering him with blood, after which he would release the player.  Sometimes the boy holding the lights would break off all the arrows which were sticking therein, instead of allowing their owners to reclaim them.

Pezhí yuskíl'skíl kutépi, They shoot at grass tied tightly in bunches.  Played by the larger boys.  Grass is wrapped around a piece of bark till it assumes an oval shape, both ends of the grass being secured together.  The grass ball thus

[a] Ogalala Games.  Bulletin of the Free Museum of Science and Art, v. 3, pp. 34, 43, Philadelphia, 1901.

[b] Sioux Games.  Journal of American Folk-Lore, v. 19, p. 32, 1906.

[c] Games of Teton Dakota Children.  The American Anthropologist, v. 4, pp. 337, 339, 340, 341, 1891.

made is thrown into the air, and all shoot at it, trying to hit it before it reaches the ground; when it is hit, the arrow generally penetrates the object very far, leaving only a small part of the feather end visible.    The one who sends his arrow near the heart or mark on the grass ball has the right to toss the ball up into the air; but he who hits the heart on the ball throws the ball on the ground, and then throws it where he pleases, when all shoot at it.    The game is generally played till dark, but there are no stakes put up.

Unkchela kutépi, Shooting at the cactus.    This game is always played for amusement, never for gain.    On the appointed day the boys assemble on the prairie.    One, who must be a swift runner, takes a cactus root into which he thrusts a stick to serve as a handle.    Grasping the cactus by this handle, he holds it aloft as he runs, and the others shoot at it.    During this game the swift runner himself is regarded as having become the cactus; so when one of the boys hits the cactus they say that it enrages the boy-cactus, who thereupon chases the others.    Whenever the boy-cactus overtakes a player he sticks his cactus into him, turns around, and returns to his former place.    Again the cactus is held aloft and they shoot at it as before, and again the players are chased.    The game is kept up till the players wish to stop it.

Ogléche kutépi, Shooting at an arrow set up.    Some boys back their favorites among the players by furnishing them with articles to be put down as stakes. On each side of a hill there is an arrow stuck upright in the ground to serve as a mark.    The players on one side shoot at the arrow set up on the other; the players at the front shoot at the arrow in the rear, and then the players in the rear shoot at the arrow set up at the front.    The nearer a player sends his arrow to the mark, the more it counts.    Sometimes one of the arrows set up is withdrawn temporarily from its place to be used for shooting at the other arrow. Only arrows are staked.

MANDAN.    North Dakota.

Catlin[a] describes a favorite amusement which they call the game of the arrow (figure 507) :

The young men who are the most distinguished in this exercise, assemble on the prairie at a little distance from the village, and having paid, each one, his entrance fee, such as a shield, a robe, a pipe, or other article, step forward in turn, shooting their arrows into the air, endeavoring to see who can get the greatest number flying in the air at one time, thrown from the same bow.    For this, the number of eight or ten arrows are clenched in the left hand with the bow, and the first one which is thrown is elevated to such a degree as will enable it to remain the longest time possible in the air, and while it is flying, the others are discharged as rapidly as possible; and he who succeeds in getting the greatest number up at once, is best, and takes the goods staked.

OMAHA.    Nebraska.

Rev. J. Owen Dorsey[b] describes the following games:

Shooting arrows at a mark is called maⁿkíde.    The mark (nacábeg¢e tĕ) may be placed at any distance from the contestants.    There must be an even number of persons on each side.    Men play with men and boys with boys.    Arrows are staked.    Sometimes when an arrow hits squarely at the mark it wins eight arrows or perhaps ten, according to previous agreement.    When no arrow

[a] The Manners, Customs, and Condition of the North American Indians, v. 1, p. 141, London, 1841.
[b] Omaha Sociology.    Third Annual Report of the Bureau of Ethnology, p. 339, 1884.

hits the mark squarely and one touches it, that arrow wins.  And if there is neither an arrow that hits the mark squarely nor one that barely touches it, then the nearest arrow wins.  Should there be no arrow that has gone nearly to the mark, but one that has gone a little beyond it and descended, that one wins. Whichever one is nearest the mark always wins.  If there are two arrows equidistant from the mark which belong to opposite sides in the game neither one wins ; but if the equidistant arrows are on the same side, both win.  Sometimes they say : " Let us finish the game whenever anyone hits the mark squarely." Then he who thus hits the mark wins all the arrows staked.

Shooting at a moccasin.—Hi$^n$be kide is a boy's game.  An arrow is stuck in the ground and a moccasin is fastened to it.  Each boy rides swiftly by and shoots at the moccasin.  The game resembles the preceding one.

Fig. 507.  Game of the arrow; Mandan Indians, North Dakota: from Catlin.

Ma$^n$-múqpe, The game of dislodging arrows, is common to the Omahas, Poncas, Iowas, Otos, and Missouris.  Arrows are shot up into a tree till they lodge among the branches ; then the players shoot up and try to dislodge them. Whoever can bring down an arrow wins it.  There are no sides or opposing parties.  Any number of boys can play.  The game has become obsolete among the Omahas, as there are no arrows now in use.

Ma$^n$-gádaze is a game unknown among the Omahas, but practised among the Poncas, who have learned it from the Dakotas.  It is played by two men.  Each one holds a bow upright in his left hand with one end touching the ground, and the bowstring toward a heap of arrows.  In the other hand he holds an arrow, which he strikes against the bowstring, which rebounds as he lets the arrow go.  The latter flies suddenly toward the heap of arrows and goes among them.  The player aims to have the feather on his arrow touch that on some other arrow which is in the heap.  In that case he wins as many arrows as the feather or web has touched, but if the sinew on his arrow touches another arrow, it wins not only that one, but all in the heap.

HAIDA.   British Columbia.

## Dr J. R. Swanton [a] describes the following game:

"Arrows stuck up" (Sq!aḷnā'da).   Some one shot an arrow up into the branches of a tree near the town until it stuck there.   Then all would try to shoot it down, and generally succeeded in getting more up.   He who knocked an arrow down owned it.

TEWA.   Santa Clara, New Mexico.

## Mr T. S. Dozier [b] writes as follows:

On the bringing in of the corn and after the dance in honor of that event the first game of the season begins.   Then the boys, from the smallest tot able to walk to well grown up ones, and the younger men may be seen at different places about the pueblo with the ah (bow) and tsu (arrow).   As you go by you ask: "Hum-bi-o" (what are you doing?) and they reply "I-vi-tsu-ah-wa" (playing the arrow).   The game is a very simple one, as played by the Tewa, the bows not being the stronger ones formerly used, nor the very excellent ones now made by the Apache, Navaho, and Ute.   A ring, varying in diameter from 5 to 6 inches to 2 or 3 feet, is made on the ground, and the arrows are placed upright in the earth.   The players take places around the ring and shoot for position. The ones coming nearest the place, generally marked by a stone or a piece of wood, from which the arrows will be shot at, will shoot first in their order. The shooting then begins, and in order to win, the arrow must be thrown entirely from the ring, and the ones winning the most arrows take positions in the next shooting and go on until the arrows in the ring are exhausted.

MAKAH.   Neah bay, Washington.

## Dr George A. Dorsey [c] describes the following games:

Tlitsaktsaudl: This game (shoot-arrow) is also played by young men and, generally, in the spring of the year.   Two goals are made, situated from 25 to 30 yards apart.   As, from the nature of these goals, no specimen could be collected, a description must suffice.   Five pieces of kelp are thrust into the earth in a row, the center piece being about 1½ feet high, the outer pieces about 3 inches high, and the two intermediate pieces midway between the center and outer pieces.   Over these is placed another piece of kelp, which is bent in a semicircular shape, with its extremities thrust into the earth about 2 feet apart. From two to six play, all standing in front of one goal and shooting at the goal opposite, the object being to hit any one of the upright pieces of kelp.   If the representative of one side or the other shoots and strikes the goal, he shoots again.   Should he miss, one of the opponents takes the arrow with which he shoots.   Should he make a hit, he retains the arrow.   The object of this . . . game is to win arrows (quilah).

---

[a] Contributions to the Ethnology of the Haida.   Memoirs of the American Museum of Natural History, whole series, v. 8, pt. 1, p. 61, New York, 1905.

[b] Some Tewa Games.   Unpublished manuscript in the Bureau of American Ethnology, May 8, 1896.

[c] Games of the Makah Indians of Neah Bay.   The American Antiquarian, v. 23, p. 70, 1901.

Tatauas. In this game a goal is also made of kelp, but instead of arrows short spears of red huckleberry, from 3 to 4 inches in length, are used. This game is played by two boys, each one sitting down on the beach facing his opponent, but at one side of him. B takes a piece of kelp stalk (wal'k-a-at) and thrusts it into the ground at his left side, at which A then hurls his spear. Failing to strike the goal, B takes A's spear and passes his piece of kelp to A, who then thrusts it into the ground by his left side, when B hurls the spear. In case he is successful he retains the spear, otherwise the kelp is returned to B and thrown at by A, and the game goes on as before. The object of the game is to win all the spears of the opponent.

## WASHOAN STOCK

WASHO. Carson valley, Nevada.

Dr J. W. Hudson describes the following game under the name of tsohotumpesh:

An arrow is stuck in the ground slanting toward the marksman, who, 60 feet away, casts at it a 3-foot blunt arrow. One or more opponents take their turn, standing in the first caster's tracks. The object is to strike the leaning arrow, or knock away an opponent's arrow. Either counts 1. To dislodge the target counts 5, or coup. Several can play, each using any number of darts agreed upon.

## YUMAN STOCK

MARICOPA. Arizona.

Mr Louis L. Meeker describes a game of grass shooting in which a wisp of grass is put upon the arrow where it crosses the bow. The bow is drawn and the wisp tossed up and shot in the air or the arrow is forfeited.

## ZUÑIAN STOCK

ZUÑI. Zuñi, New Mexico.

Mr John G. Owens [a] describes the following game:

Shō-wĕ-es-tō-pa. The number of players is unlimited. Each one has several arrows. One throws an arrow on the ground 8 or 10 feet in front of him, the others follow in turn, and, should the arrow thrown by any one cross that of another at the beginning of the feathers, he takes it. The limits of success are very small, and skillful throwing is required to win the arrows of another. This game is but little played at present, and I am doubtful whether the younger men of the tribe know how to play it. . . . The decline of the game is probably due to the decline of the use of the bow and arrow, but I think it has left a descendant in lō-pō-chē-wā. This is played only by the boys. Instead of arrows they use pieces of bone 2 or 3 inches long with feathers tied to them. You may see five or six boys playing this game in all parts of the pueblo at any time during the summer. They generally touch the bone to the tongue before throwing it, to make it stick. The principle of the game is the same as that of the one just described.

Mrs Matilda Coxe Stevenson [b] describes the preceding game as follows:

---

[a] Some Games of the Zuñi. Popular Science Monthly, v. 39, p. 40, New York, 1891.
[b] Zuñi Games. American Anthropologist, n. s., v. 5, p. 490, 1903.

Shówiältowe may be played by any number of persons, each one being provided with several arrows. Holding it between his index and middle finger and

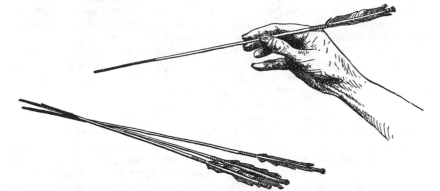

FIG. 508. Method of holding arrows in playing shówiältowe; Zuñi Indians, Zuñi, New Mexico; from Mrs Stevenson.

thumb, the first player throws an arrow a distance of some 10 or 12 feet [figure 508]. Then a second player throws, aiming to have the feathers on his arrow-

FIG. 509. Plumed sticks used in playing lápochiwe; Zuñi Indians, Zuñi, New Mexico; from Mrs Stevenson.

shaft touch those of the one already on the ground. If he is successful he takes both arrows and makes another throw, when the next player aims at the arrow on the ground; if he fails, the arrows remain in place and another player throws; and so on, each man taking the arrows which are touched by his own. Sometimes considerable dispute arises as to whether the feathers are really in contact, the men stooping and examining the arrows with the closest scrutiny.

If the arrows fall apart, each player takes his own from the ground, and a new game is begun. The taker of the full number of arrows wins the game.

Lápochiwe.—Implements [figure 509], three pencil-like sticks; three reeds the length of the sticks, one of them with a sharpened stick projecting, and one longer reed (designated the chief) having a pointed stick attached to the end. Two fluffy feathers are attached to each reed and stick.

Three sometimes play with the number of reeds and sticks mentioned, but when more than two play it is usual to increase the number of sticks, although in the genuine game of the Gods of War the number can not exceed seven.

The one proposing the game divides the six smaller reeds and sticks between his opponent and himself, and throws "the chief." The game is played like shówiältowe, except that the players are seated and throw a comparatively short distance. Lápochiwe is one of the favorite indoor games.

ZUÑI. Zuñi, New Mexico. (Cat. no. 3093, Brooklyn Institute Museum.)

Twelve feathered darts, made of slips of twig (figure 510), about 2½ inches in length, each with three feathers inserted; total length, 8½ inches. The set was collected by the writer in 1903. The name given was lapochiwe.

—— Zuñi, New Mexico. (Cat. no. 3065, Brooklyn Institute Museum.)

Miniature bows, 18½ inches in length, two arrows, and a target made of grass, 5½ inches in length (figure 511). Collected by the writer in 1903.

FIG. 510. Lápochiwe; length of darts, about 8½ inches; Zuñi Indians, Zuñi, New Mexico; cat. no. 3093, Brooklyn Institute Museum.

The name of the game was given as hapoanpiskwaiwe, from ha-po-an, bunch of grass, and pis-kwai-we, shooting. Two men or two boys play it in summer in the cornfields. The target is covered with sand, which is smoothed over so that the ha-po-an does not show. They shoot in turn, leaving the arrows in the ground. Then they pull out the arrows together, and if neither has pierced the target, it is bad luck; but if one has hit the target and lifts it out on his arrow, he is sure to kill deer. The arrows are old style, not feathered and made of cane with hard-wood foreshafts.

Mrs Matilda Coxe Stevenson [a] describes hapoanne pihlkwanawe:

Implements.—Bow and arrows; an oval roll of green cornhusks.

Any number may play this game. A hä'poännĕ (roll of husks) is placed upon the ground and arrows are shot at it from a distance of 40 or 50 feet. The first player to strike the roll covers it with a mound of earth, very much larger than the roll itself, while the others turn their backs. The one who places the hä'poännĕ is almost sure to mark the exact location of it, hence he resorts to various devices to mislead the players. A favorite deception is to leave the

---

[a] Zuñi Games. American Anthropologist, n. s., v. 5, p. 488, 1903.

mound low where the roll is actually buried, having it more elevated at some other point. The players aim to shoot their arrows into the hä'poänně, and the one who strikes wins the game. The winner draws the husk from beneath the earth with the arrow. When the arrow strikes the mound, but does not touch the hä'poänně, it is removed by the one who secretes the object, and a

Fig. 511. Target and bow and arrows; length of target, 5¼ inches; length of bow, 18¼ inches; Zuñi Indians, Zuñi, New Mexico; cat. no. 3065, Brooklyn Institute Museum.

second player shoots his arrow. Each player takes his turn until the hä'poänně is struck, the one having the arrangement of it being the last one to shoot, and he is naturally the most frequent winner. This game affords great amusement to the younger men.

## SNOW-SNAKE

I have included under the general name of snow-snake all that class of games in which darts or javelins are hurled along snow or ice or free in the air in a competition to see whose dart will go the farthest. They appear to be confined to the northern range of tribes, within the limit of ice and snow.

There are three principal types: First, the snow-snake proper, in which a long polished rod is made to glide on the snow or ice; second, the bone slider, in which a piece of bone or horn, stuck with two feathers, is made to slide along the ice; third, a game in which a javelin, sometimes feathered and commonly tipped with horn, is made to slide along the ground or to dart through the air, after being made to glance by striking the earth or some other obstacle.

The game of snow-snake is played with rods up to 10 feet in length, round or flat, usually highly polished, and not infrequently carved at the end. Shorter sticks, simple javelins or darts with carved heads, are also used. They are made to slide along the frozen crust, or in a rut in the snow. Sides are chosen and stakes bet upon the result, a snake which outdistances all on the opposite side counting a point. Snow-snake is distinctly a man's game, but special forms exist for women.

As suggested by the Omaha game, the first form appears to have been originally a game of sliding bows, and these may be referred to the two bows of the twin War Gods. The hurled snakes may be referred to their war clubs. The bone sliders which have been collected from a number of tribes—Algonquian, Kiowan, and Siouan—remain unexplained. They are all alike, with two feathers stuck on pegs, and suggest a bird in their form. The third form of darts is probably derived from arrows.

ARAPAHO.   Cheyenne and Arapaho reservation, Oklahoma.

Mr James Mooney [a] says:

The băti'qtûba (abbreviated ti'qtûp) game of the Arapaho and other prairie tribes somewhat resembles the Iroquois game of the snow-snake, and is played by children or grown persons of both sexes. It is a very simple game, the contestants merely throwing or sliding the sticks along the ground to see who can send them farthest. Two persons or two parties play against each other, boys sometimes playing against girls, or men against women. It is, however, more especially a girls' game. The game sticks (bătĭqta'wa) are slender willow rods, about 4 feet long, peeled and painted, and tipped with a point of buffalo horn to enable them to slide more easily along the ground. In throwing, the player holds the stick at the upper end with the thumb and fingers, and, swinging it like a pendulum, throws it out with a sweeping motion. Young men throw arrows about in the same way, and small boys sometimes throw ordinary reeds or weed stalks.

CHEYENNE.   Oklahoma.   (Cat. no. 21943, Free Museum of Science and Art, University of Pennsylvania.)

Feathered bone (figure 512) for throwing on the ice, called hekone-natsistam, or bone game, consisting of a piece of buffalo or beef rib, 7 inches in length, with two sticks fitted at one end, each bearing a hawk feather, dyed red; total length, 25 inches.

It was collected by Mr Louis L. Meeker, who has kindly furnished the following particulars:

The thumb is placed on one side of the bone, the forefinger between the sticks, with the end against the end of the bone, and the other three fingers opposed to the thumb against the other side of the rib, the convex side of which is down. It is then thrown down and forward against a smooth surface, preferably ice, so that it glances forward as throwing-sticks and snow-snakes do.

FIG. 512. Feathered bone slider: length, 7 inches; Cheyenne Indians, Oklahoma; cat. no. 21943, Free Museum of Science and Art, University of Pennsylvania.

The marks etched on the bone represent a horned toad, a tarantula, the milky way, and the moon. The four marks invoke the four winds, while the six legs of the tarantula represent up and down and the cardinal points.

——— Oklahoma.   (Cat. no. 67358, Field Columbian Museum.)

Dart points, made of polished horn 3⅝ inches in length, mounted on sticks 34 and 32 inches in length. The shorter one is notched at the end like an arrow.

[a] The Ghost-dance Religion. Fourteenth Annual Report of the Bureau of Ethnology, p. 1007, 1896.

Collected by Rev. H. R. Voth in 1890, who gave the following information:

The points are of buffalo horn and are employed as points for sticks from 4 to 6 feet long. The arrows thus formed are used in a game in which a number of girls shoot or hurl the darts along the road or other smooth ground. The object of the contest is to determine who can make the dart go farthest.

CHEYENNE. Cheyenne reservation, Montana. (Field Columbian Museum.)

Cat. no. 69985. Javelin, with conical bone head, 5 inches in length, and wooden shaft painted blue; total length, 66 inches.

This was collected in 1901 by Mr. S. C. Simms, who describes it as used in a woman's game, played on the ice or hard crust of snow and called majestum.

Cat. no. 69984. Arrow tipped with a conical bone point, 4 inches in length, with wooden shaft, painted yellow, and having feathers tied at the end; total length, 27½ inches.

This was collected in 1901 by Mr S. C. Simms, who describes it as used in a man's game.

The stick is seized by one end, whirled rapidly around with a vertical motion, and released when it gains momentum. The object is to make it go as far as possible.

CHIPPEWA. Apostle islands, Wisconsin.

J. G. Kohl [a] says:

The Indians are also said to have many capital games on the ice, and I had the opportunity, at any rate, to inspect the instruments employed in them, which they called shoshiman (slipping sticks). These are elegantly carved and prepared; at the end they are slightly bent, like the iron of a skate, and form a heavy knob, while gradually tapering down in the handle. They cast these sticks with considerable skill over the smooth ice. In order to give them greater impulsion, a small, gently rising incline of frozen snow is formed on the ice, over which the gliding sticks bound. In this way they gain greater impetus, and dart from the edge of the snow mound like arrows.

——— Wisconsin.

Prof. I. I. Ducatel [b] says:

They have their shosehman, or snow stick, about the length of a common walking cane, cut out in the shape of a sledge, which they cause to slide over the snow or ice.

——— Mille Lacs, Minnesota. (Cat. no. 204597, United States National Museum.)

A wooden club, 26½ inches in length, flat on one side and round on the reverse, one end wedge-shaped, with its upper face burned and marked with incised lines painted red and yellow, as shown in figure 513. Collected by Mr G. H. Beaulieu.

[a] Kitchi-Gami, Wanderings round Lake Superior, p. 90, London, 1860.
[b] A Fortnight among the Chippewas. The Indian Miscellany, p. 368, Albany, 1877.

This object is stated by the collector to be a rabbit club, which is glanced or thrown along the surface of the snow to kill the animal, "like a snow-snake."

FIG. 513.  Snow-snake; length, 26¼ inches; Chippewa Indians, Mille Lacs, Minnesota; cat. no. 204597, United States National Museum.

CHIPPEWA. Bear island, Leech lake, Minnesota. (American Museum of Natural History.)

Cat. no. $\frac{50}{4733}$. Snow-snake (figure 514a), a straight stick, pointed at one end, 26 inches in length.

Cat. no. $\frac{50}{4732}$. Snow-snake (figure 514b), curved upward and expanding at the farther end, 29½ inches in length.

These specimens were collected in 1903 by Dr William Jones, who describes them as played on the snow and called shoshiman, sliders.

FIG. 514 a, b.  Snow-snakes; lengths, 26 and 29½ inches; Chippewa Indians, Bear island, Leech lake, Minnesota; cat. no. $\frac{50}{4733}$, $\frac{50}{4732}$, American Museum of Natural History.

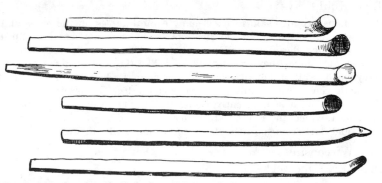

FIG. 515.  Snow-snakes; length, 12¼ inches; Chippewa Indians, Bear island, Leech lake, Minnesota; cat. no. $\frac{50}{4719}$, American Museum of Natural History.

Cat. no. $\frac{50}{4719}$.  Six snow-snakes (figure 515), 12¼ inches in length, with fore ends turned upward and carved differently.

Collected by Dr William Jones, who describes them under the name of shoshiman, sliders:

A small boy's game. Each has an equal number. Played on a ridge of snow, down which a little groove is made. The object is to send the stick the farthest.

CHIPPEWA. Bois fort, near Rainy river, Minnesota. (Cat. no. $\frac{50}{4714}$, American Museum of Natural History.)

Wooden club (figure 516), made of white cedar, tapering to the point and burned black; 22 inches in length. Collected by Dr William Jones in 1903.

FIG. 516. Snow-snake; length, 22 inches; Chippewa Indians, Bois fort, Minnesota; cat. no. $\frac{50}{4714}$, American Museum of Natural History.

———— Turtle mountain, North Dakota. (Cat. no. $\frac{50}{4734}$, American Museum of Natural History.)

Wooden club (figure 517), 21½ inches long, expanded at the upper end and painted red.

Collected in 1903 by Dr William Jones, who describes it as thrown on the snow with a wrist movement and gives the name as kwashkwashiman, bounding slider.

FIG. 517. Snow-snake; length, 21½ inches; Chippewa Indians, Turtle mountain, North Dakota; cat. no. $\frac{50}{4734}$, American Museum of Natural History.

CREE. Muskowpetung reserve, Qu'appelle, Assiniboia. (Field Columbian Museum.)

Cat. no. 61989. Wooden dart (figure 518), 7¾ inches in length, the shaft decorated with a burnt design; described by the collector, under the name of puckitseeman.

Played by any number of persons, of either sex or any age, either singly or by partners. A narrow track is made down the side of a hill covered with snow for a distance of 60 feet or more. This track is iced. The puck is started at the top of the track; it is not shoved, but must start off by its own weight. The track is barred at four points, about 10 feet apart, by

FIG. 518. Snow-dart (puckitseeman); length, 7¾ inches; Cree Indians, Assiniboia; cat. no. 61989, Field Columbian Museum.

snow barriers. The object is to pass the puck through as many as possible or all of the four barriers, and at the same time to have it not leave the track.

To win, the dart must be passed through all four barriers four times by the same person or partners. Count is kept, however, according to the number of barriers passed through. Considerable skill is acquired in this game in the handling of the puck.

Cat. no. 61991. Wooden dart (figure 519), similar to the preceding, but longer; length, 18¼ inches.

This is described by the collector, under the name of shooceeman, throwing to slide:

Played by men only, either singly or in partnership. Four barriers of loose snow are constructed at distances of a few feet apart and immediately behind each other.

The players stand about ten feet distant from the nearest barrier, and the stick is thrown, as in underhand bowling, directly at the nearest barrier, which it approaches with a gliding motion. The object of the game is to pass the stick through the entire set of barriers at one throw, which wins the game; points may be counted, however, according to the number of barriers penetrated by the dart.

In the case of a tie between players, the winner in the play-off must pass his dart through all barriers four times.

FIG. 519.  Snow dart (shooceeman); length, 18¼ inches; Cree Indians, Assiniboia; cat. no. 61991, Field Columbian Museum.

Cat. no. 61990.  Flat stick (figure 520), one end pointed and curved upward; length, 14¼ inches.

It is described by the collector under the name of esquayopuckit-seeman:

Game played by women exclusively.  Similar to game cat. no. 61989, except that the ice path is made with numerous turnings and is not impeded by barriers.  The ice path is also made much narrower, being but little wider than the dart itself.  The passage of the dart around the several turnings is equivalent to the passing of the dart through the snow barriers in the men's games.

FIG. 520.  Snow-dart (esquayopuckitseeman); length, 14¼ inches; Cree Indians, Assiniboia; cat. no. 61990, Field Columbian Museum.

All of the preceding specimens were collected by Mr J. A. Mitchell.
GROSVENTRES.  Fort Belknap, Montana.  (Cat. no. $\frac{50}{1823}$, American Museum of Natural History.)
End of beef rib, having two wooden pegs inserted at one end, upon which feathers are stuck; length, 24 inches.  A model collected by Dr A. L. Kroeber.

MENOMINEE.  Wisconsin.
Dr Walter J. Hoffman [a] describes the following game:

Another game for both amusement and gambling was termed the snow-snake, and was undoubtedly derived from the Ojibwa.  It was played during the winter, either in the snow or on the ice, and the only article necessary consisted of a piece of hard wood, from 5 to 6 feet long and from one-half to three-fourths of an inch thick.  The head was bulb-like and shaped like a snake, with eyes and a cross cut to denote the mouth.  This rounded end permitted it to pass over slight irregularities in its forward movements.  The player would grasp the end, or tail, of the snake by putting the index finger against the end and the thumb on one side, opposite to which would be the remaining three fingers; then stooping toward the ground the snake was held horizontally from

[a] The Menomini Indians.  Fourteenth Annual Report of the Bureau of Ethnology, p. 244, 1896.

right to left and forced forward in the direction of the head, skimming along
rapidly for a considerable distance. [See figure 521.]

The Ojibwa play the game in a similar manner, but they sometimes place a
ridge of snow slightly inclined away from the player in order to give the
snake an upward curve as it leaves the hands, thus propelling it a considerable
distance before touching the snow or ice.

FIG. 521. Menominee Indian holding snow-snake preparatory to throwing; Wisconsin; from
Hoffman.

MISSISAUGA. New Credit, Ontario.

Rev. Peter Jones [a] says:

Their principal play during the winter season is the snow-snake, which is
made of hard smooth timber, about 6 feet long, having eyes and mouth like a
snake. The manner of playing is to take the snake by the tail, and throw it
along the snow or ice with all their strength. Whoever sends his snake the
farthest a certain number of times gains the prize.

[a] History of the Ojebway Indians, p. 134, London, 1861.

NORRIDGEWOCK.  Norridgewock, Maine.

Rasles [a] gives, under joüets des enfans:

Sŝhé, c'est un bois plat qu'ils font glisser sur la nége, glace.

PASSAMAQUODDY.  Maine.

Mrs W. W. Brown [b] describes the following game (figure 522):

T'so-hâ-ta-ben, or t'so-hē-āc, requires more skill, both in construction and playing, than other outdoor games.  It is played on the crust or hard-drifted snow of
the hillside.  If this is the game spoken of by other writers as snow-snakes,
there is nothing in the name to so indicate.  Each player is supposed to supply
himself with the required few t'so-hē-āc, sticks.  In that case all the sticks are
bunched and thrown up, except five sticks, though it sometimes happens that
quite a number will join in the game, each contestant catching what he can as
they fall.  These sticks have different values, and as distance is what is aimed
at, the one going furthest wins all the others of
the same kind.  They are set in motion by that
peculiar movement which boys use in skipping
stones on the water.  The shouts of the players,
as the stick flies over the snow to the goal of
success, or buries itself in the drift of defeat,
are deafening.  As the sticks are, one by one,
set in motion, the player sings "la-hâ-wâ, la-
hâ-wâ," calling the stick by name, and this,
echoed and reechoed from the valley, is not altogether unmusical.  The sticks, or t'so-he-āc,
are named m-quon, āt'ho-sis, p-tqûk whol-êik,

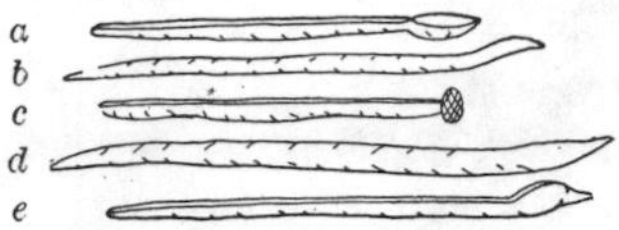

FIG. 522.  Snow darts: (a) m-quon,
the spoon; (b) at-ho-sis, the snake;
(c) ske-gä-weis, the wart; (d)
p't'gukwhol-ük; (e) be-dupk-t-s,
the duck; Passamaquoddy Indians, Maine; from Mrs W. W.
Brown.

ske-ga-weis, and be-dupk-ts.  M'quon, the spoon, is about 2 feet long, flat at
top and bottom, with one end concave like the bowl of a spoon.  A-t'ho-sis,
the snake, is long, slender, and round, one end resembling a snake's head, the
other pointed.  Ske-ga-weis is flat underneath, round on top, about 2 feet in
length, one end notched to resemble its name of wart.  P't'gûk-whol-ûk is the
largest of all.  From 5 to 7 feet long and nearly round, both ends raised slightly
and pointed, going with great force and speed, it drives in and out through the
snow, causing much merriment and noisy betting.  Be-dupk't's, the duck, is about
3 feet [long], flat on top, round underneath, with an end like the head of a duck.
Sometimes these t'so-he-ac are clever imitations, the coloring being also effective.
Though this game is not played as much as formerly, even the young boys seem
to understand whittling the sticks into a recognizable resemblance to the duck.

PENOBSCOT.  Oldtown, Maine.  (Cat. no. 48233 to 48235, Peabody
Museum of American Archæology and Ethnology.)

Three carved sticks, flat on the under side and curving upward in
front, one (48233), snake head, 21 inches in length (figure 523a);
another (48234), spoon mouth, 18 inches in length (figure 523b);
and the third (48235), 14½ inches in length (figure 523c).

These specimens were made by Big Thunder and collected by Mr
C. C. Willoughby, who furnished the following account of the game,
which is called suha:

[a] Memoirs of the American Academy of Arts and Sciences, n. s., v. 1, p. 472, Cambridge, 1833.
[b] Some Indoor and Outdoor Games of the Wabanaki Indians.  Proceedings and Transactions of the Royal Society of Canada, v. 6, sec. 2, p. 44, Montreal, 1889.

When a man wanted to play this game he took a number of his su-ha sticks and went through the village calling " su ha! su ha! " One or more of the players would take a boy by the feet and drag him down some incline, thus making a track, or path, in the snow. Down this path each player in turn, calling out " su ha! " threw one of his sticks, as a spear is thrown. To mark the distance this stick was stuck up in the snow beside the path, opposite the

FIG. 523 a, b, c. Snow-snakes; lengths, 21, 18, and 14¼ inches; Penobscot Indians, Oldtown, Maine; cat. no. 48233 to 48235, Peabody Museum of American Archæology and Ethnology.

place where it stopped. When all the sticks had been thrown, they became the property of the man whose stick had covered the greatest distance. He would gather them all up and selecting such as he wanted, calling out at the same time " su ha! " throw the others up in the air, and they became the property of those strong and quick enough to secure them. This game has not been played since 1842.

SAUK AND FOXES. Iowa. (Cat. no. $\frac{50}{2201}$, American Museum of Natural History.)

Slender stick of hard wood (figure 524), 25½ inches in length, with an egg-shaped end hardened by fire.

Collected by Dr William Jones, who describes it as snow-snake. Prof. Frederick Starr informed the writer that it was swung by the small end to give it impetus.

FIG. 524. Snow-snake; length, 25½ inches; Sauk and Fox Indians, Iowa; cat. no. $\frac{50}{2201}$, American Museum of Natural History.

────── Iowa. (American Museum of Natural History.)

Cat. no. $\frac{50}{3503}$. Three pointed sumac sticks, 46 to 52 inches in length.

Collected by Dr William Jones, who gives the name as shoskwihani, sliders.

FIG. 525. Snow-snakes; length, 30 inches; Sauk and Fox Indians, Iowa; cat. no. $\frac{50}{3502}$, American Museum of Natural History.

Cat. no. $\frac{50}{3502}$. Two narrow, flat sticks (figure 525), rounded on the upper side, 30 inches in length; one burned black for the entire length on the upper side, the other burned only at the head.

Collected by Dr William Jones, who gives the name as manetowagi, snakes.

They are played on the ice or frozen ground by men, and are thrown with a wrist movement, flat side down, so that they glide along for a great distance.

Cat. no. $\frac{5\,0}{3\,5\,0\,1}$, $\frac{5\,0}{3\,5\,0\,0}$. Two sets of sticks, one of each white and the other black, one (figure 526a) having an ovate head, 31 inches in length, and the other (figure 526b) a conical head, 33½ inches in length.

These were collected by Dr William Jones, who gives the name of both as miskwapi and states that they are played on the frozen ground or on the ice.

In throwing they are whirled around the head, and when played on the ground are made to glance from an incline.

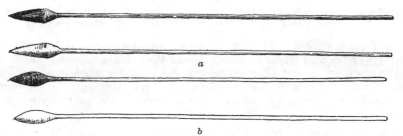

b

FIG. 526 a, b.  Snow-snakes; lengths, 31 and 33½ inches; Sauk and Fox Indians, Iowa; cat. no. $\frac{5\,0}{3\,5\,0\,1}$, $\frac{5\,0}{3\,5\,0\,0}$, American Museum of Natural History.

SAUK AND FOXES. Iowa.  (Cat. no. $\frac{5\,0}{3\,5\,0\,7}$, American Museum of Natural History.)

Two darts (figure 527), 26 inches long, with flat wooden heads, one painted blue and the other plain, with a stick 24½ inches long, having a bark cord attached with which the darts are slung. Collected by Dr William Jones.

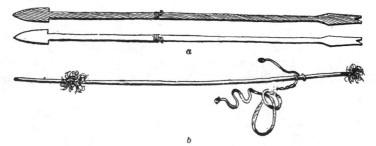

b

FIG. 527 a, b.  Slinging-darts and stick; length of darts, 26 inches; length of stick, 24¼ inches; Sauk and Fox Indians, Iowa; cat. no. $\frac{5\,0}{3\,5\,0\,7}$, American Museum of Natural History.

A summer game.  The one whose dart goes farthest wins.  The game is called nāneskwapuchuweni, and the darts nāneskwapuchi.

——— Tama, Iowa.  (Cat. no. 36756, Free Museum of Science and Art, University of Pennsylvania.)

Two peeled saplings of box elder, 66½ inches in length.

These were collected by the writer in 1900, and described to him as javelins for a game under the name of maskwapihok.

TAKULLI.  Stuart lake, British Columbia.

Reverend Father A. G. Morice[a] describes a game called tətquh:

A rod [figure 528] 5 or 6 feet long . . . is thrown through the air so as to fall as far as possible from the initial point of launching, the distance reached determining the measure of success attained.  This game . . . is now obsolescent.

A great rival is nəzəz, which is played with sticks of almost the same shape [figure 529], though much stouter near their fore end.  As they do duty on the frozen surface of the snow, the finest polish possible is aimed at in their prep-

FIG. 528.  Game dart (tətquh); Takulli Indians, Stuart lake, British Columbia; from Morice.

FIG. 529.  Snow-snake (nəzəz); Takulli Indians, Stuart lake, British Columbia; from Morice.

aration.  These sticks vary in length from 3 to 6 or 7 feet, according to the strength, possessed or assumed, of the player.  The Carriers are to-day passionately fond of this game, which is played, as a rule, by adverse bands, the stake going over to the party which first attains the fixed number of points.[b]

PAWNEE.  Oklahoma.

Dr George A. Dorsey[c] says:

In former times, a game was in vogue among the boys somewhat similar to the so-called " snow-snake," common in the central region of the United States. The prize in this game was the javelin itself; and when an individual had won a sufficient number of these long willow javelins they were made up into a mat for him by his grandmother.

HURON.  Ontario.

Bacqueville de la Potherie[d] says:

Girls play with spindles (fuseaux), which they shove beneath a small piece of wood raised above the ground.  The game is to push the spindle the farthest. There are games for the winter and games for the summer.  Those for all seasons are fruit stones and straws; those for winter are spindles for children. The boys add a tail two feet and a half long to the latter, while the girls use actual spindles.  They moisten them with saliva or put them in freezing water, so that they are covered with a slippery coat, and then they push them down the slope of a frozen hill that they may go far.  They also use for this purpose long, flat sticks.  They paint both the spindles and the sticks.

---

[a] Notes on the Western Dénés.  Transactions of the Canadian Institute, v. 4, p. 112, Toronto, 1895.

[b] See also The Western Dénés.  Proceedings of the Canadian Institute, 3d ser., v. 7, p. 154, Toronto, 1889.

[c] Traditions of the Skidi Pawnee, p. xvi, New York, 1904.

[d] Histoire de l'Amérique Septentrionale, v. 3, p. 23, Paris, 1753.

SENECA. New York.

Morgan [a] describes the game of gawàsa, or snow-snake, as follows:

Among the amusements of the winter season in Indian life was the game with snow-snakes [figure 530]. It was primarily designed as a diversion for the young; but it was occasionally made a public game between the tribes like the other, and aroused a great degree of spirit and the usual amount of betting. The snake was thrown with the hand, by placing the forefinger against its foot and supporting it with the thumb and remaining fingers. It was thus made to run upon the snow crust with the speed of an arrow, and to a much greater distance, sometimes running 60 or 80 rods. The success of the player depended upon his dexterity and muscular strength.

The snakes were made of hickory, and with the most perfect precision and finish. They were from 5 to 7 feet in length, about a fourth of an inch in thickness, and gradually diminishing from about an inch in width at the head to about half an inch at the foot. The head was round, turned up slightly, and pointed with lead to increase the momentum of the snake. This game, like that of ball, was divided into a number of separate contests; and was determined when either party had gained the number of points agreed upon, which was generally from 7 to 10. The players were limited and select, usually not more than six. A station was determined upon, with the line, or general direction in which the snake was to be thrown. After they had all been

FIG. 530.  Snow-snake; Seneca Indians, New York; from Morgan.

thrown by the players on both sides, the next question was to determine the count. The snake which ran the greatest distance was a point for the side to which it belonged. Other points might be won on the same side, if a second or third snake was found to be ahead of all the snakes upon the adverse side. One count was made for each snake which outstripped all upon the adverse side. These contests were repeated until one of the parties had made the requisite number of points to determine the game.

With the snow boat [da-ya-no-tä-yen-da-quä] was played one of the winter games of the Iroquois, in which the object was to discover which boat would run the farthest in an iced trench or path. The boat was about 15 inches in length, and made of beech or other hard wood, something in the fashion of a canoe. It was solid, with the exception of an oblong cavity in the center, designed to suspend bells or other rattles upon. In the stern of this little vessel a white feather was inserted for a flag, by which to follow it in its descent. On the bottom the boat was rounded, but with a slight wind lengthwise, as shown in the figure [531], to give it a true direction. A side hill, with an open plain below, was the kind of place selected to try the speed of the boats. Trenches in a straight line down the hill, and about a foot wide, were made by treading down the snow; after

---

[a] League of the Iroquois, p. 303, Rochester, 1851.

which water was poured into them that it might freeze and line the trenches throughout their whole extent with ice. These trenches to the number of a dozen, side by side, if as many individuals intended to play, were finished with the greatest care and exactness, not only down the hillside, but to a considerable distance across the plain below. At the same time the boats themselves were dipped in water, that they might also be coated with ice.

The people divided by tribes in playing this, as in all other Iroquois games, the Wolf, Bear, Beaver, and Turtle tribes playing against the Deer, Snipe, Heron, and Hawk. At the time appointed the

people assembled at the base of the hill and divided off by tribes, and then commenced betting on the result, a custom universally practised on such occasions. The game was played by select players who were stationed at the top of the hill, each with two or

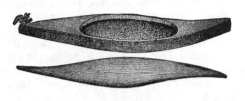

FIG. 531. Snow boat; Seneca Indians, New York; from Morgan.

three boats, and standing at the head of his own trench. When all was in readiness the boats were started off together at the appointed moment, and their rapid descent was watched with eager interest by the people below. . . . If the game was 20 it would be continued until one side had made that number of points. A count of one was made for every boat which led all upon the adverse side, so that if there were six players upon a side it was possible for that number to be made at one trial. On the contrary, if all the boats but one upon one side were in advance of all but one on the adverse side, and the latter was in advance of all, this head boat would win and count one. The principles of the game are precisely the same as in the snow-snake game.

Morgan says also:[a]

There was another game of javelino, gä-ga-dä-yan'-duk, played by shooting them through the air. In this game the javelin used was made of sumac, because of its lightness, and was of the same length and size as in the former [see page 410]. This game was divided into contests, as the ball game, and was won by the party which first made the number agreed upon. The game was usually from 15 to 20, and the number of players on a side ranged from five to ten. When the parties were ready, the one who had the first throw selected the object upon which the javelin was to be thrown, to give it an upward flight, and also its distance from the standing point. If, for example, it was a log, at the distance of a rod, the player placed his forefinger against the foot of the javelin, and, supporting it with his thumb and second finger, he threw it in such a manner, that it would strike the upper part of the log, and thus be thrown up into the air, and forward, until its force was spent. In this manner all the

---

a League of the Iroquois, p. 301, Rochester, 1851.

players, in turn, threw their javelins. The one which was thrown the greatest distance won a point. If another upon the same side was in advance of all upon the opposite side, it counted another, and so on for every one which led all those upon the opposite side. In the next contest, the second party chose the object over which to throw the javelin, and the distance. The game was thus continued, until the number of points were gained which were agreed upon for the game.

SENECA. Seneca reservation, Cattaraugus county, New York.

Dr Walter Hough [a] published the following account from information furnished by Andrew John, jr, a member of the tribe:

The game of kow-a-sa, or snow-snake, the national game of the Iroquois it may be called, is still played. A straight well-beaten road is now usually chosen, though sometimes it is played in the open, as formerly. The snakes are brought out, to the great glee of the boys, whose ears are on the alert, when some one says, " dan-di-wa-sa-ye," " let's play snow-snake," because they have the honor to run and bring back for the throwers. The snake is a thin rounded strip of hard wood, from 7 to 10 feet long and 1½ inches wide at most, made very smooth, shod at the forward end with a pewter nose piece, and not curved upward, Mr John says. It is balanced on the left hand and held by the tail in the right hand, the fingers being beneath and the thumb above. Holding it thus, the player runs 3 or 4 rods and, just before he throws he jumps. The stick skips away over the snow like an arrow, or perhaps one could better say like a snake. The skill in the game is in delivering the snake at the best slant, so that none of the original impetus given by the powerful right arm is lost.

The game is usually of four snakes—that is, the best three throws in four.

When skillful players contend, the excitement is very great among the Indians, and there is much betting, sometimes for high stakes; in fact, the game is for betting purposes entirely.

—— New York.    (Cat. no. 52241, Peabody Museum of American Archæology and Ethnology.)

Snow-snake, consisting of a highly polished hickory sapling, 7 feet 8 inches in length, the forward end tipped with lead.

This specimen was formerly owned by Chief Two Guns, who won several prizes with this snake, and whose totem, a fish, is cut on one face. Collected by Mr John W. Sanborn.

Another specimen in this collection (cat. no. 52242), made by Indians, has not been used.

—— Grand River reserve, Ontario.    (Cat. no. 55798, Field Columbian Museum.)

Snow-snake, made of polished hickory sapling, 7 feet 11 inches in length, shod with lead at forward end for a length of 4½ inches. Collected by Mr S. C. Simms, who gives the following account of the method of play:

The snake, gä-wa-sa, is thrown along a narrow shallow rut in the snow, made by the dragging of a log. The player grasps the end, or tail, of the snake by putting the index finger against the end and the thumb to one side, opposite to

[a] Games of Seneca Indians. The American Anthropologist, v. 1, p. 134, 1888.

which would be the remaining three fingers ; then, stooping toward the ground, the snake is held horizontally over the rut in the snow, and with a few quick short steps is thrown with considerable force along the rut. Sides are chosen to play the game. The snake which runs farthest wins, and a count is made by each snake which leads all upon the opposite side.

TUSCARORA. New York. (Cat. no. 16340, Free Museum of Science and Art, University of Pennsylvania.)

Four sticks of hard wood, shaved to a point, 41½ inches in length; designated as throwing sticks, ka-te nyä-ta.

KIOWAN STOCK

KIOWA. Oklahoma. (Cat. no. 152906, United States National Museum.)

Bone slider, consisting of a piece of rib bone (figure 532), 4½ inches in length, the upper concave face marked with small holes, having two feathers stuck on wooden pegs in one end; total length, 17 inches. Collected by Mr James Mooney.

FIG. 532. Feathered bone slider; length, 17 inches; Kiowa Indians, Oklahoma; cat. no. 152906, United States National Museum.

KULANAPAN STOCK

POMO. Seven miles south of Ukiah, Mendocino county, California. (Cat. no. 70945, Field Columbian Museum.)

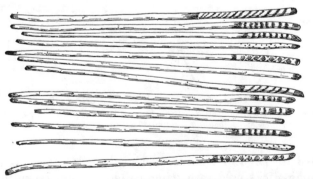

FIG. 533. Ground-coasting arrows; average length, 3 feet; Pomo Indians, Mendocino county, California; cat. no. 70945, Field Columbian Museum.

Thirteen sticks (figure 533), with butt ends marked in pairs with burned devices; average length, 3 feet.

Collected by Dr J. W. Hudson, who describes them as ground-coasting arrows, called mului, a name also applied to a process of etching a rod by holding it in a blaze after it is bound or protected in part by withes of another material, as grapevine, hazel, etc.

The darts are about the size of arrows. Distance only counts. There are five distinct mulu'-i symbols placed on the darts, all named for or as symbols for certain animals.

### MARIPOSAN STOCK

Yokuts. Tule River reservation, Tulare county, California. (Cat. no. 70405, Field Columbian Museum.)

Lance of peeled sapling (figure 534), 66½ inches in length. It is described by the collector, Dr J. W. Hudson, as a snow-snake or ground dart. The butt is weighted by being wound with iron wire.

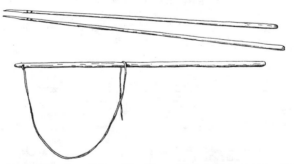

Fig. 534. Snow-snake; length, 66½ inches; Yokuts Indians, Tule River reservation, Tulare county, California; cat. no. 70405, Field Columbian Museum.

### MOQUELUMNAN STOCK

Topinagugim. Big creek, Tuolumne county, California. (Cat. no. 70230, 70231, Field Columbian Museum.)

Two flat, tapering sticks of wild cherry (figure 535), 38 inches in length, with tips burned with two rings; and whip, with buckskin thong and stock, 31½ inches in length.

Fig. 535. Throwing- or whipping-sticks, with whip and lash; length of sticks, 38 inches; length of whipstock, 31¼ inches; Topinagugim Indians, Tuolumne county, California; cat. no. 70230, 70231, Field Columbian Museum.

Collected by Dr J. W. Hudson, who describes them as throwing- or whipping-sticks used in a game called kuitumsi (kuitu, farthest one).

The lance, la-ma-ku-yi-ta, is one-fourth of an inch in diameter at the butt, expanding to five-eighths of an inch at the tip. The different ones are marked to distinguish them. A buckskin thong, pe-hu-na-ha-a-ta (buckskin to whip), is tied to a wooden handle. The farthest cast wins.

Dr J. W. Hudson describes also these Indians as casting along the ground sticks, 4 feet long, made of willow or calacanthus. Each player has one cast. The one throwing the farthest, wins. The loser is thumped on the head with the knuckles. The game is called pakumship; pakür, lance.

SIOUAN STOCK

ASSINIBOIN. Fort Union, Montana.

Mr Edwin T. Denig [a] says:

The women slide long sticks on the snow.

CROWS. Crow reservation, Montana. (Field Columbian Museum.)
Cat. no. 69657. Feathered dart, a piece of beef rib, painted red and incised with crossed lines, 6½ inches in length, having two long twigs inserted at the squared end, upon which feathers dyed red are stuck; total length, 29 inches.

Collected in 1901 by Mr S. C. Simms, who describes it as played by boys on the ice.

FIG. 536. Game dart; length, 32¼ inches; Crow Indians, Montana; cat. no. 69653, Field Columbian Museum.

Cat. no. 69653. Javelin (figure 536), a thin sapling, painted red and tipped with horn; length, 32½ inches.

Collected in 1901 by Mr S. C. Simms, who describes it as used in a man's game.

The stick is seized by the end, whirled rapidly with a vertical motion, and released when it gains momentum. The object is to make it go as far as possible.

DAKOTA (OGLALA). Pine Ridge reservation, South Dakota. (Free Museum of Science and Art, University of Pennsylvania.)

FIG. 537. Feathered bone-slider; length, 25 inches; Oglala Dakota Indians, Pine Ridge reservation, South Dakota; cat. no. 22129, Free Museum of Science and Art, University of Pennsylvania.

Cat. no. 22129. A fragment of beef rib (figure 537), 8 inches in length, with feathers stuck on two wooden pegs inserted in one end of the bone; total length, 25 inches.

<hr>

[a] Unpublished manuscript in the Bureau of American Ethnology.

Collected by Mr Louis L. Meeker,[a] who describes the implement under the name of paslo hanpi, as thrown by boys on the ice.

Cat. no. 22128.   A thin straight dart (figure 538), 29¾ inches in length, tipped with a cone of horn and having a bunch of feathers secured with sinew at the shaftment.

FIG. 538.  Boys' throwing-arrow; length, 29¼ inches; Oglala Dakota Indians, Pine Ridge reservation, South Dakota; cat. no. 22128, Free Museum of Science and Art, University of Pennsylvania.

Described by the collector, Mr Louis L. Meeker,[b] under the name of pte heste, as thrown underhand by boys against the ground to glance to a great distance.   The one whose stick goes farthest takes all the other sticks.   This game is described by Dr J. R. Walker [c] among the Tetons under the name of woskate pte heste, game of the young cow.

Any number of persons may play.  Each player may have any number of arrows, but all players should have the same number.  Two parallel lines are drawn from 20 to 30 feet apart.  The players take their position on one side of these lines.  A player must throw his horned arrow so that it may strike between the two lines and slide beyond them.  The players throw alternately until all the arrows are thrown.  At the end the player whose arrow lies farthest from the lines wins the game.

Cat. no. 22132.   A slender sapling (figure 539) tipped with a horn point, 63 inches in length.

Described by the collector, Mr Louis L. Meeker,[d] under the name of winyanta paslo hanpi, the girls' throwing-stick.

The sticks, held by the extreme end, with forefinger behind, are cast high in the air.  The game is played for small sticks about the size of lead pencils, or larger, the same as are used for counters by the men in the moccasin game.

This game is described by Dr J. R. Walker [e] under the name of woskate hepaslohanpi, game of horned javelins, and the implement he gives as hewahukezala, horned javelin.

The game is played by throwing the javelin so that it will strike and slide on the snow or ice, and the one whose javelin slides the farthest wins.

DAKOTA (TETON).   Pine Ridge reservation, South Dakota.   (American Museum of Natural History.)

Cat. no. $\frac{50}{4229}$.   Two pairs of sticks (figure 540), flat on one side and rounded on the other, slightly expanded, and turned up at the end, one set 48 inches and the other 44 inches in length; one set plain and the other with three dragon flies painted on the upper

[a] Ogalala Games.   Bulletin of the Free Museum of Science and Art, v. 3, p. 35, Philadelphia, 1901.
[b] Ibid., p. 34.
[c] Sioux Games.   Journal of American Folk-Lore, v. 19, p. 32, 1906.
[d] Ogalala Games.   Bulletin of the Free Museum of Science and Art, v. 3, p. 36, Philadelphia, 1901.
[e] Sioux Games.   Journal of American Folk-Lore, v. 19, p. 36, 1906.

face.  Collected by Dr J. R. Walker, who describes them under the name of canpaslohanpi, used in the game of throwing sticks, woskate canpaslohanpi.[a]

FIG. 539.  Girls' throwing-stick; length, 63 inches; Oglala Dakota Indians, Pine Ridge reservation, South Dakota; cat. no. 22132, Free Museum of Science and Art, University of Pennsylvania.

Each player has but one throwing stick.  Any number of persons may play. The game is played by grasping the stick at the smaller end, between the thumb and second, third, and fourth fingers, with the first finger across the smaller end, the flat side of the stick held uppermost.  Then by swinging the hand below the hips the javelin is shot forward so that it will slide on the snow or ice.  The game is to see who can slide the stick farthest.

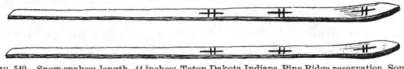

FIG. 540.  Snow-snakes; length, 44 inches; Teton Dakota Indians, Pine Ridge reservation, South Dakota; cat. no. $\frac{50}{422}$, American Museum of Natural History.

DAKOTA (TETON).  South Dakota.

Rev. J. Owen Dorsey [b] describes the following games as played by boys in winter:

Ptehéshte un'pi, buffalo horn game: The boys assemble at the corral or some other place where the cattle have been slaughtered, and gather the horns which have been thrown away.  They kindle a fire and scorch the horns, noticing how far each horn has been burnt.  That part of the horn is cut off, as it is brittle, and they make the rest of the horn very smooth by rubbing.  They cut off all the small and pliable branches and twigs of a plum tree and insert the root end into a hole in the horn, tightening it by driving in several small wedges around it. At the small end of the plum stock they fasten a feather by wrapping deer sinew round and round it.  The pteheste is then thrown along the surface of the snow, or it often goes under the surface, disappearing and reappearing at short intervals.  Sometimes they make it glide over the ice.  Stakes are frequently put up by or for the players.

Itázipa kaslóhan iyéya echun'pi, making the bow glide by throwing.  They do not use real bows, but some kind of wood made flat by cutting with an ax, with a horizontal curve at the lowest part, and sharpened on the other side.  At the head a snake's head is usually made, or else the head of some other object. At the other end the player grasps it and hurls it, making it glide rapidly over the snow or grass.  This is a game of chance, but the " bows " are never staked, as they are too expensive.  It takes so long to make one that the owner does not sell it, preferring to keep it as long as possible.

The following is played by boys and young men: [c]

In the winter the boys collect the good ribs of animals that are near the village.  They make gashes across them, and on one side of each rib they

---

[a] Sioux Games.  Journal of American Folk-Lore, v. 19, p. 32, 1906.
[b] Games of Teton Dakota Children.  The American Anthropologist, v. 4, p. 338, 1891.
[c] Ibid., p. 343.

make a hole in which they insert two plum sticks. The small end of each plum stick they insert into the hole of a quill feather of some bird. The small end of each plum stick is bent backwards. Just at the fork of the two plum sticks the player grasps the toy, called hutanachute, making it glide over the snow or ice. Stakes are put down when desired, but sometimes they play just for amusement. Occasionally young men join the boys in this game.

The following is an autumnal game of the boys or women:

Paslóhanpi, they shove it along. The boys play this game when the leaves become a rusty yellow. They go to a place where the smallest kind of willow abounds, and there they make a fire. They cut down the straightest of the willows, shaving off the bark with knives. Some color the willow in stripes. Others change the willows into what they call chan kablaskapi, i. e., wood flattened by beating, but what these are Bushotter does not explain. Much of this text is very obscure. Sometimes the young women play the game, at other times the men do; but each sex has its peculiar way of making the paslohanpi glide along. Sometimes they play for stakes.

Dr J. R. Walker [a] gives the following rules for the game with winged bones, woskate hutanacute:

Any number may play. Each player may have from two to four winged bones, but each player should have the same number. A mark is made from which the bones are thrown. The bones are thrown so that they may strike or slide on the ice or snow. The players throw alternately until all the bones are thrown. When all the bones are thrown the player whose bone lies the farthest from the mark wins the game.

Doctor Walker describes woskate paslohanpi as the game of javelins (wahukezala) played by Sioux boys in the springtime, and states that there are two ways of throwing: One to lay the javelin across something, as the arm, or the foot, or another javelin, or a stump of log, or a small mound of earth, or anything that is convenient, and grasping it at the smaller end, shoot it forward; the other way is to grasp the javelin near the middle and throw it from the hand.

DAKOTA (YANKTON).   Fort Peck, Montana.   (Free Museum of Science and Art, University of Pennsylvania.)

Cat. no. 37610.   Three peeled saplings, burnt near the larger end with spiral bands and marks; length, 46½ inches.

Collected by the writer in 1900.   The name is pasdohanpi.[b]

FIG. 541.   Feathered bone slider; length, 21 inches; Yankton Dakota Indians, Fort Peck, Montana; cat. no. 37612, Free Museum of Science and Art, University of Pennsylvania.

Cat. no. 37612.   Two pieces of beef rib, 6¼ inches in length, each with two feathers inserted on pegs in one end; total length, 21 inches. One bears incised marks, as shown in figure 541.

---

[a] Sioux Games.   Journal of American Folk-Lore, v. 19, p. 31, 1906.
[b] From pa-sdo'-han, to push or shove along.

Collected in 1900 by the writer, to whom they were designated as hutinacute.[a]

MANDAN.   Fort Clark, North Dakota.

Maximilian, Prince of Wied,[b] says:

The children of the Mandans and Manitaries play with a piece of stag's horn [figure 542], in which a couple of feathers are inserted; this is thrown forward, the piece of horn being foremost.

FIG. 542.  Feathered horn dart; Mandan Indians, North Dakota; from Maximilian, Prince of Wied.

OMAHA.   Nebraska.

Mr Dorsey [c] describes the following games:

Man¢in'-bagí, wahí-gasnug'-i¢e (Omaha names), or man-íbagí' (Ponca name) is a game played by an even number of boys. The tall sticks of the red willow are held in the hand, and when thrown towards the ground so as to strike it at an acute angle, they glance off, and are carried by the wind into the air for some distance. Whichever one can throw his stick the furthest wins the game, but nothing is staked. Man'dĕ-gasnug'-i¢e is a game similar to man¢in'-bagi, but bows are used instead of the red willow sticks, and arrows are staked, there being an even number of players on each side. Each bow is unstrung, one end being nearly straight, the other end, which is to hit the ground, being slightly curved. When snow is on the ground, the bows glide very far. Sometimes the bow rebounds and goes into the air, then alights and glides still further. The prize for each winning bow is arranged before each game. If the number be two arrows for each and three bows win, six arrows are forfeited by the losing side; if four bows win, eight arrows are lost. If three arrows be the prize for each, when two bows win, six arrows are forfeited; when three win, nine arrows; and so on.

In'-tinbúta, a boy's game among the Omahas, is played in winter. It is played by two, three, or four small boys, each having a stick, not over a yard long, shaped like the figure [543]. The stakes are necklaces and earrings; or, if they have no stakes, they agree to hit once on the head the boy whose stick goes the shortest distance. The sticks are thrown as in man¢in'-bagi.

FIG. 543.  Game dart; Omaha Indians, Nebraska; from Dorsey.

Mr Francis La Flesche described a game to the writer under the name of "wahegusungithae," or bone sliders, in which a bone with a

[a] A long stick with a large head which the Dakotas make slide on the snow or ice. (Riggs.)  Also, hu-ta'-na-ku-te, v. n., to play with the hutina¢ute; to throw a stick so as to make it slide along on the snow, hutanawakute.

[b] Travels in the Interior of North America, translated by H. Evans Lloyd, p. 358, London, 1843.

[c] Omaha Sociology.  Third Annual Report of the Bureau of Ethnology, p. 340, 1884.

feather stuck in it is slid along the ice.   He said also another game is played in summer, to which the same name is given, with sticks about 3 feet long by one-half of an inch in diameter, which are peeled and burned.   They are forcibly thrown down on the ground and fly a great distance.   Mr La Flesche described also a game played by Omaha boys under the name of intimbuta, in which a stick of hickory, scraped, polished, and whittled down, is thrown on the frozen ground so that it flies like an arrow.

## HOOP AND POLE

The game of hoop and pole, like the dice game, was played throughout the entire continent north of Mexico.   It consists essentially in throwing a spear, or shooting or throwing an arrow at a hoop or ring, the counts being determined by the way in which the darts fall with reference to the target.

The game is remarkable for the wide diversity in the form of the implements employed, as well as in the method of play.   A number of distinct types may be recognized, of which as many as three are found at the present day among the same tribe.   The essential unity of all of these, however, is plainly manifest.

The implements for hoop and pole consist of the hoop or target, the darts or poles, and, in some instances, especially made counting sticks. A common and most widely distributed form of the hoop is twined with a network resembling a spider web, the counts being determined by the particular holes which are penetrated by the darts.   In another hoop the net, with the exception of an inner ring, which is attached by cords to the hoop, has disappeared.   In still others, among the Ta-kulli, Wasco, Omaha, and Tigua, there remain only four radial spokes or strands.   In the Apache game these are reduced to a single median thong or cord, but notches on the hoop suggest the points of contact of the thong lashings.   One of the Siouan hoops, known also to the Arapaho, has four sets of equidistant notches on its circumference. These notches agree with the marks of the world quarters on the cane dice and on the tubes of the hidden-ball game.

In another group of the hoop games we find a small ring with beads of different colors set at equidistant points around its inner side. Different values are attributed to these beads, which count accordingly.   On other small rings, as among the Pawnee, a single small bead is threaded on the interior of the ring.   Marks indicating the quarters are found upon some hoops, while others are entirely plain.

The materials of the rings are equally varied.   The netted hoop usually consists of a sapling lashed with rawhide.   Other hoops are twined with cord (Mohave) or beads (Ute), and still others have a central core wrapped with rawhide (Navaho, Shoshoni, Tigua) or with bark (Umatilla, Kwakiutl, Makah). The Hopi have rings of corn husks. Again, there are rings of stone (Santa Barbara, Choctaw, Muskogee, Bellacoola, Mandan, Kwakiutl), some of rough lava, as among the tribes of the Pacific, and others of finely finished quartzite, as in the states of the south Atlantic and Gulf coasts. These stone rings are both with and without perforations, and among the Cherokee we read of them being flat on one side and convex on the other. The diameter of the hoop also varies, from 25 inches among the Oglala to 2¾ inches among the Paiute.

The darts employed are of several varieties. Arrows shot from a bow or thrown by hand are common. Simple straight shafts are frequently used, as well as plain long poles made of a single piece. The Hopi and the Thompson have feather darts. For the netted hoop, a sapling with a forked end is commonly employed. The Apache have long jointed poles, the ends marked with rings, which count in accordance with the way they fall upon the hoop. The Navaho use similar jointed poles with a thong attached, the divided ends of which count as they catch in the ring. Among the Tigua (Isleta), the Keres (Laguna), and the Mandan the darts had thongs which caught in the ring. In an Omaha game there is a curved strip of rawhide forming a kind of trident at the end of the pole.

Two short darts attached in the middle by a thong were used with the large hoop of the Dakota, and in a game played by the Caddoan and Siouan stocks the throwing sticks were complicated with arcs and crossbars.

The game was always played by males. There is no record of women participating. The number of players varied from two upward, but two appears to have been the primal number. In the ceremonial forms of the game a complete set of implements consisted of .a single ring and two poles. The latter may be explained in many instances as the bows of the twin War Gods. The jointed poles of the Navaho and the Apache may be regarded as the two bows tied together, and the same explanation may be offered for the tied darts used with the large hoop by the Dakota. The implement used by the Caddoan tribes is explained by them as representing a buffalo, the projecting curved head symbolizing the masculine organ. In playing, the long poles were ordinarily thrown after the moving ring by the two contestants; the beaded ring was commonly rolled against some kind of barrier. In the Delaware, Seneca, and Niska games the players stood in two parallel lines, shooting at the hoop as it rolled between them. Among the Makah the lines converge.

For the playing field a level place was selected, and among some tribes especially prepared. Among the Mandan we read of timber floors 150 feet long.  The Apache play on a level ground, 100 feet long, with a rock in the center, from which the poles are hurled.

The Creeks had large inclosed courts with sloping sides, on which the spectators were seated.  Among the Apache and the Navaho, the direction of the track is from north to south.  In reference to the season of the game, we learn that among the Wasco it is played at the time of the first run of salmon, and among the Umatilla in the spring.

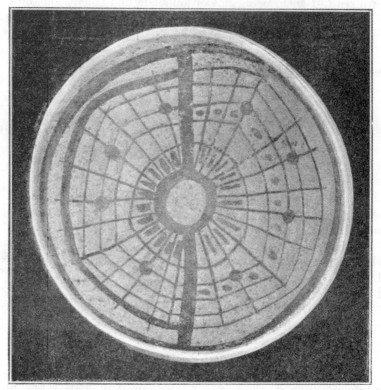

FIG. 544.  Pottery bowl with spider-web decoration; diameter, 9¼ inches; Hopi Indians, Mishongnovi, Arizona; cat. no. 75766, Field Columbian Museum.

Morgan describes it as played between different communities among the Iroquois.

Information concerning the counts is meager.  The Arapaho used one hundred and the Shoshoni six tally sticks.  Among the Apache it is the principal gambling game.  It is commonly played for stakes of value, but not infrequently for the arrows and darts used in the play.

The explanation of the origin and significance of the game of hoop and pole rests largely upon the identification of the hoop.  The netted gaming hoop is readily seen to be the same as the netted shield, one of the attributes of the twin War Gods, Ahaiyuta and Matsailema, of Zuñi mythology. Mr Cushing had explained this shield as a framework, once padded with cotton, and anciently used by the Zuñi as an actual shield in warfare.[a] Upon the basis of this account the writer assumed that the game arose from the employment of this

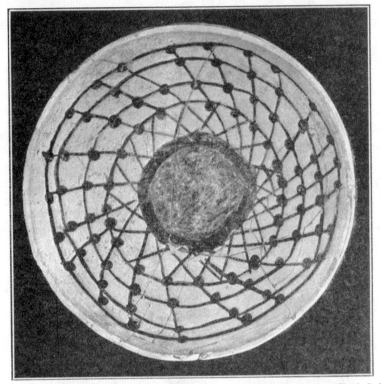

FIG. 545. Pottery bowl with spider-web decoration; diameter, 10 inches; Hopi Indians, Mishongnovi, Arizona; cat. no. 75675, Field Columbian Museum.

practical shield in connection with the arrow or javelin. A passage in Cushing's Zuñi Folk Tales,[b] where this netted shield, made only of nets and knotted cords, is described as the kiaalan, water shield, a

---

[a] The warrior carried also targets or shields of yucca or cotton cord, closely netted across a strong, round hoop frame and covered with a coarser and larger net, which was only a modification of the carrying net (like those still in use by the Papago, Pima, and other Indians of southern Arizona), and which was turned to account as such, indeed, on hunting and war expeditions. (Outlines of Zuñi Creation Myths. Thirteenth Annual Report of the Bureau of Ethnology, p. 358, 1896.) Elsewhere (A Zuñi Folk Tale of the Underworld. Journal of American Folk-Lore, v. 5, p. 52) Mr Cushing speaks thus of their shields:

"Cord shields.—Pi-a-la-we (cord or cotton shields), evidently an ancient style of shield still surviving in the form of sacrificial net shields of the priesthood of the Bow. But the shields of these two gods [the twin War Gods] were supposed to have been spun from the clouds, which, supporting the sky-ocean, that in turn supported the sky-world as this world is believed to be supported by under waters and clouds, were hence possessed of the power of floating—upward when turned up, downward when reversed." This refers to the War Gods covering their heads with their cord shields when descending into the under-world.

[b] P. 337, 376, New York, 1901.

magical implement, led the writer, however, to reconsider the probable
identity of this object, with the resulting conclusion that it was never
used as a means of physical defense; that it was, in fact, an adaptation

Fig. 546.

Fig. 547.                          Fig. 548.

FIG. 546.   Netted shield, bow, and arrows attached to plume offering; diameter of shield, 2⅞
    inches; Zuñi Indians, Zuñi, New Mexico; cat. no. 22678, Free Museum of Science and Art,
    University of Pennsylvania.
FIG. 547.   Plume offering; length, 21 inches; Zuñi Indians, Zuñi, New Mexico; cat. no. 22678,
    Free Museum of Science and Art, University of Pennsylvania.
FIG. 548.   Baho stand with netted shield; length, 5¼ inches; Hopi Indians, Oraibi, Arizona; cat.
    no. 38790, Free Museum of Science and Art, University of Pennsylvania.

of the magical spider web spun by the Spider Woman, the mother of
the Twins, the symbol of her protection.   Bowls painted with a web
are not uncommon among the ancient fictile ware of the Hopi in Arizona, as shown in figures 544, 545, from Mishongnovi.   The net some-

times appears more or less regularly dotted with spots.[a]  Such figures I regard as representing the spider web with the dew upon it.  The "water shield" of Ahaiyuta, from which he shook the torrents, was suggested, no doubt, by dew on the web.

A miniature netted shield, with or without a tiny bow and arrows, is of frequent occurrence on objects employed in Zuñi ceremonials. Such a shield with arrows is represented in figure 546 on a plume offering secured by the writer in 1902 from the shrine of the War God on Corn mountain.  As described in the introduction, a similar netted shield is also seen associated with a male baho attached to each of the four baho stands (figure 548) placed upon the Hopi Powalawu altar [b] and the effigy of Pöokong, the lesser War God on the Oraibi snake altar, has a netted shield on his back.  Feather darts, precisely like those

Fig. 549.  Sacrificial feather darts from altar of War God; length, 18 inches; Zuñi Indians, Zuñi, New Mexico; cat. no. 22683, Free Museum of Science and Art, University of Pennsylvania.

used in connection with a ring of corn husk among the Hopi (figure 648), are sacrificed upon the altar of the Zuñi War God.  Figure 549 represents a set of four made for the writer in Zuñi in 1902, identical with those he saw upon the shrine on Corn mountain.  In the Hopi Oáqöl ceremony at Oraibi, the manas discharge corncob feather darts at a netted wheel,[c] and in the Oraibi Marau ceremony women shoot arrows in a similar way into a bundle of vines.[d]  Figure 552 repre-

[a] These two bowls were excavated from ancient Hopi graves, at Mishongnovi, by Mr Charles L. Owen, in 1900.  In one this web is inclosed in a broken circle of brown paint and divided into two segments by a median line of similar brown paint.  On one side there are eleven brown strokes in the first set of spaces nearest the center, and on the other nine red strokes in the corresponding spaces.

[b] Mr Voth states that this particular netted shield is asserted to represent simply a wheel (ngölla) and the feather with the wheel also serves as a protection against the destructive sand storms.  It is called hŭkuhtsi, sand storm shutter.  (The Oraibi Powamu Ceremony, p. 77, Chicago, 1901.)

[c] See H. R. Voth, The Oraibi Oáqöl Ceremony, p. 23 and 42, Chicago, 1903.  Mr Voth relates that on the fifth day of the Oáqöl ceremony, Masátoiniwa, the chief priest, held a netted wheel, about 12 inches in diameter, of the same pattern as the wheels used on the last day by the two Oáqöl manas [figure 550], consisting of a wooden ring, about three-quarters of an inch thick, which was filled with a network of small meshes.  This is called báchaiyanpi, water sieve, because the cloud deities have such strainers through which they sift or drop the rain.

[d] Doctor Fewkes, in describing this ceremony at Walpi, says a "small package of cornhusks."  The two women who shoot the package are called Waühitaka, and their act of shooting is said to typify lightning striking in the cornfield, an event which is regarded as the acme of fertilization.  (Hopi Basket Dances.  Journal of American Folk-Lore, v. 12, p. 91, 1899.)

sents four Marau arrows, Marau hohohu, in the Free Museum of Science and Art of the University of Pennsylvania (cat no. 38810). They are made of reed, 18¼ to 21 inches in length, with wooden points; the feathers are obtained from the wing of the golden eagle. These arrows are described by the collector, Rev. H. R. Voth, as follows:

These arrows are made in the kiva on the 8th day of the Marau ceremony by a man belonging to the Pakat (Reed) clan. In the public ceremony, on the ninth day, they are used by two of the Marau takas, who act as archers in the plaza. The arrows are shot into the bundle, consisting of squash, melon, bean, cotton,

FIG. 550. Netted hoops and feather darts used by the Oáqöl manas; Hopi Indians, Oraibi, Arizona; from H. R. Voth.

and other vines. At the close of the ceremony they are deposited in a shrine north of the village, in which four old stone Pöokong fetiches are sitting on projecting rocks.

Again, in the Lalakonti ceremony, as witnessed by the writer at Walpi in the summer of 1901, the Lakone mana threw feather darts, made of ears of corn, into cloud symbols which the priest, or Lakone taka, traced with meal upon the ground.[a]

---

[a] See Dr J. Walter Fewkes, Hopi Basket Dances. Journal of American Folk-Lore, v. 12, p. 81, 1899. Doctor Fewkes describes corncobs, instead of ears of corn, stuck with eagle feathers as used in the Lalakonti ceremony at Walpi in 1898. He witnessed also the ceremony at Oraibi, mentioning corncobs as used there, and the one at Shipaulovi, where two halves of corncobs were employed.

Similar ceremonies or games were practised by the cliff-dwellers, as is attested by a number of objects from Mancos canyon, Colorado, in the Free Museum of Science and Art of the University of Pennsylvania. Figure 553 represents a corncob shuttlecock stuck with a grouse feather; figure 554 a feather dart, with a hard-wood point to which a hawk feather is secured by a wrapping of yucca fiber; and figure 555 a ball of coarse yucca stems, the latter identified by Mr Cushing as used in the " arrow-spearing game," all from this locality.

FIG. 551.  Oáqöl manas throwing darts into netted hoops; Hopi Indians, Oraibi, Arizona; from H. R. Voth.

The use of the miniature netted shield as a protective amulet is widely distributed. J. G. Kohl[a] describes a wooden ring over which thongs are drawn as a cradle amulet among the Chippewa at Apostle islands, Wisconsin, and an actual cradle charm from the Chippewa, exhibited in the Columbian Exposition at Chicago, was practically identical with the miniature netted shields of the Zuñi and the Hopi. The Hupa employ a similar charm (figure 556) on

[a] Kitchi-Gami, Wanderings round Lake Superior, p. 8, London, 1860.

their wicker cradles, a small hexagonal object made by twisting white and black straw around three sticks placed crosswise, with ends equidistant. Netted shields are also common among the amulets

FIG. 552. Marau arrows; length, 18¼ to 21 inches; Hopi Indians, Oraibi, Arizona; cat. no. 38810, Free Museum of Science and Art, University of Pennsylvania.

FIG. 553. Corncob feather dart; length, 7¼ inches; cliff-dwelling, Mancos canyon, Colorado; Free Museum of Science and Art, University of Pennsylvania.

FIG. 554. Feather dart; length, 10¼ inches; cliff-dwelling, Mancos canyon, Colorado; Free Museum of Science and Art, University of Pennsylvania.

and personal adornments of many of the Plains tribes. Figure 557 represents a hair ornament collected by Rev. H. R. Voth from the Cheyenne of Oklahoma, in the United States National Museum (cat.

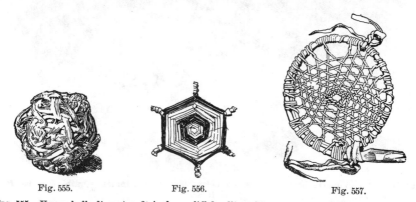

Fig. 555.               Fig. 556.                    Fig. 557.

FIG. 555. Yucca ball; diameter, 2½ inches; cliff-dwelling, Mancos canyon, Colorado; Free Museum of Science and Art, University of Pennsylvania.

FIG. 556. Cradle charm; diameter, 3 inches; Hupa Indians, Hupa valley, California; cat. no. 37166, Free Museum of Science and Art, University of Pennsylvania.

FIG. 557. Hair ornament (netted hoop); diameter, 4 inches; Cheyenne Indians, Oklahoma; cat. no. 165859, United States National Museum.

no. 165859), and figure 558 a similar object from the Crows of Montana, in the Free Museum of Science and Art of the University of Pennsylvania (cat. no. 38505). The latter has a flint arrowhead and a long down feather attached to the face of the net. Of two similar charms from the Grosventres (Algonquian) of Fort Belknap, Montana, in the Field Columbian Museum (cat. no. 60337, 60334), one is netted (figure 559), while the other is a simple hoop (figure 560) with buckskin thongs crossing at right angles. These are described by Doctor Dorsey, the collector, as hachieb, formerly much worn on the head and hair as a protection against dangers of various sorts. Analogous hoops are attached to two "medicine cords" (figures 561, 562) from the Chiricahua Apache, figured by Capt. John G. Bourke.[a]

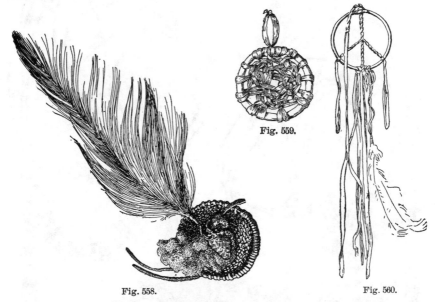

Fig. 559.

Fig. 558.　　　　　　　　　　　　　　　　　　　Fig. 560.

FIG. 558. Hair ornament (netted hoop); diameter, 2¼ inches; Crow Indians, Montana; cat. no. 38505, Free Museum of Science and Art, University of Pennsylvania.
FIG. 559. Protective amulet (netted hoop); diameter, 2¼ inches; Grosventre Indians, Montana; cat. no. 60337, Field Columbian Museum.
FIG. 560. Protective amulet (hoop); diameter, 2 inches; Grosventre Indians, Montana; cat. no. 60334, Field Columbian Museum.

Small rings of twisted grass are used as amulets by the Navaho, as illustrated by specimens collected by Dr Edward Palmer (figure 563 a, b), in the United States National Museum (cat. no. 9539). Similar illustrations of netted hoops and related rings might be multiplied almost indefinitely, and specimens may be found in every considerable collection of modern Indian ceremonial costume. From a suggestion made by Mr Louis L. Meeker, some, if not all, of these objects may be identified with gaming rings. He writes that the Cheyenne in Oklahoma use a hair ornament, consisting of a small ring, which

---
[a] The Medicine Man of the Apache. Ninth Annual Report of the Bureau of Ethnology, p. 551, 1892.

they wear as a token of prowess in a game called hohtsin, in which a rolling target, consisting of a netted wheel, is used. Later he transmitted to the writer from the Oglala of Pine Ridge reservation, South Dakota, such a hair ornament, tahosmu, which the Indians of this tribe wear as a token of prowess in the elk game, kaga woskate. It consists of a ring of bent twig (figure 564), 2¼ inches in diameter, wrapped with colored porcupine quills, with an internal cross, and thongs for fastening.[a]

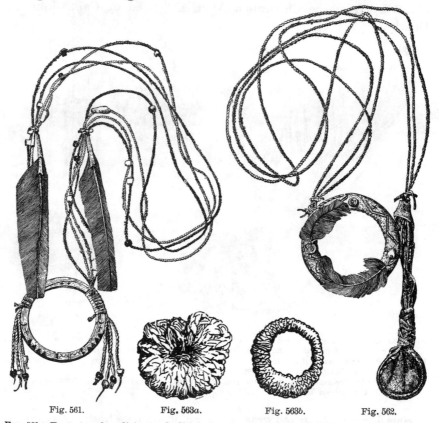

Fig. 561.          Fig. 563a.          Fig. 563b.          Fig. 562.

FIG. 561.   Four-strand medicine cord; Chiricahua Apache Indians, Arizona; from Bourke.
FIG. 562.   Three-strand medicine cord; Chiricahua Apache Indians, Arizona; from Bourke.
FIG. 563a, b.   Amulets of scented grass; diameters, 1¼ and 1½ inches; Navaho Indians, New Mexico; cat. no. 9539, United States National Museum.

An examination of two similar hair ornaments collected by the writer in 1900 from the Arapaho of the Wind River reservation, Wyoming, reveals the fact that they are miniature gaming hoops, one (figure 565: cat no. 37003, Free Museum of Science and Art of the

---

[a] Mr Charles L. Owen informs the writer that the miniature gaming hoops in the Field Columbian Museum, collected by him from the White Mountain Apache in Arizona in 1904, were worn by men who played the pole game, as amulets to secure success in that game.

University of Pennsylvania) a simple hoop with notches, like that
used by the Oglala and Yankton Dakota, and the other (figure 566;

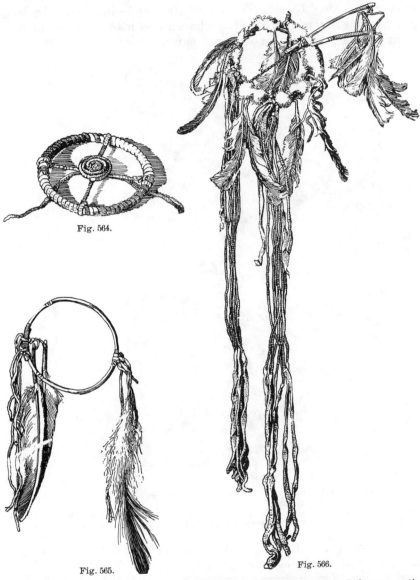

Fig. 564.

Fig. 565.

Fig. 566.

FIG. 564.  Hair ornament; diameter, 2¼ inches; Oglala Dakota Indians, Pine Ridge reservation,
South Dakota; cat. no. 21942, Free Museum of Science and Art, University of Pennsylvania.
FIG. 565.  Hair ornament; diameter, 4½ inches; Arapaho Indians, Wind River reservation, Wyo-
ming; cat. no. 37003, Free Museum of Science and Art, University of Pennsylvania.
FIG. 566.  Hair ornament; diameter, 3 inches; Arapaho Indians, Wind River reservation, Wyo-
ming; cat. no. 37004, Free Museum of Science and Art, University of Pennsylvania.

cat. no. 37004) with a median cord, like the gaming hoop of the
Apache, and having the two darts secured on the rim.

The ring and feather dart, the netted hoop, and the large buckskin ring constantly recur in the masks used in the Hopi and Zuñi ceremonials. The nose and mouth of the Hopi Hehea uncle katcina (figure 567) may be regarded as the dart and ring,[a] and the large painted rings which surround the base of so many masks are to be identified with the leather-wrapped gaming hoop.

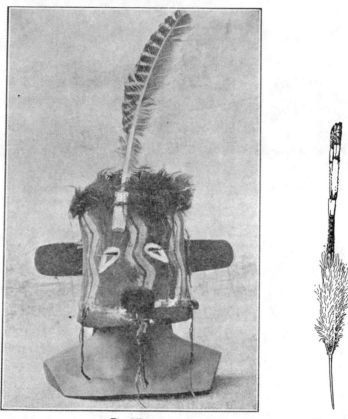

Fig. 567.                                    Fig. 568.

FIG. 567. Mask of Hehea tahaamu, or Hehea uncle katcina; Hopi Indians, Arizona; cat. no. 66452, Field Columbian Museum.
FIG. 568. Deerskin plume worn with head ring; length, 18 inches: Hupa Indians, Hupa valley, California; cat. no. 37213, Free Museum of Science and Art, University of Pennsylvania.

We discover a similar object in the heavy ring covered with buckskin and red woodpecker crests, worn on the head by the Hupa

---

[a] It is not an unreasonable conclusion that the corn-husk rings which supply the place of mouths on other masks, as, for example, the Qötca mana (cat. no. 56288, Field Columbian Museum), are also gaming rings. Again, the ring of network forming part of the Hopi ceremonial head tablet (cat. no. 16993, Field Columbian Museum) may be identified with the netted wheel, and the checkered bands at the base of the Hopi face masks, such as that of the Ana katcina (cat. no. 66286, Field Columbian Museum), with the simple ring which exists entire at the base of the other Zuñi and Hopi masks.

(Athapascan) in northern California. Its derivation from the gaming ring is further borne out by the two long plumes, covered with white deerskin and woodpecker crests, on wooden fore shafts (figure 568) that are stuck on either side in front of the ring.

The Flute priests at Oraibi wear a headdress consisting of a cornhusk ring (figure 569), pierced with two wooden darts, baho, and with four pins, on the ends of which are fastened four gaming cups of four colors.[a]

FIG. 569.  Flute priest's headdress; Hopi Indians, Oraibi, Arizona; cat. no. 65789, Field Columbian Museum.

Before returning to the final discussion of the significance of the hoop-and-pole game, let us consider some of the ceremonial uses of rings analogous to the gaming ring. One of the most notable is the conjurer's hoop (figure 570) of the Oglala Dakota. A specimen in the Free Museum of Science and Art of the University of Pennsylvania (cat. no. 22241) consists of a hoop, cangleska, "spotted wood," made of

[a] Worn at the fall ceremony of the Flute society. The cup-shaped objects symbolize blossoming, hence the headdress is sometimes called lansi, "flute blossoms." This headdress is worn also by the Flute katcina and by a few others.

24 ETH—05 M——28

a peeled branch about half an inch in diameter, tied with sinew, to form a ring 10 inches in diameter, and painted in four segments—yellow, red, blue, and black. It is accompanied with four sticks, 11½ inches in length, painted like the hoop, one yellow, one red, one blue, and one black. A small calico bag, painted to correspond with the stick and containing tobacco, is tied at the blunt end of each stick. These objects were made for the donor, Mr Louis L. Meeker, by Cangleska Luta, or Red Hoop, an Indian or mixed Cheyenne and Kiuksa Oglala parentage. I append Mr Meeker's [a] account:

According to Indian belief the hoop represents the ecliptic, or zodiac, or, as the Indian would say, the circle of day and night. The yellow segment represents the part between the eastern horizon and the zenith, over which the sun seems to pass between sunrise and noon. The red segment represents the part between the western horizon and the zenith, over which the sun seems to pass from noon to sunset. The blue represents the part from the western horizon to the nadir, the supposed course of the sun from sunset to midnight. The black represents the part from the nadir to the horizon, the supposed path of the sun from midnight to sunrise. The colors ordinarily used are yellow, from the juice of the prickly poppy; red, from blood or red clay; blue, from blue earth; and black, from charcoal. Each color represents a quarter of the globe, or, as an Indian would say, the colors denote the places of the four winds. If the hoop is set up perpendicularly, with the juncture of the red and yellow above, the former to the west and the latter to the east on the plane of the ecliptic, each color will be in its proper position, as above described. If the hoop is laid upon the ground in a horizontal position, with the juncture of the yellow and red to the north, it will give each of the four winds its proper color—from north to east will be yellow; east to south, black; south to west, blue; and west to north, red.

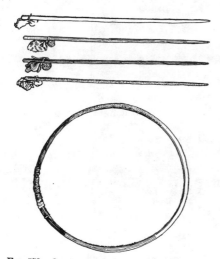

FIG. 570. Conjurer's hoop and sticks; diameter of hoop, 10 inches; Oglala Dakota Indians, South Dakota; cat. no. 22241, Free Museum of Science and Art, University of Pennsylvania.

Each stick belongs to one of the four winds, as indicated by its color. In case of sickness, the hoop, sticks, and tobacco borne by the sticks are offered in the following manner to secure recovery: The hoop is laid in the center of the lodge or on the ground in the position described above. The performer takes each stick and sets it upon its color on the hoop, point down, at the same time chanting the syllables he and e, he e, she, and e e, with or without improvised words of his own, relating to morning or forenoon, hanhanna; dawn, anpao; noon, wicokala; evening, htayetu; midnight, hancokaya; and tate, wind, with or without the name of the color of the stick—zi, yellow; sa, red; to, blue; and sapa, black.

[a] Bulletin of the Free Museum of Science and Art, v. 3, p. 252, Philadelphia, 1902.

*Chant*

Hi ya ye, hi ye ye, hi ya ye, ya-hi ye ye.
Hi ya ye, hi ye ye, hi ya ye, ya-hi ye ye.

Hi ya ya, hi ye ye, hi ya ye, ya-hi ye ye.
Hi ya ya, hi ye ye, hi ya ye, ya-hi ye ye.

*Improvisation*

Ta te zi, hi ya ye, ta te sa, ya-hi ye ye.
Ta te to, hi ye ya, ya hi ye, ta-te sa pa.

An pa o, hi ya ya, han han na, wi-co ka la.
Hta ye tu, hi ya ya, ya hi ya, han-co ka ya.

Both chorus and improvisation are repeated and continued at pleasure. The scale is in a minor key and the chant rises and falls, beginning low, becoming higher, and again low. The pupils in the schools say the syllables hi ya ye and hi ye ye are correctly rendered in English by the kindergarten chorus, " Hence this way, hence that way." I believe, however, that " Hence this one, hence that one " is more nearly correct, if, indeed, they have any meaning. Most Indians say they have none.

Two of the sticks laid across the hoop are from north to south; the others from east to west. A light-colored stick is laid from north to south, and a dark-colored one from east to west, either red and black, or yellow and blue. If red and blue are used, and recovery does not take place, red and black will be used when the ceremony is repeated. The other two sticks are held in the hand of the performer, who continues to chant he and e with variations until well-nigh exhausted. The hoop and sticks are then carried away and left on some hill as far away from all forms of animal life as possible.

According to their explanations, the Indians believe the four winds carry incense to the four powers of the universe. The efficacy of the rite is supposed to depend upon the mysterious power of the performer, the weirdness and length of the chant, and the height and solitude of the place where the offering is left. Remains of these hoops may be found on the tops of remote and lonely hills in every Indian community where I have been stationed.

The account here given describes the most common use of the hoop. I have learned that it is used in many ceremonies by the medicine men. In July last I saw one of the hoops and supposed it was used in a game. Evasive answers were given to my inquiries, but there was a young man on his death-bed, and month after month many hoops were required. In order to obtain coloring matter for them it was at last admitted that the hoops were for the benefit of the invalid, and I at last saw the performance, which took place at night. The Indians are unwilling to tell their customs, partly because the medicine men do not approve, and partly because they do not care to have their sacred customs made the object of ridicule.

The Navaho make rings which Col. James Stevenson refers to as gaming rings (figure 571), on the first day of the ceremony commonly called Yebitchai, performed as a healing rite for a member of the tribe. He gives the following account [a] of a performance which he witnessed in October, 1888, at Keams canyon, Arizona:

---

[a] Ceremonial of Hasjelti Dailjis and Mythical Sand Painting of the Navajo Indians. Eighth Annual Report of the Bureau of Ethnology, p. 237, 1891.

During the afternoon of the 12th those who were to take part in the ceremonial received orders and instructions from the song priest. One man went to collect twigs, with which to make twelve rings, each 6 inches in diameter. These rings represented gaming rings, which are not only used by the Navajo, but are thought highly of by the genii of the rocks. [Figure 571.] Another man gathered willows with which to make the emblem of the concentration of the four winds.

The square was made by dressed willows crossed and left projecting at the corners each 1 inch beyond the next. The corners were tied together with white cotton cord, and each corner was ornamented with the under tail feather of the eagle. These articles were laid in a niche behind the theurgist, whose permanent seat was on the west side of the lodge facing east. The night ceremony commenced shortly after dark. All those who were to participate were immediate friends and relatives of the invalid, excepting the theurgist or song priest, he being the only one who received direct compensation for his professional services. The cost of such a ceremony is no inconsiderable item. Not only the exorbitant fee of the theurgist must be paid, but the entire assemblage must be fed during the nine days' ceremonial at the expense of the invalid, assisted by his near relatives.

A bright fire burned in the lodge, and shortly after dark the invalid appeared, and sat upon a blanket, which was placed in front of the song priest. Previously, however, three men had prepared themselves to personate the gods—Hasjelti, Hostjoghon, and Hostjobokon—and one to personate the goddess, Hostjoboard. They left the lodge carrying their masks in their hands, went a short distance away, and put on their masks. Then Hasjelti and Hostjoghon returned to the lodge, and Hasjelti, amid hoots, "hu-hoo-hu-huh!" placed the square which he carried, over the invalid's head, and Hostjoghon shook two eagle wands, one in each hand, on each side of the invalid's head and body, then over his head, mean-

FIG. 571. Gaming ring used in the ceremony called Yebitchai; Navaho Indians, Arizona; from James Stevenson.

while hooting in his peculiar way, " hu-u-u-u-uh ! " He then followed Hasjelti out of the lodge. The men representing Hostjobokon and Hostjoboard came in alternately. Hostjobokon took one of the rings, which had been made during the afternoon, and now lay upon the blanket to the right of the invalid, and placed it against the soles of the feet of the invalid, who was sitting with knees drawn up, and then against his knees, palms, breast, each scapula, and top of his head ; then over his mouth. While touching the different parts of the body the ring was held with both hands, but when placed to the mouth of the invalid it was taken in the left hand. The ring was made of a reed, the ends of which were secured by a long string wrapped over the ring like a slip noose. When the ring was placed over the mouth of the invalid the string was pulled, and the ring dropped and rolled out of the lodge, the long tail of white cotton yarn, with eagle plume attached to the end, extending far behind. Hostjoboard repeated this ceremony with a second ring, and so did Hostjobokon and Hostjoboard alternately, until the twelve rings were disposed of. Three of the rings were afterward taken to the east, three to the south, three to the west, and three to the north, and deposited at the base of piñon trees. The rings were placed over the invalid's mouth to give him strength, cause him to talk with one tongue, and to have a good mind and heart. The other portions of the body were touched with them for physical benefit. When the rings had all been rolled out of the lodge Hasjelti entered, followed by Hostjoghon.  He passed the square (the concentrated winds) four times over the head of the invalid during his

hoots.  Hostjoghon then waved his turkey wands about the head and body of the invalid, and the first day's ceremony was at an end.

A stone ring from the Cheyenne of Oklahoma, in the United States National Museum (cat. no. 166029) is described by the collector, Rev. H. R. Voth, as a medicine wheel (figure 572).  It consists of a flat ring of limestone, 4½ inches in diameter, painted red, and inscribed with deep grooves, simulating wrappings, extending around it.  On the face are engraved a star and opposite to it a moon.  This ring serves to illustrate the transformation of the cloth- or buckskin-wrapped ring into one of stone.

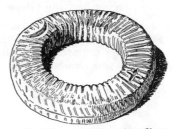

FIG. 572.  Stone medicine ring; diameter, 4½ inches; Cheyenne Indians, Oklahoma; cat. no. 166029, United States National Museum.

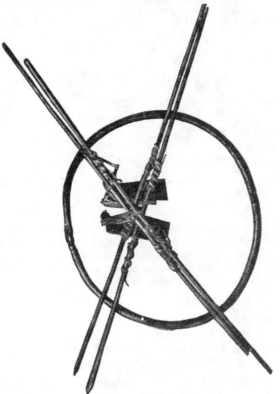

FIG. 573.  Gaming wheel and sticks used in Ghost dance; Dakota Indians, South Dakota; from Mooney.

Actual practical game rings are used ceremonially at the present day.  The writer saw a practical netted hoop worn on the back of a Yanktonai Dakota at a grass dance at Fort Peck, Montana, in the summer of 1890.   Mr James Mooney [a] also relates several instances in his account of the Ghost dance among the Sioux.

At a Ghost dance at No Water's camp, near Pine Ridge  .  .  .   four arrows, headed with bone in the olden fashion, were shot up into the air from the center of the circle and afterward gathered up and hung upon the tree, together with the bow, a gaming wheel and sticks [figure 573], and a staff of peculiar shape.

FIG. 574.   Arapaho Sun Dance altar with wheel, Oklahoma; from Dorsey.

Elsewhere [b] he says:

In the Ghost dance at Rosebud and Pine Ridge, as usually performed, a young woman stood in the center of the circle, holding out a pipe toward the messiah in the west, and remained thus throughout the dance.   Another young woman usually stood beside her holding out a bäqati wheel  .  .  .   in the same way. This feature of the dance is said to have been introduced by Short Bull.

Mr Mooney [c] states further:

It is said that the medicine man of Big Foot's band carried such a hoop with him in their flight from the north, and displayed it at every dance held by the band until the fatal day of Wounded Knee.  .  .  .   To the Indian it symbolizes the revival of the old-time games.

The ring, or wheel, plays a very considerable part in the ceremony of the Sun dance among the Plains tribes.   Dr George A. Dorsey [d]

[a] The Ghost-dance Religion.   Fourteenth Annual Report of the Bureau of Ethnology, p. 915, 1896.
[b] Ibid., p. 1064.   [c] Ibid., p. 1075.   [d] The Arapaho Sun Dance, p. 12, Chicago, 1903.

describes it as the object esteemed next after the great tribal medicine, the flat pipe, among the northern Arapaho. The wheel used by them in their Sun dance is described by him as follows:

The object (hehotti) is about 18 inches in diameter [figure 574]. It is made of a rectangular piece of wood, one end of which tapers like the tail of a serpent, the other being rudely fashioned to represent a serpent's head. Near the head of the serpent are several wrappings of blue beads, which have replaced small red berries which formerly occupied this place. At four opposite sides of the wheel are incised designs, two of them being in the form of crosses, the other two resembling the conventionalized Thunderbird. These designs are similar to those found on gaming wheels, used by Arapaho and other Plains tribes. Attached by means of short buckskin thongs are also four complete sets of the tail feathers of an eagle. The spacing of these feathers is not now uniform, but, according to Háwkan, they should have been grouped in equal numbers near the four incised markings on the wheel. As an eagle tail has 12 feathers, there would thus be, in all, 48 feathers on the wheel. At times, however, the wheel does not possess such a large number of eagle tail feathers, but a single tail is divided into four, and there are thus three feathers for each marking. . . . The feathers on the wheel at the present time number 24, there being thus two eagle tails represented, with six feathers to each marking. The inside of the wheel is painted red, while the outer periphery is stained black.

Referring to the symbolism of the wheel, Doctor Dorsey says:

According to Háwkan and one or two other authorities, the disk itself represents the sun, while the actual band of wood represents a tiny water-snake, called henigĕ, and which is said to be found in rivers, in lakes, near ponds, and in buffalo wallows. Later in the ceremony, this lake or pool of sweet water is represented, while near by on a forked stick, is the owner of the pool, a little bird. . . . This serpent is said to be the most harmless of all snakes. The wheel thus, representing this snake, has a derived meaning, and represents the water which surrounds the earth. The additional idea was also put forth that while the wheel represents a harmless snake, all snakes are powerful to charm, and hence the wheel is a sign of gentleness and meekness. The blue beads around the neck of the snake represent the sky or the heavens, which are clean and without blemish; the color blue among the Arapaho is also typical of friendship. The four inside markings (hítanni) on the wheel represent the Four-Old-Men who are frequently addressed during the ceremony, and who stand watching and guarding the inhabitants of this world. The Four-Old-Men may also be called the gods of the four world quarters and to them the Sun Dance priest often makes supplication that they may live to a great age. The Four-Old-Men are also spoken of as the Thunderbird, having power to watch the inhabitants, and in their keeping is the direction of the winds of the earth. They therefore represent the living element of all people. If the wind blows from the north, it is said to come from the Old-Man-of-the-North, who controls the wind of that end or quarter of the world. Another priest states more definitely that the Four-Old-Men are Summer, Winter, Day, and Night, who though they travel in single file, yet are considered as occupying the four cardinal points. Thus, according to direction and the Arapaho color scheme, Day and Summer are the Southeast and Southwest, respectively, and are black in color, while Winter and Night are the Northwest and Northeast, respectively, and are red in color. Inasmuch as Sun is regarded as the grandfather of the Four-Old-Men, it is more than likely that the wheel may be regarded as the emblem of the

Sun.  The Four-Old-Men are considered as ever- resent, ever-watching sentinels, always alert to guard the people from harn and injury.  The same word, hîtanni, is also applied to certain markings ,sed in the Old-Woman's lodge, the meaning of which is given variously as tl e four elements of life, the four courses, the four divides.  Thus it is said the when one traveling the trail of life gets over the fourth divide he has reached the winter of old age.  The Morning Star is the messenger of the Four-Old-Men, as are also the young men during ceremonies.

The four clusters of feathers also represent the Four-Old-Men.  The feathers collectively represent the Thunderbird, which gives rain, and they therefore represent a prayer for rain, consequently for vegetation. . . .   The wheel, as a whole, then, may be said to be symbolic of the creation of the world, for it represents the sun, earth, the sky, the water, and the wind.  In the great Sun Dance dramatization the wheel itself is represented in the person of the grandfather of the Lodge-Maker, or the "Transferer" as he is called..

In the course of the same paper Doctor Dorsey tells how the wheel is wrapped in calico and buckskin and suspended on a pole or tripod at the back of the lodge of the owner or keeper.  It is his duty to preserve the wheel inviolably sacred.  The wheel under certain circumstances may be unwrapped by the keeper.  This is usually done at the instance of some individual who has made a vow.  A new wrapper must be furnished by the person making the vow; hence the term "wrap the wheel" applied to the ceremony.  A detailed account is given of this performance.  Stories are told of the miraculous movements of the wheel.  On one occasion it was seen flying, and changed into an eagle.[a]

The wheel was first kept in the Rabbit tipi.[b]  On the second day of the ceremony the wheel was carried into the sweat lodge and placed to the west of the fireplace, the head of the snake facing the east.[c]  Later it was carried back to the Rabbit tipi.[d]  Here it was placed on its support, a small willow stick, sharpened at one end and split at the other to form a crotch.[e]  While it was in the Rabbit tipi a healing ceremony was performed by its aid.[f]  On the fifth day it was placed on its support behind the buffalo skull on the sod altar (figure 574).[g]  Here, on the seventh day, it was held up to the center pole during the dance, and placed over the head of one of the chief participants.[h]  In the origin myth of the wheel [i] the maker of the original is said to have painted it and placed the Four-Old-Men at the cardinal points.  Not only were these Old-Men located upon the wheel, but also the morning star (cross); a collection of stars sitting together, perhaps the Pleiades; the evening star (Lone Star); chain of stars (seven buffalo bulls); five stars called a "hand," and a chain of stars which is the lance; a circular group of seven stars overhead, called the "old camp;" the sun, moon, and Milky Way.

[a] The Arapaho Sun Dance, p. 21, Chicago, 1903.   [d] Ibid., p. 49.   [g] Ibid., p. 122.
[b] Ibid., p. 38.                                  [e] Ibid., p. 68.   [h] Ibid., p. 142.
[c] Ibid, p. 47.                                   [f] Ibid., p. 87.   [i] Ibid., p. 205.

Taking into consideration all the above facts concerning the hoop or ring, the writer regards the gaming hoop as referable to the netted hoop, which in turn may be regarded as the net shield of the twin War Gods. This object, which the Twins derived from their grandmother, the Spider Woman, is naturally employed, with or without the bows or darts, as a protective amulet. The hoop or ring stands as the feminine symbol, as opposed to the dart or arrows, which are masculine. The implements of the game together represent the shield and the bows or darts of the War Gods.

ALGONQUIAN STOCK

ARAPAHO. Wind River reservation, Wyoming. (Free Museum of Science and Art, University of Pennsylvania.)

Cat. no. 36927. Hoop of sapling (figure 575), 10 inches in diameter,

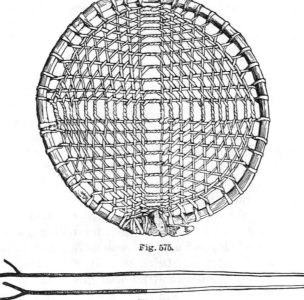

Fig. 575.

Fig. 576.

FIG. 575. Netted hoop; diameter, 10 inches; Arapaho Indians, Wyoming; cat. no. 36927, Free Museum of Science and Art, University of Pennsylvania.

FIG. 576. Darts for netted hoop; length, 42 inches; Arapaho Indians, Wyoming; cat. no. 36973, Free Museum of Science and Art, University of Pennsylvania.

covered with a network of rawhide, which passes over the edge of the hoop forty-five times. The hoop has been painted blue; an old specimen.

Cat. no. 36973. Darts (four), consisting of willow saplings (figure 576) forked at the end; length, about 42 inches.

Collected by the writer in 1900.

ARAPAHO.   Cheyenne and Arapaho reservation, Oklahoma.

Mr James Mooney [a] describes the game of the bäqati, wheel, among the Arapaho, which, he says, " was practically obsolete among the Prairie tribes, but which is being revived since the advent of the Ghost dance.  As it was a favorite game with the men in the olden times, a great many of the songs founded on these trance visions refer to it, and the wheel and sticks are made by the dreamer and carried in the dance as they sing."

The game is played with a wheel (bä′qati, large wheel) and two pairs of throwing-sticks (qa′qa-u′nûtha).  The Cheyenne call the wheel ä′ko′yo or äkwi′u, and the sticks hoo′isi′yonots.  It is a man's game, and there are three players, one rolling the wheel, while the other two, each armed with a pair of throwing sticks, run after it and throw the sticks so as to cross the wheel in a certain position. The two throwers are the contestants, the one who rolls the wheel being merely an assistant.  Like most Indian games, it is a means of gambling, and high stakes are sometimes wagered on the result.  It is common to the Arapaho, Cheyenne, Sioux, and probably to all the northern Prairie tribes, but is not found among the Kiowa or the Comanche in the south.

The wheel is about 18 inches in diameter, and consists of a flexible young tree branch, stripped of its bark and painted, with the two ends fastened together with sinew or buckskin string.  At equal distances around the circumference of the wheel are cut four figures, the two opposite each other constituting a pair, but distinguished by different colors, usually blue or black and red, and by lines or notches on the face.  These figures are designated simply by their colors.  Figures of birds, crescents, etc., are sometimes also cut or painted upon the wheel, but have nothing to do with the game.

The sticks are light rods, about 30 inches long, tied in pairs by a peculiar arrangement of buckskin strings, and distinguished from one another by pieces of cloth of different colors fastened to the strings. There is also a pile of tally sticks, usually a hundred in number, about the size of lead pencils and painted green, for keeping count of the game.  The sticks are held near the center in a peculiar manner between the fingers of the closed hand.  When the wheel is rolled, each player runs from the same side, and endeavors to throw the sticks so as to strike the wheel in such a way that when it falls both sticks of his pair shall be either over or under a certain figure.  It requires dexterity to do this, as the string has a tendency to strike the wheel in such a way as to make one stick fall under and the other over, in which case the throw counts for nothing.  The players assign

[a] The Ghost-dance Religion.  Fourteenth Annual Report of the Bureau of Ethnology, p. 994, 1896.

their own value to each figure, the usual value being 5 points for one and 10 for the other figure, with double that number for a throw which crosses the two corresponding figures, and 100 tallies to the game.

The wheel-and-stick game, in some form or another, was almost universal among our Indian tribes. Another game among the Prairie tribes is played with a netted wheel and a single stick or arrow, the effort being to send the arrow through the netting as nearly as possible to the center or bull's-eye. This game is called ana'wati'n-hati, playing wheel, by the Arapaho.

In a myth entitled "Light-Stone," related by Dr George A. Dorsey,[a] the following wheel games are enumerated: Big wheel, running-wheel, and medicine-wheel.

In the story of "The White Crow," related by Dr A. L. Kroeber,[b] there is the following reference to the wheel game:

Close to the camp the people were playing with the sacred arrows and the sacred wheel. Two young men threw the wheel towards an obstacle and then followed it just as if they were running a race.

In Doctor Dorsey's[c] story, entitled "Found-in-Grass," are two twins, Spring-Boy and By-the-Door, who correspond with the twin War Gods. Spring-Boy is blown away by a terrific wind and is found by an old woman, who names him Found-in-Grass. He induces her to make him a bow and arrows and a netted wheel. She went out and cut a green stick and bent it into a ring, and also cut rawhide into small strips. From these articles she made a small netted wheel. One morning he gave his netted wheel to his grandmother and directed her to roll it toward him and say that a fat buffalo cow was running toward him. Sure enough there came running to him a red cow. This cow he shot with his arrows. The operation was repeated, resulting in his shooting a fat buffalo steer and a big fat bull; in this way a supply of meat was procured.

BLACKFEET. Blood reserve, Alberta. (Cat. no. 51641, Field Columbian Museum.)

Ring, 3 inches in diameter, covered with buckskin, painted red, with eight spokes attached inside the rim at equidistant points, four being spirals of brass wire and four alternate ones of beads. Of the latter, one consists of two beads, one red and one blue; another of three, two green and one brass; and the third, of three, one red, one blue, and one red; and the fourth of three red. Collected by Dr George A. Dorsey.

———— Montana. (Cat. no. 22768, Free Museum of Science and Art, University of Pennsylvania.)

Ring (figure 577), 2⅛ inches in diameter, wrapped with buckskin painted red, and having six interior spokes, three consisting

---

[a] Traditions of the Arapaho, p. 181, Chicago, 1903.    [b] Ibid., p. 275.    [c] Ibid., p. 364.

of two dark-blue glass beads with a bead of spiral brass wire next the center, and three consisting of pyramidal spirals of brass wire, two with red glass beads and one with a yellow glass bead next the center.

This specimen was collected in 1900 by Dr George A. Dorsey, who states that the game is played with two iron-pointed arrows shot from a bow toward the ring, the count being determined by the proximity of the arrow to the ring.

### BLACKFEET. Montana.

Dr George Bird Grinnell [a] says:

FIG. 577. Gaming ring; diameter, 2¼ inches; Blackfoot. Indians, Montana; cat. no. 22768, Free Museum of Science and Art, University of Pennsylvania.

A favorite pastime in the day was gambling with a small wheel called it-se'-wah. This wheel was about 4 inches in diameter, and had five spokes, on which were strung different-colored beads, made of bone or horn. A level, smooth piece of ground was selected, at each end of which was placed a log. At each end of the course were two men, who gambled against each other. A crowd always surrounded them, betting on the sides. The wheel was rolled along the course, and each man at the end whence it started, darted an arrow at it. The cast was made just before the wheel reached the log at the opposite end of the track, and points were counted according as the arrow passed between the spokes, or when the wheel, stopped by the log, was in contact with the arrow, the position and nearness of the different beads to the arrow representing a certain number of points. The player who first scored 10 points won. It was a very difficult game, and one had to be very skillful to win.

――――――― Southern Alberta.

Rev. John MacLean [b] describes the hoop-and-arrow game as follows:

A board, 8 or 10 inches in width, is placed on its edge upon the ground, held in place by small stakes driven into the ground; and another, in the same fashion, about 12 feet distant. The contestants play in pairs. Each holds in his right hand an arrow, and one of them a small wheel, having fastened to it a bead, or special mark placed upon it. Standing at one end and inside the board, they run together toward the other board. The contestant having the wheel rolls it on the ground, throwing it with such force that it strikes the board. As the two men run they throw their arrows against the board, and as near the wheel as they can. When the wheel falls, they measure the distance between the point of the arrows and the bead or special mark on the wheel, and the arrow which lies nearest to this point has won the throw. They continue this running and throwing until the one who has reached the number agreed upon as the end of the game has won. The number of points made by the contestants are kept by means of small sticks held in the hands. Several pairs of contestants sometimes play after each other, and for days they will continue the game, surrounded by a large number of men, old and young, who are eagerly betting upon the result.

[a] Blackfoot Lodge Tales, p. 183, New York, 1892.
[b] Canadian Savage Folk, p. 55, Toronto, 1896.

Cheyenne and Arapaho. Oklahoma. (Cat. no. 203789, United
States National Museum.)

Hoop (figure 578), 12 inches in diameter, laced with rawhide, the
leather passing forty-eight times around the edge. Half the net
on one side of the principal division is painted blue and the
other half red; the colors are reversed on the opposite side.
Collected by E. Granier.

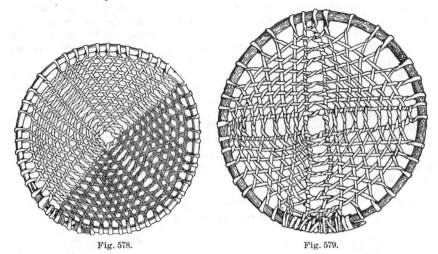

Fig. 578.　　　　　　　　　　　　　　Fig. 579.

Fig. 578. Netted hoop; diameter, 12 inches; Cheyenne and Arapaho Indians, Oklahoma; cat. no.
203789, United States National Museum.
Fig. 579. Netted hoop; diameter, 13¼ inches; Cheyenne Indians, Oklahoma; cat. no. 165845, United
States National Museum.

Cheyenne. Oklahoma. (Cat. no. 165845, United States National
Museum.)

Hoop, a bent sapling laced with a net of rawhide, as shown in figure
579; diameter, 13½ inches; the thong passes over the edge thirty-
six times. Collected by Rev. H. R. Voth.

Two other Cheyenne gaming hoops in the United States National
Museum (cat. no. 152814), diameters, 12 and 13 inches, collected by
Mr Mooney, appear to be models. The net is irregular, and does
not seem to be put on with the system and care that characterize the
old hoops.

——— Darlington, Oklahoma. (Cat. no. 18735, Free Museum of
Science and Art, University of Pennsylvania.)

Hoop, a bent sapling 7 inches in diameter, with a network of rawhide. A red down feather is attached to the hoop by a sinew.
Apparently a model. The netting, which is coarse, passes over
the hoop eighteen times. Collected by Mr George E. Starr.

——— Oklahoma.

Mr Louis L. Meeker thus describes the hoop game, ha-ko-yu-tsist:

The player holds a stick, and thrusts it through a wheel with four spokes, made of very light material, and so notched that different counts are made by thrusting in different places.

CHEYENNE.  Oklahoma.

Dr A. L. Kroeber [a] in his Cheyenne Tales gives the following account:

There was a large camp near a spring called Old-woman's spring. The people were amusing themselves by games, and were playing the "buffalo game" with rolling hoops. Two young men were standing by, watching. They were painted alike and dressed alike and wore the same headdresses, and both wore buffalo-robes. Finally one of them told the people to call every one and that all should watch him; that he would go into the spring, and bring back food that would be a great help to the people ever after. The other young man also said that he would bring them food. There was an entrance to the spring, formed by a great stone, and by this the two young men descended into the spring, both going at the same time. They found an old gray-headed woman sitting, and she showed them on one side fields of corn, and on the other herds of buffalo. Then one of the young men brought back corn, and the other buffalo meat, and the people feasted on both. And that night the buffalo came out of the spring; and there have been herds of them ever since, and corn has been grown too.

CHIPPEWA.  Turtle mountain, North Dakota.  (Cat. no. $\frac{50}{4731}$, American Museum of Natural History.)

FIG. 580.  Netted hoop and dart; diameter of hoop, 11¼ inches; length of dart, 36 inches; Chippewa Indians, Turtle mountain, North Dakota; cat. no. $\frac{50}{4731}$, American Museum of Natural History

Hoop (figure 580), 11¾ inches in diameter, netted with buckskin thongs, the thongs painted red, the edge of the hoop wrapped with black cloth, a square orifice in the center of the thongs wrapped with red cloth; accompanied by a straight dart made of a sapling 3 feet long, painted red, with a black band, and a feather tied to the handle end.

This specimen was collected in 1903 by Dr William Jones, who gives the name of the game as tititipanatuwanagi, rollers, and says that it is played by anyone.

DELAWARES.  Ontario.

Dr Daniel G. Brinton [b] gives the following account from conversations with Rev. Albert Seqaqkind Anthony:

[a] Journal of American Folk-Lore. v. 13, p. 163, Boston, 1900.
[b] Folk-lore of the Modern Lenape. Essays of an Americanist, p. 186, Philadelphia, 1890.

A very popular sport was with a hoop, tautmusq, and spear or arrow, allunth. The players arranged themselves in two parallel lines, some 40 feet apart, each one armed with a reed spear. A hoop was then rolled rapidly at an equal distance between the lines. Each player hurled his spear at it, the object being to stop the hoop by casting the spear within its rim. When stopped, the shaft must lie within the hoop, or the shot did not count.

GROSVENTRES.  Fort Belknap reservation, Montana.  (Cat. no. 60350, Field Columbian Museum.)

Hoop (figure 581), a bent sapling 10 inches in diameter, netted with hide, which passes over the ring thirty-four times.

Collected in 1900 by Dr George A. Dorsey, who describes it as employed in the game of hatchieb.

In playing, the wheel is rolled forward on the ground, when the players hurl toward it slender spears, or darts, the object being to

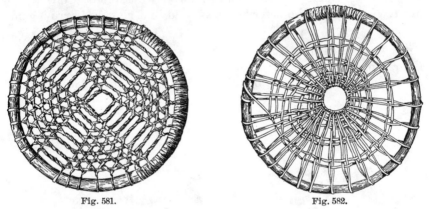

Fig. 581.                                        Fig. 582.

FIG. 581. Netted hoop; diameter, 10 inches; Grosventre Indians, Montana; cat. no. 60350, Field Columbian Museum.
FIG. 582. Netted hoop; diameter, 16½ inches; Piegan Indians, Alberta; cat. no. 69353, Field Columbian Museum.

pierce one of the holes formed by the buckskin lacing of the wheel. These holes vary in size, and each has its own proper name and value; the latter, however, could not be learned. The holes are named as follows: Large hole in center, ita, or heart; holes inclosed within the parallel lines crossing at right angles, anatayan, or buffalo bulls; large holes outside the parallel lines, behe, or buffalo cows; small triangles formed at points of cross lacing, wuuha, or buffalo calves; large holes next to the wooden ring, chadjitha, or wolves; small holes formed by the crossing of the thongs next to the wooden ring, caawu, or coyotes.

This game is played by men and formerly stakes of much value were wagered on the result.

PIEGAN.  Alberta.  (Cat. no. 69353, Field Columbian Museum.)

Hoop of cherry sapling (figure 582), 16½ inches in diameter, laced with a network of rawhide, which passes around the edge twenty-eight times.  Collected by Mr R. N. Wilson.  In another similar specimen in the same museum, cat. no. 69352, the thong passes thirty times around the edge.

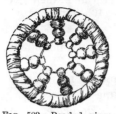

PIEGAN.  Alberta.  (Cat. no. 64350, Field Columbian Museum.)

Iron ring (figure 583), $3\frac{1}{8}$ inches in diameter, wrapped with buckskin and having eight rows of colored glass beads of three each, arranged within, like the spokes of a wheel. The beads are of different colors, as follows: Three white; three red; two black and one dark blue; two green and one black; three yellow; three light blue; two black and one red; two green and one blue.  Collected by Mr R. N. Wilson, who describes it as used in a ring-and-arrow game.

FIG. 583.  Beaded ring; diameter, $3\frac{1}{8}$ inches; Piegan Indians, Alberta; cat. no. 64350, Field Columbian Museum.

SAUK AND FOXES.  Iowa.   (Cat. no. $\frac{50}{3504}$, American Museum of Natural History.)

Four rings of elm bark (figure 584), 2, $2\frac{1}{2}$, 3, and $3\frac{1}{2}$ inches in diameter, and a little bundle of elm bark (figure 585), 3 inches

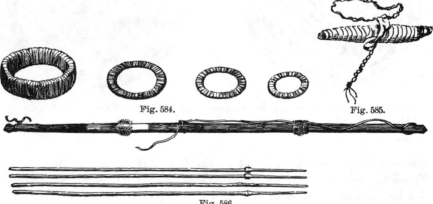

Fig. 584.

Fig. 585.

Fig. 586.

FIG. 584.  Game rings; diameters, $3\frac{1}{2}$, 3, $2\frac{1}{2}$, and 2 inches; Sauk and Fox Indians, Iowa; cat. no. $\frac{50}{3504}$, American Museum of Natural History.

FIG. 585.  Bundle of elm bark used as target; length, 3 inches; Sauk and Fox Indians, Iowa; cat. no. $\frac{50}{3504}$, American Museum of Natural History

FIG. 586.  Bow and arrows used in ring game; length of bow, 38 inches; length of arrows, 25 inches; Sauk and Fox Indians, Iowa; cat. no. $\frac{50}{3504}$, American Museum of Natural History.

long.  Bow (figure 586), 3 feet 2 inches in length, with two bands of rabbit fur, designated by its color as the property of the Blacks, one of the two divisions of the people (White and Black) ; four arrows, 25 inches in length.

The players, men or boys, divide into two sides, each side having four rings and each player four arrows.  The rings are rolled, and shot at with the arrows; each arrow must pierce the ring and hang on.   The side that hits all the rings first has the right to roll the rings at the arrows.   The arrows that have been shot are stuck up in a row, and the winning side rolls the rings at them.   Each time that the ring hits an arrow it wins that arrow.

The little bundle of bark is held with the guiding forefinger on the bow, tossed into the air, and shot at in lieu of the ring.   In another form of the game the bundle of elm bark or the rings are buried in the sand and shot at with arrows.   The game is to hit the concealed bundle or ring so that the arrow shall be held by it.   The game is called topagahagi, rings; the little bundle of bark, otawahi; the bow, metaha, and the arrows, owipanoni.

The game is played about the house.   People believe there is a spirit of sickness, Apenaweni, always hovering about to get into the lodges, and this game is encouraged in order to keep it away.

ATHAPASCAN STOCK

APACHE (CHIRICAHUA).   Arizona.

Mr E. W. Davis gave the writer the following account of a game played by Geronimo's band at St Augustine, Florida, in 1889:

Another game which interested me was played with hoops and poles, and, as I remember, always by two men.   The hoops were ordinary pieces of flexible wood, tied into a circle of about 12 inches with leather thongs, and the poles were reeds 10 or 12 feet long.   A little heap of hay was placed on the ground and parted in the center.   The players stood about 15 feet away, and each in his turn would roll his hoop into the little valley in the hay mound.   Waiting until the hoop had nearly reached the hay he would toss the staff through the hay, the object being to pass the hoop so that it might encircle the end of the pole when the hoop reached the hay.   This game was very difficult, and misses were more frequent than scores.

APACHE (JICARILLA).   Northern New Mexico.

Mr James Mooney,[a] in The Jicarilla Genesis, describes the wheel-and-stick game as having been made by Yolkaiistsun, the White-bead woman, for her two sons, children by her of the Sun and the Moon. She told them not to roll the wheel toward the north.   They played for three days, when the Sun's son rolled the wheel toward the east, south, and west.   His brother then persuaded him to roll it toward the north.   An adventure with an owl follows, and the two boys were set to perform a succession of dangerous feats, which accomplished, they went to live in the western ocean.

APACHE (MESCALERO).   Fort Sumner, New Mexico.

Col. John C. Cremony [b] says:

There are some games to which women are never allowed access.   Among these is one played with the poles and a hoop.   The former are generally about

---

[a] The American Anthropologist, v. 11, p. 201, 1898.
[b] Life Among the Apaches, p. 302, San Francisco, 1868.

10 feet in length, smooth and gradually tapering like a lance. It is [*sic*] marked with divisions throughout its whole length, and these divisions are stained in different colors. The hoop is of wood, about 6 inches in diameter, and divided like the poles, of which each player has one. Only two persons can engage in this game at one time. A level place is selected, from which the grass is removed a foot in width, and for 25 or 30 feet in length, and the earth trodden down firmly and smoothly. One of the players rolls the hoop forward, and after it reaches a certain distance, both dart their poles after it, overtaking and throwing it down. The graduation of values is from the point of the pole toward the butt, which ranks highest, and the object is to make the hoop fall on the pole as near the butt as possible, at the same time noting the value of the part which touches the hoop. The two values are then added and placed to the credit of the player. The game usually runs up to a hundred, but the extent is arbitrary among the players. While it is going on no woman is permitted to approach within a hundred yards, and each person present is compelled to leave all his arms behind. I inquired the reason for these restrictions, and was told that they were required by tradition; but the shrewd old Sons-in-jah gave me another, and, I believe, the true version. When people gamble, said he, they become half crazy, and are very apt to quarrel. This is the most exciting game we have, and those who play it will wager all they possess. The loser is apt to get angry, and fights have ensued which resulted in the loss of many warriors. To prevent this, it was long ago determined that no warrior should be present with arms upon his person or within near reach, and this game is always played at some distance from camp. Three prominent warriors are named as judges, and from their decision there is no appeal. They are not suffered to bet while acting in that capacity. The reason why women are forbidden to be present is because they always foment troubles between the players, and create confusion by taking sides and provoking dissension.

APACHE (SAN CARLOS). San Carlos agency, Gila county, Arizona. (Cat. no. 63535, Field Columbian Museum.)

Hoop of sapling, 9¾ inches in diameter, painted red, divided in half with thong wound with buckskin cord, and having four equidistant notches on both faces on opposite sides of the median thong. Collected by Mr S. C. Simms, who describes it as used in the game of nahlpice (figure 587).

APACHE (WHITE MOUNTAIN). Arizona. (Cat. no. 61246, Field Columbian Museum.)

Two jointed poles in three pieces, 14 feet and 15 feet 4¼ inches in length, and a hoop made of sapling, 9¾ inches in diameter, the latter having a thong wound with cord stretched across the middle. Collected by Rev. Paul S. Mayerhoff, who describes the game under the name of na-a-shosh.

The game is played with two poles, each of which is made up in three sections, and a hoop. The butt end of each pole is marked off into nine divisions or counters. The ring also has marked on its circumference eleven divisions or counters. The spoke bisecting the hoop and wrapped with cord is also used in counting, there being one hundred and four winds of cord, or plus the knot or bead in the center, one hundred and five in all. The total number of points on pole and hoop is one hundred and twenty-five in the average game, but exceeding that in some. The two poles represent the two sexes— yellow representing the male, red the female. They are called mbăshgah. Their three sections are, respectively: Butt, egie-shĕ dĕs-tăh-nēē; middle section, indēē dĕs-tăh-nēē; tip, bĭllăh tăh shĕ dĕs-tăh nēē. The joints are made by wrapping with sinew.

Fɪɢ. 587.  San Carlos Apache Indians playing hoop and pole; San Carlos agency, Arizona; from photograph by Mr S. C. Simms.

The hoop is called băh say; the bead on the center of the bisecting spoke, băh say-bi-yō. The playground (figure 588) is 75 to 100 feet long; the home goal (dō-thēē′-shay-tsay-nee-say-ah) is marked by a flat rock midway between the two ends (dō-thēē′-shay-his-tso).

The ends, toward which the game proceeds alternately, are so built up by means of hay or grass that three parallel ridges, 8 to 10 feet

Fɪɢ. 588.  Plan of pole grounds; White Mountain Apache Indians, Arizona.

in length, are formed. The hoop and poles must be propelled in such a way as to pass into the depressions between the ridges and come to a stop before they have passed to the extreme ends of the ridges. The throw counts only when the hoop falls upon the marked butt of the pole. In playing, one of the two opponents rolls the hoop forward from the home goal toward one of the ends; just as it begins to lose its inertia the opponents throw forward their poles so that they will slide along into the depression in which the hoop has rolled. The same proceeding is repeated in the opposite direction. Then comes the next pair of players, and so on until all have had their turn, when the first set takes its turn once more, the rotation keeping up until the agreed number of points has been made by one opponent or one side.

The method of counting is simple, every mark or counter on pole or hoop counting but one. If the hoop falls against the extreme butt of the pole so that they just touch, it counts 1; if it falls on the

FIG. 589. San Carlos Apache Indians playing hoop and pole, Arizona; from a photograph.

butt, as many points are counted as are inclosed by the hoop; e. g., if it touches the first mark above the butt end, it counts 2; the next higher, 3; the next, 4, etc.

Should marks on the circumference of the hoop touch the pole, points are added to the enclosed points on the butt of the pole, 1 point if one mark, 2 if two marks, etc. Where the spoke of the hoop also crosses the pole, as many points are added to the throw as it takes winds of the cord to cross the thickness of the butt. If the hoop falls upon the pole so that the bar or spoke in it lies exactly above and parallel with the pole, covering all the counters on the pole, such a throw wins the game.

The game has a religious character with the Apache Indians, no festivity being complete without it, and is played with great fervor and persistency. Only those medicine men (called Dēē-yín) deeply versed in their folklore and traditions can give a minute explanation of the original meaning and symbolism of this game, and they are very reluctant to part with their knowledge. Tradition says that one of the Ghons (the minor deities to whom these Indians ascribe their instruction and knowledge in handicrafts and arts, as tilling the soil, raising crops, preparing food, weaving, and manufacturing implements and utensils for camp, chase, or war, the use of medicines, etc.) taught their forefathers the game, with its symbolism.

Fig. 590.  White Mountain Apache Indians playing hoop and pole, Arizona; from photograph
by George B. Wittick.

There are several short prayers or charms, some sung, some spoken, used by players to neutralize the efforts of their opponents and bring success to themselves. The following may be given as an example:

Hǐllchee be-tä hà hǐs ēē.
Hǐll chēé shä-ō-Ka'-shay näh-ēē-gáy yūl-tláthl.
Dēē-djáy i-děs-ä̂-go shǐ-dáy gush;
Nä-gō-tláy-gō Kä-shay-day-äh.

[Translation.]

The wind will make it miss yours;
The wind will turn it on my pole.
To-day at noon I shall win all;
At night again to me will it fall.

Apache (White Mountain).   White river, Arizona.

Mr Albert B. Reagan gave the following account of the game in a communication to the Bureau of American Ethnology in 1901:

The pole game is the Apache national game.   It is played by the men every day from early morn to late in the afternoon; sometimes to pass the time only,

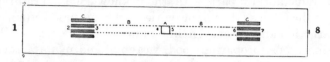

Fig. 591.   Plan of pole ground; White Mountain Apache Indians, Arizona; from sketch by Albert B. Reagan.   A, base; B B, sliding grounds, length 9 steps; C C, counting fields, length, 3 steps, width 5 feet; spaces between counting fields and end of playground, 1-2, 7-8, length, 6 steps; total length, 1-8, 36 yards; width, 9-10, 6 yards.

sometimes for "medicine," but almost always for gain.   They sometimes bet all they have on it, in former times even their women and children.

The pole ground is a level space 36 yards long and 6 wide, laid off in the directions north and south [figure 591].   In its center is the base, usually a rock, from which the poles are hurled.   Nine yards from this base, both north and south, are three hay-covered ridges, the center ridge lying on the

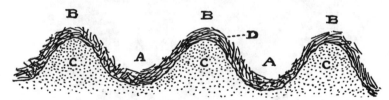

Fig. 592.   Cross section of counting field in pole game; White Mountain Apache Indians, Arizona; from sketch by Albert B. Reagan.   A A, furrows into which the wheel runs; B B B, ridges on sides of furrows; C C C, earth; D, hay or straw.

center line of the pole ground [figure 592].   These ridges are 3 yards long, with a total width of 5 feet.   There are two narrow furrows between the ridges, into which the wheel is rolled.

The two poles are willow, about 15 feet long, made in three sections, which are spliced and tied with sinew.   They taper from the butt to a point, being about 1¼ inches in diameter at the butt end.   The first 9 inches of the butt,

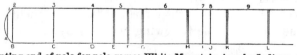

Fig. 593.   Counting end of pole for pole game; White Mountain Apache Indians, Arizona; from sketch by Albert B. Reagan.

called the "counting end" [figure 593], is marked with grooves.   The counts on this butt are nine in number: The little circular knot, A; the edge, B, of the pole; the lightly cut groove, C; the lightly cut groove, D; the space between the two heavily cut grooves, E F; the space between the two heavily cut grooves, G H; the lightly cut groove, I; the lightly cut groove, J; the space between the two heavily cut grooves, K L.   The hoop or wheel [figure 594] is made of willow, about a foot in diameter, the ends being bound with sinew.   A buckskin thong, stretched across the ring, is wound its entire length with cord. The center wrap is made larger than the others. These wraps are called beads, because originally beads were used instead of the wrapping cords. These beads

are counted to 50 in descending order on each side of the center. Sometimes there are more than fifty turns, but only this number is counted. They are not touched by the hand in counting, but are pointed to with a straw by the player. They are always counted by twos. With the center bead the fifty beads on each side make 101 counts on the diameter of the wheel. The edges on both sides of the circumference of the hoop are notched with nine cuts, which, with the two sinew wrappings, are used in counting. The space, A–B, between the places where the ends are lashed counts 1; and each of the notches, 2, 3, 4, 5, 6, 7, 8, 9, 10, 11, around the ring, 1; making 11 counts, or a total of 112 counts on the hoop.

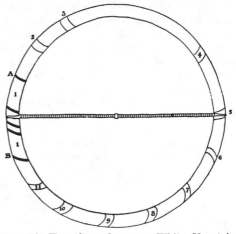

Fig. 594. Hoop for pole game; White Mountain Apache Indians, Arizona; from sketch by Albert B. Reagan.

With the 9 counts on the butt there is a total of 121 counts in the game; the players learn to count, most of them being able to count to 1,000 in their own language. In rolling the hoop, it is held vertically between the thumb and second finger of the right hand, resting on the

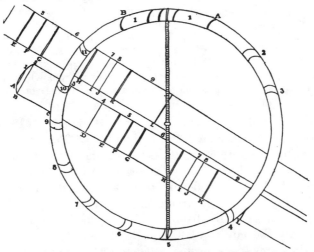

Fig. 595. Counting points in pole game; White Mountain Apache Indians, Arizona; from sketch by Albert B. Reagan.

extended index finger, over which it rolls when it is dispatched. If it is seen to be rolling wide of the furrows, it is sometimes guided to its place by one of the poles. On entering a furrow the loose hay retards its speed and it falls over, only to be slid under the hay by the well-directed poles. If it fails to enter a furrow, which is called a break in the game, it is brought back and rolled again.  It is always rolled first to the south and then to the north, and so on for hours until the game is finished.

In throwing the poles, they are propelled by the right hand and guided with the left, the index finger of the right hand being placed against the end of the pole, which is held between the thumb and index finger.  The pole, if hurled successfully, slides into the furrow beneath the wheel, and stops with its butt beneath it.  If it passes entirely through the furrow or goes to the side this is also called a break in the game, and the poles are taken back to the base and hurled again, the wheel being rolled as before.  It takes long practice and much skill to hurl the poles successfully.

In carrying back the poles after they have been hurled they are thrown over the right shoulder.  They are then stood on end upon the ground for a moment only, then hurled as before.

In counting, all points on each pole that fall on or within the rim of the hoop are counted, also all the points on the rim of the hoop and all the beads on the cord which fall within the edges of the pole.  The points being counted, the game proceeds as before.  This is continued for hours, until one side or the other gets the number of points agreed upon as deciding the game.  There may be any odd number from 37 to 1,001.  The game is sometimes played for the best two out of three or three out of five rounds, etc., two hurls south and one north constituting a play.

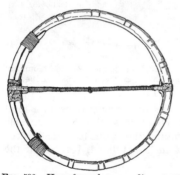

FIG. 596.  Hoop for pole game; diameter, 10 inches; White Mountain Apache Indians, Arizona; cat. no. 18618, Free Museum of Science and Art, University of Pennsylvania.

Vocabulary: Bâ-na′-e-jōsh′, let us play pole; bas′-sā, or pas′-sā, the hoop; bas′-sā-hēū′, the counting end of the pole; bas′-sā-hewk′, hoop heads, the closely wrapped cord; dá′-des-kĭsh′, the points on the hoop rim; klō-hō-ká′-nil′-dĭsh, the counting field, the three-ridged space; ná′-ē-jōsh′, the pole; ná′-ē-jōsh′-ka, the pole ground; sā kō′-shē-wal′-chēl-kŏt, the base, or center, of the pole ground, from which the hoop is rolled and the poles are hurled; ūk, one of the wraps (beads) on the cord; uk′-chō, the center bead on the cord.

APACHE (WHITE MOUNTAIN).  Arizona.  (Cat. no. 18618, Free Museum of Science and Art, University of Pennsylvania.)

Hoop of sapling (figure 596), 10 inches in diameter, painted red, the overlapping ends lashed with cords, with a thong lashing between.  A thong wound with cord is fastened across the middle of the ring, the outer circumference of which is notched with eleven notches equally disposed in the space between the lashings.

Collected by the late Capt. C. N. B. Macauley, U. S. Army, who described the game to the writer under the name panshka, pole game:

Two men play.  The ground is leveled and covered with hay or dried grass.  One rolls the wheel and both throw their poles, points first, along the ground beside it, endeavoring to make the wheel fall on the butt of the pole.  The counts are most intricate, depending upon the way in which the pole falls in reference to the wheel, the periphery of which is marked with rings of sinew. The details are so complicated that no civilized game nearly compares in complexity with this apparently simple sport.

COLVILLE (CHUALPAY).   Fort Colville, Washington.

Paul Kane [a] says:

The principal game here is called Al-kol-lock, and requires considerable skill. A smooth level piece of ground is chosen, and a slight barrier of a couple of sticks, placed lengthwise, is laid at each end of the chosen spot, being from 40 to 50 feet apart and only a few inches high. The two players, stripped naked, are armed each with a very slight spear about 3 feet long, and finely pointed with bone; one of them takes a ring made of bone, or some heavy wood, and wound round with cord; this ring is about 3 inches in diameter, on the inner circumference of which are fastened six beads of different colors at equal distances, to each of which a separate numerical value is attached. The ring is then rolled along the ground to one of the barriers, and is followed at a distance of 2 or 3 yards by the players, and as the ring strikes the barrier and is falling on its side the spears are thrown, so that the ring may fall on them. If only one of the spears should be covered by the ring, the thrower of it counts according to the colored bead over it. But it generally happens, from the dexterity of the players, that the ring covers both spears, and each counts according to the color of the beads above his spear; they then play towards the other barrier, and so on until one party has attained the number agreed upon for game.

NAVAHO.   Keams canyon, Arizona.   (Cat. no. 62535, Field Columbian Museum.)

Ring (figure 597) wrapped with sheep hide, 6½ inches in diameter, and two poles (figure 598), about 9 feet in length, made in two pieces lashed together with hide, the sticks overlapping about a foot, and the ends of the lashing (figure 599) having crosspieces of hide fastened to them by bands of sheepskin. Collected by Mr Thomas V. Keam.

————— St Michael, Arizona.

The Reverend Father Berard Haile writes in a personal letter:

Ná'azhôzh, stick and hoop. The pole is decorated with buckskin strings, called "turkey feet." The hoop is set in motion and the stick thrown through the rolling hoop. Points score as the stick falls on the turkey feet. Some sticks are decorated with claws of wildcats or of the mountain lion, bear, eagle, etc., which are attached to the strings, and as the claws catch the hoop a point is scored.

Later Father Berard writes:

I find that there were four different forms of ná'azhôzh: First, ná'azhôzh aqà'dest'loni, bound together, in which the stick or pole was cut in two and tied with buckskin, allowing the ends of the string to hang down; second, ná'azhôzh

---

[a] Wanderings of an Artist among the Indians of North America, p. 310, London, 1859. See also The Canadian Journal, p. 276, Toronto, June, 1855, where Kane describes this game in about the same words under the name of al-kol-loch as one that is universal along the Columbia river. There is a good picture of this game in Kane's collection, no. 65, at Toronto. The original sketches were made at Fort Colville.

dilkô"i, slick or polished, in which the pole was left intact and provided with
three strings, one at the point and two at the butt; third, ná'azhôzh dit'lói,
strung profusely, in which the pole was profusely decorated with strings, etc.;
fourth, ná'azhôzh dilkô', polished, in which the hoop, or wheel, was only about
an inch in diameter and thrown toward a mark or point. The players were
each provided with a stick, each the length of an arm. In a stooped position
they strive to throw the stick through the ring. How many points the winner
had to score I could not ascertain, as Mr Big Goat, my informant, claims that in

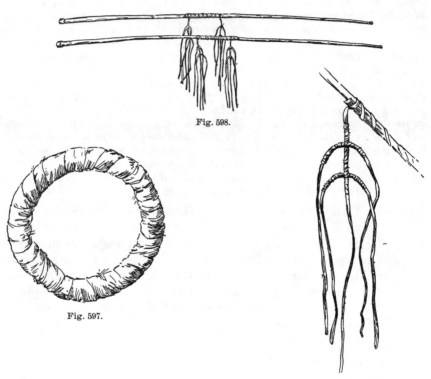

Fig. 598.

Fig. 597.

Fig. 599.

FIG. 597.  Ring for pole game; diameter, 6¼ inches; Navaho Indians, Keams canyon, Arizona;
    cat. no. 62535, Field Columbian Museum.
FIG. 598.  Pole for pole game; length, about 9 feet; Navaho Indians, Keams canyon, Arizona;
    cat. no. 62535, Field Columbian Museum.
FIG. 599.  Ends of lashing of pole for pole game; Navaho Indians, Keams canyon, Arizona; cat.
    no. 62535, Field Columbian Museum.

all these games the points were agreed upon beforehand, and a variation
naturally took place according to the value of the article put at stake. To
distinguish the first from the fourth game here mentioned, they also called
the latter laazē', which means as much as that the pole was varnished (with
juice of yucca and paint).

This game is intimated by Dr Washington Matthews in his Navaho Legends
[page 219] where he mentions dilkón, played with two sticks, each the length of
an arm, as among the four games which the Navaho brought with them from the
lower world.

Concerning another game mentioned by Doctor Matthews in this connection, atsa, played with forked sticks and a ring, Father Berard writes:

Atsá also means an eagle, whilst tsā' signifies a needle, awl, or anything similar, ergo, forked sticks? (ts'ā, basket). It was impossible for me to find any clue to this game, unless we assume that it is another form of ná'azhózh. Many of the games of the legends of the Navaho, they say, are purely mythical or artificial and have not been played by them.

NAVAHO.   Arizona, New Mexico.

Dr Washington Matthews [a] refers to the game of nanzoz, as played by the Navaho, as much the same as the game of chungkee played by the Mandan, described and depicted by Catlin (see p. 512).

A hoop is rolled along the ground, and long poles are thrown after it. The Mandan pole was made of a single piece of wood. The pole of the Navaho is made of two pieces, usually alder, each a natural fathom long; the pieces overlap and are bound together by a long branching strap of hide called thágibĭke, or turkey-claw.

Nanzoz was the second of the four games played by young Hastséhogan with the divine gambler or Gambling god named Nohoílpi, or " He Who Wins Men " (at play).

Doctor Matthews [b] says that the game is played with two long sticks or poles of peculiar shape and construction, one marked with red and the other with black, and a single hoop. A long, many-tailed string, called the " turkey claw," is secured to the end of each pole. In this contest the Great Snake came to the assistance of young Hastséhogan. Nanzoz was played out of doors.

The track already prepared lay east and west, but, prompted by the Wind God, the stranger insisted on having a track made from north to south, and again, at the bidding of Wind, he chose the red stick. The son of Hastséhogan threw the wheel; at first it seemed about to fall on the gambler's pole, in the " turkey claw " of which it was entangled; but to the great surprise of the gambler it extricated itself, rolled farther on, and fell on the pole of his opponent. The latter ran to pick up the ring, lest Nohoílpi in doing so might hurt the snake inside; but the gambler was so angry that he threw his stick away and gave up the game, hoping to do better in the next contest, which was that of pushing down trees.

Elsewhere [c] Doctor Matthews describes the personator of Hatdastsisi as carrying on his back a ring about 12 inches in diameter, made of yucca leaves, and, suspended from this by the roots, a complete plant of the *Yucca baccata*. The ring is like that used in the game of nanzoz and indicates that the god is a great gambler at nanzoz.

---

[a] Navaho Legends, note 76, Boston, 1897.
[b] Ibid., p. 85.
[c] The Night Chant, a Navaho Ceremony. Memoirs of the American Museum of Natural History, whole series, v. 6, p. 15, New York, 1902.

Speaking of the Navaho, Maj. E. Backus, U. S. Army, wrote as follows, in Schoolcraft:[a]

Their favorite game consists in throwing a lance or pole at a rolling hoop, in which they are said to exhibit much skill. I have never seen the game played and can not describe its details.

SARSI. British Columbia.

Rev. E. F. Wilson [b] gives the following account:

The Sarcees, like most other wild Indians, are inveterate gamblers. They will gamble everything away—ponies, teepees, blankets, leggings, moccasins—till they have nothing left but their breech-clout. In my report of the Blackfoot last year I mentioned the use of a little hoop or wheel for gambling purposes. I find that the Sarcees also use this, and two of them showed me how they play the game. A little piece of board, if procurable, or two or three flattened sticks, laid one on the other, are put for a target, at a distance of 18 or 20 feet from the starting-point, and the two players then take their places beside each other; one has the little wheel in his left hand, an arrow in his right; the other one has only an arrow. The play is to roll the wheel and to deliver the two arrows simultaneously, all aiming at the mark which has been set up. If the wheel falls over on one of the arrows, it counts so many points, according to the number of beads on the wire spoke of the wheel that touch the arrow. Nothing is counted unless the little wheel falls on one of the arrows. The articles for which they play are valued at so many points each. A blanket is worth, perhaps, 10 points, a pony, 50, and so on.

FIG. 600. Hoop for game; Takulli Indians, Stuart lake, British Columbia; from Morice.

TAKULLI. Stuart lake, British Columbia.

The Reverend Father A. G. Morice [c] describes the game of keilapəs, encircling willow, or arrow target-shooting, named from the implement required for its performance:

This is a sort of open work disk or wheel [figure 600], principally made of willow-bark strings, though the frame of the hoop is composed of three or four switches very closely fitting each other and kept in position by a strong lacing of strips of bark. Radiating from the axis, or heart, as it is called, are four cords of similar material, stretched so as to form a cross. As this was formerly the great national game of the Carriers, I may be pardoned for giving its rules in full.

A team of five or six men was matched against another of presumed equal force, and after each player had been provided with a given number of pointed arrows, the disk was set wheeling away by one team to the cry of tlép! flép!

[a] Information respecting the History, Condition, and Prospects of the Indian Tribes of the United States, pt. 4, p. 214, Philadelphia, 1856.

[b] Fourth Report on the North-Western Tribes of Canada. Report of the Fifty-eighth Meeting of the British Association for the Advancement of Science, p. 246, London, 1889.

[c] Notes on the Western Dénés. Transactions of the Canadian Institute, v. 4, p. 113, Toronto, 1895.

This was the signal for the other to shoot at it while it was in motion. Should they fail to hit it, it was returned rolling to the first team, so as to give them an equal chance of making at it with their arrows. As soon as the disk had been shot, the real competitive game commenced. The arrows which had hit it, two, three, or more, became the stake for the rival team to win over. For this purpose the disk was hung upon a short stick planted in the ground near the team who had succeeded in sending home the arrows, and it was aimed at successively by each member of the opposite party. Should anyone be lucky enough to shoot it with his first arrow, the stake played for became his irrevocable property. When the target was hit, but on a subsequent attempt of the marksman, the stake was thereby won over, subject to its being redeemed by any member of the opposing team performing the same feat. In this case the game became a draw; the wheel was set rolling anew, and the nature of the stake was determined as in the first instance.

I have never seen 'keilapəs played by other than children and young men. But in times past it had a sort of national importance, inasmuch as teams from distant villages were wont to assemble in certain localities more favorable to its performance in good style. Indeed, until a few years ago the sporting field of some was literally dotted with small cavities resulting from the fall of the arrows.

### CADDOAN STOCK

ARIKARA. South Dakota.

John Bradbury [a] says:

We amused ourselves some time by watching a party who were engaged in play. A place was neatly formed, resembling a skittle alley, about 9 feet in breadth and 90 feet long: a ring of wood, about 5 inches in diameter was trundled along from one end, and when it had run some distance, two Indians, who stood ready, threw after it, in a sliding manner, each a piece of wood, about 3 feet long and 4 inches in breadth, made smooth on one edge, and kept from turning by a crosspiece passing through it, and bended backwards so as to resemble a crossbow. The standers-by kept an account of the game, and he whose piece, in a given number of throws, more frequently came nearest the ring after it had fallen, won the game.

## H. M. Brackenridge [b] says:

Their daily sports, in which, when the weather is favorable, they are engaged from morning till night, are principally of two kinds. A level piece of ground appropriated for the purpose, and beaten by frequent use, is the place where they are carried on. The first is played by two persons, each armed with a long pole; one of them rolls a hoop, which, after having reached about two-thirds of the distance, is followed at half speed, and as they perceive it about to fall, they cast their poles under it; the pole on which the hoop falls, so as to be nearest to certain corresponding marks on the hoop and pole, gains for that time. This game excites great interest, and produces a gentle, but animated exercise. The other differs from it in this, that instead of poles, they have short pieces of wood, with barbs at one end, and a cross piece at the other, held in the middle with one hand; but instead of the hoop before mentioned, they throw a small ring, and endeavor to put the point of the barb through it. This is a much more violent exercise than the other.

---

[a] Travels in the Interior of America in the years 1809, 1810, and 1811, p. 126, Liverpool, 1817.
[b] Views of Louisiana, together with a Journal of a Voyage up the Missouri River, in 1811, p. 255, Pittsburg, 1814.

ARIKARA.

Dr George A. Dorsey,[a] in The Origin of the Arikara, describes them as coming in their journeyings to a great lake where they had their village for some time. They made games at this place. Shinny is specified.

At other places they had long javelins to catch a ring with. The side that won began to kill the people who were on the other side, and whose language they could not understand.

Doctor Dorsey,[b] in the story of " The Buffalo Wife and the Javelin Game," relates also the following:

Young man out hunting dreams of two buffalo bulls turning into sticks and of buffalo cow turning into ring. In morning he sees cow and lies with her. Finds ring in grass and wears it on his wrist. He makes sticks and plays game with young men, winning many things. Goes hunting and sees old woman, who induces him to carry her across river on his back. He can not throw her off, and he goes home with her fast to his back. Medicine-men are sent for, but they can do nothing. Poor boy puts on old robe and goes to young man's lodge with bow and four arrows of different colors. He shoots black arrow and splits woman in two. With red arrow he takes her off boy. The other arrows he places on boy's back to remove sore spot. Old woman is then burned. Next day crying and voice are heard near where woman burned. Young man finds ring has gone. White tipi with woman and child inside appears where others were. Young man goes to see it and woman with new buffalo robe passes by him, having child. Young man makes bundle of eagle feathers and follows them. They become buffalo. Calf communicates with father, and woman finally becomes reconciled to him. They come to hill on which Buffalo bull, boy's grandfather, is waiting for them. Man puts two eagle feathers on his horns. He sends them on to next hill and at last they come to hill with four Buffalo bulls, chiefs of Buffalo camp. Man puts feathers on their heads. They are sent into village and Buffalo become mad because man has not feathers enough to go round. Man made to sit on hill until they decide what to do with him. He sticks flint knife into ground and asks gods to form stone around where he sits. Buffalo devise various ways for killing him, but do not succeed in doing so. They decide to send man with Buffalo cow and calf to Indian village with presents. Buffalo bull turns man into Buffalo. Buffalo follow them. Man finds village and tells errand. People bring eagle feathers and native tobacco, which man takes to Buffalo. Buffalo willing to be slaughtered and man tells chiefs. Four times people go and kill Buffalo. Leader of Buffalo gives man sticks to play with. Sticks and ring different kinds of people. Man lives long life. Buffalo calf starts Buffalo ceremony among people.

CADDO. Oklahoma.

In the story of the " Brothers Who Became Lightning and Thunder" Doctor Dorsey [c] tells of two brothers, the elder of whom made two arrows for his young brother; one he painted black and the other he painted blue. They then made a small wheel out of the bark of the elm tree. One of the boys would stand about fifty yards away from the

a Traditions of the Arikara, p. 15, Washington, 1904.      b Ibid., p. 189.
c Traditions of the Caddo, p. 35, Washington, 1905.

other and they would roll this little wheel to each other and would shoot the wheel with the arrows. They played with the wheel every day until finally the younger brother failed to hit the wheel, when the wheel kept on rolling and did not stop. They followed its traces and, after a series of adventures, recovered the wheel from an old man, whom they killed. Later they ascended to the sky and became the Lightning and Thunder.

PAWNEE. Nebraska.

Maj. Stephen H. Long [a] wrote as follows:

About the village we saw several parties of young men eagerly engaged at games of hazard. One of these, which we noticed particularly, is played between two persons, and something is staked on the event of each game. The instruments used are a small hoop, about 6 inches in diameter, which is usually wound with thongs of leather, and a pole 5 or 6 feet long, on the larger end of which a limb is left to project about 6 inches. The whole bears some resemblance to a shepherd's crook. The game is played upon a smooth beaten path, at one end of which the gamester commences, and, running at full speed, he first rolls from him the hoop, then discharges after it the pole, which slides along the path pursuing the hoop until both stop together, at the distance of about 30 yards from the place whence they were thrown. After throwing them from him the gamester continues his pace, and the Indian, the hoop, and the pole arrive at the end of the path about the same time. The effort appears to be to place the end of the pole either in the ring, or as near as possible, and we could perceive that those casts were considered best when the ring was caught by the hook at the end of the pole. What constitutes a point, or how many points are reckoned to the game, we could not ascertain. It is, however, sufficiently evident that they are desperate gamesters, often losing their ornaments, articles of dress, etc., at play.

John T. Irving, jr,[b] says:

One of the principal games of the Pawnees, and the one on which the most gambling is carried on, is played by means of a small ring and a long javelin. The ring is about 4 inches in diameter, and the object of the player is to hurl his javelin through the ring, while it is sent rolling over the ground, with great speed, by one of his companions in the game. The javelin is filled with barbs nearly the whole length so that when it has once passed partly through the ring, it can not slide back. This is done to ascertain how far it went before it struck the edges of the ring, and the farther the cast the more it counts in favor of the one who hurled it. It is practiced by the children, young men, and chiefs. The first gamble for single arrows—the second for a bow and quiver— and the last for horses.

John B. Dunbar says: [c]

The most usual game with men was stŭts-au′-ĭ-ka-tus, or simply stŭts-au′-ĭ, played with a small hoop or ring, and stick. The hoop was about 4 inches in diameter, made of several coils of a small strip of rawhide wrapped tightly together with a stout string. At one point on the exterior of the hoop was a bead

---

[a] Account of an Expedition from Pittsburgh to the Rocky Mountains, v. 1, p. 444, Philadelphia, 1823.
[b] Indian Sketches, v. 2, p. 142, Philadelphia, 1835.
[c] The Pawnee Indians. Magazine of American History, v. 8, p. 749, New York, Nov., 1882.

threaded on the wrapping string.  The stick was of peculiar structure.  Its general shape is shown in the cut . . . [figure 601].  The entire length of the stick was about 5½ feet.  It was flattened somewhat in the direction of the crosspieces, and tapered slightly from the heel, *a*, to the point *b*.  Directly over the intersection of the crosspieces *c* and *d*, which were upon the upper side, was a small crooked projection (not shown) about the length of a finger, curving over the part of the crosspieces on the same side as the curved heelpiece, *a–e*, i. e., to the right.  The entire stick was firmly wrapped with buckskin or rawhide, and the crosspieces and curved attachments held in place by the same means.

At each village there were two or more grounds, about 60 paces long and 15 wide, cleared and smoothed for this game.  Two sticks and one hoop were necessary, and the players were arranged by pairs.  Two players took the sticks, one of them having also the hoop, and started at full speed from one end of the ground toward the other.  When about halfway across, the one carrying the hoop hurled it violently forward, so that it should speed along the ground before them; then instantly changing his stick from his left hand to the right, they simultaneously cast them both at the rolling hoop, in such way that striking flat upon the ground, they should glide along point forward and overtake it.  The best throw was to catch the hoop upon one of the small projections over the intersections of the crosspieces.  To catch it upon the point of the stick, upon the extremities of the crosspieces or of the curved

Fig. 601.                                    Fig. 602.

FIG. 601.   Dart for ring game; length, about 5¼ feet; Pawnee Indians, Nebraska; from Dunbar.
FIG. 602.   Dart for boys' ring game; length, about 4 feet; Pawnee Indians, Nebraska; from Dunbar.

heelpiece, was also a good throw.  If the hoop was not caught at all, as was usually the case, the value of the throw was determined by its contiguity to certain parts of the stick, and each player was provided with a straw for measuring in such cases.  The bead upon the hoop was the point from which every measurement was made.  Sometimes spirited debates were had upon the question of the correct measurement, as to whose the throw should properly be.  In such case one of the numerous spectators was called in to act as umpire.  The value of each throw was reckoned by points, so many points constituting a game.  If there were more than two players, the couples alternated in making throws.

By boys this game was played with a smaller and simpler stick [figure 602], about 4 feet long.  The aim in their game was to dart the point of the stick directly through the hoop and catch it upon the two prongs at the heel.

The Hon. Charles Augustus Murray [a] describes the hoop-and-dart game as follows:

It is played by two competitors, each armed with a dart, on the smoothest plot of grass they can find.  The area is about 50 yards long.  They start from one end at full speed; one of the players has a small hoop of 6 inches diameter, which, as soon as they have reached the middle of the course, he rolls on before them, and each then endeavors to dart his weapon through the hoop.  He who

[a] Travels in North America, p. 321, London, 1839.

succeeds, counts so many in the game; and if neither pierces it, the nearest javelin to the mark is allowed to count, but, of course, not so many points as if he had ringed it. The game is exceedingly hard exercise; they play with many on a side, and sometimes for five or six hours, in the mid-heat of an August day without intermission. It is made subservient to their taste for gambling, and I have seen them lose guns, blankets, and even one or two horses in a morning.

Zebulon M. Pike [a] says:

They are extremely addicted to gaming, and have for that purpose a smooth piece of ground cleared out on each side of the village for about 150 yards in length, at which they play the following games, viz: one is played by two players at a time, and in the following manner: They have a large hoop of about 4 feet in diameter, in the center of which is a small leather ring attached to leather thongs, which is extended to the hoop, and by that means keeps it in its central position; they also have a pole of about 6 feet in length, which the player holds in one hand, and then rolls the hoop from him, and immediately slides the pole after it, and the nearer the head of the pole lies to the small ring within the hoop (when they both fall) the greater is the cast. But I could not ascertain their mode of counting sufficiently to decide when the game was won.

Another game is played with a small stick, with several hooks, and a hoop about 4 inches in diameter, which is rolled along the ground and the forked stick darted after it, when the value of the cast is estimated by the hook on which the ring is caught. This game is gained at 100.

Dr George Bird Grinnell [b] writes:

Of all the games played by men among the Pawnee Indians, none was so popular as the stick game. This was an athletic contest between pairs of young men, and tested their fleetness, their eyesight, and their skill in throwing the stick. The implements used were a ring, 6 inches in diameter, made of buffalo rawhide, and two elaborate and highly ornamented slender sticks, one for each player. One of the two contestants rolled the ring over a smooth prepared course, and when it had been set in motion the players ran after it side by side, each one trying to throw his stick through the ring. This was not often done, but the players constantly hit the ring with their sticks and knocked it down, so that it ceased to roll. The system of counting was by points, and was somewhat complicated, but in general terms it may be said that the player whose stick lay nearest the ring gained one or more points. In the story which follows, the Buffalo by their mysterious power transformed the girl into a ring, which they used in playing the stick game.

The story related by Dr Grinnell is that of a girl who lived with her four brothers in a lodge by the banks of a river. To the branch of a tree in front of the lodge they had hung a rawhide strap, such as women use for carrying wood, so as to make a swing for the girl. The brothers would swing the girl in the swing to make the buffalo come.

The story relates how, in the brothers' absence, a coyote persuaded the girl to let him swing her, and when the buffalo came they turned her into a ring.

---

[a] An Account of Expeditions to the Sources of the Mississippi, appendix to pt. 2, p. 15, Philadelphia, 1810.

[b] The Girl Who was the Ring. Harper's Magazine, v. 102, p. 425, February, 1901.

PAWNEE.   Oklahoma.   (Field Columbian Museum.)

Cat. no. 59400.   Hoop of sapling (figure 603), 7½ inches in diameter, with inner concentric ring, 3¼ inches in diameter, attached with cord network; all painted green and having an eagle-down feather tied with a thong to the middle.

Fig. 603.          Fig. 604.

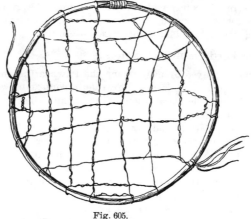

Fig. 605.

FIG. 603.  Netted hoop;  diameter, 7¼ inches;  Pawnee Indians, Oklahoma;  cat. no. 59400, Field Columbian Museum.

FIG. 604.  Netted hoop;  diameter, 5¼ inches;  Pawnee Indians, Oklahoma;  cat. no. 59398, Field Columbian Museum.

FIG. 605.  Netted hoop;  diameter, 10 inches;  Pawnee Indians, Oklahoma;  cat. no. 59392, Field Columbian Museum.

Cat. no. 59398.   Hoop (figure 604) of sapling, 5½ inches in diameter, netted with fine cord, painted yellow in the center and green outside.

Cat. no. 59392.   Hoop (figure 605) of sapling, 10 inches in diameter, netted with twine.

Cat. no. 59394.   Hoop (figure 606) of sapling, 13 inches in diameter, bisected by a thong, half the ring on one side of the hoop painted red and the other half black.   An eagle tail is tied at each end of the bisecting thong and a piece of otter fur midway between.

Cat. no. 71646. Hoop of sapling, 15 inches in diameter, similar to that last described, but painted in four colors—green, red, blue, and yellow—and having owl and flicker, instead of eagle, feathers.

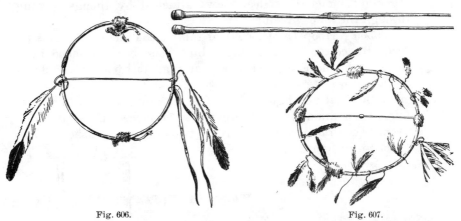

Fig. 606.                                Fig. 607.

FIG. 606. Game hoop; diameter, 13 inches; Pawnee Indians, Oklahoma; cat. no. 59394, Field Columbian Museum.

FIG. 607. Hoop and poles; diameter of hoop, 25 inches; length of poles, 50 inches; Pawnee Indians, Oklahoma; cat. no. 59390, Field Columbian Museum.

Cat. no. 59390. Hoop (figure 607) of sapling, 25 inches in diameter, with a buckskin thong bisecting it and a shell bead strung in the center. Twenty-four single feathers and bunches of feathers

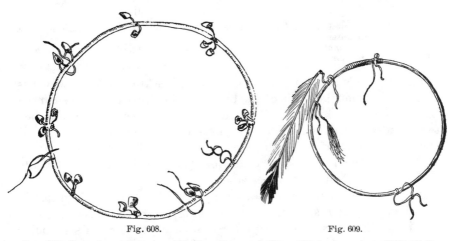

Fig. 608.                                Fig. 609.

FIG. 608. Game hoop; diameter, 13 inches; Pawnee Indians, Oklahoma; cat. no. 59393, Field Columbian Museum.

FIG. 609. Game hoop; diameter, 8½ inches; Pawnee Indians, Oklahoma; cat. no. 59395, Field Columbian Museum.

are tied with thongs around the circumference. Accompanied by two poles, 50 inches in length, made in two pieces, joined with thongs and tapering from butt to tip.

Cat. no. 59393.  Hoop (figure 608) of sapling, 13 inches in diameter, entirely covered with hide sewed with the seam on the inner side, one-half of the hoop painted red and the other half black, having eight bunches of deer claws attached by thongs passing through the hide covering.

Cat. no. 59395.  Hoop (figure 609) of sapling, 8½ inches in diameter, tied with cotton cord, having a blue glass bead attached by a thong at the place of juncture and an eagle tail feather and down feather also fastened on by thongs.

Cat. no. 59409.  Ring (figure 610) of hide, wrapped with buckskin, 4 inches in diameter, and two poles, 54 inches in length, each wrapped with buckskin and having two crosspieces lashed across, as shown in figure 611.

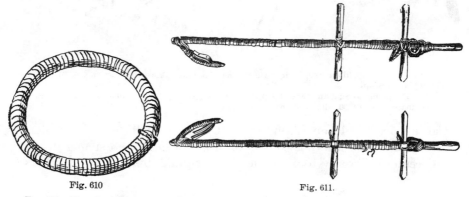

Fig. 610                                    Fig. 611.

FIG. 610.  Ring for buffalo game; diameter, 4 inches; Pawnee Indians, Oklahoma; cat. no. 59409, Field Columbian Museum.

FIG. 611.  Poles for buffalo game; length, 54 inches; Pawnee Indians, Oklahoma; cat. no. 59409, Field Columbian Museum.

The fore ends of the poles are carved with a kind of knob which is said to represent the penis of the buffalo.  The rear ends have curved pieces attached, which turn forward.  Small wooden forks are lashed to the sides of the crosspieces and a handle-shaped piece in front of the forward fork of each pole.

Another ring in the same collection (cat. no. 71602) has a white shell bead attached to the outer edge.

Cat. no. 71682.  Ring of cloth, wrapped with buckskin, 5 inches in diameter, and a pole, 47 inches long, with two prongs, made of sapling, wrapped with buckskin, each prong with six double strips and one single strip of rawhide wrapped in the buckskin and projecting inward, as shown in figure 612.  These are designated by the collector as implements for the buffalo game.

All of the preceding were collected by Dr George A. Dorsey.

In the story of " Blood-clot Boy " [a] Doctor Dorsey describes the boy

---

[a] Traditions of the Skidi Pawnee, p. 84, New York, 1904.

as making a ring of ash stick, which he wound with a string made of boiled buffalo hide, so that it looked like a spider's web. The grandmother rolled the ring and the boy shot it with arrows and killed buffalo.

FIG. 612. Ring and pole; diameter of ring, 5 inches; length of pole, 47 inches; Pawnee Indians, Oklahoma; cat. no. 71682, Field Columbian Museum.

Commenting on the above, Doctor Dorsey [a] says:

One of a number of ways for the magic production of a buffalo common to the Plains tribes, the significance of this form resting in the fact that the ring represented the spider-web, thus referring to the belief that the Spider-Woman controlled the buffalo and produced them from her web.

The ring-and-javelin game, according to the Skidi, was originally played for the direct purpose of calling the buffalo, and I have a long account of its origin. According to this account the two sticks represent young buffalo bulls, which turned into the gaming sticks, leaving first full instructions as to how they were to be treated, how the game was to be played, how the songs were to be sung, and how they were to be anointed with the buffalo fat. The ring, according to the story, was originally a buffalo cow, and those in the tribe to-day are said to be made from the skin of the vulva of the buffalo. For the two forms of this so-called buffalo game see figures [610 and 611 in this paper].

In the story "The Coyote Rescues a Maiden"[b] the coyote is described as seeing buffalo playing with sticks and a ring:

A lot of buffalo would line up on the south side of the playing ground. Coyote sat down at the north end of the playing ground. Two buffalo would rise up and take the sticks, one of them taking the ring, and as they ran to the north end, the one with the ring would throw it and both of them would throw their sticks at the ring to see if they could catch it. At the north end they picked up the sticks and the ring, and the one with the ring would throw it again toward the south end of the playing ground, and the two buffalo would throw the sticks at the ring to try to catch it. The two would sit down, and two other buffalo would rise and take up the sticks and ring, and they, too, would run down to the north end of the ground and throw the ring and sticks. They would shout at Coyote to get away, as they might hit him with the sticks. Coyote would rise and limp around, and then would sit down close to the end of the playing ground.

Now, the ring with which they were playing was a girl who had been carried off by the buffalo and transformed by them. During the course of the game the ring rolled toward the Coyote and he took it in his mouth and ran away with it, and finally by the aid of the badger, the fox, the crow, the hawk, and the blackbird the ring was carried back and transformed into a girl again in her brothers' lodge.

[a] Traditions of the Skidi Pawnee, p. 343, New York, 1904.          [b] Ibid., p. 257.

WICHITA.  Oklahoma.  (Field Columbian Museum.)

Cat. no. 59365.  Wooden hoop (figure 613), 18½ inches in diameter, with an interior network of sinew, which is wrapped around the hoop at thirty points and incloses an inner hoop, 9½ inches in diameter, having also an interior sinew net, accompanied by a dart made of sapling, 35½ inches in length, with a fork at the end.  Collected by Dr George A. Dorsey.

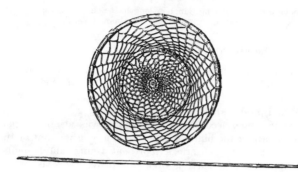

FIG. 613.  Netted hoop and dart; diameter of hoop, 18¼ inches: length of dart, 35¼ inches; Wichita Indians, Oklahoma; cat. no. 59365, Field Columbian Museum.

Cat. no. 59315.  Wooden hoop (figure 614), 25¾ inches in diameter, with connecting ends bound with sinew.  Collected by Dr George A. Dorsey.

Doctor Dorsey makes several references to the hoop game among the Wichita.  In the story of " The Seven Brothers and the Sister," [a]

FIG. 614.  Game hoop; diameter, 25¾ inches; Wichita Indians, Oklahoma; cat. no. 59315, Field Columbian Museum.

the chief game of the brothers is described as with the hoop.

In the story of " The Deeds of the After-birth-Boy " [b] the father is described as making a netted ring for his two sons, which he told them not to roll toward the west.  They disobeyed him, and were compelled to follow the ring, and ran on until they went into the water of a great lake and found themselves inside of a great monster.

In the story of " Half-a-Boy who Overcame the Gambler," [c] the hero visits a village a two-days' journey north of his own, where there was a cruel gambler who played the wheel game and won the lives of all who visited the village.  The village extended east and west and had in the middle an open space, in which he saw many people playing some kind of game.  The next morning he commenced to play the game with the gambler.  In the game that

---

[a] The Mythology of the Wichita, p. 69, Washington, 1904.    [b] Ibid., p. 95, 101.    [c] Ibid., p. 194.

they played they used two long sticks and a wheel. First they threw the wheel a long way, then they ran to it and pitched the sticks into the ring. The boy lost from the start and finally staked his life, being told his body was equal to three bets. He lost two of these when it became dark, and the gambler was persuaded by the boy to leave the third part until the next day. From this the man called the boy Half-a-Boy. The boy went to sleep on the ground and was awakened by two women, who revealed themselves as buffalo cows. He ran with them and they traveled part of the night, until they saw a light, which they said was their grandfather and grandmother taking a smoke. When they came up the young women asked the old people to make haste and give the boy powers so that he could get out of his trouble.

Deinde puero præceptum est ut ad tergum tauri iret, et, cum eius membrum semel prehendisset, " palum atrum " posceret; membro iterum prehenso, " palum rubrum " posceret. Hæc igitur fecit. Deinde ei præceptum est ut ad bovem profectus eius volvam prehenderet, anulumque posceret. Hoc facto, puer iam palos duos anulumque habebat.

The black stick remaining in the ring represented the old man and the old woman. He was requested to let the black stick remain in the ring where it belonged and to give the red stick to his opponent. In the game that followed, in which the boy's sticks and ring were employed, the black stick which the boy used never failed to find the wheel, and the boy won back everything in the village and finally the life of the gambler himself. This man was a shadow, and his name was Shadow-of-the-Sun. When the boy won the third and last part of him, he jumped out of the way as he pitched the last stick, and when the stick entered the wheel there arose two great big buffalo, who set after Shadow-of-the-Sun and hooked him until they tore him to pieces. Half-a-Boy burned the gambler's body and ordered all the bones of his victims to be placed in the fire. Then they all came to life in the same manner related in other stories.

CHIMMESYAN STOCK

NISKA. Nass river, British Columbia.

Dr Franz Boas[a] describes the following games:

Smênts, A hoop is placed upright. The players throw at it with sticks or blunt lances, and must hit inside the hoop.

Matldii', A hoop wound with cedar bark and set with fringes, is hurled by one man. The players stand in a row, about 5 feet apart, each carrying a lance or stick. When the ring is flying past the row, they try to hit it.

---

[a] Fifth Report on the Indians of British Columbia. Report of the Sixty-fifth Meeting of the British Association for the Advancement of Science, p. 583, London, 1895.

## CHINOOKAN STOCK

WASCO.   Washington.   (Cat. no. 37501, Free Museum of Science and Art, University of Pennsylvania.)

Ring (seckseck) made of strips of inner bark (figure 615), with an internal cross, 4½ inches in diameter.

Collected by Dr George A. Dorsey, who gives the following account of the game:

Shot at with arrows and played by youths on the appearance of the first run of salmon. When struck on the cross, the play is called tlia-mag-elo, to hit on the tlia-han, the cross; when struck on the periphery, ia-ma-aihth, hits one. The game is played for arrows.

FIG. 615.  Game ring; diameter, 4¼ inches; Wasco Indians, Washington; cat. no. 37501, Free Museum of Science and Art, University of Pennsylvania.

## CHUMASHAN STOCK

SANTA BARBARA.   California.

Dr Walter J. Hoffman [a] says that the Indians of Santa Barbara played a game with a barrel-shaped stone ring 3 inches in diameter and 4 in length, at which the players shot arrows, the object being to penetrate the hole while the ring was in motion. The players stood on either side of the course.

## COSTANOAN STOCK

RUMSEN.   Monterey, California.

J. F. G. de la Pérouse [b] says:

They have two games to which they dedicate their whole leisure. The first, to which they give the name of takersia, consists in throwing and rolling a small hoop, of 3 inches in diameter, in a space of 10 square toises, cleared of grass and surrounded with fascines. Each of the two players holds a stick. of the size of a common cane, and 5 feet long; they endeavor to pass this stick into the hoop whilst it is in motion; if they succeed in this they gain 2 points; and if the hoop, when it stops, simply rests upon their stick, they gain 1 by it; the game is 3 points. This game is a violent exercise, because the hoop or stick is always in action.

## ESKIMAUAN STOCK

ESKIMO (CENTRAL).   Cumberland sound, Baffin land, Franklin.

Dr Franz Boas says: [c]

A favorite game is the nuglutang [figure 616]. A small, rhomboidal plate of ivory with a hole in the center is hung from the roof and steadied by a heavy stone or a piece of ivory hanging from its lower end. The Eskimo stand

---

[a] Bulletin of the Essex Institute, v. 17, p. 32, note 12, Salem, 1885.

[b] A Voyage around the World in the years 1785, 1786, 1787, and 1788, v. 2, p. 223, London, 1798. La Pérouse refers to two tribes of Monterey, the Achastians (Rumsen) and Ecclemachs (Esselen), the latter belonging to the Esselenian family.

[c] The Central Eskimo. Sixth Annual Report of the Bureau of Ethnology, p. 568, 1888.

around it, and when the winner of the last game gives a signal everyone tries to hit the hole with a stick. The one who succeeds has won. This game is always played amid great excitement.

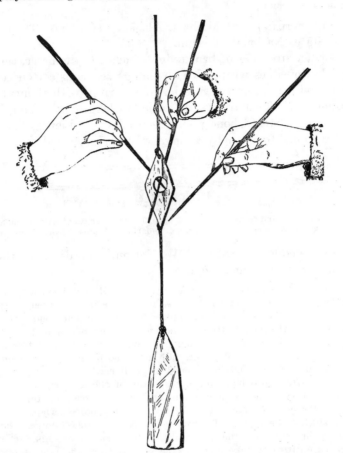

FIG. 616. Game of nuglutang; Central Eskimo, Cumberland sound, Baffin land, Franklin; cat. no. IV A 6821, Berlin Museum für Völkerkunde; from Boas.

CENTRAL ESKIMO (AIVILIRMIUT and KINIPETU). West coast of Hudson bay, Keewatin.

Dr Franz Boas[a] thus describes the game of nugluktuq:

A piece of ivory with a hole in the center is suspended from the top of the snow house. To its lower end a line with a heavy weight is attached, which serves to hold the piece of ivory steady. The men gather around this implement, each holding a small stick with a sharp point. A knife is laid down, which forms the stake of the game; and at the word " a'tē " all the men try to hit the hole in the tooth with their little sticks. Whoever succeeds in hitting the hole wins the knife. Then he places another stake near by, and the play is

[a] Eskimo of Baffin Land and Hudson Bay. Bulletin of American Museum of Natural History, v. 15, p. 110, New York, 1901.

resumed, while he himself is barred from taking part in the game. Anyone has the right to take hold of the ivory with his naked hand at the risk of having it gashed with the darts of the spears. If two persons hit the hole at the same time, it does not count.

ESKIMO (WESTERN).  St Michael, Alaska.  (Cat. no. 33970, United States National Museum.)

Oval hoop (figure 617) of bent twig, 3 inches in diameter, the upper and lower edges wrapped with thongs securing cotton cord network, which covers the interior of the ring, with thong loop for suspension. Two arrows, 22 inches in length, with simple wood shafts and barbed bone points secured with sinew. The arrows are fastened together by a long, twisted sinew cord.

FIG. 617.  Netted hoop and darts; diameter of hoop, 3 inches; length of darts, 22 inches; Western Eskimo, St Michael, Alaska; cat. no. 33970, United States National Museum.

These were collected by Mr E. W. Nelson,[a] who describes the game under the name of nugohliganuk:

This is played in the kashim by men only. A small oval wooden frame, about 3 inches long by an inch and a half wide, having the interior finely netted with cord, is hung from the roof and held in place by a cord at each end. It is placed about 4 feet from the floor in front of the summer entrance or under the smokehole in the roof. Each player has a long, slender dart, about 3 feet in length and a quarter of an inch in diameter, with a barbed point of bone or deer horn. To the butt end of the dart is fastened a small cord, so that the player can draw it back after throwing. When the point of the dart enters the wooden ring it is held fast by the barbs on the point, and this scores one for the successful player. Under this target each player places some object as a prize. Then all go to one side of the room and throw three darts in succession at the target. Whenever a player pierces the target so that he must remove his dart with his hands, he is entitled to take anything he wishes from the pile of prizes. In this way the game continues until all the articles are disposed of.

IROQUOIAN STOCK

CAUGHNAWAGA.  Quebec.

J. Long [b] says:

The boys are very expert at trundling a hoop, particularly the Cahnuaga Indians, whom I have frequently seen excel at this amusement. The game is played by any number of boys who may accidentally assemble together, some driving the hoop, while others with bows and arrows shoot at it. At this exercise

---

[a] The Eskimo about Bering Strait. Eighteenth Annual Report of the Bureau of American Ethnology, p. 334, 1899.

[b] Voyages and Travels of an Indian Interpreter and Trader, p. 53, London, 1791.

they are surprisingly expert, and will stop the progress of the hoop when going with great velocity, by driving the pointed arrow into its edge; this they will do at a considerable distance, and on horseback as well as on foot.

CHEROKEE.   Tennessee.

Lieut. Henry Timberlake (1762)[a] describes the game under the name of nettecawaw:

. . . each player having a pole about 10 feet long, with several marks or divisions, one of them bowls the round stone, with one flat side, and the other convex, on which the players all dart their poles after it, and the nearest counts according to the vicinity of the bowl to the marks on his pole.

—— North Carolina.

Mr James Mooney [b] describes the wheel-and-stick game played with a stone wheel, or circular disk, under the name of gatayusti.

John Ax, the oldest man now living among the East Cherokee, is the only one remaining in the tribe who has ever played the game, having been instructed in it when a small boy by an old man who desired to keep up the memory of the ancient things. The sticks used have long since disappeared, but the stones remain, being frequently picked up in the plowed fields, especially in the neighborhood of the mounds.

This was the game played by the great mythic gambler Uñtsaiyi, Brass.[c]

It was he who invented the gatayûstĭ game that we play with a stone wheel and a stick.

He lived at Uñtiguhi on the south side of the Tennessee river, and made his living by gambling.

The large flat rock, with the lines and grooves where they used to roll the wheel is still there, with the wheels themselves, and the stick turned to stone.[a]

Mr Mooney relates the story of a boy, the son of Thunder, who played the wheel-and-stick game with Uñtsaiyi, and vanquished him by the aid of his father's magic. The gambler at last staked his life, and was pursued to the edge of the great water, where he was caught by the boy and his brothers, whom he got to help him.

They tied his hands and feet with a grapevine and drove a long stake through his breast, and planted it far out in the deep water. They set two crows on the end of the pole to guard it and called the place Kâgûñ'yĭ, Crow place. But Brass never died, and can not die until the end of the world, but lies there always with his face up. Sometimes he struggles under water to get free, and sometimes the beavers, who are his friends, come and gnaw at the grapevine to release him. Then the pole shakes and the crows at the top cry Ka! Ka! Ka! and scare the beavers away.[d]

---

[a] Memoirs, p. 77, London, 1765.
[b] Myths of the Cherokee. Nineteenth Annual Report of the Bureau of American Ethnology, p. 434, 1902.
[c] Ibid., p. 311.
[d] Ibid., p. 314.

SENECA.  New York.

Lewis H. Morgan [a] describes the game as follows:

The game of javelins, gä-na'-gä-o, was very simple, depending upon the dexterity with which the javelin was thrown at a ring, as it rolled upon the ground. They frequently made it a considerable game, by enlisting skillful players to prepare for the contest and by betting upon the result. The people divided by tribes, the four brothers playing against their four cousin tribes, as in the last case [ball], unless the game was played on a challenge between neighboring communities.

The javelin was 5 or 6 feet in length by three-fourths of an inch in diameter, and was usually made of hickory or maple. It was finished with care, sharpened at one end, and striped as shown in the figure [618]. The ring was about 8 inches in diameter, made either into a hoop or solid like a wheel, by winding with splints. Sometimes the javelin was thrown horizontally, by placing the forefinger against its foot, and supporting it with the thumb and second finger; in other cases it was held in the center, and thrown with the hand raised above the shoulder.

On either side from fifteen to thirty players were arranged, each having from three to six javelins, the number of both depending upon the interest in the game and the time they wished to devote to the contest. The javelins themselves were the forfeit, and the game was gained by the party which won them.

Among the preliminaries to be settled by the managers, was the line on which the ring was to be rolled, the distance of the two bands of players from each other, and the space between each and the line itself. When these points

FIG. 618. Hoop and pole; diameter of hoop, 6 inches; length of pole, 5½ feet; Seneca Indians, New York; from Morgan.

were adjusted and the parties stationed, the ring was rolled by one party on the line, in front of the other. As it passed the javelins were thrown. If the ring was struck by one of them the players of the adverse party were required, each in turn, to stand in the place of the person who struck it, and throw their javelins in succession at the ring, which was set up as a target, on the spot where it was hit. Those of the javelins which hit the target when thus thrown were saved; if any missed, they were passed to the other party, and by them were again thrown at the ring from the same point. Those which hit were won, finally, and laid out of the play, while the residue were restored to their original owners. After this first contest was decided, the ring was rolled back, and the other party, in turn, threw their javelins. If it was struck, the party which rolled it was required, in the same manner, to hazard their javelins, by throwing them at the target. Such as missed were delivered to the other party, and those which hit the target when thrown by them, were won also, and laid

[a] League of the Iroquois, p. 298, Rochester, 1851. See also Report to the Regents of the University upon the Articles furnished to the Indian Collection by Lewis H. Morgan. Third Annual Report of the Regents of the University on the Condition of the State Cabinet of Natural History and the Historical and Antiquarian Collections annexed thereto, p. 79, Albany, 1850.

out of the play. In this manner the game was continued until one of the parties had lost their javelins, which, of itself, determined the contest.

Mr Andrew John, of Iroquois, New York, described the hoop-and-dart game as played at the present day by the Seneca as follows:

The implements for the game consist of a hoop, gah-nuk-gah, made of sapling, without marks; and darts, gah-geh-dok, 4 or 5 feet in length, of which each player has usually two.

The players line up equally on two sides about 10 feet apart. One party throws the hoop and the others launch their darts at it. The object is to stop the hoop as it rolls by impaling it. If a player misses, his dart is forfeited, but if it goes under the hoop, he retains it.

TUSCARORA. New York. (Cat. no. 16338, Free Museum of Science and Art, University of Pennsylvania.)

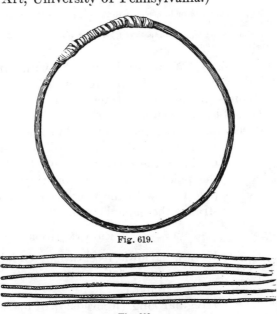

Fig. 619.

Fig. 620.

FIG. 619. Game hoop; diameter, 16 inches; Tuscarora Indians, New York; cat. no. 16338, Free Museum of Science and Art, University of Pennsylvania.
FIG. 620. Poles for hoop game; length, 7 feet; Tuscarora Indians, New York; cat. no. 16338, Free Museum of Science and Art, University of Pennsylvania.

Hoop (figure 619) made of an unpeeled bent sapling, tied with bark, 16 inches in diameter, and six poles (figure 620), 7 feet in length.

Collected in 1893 by the writer, who was informed that they were used in the game of nayearwanaqua.

The ring is called okakna and the poles are called oota. Five or six play. The ring is rolled and all discharge their poles. The one whose pole stops the ring owns it. The others then shoot in turn, and the owner of the ring takes all the poles that miss it and shoots them at the ring, winning those that he puts through it. If two men stop the ring, they divide the poles.

KERESAN STOCK

KERES. Laguna, New Mexico. (Cat. no. 3007, Brooklyn Institute
    Museum.)

Ring (figure 621), covered with buckskin, sewed on inner side with
    thong and painted white, 8 inches in diameter; and two painted

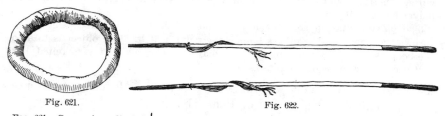

Fig. 621.                                 Fig. 622.

FIG. 621. Game ring; diameter, 8 inches; Keres Indians, Laguna, New Mexico; cat. no. 3007,
Brooklyn Institute Museum.
Fig. 622. Poles for ring game; length, 75 inches; Keres Indians, Laguna, New Mexico; cat. no.
3007, Brooklyn Institute Museum.

poles (figure 622), 75 inches in length, with tips and butts
white, middle part red. The tips are pointed, and each has four
buckskin thongs, painted red, attached some 15 inches from its
end. Collected by the writer in 1903.

Mr John M. Gunn, of Laguna, stated that the game is called
maskurtsh. The ring is rolled and the game is
to throw the poles inside of it. The thongs on
the poles are used in counting, and when the
pole falls with the ring between the two sets of
strands the game is won.

KIOWAN STOCK

FIG. 623. Game ring; di-
ameter, 3 inches; Kio-
wa Indians, Oklahoma;
cat. no. 152907, United
States National Mu-
seum.

KIOWA. Kiowa reservation, Oklahoma. (Cat.
    no. 152907, United States National Mu-
    seum.)

Irregular ring (figure 623) of buckskin, 3 inches
    in diameter, set with four double rows of
beads at equal distances on its outer edge, two opposite ones
    white, and two opposite ones dark blue.

Collected by Mr James Mooney, who furnished the following state-
ment:

Warriors or hunters purchase the privilege of throwing a dart at the ring, and
derive auguries from success or failure in sending their darts through the circle.

KULANAPAN STOCK

POMO. Seven miles south of Ukiah, Mendocino county, California.
    (Cat. no. 70939, 70940, Field Columbian Museum.)

Wooden hoop (figure 624), 20 inches in diameter, with grape binding
    at joint; and forked-end lance, 8 feet long. Collected by Dr
    J. W. Hudson.

Doctor Hudson describes the following games:

Da-ko′ kă, da-ko′, the hoop and kă, game. Played with a 16-inch hoop [figure 624] bound with Apocynum cord, by four men usually, each armed with a 9-foot pole. A races the hoop swiftly to B [figure 625], who tries to impale

FIG. 624. Hoop and dart; diameter of hoop, 20 inches; length of dart, 8 feet; Pomo Indians, Mendocino county, California; cat. no. 70939, 70940, Field Columbian Museum.

it as it passes. (The spear does not leave his hands in the thrust, else he passes out of the game.) If B misses, his place is at once taken by one of the substitutes behind him, who catches the hoop. The player at B rolls to C, who attempts to impale it, thence C to D, and D to A. The player last to miss wins the stakes. When a player misses he forfeits his position and stake money at once, and his chances and stakes are appropriated by his substitute.

In another game a 4-inch hoop is laid upon the ground, and lances 4 feet long are cast upon it from a distance of 50 feet. A transfix counts 5 and a ring strike 2. Twelve counters are used. The game is called da-ko nĭt′-ak or javelin-spearing hoop.

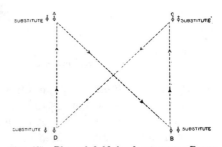
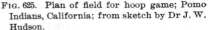

FIG. 625. Plan of field for hoop game; Pomo Indians, California; from sketch by Dr J. W. Hudson.

A tule butt is erected and a 1-inch ring of twisted fiber hung in its center. Archers stand 60 feet away. A center stroke counts 5, a hoop stroke 2. There are ten counters. This is called da-ko tcox′-tau, ring target.

LUTUAMIAN STOCK

KLAMATH. Upper Klamath lake, Oregon. (Cat. no. 61682, Field Columbian Museum.)

Ring (figure 626) made of the inner fiber of the tule rush, wrapped with tule bark, 11 inches in diameter.

Collected by Dr George A. Dorsey, who describes it as used in the game of wóshakank.[a] The ring is shot at with arrows, not differing from those used by boys in their hunting. The object of the game is to hit the ring with an arrow.

Another specimen (cat. no. 61681) is 6 inches in diameter. Rings of this size are used chiefly by boys.

---

[a] Certain Gambling Games of the Klamath Indians. American Anthropologist, n. s., v. 3, p. 17, 1901.

KLAMATH.   Oregon.   (Cat. no. 37479, Free Museum of Science and
        Art, University of Pennsylvania.)
Ring (figure 627) of bast, 7 inches in diameter.
   Collected in 1900 by Dr George A. Dorsey, who describes it as a
ring for woshakank, the kind used by boys.

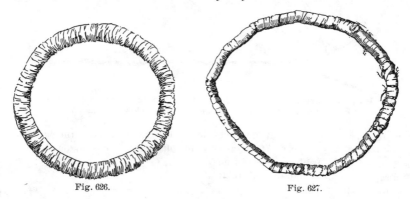

Fig. 626.                              Fig. 627.

FIG. 626.   Game ring; diameter, 11 inches; Klamath Indians, Oregon; cat. no. 61682, Field Colum-
   bian Museum.
FIG. 627.   Game ring (boy's); diameter, 7 inches; Klamath Indians, Oregon; cat. no. 37479, Free
   Museum of Science and Art, University of Pennsylvania.

——— Upper Klamath lake, Oregon.   (Field Columbian Museum.)
   Cat. no. 61641.   Two rings, diameters, 3 and 4 inches, made of flexible
        bast; a small bow, 2 feet in length, and three small reed arrows,
        with long, sharp wooden points, of sage (figure 628).
   Collected in 1900 by Dr George A. Dorsey, who describes the
game under the name of shü'kshuks.[a]

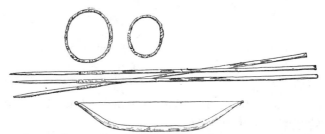

FIG. 628.   Rings, bow, and arrows for ring game; diameter of rings, 3 and 4 inches; length of
   bow, 2 feet; Klamath Indians, Oregon; cat. no. 61641, Field Columbian Museum.

   It is usually played in a wickiup, by either men or boys, most
commonly in winter, in the following manner: One of two boys sitting from 8 to 10 feet apart rolls a ring toward the other, who shoots
at it with an arrow (ntē'kish).   In case he hits the ring the one who
rolled it endeavors, by shooting, to dislodge the arrow therefrom.

[a] Certain Gambling Games of the Klamath Indians.   American Anthropologist, n. s.,
v. 3, p. 17, 1901.

Should he succeed, there is no count; otherwise the one who first shot gains an arrow, the object of the game being to win arrows.

Cat. no. 61717. Ring, one-half of an inch in diameter, and a small

awl-like object, consisting of a bone point mounted in a sharp wooden handle, 3½ inches in length (figure 629).

This was collected in 1900 by Dr George A. Dorsey, who describes the game under the same name as the preceding—shü′kshuks—which is applied also to the ring. He describes this game as played by persons of both sexes and by

FIG. 629. Game ring and awl; diameter of ring, one-half of an inch; length of awl, 3¼ inches; Klamath Indians, Oregon; cat. no. 61717, Field Columbian Museum; from Dorsey.

all ages, generally in the wickiup. The players sit facing each other, and as one rolls the ring in front of him his opponent endeavors to pierce one or both sides of the ring with the point of his awl. To pierce one side counts 1; both sides, 2.

Cat. no. 61674. Tule fiber ring (figure 630), 11 inches in diameter. Collected in 1900 by Dr George A. Dorsey, who describes the game as follows:

This is an interesting variation of the ring game, for which I could get no native name to distinguish it from the ones just described. . . . The ring measures 11 inches in diameter and is an inch thick. Across one side of it is fastened a crossbar, measuring 17 inches in length, projecting 3 inches beyond the ring on each side. Both ring and crossbar are made of the inner fiber of the tule rush, closely wrapped with tule bark, the inner surface being placed outside, giving the ring a whitish color. In playing the game two rings of equal size are used; these are placed in an

FIG. 630. Game ring; diameter, 11 inches; Klamath Indians, Oregon; cat. no. 61674, Field Columbian Museum.

upright position, one end of the crossbar resting on a sharp wooden pin firmly fixed in the ground. The interval between the two goals varies according to agreement between the players. There are always two opposing sides, each consisting of one or more individuals. The ring is shot at with arrows from a bow, the object being to pierce both sides of the goal, which is always placed at right angles. Two specimens . . . of this game were collected, the only difference being in the size of the diameter of the ring and the length of the crossbar. This game, I was informed, has not been played for many years, and satisfactory information concerning the method of playing could not be obtained.

Doctor Dorsey describes also a variation called shíkna:

This interesting variation of the ring game is played only by men. It consists of as many spears (shíkna) as there are individual players and two goals (tchedalk), each of which is simply a forked stick thrust in the ground at such interval as may be mutually agreed upon. The spears are of willow, measuring 6 feet in length, and sharpened at one end. They are decorticated, except at the lower extremity. The spears are hurled from the hand, the object being to cause them to fall in such manner that the end of the spear will rest on the fork of the goal. Such a throw counts 5, otherwise the one whose spear falls nearest the goal counts 1; ten usually constitutes the game. The game is still practised to some extent by the Klamath, and in playing they exhibit great skill, one of the players whom I saw not failing to strike the goal oftener than once in six or eight throws. One set of this game (61710) consists of two spears and a pair of forked sticks.

See the Pima game, p. 489.

See the Pima game, p. 489.

### MARIPOSAN STOCK

CHUKCHANSI. Pickayune, Madera county, California. (Cat. no. 70891, Field Columbian Museum.)

Ring (figure 631), wrapped with buckskin, 3½ inches in diameter, and two maple-wood lances, the longer about 8 feet in length. Collected by Dr J. W. Hudson.

FIG. 631.  Ring and poles; diameter of ring, 3½ inches; length of poles, the longer, about 8 feet; Chukchansi Indians, Madera county. California; cat. no. 70891, Field Columbian Museum.

A player rolls the ring along the ground and follows it with the lance, trying to impale it. If he fails, the next tries. One ring is used. Impaling the ring counts 5; if it falls on the pole, the count is 3.

KOYETI.[a]  Tule River reservation, California.

Dr J. W. Hudson describes the following game under the name of hoturx:

A lance-and-target game played with a hoop of willow about 3 inches in diameter, laced over with Apocynum with radial cords called ta-koi, and a lance, im-mak, 10 feet long. Two play, using one ring and two poles or lances, one for each. The caster tries to strike the rolling target, and if successful tallies 6. In such case he is allowed to put his hand over the second player's eyes, so that he can not see when he throws. The score is 10, and is kept with sticks.

PITKACHI.  Table mountain, Fresno county, California. (Cat. no. 70892, Field Columbian Museum.)

---

[a] Three members only of this tribe are alive.

Ring (figure 632), wrapped with bast cord, 2½ inches in diameter, described by the collector, Dr J. W. Hudson, as used as a moving target for arrows under the name of takumship,[a] " wheel roll."

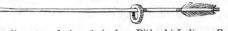

FIG. 632.   Ring and arrow; diameter of ring, 2½ inches; Pitkachi Indians, Fresno county, California; cat. no. 70892, Field Columbian Museum.

Four play.   One man rolls the ring by two opponents, one of whom shoots at it with a blunt arrow with a bow, tä-lĭp.   If he knocks it over, it counts 1 point ; if he transfixes it, 10.   Each part of the arrows used in this game, which are 30 inches long, has a name quite different from those of war, small game, or flight arrows.   The foreshaft is literally "come to us."   The shaft is literally " tied together " or " links."   The feathers are literally " appointed season." I could get no light on the reason for so naming them.

————.[b]   Table mountain, Fresno county, California.

Dr J. W. Hudson describes the following game under the name of xalau :

Two or more men stand before a brush wall or strip of matting. etc., some 10 feet tall, each armed with a 7-foot spear of *Prunus demissa* wood.   Each spear is highly decorated with covert feathers from the gray-head eagle and painted.   The umpire casts over his spear which sticks in the ground.   A player casts after it, trying to make his spear-feathers strike those of the umpire.   All follow in order, and the successful caster is assured luck in war or hunting.   A wide cast implies catastrophe or death to the caster, who at once makes a new spear and tries " stronger " medicine feathers.   This is a ceremonial game of much significance to warriors.

YAUDANCHI.   (See page 501.)

YOKUTS. Tule River reservation, Tulare county, California.   (Cat. no. 70402, 70403, Field Columbian Museum.)

Hoop of fiber, wrapped with buckskin, 4½ inches in diameter; and maple-wood lance (figure 633), about 8 feet long, sharpened at the point and marked with red stripes at the end.   Collected by Dr J. W. Hudson, who thus describes the game under the name of hotush :

FIG. 633.   Ring and pole; diameter of ring, 4½ inches; length of pole, 8 feet; Yokuts Indians, Tule River reservation, Tulare county, California; cat. no. 70402, 70403, Field Columbian Museum.

Played by four players, two on a side.   One player casts the hoop, to-ko-in ho-tush, and his partner casts his lance so that the hoop will fall on it.   If he is successful, and the hoop rests entirely on the lance, not touching the ground, he wins the game.   If the hoop rests half on the ground, it counts 1.   The game is also won at a throw by impaling the ring.   Twelve counters are used.   The

---

[a] The etymology of this name is probably not pure Mariposan, part of which seems derived from a northern stock.   (J. W. H.)

[b] Tribe extinct.

lance, hoat, is thrown underhand with both hands.  The ring is covered either with buckskin or bark.

Doctor Hudson describes also a ring-and-arrow game under the name of tokoinawas:

This game is played with a hoop or ring, to-ko-in, 6 inches, more or less, in diameter and wrapped with buckskin.  One player rolls the ring to another opposite him, while two others on opposite sides, at right angles to the course, shoot at it with arrows.  The one who transfixes the ring or strikes it oftenest in ten rolls wins.

Yokuts.   Tule River reservation, Tulare county, California.  (Cat. no. 70404, Field Columbian Museum.)

Wooden lance, 8 feet 3 inches long, and a small round wooden block or peg (figure 634).

Fig. 634.   Implements for lance-and-peg game; length of lance, 99 inches; Yokuts Indians, Tulare county, California; cat. no. 70404, Field Columbian Museum.

Collected by Dr J. W. Hudson, who thus refers to them as used in a lance-throwing game, aikiwitch:

Each player casts two lances at a peg lying loose on the ground 50 feet away. Six or less play.  The lance is call ai-yak-ta-ka and the peg kets-ma-na witch-it. The last man is thumped on the head with the bare knuckles, and the one making the highest score may strike as often as he desires.

MOQUELUMNAN STOCK

Chowchilla.   Chowchilly river, Madera county, California.

Dr J. W. Hudson describes the following game under the name of pachitu:

A ring of Asclepias, 2½ inches in diameter, called he-wi'-ta, is rolled, the caster racing, and casting after the ring a 10-foot lance, called hu-wo'-ta.  A "lean" counts 3, a "balance" 5, and a "transfix" 12.

Topinagugim.   Big creek, 2 miles north of Groveland, Tuolumne county, California.  (Cat. no. 70234, Field Columbian Museum.)

Darts and hoop for a game.

Collected by Dr J. W. Hudson, and described as follows by the collector, under the name of teweknumsia:

The implements consist of a plain lance, ho-cha, 10 feet in length, marked on the butt end with proprietary marks, in paint, and a hoop of oak, 30 inches in diameter, bound with buckskin, te-weknum-sia.  The game is played by four players, who face each other on opposite sides of a square 90 feet across.  The casters [figure 635], each of whom have four lances, stand opposite to each other, while two assistants, one for each side, roll the hoop across.  As the wheel rolls, both casters throw at it, each trying to transfix it.  If one is successful his opponent comes across to his place,

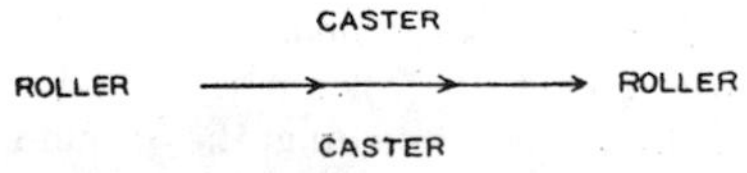

Fig. 635.  Plan of field for hoop-and-lance game; Topinagugim Indians, Tuolumne county, California; from sketch by Dr J. W. Hudson.

and, standing in the successful caster's tracks, tries to transfix the fallen hoop. After him, the first player tries at the same mark and from the same position. They cast alternately until all have thrown their four lances. The greater number of transfixing spears decides. There are 30 counting-sticks, 15 to a side. The buckskin is to keep the hoop from bounding.

WASAMA.  Madera county, California.

Dr J. W. Hudson describes the following game under the name of hewitu numhe:

A hoop, he-wi'-ta, 10 inches in diameter, of Fremontii californica bark bound with buckskin, is rolled toward an opponent, who shoots at it with arrows in passing.  A "strike" counts 3 and a "transfix" 10, or coup.

MUSKHOGEAN STOCK

BAYOGOULA and MUGULASHA.  Louisiana.

The officer who kept the journal of the frigate [a] when Iberville arrived at the mouth of the Mississippi, 1698–1699, says:

They pass the greater part of their time in playing in this place with great sticks, which they throw after a little stone which is nearly round, like a bullet.

CHOCTAW.  Mississippi.

James Adair [b] says:

The warriors have another favorite game called chungke; which, with propriety of language, may be called "running hard labor." They have near their statehouse a square piece of ground well cleaned, and fine sand is carefully strewed over it, when requisite, to promote a swifter motion to what they throw along the surface.  Only one or two on a side play at this ancient game. They have a stone about 2 fingers broad at the edge, and 2 spans round: Each party has a pole of about 8 feet long, smooth, and tapering at each end, the points flat.  They set off abreast of each other at 6 yards from the end of the playground; then one of them hurls the stone on its edge, in as direct a line as he can, a considerable distance toward the middle of the other end of the square: When they have ran a few yards, each darts his pole anointed with bear's oil, with a proper force, as near as he can guess in proportion to the motion of the stone, that the end may lie close to the stone—when this is the case, the person counts 2 of the game, and, in proportion to the nearness of the poles to the mark, 1 is counted, unless by measuring both are found to be at an equal distance from the stone.  In this manner the players will keep running most part of the day, at half speed, under the violent heat of the sun, staking their silver ornaments, their nose, finger, and ear rings; their breast, arm, and wrist plates, and even all their wearing apparel, except that which barely covers their middle.  All the American Indians are much addicted to this game, which to us appears to be a task of stupid drudgery.  It seems however to be of early origin, when their fore-fathers used diversions as simple as their manners.  The hurling stones they use at present were time immemorial rubbed smooth on the rocks, and with prodigious labor; they are kept with the strictest religious care

---

[a] Journal de la Frégate Le Marin, Margry's Découvertes, v. 4, p. 261, Paris, 1880.
[b] The History of the American Indians, p. 401, London, 1775.

from one generation to another, and are exempted from being buried with the dead. They belong to the town where they are used, and are carefully preserved.

### Capt. Bernard Romans [a] says:

Their favorite game of chunké is a plain proof of the evil consequences of a violent passion for gaming upon all kinds, classes, and orders of men; at this they play from morning to night, with an unwearied application, and they bet high; here you may see a savage come and bring all his skins, stake them and lose them; next his pipe, his beads, trinkets and ornaments; at last his blanket, and other garment, and even all their arms, and, after all it is not uncommon for them to go home, borrow a gun and shoot themselves; an instance of this happened in 1771 at East Yasoo a short time before my arrival. Suicide has also been practised here on other occasions, but they regard the act as a crime, and bury the body as unworthy of their ordinary funeral rites.

The manner of playing this game is thus: They make an alley of about 200 feet in length, where a very smooth clay ground is laid, which when dry, is very hard; they play two together, each having a straight pole of about 15 feet long; one holds a stone, which is in the shape of a truck, which he throws before him over his alley, and the instant of its departure, they set off and run; in running they cast their poles after the stone; he that did not throw it endeavors to hit it; the other strives to strike the pole of his antagonist in its flight, so as to prevent its hitting the stone; he counts 1, but should both miss their aim the throw is renewed; and in case a score is won the winner casts the stone and 11 is up; they hurl this stone and pole with wonderful dexterity and violence, and fatigue themselves much at it.

### Huma. Mississippi.

### Father James Gravier [b] says:

. . . . in the middle of the village a fine level square, where from morning to night there are young men who exercise themselves in running after a flat stone, which they throw in the air from one end of the square to the other, and which they try to have fall on two cylinders that they roll where they think that the stone will fall.

### Muskogee. Georgia.

### Col. Benjamin Hawkins [c] says:

The Micco, counselors and warriors, meet every day in the public square, sit and drink ā-cee, a strong decoction of the cassine yupon, called by the traders black drink; talk of news, the public, and domestic concerns, smoke their pipes, and play thla-chal-litch-cau, "roll the bullet."

### William Bartram, in a manuscript work on the Southern Indians, cited by Squier and Davis,[d] wrote as follows:

Chunk yards.—The 'chunk yards' of the Muscogulges, or Creeks, are rectangular areas, generally occupying the center of the town. The public square and rotunda, or great winter council house, stand at the two opposite corners of them. They are generally very extensive, especially in the large old towns: some of them are from 600 to 900 feet in length, and of proportionate breadth.

---

[a] A Concise Natural History of East and West Florida, v. 1, p. 79, New York, 1775.

[b] Journal of the Voyage of Father Gravier (1700), in Early Voyages Up and Down the Mississippi, p. 143, John Gilmary Shea, Albany, 1861.

[c] A Sketch of the Creek Country. Collection of the Georgia Historical Society, v. 3, p. 71, Savannah, 1848.

[d] Aboriginal Monuments of the State of New York. Smithsonian Contributions to Knowledge, v. 2, p. 135, 1849.

The area is exactly level, and sunk 2, sometimes 3 feet below the banks or terraces surrounding them, which are occasionally two in number, one behind and above the other, and composed of the earth taken from the area at the time of its formation. These banks or terraces serve the purpose of seats for the spectators. In the center of this yard or area there is a low circular mound or eminence, in the middle of which stands erect the chunk pole, which is a high obelisk or four-square pillar declining upwards to an obtuse point. This is of wood, the heart or inward resinous part of a sound pine tree, and is very durable; it is generally from 30 to 40 feet in height, and to the top is fastened some object which serves as a mark to shoot at, with arrows or the rifle, at certain appointed times. Near each corner of one end of the yard stands erect a less pole or pillar, about 12 feet high, called a "slave post," for the reason that to them are bound the captives condemned to be burnt. These posts are usually decorated with the scalps of slain enemies, suspended by strings from the top. They are often crowned with the white dry skull of an enemy.

It thus appears that this area is designed for a public place of exhibition, for shows, games, etc. Formerly, there is little doubt, most barbarous and tragical scenes were enacted within them, such as the torturing and burning of captives, who were here forced to run the gauntlet, bruised and beaten with sticks and burning chunks of wood. The Indians do not now practise these cruelties; but there are some old traders who have witnessed them in former times. I inquired of these traders for what reason these areas were called "chunk yards:" they were, in general, ignorant, yet, for the most part, concurred in a lame story that it originated in the circumstance of its having been a place of torture, and that the name was but an interpretation of the Indian term designating them.[a]

I observed none of these yards in use in any of the Cherokee towns; and where I have mentioned them, in the Cherokee country, it must be understood that I saw only the remains or vestiges of them among the ruins of the ancient towns. In the existing Cherokee towns which I visited, although there were ancient mounds and signs of the yard adjoining, yet the yard was either built upon or turned into a garden plat, or otherwise appropriated. Indeed, I am convinced that the chunk yards now or lately in use among the Creeks are of very ancient date, and not the work of the present Indians; although they are now kept in repair by them, being swept very clean every day, and the poles kept up and decorated in the manner I have described.

The following plan [figure 636] will illustrate the form and character of these yards: A. The great area, surrounded by terraces or banks. B. A circular eminence at one end of the yard, commonly 9 or 10 feet higher than the ground round about. Upon this mound stands the great rotunda, hothouse, or winter council house of the present Creeks. It was probably designed and used by the ancients, who constructed it for the same purpose. c. A square terrace or eminence, about the same height with the circular one just described, occupying a position at the other end of the yard. Upon this stands the public square. The banks inclosing the yard are indicated by the letters b, b, b, b; c indicates the "chunk pole"; and d, d, the "slave posts."

---

[a] According to Adair, Du Pratz, and other writers, the Cherokees and probably the Creeks were much addicted to a similar game, played with a rod or pole and a circular stone, which was called chungke. Mr Catlin describes this game as still existing under the name of tchung-kee among the Minitarees and other tribes on the Missouri. It also prevailed among some of the Ohio Indians. It has been suggested that the areas called chunk, or chunky yards, by Bartram, derived their names from the circumstance, that they were, among other objects, devoted to games, among which, that of chungke was prominent. This suggestion derives some support from Adair. . . . It is therefore not improbable that these square areas were denominated chungke yards.

Sometimes the square, instead of being open at the ends, as shown in the plan, is closed upon all sides by the banks. In the lately built or new Creek towns, they do not raise a mound for the foundation of their rotundas or public squares. The yard, however, is retained, and the public buildings occupy nearly the same position in respect to it. They also retain the central obelisk and the slave posts.

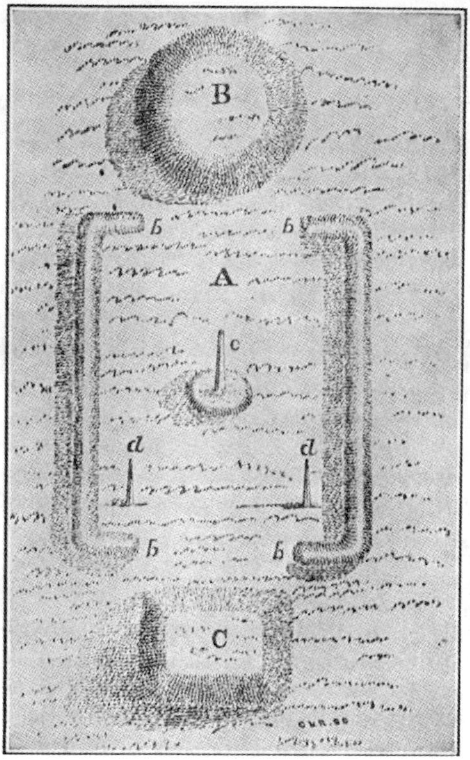

FIG. 636.  Chunk yard; Muskogee Indians, Georgia; from William Bartram.

NATCHESAN STOCK

NATCHEZ.   Louisiana.

Le Page du Pratz [a] wrote as follows:

The natives of Louisiana have invented but a very few diversions, and these perhaps serve their turn as well as a greater variety would do. The warriors practice a diversion which is called the game of the pole, at which two only play together at a time. Each has a pole, about 8 feet long, resembling a Roman f, and the game consists in rolling a flat round stone, about 3 inches in diameter and an inch thick, with the edge somewhat sloping, and throwing the pole at the same time in such a manner that when the stone rests the pole may touch it or be near it. Both antagonists throw their poles at the same time, and he whose pole is nearest the stone counts 1, and has the right of rolling the stone. The men fatigue themselves much at this game, as they run after their poles at every throw; and some of them are so bewitched by it that they game away one piece of furniture after another. These gamesters, however, are very rare, and are greatly discountenanced by the rest of the people.

---

[a] Historie de la Louisiane, v. 3, p. 4, Paris, 1768.

PIMA. Arizona. (Cat. no. 76020, United States National Museum.)
Stick or arrow with a feather at one end and a corncob at the other,
　　sent by the National Museum, as an exchange, to the Peabody
　　Museum, Salem, Mass.•

Collected by Dr Edward Palmer, who thus describes it as used in
the game of quins:

Any number can play. A short split stick is first thrown in a slanting direction. Then each one pitches his arrow to see who can come nearest to it. The
one who does so holds the stick up while the others pitch. If the arrow touches
the split stick and does not catch, the thrower loses nothing. If, however, the
arrow remains in the split stick, it becomes the property of the holder. The
game ends when one has all the arrows or when the players tire out.

This is the only record of a game analogous to hoop and pole
which I find among the tribes of the Piman stock.

PUJUNAN STOCK

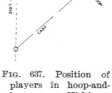

NISHINAM. Mokelumne river, 12 miles south of
　　Placerville, California.

Dr J. W. Hudson describes a hoop-and-lance
game under the name of nunt:

FIG. 637. Position of
players in hoop-and-
lance game; Nishinam
Indians, California;
from a sketch by Dr
J. W. Hudson.

　The hoop, künûn', consists of an outer hoop of oak
wrapped with rawhide, 24 inches in diameter, with a
center hoop of rawhide. The former has ten radii of
rawhide attached to the inner hoop. The players [fig-
ure 637] roll the hoop in turn, and cast a 9-foot lance
at it, after springing quickly to right angles of the hoop's course. A bull's-eye
counts coup, or 10; between spokes, 5; lean up (by hoop), 2. The dead line
and course is laid out previous to play.

SALISHAN STOCK

BELLACOOLA. Dean inlet, British Columbia. (Cat. no. $\frac{16}{1546}$ and
　　$\frac{16}{1551}$, American Museum of Natural History.)

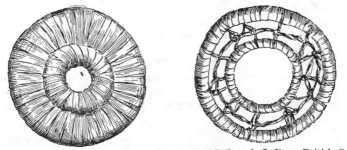

FIG. 638. Cedar-bark game rings; diameter, 7¼ inches; Bellacoola Indians, British Columbia;
cat. no. $\frac{16}{1546}$, $\frac{16}{1551}$, American Museum of Natural History.

Two rings (figure 638), wrapped with cedar bark, 7½ inches in
　　diameter. Collected by Mr George Hunt and Dr Franz Boas.

BELLACOOLA.    Dean inlet, British Columbia.    (Field Columbian Museum.)

Cat. no. 18490.    Lava ring (figure 639), 3½ inches in diameter, with hole in the center.

Cat. no. 18494.    Lava ring (figure 639), similar to the one last described, but smaller, 2½ inches in diameter.

FIG. 639.   Lava game rings; diameters, 3½ and 2½ inches; Bellacoola Indians, British Columbia; cat. no. 18490, 18494, Field Columbian Museum.

PEND D'OREILLES.    Flathead reservation, Montana.    (Cat. no. 51793, Field Columbian Museum.)

Ring, wound with buckskin, 2½ inches in diameter, the interior set with colored beads; and two arrows (figure 640), 23½ inches in length, with iron spike points, the shaft of the arrow being wound with buckskin at ends and middle.    Collected by Dr George A. Dorsey.

FIG. 640.   Beaded game ring and arrows; diameter of ring, 2½ inches; length of arrows, 23½ inches; Pend d'Oreille Indians, Montana; cat. no. 51793, Field Columbian Museum.

The Dictionary of the Kalispel [a] gives the following:

Szgolkólégu, the playing at wheels; chgolkoléguten, the play wheels, la roulette; chines golkólégui, I play with small wheels or circles; jouer à la roulette, an Indian play; golkoleguèmen, a gambler at wheels; golko, wheel, wagon.

---

[a] Dictionary of the Kalispel or Flat-head Indian Language, compiled by the Missionaries of the Society of Jesus, St Ignatius Print, Montana, 1877–8–9.

SALISH.  Comox, British Columbia.

Dr C. F. Newcombe writes: [a]

I was told of a game called xānăni, played by two sides with a quoitlike disk of twigs, bound with willow or cedar bark, and thrown in the air to be caught on a stick while skimming.  At Alert bay (Kwakiutl), the game is called kāni.

SHUSWAP.  Kamloops, British Columbia.

Dr Franz Boas [b] says:

A peculiar gambling game is played in the following way: A long pole is laid on the ground, about 15 feet from the players; a ring about 1 inch in diameter, to which four beads are attached at points dividing the circumference into four equal parts, is rolled toward the pole, and sticks are thrown after it before it falls down on touching the pole.  The four beads are red, white, blue, and black.

The ring falls down on the stick that has been thrown after it, and, according to the color of the bead that touches the stick, the player wins a number of points.

SONGISH.  Vancouver island, British Columbia.

Dr Franz Boas [c] says:

Throwing and catching of hoops is a favorite game.

THOMPSON INDIANS (NTLAKYAPAMUK).  British Columbia.

Mr James Teit [d] says:

This game [referring to the stick game] has been out of use for many years, as well as another game, greatly in vogue at one time among the Indians, which was played altogether by men.  They found it warm work, and used to strip off all their clothes except the breechcloth when playing.  The chief implement in this game was a ring [figure 641] from 2 inches to 4½ inches in diameter, and sewed over with buckskin, the framework often being made of a stick bent round.  The buckskin covering was loose, and the space inside not taken up by the stick was filled with sand to make the ring solid and heavy. The player set this ring rolling.  Then he followed it, running, and threw a small spear at it.  The object of the game was to throw the spear in front of the ring and make the latter fall on it.  Generally the playing-ground was marked by two long poles, which prevented the ring from rolling too far. Six different marks, which determined the number of points, were sewed on the buckskin inside of the circle.  In later times these were made with different colored beads.  The number of beads was six or four.  Four were always blue or some other dark color, and two were some light color, generally light blue, but frequently white or red.  The light beads counted 10 points each.  If both fell on top of the stick, it counted 20.  The dark beads counted 5 each.  If two fell on top of the stick, it counted 10; if one dark and one light, 15.  If the ring did not fall on top of the throwing stick, but stood up against it, it counted 40, which was the highest.  The beads were not then counted.  Before beads were known, porcupine quills were used as marks on the rings.  The two light marks

[a] In a letter, March 11, 1901.

[b] Second General Report on the Indians of British Columbia.  Report of the Sixtieth Meeting of the British Association for the Advancement of Science, p. 641, London, 1891.

[c] Ibid., p. 571.

[d] The Thompson Indians of British Columbia.  Members of the American Museum of Natural History, v. 2, p. 273, New York, 1900.

were in white or yellow, and the four dark marks were black. It seems, therefore, that the colors were not exactly fixed, further than that they had to be light and dark.

Another game was played with the same ring and throwing-stick, and the points were counted as in the game just described. In fact, this game was like that, except that in this the players sat facing each other, and rolled the ring from one to the other. One man started the ring rolling, and then threw his stick in front of it, so as to stop it, if possible, before it reached the other man. Sometimes one man rolled and the other threw, in turn, instead of both men running abreast and throwing their sticks in front of the ring, as in the other game, one after the other. If the player missed, the other man took his turn.

Another game was generally played by boys and girls, but occasionally by adults. It was played out of doors, but also, in cold weather, inside the winter houses. In this a ring from 6 to 10 inches in diameter was used. It was made of pliable sticks, around which bark or dried grass was thickly twisted. Sometimes it was made of reeds (the same as those used in tent-mats) bent in the form of a circle, around which other reeds were twisted. The players sat in two lines, some distance apart, facing one another. At each end of the lines sat a person who set the ring rolling from one to the other between the two lines of players. When the ring was in motion, the players threw darts at it, the object being to make these darts hit the ring. If they passed through the ring without touching, it counted nothing. The darts were about 6 or 7 inches in length, some thick in the middle and small at both ends [figure 642]. One end was feathered, while the other end was brought to a very sharp point. Many darts had the shaft all one thickness to near the point, where it was forked into two sharp points. These darts had property-marks, consisting of notches, dots, circles, or paintings, to indicate the owner. The wood used was that of the wăx·esê'lp-bush.

A peculiar custom in connection with this game was that sometimes the old people would put some of the darts which the boys used for throwing at the ring into the fire of the winter house, the lads not being allowed to get them except by catching the ends of them with their teeth. Sometimes all the darts were gathered together and thrown outside. The boys were made to scramble

FIG. 641. Beaded game ring and spear; diameter of ring, 2 to 4¼ inches; length of spear, 29¼ inches; Thompson Indians, British Columbia; cat. no. $\frac{16}{1255}$, $\frac{16}{1255}$, American Museum of Natural History.

FIG. 642. Game dart; length, 12 inches; Thompson Indians, British Columbia; cat. no. $\frac{16}{1255}$, American Museum of Natural History.

for them. The one that obtained the most was the victor. A boy who was unlucky in playing, and lost all his darts, could get them back again by putting up his back as a target, every arrow fired at it becoming his property. This game, like the preceding one, has now gone out of use.

In another game a ring the size of a finger ring was placed on the ground about 9 or 10 feet away from the players. Each player had two darts, which he threw so as to hit the center of the ring, if possible. The darts were feathered, had sharp points, and were made rather thin. Boys and girls, in playing these games, won or lost their darts. They did not gamble for anything else. There were no special months for certain games, excepting that some games were better adapted for special seasons than others, and consequently were played only in those seasons.

### SHAHAPTIAN STOCK

Nez Percés.  Southern Alberta.

Rev. John MacLean[a] mentions "throwing the arrow and wheel" among the games of the tribe.

Umatilla.  Oregon.  (Free Museum of Science and Art, University of Pennsylvania.)

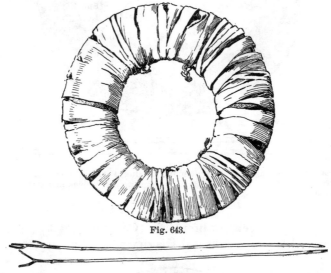

Fig. 643.

Fig. 644.

Fig. 643.  Game hoop; diameter, 11¼ inches; Umatilla Indians, Oregon; cat. no. 37538, Free Museum of Science and Art, University of Pennsylvania.

Fig. 644.  Poles for hoop game; lengths, 68 and 69 inches; Umatilla Indians, Oregon; cat. no. 37538, Free Museum of Science and Art, University of Pennsylvania.

Cat. no. 37538.  Flat hoop (figure 643) made of twigs covered with bark, 11¼ inches in diameter, and two poles (figure 644), 68 and 69 inches in length, forked and painted red at the ends. Collected by the writer in 1900.

The game is played in the spring. The ring is called pasa-pow-i-low-wikes and the poles are designated wai-hutz.

Cat. no. 37539.  Ring, wrapped with buckskin, 4 inches in diameter, its interior set with colored beads, as shown in figure 645, and two darts, slender twigs, painted red, 11 inches in length. Collected by the writer in 1900.

---

a Canadian Savage Folk, p. 42, Toronto, 1896.

Two men play.  The ring is called sow-lai-kai-kas and the darts are known as tuk-tai-pow-ma.  The counts depend on the way in which the darts fall in the ring—1, 2, 5, 10, 15, 20, according to the beads to which they are adjacent.

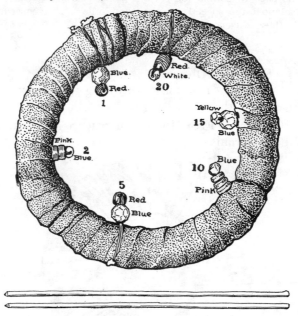

Fig. 645.  Beaded game ring and darts; diameter of ring, 4 inches; length of darts, 11 inches; Umatilla Indians, Oregon; cat. no. 37539, Free Museum of Science and Art, University of Pennsylvania.

## SHASTAN STOCK

ACHOMAWI.  Hat creek, California.  (Cat. no. $\frac{50}{4146}$ to $\frac{50}{4148}$, American Museum of Natural History.)

Fig. 646.  Bark game disk; diameter, 10 inches; Achomawi Indians, Hat creek, California; cat. no. $\frac{60}{4148}$, American Museum of Natural History.

Bark disk (figure 646), 10 inches in diameter, a bow and ten arrows.
Collected in 1903 by Dr Roland B. Dixon, who describes the disk as used as a rolling target.

SHOSHONEAN STOCK

BANNOCK.　Rossfork, Idaho.

Mr Thomas Blaine Donaldson has given the writer a photograph of the Bannock playing the hoop game, taken by him in 1890. He says:[a]

The picture [figure 647] shows a boy hurling a spear at a rolling hoop and a smaller youngster watching him. There were about ten full-grown bucks watching the youngsters playing, and the older men would take the hoop and hurl it along the ground and try to spear it. They took regular turns, and when they failed to spear the hoop, which was usual, because it took some skill, the other contestants laughed uproariously.

Fig. 647.

Fig. 648.

FIG. 647.　Bannock Indian boy playing hoop and pole, Idaho; from photograph by Mr Thomas Blaine Donaldson.
FIG. 648.　Corn-husk game ring; diameter, 5 inches; Hopi Indians, Arizona; cat. no. 128904, United States National Museum.

HOPI.　Arizona.　(United States National Museum.)

Cat. no. 128904.　Ring of corn husk (figure 648), 5 inches in diameter; accompanied by a number of corncob darts, each with two feathers and sharp points of hard wood. Collected by Mrs Matilda Coxe Stevenson.

FIG. 649.　Corncob darts; Hopi Indians, Arizona; cat. no. 69024, United States National Museum.

Cat. no. 69024.　Corncob darts (figure 648), similar to the above. Collected by Maj. J. W. Powell.

---

[a] In a letter to the writer, under date of February 25, 1901.

HOPI.   Oraibi, Arizona.   (Field Columbian Museum.)

Cat. no. 66927 to 66932.   Ring of corn husk, 7 inches in diameter,
    half overwrapped with white and half with red cord, and four
    corncob darts, each with two feathers and wooden points, from
    10¼ to 12¼ inches in length (figure 650).

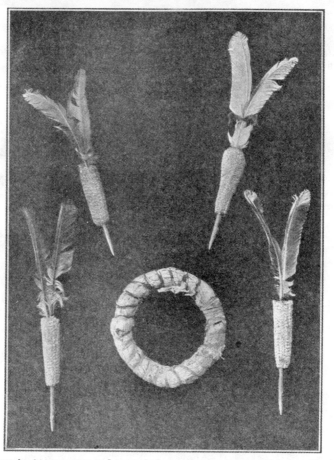

FIG. 650.   Corn-husk game ring and corncob darts; diameter of ring, 7 inches: Hopi Indians,
    Oraibi, Arizona; cat. no. 66927-66932, Field Columbian Museum.

Collected in 1898 by Rev. H. R. Voth, who furnishes the following
account:

This game is generally designated by the term "throwing the wheel" or
"throwing at the wheel" and is usually played by boys.  The wheel is thrown
on the ground, and the spears or arrows, which are held so that the middle
finger runs between the two arrows, are thrown at it.  The arrows are often
also thrown into the air; when they descend, the pressure of the air causes them
to rotate rapidly.  In the Oáqöl ceremony the women shoot with similar but
somewhat larger arrows at wheels, which are said to represent shields.  It was

noticed on several occasions that shortly before and after the Oáqöl ceremony the game was played more than at any other time.

Cat. no. 63176.　Corn-husk ring $2\frac{1}{4}$ inches in diameter; and corncob feather dart, 12 inches in length, with wooden pin (figure 651). Collected by Dr George A. Dorsey in 1897.　The label reads as follows:

The Hopi variant of a game which has a wide distribution throughout the western part of the United States and Canada.

FIG. 651. Corn-husk ring and corncob dart; diameter of ring, $2\frac{1}{4}$ inches; length of dart, 12 inches; Hopi Indians, Oraibi, Arizona; cat. no. 63176, Field Columbian Museum.

Among the Hopi tribes the game is played almost exclusively by boys.　Among other aboriginal tribes of the West men play, often for stakes of considerable magnitude.　The wheel used by the Hopi is called wipo-nölla, which simply means corn-husk wheel.　The same wheel is also used for many other purposes and in certain ceremonies.　At times the arrow is the usual one owned by every Hopi boy, and is shot from a bow.　More often a special form of double arrow, passing into a corncob and terminating in a single point, is used.　This is thrown at the wheel by hand. The special arrow is called mötöwu. There is no special name for this game, but they say "play with the wheel," or "shoot the wheel," mötöwu.

MONO. Hooker cove, Madera county, California. (Cat. no. 71432, Field Columbian Museum.)

FIG. 652. Lance-and-peg game; length of lances, 6 feet; length of peg, 3 inches; Mono Indians Madera county, California; cat. no. 71432, Field Columbian Museum.

Four lances (figure 652), about 6 feet in length, with butts unpeeled, and a small cylindrical wooden block, 3 inches in length. Collected by Dr J. W. Hudson, who describes them as implements for the lance-and-peg game.

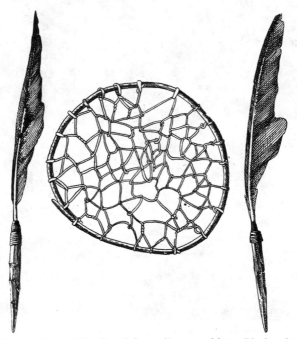

FIG. 653. Netted game hoop and feathered darts; diameter of hoop, 7 inches; length of darts, 12 inches; Paiute Indians, southern Utah; cat. no. 9428, 9429, Peabody Museum of American Archæology and Ethnology.

PAIUTE. Southern Utah. (Cat. no. 9428, 9429, Peabody Museum of American Archæology and Ethnology.)

Small hoop made of a bent twig, about 7 inches in diameter, covered with a net of yucca fiber, as shown in figure 653, and two feather darts, 12 inches in length, consisting of pins of hard wood

about 4 inches in length, to which single feathers, twisted somewhat spirally, are bound with fiber. Collected by Dr Edward
Palmer.

PAIUTE. Pyramid lake, Nevada. (Cat. no. 19059, United States National Museum.)

Small wooden hoop (figure 654), $2\frac{3}{4}$ inches in diameter, tightly wound
with a strip of buckskin; and a straight, peeled twig, 19 inches in
length.

FIG. 654. Game ring and dart; diameter of ring, $2\frac{1}{4}$ inches; length of dart, 19 inches; Paiute
Indians, Pyramid lake, Nevada; cat. no. 19059, United States National Museum.

The collector, Mr Stephen Powers, gives the following account of
the game in his catalogue:

Peisheen, ring play. The ring is rolled on the ground, and a rod shot after it
in such a way as to have the ring fall and lie on it.

SHOSHONI. Wyoming. (Cat. no. $\frac{50}{2441-2444}$, American Museum of
Natural History.)

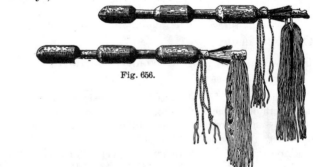

Fig. 656.

Fig. 655.

FIG. 655. Game ring; diameter, $13\frac{1}{2}$ inches; Shoshoni Indians, Wyoming; cat. no. $\frac{50}{2441}$, American
Museum of Natural History.
FIG. 656. Darts for ring game; length, 26 inches; Shoshoni Indians, Wyoming; cat. no. $\frac{50}{2442-2443}$,
American Museum of Natural History.

Hide-covered ring (figure 655), sewed with sinew, the interior filled
with cotton cloth. Diameter of ring, $13\frac{1}{2}$ inches; of section, $2\frac{1}{4}$
inches. Two wooden clubs (figure 656), 26 inches in length and
about $1\frac{1}{2}$ inches in diameter, with three knobs, 4 inches in length,
one at the extreme end and the others about equidistant along the
body of the club. The first of these knobs is covered with buckskin painted red, the second with buckskin painted yellow, and
the third red. The handle of one is covered with yellow-painted
buckskin and is perforated by a hole through which a thong
is attached, terminating in two long tassels of yellow-painted

cut-buckskin fringe. Black and white horsehair is bound by a strip of buckskin to the handle, four twisted buckskin thongs being attached to this band on the side nearest the knob. The other club is similar, except that the cover of the handle and the cut-leather fringe are stained red. They are accompanied by six willow counting sticks (figure 657), 13¾ inches in length, two painted yellow, two red, and two green.

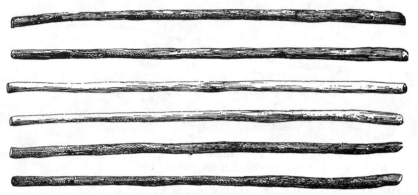

Fig. 657. Counting-sticks for ring game; length, 13¾ inches; Shoshoni Indians, Wyoming; cat. no. ₂⁵₄⁹₄₄, American Museum of Natural History.

The above-described specimens were collected by Mr H. H. St Clair, 2d, in 1901.

Tobikhar. Los Angeles county, California.

Hugo Ried [a] says:

Another game, called hararicuar, consisted in throwing rods or canes of the length of a lance, at a ring put in motion, and see who could insert it. The ring was made of buckskin with a twig of willow inside, and 4 inches in diameter. This is not played now.

The same narrative describes divination with rings of willow twigs, which were thrown in turn in the four directions to discover a missing daughter, in a legend of this region.

Uinta Ute. White Rocks, Utah. (Cat. no. 37120, Free Museum of Science and Art, University of Pennsylvania.)

Fig. 658. Game arrow; length, 32¼ inches; Uinta Ute Indians, White Rocks, Utah; cat. no. 37120, Free Museum of Science and Art, University of Pennsylvania.

Arrow (figure 658) with wooden shaft and heavy nail point, the shaftment banded with blue and red paint, with three feathers; length, 32½ inches. Collected by the writer in 1900.

[a] Account of the Indians of Los Angeles Co., Cal. Bulletin of the Essex Institute, v. 17, p. 18, Salem, 1885.

The use of this arrow was not ascertained, but from its identity in form with arrows used with the beaded ring, and the fact that it was one of a pair, it was probably used in that game.

UNCOMPAHGRE UTE. Utah. (Cat. no. $\frac{50}{1300}$, American Museum of Natural History.)

FIG. 659. Darts for ring game; length, 14¼ inches; Uncompahgre Ute Indians, Utah; cat. no. $\frac{50}{1300}$, American Museum of Natural History.

Two sticks (figure 659), wrapped with buckskin, with buckskin thongs in three sets of three each near one end, length 14¼ inches. Used with a ring 1¼ inches in diameter.

Collected by Dr A. L. Kroeber, who gives the following account:

Two players throw the sticks at the rolling ring, each attempting to make the ring come to rest touching his stick.

UTE. (Cat. no. 200582, United States National Museum.)

Wooden ring (figure 660), 6 inches in diameter, closely wound with a string of fine colored beads, in four segments, two blue and two white, and having a piece of ermine fur attached. In the E. Granier collection.

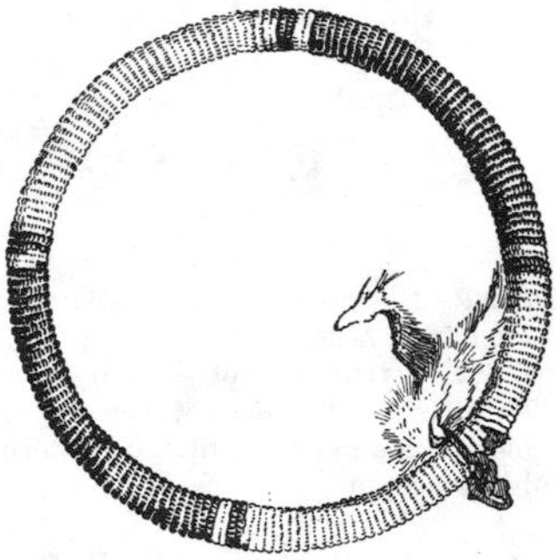

YAUDANCHI.[a] Tule River Indian reservation, California. (Cat. no. 71433, Field Columbian Museum.)

Lances and peg for lance-and-peg game. Collected by Dr J. W. Hudson, who furnishes the following description:

FIG. 660. Game ring; diameter, 6 inches; Ute Indians; cat. no. 200582, United States National Museum.

The peg is stuck in the ground, and the lance thrown at it. Played by men and boys. The smaller implements are for boys. The game is called "hot," and is played by young men, not children, and perhaps male adults.

---

[a] This tribe belongs to the Mariposan family, hence the description properly belongs on page 483.

SIOUAN STOCK

ASSINIBOIN. Southern Alberta.

Rev. John Maclean [a] says:

The Stoneys have several games similar to the Blackfeet, including the hoop and arrow game.

CROWS. Wyoming.

Prof. F. V. Hayden [b] mentions the following:

A-ba-tsink'-i-sha, a game somewhat like billiards.

—————— Crow reservation, Montana. (Field Columbian Museum.)

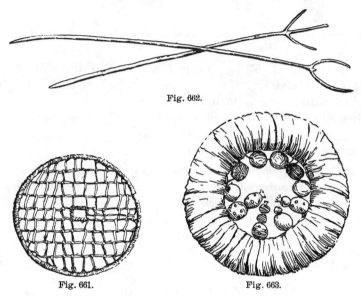

Fig. 662.

Fig. 661.　　　　　Fig. 663.

FIG. 661. Netted game hoop; diameter, 11 inches; Crow Indians, Montana; cat. no. 69651, Field Columbian Museum.
FIG. 662. Darts for netted hoop; length, 44¼ and 57 inches; Crow Indians, Montana; cat. no. 69651, Field Columbian Museum.
FIG. 663. Beaded ring; diameter, 2¼ inches; Crow Indians, Montana; cat. no. 69650, Field Columbian Museum.

Cat. no. 69651. Hoop of sapling (figure 661), covered with a thong network which is attached to the hoop thirty-four times; diameter, 11 inches; accompanied by two darts (figure 662), saplings with trident ends, 44¼ and 57 inches in length. Collected by Mr S. C. Simms in 1901.

Cat. no. 69650. Iron ring (figure 663), thickly wound with buckskin, thickly set inside with colored glass beads; diameter, 2½ inches. Collected by Mr S. C. Simms in 1901.

[a] Canadian Savage Folk, p. 26, Toronto, 1896.
[b] Contributions to the Ethnography and Philology of the Indian Tribes of the Missouri River, p. 408, Philadelphia, 1862.

DAKOTA (OGLALA).  Pine Ridge reservation, South Dakota.  (Free
     Museum of Science and Art, University of Pennsylvania.)
Cat. no. 21945.  Hoop of sapling, 25 inches in diameter (figure 664),
     with incised marks on both sides, as shown in figure 665.

The first, *a*, nearest the junction, consists of three incised rings
painted red; the next, *b*, is cut on both sides for about 1¼ inches and
marked with black, burnt scratches; the third, *c, c*, has a cut on both
sides, marked on one with a cross and on the other with a single notch

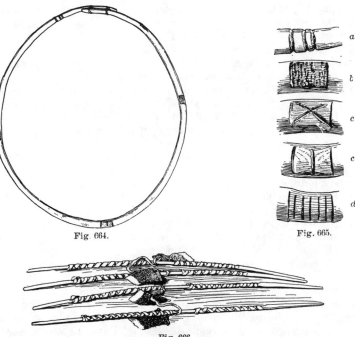

Fig. 664.                                          Fig. 665.

Fig. 666.

FIG. 664.  Game hoop; diameter, 25 inches; Oglala Dakota Indians, Pine Ridge reservation, South
     Dakota; cat. no. 21945, Free Museum of Science and Art, University of Pennsylvania.
FIG. 665.  Marks on game hoop; Oglala Dakota Indians, Pine Ridge reservation, South Dakota;
     cat. no. 21945, Free Museum of Science and Art, University of Pennsylvania.
FIG. 666.  Darts for hoop game; length, 39¼ inches; Oglala Dakota Indians, Pine Ridge reser-
     vation, South Dakota; cat. no. 21945, Free Museum of Science and Art, University of
     Pennsylvania.

in the middle, the faces being painted red;  the fourth, *d*, is cut with a
similar flat face on both sides, 1¼ inches in length, with five transverse equidistant notches, all painted red.

Four rounded sticks, 39½ inches in length, slightly larger at the butt,
     wrapped with thongs, as shown in figure 666, and held in pairs
     by thongs 11 inches in length.

One pair has the butts painted red and a small strip of red flannel
tied to the connecting thong, and the other has black butts with a blue

flag. The game is called painyankapi, and is described by the collector, Mr Louis L. Meeker,[a] as follows:

The implements consist of a hoop rather more than 2 feet in diameter, cangleska [figure 664], bent into shape and fastened when green, and two pairs of throwing sticks [figure 666], painyankapi, about 40 inches in length, wrapped with thongs, by which each pair is loosely coupled together, so that in the middle they are about a span apart. Each pair bears a small flag, blue or black on one pair, and red or yellow on the other. The hoop is made of a straight ash stick, 1¼ inches in diameter at the larger end, and is " as long as the tallest man." The hoop bears four flattened spaces on each side at equidistant points. [Figure 665.] Two players, representing two sides, throw two pairs of sticks at the hoop as it rolls past, and the counting is according to the marked or flattened space that lies upon the javelin after the hoop falls. The first mark from the junction, a, is called the butt or stump (can huta), and counts 10; the next, b, is black (sapa), and counts 20; the next, cc, the fork (okaja), counts 10, and the next, d, called marks (icazopi), counts 20. When the stick falls across the butt and the fork, it is called sweepstakes. The game is for 40 points. Painyankapi was sometimes called the buffalo game. It is said to have been played to secure success in the buffalo hunt. The hoop figuratively represents the horns of a buffalo and the bone that supports them.

Playing the game is called "shooting the buffalo." Again the hoop represents an encampment of all the Dakota tribes, and the chief's family learn to locate all different tribes upon it. Or it was supposed to represent the rim of the horizon and the four quarters of the earth. The spaces marked are the openings or passes into the circle of the camp. They also represent the four winds and are invoked as such by the thrower before he throws.

In time of much sickness the camp was ranged in two columns, the hoop painted black on one side and red on the other, the sticks painted, two red and two black, and the hoop rolled between the two ranks four times, and then carried away and left in some remote place to bear away the sickness. It was rolled "toward the whites," i. e., south.

The Lakota word for hoop is cangleska. It means spotted wood. No other term for hoop is in use. It follows that the hoop for which all other hoops are named, was spotted. This applies especially to the conjurer's hoop, colored in yellow,[b] red, white, and blue or black as is convenient, to represent the four quarters of the earth. This hoop is laid upon the ground in the medicine lodge, and after necessary ceremonies, the lights are extinguished, when a noise of eating is heard, and a ring cut from a pipe pumpkin, previously placed within the hoop for the purpose, is supposed to be devoured by the Wasicun[c] conjured up by the ceremonies.

Cat. no. 22109.   Ring of sinew (figure 667), wrapped with a thong, 3½ inches in diameter, painted red.

Cat. no. 22110.   A stick 39½ inches in length, the end lashed with a curved piece of sapling with the points turned toward the

[a] Ogalala Games.   Bulletin of the Free Museum of Science and Art, v. 3, p. 23, Philadelphia, 1901.

[b] The yellow is always placed north, but the other colors vary.

[c] The term Wasicun, now universally given to white men, means a superior and mysterious being.

handle (figure 668). Two bars of wood, 11½ inches in length, are lashed across the stick, each with a smaller piece of curved wood with points turning toward the handle, as shown in the figure. The curved piece at the end and the body of the stick are wrapped with a thong, and the bars, arcs, and exposed end of stick are painted black. There is a projection above the cross-bar, nearest the end to which the curved piece is affixed, against which the forefinger is pressed. A small square of black cloth is tied to the curved end of the stick.

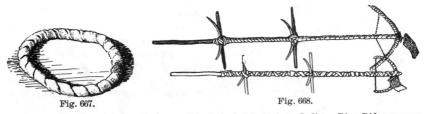

Fig. 667.　　　　　　　　　　　　　　　　　　　Fig. 668.

FIG. 667. Ring for Elk game; diameter, 3¼ inches; Oglala Dakota Indians, Pine Ridge reservation, South Dakota; cat. no. 22109, Free Museum of Science and Art, University of Pennsylvania.

FIG. 668. Darts for elk game; lengths, 39¼ and 36 inches; Oglala Dakota Indians, Pine Ridge reservation, South Dakota; cat. no. 22110, 22110a, Free Museum of Science and Art, University of Pennsylvania.

Cat. no. 22110a. A stick similar to the preceding, 36 inches in length, but painted red instead of black, and with a red instead of a black flag. The ends of the arc at the tip are united to the body of the stick by a cord of sinew. The crossbars are 6¼ inches in length.

These are implements for the game of kaga woskate, or haka heciapi, the elk game. Collected by Mr Louis L. Meeker,[a] who states that the ring is tossed into the air, and the player tries to catch it on his stick.

It is held in the hand with the forefinger pressing against a small projection that the best-made sticks bear near the center. Caught upon the point, it counts 10; if on the spur nearest the point, 5; on any other point, 1. The game is for any number of points agreed upon by the players. The Elk Game was played to secure success in the elk hunt.

He continues:

The Lakotas use a special hair ornament as a reward for victory in this game. The Cheyenne award it in the game next described (tahuka cangleska). The ornament [figure 564] is a miniature gaming hoop or wheel, tohogmu, as small as the matter can make it well, with spokes like a wheel, ornamented with porcupine quills and tied to a small lock of hair on one side of the crown by a buckskin string fastened to the center of the ornament.

Col. Garrick Mallery,[b] in his Picture-writing of the American In-

[a] Ogalala Games. Bulletin of the Free Museum of Science and Art, v. 3, p. 26, Philadelphia, 1901.

[b] Tenth Annual Report of the Bureau of Ethnology, p. 547, 1893.

dians, gives the accompanying figures referring to the preceding
game:

A dead man was used in the ring-and-pole game [figure 669]. American-
Horse's Winter Count, 1779–'80. The figure
represents the stick and ring used in the
game of haka, with a human head in front
to suggest that the corpse took the place of
the usual stick.

It was an intensely cold winter and a
Dakota froze to death [figure 670]. American-Horse's Winter Count, 1777–'78.

FIG. 669. Haka game; Oglala Dakota
pictograph from American-Horse's
Winter Count, 1779–80; from Mallery.

The sign for snow or winter, i. e., a cloud
with snow falling from it, is above the
man's head. A haka stick, which is used in playing that game, is represented
in front of him. Battiste Good's record further explains the illustration by the
account that the Dakota was killed in a fight with the Pawnees, and his companions left his body where they supposed it would not be found, but the
Pawnee found it, and, as it was frozen stiff, they dragged it into their camp and
played haka with it.

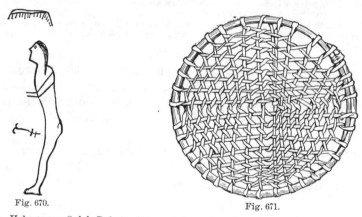

Fig. 670.                                                        Fig. 671.

FIG. 670.  Haka game; Oglala Dakota pictograph from American-Horse's Winter Count, 1779–80;
   from Mallery.
FIG. 671.  Netted hoop; diameter, 11¼ inches; Oglala Dakota Indians, Pine Ridge reservation,
   South Dakota; cat. no. 22112, Free Museum of Science and Art, University of Pennsylvania.

DAKOTA (OGLALA).  Pine Ridge reservation, South Dakota.  (Cat.
   no. 22111–22113, Free Museum of Science and Art, University of Pennsylvania.)

FIG. 672.  Dart for netted hoop; length, 46 inches; Oglala Dakota Indians, Pine Ridge reservation,
   South Dakota; cat. no. 22113, Free Museum of Science and Art, University of Pennsylvania.

Hoop (figure 671) of sapling, 11½ inches in diameter, lashed with a
   rawhide thong, which is passed around the hoop twenty-four
   times.

Another hoop, also 11½ inches in diameter, the thong passing around the edge thirty-five times. Both hoops have the edge and the thong net smeared with red paint.

A forked stick (figure 672), consisting of a peeled sapling, 46 inches in length, painted red, with a feather tied at the ends of the forks.

The specimens just described are implements for the game of the buckskin hoop, tahuka cangleska, and were collected by Mr Louis L. Meeker,[a] who describes the game as follows:

Played with several small hoops about a foot in diameter, woven with buckskin thongs with one opening more prominent than the rest, intended to be in the center, called the "heart" [figure 671]. The game is to thrust a small spear [figure 672], with a fork at one end to admit the top of the forefinger, through the "heart" as the hoop is rolled by or flung into the air. When one succeeds, he chases the one who threw the hoop, and endeavors to hit him with it. The one who oftenest pierces the "heart" wins. This is said to be a Cheyenne game played, like the other hoop games, only at the annual summer gatherings, camp against camp, from morning until a crier calls noon, when the victorious camp is feasted by the losers and the individual victor adorned with the hair ornament, good for one year.

The writer has not witnessed the game played in this way, a rain preventing when arrangements were made. The following, however, played by large boys and young men, he has seen as many as fifty times: Two forked sticks, about 4 feet high, to represent men, were set up 30 or 40 paces apart. A prop was placed across, from one foot to the other, both to make them stand erect and to make them easier marks.

Properly, the forks should not be more than an inch or so in diameter at the point and should be split up for a few inches, with a cross stick in the splits, so as to make four points come in contact with the ground and a stick for the hoop to strike, if it rolls under.

Two companies, stationed a very little in front and a little to one side of each "man," take turns rolling the hoops by throwing them against the ground to make them roll towards the "man" on the opposite side, the players of which defend their "man" by thrusting their spears through the rolling hoops.

The side is victorious that oftenest knocks down the "man." The player is victorious who oftenest pierces the heart of the hoop, so the victorious player may not be on the victorious side. My informants do not count this game with their regular hoop games, nor take any pride in the buckskin hoop generally. It was contributed by a full-blood Lakota, but definite knowledge of the manner of playing can not be obtained here.

The name tahuka cangleska means "neck hoop" rather than "deerskin hoop," though it may have the latter meaning, as my informants affirm.

Women say taoga cangleska instead of tahuka cangleska. This would mean "web-hoop" game and make it sacred to Inktomi (the Spider). Women's speech is somewhat different from men's.

The makers of the hoops for the hoop games are not selected at random. White-buffalo-cow River, Pte-sa Wakpa, makes hoops for the "buffalo game." Red Hoop, Cangleska luta, makes the hair-ornament hoop.

The hoops sent herewith were made by these men and by Crazy Horse, Ta-sunk-witko, brother of the desperado Crazy Horse who lost his life while a prisoner some years ago.

[a] Ogalala Games. Bulletin of the Free Museum of Science and Art, v. 3, p. 27, Philadelphia, 1901.

DAKOTA (TETON).   South Dakota.

Rev. J. Owen Dorsey,[a] in his account of the games of the Teton Dakota children, describes the game with a rawhide hoop, tahuka changleshka unpi, among those played by boys in the spring:

Occasionally in the early spring the people fear a freshet, so they leave the river bank and camp in the level prairie away from the river. The men hunt the deer, and when they return to camp the boys take part of the hides and cut them into narrow strips, which they soak in water; they make a hoop of ash wood, all over which they put the strips of rawhide, which they interweave in such a way as to leave a hole in the middle, which is called the "heart." The players form sides of equal numbers, and ti-oshpaye or gens usually plays against gens. The hoop is thrown by one of the players toward those on the other side. They are provided with sharp-pointed sticks, each of which is forked at the small end. As the hoop rolls they throw at it, in order to thrust one of the sticks through the heart. When one hits the heart he keeps the hoop for his side, and he and his companions chase their opponents, who flee with their blankets spread out behind them in order to deaden the force of any blow from a pursuer. When the pursuers overtake one of the fugitives they strike him with the hoop as hard as they can; then they abandon the pursuit and return to their former place, while the one hit with the hoop takes it and throws it, making it roll towards the players on the other side. As it rolls he says to them: "Ho! tatanka he gle, Ho! there is a buffalo returning to you." When the stick does not fall out of the heart, they say the hoop belongs to the player who threw the stick. This is not a game of chance, but of skill, which has been played by large boys since the olden times. Bushotter [b] says that it is obsolescent.

DAKOTA (TETON).   Pine Ridge reservation, South Dakota.

Dr J. R. Walker [c] describes the game of "wands and hoops" under the name of woskate pain yankapi.

The name of the wands made of ash or choke-cherrywood, he gives as cansakala, and he says that while anyone may make these wands, it is believed that certain men can make them of superior excellence and give them magic powers, which may be exercised in favor of those who play with them. The rules of the game, with a story of its making and of its use to cause buffalo to come, are given by Dr Clark Wissler.

DAKOTA (YANKTON).   Fort Peck reservation, Montana.   (Cat. no. 37606, Free Museum of Science and Art, University of Pennsylvania.)

Hoop of sapling (figure 673), 13 inches in diameter, with four marks at equal distances on both sides of its circumference. These marks are incised, and painted red and blue, as follows: Cross, painted blue, okizati, fork; longitudinal band, painted blue, sapapi, black spot; longitudinal band with transverse cut,

---

[a] The American Anthropologist, v. 4, p. 334, 1891.
[b] George Bushotter, a full-blood Dakota, Mr Dorsey's informant.
[c] Sioux Games. Journal of American Folk-Lore, v. 18, p. 278, Boston, 1905.

painted blue, ska, white; seven transverse notches, the outside and the middle ones blue, the others red, bahopi, notches.

Two pairs of sticks (figure 674), made of saplings, 25 inches in length, wrapped on both sides of the middle with cotton cloth and secured in pairs by a strip of cotton cloth fastened in the middle. One pair is painted red and has a small piece of red flannel fastened to each of the sticks. The other pair is blue, with similar black flags. Collected by the writer in 1900.

These implements were made by Siyo Sapa, Black Chicken, a renegade Hunkpapa and a former member of Sitting Bull's band. He gave the name of the game as pain yanka ichute and that of the darts as ichute.[a]

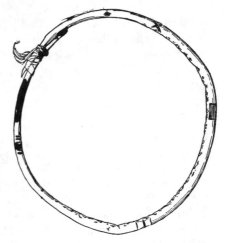

Fig. 673. Game hoop; diameter, 13 inches; Yankton Dakota Indians, Montana; cat. no. 37606, Free Museum of Science and Art, University of Pennsylvania.

The maker stated also that in the old time buffalo hide and deer skin were never employed in making the implements for this game; always, instead, something of no value, as old rags. He said that many years ago the Indians saw two buffalo bulls rolling this ring.

Fig. 674. Darts for hoop game; length, 25 inches; Yankton Dakota Indians, Montana; cat. no. 37606, Free Museum of Science and Art, University of Pennsylvania.

DAKOTA (YANKTON). Fort Peck, Montana. (Cat. no. 37607, Free Museum of Science and Art, University of Pennsylvania.)

A ring made of cotton cloth, wrapped round and round, and painted red; diameter, 3 inches. Two sticks, 32 inches in length, wrapped with rags, and having a curved piece fastened at one end and a cord stretched across like the string of a bow, connecting it with the stick; also two crosspieces, fastened at about equal distances from the ends, across the stick. These

---

[a] Pa-iⁿ'-yaⁿ-ka, to shoot or throw a stick through a hoop when rolling; painyanka kiċuⁿpi, the game of shooting through a hoop; i-cu'-te, something to shoot with, as the arrows one uses in a game. (Riggs's Dakota-English Dictionary, Washington, 1890.)

crosspieces are secured by a stout peg placed between them and the stick, and a piece of twig is bent and fastened so that its ends project upward for a distance of about 1½ inches, just above the crossbars. One of the sticks is painted red and has a piece of red flannel attached to the bow, and the other is painted blue, with a black cloth flag.

Collected by the writer in 1900.

The game is called ha-ka'-ku-te, or ha-ka' shooting, receiving its name from the sticks, ha-ká. Each man has a stick; the ring, can-hde'-ska, is rolled and it must go on one of the points to count. The name ha-ka' means branching, having many prongs, like some deer horns.[a] My informant defined it as forked.

ENO.[b]  North Carolina.

John Lederer [c] says:

Their town is built round a field, where in their sports they exercise with so much labor and violence, and in so great numbers, that I have seen the ground wet with the sweat that dropped from their bodies; their chief recreation is slinging of stones.

John Lawson [d] says:

These Indians are much addicted to a sport they call chenco, which is carried on with a staff and a bowl made of stone, which they trundle upon a smooth place, like a bowling green, made for that purpose, as I have mentioned before.

——— (?) Camden, South Carolina.   (Free Museum of Science and Art, University of Pennsylvania.)

Cat. no. 13602.  Biconcave disk of white quartzite (figure 675a), finely polished, 5¼ inches in diameter.

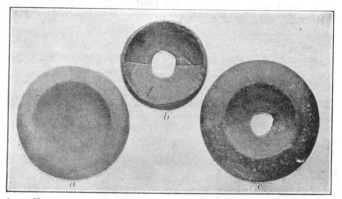

FIG. 675 a, b, c.  Chunkee stones; diameters, 5¼, 4, and 4⅜ inches; Eno (?) Indians, Camden, South Carolina; cat. no. 13602, 13556, 13603, Free Museum of Science and Art, University of Pennsylvania.

Cat. no. 13556.  Biconcave disk of quartzite, stained yellow and

[a] Riggs's Dakota-English Dictionary, Washington, 1890.
[b] It is doubtful whether the Eno were of Siouan stock; they may have been Iroquoian.
[c] Discoveries of John Lederer, p. 18, London, 1672; Rochester, 1902.
[d] History of Carolina, p. 57, London, 1714.

HIDATSA INDIANS PLAYING HOOP AND POLE; FORT CLARK, NORTH DAKOTA; FROM MAXIMILIAN, PRINCE OF WIED

highly polished by use, 4 inches in diameter and $1\frac{1}{8}$ inches thick at the edge, the edge slightly convex, the interior hollowed in symmetrical cup-shaped cavities, with a hole $1\frac{1}{4}$ inches in diameter in the middle. On one side there are two incised forked marks, as shown in figure 675b.

Cat. no. 13603.  Biconcave disk of yellow quartzite (figure 675c), $4\frac{5}{8}$ inches in diameter.

HIDATSA.  Fort Clark, North Dakota.

Maximilian, Prince of Wied,[a] describing a visit to a village of this tribe on the 27th of November, 1833, says:

We observed many very handsome young men, in fine new dresses, some of whom were playing the game called billiards [plate x].

────── Fort Atkinson, North Dakota.

Mr Henry A. Boller says:[b]

The favorite game appeared to be one which we called billiards, and a space outside the pickets of the village was beaten as smooth and hard as a floor by those who engaged in it. This game is played by couples; the implements are a round stone and two sticks 7 or 8 feet long, with bunches of feathers tied on at regular intervals. The players start together, each carrying his pole in a horizontal position, and run along until the one who has the stone, throws it, giving it a rolling motion, when each watching his chance, throws the stick. The one who comes nearest (which is determined by the marks on the stick) has the stone for the next throw. Horses, blankets, robes, guns, etc., are staked at this game, and I have frequently seen Indians play until they had lost everything.

Subsequently, in describing a winter camp, he says:[c]

In order to enjoy their amusement of "billiards," some of its devotees cleared off a level piece of ground, between the two lower camps, and planted a line of bushes and underbrush, to form a partial barrier against the wind. Logs were placed on each side of the "alley" to keep the sticks (or cues) from glancing off.

MANDAN.  Missouri river, North Dakota.

Lewis and Clark [d] say:

Notwithstanding the extreme cold, we observed the Indians at the village engaged out in the open air at a game which resembled billiards more than anything we had seen, and which we incline to suspect may have been acquired by ancient intercourse with the French of Canada. From the first to the second chief's lodge, a distance of about 50 yards, was covered with timber smoothed and joined so as to be as level as the floor of one of our houses, with a battery at the end to stop the rings; these rings were of clay-stone and flat, like the chequers for drafts, and the sticks were about 4 feet long, with two short pieces at one end in the form of a mace, so fixed that the whole will slide along

──────────

[a] Travels in the Interior of North America, translated by H. Evans Lloyd, p. 422, London, 1843.

[b] Among the Indians: Eight Years in the Far West, 1858–1866, p. 159, Philadelphia, 1868.

[c] Ibid., p. 196.

[d] History of an Expedition under the Command of Captains Lewis and Clark to the Sources of the Missouri, v. 1, p. 143, Philadelphia, 1814.

the board.   Two men fix themselves at one end, each provided with a stick, and one of them with a ring; then they run along the board, and about halfway slide the sticks after the ring.

Catlin [a] says:

The game of tchung-kee, a beautiful athletic exercise, which they seem to be almost unceasingly practicing whilst the weather is fair and they have nothing else of moment to demand their attention.   This game is decidedly their favorite amusement, and is played near to the village on a pavement of clay, which has been used for that purpose until it has become as smooth and hard as a floor. For this game two champions form their respective parties, by choosing alternately the most famous players, until their requisite numbers are made up. Their bettings are then made, and their stakes are held by some of the chiefs or others present.   The play commences [figure 676] with two (one from each

FIG. 676.   The game of tchung-kee; Mandan Indians, North Dakota; from Catlin.

party), who start off upon a trot, abreast of each other, and one of them rolls in advance of them, on the pavement, a little ring of 2 or 3 inches in diameter. cut out of a stone; and each one follows it up with his "tchung-kee" (a stick of 6 feet in length, with little bits of leather projecting from its sides of an inch or more in length), which he throws before him as he runs, sliding it along upon the ground after the ring, endeavoring to place it in such a position when it stops, that the ring may fall upon it, and receive one of the little projections of leather through it, which counts for game 1, or 2, or 4, according to the position of the leather on which the ring is lodged.   The last winner always has the rolling of the ring, and both start and throw the tchung-kee together; if either fails to receive the ring or to lie in a certain position, it is a forfeiture of the amount of the number he was nearest to, and he loses his throw; when another steps into his place.   This game is a very difficult one to describe, so as to give an exact

[a] The Manners, Customs, and Condition of the North American Indians, v. 1, p. 132, London, 1841.

idea of it, unless one can see it played—it is a game of great beauty and fine bodily exercise, and these people become excessively fascinated with it, often gambling away everything they possess and even, sometimes, when everything else was gone, have been known to stake their liberty upon the issue of these games, offering themselves slaves to their opponents in case they get beaten.[a]

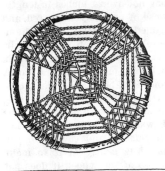

MANDAN.   Fort Clark, North Dakota.

Maximilian, Prince of Wied, says:[b]

The game called billiards, by the French Canadians, is played by two young men, with long poles, which are often bound with leather, and have various ornaments attached to them. On a long, straight, level course, or a level path in or near the village, they roll a hoop, 3 or 4 inches in diameter, covered with leather, and throw the

FIG. 677.   Netted hoop and pole; Mandan Indians, North Dakota; from Maximilian, Prince of Wied.

pole at it; and the success of the game depends upon the pole passing through it. This game is also practiced among the Manitaries [Hidatsa], and is described in Major Long's Travels to the Rocky Mountains as being played by the Pawnees, who, however, have hooked sticks, which is not the case with the tribes mentioned.

About the middle of March, when the weather is fine, the children and young men play with a hoop, in the interior of which strips of leather are interwoven; its diameter is about a foot [figure 677]. This hoop is either rolled or thrown, and they thrust at it with a pointed stick; he who approaches the center most nearly is the winner. . . .

As soon as the ice in the rivers breaks up, they run to the banks and throw this interlaced hoop into the water.

---

[a] The following account by the Abbé E. H. Domenech, who does not specify the tribe or locality, is probably taken from Catlin. (Seven Years' Residence in the Great Deserts of North America, v. 2, p. 197, London, 1860.)

"Their game of Spear and Ring is extremely curious and difficult. The players are divided into two camps, for Indians are fond of collective parties in which are many conquerors, and consequently many conquered. The stakes and bets are deposited in the care of an old man; then a hard smooth ground, without vegetation of any kind, is chosen, in the middle of which is placed perpendicularly a stone ring of about 3 inches diameter. When all is prepared the players (armed with spears 6 or 7 feet long, furnished with small shields a little apart from each other, sometimes with bits of leather) rush forward, two at a time, one from each camp; they stoop so as to place their spears on a horizontal level with the ring, so that they may pass through it, the great test of skill being to succeed without upsetting it. Each small shield or bit of leather that passes through counts for a point: the victory remains to the player who has most points, or he who upsets the ring at the last hit."

"Some Indians render the game still more difficult by playing it as follows. One of the players takes the ring in his hand and sends it rolling, with all his strength, as far as possible on the prepared ground; his adversary, who is by his side, starts full speed after it to stop it, so as to string it on his spear as far as the last little shield."

[b] Travels in the Interior of North America, translated by H. Evans Lloyd, p. 358, London, 1843.

OMAHA.  Nebraska.

Rev. J. Owen Dorsey [a] describes the following game:

Banañ'ge-kíde, Shooting at the banañge, or rolling wheel.  This is played by two men.  Each one has in his hand two sticks, about as thick as one's little finger, which are connected in the middle by a thong not over 4 inches in length.  These sticks measure about 3½ feet in length.  Those of one player are red, and those of the other are black.  The wheel which is rolled is about 2½ feet in diameter, its rim is half an inch thick, and it extends about an inch from the circumference toward the center.  On this side of the rim that measures an inch, are four figures [figure 679].  The first is called máxu, marked with a knife, or mágɛeze, cut in stripes with a knife.  The second is sábĕ tĕ, the black one.  The third is ákiɛítĕ, crossing each other.  The fourth is jiñgá tcē, the little one, the little one, or máxu jiñgá tcĕ, the little one marked with a knife.  The players agree which one of the figures shall be waqúbe for the game; that is, what card players call trumps.  The wheel is pushed and caused to roll along, and when it has almost stopped, each man hits gently at it to make it fall on the sticks.  Should the sticks fall on the top of the wheel, it does not count.  When a player succeeds in lodging his sticks in such a way that he touches the waqúbe, he wins many sticks or arrows.  When figures are touched by one or both of his sticks, he calls out the number.  When any two of the figures have been touched, he says: "Naⁿbaⁿ' a-ú hă," "I have wounded it twice."  If three figures have been hit, he says, "ɛáb ɛiⁿ a-ú hă," "I have wounded three."  Twenty arrows or sticks count as a blanket, twenty-five as a gun, and one hundred as a horse.

In the story of " The Man who had a Corn-woman and a Buffalo-woman as wives," translated by Doctor Dorsey,[b] it is related that the " buffalo bulls were playing this game."  He defines the name as " to shoot at something caused to roll by pushing."

Doctor Dorsey describes also—

ɟáɛiⁿ-jáhe, or Stick and Ring.  ɟáɛiⁿ-jáhe is a game played by two men.  At each end of the playground are two búʒa, or rounded heaps of earth.

A ring [figure 678] of rope or hide, the waɛígije, is rolled along the ground, and each player tries to dart a stick through it as it goes.  He runs very swiftly after the hoop and thrusts the stick with considerable force.  If the hoop turns aside as it rolls it is not difficult to thrust a stick in it.  The stick [figure 678A] is about 4 feet long.  D is the end that is thrust at the hoop.  B B are the gaqa or forked ends for catching at the hoop.  C C are made of ha násage, wéabasta násage íkaⁿ taⁿ, stiff hide, fastened to the forked ends' with stiff wéabasta, or material used for the soles of moccasins.  These ha násage

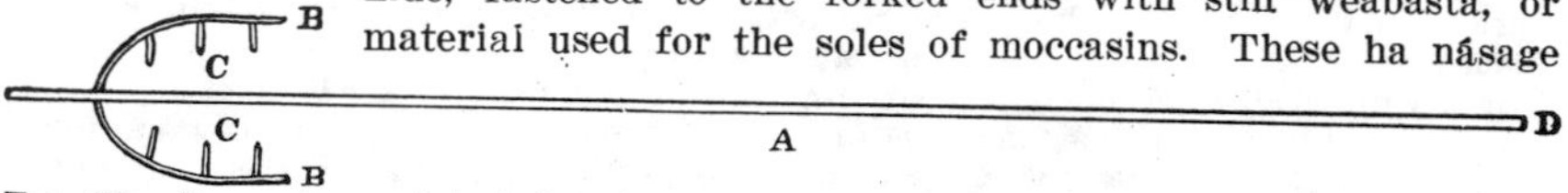

FIG. 678.  Game ring and dart; length of dart, about 4 feet; Omaha Indians, Nebraska; from Dorsey.

often serve to prevent the escape of the hoop from the forked ends.  Sometimes these ends alone catch or hook the loop.  Sometimes the end D is thrust through it.  When both sticks catch the hoop neither one wins.

The stakes are eagle feathers, robes, blankets, arrows, earrings, necklaces, etc.[c]

---

[a] Omaha Sociology.  Third Annual Report of the Bureau of Ethnology, p. 335, 1884.

[b] The Ƈegiha Language.  Contributions to North American Ethnology, v. 6, p. 162, Washington, 1890.

[c] Omaha Sociology.  Third Annual Report of the Bureau of Ethnology, p. 337, 1884.

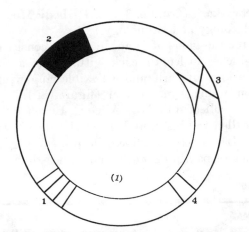

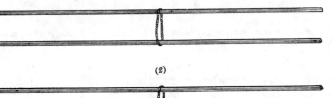

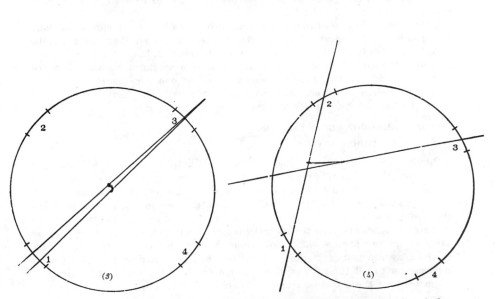

FIG. 679.  Ring-and-dart game; Omaha Indians, Nebraska; 1, the wheel, or banañge; 2, the sticks; 3, nan-ban a-ú hă; 4, ¢ábe¢in a-ú hă; from Dorsey.

OMAHA.  Nebraska.  (Cat. no. 37776, Peabody Museum of American Archæology and Ethnology.)

Implements for the game of bhadhiñ zhahe, consisting of two sticks 4 feet 2 inches in length, each with an arc attached to one end to form a kind of barb, and a flexible ring wrapped with deerskin, about 6 inches in diameter (figure 680).

These were collected by Miss Alice C. Fletcher.

The hoop is called wadhigizi and the sticks are known as wízhahe.

Mr Francis La Flesche described the preceding game to the writer under the name of pauthin zhahae, or Pawnee zhahae, as played with

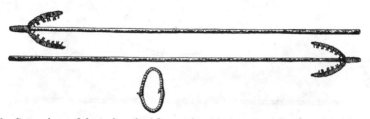

FIG. 680.  Game ring and darts; length of darts, 4 feet 2 inches; diameter of ring, about 6 inches; Omaha Indians, Nebraska; cat. no. 37776, Peabody Museum of American Archæology and Ethnology.

a hoop of buckskin, wathegezhae, about 4 inches in diameter, and a javelin, waijhahe, about 5 feet long:

The latter has two little branches about 4 inches in length and bent backward at the point.  Four pieces of rawhide are fastened to each of these, turned inward to form a kind of barbs.

There are two contestants, one of whom throws the hoop, and, as it rolls along the ground, both endeavor to drive their javelins, which they grasp in the middle, through it.  If the hoop is penetrated it counts 2, but if the hoop catches on one of the barbs it only counts 1.  If the hoop is caught on both of the barbs it counts nothing.  The game is usually 10.  The one who scores throws the hoop.  There is a long track, and the players run back and forth.  The Omaha originally had the game under another name.

OSAGE.  Missouri and Arkansas.

John D. Hunter says:[a]

Playing the hoop is performed on an oblong piece of ground, prepared for the purpose.  Three parallel lines run the whole length of the plot, at about 15 yards distance from each other.  On the exterior ones, the opposing parties, which generally consist of from twelve to eighteen persons, arrange themselves about 10 paces apart, each individual fronting intermediate to his two opposite or nearest opponents.  On the central line, extended to a few paces beyond the wings of the two parties, stand two persons facing each other.  It is their part of the play alternately to roll a hoop of about the diameter of a common hogshead, with all their strength, from one to the other.  The object for triumph between these two is, who shall catch the opponent's hoop the oftenest,

[a] Manners and Customs of Several Indian Tribes located West of the Mississippi, p. 273, Philadelphia, 1823.

and of the contending parties, which shall throw the greatest number of balls through the hoop as it passes rapidly along the intervening space. Judges are appointed, usually from among the old men, to determine which party is victorious, and to distribute the prizes, which, on some particular occasions consist of beaver and deer skins, moccasins, leggings, etc. but more usually of shells, nuts, and other trifles.

PONCA.   Fort Pierre, South Dakota.

Maximilian, Prince of Wied,[a] thus refers to a young Ponca Indian named Ho-Ta-Ma, among the Dakota at Fort Pierre, a handsome, friendly man, who often amused himself with different games:

Frequently he was seen with his comrades playing what was called the hoop game, at which sticks covered with leather are thrown at a hoop in motion.

### SKITTAGETAN STOCK

HAIDA.   Prince of Wales island, Alaska.

Dr C. F. Newcombe described a game which the Kaigani Haida call k'istaño and the Masset, tulstaonañ. The implements are a flat disk of hemlock twigs bound with cedar bark and a spear of salmon berry.

It is played with a ring. Two sides are chosen and the ring is thrown into the air, the object being to catch it on the point of a stick 9 feet long.

Another game the Kaigani Haida call kokankijao and the Masset, kokijao. A small ring of hemlock twig, with quite a long string tied to the edge, is placed anywhere in a circle of 3 feet drawn on a sandy place. The game is for the opposite player to put a stick, of which ten are given him, inside the ring, which, with the string, is hidden under earth when he is not looking.

Doctor Newcombe describes also the following game:

Ten pieces of kelp, 1 foot long, are placed in the ground at each end of a playing ground 20 feet long. There are two players on each side, each armed with a very sharp spear of salmon berry. The game is to pierce the kelp at the end opposite with the spears. One piece is very small, and if struck, the striker gets all the sticks. The players throw from a crouching position. The game is called hlqamginhlE.

HAIDA.   British Columbia.

Dr J. R. Swanton [b] describes the following games:

"A woman's pubic bones" (Gao skū′ dji).—This was a boy's game. Late in the spring, when a tall, slim plant called L!al, the pith of which was eaten, was at its best, the boys would collect a great quantity of the stalks. Then two would each drive a couple of sticks into the ground about 5 yards apart. After that, each would take about twenty sticks of the salmon-berry bush, and,

[a] Travels in the Interior of North America, translated by H. Evans Lloyd, p. 160, London, 1843.

[b] Contributions to the Ethnography of the Haida. Memoirs of the American Museum of Natural History, whole series, v. 8, p. 60, New York, 1905.

using them as spears, alternately try to drive one of them between the adversary's posts, or stick it into the ground beyond, so that it would rest on their tops. Each boy would then bid a certain number of L!al stalks, and after they had used up all of their spears, he who scored the most hits won all that had been put up by his adversary. If he were one point ahead, he got nothing more; but if he were two points ahead, he won as much again; if he were three points ahead, twice as much, and so on.

"Knocking something over by shooting" (Tc!îtgada'ldaña).—This was played by older people. Toward the end of spring a crowd would go out and set up a piece of board about 3 inches wide and 4 feet high. Then, forming a line some distance away, they would shoot at it with blunt arrows in succession, beginning at one end. He who struck the stake first won all of the arrows shot at that time around, except the others that struck. Each person had one shot at every round. Sometimes they played against each other by companies, of which there might be as many as five or six. Indeed, a whole town often seems to have turned out, and the resulting contests to have extended over a long period of time. Toward the end some of the players, their supply of arrows being exhausted, would be compelled to manufacture new ones, often of inferior make. Two of these had to be paid in as an equivalent for one of the better class. For some religious reason they ceased playing with arrows as soon as winter began.

Xatxadī'da (perhaps a name for the pieces of spruce bark used in it).—This game was played in the spring. Two boys provided themselves with ten pieces of spruce bark apiece, each of which was doubled over and fastened along one edge. The opposite edge was the one on which they were to stand. Then they were set up in a row upon the ground, and the players endeavored to drive the same spears as those used in the previous game into each of them. He who first sent a spear into each of his opponent's pieces of bark won, although the opponent was sometimes allowed to have additional pieces.

### TANOAN STOCK

TIGUA. Isleta, New Mexico. (Cat. no. 22727, Free Museum of Science and Art, University of Pennsylvania.)

Ring of cotton cloth (figure 681), closely wrapped with a buckskin thong, 9½ inches in diameter and 1¼ inches thick. The interior is divided into four quarters by two two-ply twisted thongs fastened to the interior and crossing at right angles. Five leather thongs are attached on each side of one of these radial thongs, above and below. The exterior of the ring is painted red, yellow, and blue; red on the sides, then a yellow band, with blue on the edge.

Two poles (figure 681), one 57 and the other 60 inches in length, painted red two-thirds of their length, with blue running zigzag over the red. Eight long buckskin thongs are fastened at a point 14 inches from the end of each pole, and again the same number at another point, 33 inches from the end.

These were collected by the writer in 1902.

The ring is called mar-kur, and the poles shi-a-fit, spears. The ring is rolled, and the poles are hurled at it. The counts are made according to the set of thongs nearest the striking end. If the pole penetrates the ring, and all the thongs pass entirely through it, it counts 10. If one thong remains caught in the ring, it counts 1; if two remain, 2, and so on. The thongs attached to the interior of

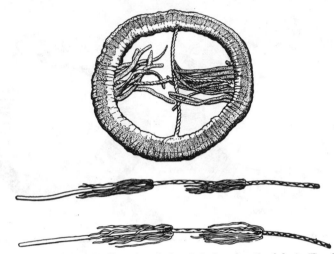

FIG 681. Game ring and darts; diameter of ring, 9¼ inches; length of darts, 57 and 60 inches; Tigua Indians, Isleta, New Mexico; cat. no. 22727, Free Museum of Science and Art, University of Pennsylvania.

the ring do not count, but serve to impede the passage of the pole and entangle its thongs. The game is played by men and boys, but it has not been played in Isleta for the past fifteen years. The writer was told that it is regarded as a Navaho game.

WAKASHAN STOCK

KWAKIUTL. British Columbia. (American Museum of Natural History.)

Cat. no. $\frac{16}{4791}$. Game ring (figure 682), wrapped with cedar bark; diameter, 9½ inches; width, 2 inches; designated as lamagikala gagayaxala, first kane, to be thrown high.

Cat. no. $\frac{16}{4792}$. Game ring like the preceding, 10 inches in diameter; designated as xwaligwagane, second kane, to be thrown high.

Cat. no. $\frac{16}{4793}$. Game ring like the preceding, 8 inches in diameter; designated as tilemyu, third kane, to be thrown very low.

Cat. no. $\frac{16}{4794}$. Game ring (figure 683), like the preceding, 1¾ wide and 8½ inches in diameter; designated as nepayu, the ring, kane, to be thrown at the other player to hurt him.

Cat. no. $\frac{16}{4795}$. Two sticks (figure 684), saplings, 53¼ inches in length; designated as tsatsigalayu, being the sticks for catching the above-mentioned rings.

Collected by Mr George Hunt, who states that the game is played by young men.

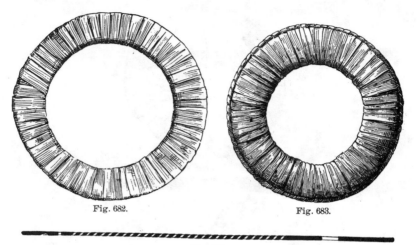

Fig. 682.  Fig. 683.

Fig. 684.

FIG. 682.  Game ring; diameter, 9½ inches; Kwakiutl Indians, British Columbia; cat. no. $\frac{16}{4791}$, American Museum of Natural History.

FIG. 683.  Game ring; diameter, 8½ inches; Kwakiutl Indians, British Columbia; cat. no. $\frac{16}{4792}$, American Museum of Natural History.

FIG. 684.  Dart for ring game; length, 53½ inches; Kwakiutl Indians, British Columbia; cat. no. $\frac{16}{4795}$, American Museum of Natural History.

KWAKIUTL.  Nawiti, British Columbia.

Dr C. F. Newcombe describes the ring-and-dart game under the name of kinxe, the ring being called kani, and the stick, dsadsigala·iu:

Each player has one ring and one stick, 4 to 8 feet long or more, according to taste, and made of willow, partly peeled to show ownership marks. There are two sides of equal numbers, who agree who shall first throw the quoit-like disk. Then each side throw alternately or altogether, as they please. The object is to catch the ring, either in the air or running along the ground, with the stick, and any or all can try at one time, but as all disks can be in the air at once this is not usual. There is no regular scoring. If one disk is caught, it is kept until the whole ten are thrown. If all ten are not caught at one flight or play, they are thrown back to the opposite side. The game is won when one side catches all ten thrown in one play, and the losers are chased by winners, who first say: " Now we have all your kani; " " Now whom will you send out to take the pay? "

If a loser steps out the winners throw their kani at this one as hard as they can from any distance. The victim usually protects himself with a blanket. If he can catch any in his blanket, he can retaliate. If no one comes out to take the penalty the whole side is chased and thrown at.

—— Blunden harbor, British Columbia.  (Cat. no. 37907, Free Museum of Science and Art, University of Pennsylvania.)

Perforated lava disk (figure 685), 5 inches in diameter and 1⅜ inches thick.

Collected in March, 1901, by Dr C. F. Newcombe, who describes it, under the name of laua·iu, as used in a game:

The Kwakiutl say that these stone disks are no longer used. According to Mr George Hunt, they were originally rolled in sets of four of different sizes and were shot at with bows and arrows.

Dr Franz Boas, in his Kwakiutl Texts,[a] describes a game played with these stones between the birds of the upper world and the myth people, i. e., "all the animals and all the birds." The four stones were called, respectively, the "mist-covered gambling stone," the "rainbow gambling stone," the "cloud-covered gambling stone," and the "carrier of the world." The woodpecker and the other myth birds played on one side, and the Thunder bird and the birds of the upper world on the other, in two

. . . . . .

rows, thus ————. The gambling

. . . . . .

stones were thrown along the middle between the two tribes of birds, and they speared them with their beaks. The Thunder bird and the birds of the upper world were beaten in this contest. This myth is given as an explanation of the reason for playing the game with the gambling stones. They are called laelae.

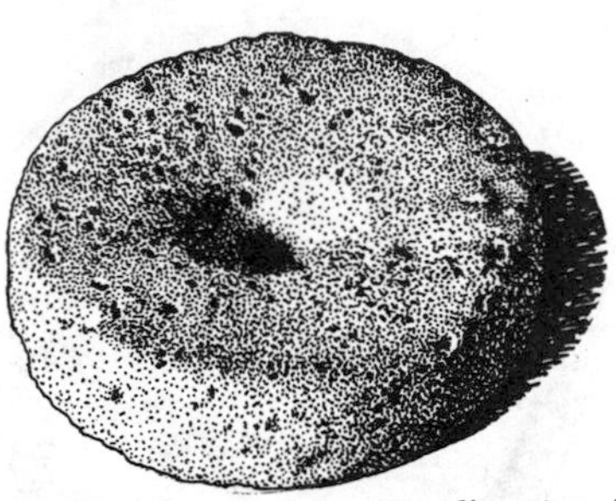

FIG. 685. Stone game ring; diameter, 5 inches; Kwakiutl (Tenaktak) Indians; cat. no. 37907, Free Museum of Science and Art, University of Pennsylvania.

KWAKIUTL. Nawiti, British Columbia. (Cat. no. 85851, Field Columbian Museum.)

Four wooden darts (figure 686), 38 inches in length, in two pairs, distinguished by burnt designs. One pair has broad flat points and the other tapering blunt points.

Collected in 1904 by Dr C. F. Newcombe, and described by him as used in the spear-and-kelp game, sakaqes.

FIG. 686. Dart for spear-and-kelp game; length, 38 inches; Kwakiutl Indians, British Columbia; cat. no. 85851, Field Columbian Museum.

The game is played by four players armed with spears, sákiåk'ŭs, or darts of yellow cedar like the above, there being two sides with two players to a side. The darts are usually pointed with deer shin bones, 6 inches long, inserted in

[a] Memoirs of the American Museum of Natural History, whole series, v. 5, p. 295, New York, 1902.

the split ends and not barbed. The targets are two piles of kelp, 10 to 15 feet apart. These consist of some twenty pieces, the largest 2½ inches in diameter, and from that down to less than the diameter of a finger, which lie transversely to the dart thrower. Standing up behind the bunch is a kelp head, which, however, is hidden by the pile from the player. If a thrower impales one or more kelp, both spear and kelp are thrown to him. If he misses, the opposite side throws. The winner is he who first gets all the kelp tubes.

MAKAH. Neah bay, Washington. (Cat. no. 37384, Free Museum of Science and Art, University of Pennsylvania.)

Ring (figure 687) made of a core of grass wrapped with braided cedar bark, 12 inches in diameter. Collected by the writer in 1900.

Dr George A. Dorsey [a] describes a game called dutaxchaias:

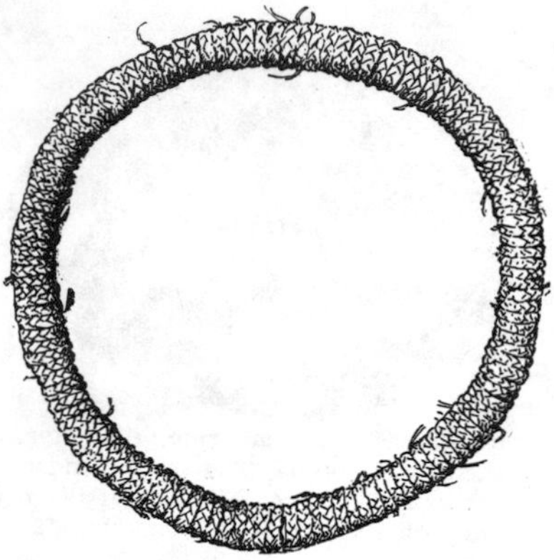

FIG. 687. Game ring; diameter, 12 inches; Makah Indians, Neah bay, Washington; cat. no. 37384, Free Museum of Science and Art, University of Pennsylvania.

This game is played by young men, generally in the spring, or it may be played at any time of the year. The ring (dutapi) is of cedar bark wound tightly and carefully braided. Two specimens were collected, one of which has seen considerable usage. In playing the game, two converging lines of from six to ten men on each side are formed. The man at the apex of the converging lines takes the ring in his hand and rolls it forward between the lines as far as he can; as the ring begins to lose its momentum, and wabbles preparatory to falling, all shoot at it with an arrow (tsik'hati) from an ordinary bow (bistati). When the ring is struck by an arrow of one side or the other (quilah = winner), the losing side pay over an arrow as forfeit. The game ends at any time by mutual consent, or when one side or the other has won all the arrows of the opposing side.

Doctor Dorsey describes also the game of katikas—sharp-stick slanting:

This game is . . . played by boys. On the side of a hill ten or more sharpened sticks are thrust into the ground at intervals of from two to three inches. Each has his individual set of sticks, or goal. One of the players rolls down the slope a large piece of kelp, 6 inches in length. If it so rolls as to impale itself on one of the sticks of one of the other players, he withdraws the stick from the earth and throws the kelp up in the air and attempts to catch it on the point of the stick. If successful, he retains the stick, which constitutes the game.

_____

[a] Games of the Makah Indians of Neah Bay. The American Antiquarian, v. 23, p. 69, 1901.

NOOTKA.  British Columbia.

Dr Franz Boas [a] says:

The games of the Nootka are identical with those of the neighboring tribes. A favorite game is played with hoops, which are rolled over the ground. Then a spear is thrown at them, which must pass through the hoop (nūtnū'tc).

WASHOAN STOCK

WASHO.  Near Truckee, Nevada.

Dr J. W. Hudson describes the hoop-and-spear game among this tribe, under the name of pululpaiyayapu, the hoop being called by the same name:

The hoop is of willow covered with buckskin, 12 inches in diameter.  One player rolls it rapidly past his opponent, who throws at it.  Impaling the hoop counts one.  Seven is the game, which is counted with sticks.  The lance is called mak.

—————— Woodfords, Alpine county, California.

Dr J. W. Hudson describes a man's game in which a rolling hoop of willow is shot at with arrows by an opponent, under the name of pululpaiyapa:

Pulul, hoop; baiyap, to shoot at.  The game is also played by casting a lance at a target hoop.

In another form of the game called pulultumpes—pulul, hoop; tumpes, to cast. the hoop is held in the hand and the opponent endeavors to catch between his fingers the small dart thrown by his opponent.  In this game the outstretched fingers occupy the center of the hoop.  In a variation of this an actual arrow is cast. the opponent being often hurt in the hand.

YUMAN STOCK

MOHAVE.  Fort Mohave, Arizona.
(Cat. no. 60264, Field Columbian Museum.)

Ring of bark, 6½ inches in diameter, wrapped with cord (figure 688); and two poles, 12
feet in length, rounded and
tapering from butt to tip.

Collected by Mr John J. Mc-
Koin, who furnishes the following
account of the game:

FIG. 688.  Game ring; diameter, 6¼ inches; Mohave Indians, Arizona; cat. no. 60264, Field Columbian Museum.

This game is played with two poles and one ring.  The poles are called co-tool-wa, and the ring cop-o-cho-ra.  These poles are respectively marked with one or two circles carved upon the larger end.  Each player chooses an umpire, who rules upon plays.  They then agree upon the pole which each is to have and as to who is to make the first trial with the ring.  Suppose a player with the pole marked with one circle gets

[a] Second General Report on the Indians of British Columbia.  Report of the Sixtieth Meeting of the British Association for the Advancement of Science, p. 590, London, 1891.

the first trial with the ring.  He then throws the pole at the ring while it is rolling or at such point as he believes the ring will fall, the object being to place the pole so that the ring will fall upon it in such a manner that the umpire, standing over the pole at the point where the ring falls and looking perpendicularly downward through the ring, can see the pole.  This counts 1 point.  If the umpire sees both poles, no points are made, and the player with the ring tries again.  He continues to try until he makes the number of points agreed upon with the player of the pole marked with two circles in such a manner that the grave and dignified umpire, making decisions as before explained, decides the point in his favor and awards the ring to him, that player No. 2 may make a trial of his skill.  The player who first makes the number of points agreed upon is declared the winner.

MOHAVE.  Colorado river, Arizona.  (Cat. no. 10116, Peabody Museum of American Archæology and Ethnology.

Implements of ring-and-pole game, consisting of three rings of bark wrapped with twine made of yucca fiber, each about 7 inches in diameter (figure 689).  One ring is overwrapped with strips

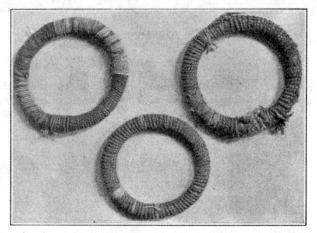

FIG. 689.   Rings for ring and pole; diameter, about 7 inches; Mohave Indians, Arizona: cat. no. 10116, Peabody Museum of American Archæology and Ethnology.

of cotton rags of different colors, white, red, and purple, for about two-thirds of its circumference.  There are two poles, one perfect, 5 feet 8 inches in length.  The other consists of parts of two poles, which have been cut in half for convenience in transportation and do not mate.  Collected by Dr Edward Palmer.

Lieut. A. W. Whipple, U. S. Army,[a] describes the following game:

Some of the young men selected a level spot, 40 paces in length, for a playground, and amused themselves in their favorite sport with hoop and poles.  The hoop is 6 inches in diameter, and made of an elastic cord.  The poles are straight, and about 15 feet in length.  Rolling the hoop from one end of the course, two

---

[a] Reports of Explorations and Surveys to ascertain the Most Practicable and Economical Route for a Railroad from the Mississippi River to the Pacific Ocean, v. 3, p. 114, Washington, 1856.

persons chase it halfway, and at the same instant throw their poles. He who succeeds in piercing the hoop wins the game.

WALAPAI. Walapai reservation, Arizona. (Cat. no. 15129, Field Columbian Museum.)

Ring (figure 690), interior core wrapped with strips of cotton cloth, with buckskin outside, 6½ inches in diameter; and two cottonwood poles, 12 feet in length. The poles taper to a point and the butts are marked differently.

Two other sets have rings wrapped with cord. One ring (cat. no. 63344, figure 691) is 7 inches in diameter, and another (cat. no. 63345), wrapped with coarse cord, is of the same diameter. Four poles (cat. no. 63344) are 13 feet 8 inches in length.

These were collected by Mr Henry P. Ewing, who gives the following account of the game, which he describes under the name of tutava:

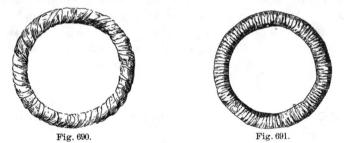

Fig. 690.                    Fig. 691.

FIG. 690. Game ring; diameter, 6½ inches; Walapai Indians, Arizona; cat. no. 15129, Field Columbian Museum.
FIG. 691. Game ring; diameter, 7 inches; Walapai Indians, Arizona; cat. no. 63344, Field Columbian Museum.

The tu-ta-va game is played with two long poles, called tu-a-a, and a hoop, called tav-a-chu-ta. To play, two persons, always men, select a piece of ground about 100 feet long and 20 feet wide, smooth, level, and clear. Standing side by side at one end of this tract, facing the other end, the men hold their poles in both hands and start to run toward the other end of the ground. As they do so the one who holds the hoop throws, or rolls, it along the ground in front of them, and as it rolls each throws his pole, end foremost, giving it a sliding motion, so that it slides along the ground for some distance ahead of the runners. The object is to get the hoop to fall so that one edge of it will rest on the pole, while the other rests on the ground. Should this happen, it counts the contestant using that pole 1. Should the hoop fall so that it rests over the point of the pole, but the pole does not go through it, that counts 4 and wins the game, 4 points constituting the game. If the pole goes through the hoop it does not count anything, and unless the hoop lies fully up on the pole it does not count. It will be seen that this is a game of skill as well as of chance, and is, or was, often played for big stakes—ponies, guns, women, anything, everything.

The game was very popular with the men, and twenty years ago, when the weather was fair, there was not a camp but a game of tu-ta-va could be seen near it all day long. It developed the muscles by running and throwing the pole. The Indians seldom play this game now.

YUMA.  Colorado river, California.

Maj. S. P. Heintzleman, U. S. Army, says[a] in 1853:

A favorite amusement is a play called mo-turp, or, in Spanish, redendo [redondo?]. It is played with two poles 15 feet long, an inch and a half in diameter, and a ring wrapped with twine, 4 inches in diameter. One rolls this ring along the ground and both run after it, projecting their poles forward. He on whose pole the ring stops counts 1, and he has the privilege to roll the ring. Four counts game. They do not count when a pole enters the ring. Old and young, chiefs and the common people, all take great delight in this game. They follow it for hours in the hot sun, raising clouds of dust, the perspiration making their dusky skins glossy.

—————— Arizona.

Dr H. F. C. ten Kate, jr,[b] says he saw a group of half-naked, painted young men who were intent in the game of otoerboek. This game is played by two men, each armed with a very long wooden pole, who run side by side. One of them rolls a wooden ring, kaptzor, rapidly ahead. At the same time they hastily throw their poles at the ring so that it is stopped. He was not certain whether the sticks had to be thrown through the ring or whether the count depended upon the particular way in which the poles lay beside it.

### ZUÑIAN STOCK

ZUÑI.  Zuñi, New Mexico.  (Cat. no. 3062, Brooklyn Institute Museum.)

Ring of bent twig (figure 692), 5 inches in diameter, wound with blue yarn, and having a piece of blue yarn, 18 inches in length, tied at the point of juncture, and a peeled twig, 30 inches in length, painted red, and tied with blue yarn at four places equidistant along its length. Collected by the writer in 1903.

The game is called tsikonai ikoshnakia, ring play; the ring is called antsikonai, and the stick, tslamtashaikoshai, long stick for play. One man has the ring, which he rolls, and the other the stick, which he throws after it. When the stick penetrates the ring it counts according to the particular string on the stick against which it lies, as shown in figure 692. In going out to play the player carries the ring suspended over his shoulder by the end and the stick held upright in his right hand.

Mrs Matilda Coxe Stevenson[c] describes the game of hotkämonne:

Implements: two slender sticks, each passed through a piece of corncob, the stick sharpened at one end and having two hawk plumes inserted in the other end; ball of yucca ribbons [figure 693].

---

[a] House of Representatives, Executive Document 76, Thirty-fourth Congress, third session, 1857, p. 49. See also Lieut. W. H. Emory in Report of the United States and Mexican Boundary Survey, v. 1, p. 111, Washington, 1857.

[b] Reizen en Onderzoekingen in Noord-Amerika, p. 108, Leiden, 1885.

[c] Zuñi Games. American Anthropologist, n. s., v. 5, p. 491, 1903.

The yucca ball is placed on the ground and the sticks are thrown at it from a short distance. The ball must be penetrated. If the first player strikes the ball, the stick is allowed to remain in place until the other party plays. If both sticks strike the ball, it is a draw. If the second stick fails to strike, it remains where it falls and the first player removes his stick from the ball and throws again. The one who strikes the ball the greater number of times wins the game.

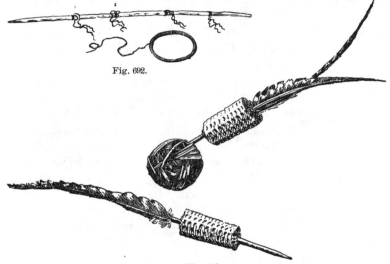

Fig. 692.

Fig. 693.

FIG. 692. Game ring and dart; diameter of ring, 5 inches; length of stick, 30 inches; Zuñi Indians, Zuñi, New Mexico; cat. no. 3062, Brooklyn Institute Museum.
FIG. 693. Yucca ball and corncob darts; Zuñi Indians, Zuñi, New Mexico; from Mrs Stevenson.

Hó⁺kämonnĕ is one of the most precious games of the Zuñi, it being among those offered to the Gods of War at the winter solstice. The game is frequently played for rains, and when it occurs in this connection sacred meal is sprinkled on the ground before the ball is placed; the one who first penetrates the ball lifts it by the stick, and, drawing a breath from it, offers thanks to the gods that the rains are soon to come.

# RING AND PIN

The game which I have designated as ring and pin has a wide distribution, similar to that of the hoop-and-pole-game, of which, as I have stated in the introduction, it may be regarded as a miniature and solitaire form. In the former game the ring or target is attached to a thong or cord by means of which it is swung in the air, the object being to catch it upon a pin or dart fastened to the other end of the thong. It is analogous to the well-known European game of cup and ball (Fr. bilboquet), in which the ball may be caught either in the cup or upon the pointed end of the catching implement. I have employed the name of ring and pin, suggested by Dr George A. Dorsey, as a matter of convenience, for the American game, although rings are among the objects least frequently used.   In point of fact, the targets are of the greatest possible variety, both in form and material, ranging from a single hide ring among the Tewa (Hano) to strings of imbricated phalangeal bones (Algonquian, Athapascan, and Siouan tribes), salmon bones (Hupa, Pomo, Umatilla, Shasta), pumpkin rinds (Pima, Mohave), and, finally, to single objects perforated with holes, such as the skulls of small rodents (Eskimo, Paiute), bone copies thereof (Eskimo), seal bones (Eskimo, Clayoquot, Kwakiutl, Makah), or balls of tule (Klamath, Thompson Indians, Paiute) and bundles of pine twigs (Micmac, Passamaquoddy, Penobscot) and moose hair (Penobscot). When we examine the games played with strings of phalangeal bones, from among the northern range of tribes (Algonquian, Athapascan, and Siouan), the most numerously represented in our present collection, we discover that the number of bones is not constant, varying from three to nine, and that not infrequently they are pierced with transverse holes and numbered by means of notches from the bones nearest the pin end.   These notches determine the count.

FIG. 694. Stick and ring; length of stick, 21⅜ inches; shrine of Little Fire society, Zuñi, New Mexico; cat. no. 4909, Brooklyn Institute Museum.

A pretty constant feature of this game is a flap of buckskin or other material attached to the extreme end of the string.   This flap is perforated with holes which vary in number, and usually has a large hole in the center.   In the Cree game (figure 705) there is the flap alone, a disk of stiff buckskin with twenty-three holes, the direct analogue of the netted hoop.   In the Siouan games the flap is replaced with strings of glass beads, which count according to the number caught.   The buckskin survives in a vestigial form in the Winnebago game (figure 740), as a piece of ribbon in that of the Sauk and Foxes (figure 713), and again as a tuft of hair in the Umatilla salmon-bone game (figure 731).   The buckskin disk survives also as the principal feature of the cedar-bough game of the Passamaquoddy.   The Eskimo game, played with a small netted hoop (figure 617), which I have included among the games of hoop and pole, occupies a position midway between the hoop game proper and the ring-and-pin games. The strings of salmon bone are directly analogous to the phalangeal bones, the same being true of the Pima and Mohave disks of pumpkin rind.   In general, the material of the target depends upon the culture.

The rabbit and hare skulls occur among both the Paiute and the Eskimo. As is natural, the greatest variation from what may be regarded as the original type is found among the latter people, who copy the hare skull in ivory and make from the same material other implements representing the polar bear and fish. The ball of tule is found among nearly contiguous tribes. The cedar-twig and moosehair target of the eastern Algonquian tribes is analogous to the archery target of the Crows and the Grosventres (figure 501).

Wire needles are now employed in the Arapaho, Cheyenne, Oglala, and other Algonquian and Siouan tribes, but originally they were all of wood or bone.

The counts are extremely varied. In the phalangeal-bone game the bones count progressively from the one nearest the pin. The loops of beads count 1 or 10; the holes in the leather, 2 or 4; the large central hole, more. The total count of the game also varies from 2, 4, 50, or 100, the commonest number, up to 2,000. The game is played both for stakes and as a child's amusement. The players are usually two in number, women and girls, or a youth and a girl, as suggested by its name of "love game" (Cheyenne) or the "lovers' game" (Penobscot). Mr Cushing informed me that in Zuñi a phallic significance was attached to the ring and pin. This corresponds with the symbolism of the hoop-and-pole game and serves to strengthen and confirm the theory I have advanced as to their interdependence. An object analogous to the ring-and-pin game of the Zuñi is found in a stick with a ring attached by a cord (figure 694), from an ancient shrine of the Little Fire society at Zuñi, in the Brooklyn Institute Museum. The ring represents the net shield of the War Gods, and the object may be considered as the ceremonial antetype of the ring-and-pin game.

ALGONQUIAN STOCK

ARAPAHO. Wind River reservation, Wyoming. (Cat. no. 36981, Free Museum of Science and Art, University of Pennsylvania.) Four phalangeal bones (figure 695), each with ten perforations,

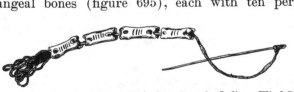

FIG. 695. Chetguetat; length of implement, 16¼ inches; Arapaho Indians, Wind River reservation, Wyoming: cat. no. 36981, Free Museum of Science and Art, University of Pennsylvania.

strung on a thong with a needle attached. The bone nearest the needle has three cuts on one side; the next, four; the next, five, and the last, six. Five beaded loops are at the end opposite the needle.

24 ETH—05 M——34

Another set (cat. no. 36982) in the same collection has three bones, each with eight lateral perforations. One bone has seven notches, another two, while the third is plain. Seven beaded loops and a similar brass ring are attached at the end opposite the needle.

Still another set (cat. no. 36983) has four bones, not perforated laterally, with two, three, four, and five transverse cuts, and three antelope hoofs at the end opposite the needle.

All these are implements for the game of chetguetat. Collected by the writer in 1900.

CHEYENNE. Oklahoma. (Cat. no. 178338, United States National Museum.)

Four phalangeal bones of the deer, perforated, and pierced with lateral perforations and marked with one, two, three. and four scratches; strung on a beaded cord with an iron needle attached, and having eight loops of red glass beads on the end opposite the needle.

These specimens were collected by Mr Louis L. Meeker, when teacher of manual training in the Cheyenne school, Darlington, Oklahoma, who furnished the following particulars concerning it in a communication on Cheyenne Games made to the United States Bureau of American Ethnology:

The ni-to-nis-dot or thrusting game of the Cheyenne is played with the four phalangeal bones from the fore or the hind feet of a deer. Sometimes two of the bones are from a fore foot and two from a hind foot, but this seems to be only when a new set is made of two old ones, part of which are broken.

Each bone is pierced with four rows of holes, four in a row, about equal distances apart, each row being on one of the faces of a bone, for the bones are somewhat quadrangular.

There is a small loop, called an earring, he-wus'-sis, attached on either side of one end of each bone by putting the cord of which it is made through one of the holes or through very small holes nearer the edge and pierced for that purpose.

Thus prepared, the four bones are strung like beads on a buckskin string or on a strand of beads strung on sinews. The larger end of each bone is toward the same end of the string, to which is attached a needle or piece of wire about 6 inches long, one end of which is coiled to make an eye to which the string is fastened. It is generally understood that originally this needle, or bodkin, was of bone and was used for piercing deerskin to sew it with sinews. Large thorns were also used.

The end of the string or strand of beads opposite that to which the needle is attached is composed of a bunch of loops, made, like the earings, of sinews, generally, if not always, strung with beads. The number of loops vary, so that the bunch may be sufficiently large to prevent the bones from slipping off. Perhaps ten loops is the proper number.

In the illustration Hi'-o-ni''-va, "Pipe woman," a camp Indian. is seated on a Government blanket with the game in her hand, ready to throw [figure 696].

The needle is held in the right hand, almost pen-fashion, but against the side of the forefinger at the joint next the nail.  The coil that forms the eye of the needle is up, and the other end or point of the needle is where the point of the pen would be, but the needle is held close to the eye that the point may project as far as possible.

The string passes along the under side of the needle; the strand of bones hang down; the tassel of loops is held by the thumb and forefinger of the left hand, which loosen it at the proper moment for a slight movement of the right hand to swing it upward and forward until the chain of bones is in a horizontal position in front of the player.  The needle is then thrust forward along the string on which the bones are strung, with the intention of catching one of the bones.

If it passes lengthwise through the first bone, it counts 10; through the second one, 20; the third, 30, and the fourth, 40.  Should it enter the end of

FIG. 696.  Cheyenne woman playing nitonisdot, Oklahoma; from photograph by Mr Louis L. Meeker.

the bone, but pass out at one of the holes, it counts but 1.  If it passes through an earring, it counts but 1.  Caught through the tassel of loops at the end it counts 50; or some say it counts 5 or 10 for each loop through which the needle passes.  This, and giving a particular value to each hole, is either an innovation or a manner of counting in use only among older players.  Children and ordinary players count the same for any hole and 50 for the end loops.

When more than two play, each side takes turns, and each player on a side, but it is not passed from one to another until there is a throw that does not count.

Each side has fifty sticks, which are passed back and forth as the play progresses.  When one side has all the sticks, the game is ended.  It is said that in olden times the sticks were redistributed and the game continued until exactly noon, when the party having fewest sticks prepared a feast for all.

CHEYENNE.    Oklahoma.    (Cat. no. 18610, Free Museum of Science
    and Art, University of Pennsylvania.)
Four phalangeal bones of a deer, perforated, and pierced with lateral
    perforations, and marked with two, three, four, and five red
    painted notches, strung on a thong, with an iron needle attached
    (figure 697).    Five loops of blue glass beads are attached to the
    end opposite the needle.
Collected by Mr George E. Starr.
Another specimen (cat. no. 18682) in the same collection is iden-
tical in form with the above, except that the bones have one, two,
three, and four notches.

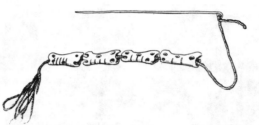

FIG. 697.   Nitonisdot; length of implement, 23¼ inches; Cheyenne Indians, Oklahoma; cat. no.
        18610, Free Museum of Science and Art, University of Pennsylvania.

Another specimen in the United States National Museum (cat. no.
165800), collected by Rev. H. R. Voth, is practically identical in its
details with the preceding.

———— Oklahoma.    (Cat. no. 67437, Field Columbian Museum.)
Four phalangeal bones of a deer, perforated and pierced and strung
    on beaded cord to which an iron needle is attached.    At the other
    end of the cord are loops of strung beads, two pink, three green,
    and one yellow.
Collected by Rev. H. R. Voth, who describes the game as follows:

These bones are used by the Arapaho as well as the Cheyenne in a game
which is sometimes called the love game.   The wire bodkin is taken in the
right hand and pointed horizontally forward.   The four bones are then swung
forward, and the bodkin is dexterously thrust through the perforations of one or
more of them, each of which represents a certain value.   The great aim of the
player is to catch all the four bones horizontally on the needle at one time.

Col. Richard Irving Dodge [a] says:

The Cheyenne women have another game of which they are passionately fond.
Small white beads are strung on a sinew, 12 or 14 inches long; at one end are
fastened in a bunch six loops, about an inch in diameter, of smaller beads similarly strung.   Four polished bones of the bear's foot are then strung on this
beaded string, the smaller ends toward the loops.   Each of these bones is perforated with sixteen holes in rows of four, and at each end are two or three

———————————
[a] Our Wild Indians, p. 331, Hartford, 1882.

very small loops of red beads. The other end of the sinew is now fastened to a sharpened piece of wire, 6 to 7 inches long, and the gambling instrument is complete.

The game is played by any number of players, each in turn. The needle is held horizontally between the thumb and fingers. The bones hanging down are steadied for an instant, then thrown forward and upward, and as they come opposite the point of the needle a rapid thrust is made. If the player be skillful the point of the needle will catch in some of the loops or perforations of the bones. For each loop at the lower extremity of the instrument caught by the needle the player counts 100. Being put together in a bunch, it is rare that more than two or three are caught, though all six may be. One of the bones caught lengthwise on the needle counts 25; two, 50. Each little loop and perforation penetrated by the needle counts 5. Though the complications are numerous, the count is simple. Thus suppose the needle passed through a little loop on the third bone (5), then through the bone (25), then through a little loop at the other end of the bone (5), then through a loop on fourth bone (5), and finally through three of the terminal loops (300), the count for the throw is the sum of all (340). I have never seen over 500 made at a throw, though it is of course possible to make over 600. If the needle misses or fails to perforate loop or orifice, there is no count. The game is usually 2,000.

CHIPPEWA. Bois fort, near Rainy river, Minnesota. (American Museum of Natural History.)

Cat. no. $\frac{40}{4111}$. Tapering bundle of cedar leaves (figure 698), tied with cotton thread, 7 inches in length, having a wooden pin attached by a cotton cord.

The game is called nāpawāgăn. Catching the bundle counts 1 point.

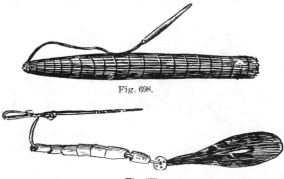

Fig. 698.

Fig. 699.

FIG. 698. Nāpawāgăn; length of bundle, 7 inches; Chippewa Indians, Bois fort, Minnesota; cat. no. $\frac{40}{4111}$, American Museum of Natural History.
FIG. 699. Nāpawāgăn; length of bones, 7½ inches; Chippewa Indians, Bois fort, Minnesota; cat. no. $\frac{50}{4709}$, American Museum of Natural History.

Cat. no. $\frac{50}{4709}$. Seven phalangeal bones (figure 699), strung on a buckskin thong having a wire needle attached at one end, and a metal button with a pear-shaped piece of buckskin, having a vertical slit in the middle and weighted with four small pieces of lead at the edge, at the other; length of bones, 7½ inches.

The game is called năpawāgăn, like the above.  Catching any bone but the one nearest the button counts 1; the last bone, 10; the hole in the leather, 1; and a hole in the button, 20.

Both specimens were collected by Dr William Jones in 1903.

CHIPPEWA.  Wisconsin.

Prof. I. I. Ducatel [a] says:

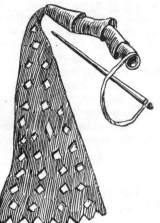

FIG. 700.  Napaăganăgi; length of implement, 15 inches; Chippewa Indians, Turtle mountain, North Dakota; cat. no. $\frac{50}{4710}$, American Museum of Natural History.

. . .  Paskahwewog, is a sort of "cup-and-ball," in which a pin is used instead of the ball, and is caught, by a similar arrangement to our game, on its point.

—————— Turtle mountain, North Dakota. (Cat. no. $\frac{50}{4710}$, American Museum of Natural History.)

Four bones (figure 700), ends of long bones painted red, strung on a thong with a wooden pin painted red, attached at one end, and a triangular piece of buckskin, cut with diamond-length, 15 inches.

Collected by Dr William Jones, who gives the name of the game as napaaganagi.

Catching a bone counts 1 point; catching the center hole in the dangle wins the game; the other holes in the dangle do not count.

—————— Ontario.

Mr David Boyle [b] describes an old Chippewa game played for gambling purposes:

FIG. 701.  Pepenggunegun; Chippewa Indians, Ontario; from Boyle.

It consists of seven conical bones strung on a leather thong about 8 inches long, which has fastened to it at one end a small piece of fur and at the other a hickory pin 3½ inches long [figure 701].  The game was played by catching the pin near the head, swinging the bones upwards, and trying to insert the point of the pin into one of them before they descended.  Each bone is said to have possessed a value of its own; the highest value being placed on the lowest bone, or the one nearest to the hand in playing.  This bone has also three holes near the wide end, and to insert the pin into any of these entitled the player to an extra number of points.  Above each hole is a series of notches numbering respectively 4, 6, and 9, which were, presumably, the value attached.  .  .  .  The one in our possession was presented by Mr J. Wood, an intelligent and influential member of the Missisauga band, near Hagersville.

---

[a] A Fortnight among the Chippewas.  The Indian Miscellany, p. 368, Albany, 1877.
[b] Fourth Annual Report of the Canadian Institute, p. 55, Toronto, 1891.

Mr Boyle gives the name as pe-peng-gun-e-gun, stabbing a hollow bone.

CREE. Coxby, Saskatchewan. (Cat. no. 15459, Field Columbian Museum.)

Eight phalangeal bones strung on a thong, with a wire needle, 6¼ inches in length, at one end, and an oblong flap of buckskin, 6¼ inches in length, perforated with 14 holes, at the other (figure 702).

These were collected by Mr Phillip Towne, who describes the game under the name of tapa whan, stringing the bone cups:

The object of the game is to catch one or more of the bone cups on the point of the bodkin or to thrust the bodkin into a hole in the buckskin thong. The game is of 50 points, which may be made as follows: One for each bone cup or hole, except the two center holes in the buckskin thong, which count 20. To cause the bodkin to enter one of the four small holes in the last bone cup is equivalent to game.

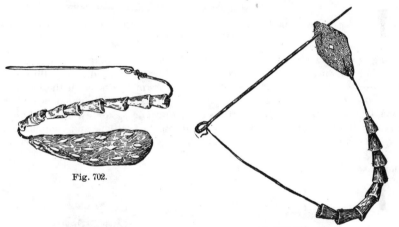

Fig. 702.

Fig. 703.

FIG. 702. Tapa whan; total length of implement, 28 inches; Cree Indians, Saskatchewan; cat. no. 15459, Field Columbian Museum.
FIG. 703. Cup and pin; total length of implement, 40 inches; Cree Indians, Saskatchewan; cat. no. 15130, Field Columbian Museum.

———— Union Lake reserve, Saskatchewan. (Cat. no. 15130, Field Columbian Museum.)

Nine phalangeal bones, painted blue, strung on a thong, with a long wire needle, 12¼ inches in length, at one end, and a diamond-shaped flap of buckskin, 5 inches in length, perforated with fifty-two small holes and a larger hole in the middle, tied at the other end (figure 703). Collected by W. Sibbold.

———— Muskowpetung reserve, Qu'appelle, Assiniboia. (Cat. no. 61993, Field Columbian Museum.)

Eight phalangeal bones strung on a thong, with a wire needle, 5¼
   inches long at one end, and a flap of buckskin, perforated with
   holes, with a large hole in the center, at the other (figure 704).
   The bone nearest the flap is stained green and has its upper edge
   serrated. The other bones are plain.

These were collected by Mr J. A. Mitchell, who furnished the following account of the game, under the name of napahwhan:

Played by either men or women, there being no limit to the number of players.
The bodkin is held in either hand, the buckskin appendage being held in the
opposite hand against the elbow with the needle pointed upward. The whole

FIG. 704. Napahwhan; total length, 24 inches; Cree Indians, Assiniboia; cat. no. 61993, Field
Columbian Museum.

string is then swung outward and upward, the object being to catch one or the
whole of the cups as they descend, on the point of the needle, or failing in this,
to cause the needle to pass through one or more of the holes in the leather tag.

Of the cups, each counts 2, except the blue-green one, which is called the
squay-chagan, last-born child; it scores game and takes all the stakes. The
holes in the tag have special values according to position, and combinations of
these holes also have certain counting values.

The game is one valued very highly by the Indians and one which they are
more loath to part with than with most others.

FIG. 705. Teheapì; length of stick, 9½ inches; Cree Indians, Wind River reservation, Wyoming;
cat. no. 37029, Free Museum of Science and Art, University of Pennsylvania.

CREE. Wind River reservation, Wyoming. (Cat. no. 37029, Free
      Museum of Science and Art, University of Pennsylvania.)
Disk of rawhide, 3¼ inches in diameter, painted yellow and perforated with holes, attached by a thong to a pointed stick, 9½
   inches in length (figure 705).

Collected by the writer in 1900 from an Indian of Riel's band, who
gave the name as teheapi:

Played indiscriminately by both sexes as a gambling game. The middle hole
counts 10 and the others 2.

DELAWARES.   Ontario.

Dr Daniel G. Brinton [a] gives an account of the following game as described to him by Rev. Albert Seqaqkind Anthony:

Qua'quallis.   In this a hollow bone is attached by a string to a pointed stick. The stick is held in the hand, and the bone is thrown up by a rapid movement, and the game is to catch the bone, while in motion, on the pointed end of the stick.   It was a gambling game, often played by adults.

GROSVENTRES.   Fort Belknap reservation, Montana.   (Cat. no. 36566, Free Museum of Science and Art, University of Pennsylvania.)

Four phalangeal bones, perforated at top and bottom, strung on a thong with five loops of colored beads at one end and a brass needle at the other (figure 706).   The bones are marked on one side with ten, nine, eight, and seven notches; length, 12½ inches.

Collected by Dr George A. Dorsey, who describes the game as follows, under the name of tsaitkusha:

A game and favorite pastime among young men and women, and so often called the matrimonial game.   The object of the game is to catch on the point of the long bodkin one or more of the bone cups made from the toe bones of

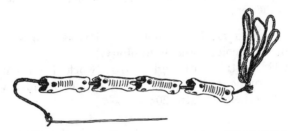

FIG. 706.  Tsaitkusha; length of implement, 22 inches; Grosventre Indians, Fort Belknap reservation, Montana; cat. no. 36566, Free Museum of Science and Art, University of Pennsylvania.

deer; or, failing in this, one or more of the loops of beaded thread.   Each cup is marked on one side with incised parallel lines; these determine its value and so the count on each cup caught, each loop also counting 1.   The number of cups and loops varies in different specimens, four being the most common number.

———— Fort Belknap reservation, Montana.   (Cat. no. 60278, 60286, 60351, Field Columbian Museum.)

Four phalangeal bones, perforated at both ends and having dotted incisions in the middle, strung on a thong with a needle at one end and a loop of colored glass beads at the other.

Three phalangeal bones, similar to the above, but with transverse notches instead of holes.

Four phalangeal bones, similar to the above.

These were collected by Dr George A. Dorsey in 1900.

---

[a] Folk-lore of the Modern Lenape.   Essays of an Americanist, p. 186, Philadelphia, 1896.

MISSISAUGA.   New Credit, Ontario.   (Cat. no. 178387, United States National Museum.)

Rev. Peter Jones [a] figures a game similar to cup and ball. The actual specimen (figure 707) exists in the United States National Museum, and consists of nine phalangeal bones strung on a thong with a wooden pin.

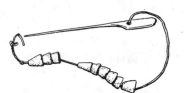

FIG. 707.  Phalangeal-bone  game; length, 16½ inches; Missisauga Indians, Ontario; cat. no. 178387, United States National Museum.

————— Rice lake, Ontario.

G. Copway [b] says:

The "Tossing Play" is a game seldom seen among the whites. It is played in the wigwam. There is used in it an oblong knot, made of cedar boughs, of length, say about 7 inches. On the top is fastened a string, about 15 inches long, by which the knot is swung. On the other end of this string is another stick, 2½ inches long, and sharply pointed. This is held in the hand, and if the player can hit the large stick every time it falls on the sharp one he wins. "Bone play" is another indoor amusement, so called because the articles used are made of the hoof-joint bones of the deer. The ends are hollowed out, and from three to ten are strung together. In playing it they use the same kind of sharp stick, the end of which is thrown into the bones.

MONTAGNAIS.   Lake St John, Quebec.   (Peabody Museum of American Archæology and Ethnology.)

Cat. no. 62326.  String of eight large worked phalangeal bones, strung on twine, with a bone pin at one end and a wild-cat tail tied at the other; length, 20½ inches.

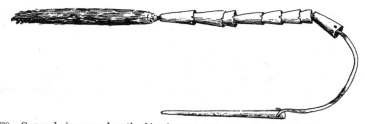

FIG. 708.  Cup-and-pin game; length of implement, 26½ inches; Montagnais Indians, Quebec; cat. no. 62327, Peabody Museum of American Archæology and Ethnology.

Cat. no. 62327.  String of phalangeal bones (figure 708), similar to the above, but strung on a thong and having a rabbit-skin roll tied at one end; length, 26½ inches. The top bone has four holes near its upper edge. Both collected by Mr Archibald Tisdale about 1892.

---

[a] History of the Ojebway Indians, fig. 7, pl. facing p. 135, London, 1861.
[b] The Traditional History and Characteristic Sketches of the Ojibway Nation, p. 55, Boston, 1851.

MONTAGNAIS.   Labrador.

Henry Youle Hind [a] writes as follows:

One evening during our return I observed Michel, who was always doing something when in camp, making some little disks of wood, with a hole in each, and stringing them on a piece of leather; he attached a thin strip of wood to the end of the string, and, with Louis, was soon engaged in a game similar to our Cup and Ball. Upon enquiry I found that the game was common among his people, and was frequently played by them at their lodges.

According to his description, the apparatus is made in exactly the same manner as the Nah-bah-wah-tah of the Ojibways, or the game of bones (the Nah-bah-wah-gun-nuk). The Nah-bah-wah-gun-nuk, or instrument with which the game is played, is constructed in the following manner:—

The bones are made from the hoof of the deer, or caribou, and made to fit one within the other to the number of twelve, the one nearest to the hand when the instrument is held for play being the largest. A hole is bored through the center of each, and the bones are strung upon sinew or a short deer-skin thong; at one end of the thong a bone needle or skewer is attached, and at the other extremity a piece of leather, 4 inches long and 1¾ wide, cut into the shape of an oval. Small holes are made

FIG. 709.  Cup and pin; length of implement, 14¼ inches; Nascapee Indians, Labrador; cat. no. 3214, United States National Museum; from Turner.

in the piece of leather, which is called the tail, and four holes are drilled into the last 'bone.' The thong is weighted with a piece of lead close to the tail, the last bone slipping over it. The players agree upon the stakes, which are placed before them in the lodge, and one of them takes the bones and begins to play. His object is to catch as many as he can on the needle or skewer in a certain number of trials; the last bone, if caught singly in one of the holes drilled in it, counts the highest; if the tail is caught it also counts next to the last bone.

The other bones count 1 each, and a skillful player will sometimes catch 8 or 10 at one throw.

NASCAPEE.   Ungava, Labrador.   (Cat. no. 3214, United States National Museum.)

Five cones of polished bone (figure 709), made of phalangeal bones, strung on a thong, with the tail of some small animal fastened

---

[a] Explorations in the Interior of the Labrador Peninsula, v. 1, p. 277, London, 1863.

at one end and a bone pin at the other. Collected by Mr Lucien Turner, who says:[a]

They also have a game corresponding to " cup and ball," but it is played with different implements from what the Eskimo use. . . . The hollow cones are made from the terminal phalanges of the reindeer's foot. The tail tied to the end of the thong is that of a marten or a mink. The player holds the peg in one hand, and tossing up the bones tries to catch the nearest bone on the point of the peg. The object of the game is to catch the bone the greatest possible number of times. It is in no sense a gambling game.

NIPISSING. Forty miles above Montreal, Quebec.

J. A. Cuoq[b] gives the following definition:

Pipindjikaneigan, toy, sort of cup and ball, made of several dew-claws of the roebuck strung on a small cord to the end of which is fastened a pointed piece of wood with which they try to catch the dew-claws thrown in the air.

PASSAMAQUODDY. Maine.

Mrs W. W. Brown[c] describes the following game (figure 710):

T'wis. This, which is also an indoor game, is at present oftenest played for amusement. The t'wis is composed of an oblong piece of moose hide, about 4 inches in length, punctured with small holes, the center one being slightly larger than the others. This piece of hide is joined to a bundle of cedar (arbor vitæ)

FIG. 710.  T'wis; Passamaquoddy Indians, Maine; from Mrs W. W. Brown.

boughs, tightly wound round with cord. To this, by about 6 inches of string, is attached a sharp-pointed stick, tied near the center and held between the thumb and finger like a pen-handle. The game consists in giving the moose-hide a peculiar upward toss and at the same time piercing one of the holes with the point of the stick. The number of points necessary for winning is usually set at 100. Each player can hold the t'wis until he misses a point.

Another kind of t'wis was made of several pieces of bone strung loosely together, each having a certain value, and being counted by catching on the point of the stick, similarly to the holes in the moose hide.

There is a tradition that the first t'wis-ūk were made from that peculiar fungus which grows out from the bark of trees and is known to the Indians as wā-be-la-wen, or squaw-oc-l'moos-wāl-dee—that is, " the swamp woman's dishes." (Squaw-oc-moos is the bête noire of the Indian legends, and even now children will not play with toadstools through the fear of the swamp woman.) " One night," so the story runs, " during a very important game of t'wis, on which everything available had been wagered, both contestants fell asleep. The one having the t'wis was carried by Med-o-lin many miles into a swamp. When he awoke he saw Squaw-oc-moos eating out of the dishes and a t'wis made of boughs in his hands."

---

[a] Ethnology of the Ungava District, Hudson Bay Territory. Eleventh Annual Report of the Bureau of Ethnology, p. 323, 1894.

[b] Lexique de la Langue Algonquine, Montreal, 1886.

[c] Some Indoor and Outdoor Games of the Wabanaki Indians. Transactions of the Royal Society of Canada, v. 6, sec. 2, p. 43, Montreal, 1889.

It seems quite impossible to get a t'wis constructed from these wal-dee. The Indians will describe such a t'wis and promise faithfully to make one, even resenting any insinuations that they are afraid to do so. Their promise, nevertheless, for whatever reason, remains unfulfilled.

PASSAMAQUODDY.  Pleasant Point, Maine.

Dr A. S. Gatschet writes from Baddeck, Nova Scotia, August 28, 1899:

The evergreen-bough game is unknown among the Micmac of Cape Breton, where I am now, but I heard of it at Pleasant Point, Me. It is called tu'tuash (plural, tutua'shek). Not only the pine species furnishing the twigs is called so, but also the twigs or needles broken off from it to play the game with, and also the game itself. The twigs, not over 4 or 5 inches long, are made to dance on a table or other level object, and a song, tu'tua, is sung while the dancing lasts.

PENOBSCOT. Kennebunkport, Maine. (Cat. no. 15406, Free Museum of Science and Art, University of Pennsylvania.)

FIG. 711.  Artoois; length of cone, 8¼ inches; Penobscot Indians, Kennebunkport, Maine; cat. no. 15406, Free Museum of Science and Art, University of Pennsylvania.

Implement for a game (figure 711), consisting of a pointed stick, 9½ inches in length, attached by a thong to a cone-shaped object 8½ inches in length, made by wrapping leaves of *Arbor vitæ* with thread. The wrapping properly should be of eelskin.

Collected by Mr Henry C. Mercer, who describes it under the name of artoois.

—————— Oldtown, Maine.  (Cat. no. 48237, Peabody Museum of American Archæology and Ethnology.)

Implement for a game (figure 712), described by the collector under the name of ahduis, and consisting of a pointed bone about 8 inches in length, attached by a thong 14 inches

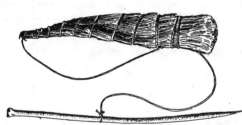

FIG. 712.  Ahdu'is; length of cone, 7 inches; Penobscot Indians, Oldtown, Maine; cat. no. 48237, Peabody Museum of American Archæology and Ethnology.

in length to the tip of a cone-shaped object of moose hair, 7 inches in length.

Collected by Mr C. C. Willoughby, who kindly furnished the following description:

Ah-du'-is is the lover's game. This game is played with a very sharp-pointed bone, some 8 inches long, and a roll of moose hair somewhat shorter, of conical form, about 1½ inches broad at base. These are fastened together by a cord about 14 inches long in the same manner as our cup and ball, which this game closely resembles in method of playing. When a man called upon a Penobscot girl to play ah-du′-is, they seated themselves, tailor-fashion, on a robe or skin. The man, taking the sharp-pointed bone, holds it spear fashion, allowing the roll of moose hair to hang down the length of the string. Then, swinging it up, he strikes at it, the object being to impale it on the point of the bone. The game consists of a given number of points. If the first attempt is successful and the bone remains impaled upon the point of the bone, it counts 1, and the player continues until he fails. Then it is passed to the girl. If his company is agreeable to her, she continues the game to the end; but if, on her first successful thrust, instead of continuing, she hands the ah-du′-is to him, it means that his company is not acceptable.

SAUK AND FOXES.   Tama, Iowa.   (Cat. no. 36755, Free Museum of Science and Art, University of Pennsylvania.)

Six perforated wooden cones (figure 713), strung on a thong with an iron needle made of an arrowhead ground down, attached to a silk ribbon fastened at the opposite end; total length, 11½ inches. Collected by the writer in 1900.

Said to be played by a boy and a girl together, and called ni-bi-quai-ha-ki.

FIG. 713.  Nibiquaihaki; length of implement, 11½ inches; Sauk and Fox Indians, Iowa; cat. no. no. 36755, Free Museum of Science and Art, University of Pennsylvania.

Two specimens of the same implement exist in the American Museum of Natural History (cat. no. $\frac{50}{3521}$, $\frac{50}{3522}$). Collected by Dr William Jones. He gave the name to the writer as nibiquihok, elm-tree eyes. When the last cone is caught on the pin, it counts 2; any other counts 1. There is a small strip of perforated leather at the extreme end. To catch one of the holes in this counts 5; to catch the thong with the pin between the pin and the first cone counts 10. The first implement has seven and the other six cones.

### ATHAPASCAN STOCK

HUPA.   Hupa valley, California.   (Cat. no. 37209, Free Museum of Science and Art, University of Pennsylvania.)

Implement for game of kiolkis. Four salmon bones (figure 714), vertebræ, perforated and strung on a cord, 17 inches long, fastened at the base or handle of a pointed stick 12 inches long, the object being to throw up and catch the bone on the point. Collected by the writer in 1900.

Men play, one against another, each using an implement. Catching one bone counts 1; two bones, 2; and so on. If a player misses, the other plays. Four points is the game.

A Crescent City Indian, whom the writer met at Arcata, Cal., gave the name of this game as tsluk, while a Mad river (Wishoskan) Indian at Blue lake called it ret-char-i-wa-ten.

FIG. 714.  Kiolkis; length of stick, 12 inches; Hupa Indians, Hupa valley, California; cat. no. 37209, Free Museum of Science and Art, University of Pennsylvania.

Dr J. W. Hudson described the preceding game under the name miltokot, " with to stab."

A bone awl held in the right hand jabs at a tightly rolled bunch of grass thrown up on the end of a string.  As long as a player succeeds, he continues. There are ten counters.  The game is common between youths and maids, and is said to symbolize the desire for a partner.  The grass ball is often replaced by fish vertebræ.

KAWCHODINNE.  Fort Good Hope, Mackenzie.  (Cat. no. 857, United States National Museum.)

Eight phalangeal bones (figure 715), worked and polished down to conical form, strung on a thong, having a heart-shaped piece of buckskin with thirty-two holes cut in it attached at one end and a polished bone needle, 7¼ inches in length, at the other; total length, 26 inches.  Collected by Maj. R. Kennicott.

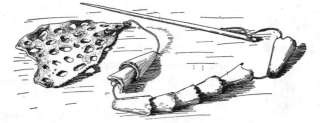

FIG. 715.  Phalangeal-bone game; length of implement, 26 inches; Kawchodinne Indians, Fort Good Hope, Mackenzie; cat. no. 857, United States National Museum.

THLINGCHADINNE.  Fort Rae, Mackenzie.  (Cat. no. 10844, Museum of the State University of Iowa.)

The late Dr Frank Russell,[a] the collector, wrote under " ecagoo " in his catalogue of ethnological material secured in the Hudson's Bay Company's territory:

No. 10,844 consists of three small pieces of bone [figure 716] rudely fashioned in hollow cones through which passes a slender thread of twisted sinew.  Each cone is 1.5 inches long and 0.8 inch in diameter at the larger end.  They are

---

[a] Explorations in the Far North.  State University of Iowa, p. 181, 1898.

hollowed at the base so that they fit into each other.  The thread is 6 inches in length and is attached to a strip of caribou skin at one end.  This leather is 4.5 inches long and has nine slits reaching within half an inch of the ends and in which the point may catch in throwing.  The needle is of bone 2 inches long and 0.1 inch in diameter.  It is attached to the end of the thread which is towards the base of the cones.  In using the ecagoo the thumb and forefinger grasp the end of the needle where it is enlarged by the sinew seizing, and the whole is swung outward and upward.  The thread is just long enough to admit the point of the needle into the base of the first cone, where they are crowded into each other.  The object to be attained is to pass the needle through the center of the cones or a slit in the leather at the top as the ecagoo falls.  In gambling, a score is kept of the points made.  Johnnie Cohoyla, from whom I obtained this, in the use of which he was an adept, said that the catching the point in the slits scored 1, on the first cone, 5, in first and second, 10, in all three, 15, and in second and third, 20.  I saw it used in his camp as a gambling device, but elsewhere merely as a child's toy.

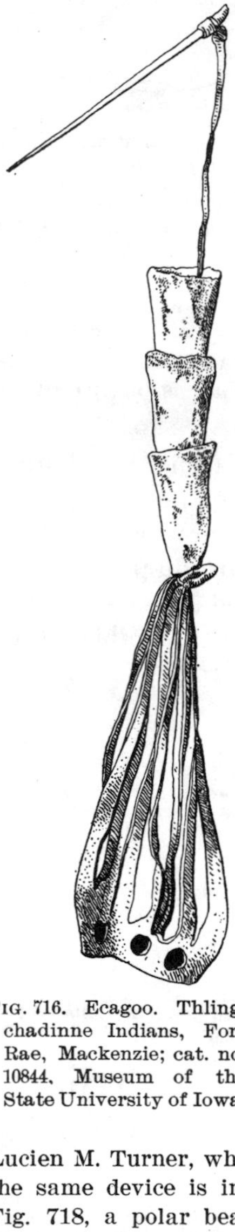

Doctor Russell precedes this account by saying:

I saw the same apparatus in use among the Stoney Indians of Morley and among the Slaveys at Providence.

ESKIMAUAN STOCK

ESKIMO (CENTRAL).  Cumberland sound, Baffin land, Franklin.

Dr Franz Boas [a] writes as follows (references to figures below follow the numbers used in this paper):

In winter, gambling is one of the favorite amusements of the Eskimo.  Figs. 717, 718, 719, 724 represent the ajegaung, used in a game somewhat similar to our cup and ball.  The most primitive device is Fig. 724, a hare's skull with a number of holes drilled through it.  A specimen was kindly lent to me by Lucien M. Turner, who brought it from Ungava bay; but in Baffin Land exactly the same device is in use.  Fig. 717 represents the head of a fox, in ivory; Fig. 718, a polar bear.  The specimen shown in Fig. 719 was brought from Cumberland sound by Kumlien.  The neck of the bear is more elaborate than the one shown in figure 718.  The attachment of the part representing the hind legs is of some interest.  The game is played as follows: First, the skull or the piece of ivory must be thrown up and caught ten times upon the stick in any one of the holes.  Then, beginning with the hole in front (the mouth), those of the

FIG. 716.  Ecagoo.  Thlingchadinne Indians, Fort Rae, Mackenzie; cat. no. 10844, Museum of the State University of Iowa.

---

[a] The Central Eskimo.  Sixth Annual Report of the Bureau of Ethnology, p. 567, 1888.

middle line must be caught. The three holes on the neck of the bear are double, one crossing vertically, the other slanting backward, but both ending in one hole on the neck. After the mouth has been caught upon the stick the vertical hole in the neck is the next, then the oblique one, and so on down the middle line of the animal's body. If, in the first part of the game, the player

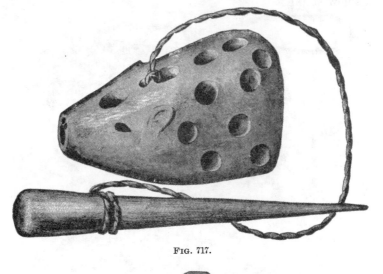

FIG. 717.

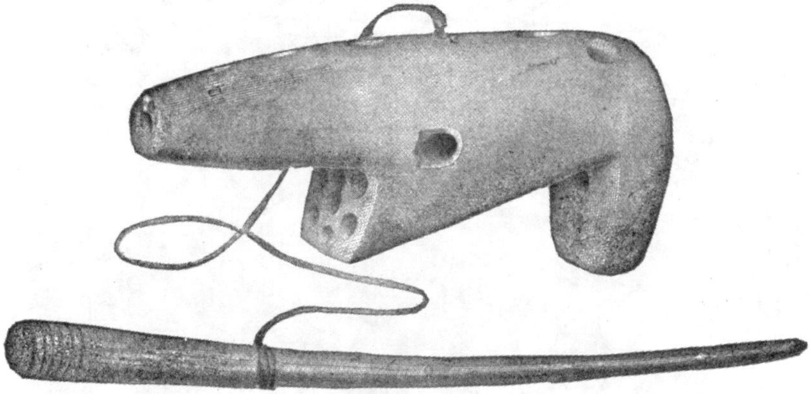

FIG. 718.

FIG. 717. Ivory carving representing head of fox, used in the game ajegaung, 1/1; Central Eskimo, Cumberland sound, Baffin land, Franklin; cat. no. IV A 6820, Museum für Völkerkunde, Berlin; from Boas.

FIG. 718. Ivory carving representing polar bear, used in the game of ajegaung, 2/3; Central Eskimo, Cumberland sound, Baffin land, Franklin; cat. no. IV A 6819, Museum für Völkerkunde, Berlin; from Boas.

misses twice, he must give up the pieces to his neighbor, who then takes his turn. In the second part he is allowed to play on as long as he catches in any hole, even if it be not the right one, but as soon as he misses he must give it up. After having caught one hole he proceeds to the next, and the player who first finishes all the holes has won the game.

ESKIMO (CENTRAL). Kings cape, Repulse bay, Keewatin. (Cat. no. 10188, United States National Museum.)

Ivory object (figure 720), 4½ inches in length, perforated with holes, and having an ivory pin, 4 inches in length, attached at top by a sinew string.

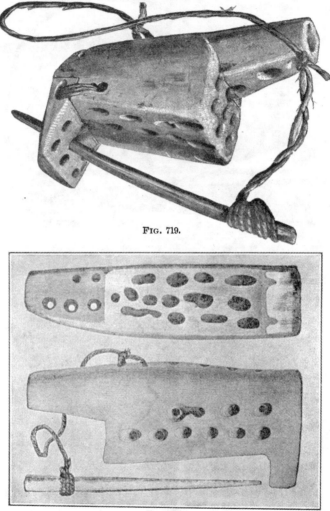

FIG. 719.

FIG. 720.

FIG. 719. Ivory carving representing polar bear, used in the game ajegaung, 2/3; length of object, 4¼ inches; length of pin, 5 inches; Central Eskimo, Cumberland sound, Baffin land. Franklin; cat. no. 34078, United States National Museum; from Kumlien.

FIG. 720. Bone game; length of implement, 4½ inches; Central Eskimo, Repulse bay, Keewatin; cat. no. 10188, United States National Museum; from Hall.

This specimen was collected by Capt. Charles Francis Hall, U. S. Navy, who says: [a]

A favorite game was that of cup and ball.

[a] Narrative of the Second Arctic Expedition, p. 96, Washington, 1879.

ESKIMO (CENTRAL). West coast of Hudson bay, Keewatin. (Cat. no. 10392, United States National Museum.)

Ivory object in the shape of a fish (figure 721), with three holes at the head end and a single hole in the flat tail; length, 4½ inches. An ivory pin, 4½ inches in length, is attached by a cord of plaited sinew to a hole in one side of the fish. The object is to catch the fish at either the head or the tail. Collected by Capt. Charles Francis Hall, U. S. Navy.

FIG. 721.  Fish game; length of fish, 4½ inches; Central Eskimo, west coast of Hudson bay, Keewatin; cat. no. 10392, United States National Museum.

ESKIMO (CENTRAL: AIVILIRMIUT AND KINIPETU). West coast of Hudson bay, Keewatin. (Cat. no. $\frac{60}{2547}$, $\frac{60}{2707}a$, American Museum of Natural History.)

Dr Franz Boas [a] describes the above objects as follows:

The game of cup-and-ball is played with an implement quite different from the one used in Cumberland sound. . . . The ball consists of a narrow

Fig. 722.

Fig. 723.

FIG. 722.  Bone game; length of bone, 2¼ inches; Central Eskimo (Aivilirmiut and Kinipetu), west coast of Hudson bay, Keewatin; cat. no. $\frac{60}{2547}$, American Museum of Natural History.

FIG. 723.  Seal-bone game; length of bone, 4 inches; Central Eskimo (Aivilirmiut and Kinipetu), west coast of Hudson bay, Keewatin; cat. no. $\frac{60}{2707}a$, American Museum of Natural History.

piece of musk-ox horn with four holes drilled into its short edge. It is caught on a wooden or bone pin [figure 722]. The game is also played with the shoulder bone of a seal [figure 723].

---

[a] Eskimo of Baffin Land and Hudson Bay. Bulletin of the American Museum of Natural History, v. 15, p. 111, New York, 1901.

ESKIMO (LABRADOR). Ungava bay, Labrador. (United States National Museum.)

Cat. no. 90227. Skull of a hare having several holes drilled in the upper part, with a radius of a hare attached by a thong (figure 724). Collected by Mr Lucien M. Turner.

Cat. no. 3478. Similar skull with bone attached, but with no perforations in the cranium.

——— Fort Chimo, Labrador.

Mr Lucien M. Turner [a] says:

A favorite game, something like cup and ball, is played with the following implements: A piece of ivory is shaped into the form of an elongate cone and

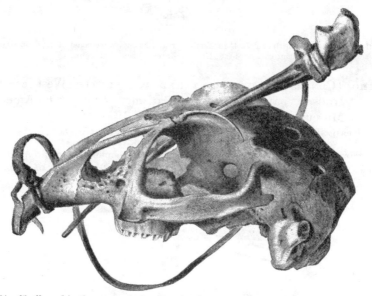

FIG. 724. Skull used in the game of ajegaung, 1/1; length, 3½ inches: Labrador Eskimo, Ungava bay; cat. no. 90227, United States National Museum: from Boas.

has two deep notches or steps cut from one side [figure 725]. In the one next the base are bored a number of small holes and one or two holes in the upper step. The apex has a single hole. On the opposite side of the base two holes are made obliquely, that they will meet, and through them is threaded a short piece of thong. To the other end of the thong is attached a peg of ivory, about 4 inches long. The game is that the person holding the plaything shall, by a dexterous swing of the ball, catch it upon the ivory peg held in the hand. The person engages to catch it a certain number of times in succession, and on failure to do so allows the opponent to try her skill. The skull of a hare is often substituted for the ivory ball, and a few perforations are made in the walls of the skull to receive the peg. It requires a great amount of practice to catch the ball, as the string is so short that one must be quick to thrust the peg in before it describes the part of a small circle.

---

[a] Ethnology of the Ungava District, Hudson Bay Territory. Eleventh Annual Report of the Bureau of Ethnology, p. 255, 1894.

Eskimo (Ita). Karma, Inglefield gulf, Greenland. (Cat. no. 18609, Free Museum of Science and Art, University of Pennsylvania.)

Implements consisting of the ulna of a seal (figure 726), 4½ inches in length, perforated at both ends; and a pin, consisting of the radius of a hare, attached by a cord of sinew. Collected by Mr Theodore Le Boutellier.

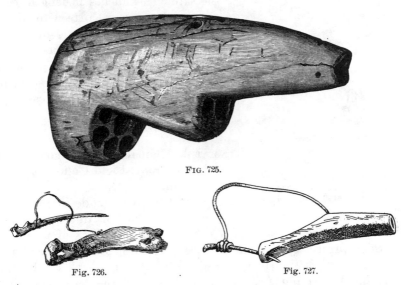

FIG. 725.

Fig. 726.                                  Fig. 727.

FIG. 725. Bone game; Central Eskimo (Koksoagmiut), Fort Chimo, Labrador; cat. no. 90228, United States National Museum; from Turner.

FIG. 726. Ajagaq; length of seal bone, 4½ inches; Ita Eskimo, Inglefield gulf, Greenland; cat. no. 18609, Free Museum of Science and Art, University of Pennsylvania.

FIG. 727. Ajagaq; length, 6½ inches; Ita Eskimo, Smith sound, Greenland; cat. no. $\frac{6\,0}{3\,3\,5}$, American Museum of Natural History.

———— Smith sound, Greenland. (Cat. no. $\frac{6\,0}{3\,3\,5}$, American Museum of Natural History.)

A bone 6½ inches in length (figure 727), with a hole bored through each socket and a thin stick tied by a short string to the bone, the latter being thrown up to be caught in either hole with the stick. Figured and described by Dr A. L. Kroeber,[a] who gives the name of the implement as ajagaq and that of the catching stick as ajautang.

### IROQUOIAN STOCK

HURON. Ontario.

Father Louis Hennepin,[b] describing the games of children, says:

They also make a ball of flags or corn leaves, which they throw in the air and catch on the end of a pointed stick.

[a] Bulletin of the American Museum of Natural History, v. 12, p. 296, New York, 1900.
[b] A Description of Louisiana, p. 303, New York, 1880.

KULANAPAN STOCK

POMO.    Ukiah,   California.    (Cat.   no.   61116,   Field   Columbian
        Museum.)

Six pointed oak forks (figure 728) set around a handle, to which they
    are bound by the bark of the *Cercis occidentales;* total length,

11⅝ inches.  Four vertebral bones of
the salmon,[a] 4 inches in length, each
composed of from thirteen to fifteen
vertebræ, tied with cords of native
flax at the base of the points.

Collected by Dr George A. Dorsey,
who designates the game as the spearing
game, dittcega; from diken, to cast up.[b]

FIG. 728. Dittcega; length, 11⅝ inches; Pomo Indians, Ukiah, California; cat. no. 61116, Field Columbian Museum.

LUTUAMIAN STOCK

KLAMATH.  Klamath lake, Oregon.  (Cat.
no. 61531, Field Columbian Museum.)

A long elliptical ball made of tule pith.
The lower end of the ball, which
remains loose, consists of a dozen or more strings of tule fiber
which project beyond the surface.  The upper portion, or body,
of the ball is tightly wrapped with the outer bark of the tule
rush.  Projecting from the upper end of the ball is a small
braided loop, one-fourth of an inch in diameter, to which is
fastened a 6-inch thread of native grass.  At the end of this
thread is attached a small bone pin a little more than 1 inch in
length.

Collected by Dr George A. Dorsey, who gives the following description of the game under the name of soquoquas:[c]

Taking the pin by the end to which the cord is attached by the thumb and
forefinger, and permitting the ball to hang loosely at the end of the string, a sudden downward thrust is given, the object being to strike the braided loop and
catch it on the point of the pin.  This is known as shapashspatcha ("to split or
punch out the moon").  The game is always played in winter and generally
only by adults.  It is believed that by "punching out the moon" in this fashion
the winter months are shortened and the advent of spring is hastened.

Another specimen, cat. no. 61673 (plate XI), is made similarly;
    the ball is 5 inches in length, while from it project several
    strands of the inner fiber of tule, also 5 inches in length; the
    knot, string, and pin are somewhat larger.

---

[a] Doctor Hudson informed the writer that sucker vertebræ are also used.
[b] Doctor Hudson gives the name as di-che-ka, to-stab-at game.
[c] Certain Gambling Games of the Klamath Indians.  American Anthropologist, n. s., v.
3, p. 21, 1901.

SOQUOQUAS; KLAMATH INDIANS, OREGON; CAT. NO. 61673, 61712, FIELD
COLUMBIAN MUSEUM; FROM DORSEY

In another specimen, cat. no. 61532, no strands of fiber project from
the ball, the two ends being finished alike. Instead of the string
being tied in a loop at the upper end, it is simply fastened in
one of the wrappings. This ball is not wound from side to side
with a circular wrapping of tule bark, but is wrapped about the
center from eight to ten times with a tightly woven thread of
that material.

The three other specimens, cat. no. 61712 (plate XI), 61713, 61715,
are much smaller than the specimens described, the largest
being not over 2½ inches in length. They are all made of bark
of tule, tightly wrapped from end to end, and are considerably
larger about the middle than at either end, thus having a sort
of lozenge shape. In each of these three specimens the thread
connecting the pin and ball is unusually well made and is very
soft and pliable, while the pin consists simply of a porcupine
quill. With all of these specimens in which no loop projects
from the ball to which the string is attached, the object of the
game is to strike the knot where the string is fastened to the ball.

PIMAN STOCK

PIMA. Gila River reserve, Sacaton agency, Pinal county, Arizona.
(Cat. no. 63290, Field Columbian Museum.)

Nineteen rings of gourd shell (figure 729), strung on cotton string,
with a wooden pin, 9 inches in length, at one end, and a triangular perforated piece of gourd shell,
3½ inches in length, at the other;
total length, 23 inches. Collected
by Mr S. C. Simms, who gives the
name as chelgwegoooot.

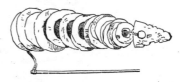

FIG. 729. Chelgwegoooot; length of
implement, 23 inches; Pima Indians,
Arizona; cat. no. 63290, Field Columbian Museum.

A specimen of the same implement
in the United States National Museum
(cat. no. 218644), collected by Dr
Frank Russell, has thirty-eight rings
of dried gourd shell, ranging from 4¼ inches to 1 inch in diameter,
with an oval pendant at the end. The catching stick is 8¼ inches in
length.

The game is described by the collector [a] under the name of tculi-
kiwe'kut:

This is the Gileño of the widespread dart-and-ring game. It is not exclusively
a woman's game, but was sometimes played by women. The younger generation
knows nothing about it. The apparatus consists of a series of rings cut from
cultivated gourds. They vary in diameter from 3 to 12 centimeters, and are
strung on a two-ply maguey fiber cord 50 centimeters long. They are kept from
slipping off at one end by a rectangular piece of gourd a little larger than the

---

[a] In a memoir to be published by the Bureau of American Ethnology.

opening in the smallest ring, which is at that end. At the other end of the string is fastened a stick 20 centimeters long, the outer end of which is sharpened. The game is to toss the rings up by a swing and, while holding the butt of the stick, thrust the dart through as many of them as possible. If the thrower fails she hands the apparatus to her opponent, but she continues throwing as long as she scores, and counts the number of rings that are caught on the dart. In the specimen collected there are 14 rings, but only a few may be caught at a single throw. A certain number of marks, 2, 3, or 4, agreed upon in advance, constitute the game. These marks are made upon a diagram laid out in the sand in the form of a whorl. The scoring commences in the center, called the tcunni ki (council house), and runs out to the last hole, called hoholdoga ki (menstrual house), which is on the west side of the diagram; then the score returns to the center before the player is entitled to one point toward game. If the player who is behind throws a number that brings her counter to the same hole as that of her opponent, she "kills" the latter and sends back her counter to the beginning point, but this is not done if she passes her opponent's position.

Two specimens were obtained at Sacaton, which were probably used in games by the Hohokam.

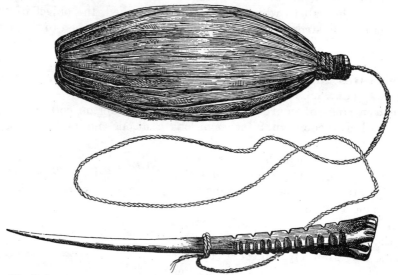

FIG. 730. Ball-and-pin game; length of ball, 4¼ inches; Thompson Indians, British Columbia; cat. no. ₈₁₂₆¹⁶, American Museum of Natural History.

SALISHAN STOCK

THOMPSON INDIANS (NTLAKYAPAMUK). British Columbia. (Cat. no. ₈₁₂₆¹⁶, American Museum of Natural History.)

Egg-shaped ball made of rushes (figure 730), 4½ inches in length, attached at one end by a twisted cord to a notched deer bone.

This specimen was collected by Mr James Teit, who says that the notches on the bone are ornamental, but some boys keep tallies of the greatest number of times they can catch without missing, by notching the pin.

Mr Teit [a] says also:

A boys' game was played as follows: A small, but rather long bail of grass was attached to the hand with a string. In the same hand was held a wooden pin. The ball was thrown away from the hand, but pulled back again by the string. On the way back, the hand was raised so as to catch the ball on the end of the pin. This was done as often as possible. After the first miss the ball had to be handed to the next boy.

FIG. 731. Pactslewitas; total length of implements, 6¼ inches; Umatilla Indians, Umatilla reservation, Oregon; cat. no. 37540, Free Museum of Science and Art, University of Pennsylvania.

### SHAHAPTIAN STOCK

UMATILLA. Umatilla reservation, Oregon. (Cat. no. 37540, Free Museum of Science and Art, University of Pennsylvania.)

Implements for the game of pactslewitas (figure 731), a piece of salmon vertebræ (seven bones) 2½ inches in length, perforated and strung on a cord with one loose bone; wooden pin at one end of the cord and a tuft of fur at the other. Collected by the writer in 1900.

The pin is held in the fingers and the bones are swung in the air. Catching the single bone counts 1; the single bone and the others, 2. The game is 100.

### SHASTAN STOCK

FIG. 732. Salmon-bone game; Shasta Indians, California; cat. no. ₃₁⁵⁰₉₂, American Museum of Natural History.

SHASTA. Hamburg bar, California. (Cat. no. $\frac{50}{3192}$, American Museum of Natural History.)

Twelve salmon bones (figure 732) strung on a cord which is tied to a pointed stick. A piece of red flannel is attached to the end of the cord. Collected in 1902 by Dr Roland B. Dixon.

### SHOSHONEAN STOCK

PAIUTE. Pyramid lake, Nevada. (Cat. no. 19058, United States National Museum.)

A bunch of tule stalks tied at the ends (figure 733), 4¾ inches in length, with a wooden needle attached with a cord. Collected by Mr Stephen Powers, who describes it in his catalogue under the name of nadohetin.

Every time the player catches it he has a right to thump his opponent on the forehead.

[a] The Thompson Indians of British Columbia. Memoirs of the American Museum of Natural History, whole series, v. 2, p. 278, New York, 1900.

PAIUTE.  Southern Utah.  (Peabody Museum of American Archæology and Ethnology.)

Cat. no. 9434.  The skull of the cottontail rabbit attached by a thong to a wooden pin (figure 734a).

The pin is held in the hand and the skull is swung and caught upon its point.

Cat. no. 9433.  A small hollow bone (figure 734b), seven-eighths of an inch in length, with a notch cut through one side, strung on a thong, to the other end of which a wooden pin is attached.  Evidently intended for a game like the preceding.

Both were collected by Dr Edward Palmer.

SHOSHONI.  Wind River reservation, Wyoming.

Dr George A. Dorsey informed me that he learned of the existence of a game of this type among the Shoshoni at Fort Washakie, but they could not be induced by any offers of money to make a specimen of the implements for him.

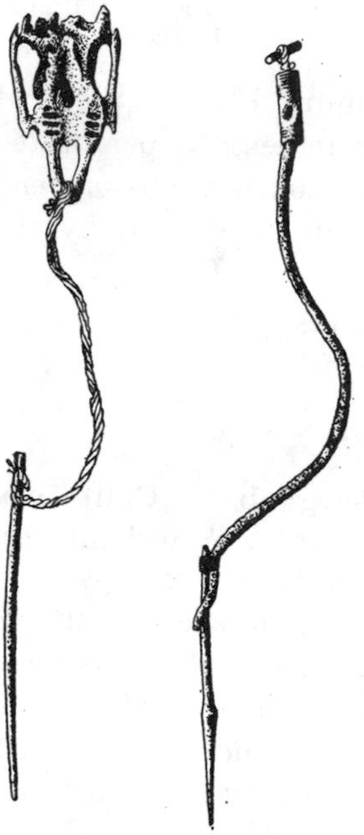

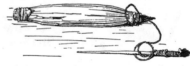

Fig. 733.

FIG. 734 a, b.                        Fig. 735.

FIG. 733.  Nadóhetin; length of reeds, 4½ inches; Paiute Indians, Pyramid lake, Nevada; cat. no. 19058, United States National Museum.
FIG. 734 a, b.  Skull and pin and bone and pin; Paiute Indians, southern Utah; cat. no. 9434, 9433, Peabody Museum of American Archæology and Ethnology.
FIG. 735.  Reed and pin; length of reed, 1½ inches; Ute Indians, St George, Utah; cat. no. 20934, United States National Museum.

UTE.  St George, Utah.  (United States National Museum.)

Cat. no. 20934.  Small tube of reed (figure 735), 1½ inches in length, with a round hole cut in the side near one end, ornamented with burned marks.

A cord passing through the reed is secured by a knot and a flat glass button at one end.  The other end has a wooden pin attached. The object appears to be to catch on the pin either the button, the hole in the side, or the hole in the end of the reed.

Cat. no. 20932.  Small bone (probably a bird bone), 1⅝ inches in
   length, marked with notches, as shown in figure 736, with a
   cotton cord passing through it having a wooden pin at one end.
   There are the traces of a tuft of rabbit fur at the end opposite the
   pin.  The object of the game is to catch the bone on the pin at
   the hollow end nearest the pin, or, possibly, also, in the tuft of
   fur.
Collected by Dr Edward Palmer.

FIG. 736.  Bone and pin; length of bone, 1⅝ inches: Ute Indians, St George, Utah; cat. no. 20932,
United States National Museum.

### SIOUAN STOCK

ASSINIBOIN.  Fort Belknap reservation, Montana.  (Field Columbian Museum.)
Cat. no. 60205.  Seven phalangeal bones, perforated and strung on a
   thong, with a bone needle at one end and a triangular piece of
   buckskin, perforated with holes, at the other end (figure 737).
Cat. no. 60263.  Seven phalangeal
   bones, like the preceding, but
   smaller, with wire needle and
   triangular piece of buckskin.

Collected in 1900 by Dr George A.
Dorsey, who describes the game under the name of taseha:

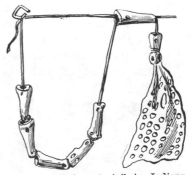

A game formerly much played by young
men and women, and known as the courting or matrimonial game.  The cups (toe
bones of the deer, perforated) are swung
forward and upward, the buckskin being
held by the thumb and forefinger.  As the
cups descend the attempt is made to catch

FIG. 737.  Taseha; Assiniboin Indians,
Montana; cat. no. 60205, Field Columbian
Museum.

one or more of them on the end of the
bodkin or to thrust the bodkin into one of the perforations in the triangular
piece of buckskin attached to the end of the cord beyond the last cup.

   The points played are generally 40, the cups having a numerical value, beginning with the first cup, counting 1; the second, 2, etc.  According to the owner of
the set no. 60263, the last cup counted 40, and so won the game, while the owner
of the set no. 60205 [figure 737] claimed that the first cup counted 5.  In both
games the small holes in the buckskin are worth 4, while the large hole (chaute,
heart) has a value of 9.

   The game as at present played is almost purely one of pastime.  That it
formerly had a deep significance there is no doubt.

ASSINIBOIN. Fort Belknap, Montana. (Cat. no. $\frac{50}{2011}$, American Museum of Natural History.)

Seven phalangeal bones strung on a thong, with a triangular piece of buckskin, perforated with holes, attached at one end and a wire needle at the other; total length, 31 inches. Collected by Dr A. L. Kroeber.

DAKOTA (BRULÉ). South Dakota. (Cat. no. 27528, Peabody Museum of American Archæology and Ethnology.)

String of five worked phalangeal bones of deer (figure 738), on a thong, to the end of which a needle is attached.

Collected by Miss Alice C. Fletcher.

They are used only by women. The bones are swung in a circle very rapidly, and caught upon the pin, which in ancient times was made of bone.

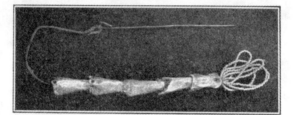

FIG. 738. Cup and pin; Brulé Dakota Indians, South Dakota; cat. no. 27528, Peabody Museum of American Archæology and Ethnology.

DAKOTA (OGLALA). Pine Ridge agency, South Dakota. (Cat. no. 22122, Free Museum of Science and Art, University of Pennsylvania.)

Six phalangeal bones of deer (figure 739), strung on a thong 11 inches in length, with a brass needle, 5 inches in length, attached at one end of the thong, and seven loops of variegated glass beads at the other end.

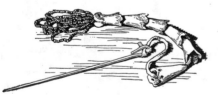

FIG. 739. Tasiha; length of implement, 23¼ inches; Oglala Dakota Indians, South Dakota; cat. no. 22122, Free Museum of Science and Art, University of Pennsylvania.

The bones are fluted at the upper edge, except the one nearest the needle, which has small holes around the edge. They were made by Winyanhopa, "Elegant Woman," and collected by Mr Louis L. Meeker, who describes it as an implement from the woman's game of tasiha.

The strand is swung in the air, and the wire thrust into one of the bones, counting from 1 to 4 (or 5) in order, or as many as the number of loops passed through. Some number as many as six bones on one string.

DAKOTA (TETON).　South Dakota.

Rev. J. Owen Dorsey [a] describes the following as a game played by boys, younger married men, or women:

Ta-síha un'pi, Game with the hoofs of a deer.—They string several deer hoofs together and throw them suddenly upward. They jerk them back again by the cord to which they are attached, and as they fall the player who has a sharp-pointed stick tries to thrust it through the holes of the hoofs, and if he succeeds he counts the number of hoofs through which his stick has gone. A number of small beads of various colors are strung together and attached to the smallest hoof at the end of the string. When a player adds a bead to those on the string he has another chance to try his skill in piercing the hoofs. When one misses the mark he hands the hoofs, etc., to the next player. Each one tries to send his stick through more hoofs than did his predecessor. Two sides are chosen by the players. Each player offers articles as stakes for the winner. The season for playing is not specified.

The women, when they play this game, bring their husbands' goods without the knowledge of the owners, and sometimes lose all of them. When the men play, they sometimes stake all of their wives' property, and occasionally they lose all. Now and then this game is played just for amusement, without any stakes.

———— South Dakota.

Dr J. R. Walker [b] describes this game under the name of woskate tasi he, game with foot bones, and gives the rules for the play.

FIG. 740.　Hokiwaxoxokke; length of implement, 15 inches; Winnebago Indians, Wisconsin; cat. no. 22158, Free Museum of Science and Art, University of Pennsylvania.

WINNEBAGO.　Wisconsin.　(Cat. no. 22158, Free Museum of Science and Art, University of Pennsylvania.)

Seven phalangeal bones strung on a thong (figure 740), with a bone needle attached at one end and two triangular pieces of buckskin at the other; length, 15 inches.

Collected by Mr T. R. Roddy, who says:

The game is called ho-ki-wa-xo-xok-ke.

SKITTAGETAN STOCK

HAIDA.　British Columbia.

Dr J. R. Swanton describes [c] the following game:

Flipping a V-shaped object over and letting it drop (Łgá sLⅠA'ñ).—A straight stick was held in one hand, while a V-shaped piece of cedar about 8 inches long was held in the other hand by one of its arms, and so thrown into the air that it would fall astride of the stick. This V-shaped piece is called the łga' sLⅠgA'ño.

---

[a] Games of Teton Dakota Children. The American Anthropologist, v. 4, p. 344, 1891.
[b] Journal of American Folk-Lore, v. 18, p. 288, 1905.
[c] Contributions to the Ethnology of the Haida. Memoirs of the American Museum of Natural History, whole series, v. 8. pt. 1, p. 60, New York, 1905.

When it fell to the ground, the one who threw it must yield to the next player; but before doing so he was at liberty to pull his opponent's hair violently or punch his knuckles as many times as he had made a catch.

### TANOAN STOCK

TEWA. Hano, Arizona. (Cat. no. 38616, Free Museum of Science and Art, University of Pennsylvania.)

Ring of rawhide (figure 741), 5 inches in diameter, attached by a thong to the end of a stick painted red, 13¼ inches in length. Collected by the writer in 1901.

FIG. 741.  Ngoila nabapi; diameter of ring, 5 inches; Tewa Indians, Hano, Arizona; cat. no. 38616, Free Museum of Science and Art, University of Pennsylvania.

The ring is swung from the end of the stick and caught on the end. The name of the game was given as ngoi-la na-ba pi.

### WAKASHAN STOCK

CLAYOQUOT. West coast of Vancouver island, British Columbia. (Cat. no. ¹⁶⁄₂₀₁₅, American Museum of Natural History.)

Femur of seal (figure 742), 4½ inches in length, with natural perforation; accompanied by a small pointed twig, 6 inches in length. Collected in 1897 by Mr F. Jacobsen. who describes it as a bilboquet.

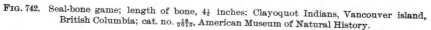

FIG. 742.  Seal-bone game; length of bone, 4¼ inches; Clayoquot Indians, Vancouver island, British Columbia; cat. no. ₇₆¹⁶₁₅, American Museum of Natural History.

The following note on a similar game in the Field Columbian Museum (cat. no. 85909) from Clayoquot, was furnished by the collector, Dr C. F. Newcombe:

The game is called shaiyixtsE. It is played with the femur of the common seal and a sharp-pointed twig of a young spruce.

Players arrange themselves in two rows, up to ten a side, opposite one-another, and consecutively toss the bone and try to catch it again by a partial rotation. Sometimes the femur is only swung by putting the stick under the projecting edge of the ball of the hip joint and then making the bone to rotate so that the point of the stick will pass into the foramen above the condyle.

The stakes and winning number are arranged according to the number and wishes of the players.

The bone is passed along the whole of one side before being thrown over to the opponents. If the player misses his first attempt he passes it to his next neighbor, but if he succeeds in catching the bone, as required, he goes on trying until he fails.

If a side fails in making 40 wins by the united efforts of all its players, the opponents try. That side which first makes 40 takes all the stake which is equally divided.

Name of femur of seal, hamut; name of stick, quiʟklɛpt.

No string is used, as reported by Dr Dorsey in a similar game amongst the Makahs.

KWAKIUTL. British Columbia. (Cat. no. $\frac{16}{6847}$, American Museum of Natural History.)

Femur of seal (figure 743), $4\frac{1}{2}$ inches in length, with small natural perforations; accompanied by a pointed stick $6\frac{3}{4}$ inches in length. Collected in 1897 by George Hunt, who describes it as a " seal bone for divining."

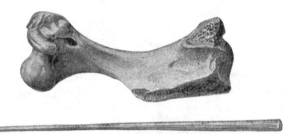

FIG. 743.   Seal bone for divining; length, $4\frac{1}{2}$ inches; Kwakiutl Indians, British Columbia; cat. no. $\frac{16}{6847}$, American Museum of Natural History.

———— Nawiti, British Columbia.

Dr C. F. Newcombe describes a game played by these Indians with a bone perforated with a small hole and a wooden pin:

The bone is not tied to the pin. The point is placed in the hole and the bone tossed up, and the object is to catch it again on the point. There is no score. Both men and women play. The name is dsīchdsk′ia.

MAKAH. Neah bay, Washington.

Dr George A. Dorsey [a] describes a game called kaskas:

This game corresponds to the well-known cup-and-pin game of the Plains Indians, which among the neighbors of the Makahs is modified into a game with a wooden pin and snake or fish vertebræ. With the Makahs a humerus (kashabs) of the hair seal, which is perforated at each end, is attached by means of a

———————————————————

[a] Games of the Makah Indians of Neah Bay. The American Antiquarian, v. 23, p. 72, 1901.

string passing through a hole in the middle of the bone to a wooden pin (ka-a-pick). The bone is tossed upward and as it falls it is caught on the end of the pin. Whatever significance this game may have had in former times has evidently been lost, for, according to Williams, it is played merely for amusement, at any time, and by both sexes.

YUMAN STOCK

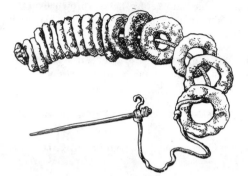

MOHAVE. Colorado river, Arizona. (Cat. no. 10086, Peabody Museum of American Archæology and Ethnology.)

Seventeen rings of pumpkin (figure 744), strung on a deerskin thong, with a wooden pin. Collected by Dr Edward Palmer.

FIG. 744. Pumpkin-rind game; Mohave Indians, Arizona: cat. no. 10086, Peabody Museum of American Archæology and Ethnology.

The wooden pin is held in the hand, and the rings, made from the shell of the pumpkin, are swung and caught upon it. A similar implement from the same tribe is contained in the United States National Museum.

ZUÑIAN STOCK

ZUÑI. Zuñi, New Mexico. (Brooklyn Institute Museum.)
Cat. no. 3061. Ring made of twig wrapped with blue yarn (figure 745), 5 inches in diameter, tied with blue yarn cord to a stick, 21 inches in length. The object is to catch the ring on the end of the stick.

FIG. 745. Ring game; length of stick, 21 inches; Zuñi Indians, Zuñi, New Mexico; cat. no. 3061, Brooklyn Institute Museum.

Cat. no. 3060. Two rings (figure 746), one $2\frac{1}{4}$ inches and the other $1\frac{1}{2}$ inches in diameter, both wrapped with blue yarn, the larger one suspended over the smaller one and having another yarn-wrapped ring inside of it, and both suspended by a blue yarn cord from the end of a twig 23 inches long; accompanied by a pointed stick, $5\frac{3}{4}$ inches in length, with a crosspiece tied at one end.

The object is to throw the dart through one or the other of the rings. The smallest ring, tsi-kon tso-na, counts 2, and the large or double ring, tsi-kon kwi-li, 4.

Cat. no. 3059.  Ring wrapped with blue yarn (figure 747), 2½ inches
  in diameter, having three smaller rings, 1½ inches in diameter,
  suspended from it, and attached to the end of a twig, 17½ inches
  long, by a blue yarn cord; accompanied by a pointed twig, 21¼
  inches in length, with a crosspiece tied near one end.

The object is to throw this dart through one of the rings.  The
large ring, called tsam-mo-so-na, counts 4.  One of the small rings,
tied with a piece of red yarn and called shi-lo-wa, red, counts 1;
another, tied with green, a-shai-na, counts 3, while the third small
ring, which is plain black, quin-a, counts 2.

All of these games were collected by the writer in 1903.  They all
bear the name of tsikonai ikoshnikia, ring play.

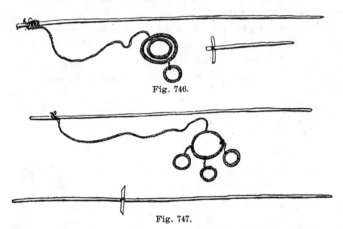

Fig. 746.

Fig. 747.

FIG. 746.  Ring game; length of stick, 23 inches; Zuñi Indians, Zuñi, New Mexico; cat. no. 3060,
  Brooklyn Institute Museum.
FIG. 747.  Ring game; length of stick, 17½ inches; Zuñi Indians, Zuñi, New Mexico; cat. no. 3059,
  Brooklyn Institute Museum.

## BALL

Under the general name of ball I have classed all ball games,
howsoever played, and all games in which an implement analogous
to a ball is employed.  In none of them, with trifling exceptions
which belong to distinct classes, is the ball ever touched with the
hand, to do so being strictly forbidden by the rules of the game.

The Indian ball games may be classified as follows: First, racket,
in which the ball is tossed with a racket; second, shinny, in which
the ball is struck with a club or bat; third, double ball, a game chiefly
confined to women, played with two balls or billets tied together,
tossed with a stick; fourth, the ball race, in which a ball or stick is
kicked.  In addition, subsidiary to the preceding and not general, being
confined to a few tribes, we have: Fifth, football; sixth, hand-and-
foot ball; seventh, tossed ball; eighth, juggling, and ninth, hot ball.

Games of the first three classes are widespread and almost universal. The ball race appears to be confined to the Southwest. The balls used vary greatly in material. The commonest form is covered with buckskin, but other balls are made of wood, of bladder netted with sinew, and of cordage, bone, or stone.

RACKET

The game of ball with rackets is distinctly a man's game, as opposed to shinny and double ball, which are commonly played by women. It is, however, sometimes played by women, and in one instance by men and women together (Santee).

Racket is less widely distributed than shinny, being confined to the Algonquian and Iroquoian tribes of the Atlantic seaboard and the region of the Great Lakes; and to their neighbors, the Dakota, on the west, and the Muskhogean tribes of the South. It occurs again among the Chinook and the Salish in the Northwest, and in a limited area in California. It is not recorded in the Southwest.

FIG. 748.  Miniature racket used by conjurers to look into futurity; length, 8¼ inches; Missisauga Indians, Ontario; cat. no. 178386, United States National Museum.

The game may be divided into two principal classes—first, those in which a single racket or bat is used; second, those in which two rackets are employed. The latter is peculiar to the southern tribes (Cherokee, Choctaw, Muskogee, Seminole), among whom the single racket is not recorded.

The racket may be regarded as a practical contrivance, akin to the throwing stick, but its origin is not clear. Morgan relates that the present netted bat of the Seneca was preceded by a simple stick, with a curved end, and Teit tells how bark strings were used by the Thompson Indians in bending ball sticks to the required crook. The strings, which were sometimes left attached to the bat, furnish an explanation of the present net. On the other hand, it is not unlikely that the racket may be related, with the drum hoop, to the spider-web shield of the twin War Gods, the probable source of the netted wheel.

Rev. Peter Jones[a] figures a miniature racket ball (figure 748), 8¼ inches long, now in his collection in the United States National Museum, as "used by conjurers to look into futurity."

The ball used with the racket was either of wood (Chippewa, Pomo, Santee, Winnebago) or of buckskin stuffed with hair. The

---

a History of the Ojebway Indians, London, 1861.

wooden ball appears to be the older and possibly the original form. Morgan states that the Seneca formerly used a solid ball of knot, for which the deerskin ball was substituted. Of the two types of covered ball, the bag-shaped form is more commonly used in racket than that with a median seam. The goals were commonly two sets of posts or poles erected at the extremities of the field, between which the ball had to be driven. Single posts were sometimes used (Miami, Missisauga, Chippewa [Minnesota], Chinook). An early account of the Muskogee describes them as setting up a square mat as a target in their ball play. An analogous object is found in the plat of the racket game at New Orleans. Among the Choctaw the goals were connected by a pole at the top. The length of the field appears to have varied greatly, from 30 rods (Mohawk) to half a league (Miami). In general it was remarkable for its extreme length. Attention appears to have been paid to the direction of the course, which is recorded as laid out from east to west or from north to south (Santee). The season varied in different localities: Summer among the Cherokee, and winter and spring among the Santee Dakota. Racket was commonly a tribal or intertribal contest. Its object, apart from mere diversion, appears to have been the stakes which were invariably wagered. Among the Huron, however, lacrosse is recorded by the Jesuit missionaries as played as a remedy for sickness. The magical rites connected with the game, the dance, scarifications, " going to water," tabus, amulets, and special features of the costume, all appear to refer to success in the contest. Attention may be called to the parallel between the Cherokee myth of ball play of the birds and animals and that of the moccasin game between the day and night animals recorded by Dr Washington Matthews.

There can be no doubt that, though the game of racket may have been modified in historic times, it remains an aboriginal invention. There are those, however, who assert the contrary. Sylva Clapin [a] says that the game of crosse, the national game of Canada since January 1, 1859, is about the same as the soule of the Ardennes mountaineers in France, and in the opinion of many is but a modification of the latter game as brought hither by the first French colonists.

ALGONQUIAN STOCK

CHEYENNE. Colorado.

Prof. F. V. Hayden [b] gives the following description:

O-ho-ni'-wo-ŏh, a ball club, with a hoop at the end to hold the ball as it is thrown.

---

[a] Dictionnaire Canadien-Français, Boston, 1894.

[b] Contributions to the Ethnography and Philology of the Indian Tribes of the Missouri Valley, p. 295, Philadelphia, 1862.

CHIPPEWA. Fort Michilimackinac, Michigan.

Alexander Henry [a] says:

Baggatiway, called by the Canadians le jeu de la crosse, is played with a bat and ball. The bat is about 4 feet in length, curved, and terminating in a sort of racket. Two posts are planted in the ground, at a considerable distance from each other, as a mile or more. Each party has its post, and the game consists in throwing the ball up to the post of the adversary. The ball, 't the beginning, is placed in the middle of the course, and each party endeavors as well to throw the ball out of the direction of its own post as into that of the adversary's.

Henry describes a game of ball played by the Ojibwa (Chippewa) and Saukies (Sauk), on the King's birthday (June 4), 1763, at Fort Michilimackinac, through which, by strategy, that fort was taken.

———— Michigan.

Baraga [b] gives the following definitions:

Playing-ball or play-ball, pikwakwad, meaning primarily knot on a tree; ball-play, pagaadowewin; pagaádowanak, Indian crozier to play with.

J. Long [c] says:

Playing at ball, which is a favorite game, is very fatiguing. The ball is about the size of a cricket ball, made of deer skn, and stuffed with hair; this is driven forwards and backwards with short sticks, about 2 feet long, and broad at the end like a bat, worked like a racket, but with larger interstices; by this the ball is impelled, and from the elasticity of the racket, which is composed of deer's sinew, is thrown to a great distance: the game is played by two parties, and the contest lies in intercepting each other and striking the ball into a goal, at a distance of about 400 yards, at the extremity of which are placed two high poles, about the width of a wicket from each other: the victory consisting in driving the ball between the poles. The Indians play with great good humour, and even when one of them happens, in the heat of the game, to strike another with his stick, it is not resented. But these accidents are cautiously avoided, as the violence with which they strike has been known to break an arm or a leg.

———— White Earth agency, Minnesota.

Dr Walter J. Hoffman [d] describes the ball play at this place, where, he says, with a population of about 2,000 Indians, it is easy to muster from 80 to 100 ball players, who are divided into sides of equal number.

If the condition of the ground permits, the two posts or goals are planted about one-third of a mile apart. . . . The best players of either side gather at the center of the ground. The poorer players arrange themselves around their respective goals, while the heaviest in weight scatter across the field between the starting point and the goals. The ball is tossed into the air in the center of

[a] Travels and Adventures in Canada, p. 78, New York, 1809.
[b] A Dictionary of the Otchipwe Language, Cincinnati, 1853.
[c] Voyages and Travels of an Indian Interpreter, p. 52, London, 1791.
[d] Remarks on Ojibwa Ball Play. The American Anthropologist, v. 3, p. 134, 1890.

the field. As soon as it descends it is caught with the ball stick by one of the players, when he immediately sets out at full speed towards the opposite goal. If too closely pursued, or if intercepted by an opponent, he throws the ball in the direction of one of his own side, who takes up the race.

The usual method of depriving the player of the ball is to strike the handle of the ball stick so as to dislodge the ball; but this is frequently a difficult matter on account of a peculiar horizontal motion of the ball stick maintained by the runner. Frequently the ball carrier is disabled by being struck across the arm or leg, thus compelling his retirement. Severe injuries occur only when playing for high stakes or when ill-feeling exists between some of the players.

Should the ball carrier of one side reach the opposite goal, it is necessary for him to throw the ball so that it touches the post. This is always a difficult matter, because even if the ball be well directed, one of the numerous players surrounding the post as guards may intercept it and throw it back into the field. In this manner a single inning may be continued for an hour or more. The game may come to a close at the end of an inning by mutual agreement of the players, that side winning the greater number of scores being declared victor.

The ball used in this game is made by wrapping thin strands of buckskin and covering the whole with a piece of the same. It is about the size of a baseball, though not so heavy.

The stick is of the same pattern as that used at the beginning of the present century by the Mississaugas, the Ojibwa of the eagle totem of the Province of Ontario.

FIG. 749. Racket; length, 26 inches; Chippewa Indians, Bear island, Leech lake, Minnesota; cat. no. $\frac{50}{4730}$, American Museum of Natural History.

CHIPPEWA. Bear island, Leech lake, Minnesota. (Cat. no. $\frac{50}{4730}$, American Museum of Natural History.)

Racket (figure 749) made of a sapling 26 inches in length, curved at the striking end to form a hoop, netted with buckskin thongs. Collected by Dr William Jones in 1903.

FIG. 750. Racket; length, 34 inches; Chippewa Indians, Wisconsin; cat. no. 22160, Free Museum of Science and Art, University of Pennsylvania.

—— Wisconsin. (Cat. no. 22160, Free Museum of Science and Art, University of Pennsylvania.)

Racket (figure 750), a sapling cut and curved to form an oval hoop at the striking end, lashed at the end, and crossed by two thongs, which are intertwined, but not knotted, in the middle; length, 34 inches. Collected by Mr T. R. Roddy.

CHIPPEWA.  Wisconsin.

Jonathan Carver [a] says:

They amuse themselves at several sorts of games, but the principal and most esteemed among them is that of ball, which is not unlike the European game of tennis.  The balls they use are rather larger than those made use of at tennis, and are formed of a piece of deer-skin; which being moistened to render it supple, is stuffed hard with the hair of the same creature, and sewed with its sinews.  The ball-sticks are about 3 feet long, at the end of which there is fixed a kind of racket, resembling the palm of the hand, and fashioned of thongs cut from a deer-skin.  In these they catch the ball, and throw it a great distance, if they are not prevented by some of the opposite party, who try to intercept it. The game is generally played by large companies, that sometimes consist of more than three hundred; and it is not uncommon for different bands to play against each other.

They begin by fixing two poles in the ground at about 600 yards apart, and one of these goals belongs to each party of the combatants.  The ball is thrown up high in the center of the ground, and in a direct line between the goals; towards which each party endeavors to strike it, and whichsoever side first causes it to reach their own goal, reckons toward the game.

They are so exceeding dexterous in this manly exercise, that the ball is usually kept flying in different directions by the force of the rackets, without touching the ground during the whole contention; for they are not allowed to catch it with their hands.

They run with amazing velocity in pursuit of each other, and when one is on the point of hurling it to a great distance, an antagonist overtakes him, and by a sudden stroke dashes down the ball.  They play with so much vehemence that they frequently wound each other, and sometimes a bone is broken; but notwithstanding these accidents there never appears to be any spite or wanton exertions of strength to effect them, nor do any disputes ever happen between the parties.

In his Chippewa vocabulary he gives ball as alewin.

———— Apostle islands, Wisconsin.

J. G. Kohl [b] says:

Of all the Indian social sports the finest and grandest is the ball play.  I might call it a noble game, and I am surprised how these savages attained such perfection in it.  Nowhere in the world, excepting, perhaps, among the English and some of the Italian races, is the graceful and manly game of ball played so passionately and on so large a scale.  They often play village against village, or tribe against tribe.  Hundreds of players assemble, and the wares and goods offered as prizes often reach a value of a thousand dollars and more.  On our island we made a vain attempt to get up a game, for though the chiefs were ready enough, and all were cutting their raquets and balls in the bushes, the chief American authorities forbade this innocent amusement.  Hence, on this occasion, I was only enabled to inspect the instruments.  They were made with great care and well adapted for the purpose, and it is to be desired that the Indians would display the same attention to more important matters.

The raquets are 2½ feet in length, carved very gracefully out of a white tough wood, and provided with a handle.  The upper end is formed into a ring, 4 or 5 inches in diameter, worked very firmly and regularly, and covered by

---

[a] Travels through the Interior Parts of North America, p. 237, Philadelphia, 1796.

[b] Kitchi-gami, Wanderings round Lake Superior, p. 88, London, 1860.

a network of leather bands. The balls are made of white willow, and cut perfectly round with the hand: crosses, stars and circles are carved upon them. The care devoted to the balls is sufficient to show how highly they estimate the game. The French call it " jeu de crosse." Great ball players, who can send the ball so high that it is out of sight, attain the same renown among the Indians as celebrated runners, hunters, or warriors.

The name of the ball play is immortalized both in the geography and history of the country. There is a prairie, and now a town, on the Mississippi known as the " Prairie de la Crosse."

CHIPPEWA. Wisconsin.

Prof I. I. Ducatel[a] described boys playing at ball " by throwing it out and catching it with a stick, the end of which is curled up and makes the opening a pocket of network. This is the pahgato-wahnak."

———— Fort William, Ontario. (Cat. no. $\frac{50}{4729}$, American Museum of Natural History.)

A wooden ball (figure 751), painted red, 3 inches in diameter, perforated with a hole, which emits a whistling noise in the air; and a wooden racket, 36 inches long, curved at the striking end to form a hoop, which is netted with buckskin thongs.

Collected in 1903 by Dr William Jones, who gives the name of the ball as pigwakwatwi and that of the racket and the game as pagatowan.

.FIG. 751. Ball and racket; Chippewa Indians, Fort William, Ontario; diameter of ball, 3 inches; length of racket, 36 inches; cat. no. $\frac{50}{4729}$, American Museum of Natural History.

DELAWARES. Pennsylvania.

In Zeisberger's Indian Dictionary [b] we find the definition:

Ball (kugel), gendsítât.

MENOMINEE. Wisconsin.

Dr Walter J. Hoffman [c] describes the following game:

When anyone prepares to have a game of ball, he selects the captains or leaders of the two sides who are to compete. Each leader then appoints his own players, and the ball sticks to be used are deposited at the ball ground on the day before the game is to occur. Then each of the leaders selects a powerful and influential mitä'[v], whose services are solicited for taking charge of the safety of the ball sticks, and to prevent their being charmed or conjured by

[a] A Fortnight Among the Chippewas. The Indian Miscellany, p. 368, Albany, 1877.
[b] Cambridge, 1887.
[c] The Menomini Indians. Fourteenth Annual Report of the Bureau of Ethnology, p. 127, 1896.

the opposing mitä'ᵛ. The mitä'ᵛ is not expected to be present at the ground during the night, because he is supposed to have the power to influence the sticks at any distance.

Should one mitä'ᵛ succeed in obtaining such necromantic power over the sticks as to carry them away from the ground—that is, to carry away the power of the sticks—then it is the duty of the opposing mitä'ᵛ to follow him and bring them back. In case the pursuing mitä'ᵛ does not succeed in catching the rival, on account of being outwitted or because of having insufficient power in overcoming him, then the pursuing mitä'ᵛ is killed by his rival's sorcery. It usually happens that the pursuer compels the rival to restore the virtue or power of the sticks before the day approaches.

Four innings are played, and usually the presents, consisting of pieces of cloth, are divided into four parts, one part being given to the victor of each inning. Sometimes, however, the presents are renewed until the end of the game.

The frames from which the presents are suspended are near the middle of the ground, but off toward the eastern side, the tobacco-tray and other accessories being placed on the ground between them and toward the center of the ball ground. The two horizontal parallel poles forming the upper part of the framework are used for the calico and blankets; before them on the ground a cloth is spread, and on this are placed tobacco, pipes, and matches, to which all the participants are at liberty to help themselves.

The accompanying plate [XII] represents the players during a run for the ball. The latter is made of thongs of buckskin tightly wrapped and covered with buckskin or leather, and measures about 2½ inches in diameter. The sticks [figure 752] are made of hickory or ash, and about 3 feet long, the wood being shaved thinner and bent into a hoop or ring at least 4 inches in diameter. Four or five thongs pass through holes in the hoop and cross in the center, forming a netted pocket in which the ball may rest half hidden.

When the ball is caught, the runner carries the stick almost horizontally before him, moving it rapidly from side to side, and at the same time turning the stick so as to keep the ball always in front and retained by the pocket. This constant swinging and twisting movement tends to prevent players of the opposing side from knocking the ball out or dislodging it by hitting the stick.

The manner of preparing for and playing the game is like that of the Ojibwa of northern Minnesota.[a]   .   .   .

FIG. 752. Racket; Menominee Indians, Wisconsin; from Hoffman.

During the intervals of rest the players approach the place of the presents and smoke. The giver of the game also awards to the successful players a part of the presents, the whole quantity being divided into four portions, so that equal portions are distributed at each of the intervals.

The players frequently hang to the belt the tail of a deer, an antelope, or some other fleet animal, or the wings of swift-flying birds, with the idea that through these they are endowed with the swiftness of the animal. There are, however, no special preparations preceding a game, as feasting or fasting, dancing, etc.—additional evidence that the game is not so highly regarded among the Ojibwa tribe.

a See p. 564.

MENOMINEE BALL GAME; WISCONSIN; FROM HOFFMAN

MIAMI.　St Joseph river, Michigan.

Charlevoix [a] says, referring to lacrosse:

It is played with a ball, and with two staffs recurved and terminated by a sort of racket. Two posts are set up, which serve as bounds, and which are distant from each other in proportion to the number of players. For instance, if there are eighty of these, there will be a half league between the posts. The players are divided into two bands, each having its own post; and it is a question of driving the ball as far as the post of the opposing party without falling upon the ground or being touched with the hand. If either of these happens the game is lost, unless he who has committed the mistake repairs it by driving the ball with one stroke to the bound, which is often impossible. These savages are so adroit in catching the ball with their crosses that these games sometimes last several days in succession.

—————— Sault de Ste Marie, Michigan.

Mr Alexander McFarland Davis [b] says:

In 1667, Nicolas Perrot, then acting as agent of the French Government, was received near Saut Sainte Marie with stately courtesy and formal ceremony by the Miamis, to whom he was deputed. A few days after his arrival, the chief of that nation gave him, as an entertainment, a game of lacrosse.[c] "More than two thousand persons assembled in a great plain each with his cross. A wooden ball about the size of a tennis ball was tossed in the air. From that moment there was a constant movement of all these crosses which made a noise like that of arms which one hears during a battle. Half of the savages tried to send the ball to the northwest the length of the field, the others wished to make it go to the southeast. The contest which lasted for a half hour, was doubtful."

MISSISAUGA.　New Credit, Ontario.

Rev. Peter Jones [d] says:

Ball playing is another favorite amusement.

—————— Rice lake, Ontario.

G. Copway [e] says:

One of the most popular games is that of ball-playing, which oftimes engages an entire village. Parties are formed of from ten to several hundred. Before they commence those who are to take part in the play must provide each his share of stakings, or things which are set apart; and one leader for each party. Each leader appoints one of each company to be stake-holder.

Each man and each woman (women sometimes engage in the sport) is armed with a stick, one end of which bends somewhat like a small hoop, about 4 inches in circumference, to which is attached a net work of raw-hide, 2 inches deep, just large enough to admit the ball which is used on the occasion. Two poles are driven in the ground at a distance of four hundred paces from each other, which serves as goals for the two parties. It is the endeavor of each to take the ball to his hole. The party which carries the ball and strikes its pole wins the game.

[a] Journal d'un Voyage dans l'Amérique Septentrionnale, v. 3, p. 319, Paris, 1744.

[b] Indian Games. Bulletin of the Essex Institute, v. 17, p. 90, Salem, 1886.

[c] Histoire de l'Amérique Septentrionale par M. de Bacqueville de la Potherie, v. 2, p. 124, Paris, 1722.

[d] History of the Ojebway Indians, p. 134, London, 1861.

[e] The Traditional History and Characteristic Sketches of the Ojibway Nation, p. 49, Boston, 1851.

The warriors, very scantily attired, young and brave, fantastically painted, and women decorated with feathers, assemble around their commanders, who are generally swift on the race. They are to take the ball either by running with it or throwing it in the air. As the ball falls in the crowd the excitement begins. The clubs swing and roll from side to side, the players run and shout, fall upon and tread each other, and in the struggle some get rather rough treatment.

When the ball is thrown some distance on each side, the party standing near instantly pick it up, and run at full speed with three or four after him at full speed. The others send their shouts of encouragement to their own party: "Ha! ha! yah!" "A-ne-gook!"—and these shouts are heard even from the distant lodges, for children and all are deeply interested in the exciting scene. The spoils are not all on which their interest is fixed, but is directed to the falling and rolling of the crowds over and under each other. The loud and merry shouts of the spectators, who crowd the doors of the wigwams, go forth in one continued peal, and testify to their happy state of feeling.

The players are clothed in fur. They receive blows whose marks are plainly visible after the scuffle. The hands and feet are unincumbered and they exercise them to the extent of their powers; and with such dexterity do they strike the ball that it is sent out of sight. Another strikes it on its descent, and for ten minutes at a time the play is so adroitly managed that the ball does not touch the ground. No one is heard to complain, though he be bruised severely or his nose come in close communion with a club. If the last-mentioned catastrophe befel him, he is up in a trice, and sets his laugh forth as loud as the rest, though it be floated at first on a tide of blood.

It is very seldom, if ever, that one is seen to be angry because he has been hurt. If he should get so, they would call him a "coward," which proves a sufficient check to many evils which might result from many seemingly intended injuries.

NIPISSING. Forty miles above Montreal, Quebec.

J. A. Cuoq [a] gives the following definitions:

Pakatowan, jeu de crosse; pakatowanak, bois du jeu de crosse; pikwatwat, balle, pelota pour le jeu de crosse; kawaatikwan, abat-bois, boule à jouer aux quilles.

FIG. 753. Ball; diameter, 3¼ inches; Passamaquoddy Indians, Eastport, Maine; cat. no. 11426, United States National Museum.

PASSAMAQUODDY. Eastport, Maine. (Cat. no. 11426, United States National Museum.)

Hide ball (figure 753), made of a single piece with a thong drawstring at the edge, forming a flattened spheroid; diameter, 3¼ inches. Collected by Dr Edward Palmer.

Mr James Mooney [b] states that the Passamaquoddy use a ball stick (figure 754) with a strong, closely woven netting, which enables the stick to be used for batting. The sticks are ornamented with designs cut or burnt into the wood, and are sometimes further adorned with paint and feathers.

[a] Lexique de la Langue Algonquine, Montreal, 1886.

[b] The Cherokee Ball Play. The American Anthropologist, v. 3, p. 114, 1890.

Mrs W. W. Brown [a] describes the game as follows:

E-bes-qua-mo'gan, or game of ball, seems to have been the most popular and universal of the outdoor games, and played by all North American tribes. Their legends are more or less indebted to it. Tradition gives it a prominent place in their wonderful mythology. The Aurora Borealis is supposed to be Wā-ba-banai playing ball. Among the Wabanaki it was played by women as well as men, but, with few exceptions, never at the same time and place, as hunters and warriors played ball to gain muscular power, to stimulate their prowess, and to augment their fleetness of foot.

The players formed in a circle, proportionate to the number engaged in the game. Each held a stick called e-bes-quā-mo'gan-a-tok. This was made of some flexible wood, about 3 feet in length, crooked to three-fourths of a circle at one end, which was interwoven with stripes of hide after the manner of snowshoes. One man was detached to stand in the centre and on his throwing into the air a chip, upon which he had spat, each one would cry, " I'll take the dry " or " I'll take the wet," thus forming opposite factions. The side of the chip which fell uppermost decided which party should commence play. The ball was never touched with the hand, but thrown and kept in motion by the e-bes-quā-mo'gan-a-tok. The goals were two rings or holes dug in the ground, the distance of the circle of players apart. The game consisted in getting the ball into opponent's goal, and regard for neither life nor limb was allowed to stand in the way of possible success. As they played with little or

FIG. 754.  Racket; Passamaquoddy Indians, Maine; from Mooney.

nothing on, few escaped unhurt, but these mishaps were taken as the fortunes of war, and no resentment was felt. The women dress very scantily while playing this game, and the men, having a strict code of honor, never go near their playground. One tradition tells of a man that did so and threw shells and pebbles at the players. They screened themselves as best they could behind bushes and rocks. At the second attack, however, they made a rush in the direction from which the missiles came. The man ran to the water, and, plunging in, was turned into a che-pen-ob-quis (large chubfish), by which transformation they knew he was a Mohawk. They look upon all Mohawks as addicted to sorcery.

PENOBSCOT.  Oldtown, Maine.  (Cat. no. 48236, Peabody Museum of American Archæology and Ethnology.)

Ball for lacrosse (figure 755), 4 inches in diameter, covered with buckskin and filled with moose hair.

The cover, a nearly circular piece of buckskin about 9 inches in diameter, is drawn up with a buckskin thong, pudding-bag fashion, around the wad of moose hair; over it is placed a second piece of buckskin, 5 inches in diameter, which closes the opening. It was purchased from Big Thunder, one of the very old men of the tribe, when he was on a visit to Cambridge.

---

[a] Some Indoor and Outdoor Games of the Wabanaki Indians.  Transactions of the Royal Society of Canada, v. 6, sec. 2, p. 45, Montreal, 1889.

SAUK AND FOXES.  Iowa.  (American Museum of Natural History.)
Cat. no. $\frac{50}{2206}$.  Racket (figure 756) made of hard wood, with the end
    shaved thin and turned around to form a circular hoop, which is
    laced with cord passing through the edge; length, 29¼ inches.
    Collected by Dr William Jones in 1901.
Cat. no. $\frac{50}{2205}$.  Buckskin-covered ball (figure 757), 2¾ inches in diam-
    eter, bag-shaped, with thong attached at the edge of the seam.

    Collected in 1901 by Dr William Jones, who describes it as a
lacrosse ball.  A bundle of twenty pieces of reed (figure 758), 9½
inches in length, in the same collection, is described as message sticks
for the lacrosse game.

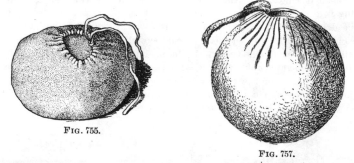

FIG. 755.

FIG. 757.

FIG. 756.

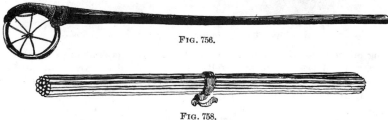

FIG. 758.

FIG. 755.  Ball; diameter, 4 inches; Penobscot Indians, Maine; cat. no. 48236, Peabody Museum
of American Archæology and Ethnology.
FIG. 756.  Racket; length, 29¼ inches; Sauk and Fox Indians, Iowa; cat. no $\frac{50}{2206}$, American
Museum of Natural History.
FIG. 757.  Ball; diameter, 2¼ inches; Sauk and Fox Indians, Iowa; cat. no. $\frac{50}{2205}$, American
Museum of Natural History.
FIG. 758.  Message sticks for ball game; length, 9¼ inches; Sauk and Fox Indians, Iowa; cat.
no. $\frac{50}{2231}$, American Museum of Natural History.

——— Tama, Iowa.  (Cat. no. 36753, Free Museum of Science and
        Art, University of Pennsylvania.)
Hickory stick (figure 759), with the end turned over to form a small
    hoop, which is netted with thong; length, 50½ inches.  Collected
    by the writer in 1900.
    These Indians stated that they no longer make their own balls.
The ball game they call bagahatuwitni, and the stick, otchi.
    Dr William Jones informed me that the ball, pekwaki, used in
this game, was bag-shaped and drawn up with a thong.

SAUK AND FOXES. Oklahoma. (Cat. no. $\frac{50}{2253}$, Amer-
    ican Museum of Natural History.)
Racket made of hickory, with the end cut thin and
    turned around to form an oval hoop, as shown
    in figure 760; length, 42 inches; the circumfer-
    ence is perforated with five holes, through which
    thongs pass to form a network, as illustrated in
    the figure. Collected by Dr William Jones.

FIG. 759. Racket; length, 50½ inches; Sauk and Fox Indians, Tama,
    Iowa; cat. no. 36758, Free Museum of Science and Art, University of
    Pennsylvania.

SHAWNEE. Indian Territory.
    Dr William Jones informs me that the lacrosse
game, while usually played by men alone, is played
also by men and women on opposite sides, the men
using the sticks and the women their hands. In this
latter case the goals, hoop wickets, are nearer together than when men play alone.

### CHINOOKAN STOCK

CHINOOK. Fort Vancouver, Washington.
    Paul Kane [a] says:

    They also take great delight in a game with a ball, which
is played by them in the same manner as the Cree, Chippewa,
and Sioux Indians. Two poles are erected about a mile
apart, and the company is divided into two bands, armed
with sticks, having a small ring or hoop at the end, with
which the ball is picked up and thrown to a great distance;
each party then strives to get the ball past their own goal.
There are sometimes a hundred on a side, and the play is kept
up with great noise and excitement. At this game they bet
heavily, as it is generally played between tribes and villages.

### IROQUOIAN STOCK

CAUGHNAWAGA. Quebec.
    Col. James Smith [b] thus describes a game:

    . . . they used a wooden ball about 3 inches in diameter,
and the instrument they moved it with was a strong staff
about 5 feet long with a hoop net on the end of it, large
enough to contain the ball. Before they begin to play, they
lay off about half a mile distance in a clear plain, and the
opposite parties all attend at the center, where a disinter-

Fig. 760. Racket; length, 42 inches; Sauk and Fox Indians, Oklahoma; cat. no. $\frac{50}{2253}$, American Museum of Natural History.

[a] Wanderings of an Artist among the Indians of North America,
p. 190, London, 1859. See also The Canadian Journal, p. 276,
Toronto, July, 1855.
    [b] An Account of the Remarkable Occurrences in the Life and
Travels of Col. James Smith, p. 78, Cincinnati, 1870.

ested person casts up the ball, then the opposite parties all contend for it.  If
anyone gets it into his net, he runs with it the way he wishes it to go, and
they all pursue him.  If one of the opposite party overtakes the person with
the ball, he gives the stay a stroke which causes the ball to fly out of the net;
then they have another debate for it; and if the one that gets it can outrun
all the opposite party, and can carry it quite out, or over the line at the end, the
game is won; but this seldom happens.  When anyone is running away with
the ball and is like to be overtaken, he commonly throws it, and with this
instrument can cast it 50 or 60 yards.  Sometimes when the ball is almost at
the one end matters will take a sudden turn, and the opposite party may quickly
carry it out at the other end.  Oftentimes they will work a long time back and
forward before they can get the ball over the line, or win the game.

CHEROKEE.  Tennessee river, North Carolina.

John Bartram [a] describes a ball dance in the council house at the Indian town of Cowe:

This assembly was held principally to rehearse the ball-play dance, this town
being challenged to play against another the next day.

The people being assembled and seated in order, and the musicians having
taken their station, the ball opens, first with a long harangue or oration, spoken
by an aged chief, in commendation of the manly exercise of the ball-play, re-
counting the many and brilliant victories which the town of Cowe had gained
over the other towns in the nation, not forgetting or neglecting to recite his
own exploits, together with those of other aged men now present, coadjutors
in the performance of these athletic games in their youthful days.  This oration
was delivered with great spirit and eloquence, and was meant to influence the
passions of the young men present, excite them to emulation, and inspire them
with ambition.

This prologue being at an end, the musicians began, both vocal and instrumental; when presently a company of girls, hand in hand, dressed in clean white
robes and ornamented with beads, bracelets, and a profusion of gay ribbands,
entering the door, immediately began to sing their responses in a gentle, low,
and sweet voice, and formed themselves in a semicircular file or line, in two
ranks, back to back, facing the spectators and musicians, moving slowly round
and round; this continued about a quarter of an hour, when we were surprised by a sudden very loud and shrill whoop, uttered at once by a company
of young fellows, who came in briskly after one another, with rackets or hurls
in one hand.  These champions likewise were well dressed, painted, and ornamented with silver bracelets, gorgets and wampum, neatly ornamented with
moccasins and highwaving plumes in their diadems: they immediately formed
themselves in a semicircular rank also, in front of the girls, when these changed
their order, and formed a single rank parallel to the men, raising their voices in
responses to the tunes of the young champions, the semicircles continually
moving round.  There was something singular and diverting in their step and
motions, and I imagine not to be learned to exactness but with great attention
and perseverance; the step, if it can be so termed, was performed after the
following manner; i. e., first, the motion began at one end of the semicircle,
gently rising up and down upon their toes and heels alternately, when the first
was up on tip-toe, the next began to raise the heel, and by the time the first
rested again on the heel, the second was on tip-toe, thus from one end of the

---

[a] Travels through North and South Carolina, Georgia, East and West Florida, p. 369,
Philadelphia, 1791.

rank to the other, so that some were always up and some down, alternately and regularly, without the least baulk or confusion; and they at the same time, and in the same motion, moved on obliquely or sideways, so that the circle performed a double or complex motion in its progression, and at stated times exhibited a grand or universal movement, instantly and unexpectedly to the spectators, by each rank turning to right and left, taking each others places: the movements were managed with inconceivable alertness and address, and accompanied with an instantaneous and universal elevation of the voice, and shrill, short whoop.

CHEROKEE. North Carolina.

Mr James Mooney described the ball game of the East Cherokee under the name of anetsa: [a]

The ball now used is an ordinary leather-covered ball, but in former days it was made of deer hair and covered with deerskin. In California the ball is of wood. The ball sticks vary considerably among different tribes. As before stated, the Cherokee player uses a pair, catching the ball between them and throwing it in the same way. The stick is somewhat less than 3 feet in length, and its general appearance closely resembles a tennis racket, or a long wooden spoon, the bowl of which is a loose network of thongs of twisted squirrel skin or strings of Indian hemp. The frame is made of a slender hickory stick, bent upon itself, and so trimmed and fashioned that the handle seems to be of one solid round piece, when, in fact, it is double. . . .

The ball season begins about the middle of summer and lasts until the weather is too cold to permit exposure of the naked body, for the players are always stripped for the game. The favorite time is in the fall, after the corn has ripened, for then the Indian has abundant leisure, and at this season a game takes place somewhere on the reservation at least every other week, while several parties are always in training. The training consists chiefly in regular athletic practice, the players of one side coming together with their ball sticks at some convenient spot of level bottom land, where they strip to the waist, divide into parties, and run, tumble, and toss the ball until the sun goes down. . . .

In addition to the athletic training, which begins two or three weeks before the regular game, each player is put under a strict gaktûnta or tabu, during the same period. He must not eat the flesh of a rabbit (of which the Indians generally are very fond) because the rabbit is a timid animal, easily alarmed and liable to lose its wits when pursued by the hunter. Hence the ball player must abstain from it, lest he, too, should become disconcerted and lose courage in the game. He must also avoid the meat of the frog (another item on the Indian bill of fare), because the frog's bones are brittle and easily broken, and a player who should partake of the animal would expect to be crippled in the first inning. For a similar reason he abstains from eating the young of any bird or animal, and from touching an infant. He must not eat the fish called the hog-sucker, because it is sluggish in its movements. He must not eat the herb called atûnka or Lamb's Quarter, (*Chenopodium album*), which the Indians use for greens, because its stalk is easily broken. Hot food and salt are also forbidden, as in the medical gaktûnta. The tabu always lasts for seven days preceding the game, but in most cases is enforced for twenty-eight days—i. e., 4×7—4 and 7 being sacred numbers. Above all, he must not touch a woman, and the player who should violate this regulation would expose himself to the summary vengeance of his fellows. This last tabu continues also for seven days after the game. As before stated, if a woman even so much as touches a

[a] The Cherokee Ball Play. The American Anthropologist, v. 3, p. 105, 1890.

ball stick on the eve of a game, it is thereby rendered unfit for use. As the white man's law is now paramount, extreme measures are seldom resorted to, but in former days the punishment for an infraction of this regulation was severe, and in some tribes the penalty was death. Should a player's wife be with child, he is not allowed to take part in the game under any circumstances, as he is then believed to be heavy and sluggish in his movements, having lost just so much of his strength as has gone into the child.

At frequent intervals during the training period the shaman takes the players to water and performs his mystic rites, as will be explained further on. They are also scratched on their naked bodies, as at the final game, but now the scratching is done in a haphazard fashion with a piece of bamboo brier having stout thorns, which leave broad gashes on the backs of the victims.

When a player fears a particular contestant on the other side, as is frequently the case, his own shaman performs a special incantation, intended to compass the defeat and even the disabling or death of his rival. As the contending sides always belong to different settlements, each party makes all these preliminary arrangements without the knowledge of the other, and under the guidance of its own shamans, several of whom are employed on a side in every hotly contested game. . . .

On the night preceding the game each party holds the ball-play dance in its own settlement. On the reservation the dance is always held on Friday night, so that the game may take place on Saturday afternoon, in order to give the players and spectators an opportunity to sleep off the effects on Sunday. . . . The dance must be held close to the river, to enable the players to " go to water " during the night, but the exact spot selected is always a matter of uncertainty up to the last moment, excepting with a chosen few. If this were not the case, a spy from the other settlement might endeavor to insure the defeat of the party by strewing along their trail a soup made of the hamstrings of rabbits, which would have the effect of rendering the players timorous and easily confused.

The dance begins soon after dark on the night preceding the game, and lasts until daybreak, and from the time they eat supper before the dance until after the game, on the following afternoon, no food passes the lips of the players.

Mr Mooney selected for illustration the last game which he witnessed on the reservation, in September, 1889. On the occasion in question the young men of Yellow Hill were to contend against those of Raven Town, about 10 miles farther up the river, and as the latter place was a large settlement noted for its adherence to the old traditions, a spirited game was expected.

Each party holds a dance [plate XIII] in its own settlement, the game taking place about midway between. The Yellow Hill men were to have their dance up the river, about half a mile from my house. . . . The spot selected for the dance was a narrow strip of gravely bottom, where the mountain came close down to the water's edge. . . . Several fires were burning. . . . Around the larger fire were the dancers, the men stripped as for the game, with their ball-sticks in their hands and the firelight playing upon their naked bodies. . . .

The ball-play dance is participated in by both sexes, but differs considerably from any other of the dances of the tribe, being a dual affair throughout. The dancers are the players of the morrow, with seven women, representing the seven Cherokee clans. The men dance in a circle around the fire, chanting responses to the sound of a rattle carried by another performer, who circles

BALL DANCE; EAST CHEROKEE INDIANS, NORTH CAROLINA; FROM PHOTOGRAPH BY MOONEY (1893)

around on the outside, while the women stand in line a few feet away and dance to and fro, now advancing a few steps toward the men, then wheeling and dancing away from them, but all the while keeping time to the sound of the drum and chanting the refrain to the ball songs made by the drummer, who is seated on the ground on the side farthest from the fire. The rattle is a gourd fitted with a handle and filled with small pebbles, while the drum resembles a small keg with a head of ground-hog leather. The drum is partly filled with water, the head being also moistened to improve the tone, and is beaten with a single stick. Men and women dance separately throughout, the music, the evolutions, and the songs being entirely distinct, but all combine to produce an harmonious whole. The women are relieved at intervals by others who take their places, but the men dance in the same narrow circle the whole night long, excepting during the frequent halts for the purpose of going to water.

At one side of the fire are set up two forked poles, supporting a third laid horizontally, upon which the ball sticks are crossed in pairs until the dance begins. As already mentioned, small pieces from the wing of the bat are sometimes tied to these poles, and also to the rattle used in the dance, to insure success in the contest. The skins of several bats and swift-darting insectivorous birds were formerly wrapped up in a piece of deerskin, together with the cloth and beads used in the conjuring ceremonies later on, and hung from the frame during the dance. On finally dressing for the game at the ball ground, the players took the feathers from these skins to fasten in their hair or upon the ball sticks, to insure swiftness and accuracy in their movements. Sometimes also hairs from the whiskers of the bat are twisted into the netting of the ball sticks. The players are all stripped and painted, with feathers in their hair, just as they appear in the game. When all is ready an attendant takes down the ball sticks from the frame, throwing them over his arm in the same fashion, and, walking around the circle, gives to each man his own. Then the rattler, taking his instrument in his hand, begins to trot around on the outside of the circle, uttering a sharp " Hĭ ! " to which the players respond with a quick " Hi-hĭ′ !" while slowly moving around the circle with their ball sticks held tightly in front of their breasts. Then, with a quicker movement, the song changes to " Ehu′ ! " and the responses to " Hăhĭ′ ! Ehu′ ! Hăhĭ′ ! Ehu′ ! Hăhĭ′ !" Then, with a prolonged shake of the rattle, it changes again to "Ahiye′ ! " the dancers responding with the same word "Ahiye′ ! " but in a higher key; the movements become more lively and the chorus louder, till at a given signal with the rattle the players clap their ball sticks together, and, facing around, go through the motions of picking up and tossing an imaginary ball. Finally, with a grand rush, they dance up close to the women, and the first part of the performance ends with a loud prolonged " Hu-ŭ ! " from the whole crowd.

In the meantime the women have taken position in a line a few feet away, with their backs turned to the men, while in front of them the drummer is seated on the ground, but with his back turned toward them and the rest of the dancers. After a few preliminary taps on the drum, he begins a slow, measured beat, and strikes up one of the dance refrains, which the women take up in chorus. This is repeated a number of times until all are in harmony with the tune, when he begins to improvise, choosing words which will harmonize with the measure of the chorus, and at the same time be appropriate to the subject of the dance. As this requires a ready wit in addition to ability as a singer, the selection of a drummer is a matter of considerable importance, and that functionary is held in corresponding estimation. He sings of the game on the morrow, of the fine things to be won by the men of his party, of the joy with which they will be received by their friends on their return from the field, and of the disappointment and defeat of their rivals.  Throughout it all the women keep up the same minor refrain, like an instrumental accompaniment to vocal music. As Cherokee songs are always in the minor key, they have a plaintive effect, even when the sentiment is cheerful or even boisterous, and are calculated to excite the mirth of one who understands the language.  This impression is heightened by the appearance of the dancers themselves, for the women shuffle solemnly back and forth all night long without ever a smile upon their faces, while the occasional laughter of the men seems half subdued.  The monotonous repetition, too, is something intolerable to anyone but an Indian, the same words, to the same tune, being sometimes sung over and over again for a half hour or more. Although the singer improvises as he proceeds, many of the expressions have now become stereotyped and are used at almost every ball-play dance. . . . .

According to a Cherokee myth, the animals once challenged the birds to a great ball play.  The wager was accepted, the preliminaries were arranged, and at last the contestants assembled at the appointed spot—the animals on the ground, while the birds took position in the tree-tops to await the throwing up of the ball.  On the side of the animals were the bear, whose ponderous weight bore down all opposition; the deer, who excelled all others in running; and the terrapin, who was invulnerable to the stoutest blows.  On the side of the birds were the eagle, the hawk, and the great Tlániwă—all noted for their swiftness and power of flight.  While the latter were preening their feathers and watching every motion of their adversaries below, they noticed two small creatures, hardly larger than mice, climbing up the tree on which was perched the leader of the birds.  Finally they reached the top and humbly asked the captain to be allowed to join in the game.  The captain looked at them a moment, and, seeing that they were four-footed, asked them why they did not go to the animals where they properly belonged.  The little things explained that they had done so, but had been laughed at and rejected on account of their diminutive size.  On hearing their story the bird captain was disposed to take pity on them, but there was one serious difficulty in the way—how could they join the birds when they had no wings?  The eagle, the hawk, and the rest now crowded around, and after some discussion it was decided to try and make wings for the little fellows. But how to do it!  All at once, by a happy inspiration, one bethought himself of the drum which was to be used in the dance.  The head was made of groundhog leather, and perhaps a corner could be cut off and utilized for wings.  No sooner suggested than done.  Two pieces of leather taken from the drumhead were cut into shape and attached to the legs of one of the small animals, and thus originated Tlameha, the bat.  The ball was now tossed up, and the bat was told to catch it, and his expertness in dodging and circling about, keeping the ball constantly in motion and never allowing it to fall to the ground, soon convinced the birds that they had gained a most valuable ally.  They next turned their attention to the other little creature; and now behold a worse difficulty!  All their leather had been used in making wings for the bat, and there was no time to send for more.  In this dilemma it was suggested that perhaps wings might be made by stretching out the skin of the animal itself. So two large birds seized him from opposite sides with their strong bills, and by tugging and pulling at his fur for several minutes succeeded in stretching the skin between the fore and hind feet until at last the thing was done and there was Tewa, the flying squirrel.  Then the bird captain, to try him, threw up the ball, when the flying squirrel, with a graceful bound, sprang off the limb and, catching it in his teeth, carried it through the air to another tree-top a hundred feet away.

When all was ready, the game began, but at the very outset the flying squirrel caught the ball and carried it up a tree, then threw it to the birds, who kept it in the air for some time, when it dropped; but just before it reached the ground the bat seized it, and by his dodging and doubling kept it out of the way of even the swiftest of the animals until he finally threw it in at the goal, and thus won the victory for the birds. Because of their assistance on this occasion, the ball player invokes the aid of the bat and the flying squirrel and ties a small piece of the bat's wing to his ball stick or fastens it to the frame on which the sticks are hung during the dance.[a] . . .

At a certain stage of the dance a man, specially selected for the purpose, leaves the groups of spectators around the fire and retires a short distance into the darkness in the direction of the rival settlement. Then, standing with his face still turned in the same direction, he raises his hand to his mouth and utters four yells, the last prolonged into a peculiar quaver. He is answered by the players with a chorus of yells—or rather yelps, for the Indian yell resembles nothing else so much as the bark of a puppy. Then he comes running back until he passes the circle of dancers, when he halts and shouts out a single word, which may be translated, "They are already beaten!" Another chorus of yells greets this announcement. This man is called the talala, or woodpecker, on account of his peculiar yell, which is considered to resemble the sound made by a woodpecker tapping on a dead tree trunk. According to the orthodox Cherokee belief, this yell is heard by the rival players in the other settlement— who, it will be remembered, are having a ball dance of their own at the same time—and so terrifies them that they lose all heart for the game. The fact that both sides alike have a talala in no way interferes with the theory.

At frequent intervals during the night all the players, accompanied by the shaman and his assistant, leave the dance and go down to a retired spot at the river's bank, where they perform the mystic rite known as "going to water," hereafter to be described. While the players are performing this ceremony, the women, with the drummer, continue the dance and chorus. The dance is kept up without intermission, and almost without change, until daybreak. At the final dance green pine tops are thrown upon the fire, so as to produce a thick smoke, which envelopes the dancers. Some mystic properties are ascribed to this pine smoke, but what they are I have not yet learned, although the ceremony seems to be intended as an exorcism, the same thing being done at other dances when there has recently been a death in the settlement.

At sunrise the players, dressed now in their ordinary clothes, but carrying their ball sticks in their hands, start for the ball ground, accompanied by the shamans and their assistants. The place selected for the game, being always about midway between the two rival settlements, was in this case several miles above the dance ground and on the opposite side of the river. On the march each party makes four several halts, when each player again "goes to water" separately with the shaman. This occupies considerable time, so that it is usually afternoon before the two parties meet on the ball ground. While the shaman is busy with his mysteries in the laurel bushes down by the water's edge, the other players, sitting by the side of the trail, spend the time twisting extra strings for their ball sticks, adjusting their feather ornaments, and discussing the coming game. In former times the player during these halts was not allowed to sit upon a log, a stone, or anything but the ground itself; neither was it permissible to lean against anything excepting the back of another player, on penalty of defeat in the game, with the additional risk of

---

[a] A somewhat different account of this myth is given by Mr Mooney in Myths of the Cherokee. Nineteenth Annual Report of the Bureau of American Ethnology, p. 286, 1900.

being bitten by a rattlesnake.   This rule is now disregarded, and it is doubtful
if any but the older men are aware that it ever existed.

On coming up from the water after the fourth halt, the principal shaman
assembles the players around him and delivers an animated harangue, exhort-
ing them to do their utmost in the coming contest, telling them that they will
undoubtedly be victorious, as the omens are all favorable, picturing to their
delighted vision the stakes to be won and the ovation awaiting them from their
friends after the game, and finally assuring them in the mystic terms of the
formulas that their adversaries will be driven through the four gaps into the
gloomy shadows of the Darkening Land, where they will perish forever from
remembrance.   The address, delivered in rapid, jerky tones like the speech of
an auctioneer, has a very inspiriting effect upon the hearers and is frequently
interrupted by a burst of exultant yells from the players.   At the end, with
another chorus of yells, they again take up the march.

On arriving in sight of the ball ground, the talala again comes to the front
and announces their approach with four loud yells, ending with a long quaver,
as on the previous night at the dance.   The players respond with another yell,
and then turn off to a convenient sheltered place by the river to make the final
preparations.

The shaman then marks off a small space upon the ground to represent the
ball field, and, taking in his hand a small bundle of sharpened stakes about a
foot in length, addresses each man in turn, telling him the position which he is
to occupy in the field at the tossing up of the ball after the first inning, and
driving down a stake to represent each player until he has a diagram of the
whole field spread out upon the ground.

The players then strip for the ordeal of scratching [plate XIV].   This painful operation is performed by an assistant, in this case by an old man named
Standing Water.   The instrument of torture is called a kanuga and resembles
a short comb with seven teeth, seven being also a sacred number with the
Cherokees.   The teeth are made of sharpened splinters from the leg bone of
a turkey and are fixed in a frame made from the shaft of a turkey quill, in such
a manner that by a slight pressure of the thumb they can be pushed out to the
length of a small tack.   Why the bone and feather of the turkey should be
selected I have not yet learned, but there is undoubtedly an Indian reason for
the choice.

The players having stripped, the operator begins by seizing the arm of a
player with one hand while holding the kanuga in the other, and plunges the
teeth into the flesh at the shoulder, bringing the instrument down with a steady
pressure to the elbow, leaving seven white lines which become red a moment
later as the blood starts to the surface.   He now plunges the kanuga in again at
another place near the shoulder, and again brings it down to the elbow.   Again
and again the operation is repeated until the victim's arm is scratched in
twenty-eight lines above the elbow.   It will be noticed that twenty-eight is a
combination of four and seven, the two sacred numbers of the Cherokee.
The operator then makes the same number of scratches in the same manner
on the arm below the elbow.   Next the other arm is treated in the same way;
then each leg, both above and below the knee, and finally an X is scratched
across the breast of the sufferer, the upper ends are joined by another stroke from
shoulder to shoulder, and a similar pattern is scratched upon his back.   By this
time the blood is trickling in little streams from nearly three hundred gashes.
None of the scratches are deep, but they are unquestionably very painful, as
all agree who have undergone the operation.   Nevertheless the young men
endure the ordeal willingly and almost cheerfully, regarding it as a necessary part of the ritual to secure success in the game.   In order to secure a

SCRATCHING A PLAYER; CHEROKEE INDIAN BALL GAME, NORTH
CAROLINA; FROM PHOTOGRAPH BY MOONEY (1893)

picture of one young fellow under the operation I stood with my camera so near that I could distinctly hear the teeth tear through the flesh at every scratch with a rasping sound that sent a shudder through me, yet he never flinched, although several times he shivered with cold, as the chill autumn wind blew upon his naked body. This scratching is common in Cherokee medical practice, and is variously performed with a brier, a rattlesnake's tooth, a flint, or even a piece of broken glass. It was noted by Adair as early as 1775. To cause the blood to flow more freely, the young men sometimes scrape it off with chips as it oozes out. The shaman then gives to each player a small piece of root, to which he has imparted magic properties by the recital of certain secret formulas. Various roots are used, according to the whim of the shaman, their virtue depending entirely upon the ceremony of consecration. The men chew these roots and spit out the juice over their limbs and bodies, rubbing it well into the scratches; then going down to the water, plunge in and wash off the blood, after which they come out and dress themselves for the game.

The modern Cherokee ball costume consists simply of a pair of short trunks, ornamented with various patterns in red or blue cloth, and a feather charm worn upon the head. Formerly the breechcloth alone was worn, as is still the case in some instances, and the strings with which it was tied were purposely made weak, so that if seized by an opponent in the scuffle the strings would break, leaving the owner to escape with the loss of his sole article of raiment. This calls to mind a similar custom among the ancient Greek athletes, the recollection of which has been preserved in the etymology of the word " gymnast." The ornament worn in the hair is made up of an eagle's feathers, to give keenness of sight; a deer tail, to give swiftness; and a snake's rattle, to render the wearer terrible to his adversaries. If an eagle's feathers can not be procured, those of a hawk or any other swift bird of prey are used. In running, the snake rattle is made to furnish a very good imitation of the sound made by the rattlesnake when about to strike. The player also marks his body in various patterns with paint or charcoal. The charcoal is taken from the dance fire, and whenever possible is procured by burning the wood of a tree which has been struck by lightning, such wood being regarded as peculiarly sacred and endowed with mysterious properties. According to one formula, the player makes a cross over his heart and a spot upon each shoulder, using pulverized charcoal procured from the shaman and made by burning together the wood of a honey-locust tree and of a tree which has been struck by lightning, but not killed. The charcoal is pulverized and put, together with a red and black bead, into an empty cocoon from which one end has been cut off. This paint preparation makes the player swift like the lightning and invulnerable as the tree that defies the thunderbolt, and renders his flesh as hard and firm to the touch as the wood of the honey locust. Among the Choctaws, according to Catlin, a tail of horse hair was also worn, so as to stream out behind as the player ran. Just before dressing, the players rub their bodies with grease or the chewed bark of the slippery elm or the sassafras, until their skin is slippery as that of the proverbial eel.

A number of precautionary measures are also frequently resorted to by the more prudent players while training, in order to make assurance doubly sure. They bathe their limbs with a decoction of the herb *Tephrosia virginiana*, or catgut, in order to render their muscles tough like the roots of that plant. They bathe themselves with a decoction of the small rush (*Juncus tenuis*), which grows by the roadside, because its stalks are always erect and will not lie flat upon the ground, however much they may be stamped and trodden upon. In the same way they bathe with a decoction of the wild crabapple or the ironwood, because the trunks of these trees, even when thrown down, are supported

and kept up from the ground by their spreading tops.  To make themselves more
supple, they whip themselves with the tough stalks of the wā'takû, or star-grass,
or with switches made from the bark of a hickory sapling which has grown up
from under a log that has fallen across it, the bark being taken from the bend
thus produced in the sapling.  After the first scratching the player renders himself an object of terror to his opponents by eating a portion of a rattlesnake
which has been killed and cooked by the shaman.  He rubs himself with an eel
skin to make himself slippery like the eel, and rubs each limb down once with
the fore and hind leg of a turtle, because the legs of that animal are remarkably
stout.  He applies to the shaman to conjure a dangerous opponent, so that he
may be unable to see the ball in its flight, or may dislocate a wrist or break a
leg.  Sometimes the shaman draws upon the ground an armless figure of his
rival, with a hole where his heart should be.  Into this hole he drops two black
beads, covers them with earth and stamps upon them, and thus the dreaded rival
is doomed, unless (and this is always the saving clause) his own shaman has
taken precautions against such a result, or the one in whose behalf the charm
is made has rendered the incantation unavailing by a violation of some one of
the interminable rules of the gaktûnta.

The players, having dressed, are now ready to go to water for the last time,
for which purpose the shaman selects a bend of the river where he can look
toward the east while facing upstream.  This ceremony of going to water is the
most sacred and impressive in the whole Cherokee ritual, and must always be
performed fasting, and in most cases also is preceded by an all-night vigil.  It is
used in connection with prayers to obtain a long life, to destroy an enemy, to
win the love of a woman, to secure success in the hunt and the ball play, and for
recovery from a dangerous illness, but is performed only as a final resort or
when the occasion is one of special importance.  The general ceremonial and
the principal formulas are nearly the same in all cases.  I have collected a
number of the formulas used on these various occasions, but it is impossible
within the limits of this paper to give more than a general idea of their nature.

The men stand side by side looking down upon the water, with their bal
sticks clasped upon their breasts, while the shaman stands just behind them,
and an assistant kneeling at his side spreads out upon the ground the cloth upon
which are placed the sacred beads.  These beads are of two colors, red and
black, each kind resting upon a cloth of the same color, and corresponding in
number to the number of players.  The red beads represent the players for
whom the shaman performs the ceremony, while the black beads stand for their
opponents, red being symbolic of power and triumph, while black is emblematic
of death and misfortune.  All being ready, the assistant hands to the shaman
a red bead, which he takes between the thumb and finger of his right hand;
and then a black bead, which he takes in the same manner in his left hand.
Then, holding his hands outstretched, with his eyes intently fixed upon the
beads, the shaman prays on behalf of his client to Yûwï Gûnahi'ta, the Long
Man, the sacred name for the river: "O, Long Man, I come to the edge of
your body.  You are mighty and most powerful.  You bear up great logs and
toss them about where the foam is white.  Nothing can resist you.  Grant me
such strength in the contest that my enemy may be of no weight in my hands—
that I may be able to toss him into the air or dash him to the earth."  In a
similar strain he prays to the Red Bat in the Sun Land to make him expert in
dodging; to the Red Deer to make him fleet of foot; to the great Red Hawk
to render him keen of sight; and to the Red Rattlesnake to render him terrible
to all who oppose him.

Then, in the same low tone and broken accents in which all the formulas
are recited, the shaman declares that his client (mentioning his name and clan)

CHEROKEE INDIAN BALL PLAYER, JOE CROW, READY FOR THE BALL
DANCE; NORTH CAROLINA; FROM PHOTOGRAPH BY MOONEY (1888)

has now ascended to the first heaven. As he continues praying he declares that he has now reached the second heaven (and here he slightly raises his hands) ; soon he ascends to the third heaven, and the hands of the shaman are raised still higher ; then, in the same way, he ascends to the fourth, the fifth, and the sixth heaven, and finally, as he raises his trembling hands aloft, he declares that the spirit of the man has now risen to the seventh heaven, where his feet are resting upon the Red Seats, from which they shall never be displaced.

Turning now to his client, the shaman, in a low voice, asks him the name of his most dreaded rival on the opposite side. The reply is given in a whisper, and the shaman, holding his hands outstretched as before, calls down the most withering curses upon the head of the doomed victim, mentioning him likewise by name and clan. He prays to the Black Fog to cover him so that he may be unable to see his way ; to the Black Rattlesnake to envelop him in his slimy folds ; and at last to the Black Spider to let down his black thread from above, wrap it about the soul of the victim, and drag it from his body along the black trail to the Darkening Land in the west, there to bury it in the black coffin under the black clay, never to reappear. At the final imprecation he stoops and, making a hole in the soft earth with his finger (symbolic of stabbing the doomed man to the heart), drops the black bead into it and covers it from sight with a vicious stamp of his foot ; then with a simultaneous movement each man dips his ball sticks into the water, and bringing them up, touches them to his lips ; then, stooping again, he dips up the water in his hand and laves his head and breast.

Below is given a translation of one of these formulas, from the collection of original Cherokee manuscripts obtained by the writer. The formulistic name for the player signifies "admirer or lover of the ball play." The shaman directs his attention alternately to his clients and their opponents, looking by turns at the red or the black bead as he prays. He raises his friends to the seventh heaven and invokes in their behalf the aid of the bat and a number of birds, which, according to the Cherokee belief, are so keen of sight and so swift upon the wing as never to fail to seize their intended prey. The opposing players, on the other hand, are put under the earth and rendered like the terrapin, the turtle, the mole, and the bear—all slow and clumsy of movement. Blue is the color symbolic of defeat, red is typical of success, and white signifis joy and happiness. The exultant whoop or shout of the players is believed to bear them on to victory, as trees are carried along by the resistless force of a torrent :

"THIS IS TO TAKE THEM TO WATER FOR THE BALL PLAY."

" Sgĕ! Now, where the white thread has been let down, quickly we are about to inquire into the fate of the lovers of the ball play.

"They are of such a descent. They are called so and so. (As they march) they are shaking the road which shall never be joyful. The miserable terrapin has fastened himself upon them as they go about. They are doomed to failure. They have become entirely blue.

"But now my lovers of the ball play have their roads lying down in this direction. The Red Bat has come and become one with them. There, in the first heaven, are the pleasing stakes. There, in the second heaven, are the pleasing stakes. The Peewee has come and joined them. Their ball sticks shall be borne along by the immortal whoop, never to fail them in the contest.

"But as for the lovers of the ball play on the other side, the common turtle has fastened himself to them as they go about. There, under the earth, they are doomed to failure.

"There, in the third heaven, are the pleasing stakes. The Red Tla′niwă has come and made himself one of them, never to be defeated. There, in the fourth heaven, are the pleasing stakes. The Crested Flycatcher has come and joined them, that they may never be defeated. There, in the fifth heaven, are the pleasing stakes. The Marten has come and joined them, that they may never be defeated.

"The other lovers of the ball play—the Blue Mole has become one with them, that they may never feel triumphant. They are doomed to failure.

"There, in the sixth heaven, the Chimney Swift has become one with them, that they may never be defeated. There are the pleasing stakes. There, in the seventh heaven, the Dragonfly has become one of them, that they may never be defeated. There are the pleasing stakes.

"As for the other lovers of the ball play, the Bear has come and fastened himself to them, that they may never be triumphant. He has caused the stakes to slip out of their hands, and their share has dwindled to nothing. Their fate is forecast.

"Sgĕ! Now let me know that the twelve (runs) are mine, O White Dragonfly. Let me know that their share is mine—that the stakes are mine. Now, he [the rival player] is compelled to let go his hold upon the stakes. They [the shaman's clients] are become exultant and gratified. Yû!"

This ceremony ended, the players form in line, headed by the shaman, and march in single file to the ball ground, where they find awaiting them a crowd of spectators—men, women and children—sometimes to the number of several hundred, for the Indians always turn out to the ball play, no matter how great the distance, from old Big Witch, stooping under the weight of nearly a hundred years, down to babies slung at their mothers' backs. The ball ground is a level field by the river side, surrounded by the high timber-covered mountains. At either end are the goals, each consisting of a pair of upright poles, between which the ball must be driven to make a run, the side which first makes 12 home runs being declared the winner of the game and the stakes. The ball is furnished by the challengers, who sometimes try to select one so small that it will fall through the netting of the ball sticks of their adversaries; but as the others are on the lookout for this, the trick usually fails of its purpose. After the ball is once set in motion it must be picked up only with the ball sticks, although after having picked up the ball with the sticks the player frequently takes it in his hand, and, throwing away the sticks, runs with it until intercepted by one of the other party, when he throws it, if he can, to one of his friends further on. Should a player pick up the ball with his hand, as sometimes happens in the scramble, there at once arises all over the field a chorus of "Uwâ′yĭ Gûtĭ! Uwâ′yĭ Gûtĭ!" "With the hand! with the hand!"—equivalent to our own "Foul! foul!"—and that inning is declared a draw.

While our men are awaiting the arrival of the other party, their friends crowd around them, and the women throw across their outstretched ball sticks the pieces of calico, the small squares of sheeting used as shawls, and the bright red handkerchiefs so dear to the heart of the Cherokee, which they intend to stake upon the game. It may be as well to state that these handkerchiefs take the place of hats, bonnets, and scarfs, the women throwing them over their heads in shawl fashion and the men twisting them like turbans about their hair, while both sexes alike fasten them about their throats or use them as bags for carrying small packages. Knives, trinkets, and sometimes small coins, are also wagered. But these Cherokee to-day are poor indeed. Hardly a man among them owns a horse, and never again will a chief bet a thousand dollars upon his favorites, as was done in Georgia in 1834. To-day, however, as then, they will risk all they have.

Now a series of yells announces the near approach of the men from Raven Town, and in a few minutes they come filing out from the bushes—stripped, scratched, and decorated like the others, carrying their ball sticks in their hands, and headed by a shaman. The two parties come together in the center of the ground, and for a short time the scene resembles an auction, as men and women move about, holding up the articles they propose to wager on the game and bidding for stakes to be matched against them. The betting being ended, the opposing players draw up in two lines facing each other, each man with his ball sticks laid together upon the ground in front of him, with the heads pointing toward the man facing him. This is for the purpose of matching the players so as to get the same number on each side; and should it be found that a player has no antagonist to face him he must drop out of the game. Such a result frequently happens, as both parties strive to keep their arrangements secret up to the last moment. There is no fixed number on a side, the common quota being from nine to twelve. Catlin, indeed, speaking of the Choctaws, says that "it is no uncommon occurrence for six or eight hundred or a thousand of these young men to engage in a game of ball, with five or six times that number of spectators;" but this was just after the removal, while the entire nation was yet camped upon the prairie in the Indian Territory. It would have been utterly impossible for the shamans to prepare a thousand players, or even one-fourth of that number, in the regular way, and in Catlin's spirited description of the game the ceremonial part is chiefly conspicuous by its absence. The greatest number that I ever heard of among the old Cherokee was twenty-two on a side. There is another secret formula to be recited by the initiated at this juncture, and addressed to the Red Yahulu, or hickory, for the purpose of destroying the efficiency of his enemy's ball sticks.

During the whole time that the game is in progress the shaman, concealed in the bushes by the water side, is busy with his prayers and incantations for the success of his clients and the defeat of their rivals. Through his assistant, who acts as messenger, he is kept advised of the movements of the players by seven men, known as counselors, appointed to watch the game for that purpose. These seven counselors also have a general oversight of the conjuring and other proceedings at the ball-play dance. Every little incident is regarded as an omen, and the shaman governs himself accordingly.

An old man now advances with the ball, and standing at one end of the lines, delivers a final address to the players, telling them that Uné'lanû'hĭ, the Apportioner—the sun—is looking down upon them, urging them to acquit themselves in the games as their fathers have done before them; but above all to keep their tempers, so that none may have it to say that they got angry or quarreled, and that after it is over each one may return in peace along the white trail to rest in his white house. White in these formulas is symbolic of peace and happiness and all good things. He concludes with a loud "Ha! Taldu-gwŭ'!" "Now for the twelve!" and throws the ball into the air.

Instantly twenty pairs of ball sticks clatter together in the air, as their owners spring to catch the ball in its descent. In the scramble it usually happens that the ball falls to the ground, when it is picked up by one more active than the rest. Frequently, however, a man will succeed in catching it between his ball sticks as it falls, and, disengaging himself from the rest, starts to run with it to the goal; but before he has gone a dozen yards they are upon him, and the whole crowd goes down together, rolling and tumbling over each other in the dust, straining and tugging for possession of the ball, until one of the players manages to extricate himself from the struggling heap and starts off with the ball. At once the others spring to their feet and, throwing away their ball sticks, rush to intercept him or prevent his capture, their black hair streaming out behind and their naked bodies glistening in the sun as they run. The scene is constantly changing. Now the players are all together at the lower end of the field, when suddenly, with a powerful throw, a player sends the ball high over the heads of the spectators and into the bushes beyond. Before there is time to realize it, here they come with a grand sweep and a burst of short, sharp Cherokee exclamations, charging right into the crowd, knocking men and women to right and left, and stumbling over dogs and babies in their frantic efforts to get at the ball.

It is a very exciting game, as well as a very rough one, and in its general features is a combination of baseball, football, and the old-fashioned shinny. Almost everything short of murder is allowable in the game, and both parties sometimes go into the contest with the deliberate purpose of crippling or otherwise disabling the best players on the opposing side. Serious accidents are common. In the last game which I witnessed one man was seized around the waist by a powerfully built adversary, raised up in the air, and hurled down upon the ground with such force as to break his collar-bone. His friends pulled him out to one side and the game went on. Sometimes two men lie struggling on the ground, clutching at each others' throats, long after the ball has been carried to the other end of the field, until the drivers, armed with long, stout switches, come running up and belabor both over their bare shoulders until they are forced to break their hold. It is also the duty of these drivers to gather the ball sticks thrown away in the excitement and restore them to their owners at the beginning of the next inning.

When the ball has been carried through the goal, the players come back to the center and take position in accordance with the previous instructions of their shamans. The two captains stand facing each other, and the ball is then thrown up by the captain of the side which won the last inning. Then the struggle begins again; and so the game goes on until one party scores 12 runs and is declared the victor and the winner of the stakes.

As soon as the game is over, usually about sundown, the winning players immediately go to water again with their shamans and perform another ceremony for the purpose of turning aside the revengeful incantations of their defeated rivals. They then dress, and the crowd of hungry players, who have eaten nothing since they started for the dance the night before, make a combined attack on the provisions which the women now produce from their shawls and baskets. It should be mentioned that, to assuage thirst during the game, the players are allowed to drink a sour preparation made from green grapes and wild crabapples.

Although the contestants on both sides are picked men and strive to win [plates xv, xvi], straining every muscle to the utmost, the impression left upon my mind after witnessing a number of games is that the same number of athletic young white men would have infused more robust energy into the play— that is, provided they could stand upon their feet after all the preliminary fasting, bleeding, and loss of sleep. Before separating, the defeated party usually challenges the victors to a second contest, and in a few days preparations are actively under way for another game.

## Of the ball game, Mr Mooney relates further:

Some old people say that the moon is a ball which was thrown up against the sky in a game a long time ago. They say that two towns were playing against each other, but one of them had the best runners and had almost won the game when the leader of the other side picked up the ball with his hand— a thing that is not allowed in the game—and tried to throw to the goal, but it struck against the solid sky vault and was fastened there, to remind players

CHEROKEE INDIAN BALL TEAM; WOLFTOWN, NORTH CAROLINA; FROM PHOTOGRAPH BY MOONEY (1888)

TWENTY-FOURTH ANNUAL REPORT   PL. XVI

BUREAU OF AMERICAN ETHNOLOGY

never to cheat. When the moon looks small and pale, it is because some one has handled the ball unfairly, and for this reason they formerly played only at the time of a full moon.[a]

In another myth Mr Mooney refers to playing ball as a figurative expression for a contest of any kind, particularly a battle.[b]

CHEROKEE. Walker county, Georgia.

Rev. George White writes: [c]

We have been favored with the following letter from a gentleman, giving an account of an Indian ball-play which took place in this county, and at which he was present:

"We started one fine morning in the month of August, for the hickory grounds, having learned that two towns, Chattooga and Chicamauga, were to have a grand ball play at that place. We found the grounds to be a beautiful hickory level, entirely in a state of nature, upon which had been erected several rude tents, containing numerous articles, mostly of Indian manufacture, which were the stakes to be won or lost in the approaching contest. We had been on the ground only a short time when the two contending parties, composed of fifty men each, mostly in a state of nudity and having their faces painted in a fantastical manner, headed by their chiefs, made their appearance. The war-whoop was then sounded by one of the parties, which was immediately answered by the other, and continued alternately as they advanced slowly and in regular order towards each other to the center of the ground allotted for the contest.

"In order that you may have an idea of the play, imagine two parallel lines of stakes driven into the ground near each other, each extending for about 100 yards and having a space of 100 yards between them. In the center of these lines were the contending towns, headed by their chiefs, each having in their hands two wooden spoons, curiously carved, not unlike our large iron spoons. The object of these spoons is to throw up the ball. The ball is made of deer skin wound around a piece of spunk. To carry the ball through one of the lines mentioned above is the purpose to be accomplished. Every time the ball is carried through these lines counts 1. The game is commenced by one of the chiefs throwing up the ball to a great height, by means of the wooden spoons. As soon as the ball is thrown up, the contending parties mingle together. If the chief of the opposite party catches the ball as it descends, with his spoons, which he exerts his utmost skill to do, it counts 1 for his side. The respective parties stand prepared to catch the ball if there should be a failure on the part of their chiefs to do so. On this occasion the parties were distinguished from each other by the color of their ribbons; the one being red, the other blue.

"The strife begins. The chief has failed to catch the ball. A stout warrior has caught it, and endeavors with all speed to carry it into his lines, when a faster runner knocks his feet from under him, wrests the ball from him, and triumphantly makes his way with the prize to his own line; but when he almost reaches the goal, he is overtaken by one or more of his opponents, who endeavors to take it from him. The struggle becomes general, and it is often the case that serious personal injuries are inflicted. It is very common during the contest to let the ball fall to the ground. The strife now ceases for a time, until the chiefs again array their bands. The ball is again thrown up, and the game is continued as above described. Sometimes half an hour elapses before either side succeeds in making 1 in the game.

---

[a] Myths of the Cherokee. Nineteenth Annual Report of the Bureau of American Ethnology, pt. 1, p. 257, 1900.

[b] Ibid., p. 245, 433.      [c] Historical Collections of Georgia, p. 670, New York, 1855.

"It is usual at these ball-plays for each party to leave their conjurers at work at the time the game is going on; their stations are near the center of each line. In their hands are shells, bones of snakes, etc. These conjurers are sent for from a great distance. They are estimated according to their age, and it is supposed by their charms they can influence the game. On this occasion two conjurers were present; they appeared to be over 100 years of age. When I spoke to one of them he did not deign even to raise his head; the second time I spoke he gave me a terrible look, and at the same time one of the Indian women came and said, 'Conagatee unaka,' 'Go away, white man.'"

## HURON.  Ontario.

### Nicolas Perrot [a] says, under jeu de crosse:

They have a certain game played with a bat, which greatly resembles our game of tennis. Their custom is to pit one nation against another, and if one is more numerous than the other, a certain number of men are withdrawn to render the sides equal. They are all armed with a bat—that is to say, a stick—the lower end of which is enlarged and laced like a racket. The ball is of wood and shaped very much like a turkey egg.

The goals are laid out in the open country, and face east and west, south and north. One of the parties, in order to win, must make the ball pass beyond the east and west goals, while the other party plays for the north and south goals. If anyone who has won once makes the ball pass beyond the wrong goal, he is obliged to begin again, taking his adversary's goal. If he happens to win again, he gains nothing. Then, the parties being equal and the game even, they begin the deciding game, and the successful side takes the stakes. Men and women, young boys, and girls all play on one side or the other, and make bets according to their means.

These games usually begin after the disappearance of the snow and ice and continue till seed time. The games are played in the afternoon, and the captain of each team harangues his players and announces the hour fixed for beginning the game. At the appointed time they gather in a crowd in the center of the field, and one of the two captains, having the ball in his hand, tosses it up in the air, each player trying to send it in the proper direction. If the ball falls to the ground, they try to pull it toward themselves with their bats, and should it fall outside the crowd of players, the most active of them win distinction by following closely after it. They make a great noise striking one against the other when they try to parry strokes in order to drive the ball in the proper direction. If a player keeps the ball between his feet and is unwilling to let it go, he must guard against the blows his adversaries continually aim at his feet; if he happens to be wounded, it is his own fault. Legs and arms are sometimes broken, and it has even happened that a player has been killed. It is quite common to see some one crippled for the rest of his life who would not have had this misfortune but for his own obstinacy. When these accidents happen the unlucky victim quietly withdraws from the game, if he is in a condition to do so; but if his injury will not permit this, his relatives carry him home, and the game goes on till it is finished, as if nothing had occurred.

As to the runners, when the sides are equal, sometimes neither side will win during the entire afternoon, and, again, one side may gain both of the two games necessary to win. In this racing game it looks as if the two sides were about to engage in battle. This exercise contributes much toward rendering the savages agile and quick to avoid adroitly a blow of a tomahawk in the hands of

[a] Mémoire sur les Moeurs, Coustumes et Relligion des Sauvages de l'Amérique Septentrionale, p. 43, Leipzig, 1864.

an enemy when engaged in war, and unless previously informed that they were at play one would truly believe them to be fighting.

Whatever accident the game may cause is attributed to luck, and there is in consequence no hard feeling between the players. The wounded seem as well satisfied as if nothing had happened to them, thus demonstrating that they have plenty of courage and that they are men.

They take what they have wagered and their winnings, and there is no dispute on either side when it comes to a question of payment, no matter what game they play. If, however, anyone who does not belong in the game, or who has bet nothing, hits the ball, thus giving any advantage to either side, one of the players on the other side will upbraid the outsider, asking him if the game is any affair of his and why he meddles with it. They often come to blows, and, if some chief does not pacify them, blood may be spilled or even some one killed. The best way to prevent such disorderly occurrences is to begin the game anew, with the consent of those who are ahead, for if they refuse to do so they have the advantage. When some prominent man takes part in the dispute, it is not difficult to arrange their differences and induce them to follow his advice.

### Baron La Hontan says: [a]

They have a third play with a ball not unlike our tennis, but the balls are very large, and the rackets resemble ours, save that the handle is at least 3 feet long. The savages, who commonly play at it in large companies of three or four hundred at a time, fix two sticks at 500 or 600 paces distant from each other. They divide into two equal parties, and toss up the ball about halfway between the two sticks. Each party endeavors to toss the ball to their side; some run to the ball, and the rest keep at a little distance on both sides to assist on all quarters. In fine, this game is so violent that they tear their skins and break their legs very often in striving to raise the ball. All these games are made only for feasts or other trifling entertainments; for 'tis to be observed that as they hate money, so they never put it in the balance, and one may say interest is never the occasion of debates among them.

### HURON. Ihonatiria, or St Joseph, near Thunder bay, Ontario.

### Jean de Brébeuf says: [b]

Of three kinds of games especially in use among these peoples—namely, the games of crosse, dish, and straw, the first two are, they say, most healing. Is not this worthy of compassion? There is a poor sick man, fevered of body and almost dying, and a miserable sorcerer will order for him, as a cooling remedy, a game of crosse. Or the sick man himself, sometimes, will have dreamed that he must die unless the whole country shall play crosse for his health; and no matter how little may be his credit, you will see then in a beautiful field, village contending against village as to who will play crosse the better, and betting against one another beaver robes and porcelain collars, so as to excite greater interest. Sometimes, also, one of these jugglers will say that the whole country is sick, and he asks a game of crosse to heal it; no more needs to be said, it is published immediately everywhere; and all the captains of each village give orders that all the young men do their duty in this respect, otherwise some great misfortune would befall the whole country.[c]

---

[a] New Voyages to North-America, v. 2, p. 18, London, 1703.

[b] Relation of 1636. The Jesuit Relations and Allied Documents, v. 10, p. 185, Cleveland, 1897.

[c] Brébeuf describes all the affairs of the Huron as included under two heads:
The first are, as it were, affairs of state—whatever may concern either citizens or strangers, the public or the individuals of the village; as, for example, feasts, dances, games, crosse matches, and funeral ceremonies. The second are affairs of war. Now there are as many sorts of Captains as of affairs. (Ibid., p. 229.)

MOHAWK. Grand river, Ontario. (Cat. no. 38513, 38514, Free Museum of Science and Art, University of Pennsylvania.)

Racket for lacrosse (figure 761), consisting of a sapling curved at one end, the bent portion woven with a network of bark cord; length, 48 inches.

FIG. 761. Racket; length, 48 inches; Mohawk Indians, Grand river, Ontario; cat. no. 38513, Free Museum of Science and Art, University of Pennsylvania.

Ball covered with buckskin (figure 762), round, 2½ inches in diameter, the cover in one piece cut and sewed like a baseball. Collected by the writer in 1901.

The name of the racket was given as ki-du-kwa-sta, and that of the ball as no-hā. The racket was explained as the old kind, with bast cords instead of twine, as is now used.

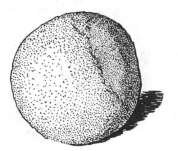

FIG. 762. Ball; diameter, 2¼ inches; Mohawk Indians, Grand river, Ontario; cat. no. 38514, Free Museum of Science and Art, University of Pennsylvania.

Mr J. N. B. Hewitt [a] informed the writer that the use of bark as a network was only to replace sinew when that article was not obtainable. The bark of the slippery elm, boiled in water to make it pliable, was employed. He says:

The network on the common Iroquois club was not drawn taut, but it was sufficiently taut to enable the player to throw the ball to a very great distance—a successful throw carrying the ball about 20 rods—and yet the netting was loose enough to enable a skillful player oftentimes to carry the ball through a crowd of opposing players. On the regulation club used in the modernized game, which is very seldom played by the Iroquois, the network is made very taut, so that the network emits a twang when it is picked by the fingers. . . .

The goals or butts for the ball game were marked by poles or stakes, from 10 to 15 feet in length, two in number, driven in the ground from 5 to 15 paces apart. The goal therefore was a square or quadrilateral space bounded on two sides by the two upright poles, on one side by the ground and on the other by a line connecting either the extreme ends of the poles or two marked points on the poles at some agreed height from the ground. The goals were placed from 40 to 80 rods apart, according to the number and skill of the players. . . .

The players to begin the game assemble on the ball-ground at a point midway between the goals, or butts. The two parties are then divided into couples, every player being paired with one of the opposite party, those paired being, as nearly as possible, of equal skill, agility, strength, and fleetness of foot. One of the players is placed immediately in front of the goal defended by his side, and another in front of the opposite goal. These two are called the door-guards. It is their duty to guard the goals against an opposing player who may attempt to

[a] See The American Anthropologist, v. 5, p. 189, 1892.

throw the ball through from a distance or to carry the ball into the goal on his club. These two are chosen rather for their skill and vigilance than for fleetness of foot.

It was considered a great feat for a player to take the ball on his bat, elude his pursuers and opponents, outplay the door-guard, and thus carry the ball into the goal, especially if he was able to walk into the goal. The side whose player did this would taunt the other side by saying, " It lay on the club when it entered."

The game was opened by the two captains holding their clubs crossed in the form of a Maltese cross with the ball placed midway between the ends of the network on each club; then by a steady push each captain endeavors to throw the ball in the direction of the goal to which his side must bear it.

Like all other public games of the Iroquois, the ball game was to the spectators a favorite opportunity for betting, and many would wager and lose all their possessions.

The Iroquois prefer the ancient to the modern style of the game, for in the former they had a greater opportunity to exhibit their skill, strength, and fleetness of foot individually, whereas in the modernized form of the game, I believe, there is more team-play.

Previous to a matched game the players would go through a course of stringent fasting, bathing, and emetics. The latter were decoctions of the bark of spotted alder and red willow.

The contending parties of ball players all carried some charm or talisman to insure their victory. Shamans were hired by individual players to exert their supernatural powers in their own behalf and for their side, and when a noted wizard openly espoused the cause of one of the parties the players of the other side felt to a certain extent disheartened.

The game was played during spring, summer, and fall; and formerly the players painted and adorned themselves in their most approved style.

The game generally begins in the afternoon; seldom, if ever, in the forenoon. It is usually followed by a dance at night, accompanied by a feast.

MOHAWK. Grand river, Ontario.

Col. William H. Stone,[a] referring to the ball game, which he erroneously declares the Six Nations adopted from the whites, describes a match played at Grand river between the Mohawk and Seneca in 1797:

The combatants numbered about six hundred upon a side. The goals, designated by two pair of byes, were 30 rods apart and the goals of each pair about 30 feet apart. Each passage of the ball between them counted a point, but the tally chiefs were allowed to check or curtail the count in order to protract the game. The ball was put in play by a beautiful girl.

——— Caughnawaga, Quebec.

J. A. Cuoq [b] gives the following definitions:

Atenno, paume, balle, pelote à jouer; atstsikwahe, crosse de jouer, baton recourbè, raquette pour le jeu de crosse; tekatsikwaheks, frapper la balle, jouer à la crosse.

---

[a] Life of Brant, v. 2, p. 447, Cooperstown, 1844.
[b] Lexique de la Langue Iroquoise, Montreal, 1882.

The last two are derived from otsikwa, meaning in general anything that has a form almost round and a certain solidity.

ONONDAGA.  New York.

The Dictionnaire Français-Onontagué [a] gives this definition:

Bale à jouer, odzikk8a deyeyendakk8a.

In Zeisberger's Indian Dictionary [b] we find:

To play at ball, waszichquaëqua; ball (kugel), ozíchqua.

ST REGIS.  St Regis, New York.  (Cat. no. 118840, United States National Museum.)

Leather-covered ball (figure 763), made of a single piece cut and stitched with thread, containing an interior core of cotton thread; diameter, 2¼ inches.  Collected by R. B. Hough.

FIG. 763. Ball; diameter, 2¼ inches; St Regis Indians, St Regis, New York; cat. no. 118840, United States National Museum.

SENECA.  New York.

Morgan [c] describes the Iroquois ball game as follows:

With the Iroquois, the ball game, o-tä-dä-jish'-quä-äge, was the favorite among their amusements of this description. This game reaches back to a remote antiquity, was universal among the red races, and was played with a degree of zeal and enthusiasm which would scarcely be credited. It was played with a small deerskin ball, by a select band, usually from six to eight on a side, each set representing its own party. The game was divided into several contests, in which each set of players strove to carry the ball through their own gate. They went out into an open plain or field and erected gates, about 80 rods apart, on its opposite sides. Each gate was simply two poles, some 10 feet high, set in the ground about 3 rods asunder. One of these gates belonged to each party; and the contest between the players was, which set would first carry the ball through its own a given number of times. Either 5 or 7 made the game, as the parties agreed. If 5, for example, was the number, the party which first carried, or drove the ball through its own gate this number of times, won the victory. Thus, after eight separate contests, the parties might stand equal, each having won 4; in which case the party which succeeded on the ninth contest would carry the game. The players commenced in the center of the field, midway between the gates. If one of them became fatigued or disabled during the progress of the game, he was allowed to leave the ranks, and his party could supply his place with a fresh player, but the original numbers were not at any time allowed to be increased. Regular managers were appointed on each side to see that the rules of the game were strictly and fairly observed. One rule forbade the players to touch the ball with the hand or foot.

---

[a] New York, Cramoisy Press, 1859.
[b] Cambridge, 1887.
[c] League of the Iroquois, p. 294, Rochester, 1851.

In preparing for this game the players denuded themselves entirely, with the exception of the waistcloth.[a] . . . They also underwent, frequently, a course of diet and training, as in a preparation for a foot-race.

When the day designated had arrived the people gathered from the whole surrounding country, to witness the contest. About meridian they assembled at the appointed place, and having separated themselves into two companies, one might be seen upon each side of the line, between the gates, arranged in scattered groups, awaiting the commencement of the game. The players, when ready, stationed themselves in two parallel rows, facing each other, midway on this line, each one holding a ball bat, of the kind represented in the figure, and with which alone the ball was to be driven. As soon as all the preliminaries were adjusted, the ball was dropped between the two files of players, and taken between the bats of the two who stood in the middle of each file, opposite to each other. After a brief struggle between them, in which each player endeavored, with his bat, to get possession of the ball, and give it the first impulse towards his own gate, it was thrown out, and then commenced the pursuit. The flying ball, when overtaken, was immediately surrounded by a group of players, each one striving to extricate it, and, at the same time, direct it towards his party gate. In this way the ball was frequently imprisoned in different parts of the field, and an animated controversy maintained for its possession. When freed, it was knocked upon the ground or through the air : but the moment a chance presented it was taken up upon the deer-skin network of the ball bat by a player in full career, and carried in a race towards the gate. To guard against this contingency, by which one contest of the game might be determined in a moment, some of the players detached themselves from the group contending around the ball, and took a position from which to intercept a runner upon a diagonal line, if it should chance that one of the adverse party got possession of the ball. These races often formed the most exciting part of the game, both from the fleetness of the runners, and the consequences which depended upon the result. When the line of the runner was crossed, by an adversary coming in before him upon a diagonal line, and he found it impossible, by artifice or stratagem, to elude him, he turned about, and threw the ball over the heads of both of them, towards his gate ; or, perchance, towards a player of his own party, if there were adverse players between him and the gate. When the flight of the ball was arrested in any part of the field, a spirited and even fierce contest was maintained around it ; the players handled their bats with such dexterity, and managed their persons with such art and adroitness, that frequently several minutes elapsed before the ball flew out. Occasionally in the heat of the controversy, but entirely by accident, a player was struck with such violence that the blood trickled down his limbs. In such a case, if disabled, he dropped his bat and left the field, while a fresh player from his own party supplied his place. In this manner was the game contested : oftentimes with so much ardor and skill that the ball was recovered by one party at the very edge of the adverse gate ; and finally, after many shifts in the tide of success, carried in triumph through its own. When one contest in the game was thus decided, the prevailing party sent up a united shout of rejoicing.

After a short respite for the refreshment of the players, the second trial was commenced, and continued like the first. Sometimes it was decided in a few moments, but more frequently it lasted an hour, and sometimes much longer, to

---

[a] The gä-kä or waist-cloth, was a strip of deerskin or broadcloth, about a quarter wide and 2 yards long, ornamented at the ends with bead- or quill-work. It was passed between the limbs and secured by a deerskin belt, passing around the waist, the embroidered ends falling over the belt, before and behind, in the fashion of an apron.

such a system had the playing of this game been reduced by skill and practice. If every trial was ardently contested, and the parties continued nearly equal in the number decided, it often lengthened out the game, until the approaching twilight made it necessary to take another day for its conclusion.

On the final decision of the game, the exclamations of triumph, as would be expected, knew no bounds. Caps, tomahawks and blankets were thrown up into the air, and for a few moments the notes of victory resounded from every side. It was doubtless a considerate provision, that the prevailing party were upon a side of the field opposite to, and at a distance from, the vanquished, otherwise such a din of exultation might have proved too exciting for Indian patience.

In ancient times they used a solid ball of knot. The ball bat, also, was made without network, having a solid and curving head. At a subsequent day they substituted the deer-skin ball and the network ball bat [figure 764] in present use. These substitutions were made so many years ago that they have lost the date.

FIG. 764. Racket; length, 5 feet; Seneca Indians, New York; from Morgan.

KULANAPAN STOCK

GUALALA.   California.

Mr Stephen Powers [a] mentions tennis among the amusements at the great autumnal games of this tribe.

POMO.   California.

Mr Stephen Powers [b] relates the following:

There is a game of tennis played by the Pomo, of which I have heard nothing among the northern tribes. A ball is rounded out of an oak-knot about as large as those generally used by schoolboys, and it is propelled by a racket which is constructed of a long, slender stick, bent double and bound together, leaving a circular hoop at the extremity, across which is woven a coarse mesh-work of strings. Such an implement is not strong enough for batting the ball, neither do they bat it, but simply shove or thrust it along the ground.

The game is played in the following manner: They first separate themselves into two equal parties, and each party contributes an equal amount to a stake to be played for, as they seldom consider it worth while to play without betting. Then they select an open space of ground, and establish two parallel base lines a certain number of paces apart, with a starting-line between, equidistant from both. Two champions, one for each party, stand on opposite sides of the starting-point with their rackets; a squaw tosses the ball in the air, and as it descends the two champions strike at it, and one or the other gets the advantage, hurling it toward his antagonist's base-line. Then there ensues a universal rush, pell-mell, higgledy-piggledy, men and squaws crushing and bumping—for the squaws participate equally with the sterner sex—each party striving to propel

---

[a] Tribes of California. Contributions to North American Ethnology, v. 3, p. 193, Washington, 1877.

[b] Ibid., p. 151; also Overland Monthly, v. 9, p. 501.

the ball across the enemy's base-line. They enjoy this sport immensely, laugh and vociferate until they are "out of all whooping"; some tumble down and get their heads batted, and much diversion is created, for they are very good-natured and free from jangling in their amusements. One party must drive the ball a certain number of times over the other's base line before the game is concluded, and this not unfrequently occupies them a half day or more, during which they expend more strenuous endeavor than they would in a day of honest labor in a squash-field.

Powers describes the Pomo as staking fancy bows and arrows on their ball games. Of these articles they frequently have a number made only for gambling purposes—not for use in hunting.

POMO. Ukiah valley, Mendocino county, California. (Cat. no. 70966, 70977, Field Columbian Museum.)

Racket (figure 765), made of a bent oak stick, 40 inches in length, with twine mesh, and ball, of pepper-wood knot, 2¼ inches in diameter. Collected by Dr J. W. Hudson.

FIG. 765. Ball and racket; diameter of ball, 2¼ inches; length of racket, 40 inches; Pomo Indians, Mendocino county, California; cat. no. 70966, 70977, Field Columbian Museum.

——— Seven miles south of Ukiah, Mendocino county, California. (Cat. no. 70946, 70947, Field Columbian Museum.)

Racket of dogwood (figure 766), with rawhide lacings, 35 inches long; and ball, a pepperwood knot. Collected by Dr J. W. Hudson, who describes the game as played by tossing the ball in the center of the field and contesting for it with netted sticks, under the name of tsitimpiyem:

FIG. 766. Ball and racket; length of racket, 35 inches; Pomo Indians, Mendocino county, California; cat. no. 70946, 70947, Field Columbian Museum.

The ball sticks, called tsi-tīm', are 3 feet in length. The goals, hui kali dako' (hui!=we win!) are 6 feet high and 25 yards apart. The ball, pikŏ', is usually of laurel (Umbellaria), but sometimes a deer knuckle bone.

### MARIPOSAN STOCK

YOKUTS. Tule River agency, Tulare county, California. (Cat. no. 70392, Field Columbian Museum.)

Two willow saplings (figure 767), 50 inches in length, with an oak loop lashed on the lower end with sinew; accompanied by two small mistletoe-root balls coated with pitch and painted red.

These are implements for a ball game, collected by Dr J. W. Hudson.

The two balls are laid side by side on the ground at the end of the course, and at a word the captains dip them up with their spoon sticks and cast them forward to their mates, who send them on to the nearest pair of opponents. The course is about 1,200 yards—around a tree and back to the first goal. There are usually eight players, three and a captain on each side.

FIG. 767.  Ball and racket; length of racket, 50 inches; Yokuts Indians, Tule River agency, Tulare county, California; cat. no. 70392, Field Columbian Museum.

The game is called wip-i-watch (to lift on the end of a stick); the ball, o-lol; the stick, wi-pat; the starting goal, to-liu, and the turning stake, tsa-lam. It is played only by men.

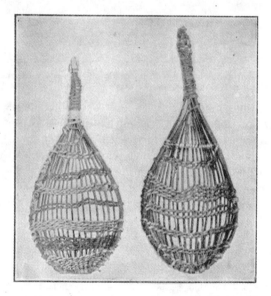

FIG. 768.  Ball baskets; lengths, 16 and 18 inches; Miwok Indians, Tuolumne county, California; in the collection of Dr C. Hart Merriam.

## MOQUELUMNAN STOCK

MIWOK.  Bald Rock, Tuolumne county, California.  (Collection of Dr C. Hart Merriam.)

Two spoon-shaped willow baskets (figure 768), one 16 and the other 18 inches in length, the longer stiffened by a crosspiece near the handle.

Collected by Doctor Merriam and described by him as used by women in catching the ball, posko, in the game called amtah.

Each woman carries a pair of these baskets, called am-mut′-nah, one in each hand. She catches the ball in the larger one and covers it with the other while she runs off with it toward the goal. The men try to kick the ball, but can not lay hands on it.

TOPINAGUGIM. Big creek, Tuolumne county, California. (Cat. no. 70220, 70226, Field Columbian Museum.)

Two oval wicker baskets (figure 769), 13 inches in length, with handle; and buckskin-covered ball, 3½ inches in diameter.

Collected by Dr J. W. Hudson, who describes them as used in the game of umta, played by both men and women. The baskets resemble the seed-flail baskets used in this region.

—— California.

Mr H. H. Bancroft [a] says:

FIG. 769. Ball and ball-casting basket; diameter of ball, 3¼ inches; length of basket, 13 inches; Topinagugim Indians, Tuolumne county, California; cat. no. 70220, 70226, Field Columbian Museum.

. . . they have one or two games which require some exertion. One of these, in vogue among the Meewocs, is played with bats and an oak-knot ball. The former are made of a pliant stick, having the end bent round and lashed to the main part, so as to form a loop, which is filled with a network of strings. They do not strike but push the ball along with these bats. The players take sides, and each party endeavors to drive the ball past the boundaries of the other.

—— Big creek, 2 miles north of Groveland, Tuolumne county, California.

Dr J. W. Hudson describes the following game under the name of sakumship:

Two women, standing 50 feet apart, throw a 4-inch ball of buckskin filled with hair, each using two baskets to throw the ball, which they may not touch with their hands. The casting baskets, called shak-num-sia, are made somewhat stronger than the a-ma-ta.

This is a great gambling game between women, and is played for high stakes. It is counted with sticks, and a player forfeits one if she fails to catch or throw the ball so that it goes beyond the other's reach.

MUSKHOGEAN STOCK

CHICKASAW. Mississippi.

Adam Hodgson [b] says:

As we were riding along toward sunset, we saw many parties of Chickasaws repairing to a dance and ball-play. The magnificence of their dresses exceeded anything we had yet seen.

---

[a] The Native Races of the Pacific Coast, v. 1, p. 393, San Francisco, 1874.
[b] Remarks during a Journey through North America, p. 283, New York, 1823.

CHOCTAW.   Mississippi.

### Capt. Bernard Romans [a] says:

Their play at ball is either with a small ball of deerskin or a large one of woolen rags; the first is thrown with battledores, the second with the hand only; this is a trial of skill between village and village; after having appointed the day and field for meeting, they assemble at the time and place, fix two poles across each other at about an 150 feet apart. Then they attempt to throw the ball through the lower part of them, and the opposite party, trying to prevent it, throw it back themselves, which the first again try to prevent; thus they attempt to beat it about from one to the other with amazing violence, and not seldom broken limbs or dislocated joints are the consequence: their being almost naked, painted, and ornamented with feathers has a good effect on the eye of the bystander during this violent diversion; a number is agreed on for the score, and the party who first gets this number wins.

The women play among themselves (after the men have done) disputing with as much eagerness as the men; the stakes or bets are generally high. There is no difference in the other game with the large ball, only the men and women play promiscuously, and they use no battledores.

### James Adair [b] says:

Ball playing is their chief and most favorite game: and it is such severe exercise, as to show it was originally calculated for a hardy and expert race of people like themselves, and the ancient Spartans. The ball is made of a piece of scraped deer-skin, moistened and stuffed hard with deer's hair, and strongly sewed with deer's sinews.—The ball-sticks are about 2 feet long, the lower end somewhat resembling the palm of a hand, and which are worked with deer-skin thongs. Between these, they catch the ball and throw it a great distance, when not prevented by some of the opposite party, who try to intercept them. The goal is about 500 yards in length: at each end of it, they fix two long bending poles into the ground, 3 yards apart below, but slanting a considerable way outward. The party that happens to throw the ball over these counts 1; but if it be thrown underneath, it is cast back, and played for as usual. The gamesters are equal in number on each side; and at the beginning of every course of the ball they throw it up high in the center of the ground, and in a direct line between the two goals. When the crowd of players prevents the one who catched the ball from throwing it off with a long direction, he commonly sends it the right course by an artful sharp twirl. They are so exceedingly expert in this manly exercise, that, between the goals, the ball is mostly flying the different ways, by the force of the playing sticks, without falling to the ground, for they are not allowed to catch it with their hands. It is surprising to see how swiftly they fly, when closely chased by a nimble-footed pursuer; when they are intercepted by one of the opposite party, his fear of being cut by the ball sticks commonly gives them an opportunity of throwing it perhaps a hundred yards; but the antagonist sometimes runs up behind, and by a sudden stroke dashes down the ball. It is a very unusual thing to see them act spitefully in any sort of game, not even in this severe and tempting exercise.

### Bossu [c] says:

The Chactaws are very active and merry; they have a play at ball, at which they are very expert; they invite the inhabitants of the neighboring villages to it.

---

[a] A Concise Natural History of East and West Florida, p. 79, New York, 1776

[b] The History of the American Indians, p. 399, London, 1775.

[c] Travels through that Part of North America formerly called Louisiana, by Mr. Bossu, Captain in the French Marines, translated from the French by John Reinhold Forster. v. 1, p. 304, London, 1771.

exciting them by many smart sayings. The men and women assemble in their best ornaments, they pass the whole day in singing and dancing; they even dance all the night to the sound of the drum and chickikois. The inhabitants of each village are distinguished by a separate fire, which they light in the middle of a great meadow. The next day is that appointed for the match; they agree upon a mark or aim about 60 yards off, and distinguished by two great poles, between which the ball is to pass. They generally count 16 till the game is up. There are forty on each side, and everyone has a battledoor in his hand, about $2\frac{1}{2}$ feet long, made very nearly in the form of ours, of walnut or chestnut wood, and covered with roe-skins.

An old man stands in the middle of the place appropriated to the play and throws up into the air a ball of roe-skins rolled about each other. The players then run, and endeavor to strike the ball with their battledoors; it is a pleasure to see them run naked, painted with various colors, having a tiger's tail fastened behind, and feathers on their heads and arms, which move as they run, and have a very odd effect; they push and throw each other down; he that has been expert enough to get the ball, sends it to his party; those of the opposite party run at him who has seized the ball, and send it back to their side; and thus they dispute it to each other reciprocally, with such ardour, that they sometimes dislocate their shoulders by it. The players are never displeased; some old men, who assist at the play, become mediators, and determine, that the play is only intended as a recreation, and not as an opportunity of quarreling. The wagers are considerable; the women bet among themselves.

When the players have given over, the women assemble among themselves to revenge their husbands who have lost the game. The battledoor they make use of differs from that of the men in being bent; they all are very active, and run against each other with extreme swiftness, pushing each other like the men, they having the same dress, except on those parts which modesty teaches them to cover. They only put rouge on their cheeks, and vermilion, instead of powder, in their hair.

## CHOCTAW.  Indian Territory.

### Catlin [a] says:

It is no uncommon occurrence for six or eight hundred or a thousand of these young men to engage in a game of ball, with five or six times that number of spectators, of men, women, and children, surrounding the ground and looking on. . . .

While at the Choctaw agency it was announced that there was to be a great ball play on a certain day, within a few miles, on which occasion I attended and made the three sketches which are hereto annexed (see plates XVII, XVIII, XIX); and also the following entry in my notebook, which I literally copy out:

"Monday afternoon at 3 o'clock, I rode out with Lieutenants S. and M., to a very pretty prairie, about 6 miles distant, to the ball-play-ground of the Choctaws, where we found several thousand Indians encamped. There were two points of timber, about half a mile apart, in which the two parties for the play, with their respective families and friends, were encamped; and lying between them, the prairie on which the game was to be played. My companions and myself, although we had been apprised, that to see the whole of a ball-play, we must remain on the ground all the night previous, had brought nothing to sleep upon, resolving to keep our eyes open, and see what transpired through the night. During the afternoon, we loitered about among the different tents and shanties of the two encampments, and afterwards, at sundown, witnessed the ceremony

---

[a] Letters and Notes on the Manners, Customs, and Condition of the North American Indians, v. 2, p. 123, London, 1841.

of measuring out the ground, and erecting the "byes," or goals which were to guide the play. Each party had their goal made with two upright posts, about 25 feet high and 6 feet apart, set firm in the ground, with a pole across at the top. These goals were about 40 or 50 rods apart; and at a point just halfway between, was another small stake, driven down, where the ball was to be thrown up at the firing of a gun, to be struggled for by the players. All this preparation was made by some old men, who were, it seems, selected to be the judges of the play, who drew a line from one bye to the other; to which directly came from the woods, on both sides, a great concourse of women and old men, boys and girls, and dogs and horses, where bets were to be made on the play. The betting was all done across this line, and seemed to be chiefly left to the women, who seemed to have martialled out a little of everything that their houses and their fields possessed. Goods and chattels—knives—dresses—blankets—pots and kettles—dogs and horses, and guns; and all were placed in the possession of stakeholders, who sat by them, and watched them on the ground all night, preparatory to the play.

FIG. 770. Choctaw ball player; Indian Territory; from Catlin.

The sticks with which this tribe play, are bent into an oblong hoop at the end, with a sort of slight web of small thongs tied across, to prevent the ball from passing through. The players hold one of these in each hand, and by leaping into the air, they catch the ball between the two nettings and throw it, without being allowed to strike it or catch it in their hands.

The mode in which these sticks are constructed and used will be seen in the portrait of Tullock-chish-ko (he who drinks the juice of the stone), the most distinguished ball-player of the Choctaw nation [figure 770], represented in his ball-play dress, with his ball-sticks in his hands. In every ball-play of these people, it is a rule of the play that no man shall wear moccasins on his feet, or any other dress than his breech-cloth around his waist, with a beautiful bead-belt, and a "tail," made of white horsehair or quills, and a "mane" on the neck, of horsehair dyed of various colors.

This game had been arranged and "made up," three or four months before the parties met to play it, and in the following manner:—The two champions who led the two parties, and had the alternate choosing of the players through the whole tribe, sent runners, with the ball-sticks most fantastically ornamented with ribbons and red paint, to be touched by each one of the chosen players; who thereby agreed to be on the spot at the appointed time and ready for the play. The ground having been all prepared and preliminaries of the game all settled, and the bettings all made, and goods all "staked," night came on without the appearance of any players on the ground. But soon after dark, a procession of lighted flambeaux was seen coming from each encampment, to the ground where the players assembled around their respective byes; and at the beat of the drums and chants of the women each party of players commenced the "ball-play dance" [plate XVII]. Each party danced for a quarter of an hour around

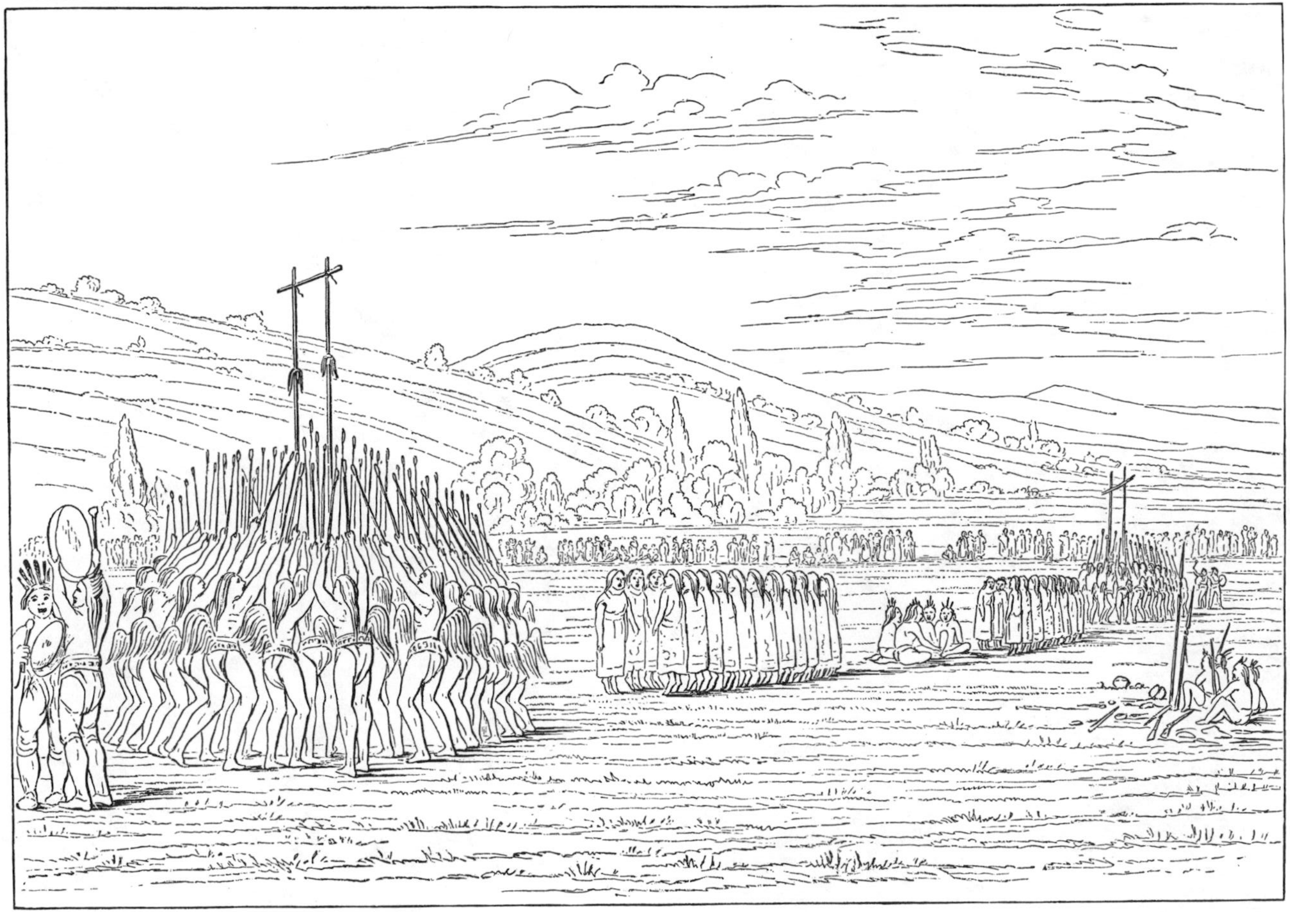

CHOCTAW INDIAN BALL-PLAY DANCE AROUND THE STAKES; INDIAN TERRITORY; FROM CATLIN

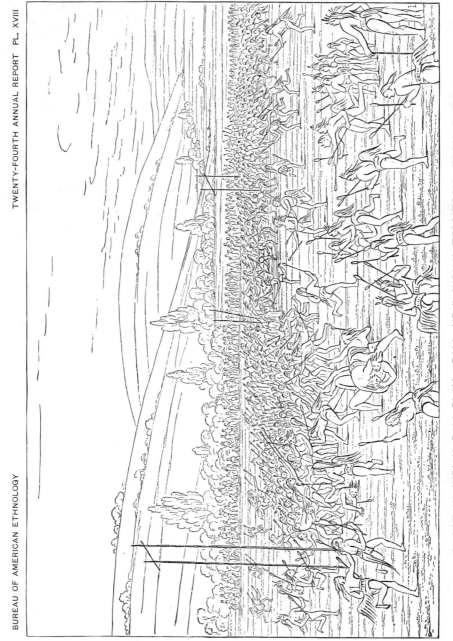

CHOCTAW INDIAN BALL-PLAY—"BALL UP;" INDIAN TERRITORY; FROM CATLIN

CHOCTAW INDIAN BALL-PLAY—"BALL DOWN;" INDIAN TERRITORY; FROM CATLIN

their respective byes, in their ball-play dress, rattling their ball-sticks together in the most violent manner, and all singing as loud as they could raise their voices; whilst the women of each party, who had their goods at stake, formed into two rows on the line between the two parties of players, and danced also, in an uniform step, and all their voices joined in chants to the Great Spirit; in which they were soliciting his favor in deciding the game to their advantage; and also encouraging the players to exert every power they possessed, in the struggle that was to ensue. In the meantime, four old medicine-men, who were to have the starting of the ball, and who were to be judges of the play, were seated at the point where the ball was to be started; and busily smoking to the Great Spirit for their success in judging rightly, and impartially, between the parties in so important an affair.

This dance was one of the most picturesque scenes imaginable, and was re-peated at intervals of every half hour during the night, and exactly in the same manner; so that the players were certainly awake all night, and arranged in their appropriate dress, prepared for the play which was to commence at 9 o'clock the next morning. In the morning, at the hour, the two parties and all their friends were drawn out and over the ground; when at length the game commenced, by the judges throwing up the ball at the firing of a gun; when an instant struggle ensued between the players, who were some six or seven hundred in numbers, and were mutually endeavoring to catch the ball in their sticks, and throw it home and between their respective stakes; which, whenever suc-cessfully done, counts 1 for game. In this game every player was dressed alike, that is, divested of all dress, except the girdle and the tail, which I have before described; and in these desperate struggles for the ball, when it is up ([plate xviii], where hundreds are running together and leaping, actually over each other's heads, and darting between their adversaries' legs, tripping and throwing, and foiling each other in every possible manner, every voice raised to the highest key, in shrill yelps and barks)! there are rapid successions of feats, and of incidents, that astonish and amuse far beyond the conception of anyone who has not had the singular good luck to witness them. In these struggles, every mode is used that can be devised, to oppose the progress of the foremost, who is likely to get the ball; and these obstructions often meet desperate individual resistance, which terminates in a violent scuffle, and some-times in fisticuffs; when their sticks are dropped, and the parties are unmolested, whilst they are settling it between themselves; unless it be by a general *stam-pedo*, to which they are subject who are down, if the ball happens to pass in their direction. Every weapon, by a rule of all ball-plays, is laid by in their respective encampments, and no man is allowed to go for one; so that the sudden broils that take place on the ground are presumed to be as suddenly settled without any probability of much personal injury; and no one is allowed to interfere in any way with the contentious individuals.

There are times when the ball gets to the ground [plate xix], and such a confused mass rushing together around it, and knocking their sticks together, without the possibility of anyone getting or seeing it, for the dust that they raise, that the spectator loses his strength, and everything else but his senses; when the condensed mass of ball-sticks, and shins, and bloody noses, is carried around the different parts of the ground, for a quarter of an hour at a time, without any one of the mass being able to see the ball; which they are often thus scuffling for, several minutes after it has been thrown off, and played over another part of the ground.

For each time that the ball was passed between the stakes of either party, one was counted for their game, and a halt of about one minute; when it was again started by the judges of the play, and a similar struggle ensued; and so on until the successful party arrived to 100, which was the limit of the game, and accomplished at an hour's sun, when they took the stakes; and then, by a previous agreement, produced a number of jugs of whisky, which gave all a wholesome drink, and sent them all off merry and in good humor, but not drunk.

CHOCTAW.   Indian Territory.   (Cat. no. 6904, United States National Museum.)

Ball stick, consisting of a stick with a round handle, the end shaved flat and curved to form a kind of spoon-shaped hoop, which is laced with thongs, one running horizontally across, and the other from end to end, the latter serving to lash the turned end of the stick to the handle; length, 30¾ inches.   Collected by Dr Edward Palmer in 1868.

——— Indian Territory.   (Cat. no. 21967, Free Museum of Science and Art, University of Pennsylvania.)

Pair of rackets (figure 771), one 30 and the other 28½ inches in length, consisting of a hickory sapling, cut flat at one end, which is curved around to form a spoon-like hoop, the turned-over end, which terminates in a small knob, being lashed to the handle.

Fig. 771.

FIG. 771.   Rackets; lengths, 30 and 28½ inches; Choctaw Indians, Indian Territory; cat. no. 21967, Free Museum of Science and Art, University of Pennsylvania.

FIG. 772.   Horse tail worn in ball game; length, 25 inches; Choctaw Indians, Indian Territory; cat. no. 18764, Free Museum of Science and Art, University of Pennsylvania.

Also, a tail (figure 772; cat. no. 18764), used in the ball game, consisting of a piece of a horse's tail attached to a strip of wood by a thong and loop at the top; length, 25 inches.   This was collected by Mr George E. Starr, who has furnished the following account of the game as witnessed by him at a place about 10 miles southwest of Red Oak, on the line of the Choctaw railroad, in Indian Territory:

Fig. 772.

The game was between Tobucksey and Sugarloaf counties of the Choctaw Nation.   On the night before, the players went into camp near the place agreed upon.   The season was the traditional one of the full moon of one of the summer months, and the company slept, without shelter, upon the ground.   On their arrival, the new players, who had never been allowed to play before on the county teams, dressed themselves in ball costume, and, while their elders were arranging rules, ran around making themselves conspicuous to their own side in the hope they would be chosen the next day. Before retiring, the managers on each side and the principal players assembled to make regulations to govern the play. They sat in a circle, and, no matter how heated the argument became, a speaker was never interrupted by one of the opposite side. There were about 250 Indians present, about evenly divided on each side, being chiefly men, with a few women and children. Each side brought with them a conjurer, or medicine man. At about 7 o'clock on the following morning the managers assembled for some purpose, after which they collected their sides, and took their places, a little apart, to prepare for the play. They stripped for the game, putting on nothing but a breech clout. Their heads were bare, with the hair cut short, without feathers. Their only ornament was a coon tail stuck up straight along the spine, or a horse tail falling on the breech clout behind. This was attached to the belt, a leather strap or revolver belt. The men carry their weapons to the ball game, but are not allowed to wear them in the field. The majority of the players were of splendid physique, spare and wiry. Several were, in part, of negro blood, and many showed the result of intermixture with the whites. The sides each numbered 30, of ages varying from 18 to 35. Among them were some that were crippled, the result, it may be, of former play.

The goal posts, which the ball must touch, were about 200 to 225 yards apart. They consisted of two trees, lashed together with ropes. They were about 8 inches in diameter, and were cut flat on one side, and were set at an angle so that they presented a face of about 12 inches to the ball. This must hit the post, to which it may be carried between a player's sticks, but it must bounce over a line in front of the posts, otherwise it does not count and is still in play.

The conjurers were conspicuous throughout the game. At the commencement, after the sides were chosen, all went to their goal posts. When within about 10 feet of the posts they broke their formation, and, uttering a cry, ran up to the posts, battering them with their ball sticks. They did this to scare the spirit of bad luck away.

Then they lined up in a kind of alley between the goals. Near the middle of the field, however, there were about eight men of each side ranged opposite to each other in a line running horizontally across the goal line. When all the others were ready, the men who were to take these places crossed the field. A medicine man put the ball in play, tossing it into the air. One of them had his face painted half red and half black, and carried in his hand a small branch of a tree resembling hickory. They both stood near their respective goals and sung and clapped their hands. The game lasted from 10 to 5, with an intermission for luncheon. The score is 12 goals, but if this number is not completed on either side, the one having the highest number is adjudged the winner. Butting with the head is prohibited, under a penalty of 5 goals.

The Indians bet everything they possess upon the game, even to their clothes and boots. The bets are made through stakeholders—four or five Indians—who constantly ride about on horseback. Whatever is bet is put with what is bet against it. If handkerchiefs, they are knotted together and thrown over the stakeholder's shoulder; if money, the sums are put together in his pocketbook. His memory is remarkable, and he never fails to turn over the stakes correctly. Much skill is shown during the game. In a scrimmage the ball is tossed backward through the bent legs of the players, and when the player secures it he utters a signal cry—hogle á! This is repeated by those along the line, and each grabs the opponent nearest to him and holds him. While they are wrestling the player with the ball tries to run with it, so that he can throw it and make a goal.

The ball, it should be observed, is about the size of a golf ball, made of rags and covered with white buckskin. Several are provided, as they are frequently lost in the tall grass. The players ón the side with the wind sometimes substitute a ball with a long tail and a loose cover that comes off during the play. The tail then impedes their opponents in throwing it against the wind. The women are extremely active in aiding their side. They are not permitted to touch the ball sticks, but they are constantly running about and giving hot coffee to the men. In one hand they carry a cup of coffee and in the other a quirt with which they whip the players when they think they are not playing hard enough. At times a player will get a woman to give him a pin, with which he will scarify his leg, making from three to five scratches from near the ankle to the middle of the calf, until the blood comes. This, they say, prevents cramps.

When the players return to the game after lunch hour they place their ball sticks in rows opposite each other in the middle of the field, where they are counted by the umpire or the leaders on each side. This is done to see that no more are playing than started in the game. The spectators cry out and encourage the sides. When a goal is made there is a shout. The most exciting point in a close game is when the last goal is neared. Then the play becomes very fast and the rules are not strictly observed. A goal may be made in a few moments or the contest may last for an hour. In wrestling, the players seize each other by the belts, dropping the ball sticks. With the exception of the prohibited butting almost everything is permitted. At the present game five men were crippled, of whom two died. The injuries inflicted upon a man during a game are frequently avenged by his relatives. The result of the game described was a victory for Tobucksey county. The conjurer on the Sugarloaf side was said to have sent his men to the creek to bathe in the morning, which weakened them. They were penalized five goals for butting at the end, and so lost the game. There was no celebration afterwards. All were tired out and went home quietly to their mud-chinked log cabins at the close of the day.

CHOCTAW.   Mandeville, Louisiana.   (Cat. no. 38476, Free Museum of
    Science and Art, University of Pennsylvania.)
Racket (figure 773), one of pair, consisting of a sapling, the end cut
    thin and turned over to form a kind of spoon, which is crossed
    and tied to the handle with cotton cord; length, 36½ inches.

FIG. 773.   Racket; length, 36¼ inches; Choctaw Indians, Louisiana; cat. no. 38476, Free Museum
of Science and Art, University of Pennsylvania.

Collected by the writer in 1901. The rackets are called kabucha. The ball game is now seldom or never played by these Indians. The game was borrowed from the Indians by the whites in Louisiana, and is still played under the name of raquette.

While in New Orleans in the summer of 1901 I was told that the old game of raquette was still played on Sunday afternoons on a vacant lot east of the town. The players, some hundreds of French-speaking negroes, had assembled in a level, uninclosed field. The majority were armed with rackets (figure 774), each consisting of a piece of hickory bent over at one end to form a spoon, which was netted with a thong, precisely like those used by the Choctaw. A racket was carried in each hand, and the ball was picked up and thrown with them in the same way as in the Indian game. The players appeared to own their own rackets, and I purchased a pair without difficulty. At the same time there was an old man who had a large number of rackets strung on a cord, which he said were reserved for the use of the clubs to which they belonged.

FIG. 774. Rackets; lengths, 21 and 24 inches; negroes, New Orleans; cat. no. 38480, Free Museum of Science and Art, University of Pennsylvania.

The goals or bases were two tall poles about 600 feet apart, having a strip of tin, about a foot wide and 10 feet long, fastened on the inner side some distance above the ground. These goals, called plats, were painted, one red with a small double ring of white near the top, the other blue with a black ring. Midway in a straight line between was a small peg to mark the center of the field, where the ball was first thrown. The players belonged to two opposing clubs, the Bayous and La Villes. Their colors agreed with those of the goals. Each side was led by a captain, who directed the play. The contest was for a flag, for which three successive games were played. The game appeared to be open, free for all, without reference to number; but in more formal matches the sides are equalized and regulated. The ball was put in play at the center flag, being tossed high in the air, and caught on the uplifted ball sticks. Then there was a wild rush across the field, the object being to secure and carry the ball and toss it against the tin plate, making a plat. The game was played with much vigor and no little violence. A blow across the shins with a racket is permissible, and broken heads are not uncommon. Play usually continues until dark, and, at the close, the winners sing Creole songs, reminding one of the custom at the close of the Choctaw game. Raquette was formerly much played by the Creoles, and the present negro clubs perpetuate the names of the opposing clubs of old Creole days.

MUSKOGEE. Eufaula, Indian Territory. (Cat. no. 38065, Free Museum of Science and Art, University of Pennsylvania.)
Pair of rackets (figure 775), 37¼ inches in length, each made of a sapling, cut thin at the end, which is curved over to form a

kind of scoop, the cut end being bound to the body of the stick by thongs. The spoon at the end is crossed by two twisted thongs, with a longitudinal thong running through the middle. Made by Matawa Karso and collected by Mr W. H. Ward in 1891.

According to Tuggle,[a] the Creeks and Seminoles have stories of ball games by birds against fourfooted animals. In one story the bat is rejected by both sides, but is finally accepted by the four-footed animals on account of his having teeth, and enables them to win the victory from the birds.

FIG. 775.   Rackets; lengths, 37¼ inches; Muskogee Indians, Indian Territory; cat. no. 38065, Free Museum of Science and Art, University of Pennsylvania.

MUSKOGEE.   Georgia.

Réné Laudonnière [b] wrote as follows in 1562:

They play at ball in this manner: they set up a tree in the midst of a place which is 8 or 9 fathoms high, in the top whereof there is set a square mat made of reeds or bulrushes, which whosoever hitteth in playing thereat, winneth the game.

John Bartram [c] says:

The ball play is esteemed the most noble and manly exercise; this game is exhibited in an extensive level plain, usually contiguous to the town; the inhabitants of one town play against another, in consequence of a challenge, when the youth of both sexes are often engaged and sometimes stake their whole substance. Here they perform amazing feats of strength and agility; the game principally consists in taking and carrying off the ball from the opposite party, after being hurled into the air, midway between two high pillars, which are the goals, and the party who bears off the ball to their pillar wins the game; each person having a racquet, or hurl, which is an implement of a very curious construction, somewhat resembling a ladle or little hoop-net, with a handle near 3 feet in length, the hoop and handle of wood, and the netting of thongs of rawhide, or tendons of an animal.

The foot-ball is likewise a favorite, manly diversion with them. Feasting and dancing in the square at evening ends all their games.

Maj. Caleb Swan [d] says:

Their ball-plays are manly and require astonishing exertion, but white men have been found to excel the best of them at that exercise; they therefore seldom or never admit a white man into the ball-ground. Legs and arms have often

---

[a] Quoted by Mooney in Myths of the Cherokee. Nineteenth Annual Report of the Bureau of American Ethnology, pt. 1, p. 454, 1900.

[b] Hakluyt's Voyages, v. 13, p. 413, Edinburgh, 1889.

[c] Travels through North and South Carolina, Georgia, East and West Florida, p. 508, Philadelphia, 1791.

[d] Schoolcraft, Information respecting the History, Condition, and Prospects of the Indian Tribes of the United States, pt. 5, p. 277, Philadelphia, 1856.

been broken in their ball-plays, but no resentments follow an accident of this kind.

The women and men both attend them in large numbers, as a kind of gala; and bets often run as high as a good horse or an equivalent of skins.

J. M. Stanley,[a] in his Catalogue of Portraits of North American Indians, describes under no. 16, Tah-Coo-Sah Fixico, or Billy Hardjo, chief of one of the Creek towns:

The dress in which he is painted is that of a ball-player as they at first appear upon the grounds. During the play they divest themselves of all their ornaments, which are usually displayed on these occasions, for the purpose of betting on the results of the play; such is their passion for betting that the opposing parties frequently bet from five hundred to a thousand dollars on a single game.

Col. Marinus Willett [b] says:

This day I crossed the Toloposa and went 5 miles to see a most superb ball play. There were about eighty players on a side. The men, women, and children, from the neighboring towns, were assembled upon this occasion. Their appearance was splendid; all the paths leading to the place were filled with people; some on foot, some on horseback. The play was conducted with as much order and decorum as the nature of things would admit of. The play is set on foot by one town sending a challenge to another; if the challenge be accepted, the time and place are fixed on, and the whole night before the play is employed by the parties in dancing, and some other ceremonious preparations. On the morning of the play, the players on both sides paint and decorate themselves, in the same manner as when they are going to war. Thus decorated, and stripped of all such clothing as would encumber them, they set out for the appointed field. The time of their arrival is so contrived, that the parties arrive near the field at the same time; and when they get within about half a mile, in a direction opposite to each other, you hear the sound of the war song and the yell; when, presently, the parties appear in full trot, as if fiercely about to encounter in fight. In this manner they meet and soon become intermingled together, dancing while the noise continues. Silence then succeeds; each player places himself opposite to his antagonist. The rackets which they use are then laid against each other, in the center of the ground appointed for the game. They then proceed to measure a distance of 300 yards, 150 each way, from the center, where they erect two poles, through which the ball must pass, to count 1. The play is commenced by the balls being thrown up in the air, from the center; every player then, with his rackets, of which each has two, endeavors to catch the ball, and throw it between the poles; each side laboring to throw it between the poles towards their own towns; and every time this can be accomplished, it counts 1. The game is usually from 12 to 20. This was lost by the challengers. Large bets are made upon these occasions; and great strength, agility, and dexterity are displayed. The whole of the present exhibition was grand and well conducted. It sometimes happens that the inhabitants of a town game away at these plays all their clothes, ornaments, and horses. Throughout the whole of the game the women are constantly on the alert, with bottles and gourds filled with drink, watching every opportunity to supply the players.

---

[a] Smithsonian Miscellaneous Collections, v. 2, p. 13, 1862.
[b] A Narrative of the Military Actions of Colonel Marinus Willett, p. 108, New York, 1831.

SEMINOLE.   Florida.   (Cat. no. 18497, 19841, Free Museum of Science and Art, University of Pennsylvania.)

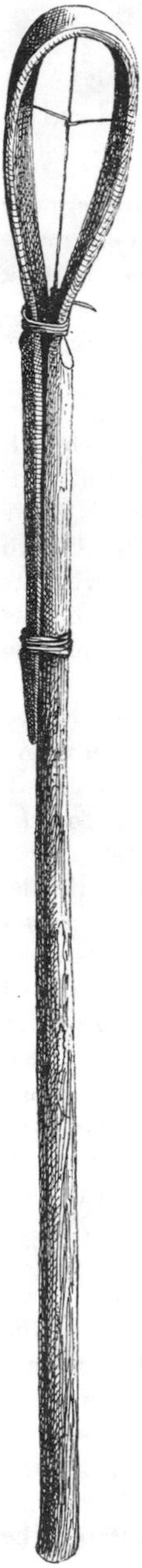

Rackets and ball, the rackets (figure 777) saplings bent to form a scoop-shaped hoop, the ends lashed together for a handle, the hoop crossed by two thongs tied at right angles: the ball (figure 776), of two colors, one hemisphere light, the other dark, made of buckskin, with median seam; diameter, 2¾ inches.

Fig. 776.

The rackets were collected by Mr Henry G. Bryant and the ball by Lieut. Hugh L. Willoughby in 1896. Mr Bryant gives the name of the rackets as tokonhay.

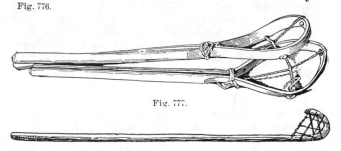

Fig. 777.

Fig. 779.

FIG. 776.  Ball; diameter, 2¾ inches; Seminole Indians, Florida; cat. no. 19841, Free Museum of Science and Art, University of Pennsylvania.
FIG. 777.  Rackets; length, 13 inches; Seminole Indians, Florida; cat. no. 18497, Free Museum of Science and Art, University of Pennsylvania.
FIG. 778.  Racket; length, 33 inches; Seminole Indians, Indian Territory; cat. no. $\frac{50}{2288}$, American Museum of Natural History.
FIG. 779.  Ball racket; length, 36 inches; Nishinam Indians, California; from sketch by Dr J. W. Hudson.

———— Indian Territory.   (Cat. no. $\frac{50}{2288}$, American Museum of Natural History.)

Ball stick (figure 778), made of hickory, one end cut flat and turned over to form a spoon-shaped receptacle, which is crossed by two thongs at right angles; length, 33 inches.   Collected by Dr William Jones in 1901.

Fig. 778.

PUJUNAN STOCK

NISHINAM.   Mokelumne river, 12 miles south of Placerville, California.

Dr J. W. Hudson describes the following game under name of patai kato:

Pä'-tai is the general name for the flail basket used in harvesting seed; ka-tüm', sling.  The implements are a ball of buckskin, 3 inches in diameter, filled with deer hair, called pâs'-ko, and a single club [figure 779], ku-nûn'-teä, 3 feet in length, with its recurved lower end netted. There are four players to a side, each side having its captain. The ball is placed in the center of the field, 20 feet distant from the captains. The umpire calls "Ha!" for the start. The goals, 500 yards apart, consist of wooden arches, 4 feet apart at bottom and 6 feet high.

No interference is permitted, under penalty of individual stakes.

### SALISHAN STOCK

Skokomish. British Columbia.

Mr Charles Hill-Tout [a] mentions two kinds of ball games, kekqua and tcquila.

The former was a kind of lacrosse, and the ball was caught and thrown with an instrument similar to the lacrosse stick.

Thompson Indians (Ntlakyapamuk). British Columbia.

James Teit [b] says:

The other game was similar to that of "lacrosse." There were two sides and a goal for each, marked by stones or wooden pegs, or by long stakes half the

Fig. 780a.

height of a man or more. The ball was like that used in the other game. It was placed in the middle of the ground, between the two goals, and the object of either party was to drive it through the other's goal. This was done by lifting and throwing it with the toe, or by striking it with the sticks which the players held in their hands. These sticks were about 3 feet long, and had a very crooked head [figure 780a], so that the players could catch the ball with them and throw it from them toward the goal of the enemy. Many men ran with the ball held in the crook of the stick until stopped by an opponent, when they threw

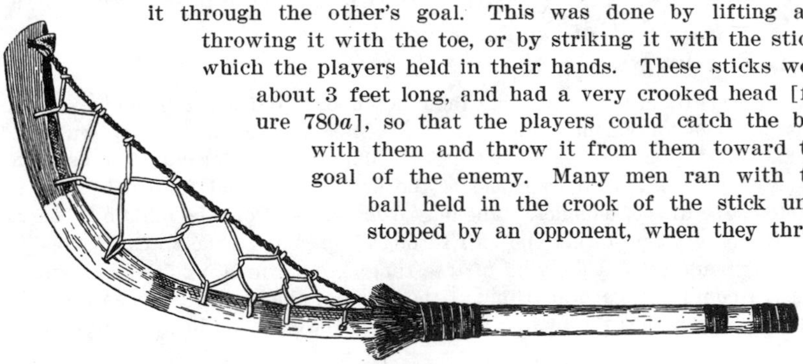

Fig. 780b.

FIG. 780 a, b. Ball sticks; lengths, 23½ and 23 inches; Thompson Indians, British Columbia; cat. no. $\frac{16}{2}\frac{9}{8}\frac{9}{7}$, $\frac{16}{2}\frac{9}{8}\frac{9}{7}$, American Museum of Natural History.

the ball toward the intended goal. Others preferred, if they had a chance, to lift the ball with the toe, and before it fell strike or catch it with their stick. One man always tried to take the ball from his opponent with his stick.

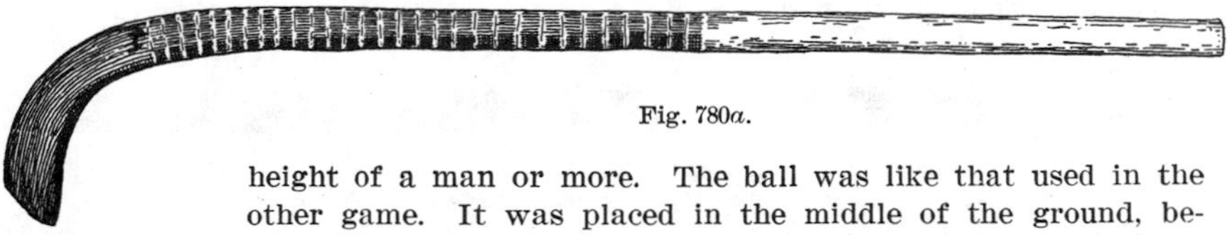

---

[a] Notes on the Sk'qō'mic of British Columbia. Report of the Seventieth Meeting of the British Association for the Advancement of Science, p. 488, London, 1900.

[b] The Thompson Indians of British Columbia. Memoirs of the American Museum of Natural History, whole series, v. 2, p. 277, New York, 1900.

When bending the end of the stick to the desired crook, bark string was used, connecting the latter to the straight part of the stick. Some Indians played with the strings still attached, thinking to get a better hold of the ball, but this was considered unfair. In some games all the players used crooks with nets similar to those of lacrosse sticks [figure 780b]. Often a guard stick was used to protect the ball from the players of the opposite party [figure 781]. Any person who touched the ball with his hands while playing went immediately out of the game. Sometimes, to the amusement of the men, the women were persuaded to play the game. Within the last few years this game has fallen altogether into disuse.

The Lower Thompsons had a ball game in which the ball was thrown up by one player. The player who caught it ran with it until overtaken by another player, who in his turn ran with it until a certain goal was reached. . . .

Another boys' game was to take a pebble about 3 inches in diameter and covered with skin, and roll it down a hillside. Other players with scoop-nets, about 1 foot long (including the handle), stood at the bottom, and each tried to catch the bounding ball as it reached him. The nets were made of a pliable stick or wand, bent over the top so as to form a circle, which was filled with a netting of bark twine. A game similar to the last was played with a skin-covered ball, to which a short toggle was attached [figure 782a]. The players held a kind of hoop with handle [figure 782 b, c], by means of which they tried to catch the ball by its toggle.

FIG. 781. Stick for protecting ball; length, 28¼ inches; Thompson Indians (Ntlakyapamuk), British Columbia; cat. no. ₄₈₈₇, American Museum of Natural History.

THOMPSON INDIANS (NTLAKYAPAMUK). Thompson and Fraser rivers, British Columbia.

Mr Charles Hill-Tout [a] says:

They were fond of games, like their neighbors, and utilized the level, grassy river benches for various games of ball. One of these games, suk'-kul-lila'-ka, was not unlike our own game of football. The players were divided, as with us, into two groups, and at each end of the field was a goal formed by two poles planted several feet asunder. The play commenced from the middle of the field, and the object was to get the ball through the goal of their adversaries. The ball was made from some kind of tree fungus, cut round, and covered with elk-hide. I could not learn anything of the rules of the game; nor was my informant certain whether the feet or hands, or both, were used in propelling the ball.

SIOUAN STOCK

ASSINIBOIN. Fort Union, Montana.

In a report to Isaac I. Stevens, governor of Washington Territory, on the Indian tribes of the upper Missouri, by Edwin T. Denig, a manuscript in the library of the Bureau of American Ethnology, after a description of the game of shinny, occurs this passage:

Another mode of playing the game is by catching the ball in a network attached to the end of the stick, over a small hoop a little larger than the ball.

[a] Notes on the N'tlapamuq of British Columbia. Report of the Sixty-ninth Meeting of the British Association for the Advancement of Science, p. 507, London, 1900.

They catch it in this net as it flies through the air and throw it from one to the other towards either goal. The man who catches can run with the ball toward the limit until he is overtaken by one on the other side, when he throws it as far as he can on its way, which is continued by the others.

CATAWBA.  South Carolina.

Mrs R. E. Dunbar, of Leslie, York county, South Carolina, informs the writer [a] that the Catawba do not play any of their old games. They used to play a game with two sticks and a ball. The sticks were hollowed out like a large wooden spoon. The ball must not touch the hand or the ground, but must be thrown and kept in the air with the sticks. Any number in excess of two could play. This game was called wahumwah.

Fig. 782a.          Fig. 782b.          Fig. 782c.

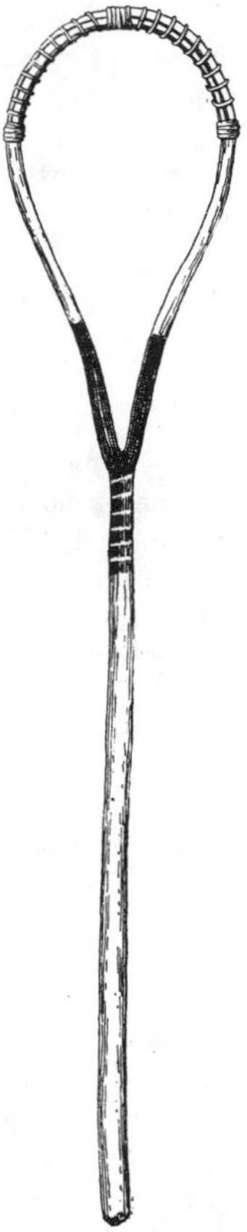

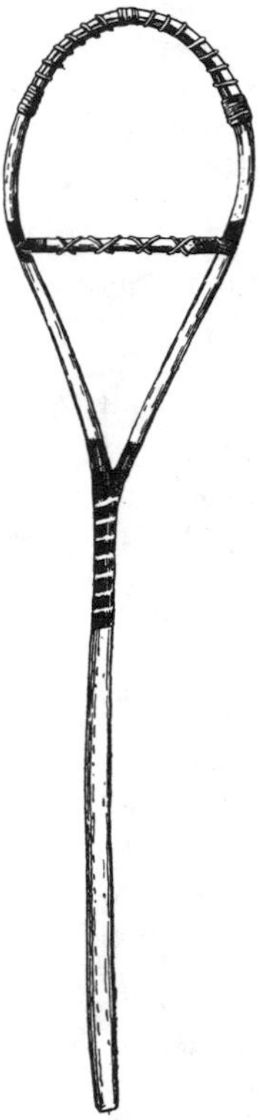

FIG. 782 a, b, c.  Balls and catching hoops; lengths of hoops, 22¼ and 20½ inches; Thompson Indians (Ntlakyapamuk), British Columbia; cat. no. $\frac{16}{4870}$, $\frac{16}{4869}$, $\frac{16}{4868}$, American Museum of Natural History.

DAKOTA (SANTEE).  Minnesota.
Dr Walter J. Hoffman [b] wrote:

The game played by the Dakota Indians of the upper Missouri was probably learned from the Ojibwa, as these two tribes have been upon amicable terms for many years; the ball sticks are identical in construction, and the game is played in the same manner. Sometimes, however, the goals at either end of the ground consist of two heaps of blankets about 20 feet apart, between which the ball is passed.

[a] In a letter, dated September 1, 1901.
[b] Remarks on Ojibwa Ball Play.  The American Anthropologist, v. 3, p. 135, 1890.

When the Dakotas play a game, the village is equally divided into sides. A player offers as a wager some article of clothing, a robe, or a blanket, when an opponent lays down an object of equal value. This parcel is laid aside and the next two deposit their stakes, and so on until all have concluded. The game then begins, two of the three innings deciding the issue.

When the women play against the men, five of the women are matched against one of the latter. A mixed game of this kind is very amusing. The fact that among the Dakota women are allowed to participate in the game is considered excellent evidence that the game is a borrowed one. Among most other tribes women are not even allowed to touch a ball stick.

The players frequently hang to the belt the tail of a deer, antelope, or some other fleet animal, or the wings of swift-flying birds, with the idea that through these they are endowed with the swiftness of the animal. There are, however, no special preparations preceding a game as feasting or fasting, dancing, etc.— additional evidence that the game is less regarded among this people.

Mr Philander Prescott [a] gives the following account of the ball game in Schoolcraft:

Ball plays are played by both men and women, and heavy bets depend on the issue. I believe there is but one kind of ball playing. One village plays against another. The boundaries are near a half mile. The ball is started from the middle. Each party strives to get the ball over the respective boundaries; for instance, the boundaries are east and west; one party or village will try to carry the ball west and the other east. If a village or party gets the ball over the eastern boundary, they change sides, and the next time they have to try and get it over the western boundary; so, if the same party propels it over the western boundary, they win one game; and another bet is played for. The ball is carved and thrown in a stick about 2 or 3 feet long, with a little circle at the end to assist in picking it up. This hoop has some buckskin cords across to keep the ball in. I have known an Indian to throw the ball over the boundaries in three throws. When it is seen flying through the air, there is a great shout and hurra by the spectators. They sometimes pick up the ball, and run over the lines without being overtaken by any of the opposite party. Then a great shout is raised again, to urge on the players. Horses, guns, kettles, blankets, wampum, calico, beads, etc., are bet. This game is very laborious and occasionally the players receive some hard blows, either from the club or ball. I once saw a man almost killed with the ball. He stood in front of the player that was going to throw the ball, who threw with great force and aimed too low. The ball struck the other in the side, and knocked him senseless for some time. As to the effects, I do not perceive that any serious evil results, if we except the gambling. Ball is generally played in May and June, and in winter.

Schoolcraft [b] says:

Ball playing.—This game is played by the northwestern Indians in the winter season, after the winter hunts are over, and during summer, when, the game being unfit to kill, they amuse themselves with athletic sports, games of chance, dances, and war. The game is played by two parties, not necessarily equally divided by numbers, but usually one village against another, or one large village may challenge two or three smaller ones to the combat. When a challenge is accepted, a day is appointed to play the game; ball-bats are made, and each party

[a] Information respecting the History, Condition, and Prospects of the Indian Tribes of the United States, pt. 4, p. 64, Philadelphia, 1856.
[b] Ibid., pt. 2, p. 78, 1852.

assembles its whole force of old men, young men, and boys. The women never play in the same game with the men. Heavy bets are made by individuals of the opposite sides. Horses, guns, blankets, buffalo-robes, kettles, and trinkets are freely staked on the result of the game. When the parties are assembled on the ground, two stakes are placed about a quarter of a mile apart, and the game commences midway between them; the object of each party being to get the ball beyond the limits of its opponents. The game commences by one of the old men throwing the ball in the air, when all rush forward to catch it in their ball-bats before or after it falls to the ground. The one who catches it throws it in the direction of the goal of the opposing party, when, if it be caught by one of the same side, it is continued in that direction, and so on until it is thrown beyond the limits; but if caught by an opponent, it is thrown back in the opposite direction. In this way, the ball is often kept all day between the two boundaries, neither party being able to get it beyond the limit of the other. When

FIG. 783. Santee Dakota Indian ball-play on the ice, Minnesota; from Schoolcraft.

one has caught the ball, he has the right, before throwing it, to run towards the limits until he is overtaken by the other party, when, being compelled to throw it, he endeavors to send it in the direction of some of his own party, to be caught by some one of them, who continues sending it in the same direction.

Figure 783 represents a ball play on the ice. The young man has the ball in his ball-bat, and is running with it toward the limits of the other side, pursued by all the other players.

Fig. 784 represents a ball play on the prairies in summer. The ball is on the ground and all are rushing forward to catch it with their ball-bats, not being allowed to touch it with their hands.

The ball is carved from a knot, or made of baked clay covered with rawhide of the deer. The ball-bat . . . is from 3 to 4 feet long; one end bent up in a circular form of about 4 inches in diameter, in which is a net-work made of rawhide or sinews of the deer or buffalo.

E. D. Neill [a] says:

The favorite and most exciting game of the Dakota is ball playing. It appears to be nothing more than a game which was often played by the writer in school-boy days and which was called shinny. A smooth place is chosen on the prairie or frozen river or lake. Each player has a stick 3 or 4 feet long and crooked at the lower end, with deer strings tied across, forming a sort of pocket. The ball is made with a rounded knot of wood, or clay covered with hide, and is supposed to possess supernatural qualities. Stakes are set at a distance of a quarter or a half a mile, as bounds. Two parties are then formed, and, the ball being thrown up in the center, the contest is for one party to carry the ball from the other beyond one of the bounds. Two or three hundred men are sometimes engaged at once. On a summer's day, to see them rushing to and fro, painted in divers colors, with no article of apparel, with feathers in their heads, bells

FIG. 784.   Santee Dakota Indian ball-play on the prairie, Minnesota; from Schoolcraft.

around their wrists, and fox and wolf tails dangling behind, is a wild and noisy spectacle. The eyewitnesses among the Indians become more interested in the success of one or the other of the parties than any crowd at a horse race, and frequently stake their last piece of property on the issue of the game.

DAKOTA (YANKTONAI). Devils lake, North Dakota. (Cat. no. 60362, 60395, Field Columbian Museum.)

Stick of hickory terminating in a ring which supports a buckskin thong net, and a buckskin ball filled with deer hair. These specimens were collected in 1900 by Dr George A. Dorsey, who gives the name of the stick as chianyankapi, and that of the ball as tahpa.

[a] Dakota Land and Dakota Life. Collections of the Minnesota Historical Society, v. 1, p. 281, St Paul, 1872.

Iowa.   Missouri.

George Catlin [a] says:

Two byes, or goals, are established, at three or four hundred yards from each other, by erecting two poles in the ground for each, 4 or 5 feet apart, between which it is the strife of either party to force the ball (it having been thrown up at a point halfway between) by catching it in a little hoop, or racket, at the end of a stick, 3 feet in length, held in both hands as they run, throwing the ball an immense distance when they get it in the stick.   The game is always played over an extensive prairie or meadow.

Catlin says also:

Previous to commencing on the exciting game of ball, as the goods of all playing are more or less at stake, each party must needs invoke the aid of supernatural influence to their respective sides ; and for this purpose they give a very pretty dance, in which, as in the Scalp Dance, the women take a part, giving neat and curious effect to the scene.   In most of the tribes this dance is given at intervals of every half hour or so, during the night previous to the play, preparing the minds and bodies of the players for this exciting scene, upon which they enter in the morning with empty stomachs and decide before they leave the ground to eat.

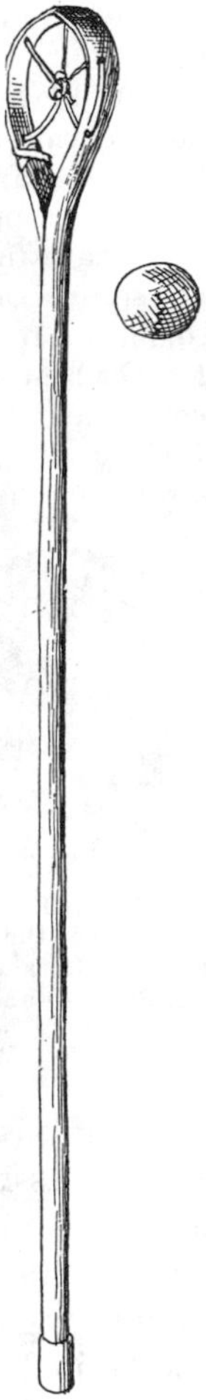

Oto.   Oklahoma.   (Cat. no. 71404, Field Columbian Museum.)

Ball covered with buckskin (figure 785), $2\frac{1}{4}$ inches in diameter, and racket, a stick 40 inches in length with end bent to form a spoon-shaped hook, which is laced with buckskin.   Collected in 1902 by Dr George A. Dorsey.

Winnebago.   Wisconsin.   (Cat. no. 22159, 22160, Free Museum of Science and Art, University of Pennsylvania.)

Wooden ball (figure 786), 3 inches in diameter, perforated with six holes at right angles, and a racket (figure 787), length $26\frac{1}{2}$ inches, consisting of a sapling cut and bent at the striking end to form a hoop, which is laced with a throng and a cord crossing at right angles.   Collected by Mr T. R. Roddy.

The ball stick is called cha-pa-nun-a.   The ball, wa-ki-hki, is perforated with holes in order to sound when flying through the air.

FIG. 785.   Ball and racket; diameter of ball, $2\frac{1}{4}$ inches; length of racket, 40 inches; Oto Indians, Oklahoma, cat. no. 71404, Field Columbian Museum.

---

[a] The George Catlin Indian Gallery, p. 151, 1887.   Annual Report of the Smithsonian Institution for 1885, 1887.

Caleb Atwater [a] (1829) says:

They also play ball, in which sport great numbers engage, on each side, and the spectators bet largely on each side. The articles played for are placed in view of those who play the game. These consist of beads, paints, jewels, etc. This game is very animated and excites great interest.

In regard to the Winnebago in Wisconsin, Mr Reuben G. Thwaites [b] says:

The vigorous game of lacrosse—nowadays familiar to patrons of state and county fairs of this section, at which professional bands of Chippewas exhibit their skill—was, in earlier days, much played by the Winnebagoes. It was usually played at La Crosse—Prairie la Crosse deriving its name from this fact—during the general rendezvous after the winter's hunt. The Winnebagoes having always clung to the water-courses and heavy timber, during their winter's trapping and hunting, would float down the rivers to La Crosse, and there have their feasts and lacrosse games, meet the traders, and indulge in a big spree. Occasionally they played lacrosse in their villages, but this was not common. It was considered to be more especially a spring festival game. I never hear, nowadays, of the Wisconsin Winnebagoes playing it, and in fact I never saw it in this state, but when I was at the mission on Turkey river I frequently saw the Indians there indulge in it. . . . These games were always for heavy stakes in goods.

Fig. 787.

Fig. 786.

FIG. 786. Ball; diameter, 3 inches; Winnebago Indians, Wisconsin; cat. no. 22159, Free Museum of Science and Art, University of Pennsylvania.

FIG. 787. Racket; length, 26½ inches; Winnebago Indians, Wisconsin; cat. no. 22160, Free Museum of Science and Art, University of Pennsylvania.

## SHINNY

Shinny is especially a woman's game, but it is also played by men alone (Assiniboin, Yankton, Mohave, Walapai), by men and women alone (Sauk and Foxes, Tewa, Tigua), by men and women together (Sauk and Foxes, Assiniboin), by men against women (Crows). It may be regarded as practically universal among the tribes throughout the United States. As in racket, the ball may not be touched with the hand, but is both batted and kicked with the foot. A single bat is ordinarily used, but the Makah have two, one for striking and the other for carrying the ball. The rackets are invariably curved, and usually expanded at the striking end. In some instances they are painted or carved.

[a] The Indians of the Northwest, p. 118, Columbus, 1850.
[b] The Wisconsin Winnebagoes. Collections of the State Historical Society of Wisconsin, v. 12, p. 426, Madison, 1892.

The ball is either of wood, commonly a knot, or of buckskin. The wooden ball occurs chiefly on the Pacific coast and in the Southwest. The buckskin ball is generally used by the Eastern and Plains tribes, and is commonly flattened, with a median seam, the opposite sides being painted sometimes with different colors. The Navaho use a bag-shaped ball. The goals consist of two posts or stakes at the ends of the field, or two blankets spread side by side on the ground (Crows); again a single post is used (Menominee, Shuswap, Omaha) or lines drawn at the ends of the field over which the ball must be forced (Navaho, Eskimo, Omaha, Makah). The distance of the goals is not recorded, except among the Miwok (200 yards), the Omaha (300 yards). Mono (1,400 yards and return), and the Makah (200 yards).

In a California form of the game the players were lined up along the course and struck their ball along the line, the game corresponding with one in which the ball was kicked, struck, or tossed, played by the same tribe.

The game of shinny is frequently referred to in the myths. It was commonly played without any particular ceremony. Among the Makah it was played at the time of the capture of a whale, the ball being made from a soft bone of that animal. The shinny stick may be regarded as analogous to the club of the War Gods.

ALGONQUIAN STOCK

ARAPAHO. Cheyenne and Arapaho reservation, Oklahoma.

Mr James Mooney [a] describes the woman's game of gugahawat, or shinny, played with curved sticks and a ball like a baseball (figure 788), called gaa-wă′ha, made of buffalo hair and covered with buckskin.

Two stakes are set up as goals at either end of the ground, and the object of each party is to drive the ball through the goals of the other. Each inning is a game.

Mr Mooney gives the Cheyenne name of this game as ohonistuts.

FIG. 788. Shinny ball and stick; Arapaho Indians, Oklahoma; from Mooney.

[a] The Ghost-dance Religion. Fourteenth Annual Report of the Bureau of Ethnology, pt. 2, p. 964, 1896.

ARAPAHO.   Wind River reservation, Wyoming.   (Cat. no. 36974, Free
    Museum of Science and Art, University of Pennsylvania.)
Ball covered with buckskin (figure 789), flattened, with median seam,
    one face painted with a cross, dividing it into quarters, the
    other with a similar cross, the quarters each containing two dots,
    with a T-shaped mark between; diameter, 4 inches.   Three
    metal dangles are attached to the center of one face.   There is
    a thong loop for suspension.   Collected by the writer in 1900.

———— Wind River reservation, Wyoming.   (Free Museum of Science
    and Art, University of Pennsylvania.)
Cat. no. 36976.   Shinny stick (figure 791), besh, curved at the end
    and painted red and blue; length, 40 inches.   Ball (figure 790)
    covered with buckskin, with median seam, one face painted red
    and one green; diameter, 3½ inches.

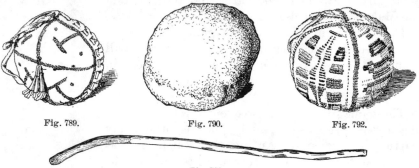

Fig. 789.             Fig. 790.             Fig. 792.

Fig. 791.

FIG. 789.   Shinny ball; diameter, 4 inches; Arapaho Indians, Wind River reservation, Wyoming;
    cat. no. 36974, Free Museum of Science and Art, University of Pennsylvania.
FIG. 790.   Shinny ball; diameter, 3½ inches; Arapaho Indians, Wind River reservation, Wyoming;
    cat. no. 36976, Free Museum of Science and Art, University of Pennsylvania.
FIG. 791.   Shinny stick; length, 40 inches; Arapaho Indians, Wind River reservation, Wyoming;
    cat. no. 36976, Free Museum of Science and Art, University of Pennsylvania.
FIG. 792.   Shinny ball; diameter, 3½ inches; Arapaho Indians, Wyoming; cat. no. 200764, United
    States National Museum.

Cat. no. 36975.   Shinny stick, besh, curved at the end and painted
    with bands of red and green; length, 34 inches.
These were collected by the writer in 1900.

———— Wyoming.   (United States National Museum.)
Cat. no. 200764.   Beaded ball (figure 792), made of buckskin, slightly
    flattened, with buckskin thong for suspension; diameter, 3½
    inches.   The ball is completely covered with a ground of white
    glass beads divided by two intersecting lines of red beads into
    four segments, each of which contains a design in colored beads,
    probably representing conventionalized animal figures.   The de-
    signs on opposite sides are alike.

Cat. no. 200765. Beaded ball, similar to the preceding, but only partially covered with beads. Two intersecting lines of white and red beads divide the ball into four segments, each of which contains a rectangular beaded design, two opposite ones alike of white and red beads with green center, and two of dark blue and white with green center. It has a loop for suspension.

Cat. no. 200763. Beaded ball, entirely covered with beadwork. Two bands of white beads surround the ball at right angles, forming four segments, two on opposite sides composed of beads of different colors—pink, white, blue, yellow, red, and green—and two, also opposite, of blue beads with a white middle line and colored figures on the blue ground.

The three preceding balls belong to the E. Granier collection.

Fig. 793. Shinny ball: diameter, 4 inches; Cheyenne Indians, Oklahoma: cat. no. 166027, United States National Museum.

ARAPAHO. Wyoming.

In the tale of " Foot-Stuck-Child " [a] Dr A. L. Kroeber relates how a miraculous girl, who is escaping from her husband, a buffalo, and from a rock who wished to marry her, threw up a ball which she was carrying. She first threw the ball, and as it came down kicked it upward, and her fathers, in turn, rose up. Then she threw and kicked it for herself. She and her fathers reached the sky in one place. They live in a tent covered with stars.

In Doctor Dorsey's [b] version of the same story the girl disobeys her father's injunction not to leave her tipi to take part in a shinny-ball game, and was captured by the buffalo bull.

CHEYENNE. Oklahoma. (United States National Museum.)

Cat. no. 166027. Hide ball (figure 793), disk-shaped, with two hide faces sewed to a strip at the edge, painted brown, with a design of a turkey drawn on one side and on the opposite side a deer, with hills and pine trees; diameter, 4 inches; thickness, 2 inches.

---

[a] Traditions of the Arapaho, p. 159, Chicago, 1903.          [b] Ibid., p. 172.

Cat. no. 165856.   Another (figure 794), a flattened sphere with median seam, encompassed with thong, with a loop for suspension; diameter, 3 inches.

Both were collected by Rev. H. R. Voth.

Cat. no. 152903.   Shinny stick (figure 795), curved and expanded at the end, with incised design of an elk and eagle, painted yellow, with half the striking end green; length, 35 inches.   Collected by Mr James Mooney.

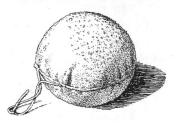

FIG. 794.   Shinny ball; diameter, 3 inches; Cheyenne Indians, Oklahoma; cat. no. 165856, United States National Museum.

C H E Y E N N E.   Oklahoma.   (Cat. no. 67443, 67445, Field Columbian Museum.)

Two shinny sticks; length 33¾ and 37¾ inches.   Collected by Rev. H. R. Voth in 1890.

The following appears on the label:

Used in an old ball game which was very seldom played, but was revived during the Ghost-dance craze among the Cheyenne and Arapaho, with other games and ceremonies that had been nearly forgotten.   The ball was rolled and struck along the ground, generally within the circle of the dancers.

FIG. 795.   Shinny stick; length, 35 inches; Cheyenne Indians, Oklahoma; cat. no. 152903, United States National Museum.

―――― Cheyenne reservation, Montana.   (Cat. no. 69979, Field Columbian Museum.)

Shinny stick and ball (figure 797); the ball of buckskin, flattened, with median seam, 3¾ inches in diameter, and painted red; the stick a sapling, curved at right angles at striking end, 31 inches in length.   Collected in 1901 by Mr S. C. Simms, who describes the game as played by young girls.

CHIPPEWA.   Turtle mountain, North Dakota.   (Cat. no. $\frac{50}{4723}$, American Museum of Natural History.)

Buckskin ball, flattened, with median seam, 4½ inches in diameter, painted with a cross in red on both faces and a red circle around the middle.   The ball is very heavy and is probably weighted with clay.

Buckskin ball (figure 798) with median seam, with a Greek cross in yellow beads on one face, a green bead cross on the other, and a band of yellow beads around the seam.

Curved stick (figure 798), painted red, 24 inches in length.

These were collected by Dr William Jones in 1903.

GROSVENTRES.    Fort Belknap reservation, Montana.    (Cat. no. 60356, Field Columbian Museum.)

Buckskin-covered ball with median seam, painted red, 3¼ inches in diameter, and stick made of sapling, curved at one end and painted red, 31 inches in length (figure 799).

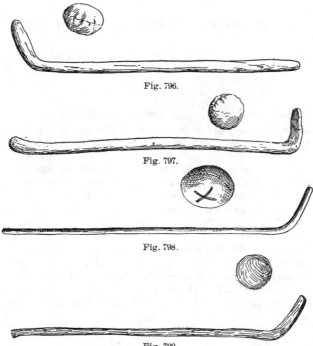

Fig. 796.

Fig. 797.

Fig. 798.

Fig. 799.

FIG. 796.   Shinny ball and stick; diameter of ball, 4 inches; length of stick, 38 inches; Cheyenne Indians, Montana; cat. no. 69648, Field Columbian Museum.

FIG. 797.   Shinny ball and stick; diameter of ball, 3¼ inches; length of stick, 31 inches; Cheyenne Indians, Montana; cat. no. 69979, Field Columbian Museum.

FIG. 798.   Shinny ball and stick; diameter of ball, 4¼ inches; length of stick, 24 inches; Chippewa Indians, Turtle mountain, North Dakota; cat. no. ₁₅⁶₂⁹₃, American Museum of Natural History.

FIG. 799.   Shinny ball and stick; diameter of ball, 3¼ inches; length of stick, 31 inches; Grosventre Indians, Montana; cat. no. 60356, Field Columbian Museum.

These were collected in 1900 by Dr George A. Dorsey, who describes them as used in the game of shinny, kakawaasethi, a game of ball played with a curved stick and a buckskin-covered ball, kawa, slightly flattened on two sides.

Formerly this was a popular game among the young men of the tribe, who played among themselves or against a team representing some rival tribe.    The object of the game was to advance the ball by batting it with sticks to some goal, against the effort of the opposing team.

GROSVENTRES. Fort Belknap reservation, Montana. (American Museum of Natural History.)

Cat. no. $\frac{50}{1728}$. Buckskin ball with median seam, painted yellow, with a bear's foot in green on one face; diameter, 3 inches.

Cat. no. $\frac{50}{1729}$. Buckskin ball with median seam, one side painted red, with a cross, the other dark; diameter, $4\frac{1}{4}$ inches.

Cat. no. $\frac{50}{1731}$. Buckskin ball with median seam, a cross in red quill work on one face, a bow and arrow on the other; diameter, $2\frac{1}{2}$ inches.

Cat. no. $\frac{50}{1910}$. Shinny stick, curved at the end; length, 2 feet 3 inches.

These specimens were collected by Dr A. L. Kroeber.

MENOMINEE. Wisconsin.

Dr Walter J. Hoffman [a] wrote:

The women formerly played a game of ball in which two sides, composed of unlimited numbers, would oppose each other. At each end of the ball ground, which was several hundred yards in length, a pole was erected, to serve as a goal. Many of the players would surround their respective goals, while the strongest and most active women, playing about the middle of the ground, would endeavor to obtain the ball and throw it toward their opponents' goal. The ball was made of deer hair tightly wrapped with thongs of buckskin, and covered with the same material. It measured about 3 inches in diameter. The women used sticks with a slight curve at the striking end, instead of a hoop, as on the sticks used by the men.

The game was more like the well-known game of shinny than anything else, with the addition of having to cause the ball to strike the goal instead of being merely knocked across a certain score line. The guardians of the goals were expected to prevent the ball from touching the post, and a good strike might send it away over the active players' heads, far toward their opponents' goal.

POWHATAN. Virginia.

William Strachey [b] wrote:

A kind of exercise they have amongst them much like that which boys call bandy in English.

SAUK AND FOXES. Iowa. (Cat. no. $\frac{50}{3505}$, $\frac{50}{3506}$, American Museum of Natural History.)

Leather-covered ball (figure 800) with median seam, flattened, 5 inches in diameter, and stick (figure 800), a sapling, curved at the striking end, 41 inches in length.

Collected by Dr William Jones, who describes them as used in the game of ice hockey. Men and women play apart or together. The goals are lines on opposite sides, across which the balls must be driven from either side to count.

---

[a] The Menomini Indians. Fourteenth Annual Report of the Bureau of Ethnology, pt. 1, p. 244, 1896.

[b] The History of Travaile into Virginia Brittania. Printed for the Hakluyt Society, p. 77, London, 1849.

ATHAPASCAN STOCK

Mɪᴋᴏɴᴏᴛᴜɴɴᴇ ᴀɴᴅ Mɪsʜɪᴋʜᴡᴜᴛᴍᴇᴛᴜɴɴᴇ.   Siletz reservation, Oregon.

A. W. Chase [a] says:

One of the national games is extremely interesting.   It is generally played by rival tribes, and is identical with that in vogue amongst our school-boys called hockey.   Sides being chosen, each endeavors to drive a hard ball of pine wood around a stake and in different directions.

Nᴀᴠᴀʜᴏ.   New Mexico.   (Cat. no. 9530, United States National Museum.)

Buckskin ball (figure 801), bag shaped, with drawstring; diameter, 1½ inches.   Collected by Dr Edward Palmer.

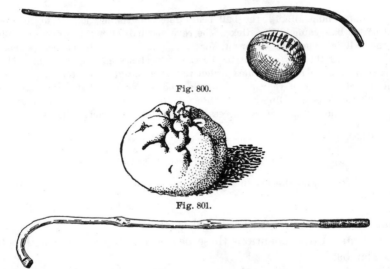

Fig. 800.

Fig. 801.

Fig. 802.

Fɪɢ. 800.   Ball and stick for ice hockey; diameter of ball, 5 inches; length of stick, 41 inches; Sauk and Fox Indians, Iowa; cat. no. $\frac{50}{3505}$, $\frac{50}{3505}$, American Museum of Natural History.

Fɪɢ. 801.   Shinny ball; diameter, 1½ inches; Navaho Indians, New Mexico; cat. no. 9530, United States National Museum.

Fɪɢ. 802.   Shinny stick; length, 32 inches; Navaho Indians, Arizona; cat. no. 3629, Brooklyn Institute Museum.

────── Chin Lee, Arizona.   (Cat. no. 3629, Brooklyn Institute Museum.)

Ball stick (figure 802), a peeled sapling curved at the striking end, with bark at the handle; length, 32 inches.   Collected by the writer in 1903.

Dr Washington Matthews describes the game of tsol, or ball, as the last of the games played by the young Hatsehogan with the gambling god Nohoilpi.[b]

───────────────────────────

[a] Overland Monthly, v. 2, p. 433, San Francisco, 1869.
[b] Navaho Legends, p. 84, Boston, 1897.

The object was to hit the ball so that it would fall beyond a certain line. " I will win this game for you," said the little bird Tsĭlkáli, for I will hide within the ball and fly with it wherever I want to go. Do not hit the ball hard; give it only a light tap, and depend on me to carry it." . . . On the line over which the ball was to be knocked all the people were assembled; on one side were those who still remained slaves; on the other side were the freedmen and those who had come to wager themselves, hoping to rescue their kinsmen. No*h*oïlpi bet on this game the last of his slaves and his own person. The gambler struck his ball a heavy blow, but it did not reach the line; the stranger gave his but a light tap, and the bird within it flew with it far beyond the line, whereat the released captives jumped over the line and joined their people.

NAVAHO. St Michael, Arizona.

Reverend Father Berard Haile writes as follows in a personal letter: [a]

In shinny, ndashdilkă'ɪ, the ball bears the same name, jol, as in the tossed and batted ball game. The stick is the reversed ball stick; however, the filling of the ball is somewhat different, for it is put in a small leather pouch and then sewed at the end and not in the center. This seems immaterial. Shinny is played according to the rules which regulate the game of tossed and batted ball regarding time of year, etc. The Navaho prefer long distances [figure 803] between the opposing lines. The object is to bring the shinny ball over the opponent's line. Whoever is successful first is the winner. The stick is also

Players | one or two miles | Players

FIG. 803. Plan of shinny ball field; Navaho Indians, St Michael, Arizona.

called be-akă'li, and the origin of the game is the same as that of tossed and batted ball.

TSETSAUT. Portland inlet, British Columbia.

Dr Franz Boas [b] mentions these people playing a game with a ball of cedar bark.

CADDOAN STOCK

ARIKARA. Oklahoma.

Dr George A. Dorsey,[c] in the origin of the Arikara, describes them as coming in their journeying to a great lake where they had their village for some time.

They made games at this place. The first game they played was the shinny ball and four sticks. The land was marked out by four sticks, which inclosed an oblong extending from east to west. Each side tried to force the ball through the other's goal. When one side was beaten it immediately began to kill those of the other side.

---

[a] June 27, 1902.

[b] Fifth Report on the Indians of British Columbia. Report of the Sixty-fifth Meeting of the British Association for the Advancement of Science, p. 568, London, 1895.

[c] Traditions of the Arikara, p. 16, Washington, 1904.

PAWNEE. Oklahoma. (Cat. no. 59384, Field Columbian Museum.)
Buckskin ball (figure 804), 3⅛ inches in diameter, flattened, with
median seam and painted with concentric rings in color on both
faces; on one face an outside ring of green, then red, black, and
white, with yellow in the center; on the other, black, yellow,
red, black, yellow, and black in the center. It has a thong for
suspension and is accompanied with four sticks (figure 805)

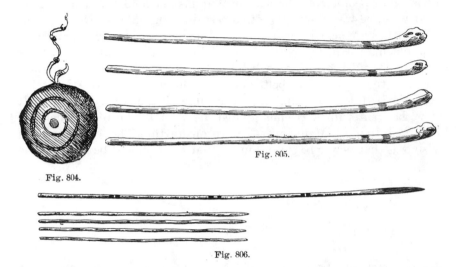

Fig. 805.

Fig. 804.

Fig. 806.

FIG. 804. Shinny ball; diameter, 3⅛ inches; Pawnee Indians, Oklahoma; cat. no. 59384, Field
Columbian Museum.
FIG. 805. Shinny sticks; length, 34 inches; Pawnee Indians, Oklahoma; cat. no. 59384, Field
Columbian Museum.
FIG. 806. Goal sticks and pole for shinny; length of sticks, 43 inches; length of pole, 85 inches;
Pawnee Indians, Oklahoma; cat. no. 59384, Field Columbian Museum.

made of saplings about 34 inches in length, curved and knobbed
at the end, and painted in pairs with bands of color near striking
end; two with a green and a red band, and two with one red and
two green bands. Also a pole (figure 806) 85 inches in length,
with a kind of ferrule at the upper end, and the lower end
pointed, and four stakes, 43 inches in length, designated as
goal posts. Collected in 1901 by Dr George A. Dorsey.

WICHITA. Wichita reservation, Oklahoma. (Cat. no. 59305, Field
Columbian Museum.)
Buckskin-covered ball (figure 807), 4 inches in diameter, with median
seam and loop for suspension; and ball stick, 34 inches in
length, curved, with a knot at the end. Collected by Dr George
A. Dorsey.

24 ETH—05 M——40

Dr A. S. Gatschet has kindly furnished the writer with the following list of words relating to ball, from the Wichita language, obtained by him in 1872:

Kasins, ball, plural kasritsa or irha kasintsa; kuyätsits, catching; kakia ti kasints kuyätsik, somebody catches a ball.

In his Wichita Tales[a] Dr George A. Dorsey relates how the first man, Darkness, who began to get power to foretell things after the creation of people, told the woman Watsikatsia, made after his image, that when he was about to go to a certain being, Man-Never-Known-on-Earth, he reached down at his left side with his right hand and brought up a ball. Then he reached down with his left hand at his right side and brought up a belt. Then he reached down in front, touched the ball to the belt, and brought up a shinny stick. He took the ball, tossed it up, and struck it with the stick. As the ball flew, he went with it. Thus guided, he went to the place where he expected to find Man-Never-Known-on-Earth. The object of his visit was that power be given him so that there should be light on the

FIG. 807.  Shinny ball and stick; diameter of ball, 4 inches; length of stick, 34 inches; Wichita Indians, Oklahoma; cat. no. 59305, Field Columbian Museum.

face of the earth. He tossed and struck the ball again, but not arriving at the place, he knew he could not depend upon the ball, and so took his bow and arrow and shot an arrow and flew with it. This he did a second, third, and fourth time, but without avail. Then he remembered he could run. He made one long run and stopped to rest. Then he ran again and a third and fourth time. He had made twelve trials and knew he was near the place of his journey.

Later, in the same narrative, it is related how Darkness, arriving at a certain village, instituted the game of shinny:

The crowd came, and he told them they were to have such a game as shinny ball. He reached down with his right hand on his left side and produced a ball, and then reached down on his right side with his left hand and brought up a shinny stick. These he showed the people and told them they were for their use. Then he commanded the people to gather just outside the village at about evening time, and then he set the time for play. They went as he told them. When they were all there he tossed the ball toward the north and traveled with it. It went a long ways. When it lit, he picked it up and struck it with the stick and drove the ball back south, then said that the point

[a] Journal of American Folk-Lore, v. 15, p. 215, 1902.

where he stood when he struck the ball would be called "flowing water" (the goal). Then he took the ball, tossed it, went with it, and again struck it southward. Where it hit was the second "flowing water," or goal. Between these two goals or bases was level ground, and in both directions as far as you could see. Then he divided the men into two parties, and placed one at each goal. Between these two parties and in the center of the field he placed two men, one from each of the two parties. He gave one man the ball and told him to toss it up. As the ball was tossed he told the other man to strike it towards the south. He did so and drove the ball towards his opponents on the south. Now they played, and the north side drove the ball to the south goal and won. Then they changed goals, and the other side won. Then Darkness said they had played enough.

Dr George A. Dorsey [a] also relates that in the Wichita creation legend the first man, Having-Power-to-carry-Light, gave the men a ball smaller than the shinny ball.

He told them this ball was to be used to amuse themselves with; that the men were to play together and the boys were to play together. Whenever a child was born, if it was a boy this kind of ball was to be given to it, that he might observe it and learn how to move around. The ball had a string to it. The farther the ball rolled—that is, the older the child should get—the faster it would move around. He went on and taught the men how to play the game, for the people were ignorant and did not know what the things were for. Finally, the men were shown how the ball should be used. He showed them the clubs for the shinny game. He told them they should be divided equally in the game, one party on one side and the other party on the other side. Many were interested, for the game was new to them. Many of the men were fast on their feet. The game was to be won by the side that should get the ball to the goal first. Having-Power-to-carry-Light also told them how to travel with the arrows and ball. This marks the time when they learned to travel fast from one place to another. The men went out hunting animals after they had been taught that animals existed for their use, and they traveled with their arrows and ball. They would shoot an arrow in the direction they wanted to go; then they would go with the arrow as it went up. This is the way they traveled. They would hit the ball, and as it flew the person would be on the ball. When the ball hit the ground they would hit it again, and so they would go from place to place.

In the story of "The Deeds of After-Birth Boy"[b] his father made his boy a shinny ball and stick. This ball was what we call "ball-for-young-boys" (kasintswiks).

Again, in the story of "The Deeds of After-birth-Boy" the father made his two boys a shinny ball and two sticks, with which they played a game against the Headless-Man, the stake to be their own

---

[a] The Mythology of the Wichita, p. 27, Washington, 1904.
[b] Ibid., p. 92.

'lives. The ball was finally knocked by After-birth-Boy over a small creek that had been selected as a goal.

The Headless-Man's ball was black and his shinny stick was black. The two boys had a green ball and green sticks, green representing the spring of the year. Since that time the shinny game is played in the spring, under the power of the After-birth-Boy.[a]

There is a similar episode in the story of "The Little Brown Hawks,"[b] in which the four brother Swift-Hawks and their father played successively against Boy-setting-Grass-on-Fire-by-his-Footsteps, lost their lives and were clubbed with a shinny club. The playground extended north and south, and it was a long way from goal to goal. The game consisted in tossing the ball and one hitting it, the first running in the direction they were headed, the other following him. A posthumous brother of the four Swift-Hawks finally overcame Boy-setting-Grass-on-Fire-by-his-Footsteps. When the ball was tossed up, hail began to fall instead of the ball coming down. All of the hail came down on Boy-setting-Grass-on-Fire-by-his-Footsteps, and on him alone, and killed him. Those whom he had killed were brought to life by burning his body.

### CHIMMESYAN STOCK

Niska. Nass river, British Columbia.

Dr Franz Boas[c] describes the following game:

Gōntl: a ball game. There are two goals, about 100 to 150 yards apart. Each is formed by two sticks, about 10 feet apart. In the middle, between the goals, is a hole in which the ball is placed. The players carry hooked sticks. Two of them stand at the hole, the other players of each party, six or seven in number, a few steps behind them towards each goal. At a given signal, both players try to strike the ball out of the hole. Then each party tries to drive it through the goal of the opposing party.

### CHUMASHAN STOCK

Santa Barbara. Santa Barbara, California.

Alfred Robinson[d] says:

In front of the house was a large square, where the Indians assembled on Sunday afternoons to indulge their favorite sports and pursue their chief amusement—gambling. Here numbers were gathered together in little knots, who appeared engaged in angry conversation; they were adjusting, as Daniel informed me, the boundary lines for the two parties who were to play that afternoon at ball, and were thus occupied till dinner time. When I returned from dinner they had already commenced; and at least two or three hundred

---

[a] The Mythology of the Wichita, p. 99, Washington, 1904.
[b] Ibid., p. 247.
[c] Fifth Report on the Indians of British Columbia. Report of the Sixty-fifth Meeting of the British Association for the Advancement of Science, p. 583, London, 1895.
[d] Life in California, p. 105, San Francisco, 1891.

Indians of both sexes were engaged in the game. It was the "Presidio" against the "Mission." They played with a small ball of hard wood, which, when hit, would bound with tremendous force without striking the ground for two or three hundred yards. Great excitement prevailed, and immense exertion was manifested on both sides, so that it was not till late in the afternoon that the game was decided in favor of the Indians of the Presidio.

## ESKIMAUAN STOCK

Eskimo (Western). St Michael, Alaska.

Mr Nelson [a] describes the game which he calls hockey—aiyutalugit or patkutalugit.

This is played with a small ball of ivory, leather, or wood, and a stick, curved at the lower end. The ball and stick are called pat-k'u'-tûk. The ball is placed on the ground or ice and the players divide into two parties. Each player with his stick attempts to drive the ball across the opponents' goal, which is established as in the football game.

## IROQUOIAN STOCK

Tuscarora. North Carolina.

John Lawson[b] says:

Another game is managed with a batoon and a ball, and resembles our trapball.

## KERESAN STOCK

Keres. Acoma, New Mexico.

A Keres Indian at Zuñi, named James H. Miller, informed the writer in 1904 that the boys played shinny—matashoku—in the fall. The stick they call hopi, and the ball matashoku.

—— Cochiti, New Mexico.

A Keres boy at St Michaels, Arizona, named Francisco Chaves (Kogit), described the Indians at Cochiti to the writer in 1904 as playing shinny under the name of oomatashia. The ball, pelota, they call matashshok, and the stick, oomatash.

## KIOWAN STOCK

Kiowa. Oklahoma. (United States National Museum.)

Cat. no. 152903. Buckskin ball (figure 808), a flattened sphere, with median seam; diameter, 3½ inches; wooden stick (figure 809), painted red, curved at the striking end, with a knob at the top; length, 30 inches.

Cat. no. 152904. Hide ball (figure 810), a flattened sphere with median seam, painted red; diameter, 3¼ inches.

These specimens were collected by Mr James Mooney.

[a] The Eskimo about Behring Strait. Eighteenth Annual Report of the Bureau of American Ethnology, pt. 1, p. 337, 1899.
[b] The History of Carolina, p. 288, London, 1714; reprint, Raleigh, N. C., 1860.

MARIPOSAN STOCK

CHUKCHANSI. Pickayune, Madera county, California. (Cat. no.
70895, Field Columbian Museum.)

Two mountain mahogany balls, 1½ inches in diameter. Collected by
Dr J. W. Hudson.

MIXED TRIBES. Tule River reservation, California.

Dr J. W. Hudson describes the following game:

The ball is called o-lol, and the stick, ka-tal. The goals, to-lin, are two pairs
of upright sticks, placed at the ends of the course, at a distance of 400 yards.

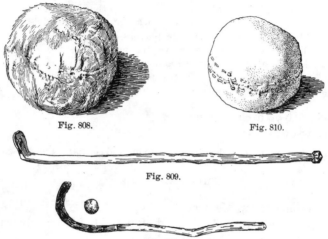

Fig. 808.                     Fig. 810.

Fig. 809.

Fig. 811.

FIG. 808. Shinny ball; diameter, 3¼ inches; Kiowa Indians, Oklahoma; cat. no. 152903, United
States National Museum.
FIG. 809. Shinny stick; length, 30 inches; Kiowa Indians, Oklahoma; cat. no. 152903, United
States National Museum.
FIG. 810. Shinny ball; diameter, 3¼ inches; Kiowa Indians, Oklahoma; cat. no. 152904, United
States National Museum.
FIG. 811. Shinny ball and stick; diameter of ball, 2¼ inches; length of stick, 40 inches; Yokuts
Indians, Tule River reservation, California; cat. no. 70399, 70400, Field Columbian Museum.

YOKUTS. Tule River reservation, Tulare county, California. (Cat.
no. 70399, 70400, Field Columbian Museum.)

Shinny stick, 40 inches in length (figure 811), made of oak, bent and
fire seasoned at the lower end, with a red stripe near the crook;
and a ball, 2½ inches in diameter, made of an oak knot, rounded
and seasoned. Collected by Dr J. W. Hudson.

MOQUELUMNAN STOCK

AWANI. Yosemite valley, Mariposa county, California. (Cat. no.
70229, Field Columbian Museum.)

Four mountain mahogany ball sticks, 4 feet in length, with recurved
ends. Collected by Dr J. W. Hudson.

CHOWCHILLA.  Chowchilly river, Madera county, California.  (Cat.
    no. 70233, Field Columbian Museum.)
Two oak-wood balls, 3 inches in diameter.  Collected by Dr J. W.
    Hudson, who describes the game as follows:

Played only by men, who are divided in two equal sides,
say fifteen on a side.  The goals, which are each some 200
yards from the center, are two trees or two posts, a long step,
or, say, 3 feet, apart.  Two men standing side by side cast
the ball up and strike it to their opponents' goal.

WASAMA.  Chowchilly river, Madera county, Cali-
    fornia.
Dr J. W. Hudson describes the following ball game
under the name of müla:

Played with a club, mu-lau' of mountain mahogany, and a
mahogany ball, o-lo'-la.
Two or more men play in couples or pairs from a start
line [figure 812].  The captains at station 1 strike their respective balls toward their respective partners at station 2.
If the ball falls short of 2, the failing striker must forward
his ball to station 2 by an additional stroke; when the ball
passes into the territory of the partner at station 2, he (no.
2) must drive it forward from where it stopped.  The last
stationed partner must drive it over the goal line.  The smallest number of aggregate strokes on a side wins.  Station
keepers must keep within their own territories.

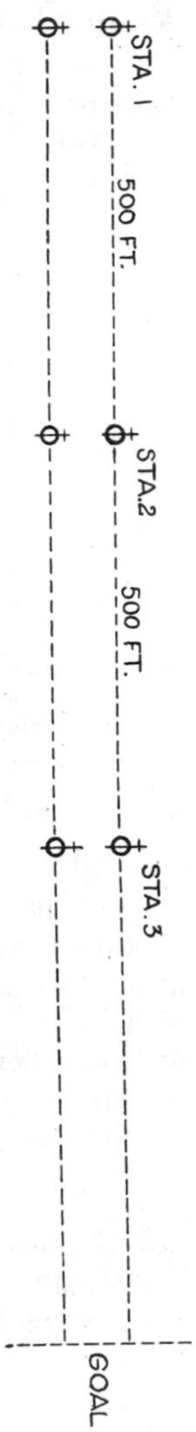

PIMAN STOCK

OPATA.  Sonora, Mexico.
Mr A. F. Bandelier [a] speaks of a game called
uachicori, or shinny.
TARAHUMARE.  Chihuahua, Mexico.
Dr Carl Lumholtz [b] states:

In a game called taquari, a ball is knocked along the ground
by one party of players toward a goal, while the opposite
party strives to beat it back to the opposite goal.

ZUAQUE.  Sonora, Mexico.  (Cat. no. 129853, United
    States National Museum.)
Irregular wooden ball (figure 813), somewhat rudely
    carved, 1⅜ inches in diameter; and a roughly
        hewn stick, curved and flattened on the inner side at the end, 23
        inches in length.
Described by the collector, Dr Edward Palmer, as a boy's shinny
stick and ball.

FIG. 812. Ball course; Wasama Indians, California; from sketch by Dr J. W. Hudson.

[a] Final Report.  Papers of the Archæological Institute of America, pt. 1, p. 240, Cambridge, 1890.
[b] Tarahumari Life and Customs.  Scribner's Magazine, v. 16, p. 311, New York, 1894.

SALISHAN STOCK

CLALLAM.  Washington.

A Clallam boy described this tribe as playing the game of shinny, skweikuklioise.  The ball, smuck, is a cedar knot.  The shinny stick is called kuklioisesun.  The word for goal is sweikkutum.

PEND D'OREILLES.  Flathead reservation, Montana.  (Cat. no. 51777, Field Columbian Museum.)

Shinny stick (figure 814), curved and expanding at the striking end into a thin blade, with a knob at the end of the handle; length, 27 inches.  Collected by Dr George A. Dorsey.

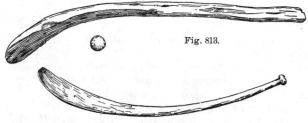

Fig. 813.

Fig. 814.

FIG. 813.  Shinny ball and stick; diameter of ball, 1⅜ inches; length of stick, 23 inches; Zuaque Indians, Sonora, Mexico; cat. no. 129853, United States National Museum.

FIG. 814.  Shinny stick; length, 27 inches; Pend d'Oreille Indians, Flathead reservation, Montana; cat. no. 51777, Field Columbian Museum.

SHUSWAP.  Kamloops, British Columbia.

Dr Franz Boas [a] says:

The following game of ball was described to me: The players stand in two opposite rows.  A stake is driven into the ground on the left side of the players of one row, and another on the right side of the players on the other row.  Two men stand in the center between the two rows.  One of these pitches the ball, and the other tries to drive it to one of the stakes with a bat.  Then both parties endeavor to drive the ball to the stake on the opposite side, and the party which succeeds in this has won the game.

SONGISH.  Vancouver island, British Columbia.

Dr Franz Boas [b] describes the following game:

K'k·oiä'ls, a game at ball; the ball, which is made of maple knots, is called smuk.  It is pitched with crooked sticks and driven from one party to the other.

SHAHAPTIAN STOCK

NEZ PERCÉS.  Idaho.

Col. Richard Irving Dodge [c] says:

Among the Nez Percés and other western tribes the women are extremely fond of a game of ball similar to our "shinny," or "hockey," and play with great spirit.

---

[a] Second General Report on the Indians of British Columbia.  Report of the Sixtieth Meeting of the British Association for the Advancement of Science, p. 641, London, 1891.
[b] Ibid., p. 571.
[c] Our Wild Indians, p. 344, Hartford, 1882.

UMATILLA. Oregon. (Cat. no. 37541, 37542, Free Museum of
   Science and Art, University of Pennsylvania.)
Ball (figure 815), a flattened spheroid of buckskin, with median
   seam, painted yellow, with the sun in red lines on one side and a
   similar design, perhaps a star, on the other; diameter, 4 inches.
Stick (figure 816), a club, flattened and curved at one end; length,
   29 inches.
These were collected by the writer in 1900. The ball is called
tkaiput, and the bat tkaila.

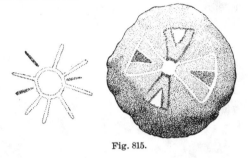

Fig. 815.

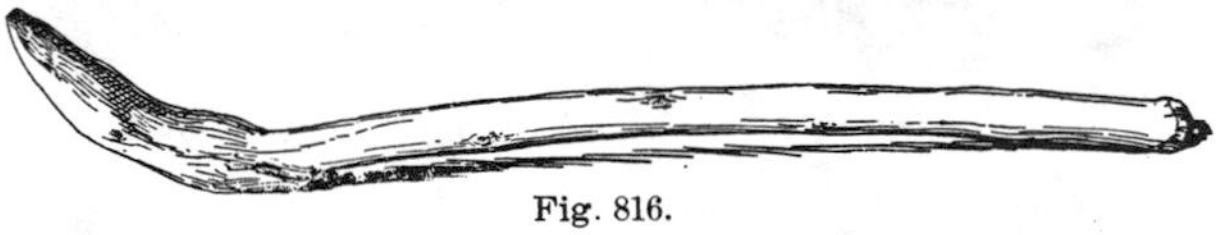

Fig. 816.

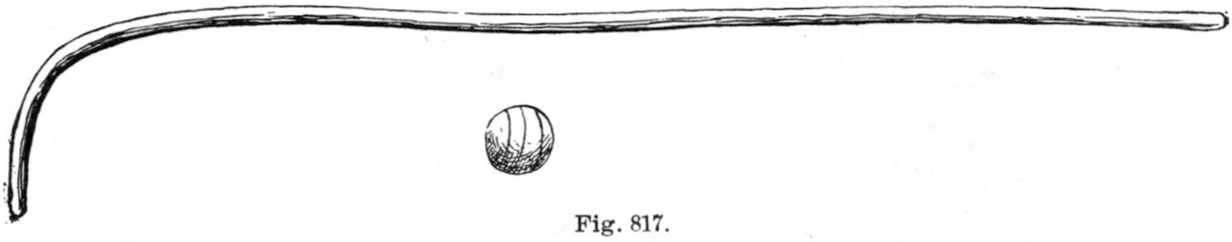

Fig. 817.

FIG. 815.  Shinny ball; diameter, 4 inches; Umatilla Indians, Oregon; cat. no. 37541, Free Museum
   of Science and Art, University of Pennsylvania.
FIG. 816.  Shinny stick; length, 29 inches; Umatilla Indians, Oregon; cat. no. 37542, Free Museum
   of Science and Art, University of Pennsylvania.
FIG. 817.  Shinny ball and stick; diameter of ball, 1⅝ inches; length of stick, 42 inches; Achomawi Indians, Hat creek, California; cat. no. $\frac{50}{4117}$, American Museum of Natural History.

SHASTAN STOCK

ACHOMAWI. Hat creek, California. (Cat. no. $\frac{50}{4117}$, American Museum of Natural History.)
Wooden ball, 1⅝ inches in diameter, and curved stick, 42 inches in
   length (figure 817). Collected in 1903 by Dr Roland B. Dixon,
   who describes them as implements for hockey, popaqwaiwi.

SHOSHONEAN STOCK

HOPI. Arizona. (United States National Museum.)
Cat. no. 23222. Buckskin ball; a flattened spheroid, with median
   seam; diameter, 3¼ inches. Collected by Maj. J. W. Powell and
   designated as a shinny ball.

Cat. no. 41765.   Buckskin ball, painted red, **ovate**, with median seam, stuffed with hair; diameter, 3¾ inches.

Cat. no. 68843.   Buckskin ball; a flattened spheroid, with median seam; diameter, 2½ inches.

Cat. no. 68869.   Buckskin ball (figure 818) ; bag-shaped, painted red, with drawstring; diameter, 5 inches.   Designated as a football.

  The three foregoing specimens were collected by Col. James Stevenson.

Cat. no. 84286.   Buckskin ball (figure 819) ; a flattened spheroid, with median seam; diameter, 3¾ inches.

Cat. no. 84287.   Buckskin ball, similar to the preceding; diameter, 2½ inches.

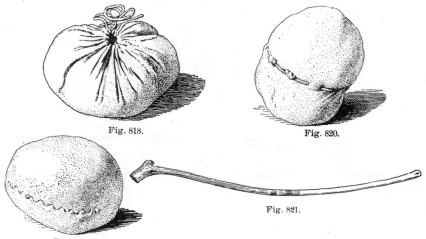

Fig. 818.

Fig. 820.

Fig. 821.

Fig. 819.

FIG. 818.   Shinny ball; diameter, 5 inches; Hopi Indians, Arizona; cat. no. 68869, United States National Museum.

FIG. 819.   Shinny ball; diameter, 3¾ inches; Hopi Indians, Arizona; cat. no. 84286, United States National Museum.

FIG. 820.   Shinny ball; diameter, 3½ inches; Hopi Indians, Arizona; cat. no. 84289, United States National Museum.

FIG. 821.   Shinny stick; length, 28 inches; Hopi Indians, Walpi, Arizona; cat. no. 166718, United States National Museum.

Cat. no. 84288.   Buckskin ball, similar to the preceding; diameter, 3 inches.

Cat. no. 84289.   Buckskin ball (figure 820), spheroidal, with median seam and drawstring around the seam; diameter, 3½ inches.

  This and the three specimens preceding were collected by Mr Victor Mindeleff.

HOPI.   Walpi, Arizona.   (Cat. no. 166718, United States National Museum.)

Peeled stick with curved end (figure 821), one-half painted red, with two bands of blue paint near the middle; length, 28 inches.   Collected by Mr James Mooney.

Mr A. M. Stephen, in his unpublished manuscript, gives the following definitions:

Ball, ta-tci; shinny, or hockey, as practiced by white boys, ta-tatc'-la-la-wŭh.

Mono. Hooker cove, Madera county, California. (Cat. no. 71435, 71436, Field Columbian Museum).

Mahogany club (figure 822), with flat end slightly curved, 54 inches in length, and small mountain mahogany ball.

Collected by Dr J. W. Hudson, who describes it as of the Yokuts type.

Five other clubs (figure 823) in the same collection (cat. no. 71434) are similar, but the striking part is narrow. Four of these are of oak and one is of mountain mahogany.

Fig. 822.

Fig. 823.

Fig. 822. Shinny ball and stick; length of stick, 54 inches; Mono Indians, Madera county, California; cat. no. 71435, 71436, Field Columbian Museum.

Fig. 823. Shinny ball and stick; length of stick, 50½ inches; Mono Indians, Madera county, California; cat. no. 71434, Field Columbian Museum.

Doctor Hudson gives the following account of the game under the name of nakwatakoina, to swing strike:

Each opponent starts his mahogany-wood ball, usually 1¾ inches in diameter, forward at a signal. Their partners at the next station forward their respective balls to the next relay station, and so on. Interference with an opponent's ball, even by accident, is protested by loud " Hip! he!!" which is at once apologized for by " He-he-he!!" If a player should forward an opponent's ball, this protesting cry recalls him to seek his own ball, while the distance made by the fouled stroke is kept by the fouled party. Every player has one or more substitute balls in his belt, so that when a ball is lost another is allowed in play. The balls must turn a goal stake, a-na'-na kwi-no hi'-na, " man's circling stake," often a tree, about 400 yards from the starting line, and return to a hole, to'-op, at the starting line. The game may be played also to a goal straight away, several miles. Once a game was played between the Hooker Cove people and Whisky Creeks, in which they started at Hooker Cove, and the goal was in a field beside the road at Whisky Creek, 7½ miles distant.

Shoshoni. Wind River reservation, Wyoming. (Cat. no. 36878, Free Museum of Science and Art, University of Pennsylvania.)

Stick (figure 825), ego, with a broad curved end and a knot at the handle; length, 24½ inches; and a ball (figure 824), covered with buckskin, with median seam, in the form of a flattened sphere, 3½ inches in diameter. Collected by the writer in 1900.

UINTA UTE. White Rocks, Utah. (Free Museum of Science and Art, University of Pennsylvania.)

Cat. no. 37114. Buckskin ball (figure 826), bag shaped, with drawstring and thong; diameter, 3¼ inches.

Cat. no. 37117. Shinny stick (figure 827), rudely whittled, with broad curved end; length, 27½ inches.

These specimens were collected by the writer in 1900. The ball is called pokunump, and the stick, beher. It is a woman's game.

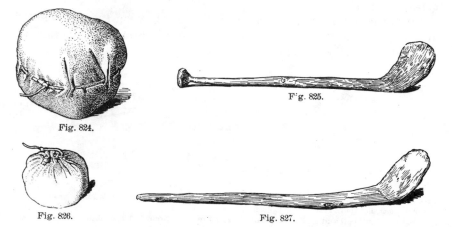

Fig. 824.

F'g. 825.

Fig. 826.

Fig. 827.

FIG. 824. Shinny ball; diameter, 3¼ inches; Shoshoni Indians, Wind River reservation, Wyoming; cat. no. 36878, Free Museum of Science and Art, University of Pennsylvania.
FIG. 825. Shinny stick; length, 24¼ inches; Shoshoni Indians, Wind River reservation, Wyoming; cat. no. 36878, Free Museum of Science and Art, University of Pennsylvania.
FIG. 826. Shinny ball; diameter, 3¼ inches; Uinta Ute Indians, White Rocks, Utah; cat. no. 37114, Free Museum of Science and Art, University of Pennsylvania.
FIG. 827. Shinny stick; length, 27¼ inches; Uinta Ute Indians, White Rocks, Utah; cat. no. 37117, Free Museum of Science and Art, University of Pennsylvania.

SIOUAN STOCK

ASSINIBOIN. Fort Union, Montana.

In a report to Isaac I. Stevens, governor of Washington Territory, on the Indian tribes of the upper Missouri, by Mr Edwin T. Denig, a manuscript in the library of the Bureau of American Ethnology, there occurs the following account:

Most of these tribes, particularly the Sioux, are fond of playing in parties. The principal game at ball is called tah-cap-see-chah, being the same denominated shinny, or bandy, by the whites. It is generally got up when two different bands are camped together, and a principal person in each having made a bet of a blanket or gun, they choose from their bands an equal number of young men, who are always the most active they can select, the number varying from fifteen to forty on each side. Sometimes the play is headed by the chief of each band betting, though they take no part in the game, which is usually played by men of 20 to 30 years of age. Each of the players stakes something against an equivalent on the part of one on the opposite side, and every bet, which consists of shirts, arrows, shells, feathers, blankets and almost every article of trade or their own manufacture, is tied together separately, and as fast as the bets are taken and tied together they are laid on a pile about the center of the playground, being given in charge of three or four elderly men, who are chosen as judges of the sport. After this has been concluded two posts are set up about three-quarters of a mile apart and the game consists in knocking the ball with sticks toward these posts, they being the outcome or limit for either party in different directions. They strip naked, except the breechcloth and moccasins, and paint their bodies in every possible variety of manner. Each is furnished with a stick about 3½ feet long, turned up at the lower end, and they range themselves in two lines, commencing at the middle of the ground and extending on either side some distance. The ball is cast into the air in the center of the course, struck as soon as it falls by some one, and the game begins, each party endeavoring to knock the ball to the post designated as their limit. The game is played three times, and whichever party succeeds in winning two courses out of the three is judged conqueror. When the players are well chosen it is often an interesting game, and some splendid specimens of foot racing can be seen; but when one of them, either intentionally or by accident, hurts another by a stroke with the play stick, a general shindy takes place, and the sticks are employed over each others' heads, which is followed by a rush for the stakes and a scramble. We have seen them, when this was the case, arm themselves and exchange some shots, when, a few being wounded, the camps would separate and move away in different directions. Supposing, however, the game proceeds in its proper spirit and humor, each bet being tied separately, the parcels are handed out to the successful party by the judges. This game is not often done by large parties of men, or, if so, it is very warmly contested and very apt to break up in a disturbance. We have seen it also played by both men and women joined, a few men aiding two parties of women; this was amongst the Sioux, but with the other tribes it is generally played by men only.

CROWS. Crow reservation, Montana. (Cat. no. 69648, Field Columbian Museum.)

Shinny stick and ball; the ball a flattened spheroid, with median seam, 4 inches in diameter; the stick an unpainted sapling, curved at the end; length, 38 inches.

Collected by Mr S. C. Simms in 1901, who says:

The game is played only in the spring, when the grass is green, the men on one side and the women on the other. The goals each consist of two blankets, spread side by side on the ground. A man or a woman selects one of the goals. The ball is tossed in the air among the crowd of players, and the object is to drive it to the goal selected.

DAKOTA (OGLALA). Pine Ridge reservation, South Dakota. (Cat. no. 22117, 22118, Free Museum of Science and Art, University of Pennsylvania.)

Stick (figure 828), made of a sapling, 39 inches in length, bent at one end by fire, and a buckskin-covered ball (figure 828), 2½ inches in diameter, the cover made of a single piece and stitched with sinew.

It is described by the collector, Mr Louis L. Meeker,[a] as used in the woman's game of shinny, takapsica:

Many players form two companies and strive to take the ball with their sticks to two different goals in opposite directions. First play is decided by kicking the ball up into the air. The one who can do so oftenest without letting the ball or the foot touch the ground plays first. This is a separate game with the Winnebago.

Shinny is played by women, large girls, and schoolboys. The women of one camp will play against the women of another camp. The boys and girls of one school will play against another school, for, although not quite up to the dignity of men, the game is scarcely limited to women.

FIG. 828. Shinny ball and stick; diameter of ball, 2½ inches; length of stick, 39 inches; Oglala Dakota Indians, Pine Ridge reservation, South Dakota; cat. no. 22117, 22118, Free Museum of Science and Art, University of Pennsylvania.

DAKOTA (OGLALA). Pine Ridge reservation, South Dakota. (Cat. no. 22124, Free Museum of Science and Art, University of Pennsylvania.)

Knobbed stick (figure 829), made of a sapling, 36 inches in length.

Described by the collector, Mr Louis L. Meeker,[b] as used in the boy's game of can takapsica, or wood shinny:

A block of wood, cut from a seasoned stick about 3 inches in diameter, is laid upon the ground. Two players, armed with sticks having a natural enlargement on one end, each paces off 50 steps in opposite directions, and each marks his opponent's goal. Giving the word to each other, they race back to the block of wood, the one who wins placing his foot upon the block to take possession. He then deliberately aims and strikes the block with all his force toward his goal, and both race after it to take possession with the foot and strike it again as before.

FIG. 829. Stick for wood shinny; length, 36 inches; Oglala Dakota Indians, Pine Ridge reservation, South Dakota; cat. no. 22124, Free Museum of Science and Art, University of Pennsylvania.

DAKOTA (TETON). Pine Ridge reservation, South Dakota.

Dr J. R. Walker [c] describes the game of shinny, woskate takapsice, and of woman's shinny, woskate takwinkapisce, and gives the rules for the play.

---

[a] Ogalala Games. Bulletin of the Free Museum of Science and Art, v. 3, p. 31, Philadelphia, 1901.

[b] Ibid., p. 33.

[c] Sioux Games. Journal of American Folk-Lore, v. 18, p. 283, 1905.

DAKOTA (TETON), Cheyenne River agency, South Dakota. (Cat. no. 168170, United States National Museum.)

Shinny stick (figure 830), a peeled sapling, turned around at one end, 28½ inches in length. The handle is cut away at the end and has four thongs wrapped with colored quill work, and a bunch of strings of glass beads attached. Collected by Mr Z. T. Daniel.

FIG. 830. Shinny stick; length, 28½ inches; Teton Dakota Indians, Cheyenne River agency, South Dakota; cat. no. 168170, United States National Museum.

DAKOTA (YANKTON). South Dakota.

George P. Belden [a] describes the ball game as follows:

A great noise of shouting is heard in the camp, and the young men, with bat, or club, 3 feet long and crooked at the end, go out on the prairie near the camp. Having found a smooth spot they halt, and two of the youths, by common consent, take opposite sides and pick out the players, first one and then the other, until enough are had.

One morning I heard the young men shouting for ball, and I went out with them to the playground. The two chiefs, A-ke-che-ta (Little Dog Soldier) and Ma-to-sac (White Bear), were picking sides, and a number of Indians were already seated facing each other, and bantering on the game. As each man was selected he spread down his buffalo robe and sat upon it, facing his opponent. I was selected by A-ke-che-ta, and silently took my place in the line. Presently all the young men who were to play were selected, and then several old men were appointed to act as umpires of the game. These advanced and seated themselves between the contestants, and then the warriors rose and commenced betting on the game. First one warrior advanced and threw down a robe before the old men; then a warrior from the other side came forward and laid a robe upon it; and so all bet, one against the other. Presently there was a great number of piles of stakes, some having bet moccasins, headdresses, beadwork, earrings, necklaces, bows and arrows, and even ponies. All these were carefully watched over by the old men, who noted each stake and the depositor on a stick. If you did not wish to bet with any particular warrior you laid your wager on the big pile, and instantly it was matched by the judges against some article of corresponding value from the pile of the other side. Thus I bet a hunting knife, half a pound of powder, a pair of moccasins, and a small hand mirror, which articles were appropriately matched with others by the judges. All was now in readiness for the game to begin, and the parties separated. The two lines were formed about 100 yards apart. In front of each side, 20 feet from each other, two stakes, smeared with paint, are driven firmly into the ground, and the object of the game is to drive the ball between the stakes. Whichever side shall first force the ball through the opposite stakes wins the game. The ball, made of rags and covered with buckskin, is carried to the center of the ground between the combatants and there deposited, by one of the old men, who then returns to his post. The judges then give the signal, and

[a] Belden, the White Chief; edited by Gen. James S. Brisben, U. S. A., p. 37, Cincinnati, 1871.

with loud shouts the players run to the ball, and commence knocking it to and fro with their crooked sticks. The ball is about the size of a large orange, and each party tries to prevent its coming toward their stakes. No warrior must touch the ball with his hands; but if it lies in a hole, he may push it out with his foot and then hit it with his stick.

In the game which I am telling you about, Ma-to-sac's party reached and struck the ball first, lifting it clear over our heads, and sending it far to our rear and close to our stakes. Then we all ran, and Ma-to-sac's and A-ke-che-ta's warriors fell over one another, and rapped each other on the shins with their clubs, and there was great confusion and excitement, but at length one of the party succeeded in hitting the ball, and sent it to Ma-to-sac's stakes. Thither we ran, but no one could find the ball. After much search I discovered it in a tuft of grass, and, bidding one of our men run quickly to the stakes, I hit it and drove the ball to him. Unfortunately it fell in a hole, and before our warrior could get it out and hit it, a dense crowd of Ma-to-sac's men were around the spot and in front of the stakes. The contest was violent, so much so, indeed, that no one could hit the ball, though it was continually tramped over. At length some one called out, "There it goes," and the warriors scattered in all directions, looking to see where it was; but one of Ma-to-sac's men, who had called out, stood fast, and when the crowd had scattered, I saw him attempting to conceal the ball beneath his foot. Running against him from behind with such force as to throw him on his face, before he could recover his feet I hit the ball, and, seeing all Ma-to-sac's men off their guard, with the aid of a young man, easily drove it between their stakes, only a few yards distant.[a]

The judges at once declared the game was ours, and many and loud were the cheers sent up by our party, in token of the victory, while Ma-to-sac's men retired sullen and disappointed. I was declared the winner, and A-ke-che-ta thanked me for my services, while the young warriors gathered around and congratulated me on my success. Then we all smoked, and went over to the stakes to receive our shares. As winner I was entitled to a general share of the spoils; but I declined in favor of the young Indian who had helped me drive the ball, saying that, as he had last hit it, and actually forced it between the stakes, he was, in reality, the most deserving. This argument was loudly applauded by the old men, and the young warrior, who had not been friendly for some time with me, was so touched by my generosity that he came and thanked me, saying, frankly, "You, and not I, won the game." However, I forced the general stakes upon him, at which he was much pleased. I found that the stakes had won a saddle, half a pound of powder, 6 yards of wampum beads, and a handsomely braided knife-scabbard. When the judges had awarded all the winnings, among which were fourteen ponies, each took up his trophies and returned to the village, where for the remainder of the day the game was fought over again and again in the tepees.

DAKOTA (YANKTON). Fort Peck, Montana. (Free Museum of Science and Art, University of Pennsylvania.)

Cat. no. 37609. Ball, tapa, covered with buckskin, slightly flattened, with median seam; diameter, 2½ inches.

---

[a] In this game everyone must keep his temper, and any stratagem is allowed, so the ball is not touched with the hands. It is not suffered, however, for anyone to hit another over the head, or on the body with sticks or the hands, but if you can upset a gamester by running against him it is esteemed fair. When either party cheats, foul is called by the opposite party, when the game ceases until the judges decide the matter. If it is a foul play the play is given to the other side. No one thinks of disputing the judges' decision, and from it there is no appeal.

Cat. no. 37608.  Flat, highly finished stick (figure 831), painted red, somewhat wide and slightly spoon-shaped at the striking end; length, 39½ inches.

Collected by the writer in 1900; the stick is one of several that were found in the grass after a woman's ball game.

HIDATSA.  Fort Atkinson, North Dakota.

Henry A. Boller [a] says:

The young squaws are playing a game of ball resembling shinny or football, insomuch as curved sticks and feet are called into service.

OMAHA.  Nebraska.  (Cat. no. IV B 2225, Berlin Museum für Völkerkunde.)

Club (figure 833), curved at end, 39 inches in length, and a buckskin ball (figure 832), with median seam, 4 inches in diameter.  Collected by Miss Alice C. Fletcher.

The ball is designated tabe, and the stick tabe gathi.

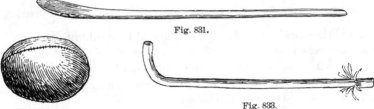

Fig. 831.

Fig. 832.

Fig. 833.

FIG. 831.  Shinny stick; length, 39½ inches; Yankton Dakota Indians, Fort Peck, Montana; cat. no. 37608, Free Museum of Science and Art, University of Pennsylvania.

FIG. 832.  Shinny ball; diameter, 4 inches; Omaha Indians, Nebraska; cat. no. IV B 2225, Berlin Museum für Völkerkunde.

FIG. 833.  Shinny stick; length, 39 inches; Omaha Indians, Nebraska; cat. no. IV B 2225, Berlin Museum für Völkerkunde.

Rev. J. Owen Dorsey [b] describes tabegasi, men's game of ball, as follows:

This is played by the Omahas and Ponkas with a single ball.  There are thirty, forty, or fifty men on each side, and each one is armed with a curved stick about 2 feet long.  The players strip off all their clothing except their breechcloths.  At each end of the playground [figure 834] are two posts from 12 to 15 feet apart.  The playground is from 300 to 400 yards in length.  When the players on the opposite side see that the ball is liable to reach A they try to knock it aside, either towards B or C, as their opponents would win if the ball passed between the posts at A.  On the other hand, if the party represented by A see that the ball is in danger of passing between the posts at D, they try to divert it either towards E or F.

The stakes may be leggings, robes, arrows, necklaces, etc.  All are lost by the losing side, and are distributed by the winners in equal shares.  One of the elder

[a] Among the Indians: Eight Years in the Far West, 1858–1866, p. 67, Philadelphia, 1868.

[b] Omaha Sociology.  Third Annual Report of the Bureau of Ethnology, p. 336, 1884.

men is requested to make the distribution. Two small boys, about 12 years old, stand at the posts A, and two others are at D. One boy at each end tries to send the ball between the posts, but the other one attempts to send it in the opposite direction. These boys are called uhé ginájiⁿ.

The game used to be played in three ways: (1.) Phratry against phratry. Then one of the players was not blindfolded. (2.) Village against village. The Omaha had three villages after 1855. . . . (3.) When the game was played neither by phratries nor by villages, sides were chosen thus: A player was blindfolded, and the sticks were placed before him in one pile, each stick having a special mark by which its owner could be identified. The blindfolded man then took up two sticks at a time, one in each hand, and, after crossing hands, he laid the sticks in separate piles. The owners of the sticks in one pile formed a side for the game. The corresponding women's game is wabaꞮnade.

FIG. 834.  Plan of shinny ball ground; Omaha Indians, Nebraska; from Dorsey.

OSAGE.  Oklahoma.   (Cat. no. 59174, Field Columbian Museum.)
Buckskin-covered ball (figure 835) 2⅝ inches in diameter, cover in one
    piece, with median seam four-fifths round; and stick, a sapling,
    bent and squared at the end, 31½ inches in length.
Collected by Dr George A. Dorsey.

FIG. 835.  Shinny ball and stick; diameter of ball, 2⅝ inches; length of stick; 31¼ inches; Osage
Indians, Oklahoma; cat. no. 59174, Field Columbian Museum.

## SKITTAGETAN STOCK

HAIDA.  Queen Charlotte islands, British Columbia.
  Mr James Deans [a] says:
  It has been common from unknown times for all the native tribes on this coast to play the game of shinny, it being played in the same way our fathers used to play it, and as I have often played it myself, with crooked stick and wooden ball.

## TANOAN STOCK

TIGUA.  Isleta, New Mexico.   (Cat. no. 22728, Free Museum of Science and Art, University of Pennsylvania.)
Ball (figure 836), covered with buckskin, flat, with median seam, 2¾
    inches in diameter; and a stick, a curved sapling, 30 inches in
    length.
Collected by the writer in 1902.

_____

[a] Games of the Haidah Indians.

An Isleta boy, J. Crecencio Lucero, described the people of this pueblo as playing a game of shinny with a soft buckskin ball, poja or pelota, which they hit with a stick, pojatu or chueco. Men and women play.

FIG. 836. Shinny ball and stick; diameter of ball, 2¼ inches; length of stick, 30 inches; Tigua Indians, Isleta, New Mexico; cat. no. 22728, Free Museum of Science and Art, University of Pennsylvania.

TEWA. Santa Clara, New Mexico.

Mr T. S. Dozier [a] writes as follows:

About the middle of January there is played a game that is to the Pueblos what baseball is to the Americans. It is nothing more or less than the old game of shinny, generally played on the ice, as with us. The pu-nam-be, or ball, used is a soft, light affair, made of rags and buckskin or wholly of buckskin. The pu-nam-be pfĕ, stick, is generally of willow, with a curved end, and is about 3 feet long. Men, boys of all sizes, and girls of all ages, and now and then a married woman engage in the pastime. The sexes do not play together, nor the boys with men. Among the men wagers of every description are made. During the past winter, in a game between the men, which lasted nearly a whole day, the side that was beaten had to dance a solemn dance for a whole day. Quite a difficulty arose on account of it.

———— Tesuque, New Mexico. (Cat. no. 23219, 23221, United States National Museum.)

Two shinny sticks (figure 837), made of bent saplings, the bark being left on the handle; lengths, 24 and 26 inches. Collected by Maj. J. W. Powell.

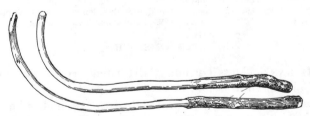

FIG. 837. Shinny sticks; lengths, 24 and 26 inches; Tewa Indians, Tesuque, New Mexico; cat. no. 23219 and 23221, United States National Museum.

WAKASHAN STOCK

MAKAH. Neah bay, Washington. (Cat. no. 37387, 37388, Free Museum of Science and Art, University of Pennsylvania.)

Ball (figure 838), an irregular spheroid, 3 inches in diameter, made of whalebone; and two sticks (figure 839), one a round club,

[a] Some Tewa Games. Unpublished manuscript, Bureau of American Ethnology.

curved at the end, 31 inches in length, used for striking the ball, ·
and the other slender, 32 inches in length, hooked at the end,
used in running away with the ball.   Collected by the writer in
1900, and described by Dr George A. Dorsey [a] as follows:

Keyuquah.—This is the well-known game of shinny, which is played, as a rule,
only by young men.   In former times it was only played at the celebration
of the capture of a whale.   Now it is played at any time.   A specimen of bat,
lok-whiuk, was collected, which differs from the shinny stick as used by the tribes
of the interior, in that it has no broad extended portion.   The bat measures
2 feet 9 inches in length, the lower 6 inches being curved out at an angle of
twenty degrees.   One side of this curved extremity is flattened.   The specimen collected of the ball (huoo) is made from the body of some large vertebra.
Williams states that in former times the ball was invariably made of whalebone.
The goals (loquatsis, for the mark) are two straight lines on the beach, about
200 yards apart, and the starting point of the game is invariably from a point
equidistant between the goal lines.

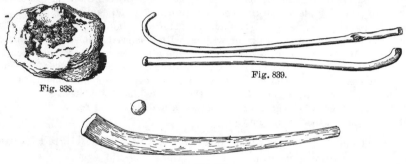

Fig. 838.

Fig. 839.

Fig. 840.

Fig. 838.   Shinny ball; diameter, 3 inches; Makah Indians, Neah bay, Washington; cat. no.
37387, Free Museum of Science and Art, University of Pennsylvania.
Fig. 839.   Shinny sticks; lengths, 31 and 32 inches; Makah Indians, Neah bay, Washington; cat.
no. 37388, Free Museum of Science and Art, University of Pennsylvania.
Fig. 840.   Shinny ball and stick; diameter of ball, 1¼ inches; length of stick, 33 inches; Mission
Indians, Mesa Grande, California; cat. no. 62539, Field Columbian Museum.

YUMAN STOCK

Mission Indians.   Mesa Grande, California.   (Cat. no. 62539, Field
        Columbian Museum.)
Ball of wood (figure 840), painted brown, 1¾ inches in diameter,
    and stick, a round club, 33 inches in length, slightly curved and
    expanding toward the end.   Collected by Mr C. B. Watkins.

Mohave.   Parker, Yuma county, Arizona.   (Field Columbian Mu-
        seum.)
Cat. no. 63395.   Ball (figure 841), made of cordage, 1¾ inches in
    diameter.   Another (cat. no. 63399) is somewhat smaller and
    unpainted.

[a] Games of the Makah Indians of Neah Bay.   The American Antiquarian, v. 23, p. 70,
1901.

Cat. no. 63357.   Ball sticks (figure 841) of cottonwood, 41 inches in
      length, slender and curved at the end.   Half the stick near the
      striking end is blackened by charring.   Another (cat. no. 63359)
      is also 41 inches in length.   The first stick has a notched cross
      mark on the handle.

Collected by Mr S. C. Simms, who gives the name of the ball as
mahlke.

MOHAVE.   Fort Mohave, Arizona.   (Cat. no. 63194, Field Columbian
      Museum.)

Slender stick, 42½ inches in length, unpainted and curved at the end.

Collected by Mr S. C. Simms, who gives the name of the stick as
unro.

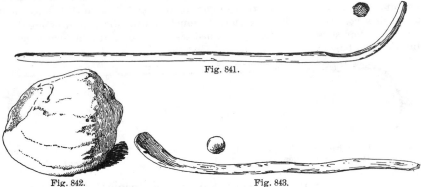

Fig. 841.

Fig. 842.                                    Fig. 843.

FIG. 841.  Shinny ball and stick; diameter of ball, 1⅜ inches; length of stick, 41 inches; Mohave
      Indians, Arizona; cat. no. 63395, 63357, Field Columbian Museum.
FIG. 842.  Shinny ball; diameter, 4¼ inches; Mohave Indians, Arizona; cat. no. 24163, United
      States National Museum.
FIG. 843.  Shinny ball and stick; diameter of ball, 2¼ inches; length of stick, 32 inches; Walapai
      Indians, Arizona; cat. no. 63140, Field Columbian Museum.

———— Colorado river, Arizona.   (Cat. no. 10098, 10117, Peabody
      Museum of American Archæology and Ethnology.)

Stick, or bat, curved at one end, length, 3 feet 2 inches, and ball con-
      sisting of large dried pumpkin stem.

Collected by Dr Edward Palmer, who describes them as a shinny
stick and ball for bandy.

———— Colorado river, Arizona.   (Cat. no. 24163, United States Na-
      tional Museum.)

Shinny ball (figure 842), a dried pumpkin or squash, an irregular
      spheroid, about 4½ inches in diameter.   Collected by Dr Edward
      Palmer.

WALAPAI.   Walapai reservation, Arizona.   (Cat. no. 63140, Field
      Columbian Museum.)

Buckskin-covered ball (figure 843), 2¼ inches in diameter, the cover
      a bag brought together by a drawstring; and ten sticks, curved
      at one end, about 32 inches in length.

They were collected by Mr Henry P. Ewing, who describes the game as follows:

The tas-a-va game is not a Walapai game, particularly, although the young men and boys still play it a good deal.   It is essentially the national game of the Mohave.   They use a more delicate stick, made of willow, slender and curved perfectly at the end.   The men all play it, young and old, and they are very expert, and it has developed them into great runners.   They make a ball with a buckskin cover sewed on it exactly like the cover on our baseballs.   Their ball is smaller and neater, their sticks trimmer and nicer, and when they play with the Walapai there is always a row about whether the Mohave ball or the Walapai ball shall be used.   The Mohave usually give in, because they know that they can win anyway.   As many can play as wish, and the distance for the grounds is usually from 300 to 500 yards.   In starting the game the ball is buried by a medicine man in sight of all halfway between the home stations, and at a signal the contestants rush in and dig out the ball with their sticks and away they go.   It is against the rules to touch it with the hands, or anything but the shinny stick.   The sticks are called tas-a-va; the ball tam-a-nat-a, meaning tied in a bundle.

FIG. 844.   Shinny ball and stick; diameter of ball, 1¼ inches; length of stick, 38½ inches: Yuma Indians, Fort Yuma, California; cat. no. 63349, Field Columbian Museum.

YUMA.   Fort Yuma, San Diego county, California.   (Field Columbian Museum.)

Cat. no. 63349.   Ball (figure 844), covered with colored yarn, red, white, and black, 1¼ inches in diameter; and slender curved stick, 38½ inches in length, the handle straight, the end crooked, the outside of the curved end painted black, the inner side red, with three sets of bands of 'colored paint—red, black, and red; black, red, and black; and black, red, and black on the lower half of the stick above the crook.

Cat. no. 63312.   Ball and stick similar to the preceding, but uncolored and unpainted.

Collected by Mr S. C. Simms, who gives the name of the ball as etsoat and that of the stick as sahtos.

ZUÑIAN STOCK

ZUÑI.   Zuñi, New Mexico.   (Cat. no. 3077, 3569, Brooklyn Institute Museum.)

Bag-shaped ball (figure 845), covered with deerskin, 2 inches in diameter; and curved stick, 35 inches in length.   Collected by the writer in 1903.

The name of the ball was given as poppun and that of the stick as poppun kapnaki tammai.

Mrs Matilda Coxe Stevenson[a] speaks of the game of popone tkapnane, ball hit, as the same as shinny or bandy, and says that the Zuñi assert that the game came from Mexico long ago.

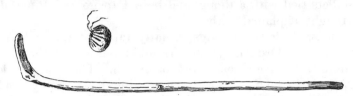

FIG. 845.  Shinny ball and stick; diameter of ball, 2 inches; length of stick, 35 inches; Zuñi Indians, Zuñi, New Mexico; cat. no. 3077, 3569, Brooklyn Institute Museum.

ZUÑI.  Zuñi, New Mexico.  (Cat. no. 4999, Brooklyn Institute Museum.)

Buckskin-covered ball (figure 846), ovate, with median seam, 8 inches in greatest diameter.  Collected by the writer in 1904.

This is used in the man's game of shinny, po-pone-kap-na-kwai. The goals consist of circles in the sand on the east and west sides of the village.  A hole is dug midway between, in which the ball is placed and covered with sand.  Each man makes a lightning mark with his stick.  The object is to drive the ball into the opponent's circle.  They bet on the game.  The smaller balls are used by boys.

FIG. 846.  Shinny ball; diameter, 8 inches; Zuñi Indians, Zuñi, New Mexico; cat. no. 4999, Brooklyn Institute Museum.

### DOUBLE BALL

The game of double ball throughout the eastern United States and among the Plains tribes is played exclusively by women, and is commonly known as the woman's ball game.  In northern California, however, it is played by men.

The implements for the game consist of two balls or similar objects attached to each other by a thong, and a curved stick with which they are thrown.

The balls vary in shape and material.  Among the Cheyenne two small slightly flattened buckskin balls are used.  The Wichita balls are smaller, with a long cut-leather fringe.  Among the Sauk and Foxes and other Algonquian tribes the balls are oblong, weighted with sand, and frequently both, with the connecting thong, are made of one piece of buckskin.  These pass by an easy transition into a single long buckskin-covered piece, somewhat narrow in the middle, as among the Paiute.

[a] American Anthropologist. n. s., v. 5, p. 496, 1903.

A distinct variation is found among the Hupa, where, instead of balls, two small bottle-shaped billets tied together at the top are employed.  The Klamath use large billets fastened together by a cord passing through a hole in the middle of each stick.  The Chippewa, Papago, Tarahumare, Achomawi, and Shasta have short cylindrical billets tied with a thong, and both Papago and Pima, double balls wrought of plaited leather.

The sticks, made of saplings, usually taper to the end and are slightly curved.  Ordinarily they are plain, but among the Shoshoni and Paiute they have a small fork or crotch.  They vary in length from 23 inches to 6 feet.  One stick is almost invariably used, but Catlin describes the Dakota as playing with one in each hand.  The bases, two in number, consist of poles (Chippewa) or of two piles of earth (Omaha), and vary in distance from 300 and 400 yards (Omaha) to a mile (Cree) apart.  The object of the game is to get the ball over the opponent's base line or to take it to one's home (Missisauga).  Bets are made upon the result.

FIG. 847. Yoke-shaped billet; height, 3⅝ inches; cliff-dwelling, Mancos canyon, Colorado; Free Museum of Science and Art, University of Pennsylvania.

Double ball as a woman's game appears at present to have no ceremonial significance.  Its implements, however, offer a possible means of identifying the wooden yoke-shaped objects found in the cliff-dwellings, such as are represented in figure 847 from Mancos canyon, Colorado.

This specimen, in the Free Museum of Science and Art of the University of Pennsylvania, was made by bending a straight piece of wood, 8½ inches in length.  The ends are cylindrical, each having three knobs, one at the extremity and two equidistant above.  The upper part of the yoke, which is 4 inches in height, is squared.  A large number of similar yokes, accompanied by many highly finished sticks, which might have been used for throwing them, were found together in a chamber in the Pueblo Bonito, Chaco canyon, New Mexico, by the Hyde exploring expedition.  The collection is now in the American Museum of Natural History, New York City.  The sticks, numbering several hundred specimens, vary in length from 3 to 4 feet, and are very finely finished.  They vary also in form.  One series terminates in a kind of hook.  Another has a curved end, on some bound with cord or sinew and on others plain.  A third series has a flat, shovel-like end.  Still others are straight, with a flat, knobbed handle.

A ceremonial analogue of the game may be observed in the tossing of the annulets and cylinder from cloud-terrace symbol to cloud-terrace symbol by the girls and boys in the procession on the ninth day of the Flute ceremony.

M. Wright Gill

FLUTE CHILDREN THROWING ANNULETS AND CYLINDERS ON RAIN-CLOUD SYMBOLS; HOPI INDIANS, MISHONGNOVI, ARIZONA; FROM FEWKES

Dr J. Walter Fewkes [a] described this performance as witnessed by him at Shipaulovi in the summer of 1891:

These annulets [figure 848] [called yo-yo-ñu-la] were made of wi'-po, a flag leaf, which is twisted into shape around a core of the same material. Into each was bound one or more live insects, bā'-chi-bi, a "skater" which lives on the surface of the water. The annulet was painted black, and to it was attached a handle made of twisted fibers of yucca leaves, forming a hoop across the annulet by which it can be carried. . . .

At the same time that the annulets were manufactured, a small cylinder [figure 849], about the length of the diameter of the annulets, or a little more, was whittled out of wood. This cylinder was painted black. . . . A small handle made of yucca fiber was securely fastened to it.

Fig. 848.

In the march to the top of the mesa from the spring two girls each cast an annulet, and the boys the cylinder, into the cloud-terrace symbol [plate xx], which the priest traced with meal on the ground, using for the purpose the long black-snake baho.

A similar cylinder and annulets are described by Doctor Fewkes [b] as employed in the Mishongnovi Flute ceremony in 1896.

A stick with a small ring stands on each side of the altar of the Drab Flute at Oraibi, these being the implements used by the girls in the ceremony described above.

The double or tied billets used in this game may be referred to the two bows of the twin War Gods, and the other forms are probably derived from them. A suggestion as to the origin of the tossing stick may be obtained from the Flute ceremony.

Fig. 849.

FIG. 848. Annulet baho, used in the Flute ceremony; Hopi Indians, Shipaulovi, Arizona; from Fewkes.
FIG. 849. Cylinder tossed in the Flute ceremony; Hopi Indians, Shipaulovi, Arizona; from Fewkes.

ALGONQUIAN STOCK

CHEYENNE. Oklahoma. (Cat. no. 50/24, American Museum of Natural History.)

Two buckskin-covered balls (figure 850), 3 inches in diameter, somewhat flattened, with median seam, painted yellow, with red bands on opposite side of the seam and green rings on opposite faces, connected by a thong 5 inches long. Collected by Mr Walter C. Roe and described as thrown with a stick.

[a] Journal of American Ethnology and Archæology, v. 2, p. 131, Boston, 1892.
[b] Nineteenth Annual Report of the Bureau of American Ethnology, pt. 2, p. 999, 1900.

CHIPPEWA.  Wisconsin.

Prof I. I. Ducatel [a] says:

The only play observed among the girls is the pahpahjekahwewog, a sort of substitute for our "graces," which simply consists in catching with two sticks a twine loaded at each end with a ball.

———— Michigan.

Baraga [b] gives the following definitions:

Passikawein, Indian women's play corresponding to the Indian ball play which is played by men only; passikawan, the stick or rod used by the squaws in playing their play.

———— Apostle islands, Wisconsin.

J. G. Kohl [c] says:

Another description of ball play, especially practiced by the women, is what is called the "papassi kawan," which means, literally, "the throwing game." It is played by two large bands, who collect round two opposite poles, and try to throw the object over their opponents' pole. In place of a ball they have two

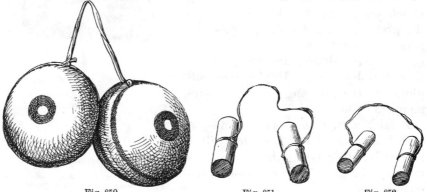

Fig. 850.                Fig. 851.                Fig. 852.

FIG. 850.  Double balls; diameter of balls, 3 inches; Cheyenne Indians, Oklahoma; cat. no. $\frac{50}{34}$, American Museum of Natural History.
FIG. 851.  Double billets; length of billets, 3¾ inches; Chippewa Indians, Bear island, Leech lake, Minnesota; cat. no. $\frac{50}{4725}$, American Museum of Natural History.
FIG. 852.  Double billets; length of billets, 4¼ inches; Chippewa Indians, Bear island, Leech lake, Minnesota; cat. no. $\frac{50}{4724}$, American Museum of Natural History.

leathern bags filled with sand, and attached by a thong. They throw them in the air by means of a staff excellently shaped for the purpose, and catch it again very cleverly. The stick is sharp and slightly bent at the end, and adorned like the raquets. I once saw a very neat model of these instruments for the women's throwing game suspended to the cradle of a little girl.

———— Bear island, Leech lake, Minnesota.  (American Museum of Natural History.)

Cat. no. $\frac{50}{4725}$.  The wooden billets (figure 851), each 3¾ inches in length, tied together with a cord of lin bark. The ends of the billets are painted red.

[a] A Fortnight Among the Chippewas.  The Indian Miscellany, p. 368, Albany, 1877.
[b] A Dictionary of the Otchipwe Language, Cincinnati, 1853.
[c] Kitchi-Gami, Wanderings round Lake Superior, p. 90, London, 1860.

Cat. no. $\frac{50}{4724}$.  Two wooden billets (figure 852), similar to the preceding, but 4¼ inches in length, diameter 1½ inches, unpainted, and tied together with a strip of the same bark.

Collected in 1903 by Dr William Jones.

CHIPPEWA.  Fort William, Ontario.  (Cat. no. $\frac{50}{4727}$, $\frac{50}{4751}$, American Museum of Natural History.)

Double ball (figure 853), two buckskin-covered bags made in one piece, 18½ inches in length; with a stick, a sapling, 44 inches in length, painted red.

Collected in 1903 by Dr William Jones.

——— Turtle mountain, North Dakota.  (American Museum of Natural History.)

Cat. no. $\frac{50}{4726}$.  Two buckskin-covered bags (figure 854), made in one piece, 20 inches in length, having Greek crosses made of green beads sewed on the opposite faces.  Accompanied by a stick 26½ inches in length, wrapped from the upper end with black

Fig. 853.                                        Fig. 854.

FIG. 853.  Double ball and stick; length of ball, 18½ inches; length of stick, 44 inches: Chippewa Indians, Fort William, Ontario; cat. no. $\frac{50}{4727}$, $\frac{50}{4751}$, American Museum of Natural History.

FIG. 854.  Double ball and stick; length of ball, 20 inches; length of stick, 26½ inches; Chippewa Indians, Turtle mountain, North Dakota; cat. no. $\frac{50}{4726}$, American Museum of Natural History.

cloth for the greater part of its length, and ornamented with a band of red and three bands of white beads.

Cat. no. $\frac{50}{4728}$.  A double ball, similar to the preceding, but decorated with white, red, and blue beads.

These were collected in 1903 by Dr William Jones, who states that the goal is the bent limb of a tree or a stick that will hold the bag, the goals being from 100 to 200 yards apart.  The stick is called wipawaganak; the bag, papasikawanag, meaning thing that is kicked.  The game is called by the same name as the bag.

CREE. Muskowpetung reserve, Qu'appelle, Assiniboia. (Cat. no. 61992, Field Columbian Museum.)

Two oblong balls covered with deerskin, connected by a strip of the same material (figure 855) ; total length, 24 inches.

They were collected by Mr J. A. Mitchell, who describes the game under the name of puseekowwahnuk, kicking game:

> The name of kicking game seems to be a misnomer, as the game is in no way played with the feet. The game is played by women only, any number, but not by the old women, as great powers of endurance are required. It is in many respects similar to lacrosse. The players are given various stations in the field and carry sticks. The goals are usually 1 mile or thereabout apart.
>
> Players gather in a circle at the beginning and the double ball is thrown aloft from the stick of one of the leaders, when the scrimmage commences and is kept up until one side passes the ball through its opponent's goal.
>
> The game is a very interesting one and develops much skill. It is, from a hygienic point of view, highly beneficial, as it develops a fine, robust class of women. As with all other Indian games, this game is invariably played for stakes of some kind.

Fig. 856.

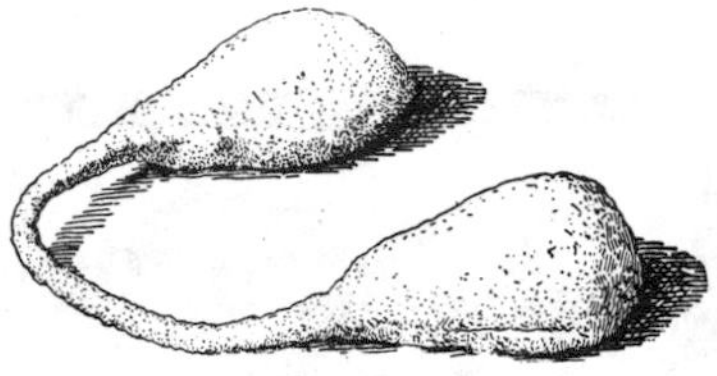

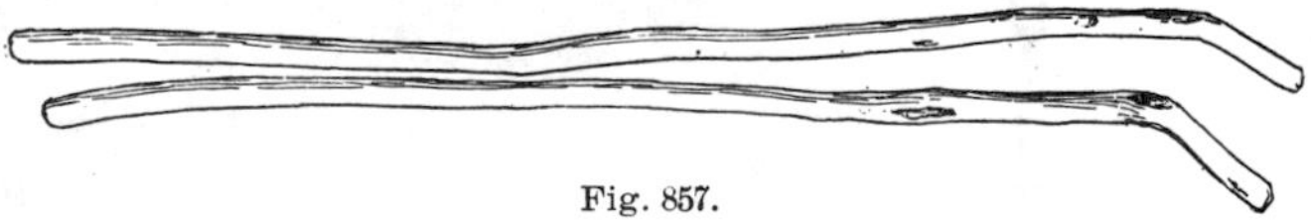

Fig. 855.                         Fig. 857.

FIG. 855. Double ball; length, 24 inches; Cree Indians, Assiniboia; cat. no. 61992, Field Columbian Museum.

FIG. 856. Double ball; length, 10 inches; Cree Indians, Wind River reservation, Wyoming; cat. no. 37030, Free Museum of Science and Art, University of Pennsylvania.

FIG. 857. Sticks for double ball; length, 31 inches; Cree Indians, Wind River reservation, Wyoming; cat. no. 37030, Free Museum of Science and Art, University of Pennsylvania.

——— Wind River reservation, Wyoming. (Cat. no. 37030, Free Museum of Science and Art, University of Pennsylvania.)

Two oblong bags of buckskin (figure 856), weighted with sand, and attached to each other by a thong made of the same piece; length, 10 inches. Two sticks (figure 857), peeled saplings, slightly curved at one end and painted yellow; length, 31 inches.

These were collected by the writer in 1900 from an Indian of Riel's band, who gave the name of the balls as wepitse and weshikanik, and the name of the sticks as wepitse kana tikwa. The game is said to be played by both men and women. The goal is placed at a distance of 50 yards.

CREE. Edmonton, Alberta. (Cat. no. 15060, Field Columbian Museum.)

A buckskin bag (figure 858), 12 inches in length, the ends filled with sand; and a curved stick, 37 inches in length. Collected by Isaac Cowie and described as used by women in playing handball.

MENOMINEE. Shawano, Wisconsin. (Cat. no. 37958, Free Museum of Science and Art, University of Pennsylvania.)

Double ball (figure 859), consisting of two slender buckskin bags, united in the center by a thong 5½ inches in length; total length, 10½ inches.

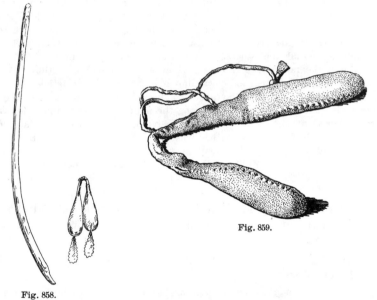

Fig. 859.

Fig. 858.

FIG. 858. Double ball and stick; length of ball, 12 inches; length of stick, 37 inches; Cree Indians, Alberta; cat. no. 15060, Field Columbian Museum.

FIG. 859. Double ball; length, 10½ inches; Menominee Indians, Shawano, Wisconsin; cat. no. 37958, Free Museum of Science and Art, University of Pennsylvania.

This was collected by F. X. Steinbrecker in 1890 and is described on an appended label as a superstitious toy used by females at joyous feasts.

A Menominee Indian informed the author in Washington that the women of this tribe play the game with the long double ball, which they call cuachiciwuk.

MISSISAUGA. Rice lake, Ontario.

G. Copway[a] says:

Doubtless the most interesting of all games is the Maiden's Ball Play, in the Ojibway language, pah-pah-se-Kah-way. The majority of those who take part in this play are young damsels, although married women are not excluded.

───────

[a] The Traditional History and Characteristic Sketches of the Ojibway Nation, p. 55, Boston, 1851.

The ball is made of deer skin bags, each about 5 inches long and 1 in diameter. These are so fastened together as to be at a distance of 7 inches each from the other.  It is thrown with a stick 5 feet long.

This play is practiced in summer beneath the shade of wide-spreading trees, beneath which each strives to find their homes, tahwin, and to run home with it. These having been appointed in the morning, the young women of the village decorate themselves for the day by painting their cheeks with vermilion and disrobe themselves of as much unnecessary clothing as possible, braiding their hair with colored feathers, which hang profusely down to the feet.

At the same time the whole village assemble, and the young men, whose loved ones are seen in the crowd, twist and turn to send shy glances to them, and receive their bright smiles in return.

The same confusion exists as in the game of ball played by the men.  Crowds rush to a given point as the ball is sent flying through the air.  None stop to narrate the accidents that befall them, though they tumble about to their not little discomfiture; they rise, making a loud noise between a laugh and a cry, some limping behind the others, as the women shout.  "Ain goo " is heard, sounding like the notes of a dove, of which it is no bad imitation.  Worked garters, moccasins, leggins, and vermilion are generally the articles at stake. Sometimes the chief of the village sends a parcel as they commence, the contents of which are to be distributed among the maidens when the play is over.

I remember that, some winters before the teachers from the pale faces came to the lodge of my father, my mother was very sick.  Many thought she could not recover her health.  At this critical juncture she told my father that it was her wish to see the Maiden's Ball Play, and gave as her reason for her request that were she to see the girls at play it would so enliven her spirits with the reminiscences of early days as to tend to her recovery.

A description of the game follows in which it is related that the goals were two large spruce trees transplanted from the woods to holes in the ice.

MISSISAUGA.  River Credit, Ontario.

Rev. Peter Jones [a] says:

The women have a game called uhpuhsekuhwon, which is played with two leather balls tied with a string about 2 feet long.  These are placed on the ground, and each woman, with a stick about 6 feet long, tries to take up uhpuhsekuhwon from her antagonist, throwing it in the air.  Whichever party gets it first to their respective goals or stakes counts 1.

FIG. 860.  Double ball; length, 18¼ inches; Sauk and Fox Indians, Tama, Iowa; cat. no. 36754, Free Museum of Science and Art, University of Pennsylvania.

SAUK AND FOXES.  Tama, Iowa.  (Cat. no. 36754, Free Museum of Science and Art, University of Pennsylvania.)

Bag of cotton cloth (figure 860), 18½ inches in length, expanded at the two ends and thin in the middle.  Collected by the writer in 1900.

Six women play on each side, some 50 yards apart.  The side that first gets the ball across wins the game.  The ball is called kunanohc .

[a] History of the Ojebway Indians, p. 135, London, 1861.

SAUK AND FOXES. Iowa. (Cat. no. $\frac{50}{2210}$, American Museum of Natural History.)

Double ball (figure 861), covered with buckskin and filled with sand, the ends ovate; length, 15 inches.

Cat. no. $\frac{50}{2209}$. Two sticks or clubs (figure 862), slightly knobbed at the end opposite the handle, 36 and 39 inches in length, one blackened and the other white.

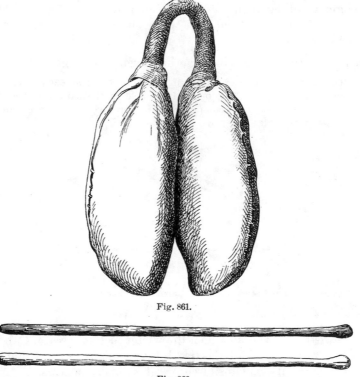

Fig. 861.

Fig. 862.

FIG. 861. Double ball; length, 15 inches; Sauk and Fox Indians, Iowa; cat. no. $\frac{50}{2210}$, American Museum of Natural History.

FIG. 862. Sticks for double ball; lengths, 36 and 39 inches; Sauk and Fox Indians, Iowa; cat. no. $\frac{50}{2209}$, American Museum of Natural History.

The foregoing specimens were collected by Dr William Jones, who describes them as used in the woman's ball game:

The game is played only by women. They have two bases, for which almost anything will answer. They like to get two trees some distance apart—say a quarter of a mile—and use outstretched limbs for the goals. The ball must be thrown on the goal. Each goal made counts a point. The color of the sticks corresponds with the division among the people into Whites and Blacks, each side using implements of its appropriate color.

The game is called ko-nen-no-hi-wag; the ball, ko-na-no-ha-ki, kidneys; the ball sticks, ot-chi.

ATHAPASCAN STOCK

HUPA.  Hupa valley, California.  (Cat. no. 37208, Free Museum of Science and Art, University of Pennsylvania.)

Implements for the game of miskatokitch: Two small bottle-shaped billets of wood (figure 863), with a knob at each end, attached to each other by a double thong 3 inches in length; and a slender stick (figure 864), or bat, of hardwood, 32 inches in length, slightly curved at the end.  Collected by the writer in 1900.

The billets are called yatomil, while the long sticks are called by the same name as the game.[a]

Dr J. W. Hudson describes another form of this game:

A dumb-bell-shaped piece of buckskin, with big knots at each end, is jerked with a rod to a tree goal.  The buckskin is held in the mouth by one captain, who finally drops it between the opponents.  There are three players to a side. The game is characterized by fierce interference.

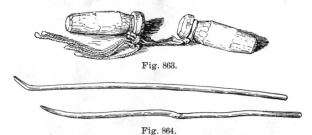

Fig. 863.

Fig. 864.

FIG. 863.  Double billets; length of each, 3 inches; Hupa Indians, Hupa valley, California; cat. no. 37208, Free Museum of Science and Art, University of Pennsylvania.
FIG. 864.  Sticks for double-billet game; length, 32 inches; Hupa Indians, California; cat. no. 37208, Free Museum of Science and Art, University of Pennsylvania.

A Crescent City Indian whom the writer met at Arcata, California, in 1900 gave the name of the tied billets as naustais and that of the long sticks, or bats, as naustaischin; let us play, natithis.

Dr Pliny Earle Goddard [b] says:

The Hupa have four games.  One of these very much resembles shinny. The contestants are not individuals, but social or ethnic units.  Village is pitted against village or tribe against tribe.  The shinny stick, called miʟkitûkûtc, is about 3 feet long, or, more exactly, the length of the leg of the player.  It has a natural turn at the end.  Two round sticks about 5 inches long tied together with a piece of buckskin are used for a ball.  They are called yademil.  A straight course is laid out with a stake at each end.  At least six players take their places in pairs, two at the middle and two at the points halfway between the middle and the stakes.  The pair at the middle have the balls.  Those at the other points stand facing each other with interlocked sticks.  They are said " to tie " each other.  One of the two at the middle of the course takes the two balls in his teeth.  Suddenly he drops them and tries to drive them toward

---

[a] Dr Pliny E. Goddard gave the writer the names as follows: Long sticks, mil-tĕ-tŭk-ketsh; tied sticks, yā-tĕ-mil.
[b] Life and Culture of the Hupa, p. 60, Berkeley, 1903.

his goal by catching the buckskin loop on the end of his stick.  If he succeeds, he runs after the balls and tries to strike them again before he is overtaken. If he is overtaken, the next pair of players release one another and start after the balls while the first couple wrestle.  The third pair take up the game if the second couple become involved in a wrestling match.  The side which succeeds in getting the balls to the stake wins.  As the game is described as played in former times, it probably rivaled modern football in roughness.

Dr Goddard [a] relates the story of a miraculous boy, Dug-from-the-ground, whose grandmother made him a shinny stick of blue-stone, with other things of the same material, for his journey to the home of the immortals, at the edge of the world, toward the east.  Arriving, he met ten brothers who greeted him, as brother-in-law.  He played shinny with them, Wildcat, Fox, Earthquake, and Thunder, and won with the aid of the stick and balls his grandmother had made.  He returned home to his grandmother and found he had been away as many years as it seemed to him he had spent nights.

Fig. 865.  Double ball and stick; length of ball, 25 inches; length of stick, 32¼ inches; Pawnee Indians, Oklahoma; cat. no. 59405, Field Columbian Museum.

CADDOAN STOCK

ARIKARA.  Fort Berthold, North Dakota.
Susan W. Hall [b] writes:

The women, in their modern Christian sewing meeting, are reviving a pretty and interesting old game of theirs, played with small deerskin-covered balls attached by a couple of inches of deerskin string and tossed by a long stick from one side to another.

PAWNEE.  Oklahoma.  (Cat. no. 59405, Field Columbian Museum.)
Two buckskin balls (figure 865), each composed of two small balls conjoined, which have bands of white and blue beads around the middle, with buckskin fringe at the ends, and a string uniting them; total length, 25 inches; accompanied by a stick, painted yellow, 32½ inches in length.  Another specimen in the same collection (cat. no. 59408) has single balls, flattened, each about 2 inches in diameter, painted yellow.  Collected in 1901 by Dr George A. Dorsey.

[a] Hupa Texts, p. 146, Berkeley, 1904.
[b] A letter to Mr Theodore J. Eastman, dated August 11, 1900.  In a subsequent letter to the writer she says that the balls were about the size of a lemon and were thrown with a stick and kept going from opposing sides.

Doctor Dorsey [a] mentions the shinny ball and double ball being used by a boy and a girl to convey them miraculously through space.

WICHITA.   Oklahoma.

Implements (figure 866) for a woman's ball game, in the possession of Mr James Mooney, consist of two balls of buckskin, each about 2 inches in the greatest diameter and having white glass beads at the median seam fastened together with a thong, 11 inches in length, with a fringe of cut buckskin attached to each; and a stick, consisting of a bent sapling, 23 inches in length.   The balls and stick are painted yellow.   These implements are models, made and presented to Mr Mooney by Wichita Indians at the Indian Congress at Omaha in 1898.

FIG. 866.   Double ball and stick; length of stick, 23 inches; Wichita Indians, Oklahoma; in the possession of Mr James Mooney.

In the Wichita tales the double ball is frequently referred to as a magical implement used in traveling.   Bright-Shining-Woman (the Moon) gave it to women among the things they should use to enjoy themselves.   She showed them how to play the game, and told them that the ball was for their use in traveling.[b]

In the story of " The Seven Brothers and the Woman " [c] the woman made her escape, aided by the double ball.   When she tossed the double ball she went with it up in the air.   Again, in " The Story of Child-of-a-Dog " [d] the woman uses the double ball in escaping from her pursuers.   The same incident occurs in the stories of " Young-Boy-Chief and his Sister " [e] and " Trouble Among the Chief's Children." [f]   In the story of " Young-Boy-Chief Who Married a Buffalo " [g] two women are described as playing the double-ball game with the other women.

COPEHAN STOCK

WINTUN.   California.

Mr Alexander MacFarland Davis [h] says:

I am indebted to Mr Albert S. Gatschet, of Washington, for information concerning a game played among the Wintún Indians, called Ka-rá, which is played by throwing up two disks of wood connected by a string about 3 inches long. They are to be caught when they come down.   Mr Gatschet refers to Mr Jeremiah Curtin, Bureau of Ethnology, for authority.

---

[a] Traditions of the Skidi Pawnee, p. 25, New York, 1904.
[b] The Mythology of the Wichita, p. 28, Washington, 1904.
[c] Ibid., p. 65.
[d] Ibid., p. 146.
[e] Ibid., p. 220.
[f] Ibid., p. 237.
[g] Ibid., p. 200.
[h] A Few Additional Notes concerning Indian Games.   Bulletin of the Essex Institute, v. 18, p. 184, Salem, 1887.

LUTUAMIAN STOCK

KLAMATH. Upper Klamath lake, Oregon. (Cat. no. 61538, Field Columbian Museum.)

Willow poles (figure 867), skuekush, 52¼ inches in length, decorated and marked throughout the greater part of their length with two burnt spiral lines, which run in opposite directions; and two wooden billets, 6 inches long and 1 inch in diameter, fastened to each other by means of a short cord, 10 inches in length, which passes through the center of each billet.

Collected in 1900 by Dr George A. Dorsey,[a] who describes them as used in the game of tchimmaash, generally played by women. Two goals, anku, are marked, about a hundred yards apart. From two to ten generally play.

Dr A. S. Gatschet [b] says:

The tchimmá-ash game is played almost exclusively by females. The tchimmá-ash is a string about 2–3 feet long, to the ends of which sticks or pieces of cloth are tied; it is taken up and thrown forward by two flexible willow rods (shuékûsh wá'hlkish) to playmates, who divide themselves into two parties. Before the commencement of the game two limits (yúash) are meted out on the ground, which serve as bases. Both of them are located between the lines of starting (shalχuétgîsh).

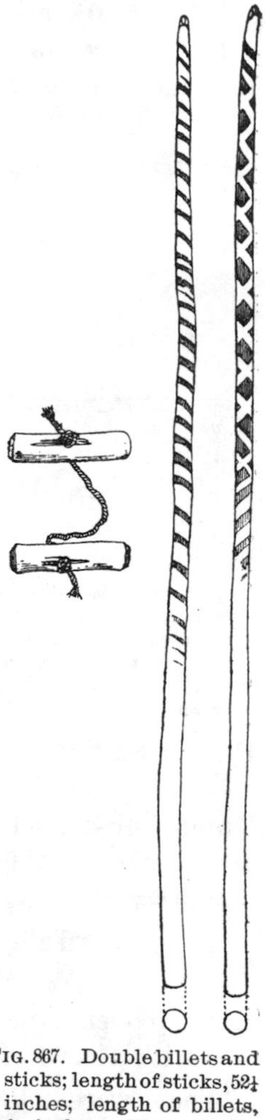

MOQUELUMNAN STOCK

WASAMA. Chowchilly river, Madera county, California.

Dr J. W. Hudson describes the following game under the name of tawilu:

Two or more women contest with 3-foot sticks for a braided buckskin strip 10 inches long. The goals are 150 feet apart.

PIMAN STOCK

PAPAGO. Mission of San Xavier del Bac, Pima county, Arizona. (Field Columbian Museum.)

Cat. no. 63543. Double ball (figure 868), consisting of two balls made of plaited hide, 1½ inches in diameter, united by a plaited

FIG. 867. Double billets and sticks; length of sticks, 52¼ inches; length of billets, 6 inches; Klamath Indians, Oregon; cat. no. 61538, Field Columbian Museum.

[a] Certain Gambling Games of the Klamath Indians. American Anthropologist, n. s., v. 3, p. 19, 1901.

[b] The Klamath Indians of Southwestern Oregon. Contributions to North American Ethnology, v. 2, pt. 1, p. 81, Washington, 1890.

thong, total length, 5 inches; and slender stick, made of sapling, tapering to a point, 44 inches in length.

Cat. no. 63506.   Double ball (figure 869), consisting of two oblong wooden balls, 1⅝ inches in longest diameter, tied together by a strip of cotton cloth.

Cat. no. 63507.   Sticks used with the above, tapering to a point, one 6 feet 10½ inches, and the other 4 feet 4 inches in length.

These were collected by Mr S. C. Simms, who describes them as implements used in the woman's game of toakata.   The Spanish call it "hobbles."

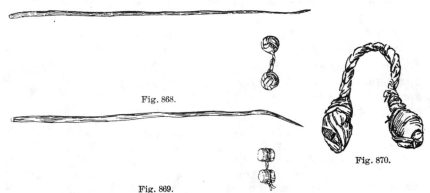

Fig. 868.

Fig. 869.

Fig. 870.

FIG. 868.   Double ball and stick; length of balls, 5 inches; length of stick, 44 inches; Papago Indians, Arizona; cat. no. 63543, Field Columbian Museum.

FIG. 869.   Double billets and stick; length of billets, 1⅜ inches; length of stick, 52 inches; Papago Indians, Arizona; cat. no. 63506, 63507, Field Columbian Museum.

FIG. 870.   Double ball; length, 9½ inches; Pima Indians, Arizona; cat. no. 63499, Field Columbian Museum.

PIMA.    Salt River reservation, Maricopa county, Arizona.   (Cat. no. 63499, Field Columbian Museum.)

Dumb-bell shaped ball (figure 870) of black painted leather; length (extended), 9½ inches.   Collected by Mr S. C. Simms, who describes it as used in a woman's game.

TEPEHUAN.   Talayote, near Nabogame, Chihuahua, Mexico.   (Cat. no. $\frac{65}{9\,1\,6}$, American Museum of Natural History.)

Two wooden billets (figure 871), 2½ inches in length, tied together with a cord of twisted white wood.

These were collected by Dr Carl Lumholtz in 1894, who gave the name of the billets as dādayar and that of the sticks as tshibukar. In case the cord of the billets should break it is mended, and the dadayar is buried under some loose earth in order to be thrown again.   Bets are made by the bystanders.

PUJUNAN STOCK

KAONI.   Cosumnes river, 12 miles south of Placerville, California.

Dr J. W. Hudson describes a game played with a buckskin strap, 24 inches long and knotted at the ends, under the name of tikili.

This is contested for by four women armed with clubs 30 inches long. The goals, which are usually trees, are 100 feet apart.

In Todds valley a dumb-bell shaped plaything consisting of pine cones thrust upon each end of a 12-inch stick [figure 872] is called hĕp'-pĕp-do'-kai. It is played by women, three to a side, with goal-lines 200 feet apart. Kicking or foot-casting only is allowed.

## Nishinam. California.

Mr Stephen Powers[a] says:

The ti'-kel is almost the only really robust and athletic game they use, and is played by a large company of men and boys. The piece is made of rawhide, or nowadays of strong cloth, and is shaped like a small dumb-bell. It is laid in the center of a wide, level space of ground, in a furrow hollowed out a few inches in depth. Two parallel lines are drawn equidistant from it, a few paces apart, and along these lines the opposing parties, equal in strength, range themselves. Each player is equipped with a slight, strong staff, from 4 to 6 feet long. The two champions of the parties take their stations on opposite sides of the piece, which is then thrown into the air, caught on the staff of one or

Fig. 871. Double billets; length, 2¼ inches; Tepehuan Indians, Chihuahua, Mexico; cat. no. ₂₆₁₆, American Museum of Natural History.

the other, and hurled by him in the direction of his antagonist's goal. With this send-off there ensues a wild chase and a hustle, pellmell, higgledy-piggledy, each party striving to bowl the piece over the other's goal. These goals are several hundred yards apart, affording room for a good deal of lively work; and the players often race up and down the champaign, with varying fortunes, until they are dead blown and perspiring like top-sawyers.

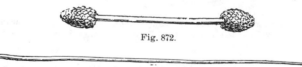

Fig. 872.

Fig. 873.

Fig. 872. Implement for tossing game; Kaoni Indians, California; from sketch by Dr J. W. Hudson.

Fig. 873. Stick for double ball; length, 62 inches; Achomawi Indians, Hat creek, California; cat. no. ₄₁₁₆, American Museum of Natural History.

### SHASTAN STOCK

Achomawi. Hat creek, California. (Cat. no. ₄₁₁₆, American Museum of Natural History.)

Stick (figure 873), a peeled sapling, 62 inches in length.

Collected in 1903 by Dr Roland B. Dixon, who describes it as used in a woman's ball game, luswalli. The tied billets, which doubtless accompanied it, are missing.

[a] Tribes of California. Contributions to American Ethnology, v. 3, p. 333, Washington, 1877.

SHASTA.   Hamburg bar, California.   (Cat. no. $\frac{50}{3194}$, American Museum of Natural History.)

Two wooden billets (figure 874), about 5 inches in length, tied together with a buckskin thong; accompanied with a stick, a peeled sapling, about 40 inches in length.   Collected in 1902 by Dr Roland B. Dixon, who describes these specimens as implements for a woman's game.

FIG. 874.   Double billets and stick; length of billets, about 5 inches; length of stick, about 40 inches; Shasta Indians, California; cat. no. $\frac{50}{3194}$, American Museum of Natural History.

### SHOSHONEAN STOCK

PAIUTE.   Pyramid lake, Nevada.   (Cat. no. 37157, Free Museum of Science and Art, University of Pennsylvania.)

Ball and stick (figure 875) for woman's game; the ball, of buckskin, nearly cylindrical, and expanding at the ends; length, 11½ inches; the stick a forked, peeled sapling, 40 inches in length. Collected by the writer, through Miss Marian Taylor, in 1900.

FIG. 875.   Double ball and stick; length of ball, 11½ inches; length of stick, 40 inches; Paiute Indians, Pyramid lake, Nevada; cat. no. 37157, Free Museum of Science and Art, University of Pennsylvania.

———— Pyramid lake, Nevada.   (Cat. no. 19053, United States National Museum.)

Leather ball for woman's game, 12 inches in length, identical with the preceding.

Collected by Mr Stephen Powers, and described by him in his catalogue under the name of tapecool:

It is laid on the ground midway between two base lines, and the contending parties of women, armed with long sticks, seek to propel it beyond each other's base line.

SHOSHONI.   Wind River reservation, Wyoming.   (Cat. no. 36875, 36876, Free Museum of Science and Art, University of Pennsylvania.)

Ball (figure 876), nazeto, and stick, hope, for a woman's ball game. The ball, a buckskin bag, shaped like a dumb-bell, 10 inches in length; the stick, a peeled willow branch (figure 877), 46½ inches in length, with a projecting twig near the end. Collected by the writer in 1900.

UINTA UTE. White Rocks, Utah. (Cat. no. $\frac{50}{1287}$, American Museum of Natural History.)

Buckskin ball, nearly rectangular, narrowing toward the middle, with padded ends, with design in blue beads on one side, as shown in figure 878; length, 7 inches. Collected by Dr A. L. Kroeber in 1900.

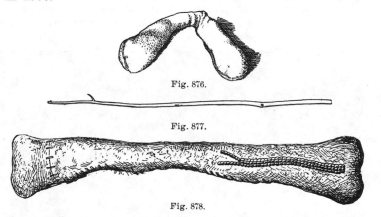

Fig. 876.

Fig. 877.

Fig. 878.

FIG. 876. Double ball; length, 10 inches; Shoshoni Indians, Wyoming; cat. no. 36876, Free Museum of Science and Art, University of Pennsylvania.
FIG. 877. Stick for double ball; length, 46¼ inches; Shoshoni Indians, Wyoming; cat. no. 36875, Free Museum of Science and Art, University of Pennsylvania.
FIG. 878. Double ball; length, 7 inches; Uinta Ute Indians, Utah; cat. no. $\frac{50}{1287}$, American Museum of Natural History.

SIOUAN STOCK

DAKOTA (SANTEE). Prairie du Chien, Wisconsin.

Catlin [a] says:

In the ball-play of the women [figure 879], they have two balls attached to the ends of a string about a foot and a half long; and each woman has a short stick in each hand, on which she catches the string with the two balls, and throws them, endeavoring to force them over the goal of her own party. The men are more than half drunk, when they feel liberal enough to indulge the women in such an amusement, and take infinite pleasure in rolling about on the ground and laughing to excess, while the women are tumbling about in all attitudes, and scuffling for the ball.

OMAHA. Nebraska.

Rev. J. Owen Dorsey [b] describes this game:

Wabáonade, the women's game of ball.—Two balls of hide are filled with earth, grass, or fur, and then joined by a cord. At each end of the playground are two gabázu, or hills of earth, blankets, etc., that are from 12 to 15 feet

[a] Letters and Notes on the Manners, Customs, and Condition of the North American Indians, v. 2, p. 146, London, 1841.
[b] Omaha Sociology. Third Annual Report of the Bureau of Ethnology, p. 338, 1884.

apart. Each pair of hills may be regarded as the "home," or "base," of one of the contending parties, and it is the aim of the members of each party to throw the balls between their pair of hills, as that would win the game.

Two small girls, about 12 years old, stand at each end of the playground and act as uhe ginaji$^n$ for the women, as the boys do for the men in ꝗabe-gasi.

Each player has a webaɔnade, a very small stick of hard or red willow, about 5 feet long, and with this she tries to pick up the balls by thrusting the end of the stick under the cord. Whoever succeeds in picking them up hurls them into the air, as in playing with grace hoops. The women can throw these balls very far. Whoever catches the cord on her stick in spite of the efforts of her opponents tries to throw it still further and closer to her "home." The stakes are buffalo hides, small dishes or bowls, women's necklaces, awls, etc. The bases are from 300 to 400 yards apart. The corresponding men's game is Labe-gasi.

FIG. 879.   Santee Dakota women playing double ball, Prairie du Chien, Wisconsin; from Catlin.

## WASHOAN STOCK

WASHO.   Carson valley and Lake Tahoe, Nevada.

Dr J. W. Hudson describes the following game played by women under the name of tsikayaka:

A buckskin strap, pĕ-tsĭl'-tsi, is contested for by the opposing players, each armed with a four-foot rod, tse-kai'-yak. The goals are stakes, two hundred feet apart.

## WEITSPEKAN STOCK

YUROK.   Klamath river, California.   (Cat. no. 37259, Free Museum of Science and Art, University of Pennsylvania.)

Two bottle-shaped wooden billets (figure 880), 5½ inches in length, with a knob at the end and two lines of bark left at the center, tied together with a piece of twine, $2\frac{1}{2}$ inches in length; accompanied by two long slender sticks (figure 881) or bats, of hard wood, pointed and slightly curved at the end, 33 and 35 inches in length. Collected by the writer in 1900.

The billets are called wat-tai; the bats, mai-num-in. The latter were obtained from an Indian named Wichapec Billy, 57 years of age, who had used them in matches. He said the game was played by three parties of three each, who stripped and painted. Money was put up, say five dollars on a side. Matches were formerly common between Hupa and Wichapec.

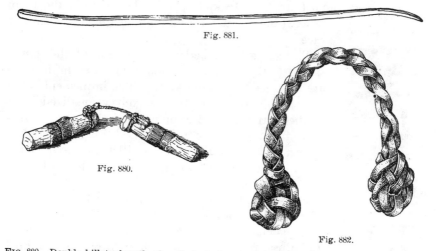

Fig. 881.

Fig. 880.

Fig. 882.

FIG. 880. Double billets; length of each, $5\frac{1}{4}$ inches; Yurok Indians, California; cat. no. 37259, Free Museum of Science and Art, University of Pennsylvania.
FIG. 881. Stick for double billets; length, 33 inches; Yurok Indians, California; cat. no. 37259; Free Museum of Science and Art, University of Pennsylvania.
FIG. 882. Double ball; length, $8\frac{1}{2}$ inches; Maricopa Indians, Arizona; cat. no. 2924, Brooklyn Institute Museum.

### WISHOSKAN STOCK

A Batawat Indian at Blue Lake, California, gave the name of the long sticks as rocosaiyok wataiwat and that of the tied billets as goshwa wik.

### YUMAN STOCK

MARICOPA. Arizona. (Cat. no. 2924, Brooklyn Institute Museum.) Double ball (figure 882), made on a plaited leather throng; length, $8\frac{1}{2}$ inches. Collected in 1904 by Mr Louis L. Meeker, who gives the name as tus-ho-al kik, and says that the ball is pitched with sticks.

### BALL RACE

The ball race appears to be confined to the Southwestern tribes, extending into Mexico and westward into California, although it was found by the writer among the Shoshonean Bannock in Idaho. It consists of a race in which the contestants kick or toss some small object before them, commonly around a circuit which has been agreed upon, back to the starting place. There are either two individual players or two parties. The object which is kicked or tossed is of three different kinds—first, a ball of stone (Pima, Mono, Tewa, Maricopa) or of wood (Opata, Papago, Pima, Tarahumare, Zuaque, Cocopa, Mohave, Yuma); second, a single billet (Navaho) or two billets (Keres, Tewa, Zuñi); third, a ring or rings (Tarahumare, Zuñi). In addition, the Bannock are said to kick a beef bladder, and the Hopi use two cubes of hair and piñon gum in a similar race.

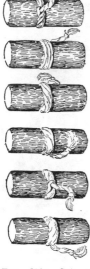

The game of kicked stick was one of the games sacred to the War God in Zuñi, and the implements are sacrificed upon his altar. The implements used may be identified readily as conventionalized bows of the War Gods, an explanation which serves likewise for the racing billets used by other tribes. Objects similar to the kicking billets are used by the Hopi in ceremonials, and may be regarded as having a similar origin.

For example, a set of six small wooden cylinders (figure 883), contained in the Field Columbian Museum, is made of cottonwood root, $2\frac{5}{8}$ inches in length and three-fourths of an inch in diameter, painted black, with green ends, and having a feather attached around the middle by cotton cord. They were collected by Rev. H. R. Voth in 1893, and described by him as oönötki. He says:

FIG. 883. Set of sacrificial wooden cylinders; length, $2\frac{5}{8}$ inches; Hopi Indians, Oraibi, Arizona; cat. no. 67049 to 67054, Field Columbian Museum.

Cylinders of this kind are made of different sizes and used in various ceremonies such as the Flute, Marau, and Soyal. They are deposited as offerings in springs and shrines, but generally not before they have been consecrated at the altar during some ceremony. This set of six was made by and obtained from the chief priest of the Marau order. The small feathers attached to them are those of the pin-tail duck.

Another set of two cylinders in the same museum (cat. no. 67086, 67087) are $2\frac{1}{2}$ inches in length, and are mentioned by Mr Voth as having been found by him in a shrine where the Soyaluna fraternity made their offerings to the sun.

The tossing-rings of the Zuñi and Tarahumare game may be explained as representing net shields, and the contest, which in Zuñi is conducted between the clowns with billets and between the women with rings, is analogous to the ceremony in the Flute dance, where the

Flute youth and the Flute maid throw annulets and cylinders, described under " Double ball," to which game the ball race is apparently closely related.

The existence of the ball race at an early period is proved by specimens of the kicking-sticks (figure 884) in the cliff-dwellings. A pair of such billets from Mancos canyon, identified by Mr Cushing, is in the Free Museum of Science and Art of the University of Pennsylvania. They are made of cottonwood, one 4½ inches in length and 1⅝ inches in diameter, marked around with sharply incised parallel lines about one-fourth of an inch apart; the other 5 inches long and 1¼ inches in diameter, with similar incised lines in diamond pattern. Another pair (figure 885) from the same place are simple sections of

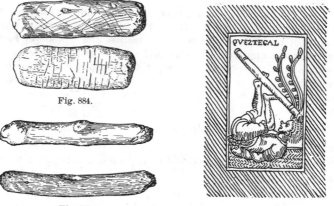

Fig. 884.

Fig. 885.

Fig. 886.

FIG. 884. Kicking billets; lengths, 4½ and 5 inches; cliff-dwelling, Mancos canyon, Colorado; Free Museum of Science and Art, University of Pennsylvania.

FIG. 885. Kicking billets; lengths, 4½ and 5 inches; cliff-dwelling, Mancos canyon, Colorado; Free Museum of Science and Art, University of Pennsylvania.

FIG. 886. Clown kicking billet; Mexico, 1583; reverse of Hispano-American playing card, impression, 2½ by 4 inches; from photograph of the original in the Archives of the Indies, Seville, Spain.

twig, 4¾ and 5 inches in length and three-fourths of an inch in diameter. Many of the unidentified stone balls found in ruins and graves at various places in the Southwest may have been used in this game.

A picture of a travesty of the kicked-stick game, identified by Mr Cushing, is printed on the reverse of an Hispano-American playing card, engraved in Mexico in 1583 and preserved in the Archives of the Indies at Seville, Spain. This curious and interesting relic represents a clown (figure 886), fantastically dressed in the native ceremonial costume, standing on his head and kicking a huge billet in the air with his feet.

The ball race has been adopted from the Indians by the Mexicans of the Rio Grande. Capt. John G. Bourke, of the United States

Army, informed the writer that they have a game of kicking a cow's horn, which they call juego del cuaco.[a]  This game, according to the authority just mentioned, corresponds with the Zuñi, Hopi, Pueblo, and Pima game of the tor stick.

ATHAPASCAN STOCK

NAVAHO.  St Michael, Arizona.

Rev. Berard Haile describes the following game in a letter to the writer:[b]

Iddi is football.  This is a gambling game, and there are two parties, five to a side at most.  There may be less than five, but not more.  The players strip themselves and agree upon a distance, which is regulated by the stake.  A stick, about 4 inches long, of green piñon or oak, cut smooth and round, is set into the ground about 2 fingers deep.  The best runner works his toes, as hands and fingers are not allowed, under the stick, and kicks it ahead of him. Should he miss, his successor is ready to bring it into his territory again.  The required distance being made, the home run begins, and whosoever has the ball at the starting point first wins the game and stake.  The game was played only in the spring of the year, because it is not too warm during that season.  At present the Navaho do not play it.  Some would not allow it, even in the springtime, as they claim it would bring a stormy season and much wind. They say the Great Earth-Winner, Ni'nahuiebî'i, taught them the game.

In a subsequent letter to the author Father Haile gives the name of the game, according to information received from another source, as baaes or iolis, which means " to hop " game, raise and throw with the foot.

The Navaho at Chin Lee, Arizona, informed the writer that this was not originally a Navaho game, but was borrowed by them from the Zuñi.

KERESAN STOCK

KERES.  Acoma, New Mexico.  (Cat. no. 4974, Brooklyn Institute Museum.)

FIG. 887.  Kicking billets; length, 2 inches; Keres Indians, Acoma, New Mexico; cat. no. 4974, Brooklyn Institute Museum.

Two billets (figure 887), 2 inches in length, one painted with black at the ends and the other with a black band in the middle.  Collected by the writer in 1904 and made by James H. Miller, an Acoma Indian, at Zuñi.

They are kicked in a racing game called a-cha-wa-i ta-wa-ka.  The one with the black bands at the end is called gosh, man, and the other tsoi-yo, woman.  This is a game of the war captains, and is played in the spring in the months from March to May to secure rain. The winning stick is buried in a cornfield.  The present sticks are such as are

---

[a] Spanish chueca, pan or hollow of the joints of bones; a small ball with which country people play at crickets.

[b] Under date of June 5, 1902.  The information was obtained from a medicine man named Qatali Natloi, Laughing Doctor.

used by boys. The regular kicking sticks are made of oak. Tsa-tio hu-chi made the game first.

KERES. Cochiti, New Mexico. (Cat. no. 4978, Brooklyn Institute Museum.)

Two wooden billets (figure 888), 2 inches in length and about seven-eighths of an inch in diameter, one painted red and the other yellow.

These were made by a Keres boy from Cochiti, named Francisco Chaves (Kogit), at St Michael, Arizona, who describes the billets under the name of tawaka and mentions them as being kicked in the race of the same name.

Boys, girls, and men play. Sides are chosen, and the sticks are kicked with the bare feet.

———— Laguna, New Mexico. (Cat. no. 3006, Brooklyn Institute Museum.)

Two wooden billets (figure 889), 1⅛ inches in length and about 1 inch in diameter. One of these billets has a band of red paint around the middle, and the other is plain, except the ends, which are painted red. These implements were collected by the writer in 1903.

Fig. 888.                                     Fig. 889.

FIG. 888. Kicking billets; length, 2 inches; Keres Indians, Cochiti, New Mexico; cat. no. 4978, Brooklyn Institute Museum.
FIG. 889. Kicking billets; length, 1⅛ inches; Keres Indians, Laguna, New Mexico; cat. no. 3006, Brooklyn Institute Museum.

The sticks are called tow-wa-ka ; the one with the red band ku-ka-ni tow-wa-ka, and the other sho-mutz tow-wa-ka. The game is called ka-tcho-wai. The blocks are kicked with the bare feet around a designated course. Sides are chosen and there is one block for each. It may not be thrown with the hands, but they may place it on the toe to give it a good kick.

MOQUELUMNAN STOCK

COSUMNI. California.

Mr James Mooney [a] writes as follows from information obtained from Col. Z. A. Rice, of Atlanta, Ga., who went to California in the

[a] Notes on the Cosumnes Tribes of California. The American Anthropologist, v. 3, p. 261, 1890.

year 1850, where he spent several years in the immediate vicinity of the tribe now under consideration, which formerly lived in the Sacramento basin:

Their football game was more properly a foot race. Two parallel tracks were laid off and each party had its own ball. Two athletic young fellows, representing the two contending parties, took their stand at one end, each with a ball on the ground in front of him, and at the signal each kicks it along his respective track towards the goal. All along the line were stationed relays of players, whose duty it was to assist in getting the ball through. It was a rough-and-tumble game, to see who should kick the ball, for no one was allowed to touch it with his hand. Two posts were put up at each end of the track, and the ball must be driven between these posts. Betting was heavy, the stakes being Indian trinkets of all kinds, and judges and stakeholders presided with a great deal of dignity. The score was kept by means of an even number of short sticks, and as each player drove the ball home, he drew out one of the sticks, and so on until the game was won. It was a very exciting play and aroused as much interest as does a horse race among the whites.

WASAMA. Near Grant Springs, Mariposa county, California.

Dr J. W. Hudson describes these Indians as playing a game with a ball made of deer hair and provided with a buckskin cover, in which two men each contest or race with their ball along a prescribed course to a certain goal.

The name of the game is tĕk'mĕ, to kick; and that ot the ball, pu'kŭ, little dog, pup.

### PIMAN STOCK

OPATA. Sonora, Mexico.

Mr A. F. Bandelier [a] says:

The Ua-ki-mari is rather a foot-race than a game of ball, for the runners toss the ball before them with their toes, and the party whose " gomi," or ball of a certain kind of wood, reaches the goal first is declared the victor. . . .

Village plays against village. The Maynates or captains of the runners are important personages on such days, and what is evidently primitive, and shows besides that there is a religious import placed upon the ceremony, is the fact that they formerly used to gather the evening before at a drinking bout, smoking at the same time the fungus of the mesquite, called in Opata to-ji, in long and big cigar-like rolls.

PAPAGO. Mission of San Xavier del Bac, Pima county, Arizona. (Cat. no. 63485, Field Columbian Museum.)

Ball of mesquite wood, 3⅛ inches in diameter, designated by the collector, Mr S. C. Simms, as a football, sonecua.

PAPAGO. Arizona.

Dr H. F. C. ten Kate, jr,[b] says:

One of the few bodily exercises they have is a sort of ball game in which they use a ball made of hard gum, which is kicked without stopping by two men

a Final Report, pt. 1, p. 240, Cambridge, 1890.
b Reizen en Onderzoekingen in Noord-Amerika, p. 29, Leiden, 1885.

who run over a great expanse of country. A large number of spectators follow the two players, either on horseback or on foot, at the same gait.

PIMA. Arizona. (United States National Museum.)

Cat. no. 76014. Two stone balls (figure 894), consisting of tufa, covered with some black vegetable substance, probably mesquite gum; diameters, 2⅛ and 2⅜ inches. Described by the collector, Dr Edward Palmer, as footballs.

Cat. no. 27847. Wooden ball (figure 895), 2½ inches in diameter, covered with mèsquite gum. Described by the collector as a football.

FIG. 890. Papago kicking-ball players, Arizona; from photograph by Mr William Dinwiddie.

Dr H. F. C. ten Kate, jr,[a] says the Pima have a football game in which the ball—sonjikjo—is made of the gum of the greasewood and sand.

———— Arizona.

The late Dr Frank Russell [b] described the kicked ball races of this tribe as follows:

These races were frequently intertribal, and in their contests with the Papagos the Pimas nearly always won. The use of these balls in foot races is very widespread in the Southwest, and even yet we hear of races taking place that exceed twenty miles in length.

The kicking ball when of wood resembles a croquet ball in size, but it is usually covered with a creosote gum. They are made of either mesquite or paloverde wood. Stone balls about 6 cm. in diameter are also used, and are covered with the same black gum.

---

[a] Reizen en Onderzoekingen en Noord-Amerika, p. 159, Leiden, 1885.
[b] In a memoir to be published by the Bureau of American Ethnology.

Each contestant kicks one of these balls before him, doing it so skillfully that his progress is scarcely delayed; indeed, the Pima declare that they can run faster with than without the balls—which, in a sense, is true. Perhaps the occurrence of the stone balls in the ruins gave rise to the idea that they possess magic power to "carry" the runner along, for all things pertaining to the Hohokam have come to have more or less supernatural significance. Two youths will sometimes run long distances together, first one and then the other kicking the ball so that it is almost constantly in the air. The custom of using these balls is rapidly disappearing, as, it is to be regretted, are the other athletic games of the Pima.

The men received thorough training in speed and endurance in running during their raids into the Apache country, but they had few sports that tended toward physical improvement except the foot races. Sometimes a woman ran in a contest against a man, she throwing a double ball by means of a long stick while he kept a kicking ball before him. But the women seldom ran in foot races, though their active outdoor life, engaged in the various tasks that fell to them, kept them in fit condition. However, they had an athletic game which corresponded in a measure to the races of the men and developed skill in running. This game was played as follows:

Âldû.—Two of the swiftest runners among the women acted as leaders and chose alternately from the players until all were selected in two groups. Two goals were fixed about 400 yards apart. One side saying, "To the trail is where we can beat you," while the other party declared, "To that mesquite is where we can beat you." Two lines were formed about 25 yards apart, and the ball was put in play by being tossed up and started toward the opponent's goal. It was thrown with sticks until some one drove it beyond the goal and won the game.[a] To touch the ball with the hands debarred the person from further play. This game was abandoned about 1885.

## TARAHUMARE.   Chihuahua, Mexico.
Dr Carl Lumholtz describes the foot race of this tribe:[b]

Two districts or pueblos always run against each other. Sometimes there are many runners on each side, and the two parties show in their apparel some distinguishing mark; for instance, one side wears red headbands, while the other wears white ones. I have seen from four to twenty runners taking part on each side. Each party has a small ball, about 2 inches in diameter, carved with a knife from the root of an oak tree, which they have to toss ahead of them as they run. The runner who happens to be ahead is the one whose duty it is to toss the ball with his toes, and at each toss it may be thrown a hundred yards or more in advance. They are not allowed to touch the balls with their hands, but their friends who follow them may point out to the runner where the ball is lying. If the ball lodges in an awkward place, as between two rocks, or in the water, the runners or their friends may pick it up and place it back on the race course. The circuits over which the race is held are circular when the country allows, but generally the course is backward and forward along the top of the ridge, the group of spectators and bettors being at the starting-point, which is always at the middle of the race-track. Each party chooses a manager to represent the runners and to arrange the day and place of the race.

---

[a] The stick in the collection is of willow, 1.230 m. long, with a maximum diameter of 18 mm. The balls are in pairs, 15 cm. apart, connected by a 4-strand, 2-ply leather thong, the balls being mere knotty enlargements of the thong.

[b] Tarahumari Life and Customs.  Scribner's Magazine, v. 16, p. 304, New York, 1894.

These managers also decide the number of circuits to be made, and get runners of equal ability, if they can, for each side, the object being to get the best runners possible.

In important races the runners may prepare for a fortnight, but as a rule they do not practice much before the race, for running comes to them as naturally as swimming to ducks. Their training chiefly consists in abstinence from native beer for two or three days before the event. On the day of the race the runners are fed with pinole only; they have tepid water to drink, and their legs are well bathed in warm water and rubbed by the managers. The medicine man also rubs them with a smooth stone to make them strong.

Fig. 891. Papago kicking-ball player, Arizona; from photograph by Mr William Dinwiddie.

A race is never won by natural means. The losers always say that they were influenced by some herb and became sleepy on the race-course, so that they had to lose. The help of the medicine man is needed in preparing the runner for the race. He assists the manager to wash the feet of the runners with warm water and different herbs, and he strengthens their nerves by making passes over them. He also guards them against sorcery. Before they run he performs a ceremony to " cure " them.

The food and the remedies he uses are put under the cross with many kinds of charms, different kinds of woods, and herbs from the barrancas. Some of the herbs are supposed to be very powerful, and they are, therefore, securely tied up in small pieces of buckskin or cotton cloth. If not so tied up, they might break away. The water which the runners drink is also placed near the

cross, upon each side of which is put a candle, and the whole outfit is on a
blanket. At the ceremony the runners stand, holding the balls in their hand.
The doctor, or medicine man, standing near the cross, burns incense (copal)
over them. He also sings about the tail of the gray fox, one of their legendary
animals, and other songs. After this he makes a speech, warning them against
eating pinole or drinking water in other people's houses, for fear of poison;
all that they eat and drink must come from their parents or relatives. They are
not allowed to eat anything sweet, nor eggs, potatoes, cheese, or fat. Three
times they drink from the water near the cross, and three times from the herbs.
The eldest and swiftest runner then leads in walking around the cross as many
times as there are to be circuits in the race, and the rest follow him. All the
things near the cross then remain untouched until morning. The runners sleep
near by to keep watch, and they also secure some old men to watch against
sorcery, for old men are supposed to discover the approach of sorcerers even
when they sleep. After the ceremonies are over the doctor takes each runner
aside and subjects him to a rigid examination.

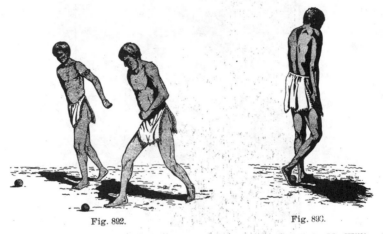

Fig. 892.                                                     Fig. 893.

FIG. 892. Papago kicking-ball race—the start, Arizona; from photograph by Mr William Dinwiddie.
FIG. 893. Papago kicking-ball race, Arizona; from photograph by Mr William Dinwiddie.

More than a hundred kinds of remedies are brought to the contest, some to
strengthen the runners and secure success, and others to weaken their rivals.
The most efficient thing against the rivals is the blood of the turtle and bat
mixed together, dried and ground, and rolled into a big cigar, with a small
amount of tobacco added to it. Its smoke makes the rivals stupid. The dried
head of a crow or eagle, hikori, a small cactus worshiped by the Tarahumaris,
and other herbs and innumerable things are carried around by all who take
part in the racing. Some of the women carry small, thin stones to protect them
against sorcerers. During the race the runners have their heads ornamented
with the feathers of the chaparral-cock, and in some parts with the feathers
of the peacock, of which bird the Indians are very fond, because it is supposed
to be light footed, and also because it is from another country. Many of them
also have their legs ornamented with chalk, and wear belts to which a great
number of deer hoofs, beads, or reeds are attached, so as to make a great
deal of noise. These belts help them to victory, because they become, as they

fancy, as light as the deer itself, and the noise keeps them from falling asleep.

In the afternoon before the race the managers and the runners meet together, the latter bringing the balls with them, to receive an omen as to which party is going to win. Water is put into a big earthen tray, and the two balls are started simultaneously from one end of the tray to the other. The party whose ball reaches the other end first will be the winner, and they repeat this as many times as there are to be circuits. Three or four hours before sunset the chief calls the runners together and makes a speech, warning them against any kind of cheating. Just as in horse racing, rascally tricks are more or less common, especially if the Indians have become half civilized. It may happen that some one will bribe the runners with a cow not to run fast; afterward he may also cheat the runner. It is not uncommon for an important runner to simulate illness. "Our rivals," he may say, "have bewitched us." The whole thing then comes to nothing, and the wagers are divided between the parties, who return to their home to await the next race.

There is no prize given to the runners themselves, and they gain nothing by it unless in helping their friends to win wagers. A good runner is also greatly admired by the women, which may be of some account to him. It is also the custom for a man who has been very lucky with his wagers to give a small part of his winnings to the successful runner, who, however, is allowed to take

Fig. 894.                              Fig. 895.

FIG. 894. Stone kicking balls; diameters, 2¼ and 2⅝ inches; Pima Indians, Arizona; cat. no. 86014, United States National Museum.

FIG. 895. Wooden kicking ball; diameter, 2¼ inches; Pima Indians, Arizona; cat. no. 27847, United States National Museum.

neither beads nor money, but only light-weight things made from wool or cotton; but his father can receive gifts for him and buy something for his son's benefit.

On the day of the race stones are laid on the ground in a row, one stone for each circuit to be run, and as the race progresses count is kept by taking away one stone for each circuit finished by the runners. It is from this practice that the tribe derives its name, Tarahumari—from tara (count), and humari (run), people who run according to count.

Trees are marked with crosses, so as to show the circuit to be run. Three to six watchmen are placed along the circuit to see that no cheating is done during the race. Each party helps the side in which it is interested, so that their runners may win the race.

The women, as the runners pass them, stand ready with dippers of warm water, or pinole, which they offer to them to drink, and for which they stop for a few seconds. The wife of the runner may throw a jar of tepid water over him as he passes, in order to refresh him, and all incite the runners to greater speed by cries and gesticulations. Drunken people must not be present, because they make the runners heavy. For the same reason pregnant women are forbidden to enter the race-course. A runner must not even touch the blanket of such a woman. As the time passes, the excitement becomes more and more intense. Most of the men and women follow the race, shouting to the runners all the time to spur them on, and pointing out to them where the ball is; and if night comes on before the contest has been decided, the men light torches made from the oily pine-wood to show the runners the road, making the scene one of extreme picturesqueness, as like demons these torch-bearers hurry through the forest.

One manager, or chochiame, from each side is appointed stakeholder. They tie the stakes, of whatever nature, together—so much ari _a_ against so many arrows, so many blankets against so many balls of yarn, etc., and hold them until the race is over. At big races, where the wagers may amount to small mountains of such articles, and may include cattle and goats, the position of the manager requires a man of decision and memory, as he carries all the bets in his head and makes no written record. The value of such wagers may exceed $1,000.

Describing a race which he witnessed near Guachochic in September, 1892, Doctor Lumholtz says:

The chief race began late, as is generally the case, about 3 o'clock. When all was ready, the two managers threw the balls in the direction in which the men were to go, the runners dropped their blankets and sped away, although not from a line, as with us. They were naked, except for a breech-cloth, and wore sandals on their feet. The race was made in two hours and twenty-one seconds, and the distance covered was 21 miles, according to my calculation. I estimated that the runners covered a distance of 290 feet in nineteen seconds on the first circuit, and in later circuits in about twenty-four seconds. A circuit may measure from 3 to 12 miles in length. They may agree upon from five to twenty circuits. The first three circuits are run at the highest speed, but the speed is never great, although constant. At a race rehearsal I have seen them making 4 miles in half an hour. Filipe, who is now dead, could run from mid-day to sunrise. He was from Marrarachic, and was the greatest runner known in the northeastern part of Tarahumari. Good runners make 40 miles in from 6 to 8 hours.

Women hold their own races, one valley against another, and the same scenes of betting and excitement are to be observed, although on a smaller scale. The women do not toss the balls with their toes, but use a species of long wooden fork, with two or three prongs, with which they propel the ball forward. It must not be touched with the hand. At other times the women use a curved stick, with which they throw before them a ring of twisted fibre, which thus replaces the ball. Neither must this be touched with the hand, although I have seen them cheat when they fancied themselves unobserved, picking it up and running with it in order to save time. This is a very ancient game, as similar rings have been excavated from the cliff-dwellings. The women get even more excited than the men, and it is a strange sight to see these stalwart Amazons racing heavily along, but with astonishing perseverance. They wear nothing but a skirt, which, when creeks or water-holes come in their way, they gather up, à la Diane, and make short work of the crossing.

TARAHUMARE. Chihuahua, Mexico. (Cat. no. 16311, 16312, Free Museum of Science and Art, University of Pennsylvania.)

_a_ Secretion of a plant-louse, which is eaten by the Indians.

Two wooden balls (figure 896), 2½ and 2⅝ inches in diameter; and two sticks (figure 897), with curved, fork-like ends, one with two and the other with three prongs; lengths, 24½ and 26 inches.

Collected by Dr Carl Lumholtz, who gives the name of the sticks as manijera,[a] and of the game as el patillo. He further says, in a letter:[b]

> The ball game of the Tarahumare women, played by two at a time, is called by the Tepehuan ke ta-tau-koard. The ball is beaten by a cuchara, or spoon, called tau-koua-le-ka-re. The game is begun by the ball being thrown up in the air and then struck to one side.

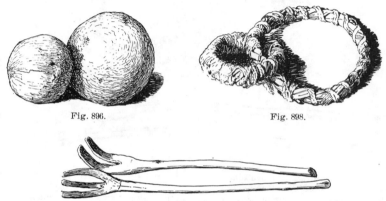

Fig. 896.　　　　　　　　　　　　　　Fig. 898.

Fig. 897.

FIG. 896. Tossing balls for women's race; diameters, 2½ and 2⅝ inches; Tarahumare Indians, Chihuahua, Mexico; cat. no. 16311, Free Museum of Science and Art, University of Pennsylvania.

FIG. 897. Tossing sticks for women's ball race; lengths, 24½ and 26 inches; Tarahumare Indians, Chihuahua, Mexico; cat. no. 16312, Free Museum of Science and Art, University of Pennsylvania.

FIG. 898. Tossing rings for women's race; diameters, 3½ and 5 inches; Tarahumare Indians, Chihuahua, Mexico; cat. no. 16314, Free Museum of Science and Art, University of Pennsylvania.

TARAHUMARE. Guachochic, Chihuahua, Mexico. (Cat. no. 16313–16315, Free Museum of Science and Art, University of Pennsylvania.)

Two rings (figure 898) made of yucca fiber, wrapped with cord made of native wool, interlinked, one 3½ and the other 5 inches in diameter, and two similar rings (figure 899), each 5 inches in diameter; accompanied by two pointed sticks (figure 900), slightly curved at the end, 28½ and 29½ inches in length.

Collected by Dr Carl Lumholtz, who describes them as used in the game of la revetta.[c]

[a] Probably manejera, from manejar, to handle.
[b] Dated July 23, 1902.
[c] Spanish, revuelta.

ZUAQUE.   Rio Fuerte, Sinaloa, Mexico.

Mr C. V. Hartman writes the author as follows:

These Indians have the same game as the Tarahumare, corrida de la bola, a race in which a wooden ball is tossed with the foot. Its name in their language is ga-hi′-ma-ri.

Their women have a game with similar wooden balls, thrown up in the air with sticks which are spoon-like in the end, not forked, as by the Tarahumare. They call the game a′-tja.

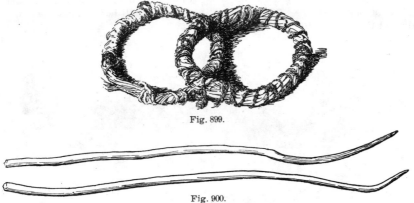

Fig. 899.

Fig. 900.

FIG. 899.   Tossing rings for women's race; diameter, 5 inches; Tarahumare Indians, Chihuahua, Mexico; cat. no. 16313, Free Museum of Science and Art, University of Pennsylvania.

FIG. 900.   Tossing sticks for women's ring race; lengths, 28¼ and 29½ inches; Tarahumare Indians, Chihuahua, Mexico; cat. no. 16315, Free Museum of Science and Art, University of Pennsylvania.

### SHOSHONEAN STOCK

BANNOCK.   Fort Hall reservation, Idaho.

A kind of foot race, in which a ball made of an inflated beef bladder, watooka, is kicked, was described to the writer in 1900 by the Indians at Rossfork, Idaho. Two sides choose, sometimes three or four men and sometimes only one on each side. Each side has its ball. The runners start at a given point, make a circuit, and return.

HOPI.   Oraibi, Arizona.   (Cat. no. 66084, 66113, Field Columbian Museum.)

Footballs consisting of nearly cubical blocks, 2⅛ inches and 1⅞ inches square, made of pitch and horsehair.

These balls, called qöonah, are described as follows by the collector, Rev. H. R. Voth:

One of the principal sports of the Hopi, in which they indulge every few days in the spring, is a football race, in which the men from different kivas participate and in which balls like these specimens are used. They are made of pitch and horsehair, to which sometimes a little rabbit fur and a few hairs growing over the big toe of men who are known as specially fast runners are added. These toe hairs are chosen because the ball is kicked with the point of the moccasin. The horsehair is taken from fast horses. The racers start on one side of the mesa, each group kicking before them their own ball around the mesa point, ascending on the opposite side. At each succeeding race the circuit is increased, until it reaches a length of from 8 to 10 miles.

Mr Voth informed the writer that the balls are distinguished by having the mark of the kiva to which they belong painted on one side.

HOPI. Oraibi, Arizona. (Cat. no. 38705, Free Museum of Science and Art, University of Pennsylvania.)

FIG. 901. Kicking balls; dimensions, 2 inches square; Hopi Indians, Oraibi, Arizona; cat. no. 38705, Free Museum of Science and Art, University of Pennsylvania.

Two black cubes made of hair and piñon gum, with rounded corners, about 2 inches square (figure 901). Collected by the writer in 1901.

They were described as sunkoiungat, footballs, and were used in the spring of the year.

———— Walpi, Arizona. (Cat. no. 38622, Free Museum of Science and Art, University of Pennsylvania.)

Ball of hard white clay stone, 2¼ inches in diameter. Collected by the writer in 1901.

Mr A. M. Stephen in his unpublished manuscript mentions "kicking a nodule ahead during a run;" Hopi, wunpaya nanamüiniwa; Tewa, tibi kwanwino. In his diary he says:

Monday, March 20 [1893]: A cold, blustering day and not many want na-na′-mü-i-nĭ-wa. Still there are a few from each kiva. They ran at usual time and place.

Tuesday, March 21: Last night was rainy and to-day is cloudy, foggy, and showery. The decorations of the different kivas engaged in the na-na′-mü-i-nĭ-wa, I should think, must have been originally of ceremonial significance, but I do not find anyone who can enlighten me on that side. The racers run in the valley. The women watch the varying positions of the men of the different kivas. When the men are clustered together kicking the nodules, others on the outside of the hurdle watch their legs and distinguish the nodules as kicked.

FIG. 902. Footballs; diameter, 4½ inches; Mono Indians, Madera county, California; cat. no. 71440, Field Columbian Museum.

The name of the stone nodule he gives as küüñü; to kick the nodule, wiñpa or wüñpa.

MONO. Hooker cove, Madera county, California. (Cat. no. 71440, Field Columbian Museum.)

Two buckskin-covered balls (figure 902) filled with hair, 4½ inches in diameter. Collected by Dr J. W. Hudson, who describes them as a pair of balls for the ball race.

Two balls are used. They are sometimes kicked as far as 15 miles.

Tobikhar (Gabrieleños).  Los Angeles county, California.

Hugo Ried[a] says:

Football was played by children and by those swift of foot.  Betting was indulged in by the spectators.

### TANOAN STOCK

Tewa.  Hano, Arizona.  (Free Museum of Science and Art, University of Pennsylvania.)

Cat. no. 38617.  Two wooden cylinders (figure 903) about 1 inch in diameter and 3¼ inches long, painted black.  One slightly smaller in the diameter than the other.  Collected by the writer in 1901.

The Hopi name of these sticks was given to the collector as kohoumpaiah.  The large one was designated as yasako kohoumpaiah and the smaller as chihoiya kohoumpaiah.  They were described as used in a racing game by two men, who kick them and run down the trail in the woman's dance, majowtikiwe, in July.

Fig. 903.                    Fig. 904.

Fig. 903.  Kicking billets; length, 3¼ inches; Tewa Indians, Hano, Arizona; cat. no. 38617, Free Museum of Science and Art, University of Pennsylvania.

Fig. 904.  Slinging ball; diameter of ball, 3½ inches; Tewa Indians, Hano, Arizona; cat. no. 38619, Free Museum of Science and Art, University of Pennsylvania.

In the summer of 1905 the writer obtained a single kicking stick from the Tewa at Hano.  It was painted red.  He was told only one was used.  They called it pai-kweh-beh, and gave the Walpi name for the stick as ko-ho-koing-i.

Cat. no. 38620, 38621.  Two balls of altered peridotite, apparently approximating closely to serpentine, 2 inches in diameter.

Cat. no. 38623.  Balls of iron concretion, slightly shaped, 2⅝ inches in diameter.

Collected by the writer in 1901.

Cat. no. 38619.  A ball (figure 904), 3½ inches in diameter, covered with a piece of an old stocking, blackened, and having a braided wool cord, 10 inches in length, with a knot at the end, attached.

This was collected by the writer in 1901, to whom it was described as used in a game in which the contestants lie on their backs and sling the ball backward overhead.  In A. M. Stephen's unpublished manuscript, he refers to a game with " a small nodule in a sling fastened to the great toe; player lies on back and kicks or slings it backward overhead;" Hopi, süñü wûñpa; Tewa, konlo kwebe.

---

[a] Account of the Indians of Los Angeles Co., Cal.  Bulletin of the Essex Institute, v. 17, p. 18, Salem, 1885.

Dr J. Walter Fewkes,[a] in his account of the Hopi Powamu, describes a curious game of ball called sunwuwinpa played by the kiva chief and the Hehea katcinas. The ball is attached to a looped string. The player lies on his back and, passing the loop over the great toe, projects the ball back over his head. The slinging-ball game would appear to be the clown's travesty of the kicked-stick race.

TEWA. Santa Clara, New Mexico.
Mr T. S. Dozier writes: [b]

The game of the kicked stick, still played at Zuñi, has been discontinued at the Tewa pueblos for some years. This is a game of sacrifice as well as of wager, and would have to be performed at the latter pueblos with too much publicity, owing to the encroachment of the settlers on all sides; the course of the race, taking Santa Clara for an example, could be preserved on the lands of the pueblo, but to the north, in accordance with the old bounds, would have to pass through or beyond thickly settled villages to the north of Española, then it would cross the tracks of the Denver and Rio Grande Railroad, and there would be one continuous obstruction of houses and fenced fields on the homestretch toward the south.

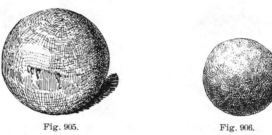

Fig. 905.                              Fig. 906.

FIG. 905.  Wooden kicking ball; diameter, 3⅜ inches; Cocopa Indians, Sonora, Mexico; cat. no. 152694, United States National Museum.
FIG. 906.  Stone kicking ball; diameter, 2⅜ inches; Maricopa Indians, Arizona; cat. no. 2925, Brooklyn Institute Museum.

YUMAN STOCK

COCOPA.  Lower Colorado river, Sonora, Mexico.  (Cat. no. 152694, United States National Museum.)
Ball of hard wood (figure 905), almost perfectly spherical, and highly polished by use; diameter, 3¾ inches. Collected by Dr Edward Palmer, who describes it as a football.

MARICOPA.  Arizona.  (Cat. no. 2925, Brooklyn Institute Museum.)
Stone ball (figure 906), 2¾ inches in diameter.
Collected in 1904 by Mr Louis L. Meeker, who describes the ball under the name of ho nyavik as kicked between goals in a game similar to shinny.

---

[a] Tusayan Katcinas.  Fifteenth Annual Report of the Bureau of Ethnology, p. 290, 1897.
[b] Some Tewa Games.  Unpublished MS. in the library of the Bureau of American Ethnology.

MOHAVE.   Fort Mohave, Arizona.   (Cat. no. 60267, Field Columbian
    Museum.)
Ball of mesquite wood, 2½ inches in diameter.

    Collected by Mr John J. McKoin, who describes it as used in a
game of football, ooy yank:

This game is played with a mesquite ball, about 2 inches in diameter. This
ball is called coon ya va. The players wager beads, ponies, wives, blankets, etc.
The game is played by two persons, each having a ball. A line is marked out
upon the ground and each player puts his ball upon this line, placing them about
5 or 6 feet apart. Then they take positions 8 or 10 feet behind the balls. Each
player has a second, who stands behind his principal and follows him throughout
the play. These seconds give the player a signal to begin the play. The players
then rush forward, each to his own ball, pushes his foot under it and tosses
it as far as he can. He continues this performance until he reaches a goal,
previously agreed upon and marked, 1 or 2 miles from the starting point.
Upon reaching this goal the players turn and play back to the starting point.
The one who first puts his ball over the mark is the winner and takes the stakes.

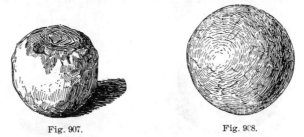

Fig. 907.                              Fig. 908.

FIG. 907.  Wooden kicking ball; diameter, 2¼ inches; Mohave Indians, Arizona; cat. no. 9980,
    United States National Museum.
FIG. 908.  Wooden kicking ball; diameter, 3¼ inches; Yuma Indians, Fort Yuma, California; cat.
    no. 63347, Field Columbian Museum.

———— Colorado river, Arizona.   (Cat. no. 9980, United States Na-
    tional Museum.)
Wooden ball (figure 907), rudely carved and slightly flattened;
    diameter, 2½ inches. Described by the collector, Dr Edward
    Palmer, as a football.

YUMA.   Fort Yuma, San Diego county, California.   (Cat. no. 63347,
    Field Columbian Museum.)
Cottonwood ball (figure 908), 3¼ inches in diameter, designated by
    the collector, Mr S. C. Simms, as a football, esor.

### ZUÑIAN STOCK

ZUÑI.   Zuñi, New Mexico.   (United States National Museum.)
Billets of hard wood, in pairs, one of each pair with a band of red
    paint in the middle and the other with bands at both ends and
    the middle.
Cat. no. 69273a.   Two billets, 3¾ inches long, 1⅛ inches in diameter.

Cat. no. 69273*b*.　Two billets (figure 909), 4½ inches long, seven-eighths of an inch in diameter.

Cat. no. 69274.　Two billets, 4 inches long, five-eighths of an inch in diameter.

Cat. no. 69275.　Two billets, 6 inches long, one-half inch in diameter.

Cat. no. 69276.　Two billets (figure 910), 5 inches long, three-eighths of an inch in diameter.

These are used in the kicked-stick race. They were collected by the late Col. James Stevenson.

Mr F. W. Hodge[a] describes the kicked-stick race as follows:

When the Sun Priest announces the arrival of planting time, and the herald proclaims from the house-tops that the planting has been done, the seasons for foot-racing in Zuñi are at hand.

The first races of the year, while interesting ceremonially, are by no means so exciting as those which follow later in the season when the planting is finished. These preliminary races are over a short course and are participated in by a representative of each of the six estufas. Six prayer-plumes and an

Fig. 909.　　　　　　　　　　　　　　　　　Fig. 910.

FIG. 909. Kicking billets; length, 4½ inches; Zuñi Indians, Zuñi, New Mexico; cat. no. 69273*b*, United States National Museum.

FIG. 910. Kicking billets; length, 5 inches; Zuñi Indians, Zuñi, New Mexico; cat. no. 69276, United States National Museum.

equal number of race-sticks are made by the Priests of the Bow, the latter of which are placed in the trail about 2 miles from the starting point. When the time for the race has been decided upon, which may not be until three or four days after the race-sticks have been deposited by the priests, the six representatives of the estufas run to the point where they are, and each man finds and kicks one of the sticks in a small circle homeward. This race is a contest between the six individuals comprising the racing party, and no betting is engaged in.

The great races of Zuñi, and those in which the chief interest is centered, occur after the planting—the time when nearly all the men are at leisure. In selecting the participants in these races, the swiftest-footed of the young men of the northern half of the pueblo are matched against those of the southern, or of the western half against the eastern. The number of racers on a side varies from three to six, and the degree of interest taken in the contest depends upon the reputation of those engaged in it, and particularly upon the extent to which betting has been indulged in.

As soon as the choice of sides has been made, the wagering begins, and increases with good-natured earnestness until the time for the foot-race arrives. Every available hide and pelt is brought to light from beneath the piles of stores secreted in the back rooms and cellars, to be converted into cash or gorgeously colored calico, and the demand upon the trader for goods is unequaled except

---

[a] A Zuñi Foot-race. The American Anthropologist, v. 3, p. 227, 1890

when a great dance is approaching. Money, silver belts, bracelets and rings, shell necklaces, turquoises, horses, sheep, blankets, in fact anything and everything of value to the Indian, are offered by a resident of one side of the pueblo in support of his favorites against something of equal value held by a champion of the opposing side.

On the evening of the day before a long race takes place, the participants repair to a secluded spot in one of the mesas some miles from the village, where a hole, a foot or two in depth, is excavated, in which is deposited, with due ceremony, a quantity of sacred meal and two cigarettes made of native tobacco (ah-na-té) rolled in the husk of corn. When this portion of the ceremony has been concluded and the hole filled, the Indians move away for a short distance and sit for a while without speaking above a whisper, when they start for the pueblo. On their way should a roosting bird become frightened and take flight, or the hoot of an owl be heard, the sign is a warning to defer the race. But if lightning be seen or a shooting-star observed, the omen is considered a favorable one and the race takes place on the day following.

The racers are greeted on their return by a priest who offers a blessing. A single cigarette is made and passed around among the number, after which one of them recites a prayer. The preparatory ceremonies being now completed, the racers retire into the house of the priest, who extends his hospitality until after the event. The following morning, the day of the race, the runners arise even earlier than usual, take a short run, and return to await the time appointed to start. In the meanwhile they make bets with one another or with anyone who may happen in. About an hour before starting they partake sparingly of paper bread (hé-we) soaked in water, after which they doff their every-day apparel and substitute breech-cloths, the color of which is either entirely white or red, dependent upon the side to which the wearer belongs. To prevent the hair being an impediment to progress, it is carefully and compactly arranged above the forehead in a knot by one of the Priests of the Bow. To this knot or coil an arrow-point is invariably attached as a symbol of flight, or perhaps as a charm to insure to the runner the swiftness of the arrow. The arrow-points having been thus placed, the same priest, holding in each hand a turkey-quill, pronounces a blessing and leads his charges to the starting point.

Without, the excitement is intense. The women discuss with one another the probable outcome, and engage in betting as spiritedly as the men. Here may be seen a fellow who has wagered all he possesses—if he wins, so much the better, and if all is lost he takes the consequences philosophically and trusts success will visit him next time. Another may be seen who has ventured all his own property as well as that of his wife, and if he fails to win a divorce is imminent. The small boys also are jubilant. When the race was first proposed they sought their companions, selected sides, and staked their small possessions on the results of their own races with a zeal that would have become their fathers.

The articles that are to change hands at the close of the race are placed in a heap in the center of the large dance-court near the old Spanish church. Around this pile of valuables a crowd gathers, on horse-back or afoot, to take advantage of the few moments that remain in which to make their final wagers. As the runners emerge from the house under the leadership of the priest, they are followed by the excited crowd to the smooth ground on the opposite side of the river, from whence they usually start.

A Zuñi foot-race is not entirely a contest of swift-footedness, although much, of course, depends upon that accomplishment. In preparing for the start

the members of one side arrange themselves several paces apart in an irregular
line in the course to be pursued, in such a manner that the movements of their
leader at the point of starting can be readily seen, those of the contesting
party posting themselves in a similar line a few feet away.  The leader of
each side places across his foot at the base of the toes a rounded stick measured by the size of the middle finger.  Just before the signal is given to proceed a mounted priest goes ahead, sprinkling the trail with sacred meal.

At the signal each of the two leaders kicks his stick as far in advance as
possible, when the racer of his side who happens to be nearest its place of falling immediately rushes for and again kicks it, his companions running ahead
in order to be in readiness to send the stick on its further flight.  This operation is continued throughout the entire course, the racers in the rear each time
running in advance as rapidly as possible that they may kick the stick as often
as their companions.

Not infrequently the first kicking of the sticks sends them flying over the
heads of the second and even the third racers in advance, and they fall near
each other.  The excitement at this occurrence is very great, for none of the
dozen young men spare themselves in scrambling over and pushing one another
in order to secure the stick and send it on its course.  No difficulty is experienced by a racer in recognizing the stick of his party, that belonging to one side
having a band of red paint around the center, the other an additional, though
narrower, stripe around both ends.

Considering the extreme lightness of the race-stick, the distance which it is
sent by a single kick, or rather toss, with the toes is remarkable.  Very often a
stick is raised aloft in this manner about 30 feet and falls at least a hundred
feet from the point at which it was lifted.  Nor is the distance which the stick
is sent the only requisite of success.  Sometimes a narrow, sandy trail bordered
by weeds is to be traversed, and a careless kick will probably send the stick
into the brush or into an arroyo, where great difficulty may be experienced in
regaining it, since a racer is never allowed to touch a stick with his hands
until he reaches the goal.  Again, throughout the rough race-trail the character of the land surface varies greatly, and long stretches of deep sand alternate with rocky passes, arroyos, and hills clothed with scrub timber or sagebrush.  Indeed, smooth ground is seldom met with over the entire course of 25
miles.

Accompanying the participants may always be seen two or three hundred
equestrians—those who, more than any others, are interested in the outcome of
the race by reason of the extent of their prospective gains or losses.  When
one side follows closely in the track of its opponent, the horsemen all ride
together; but when, by reason of accident or inferiority in speed, a party falls
considerably in the rear, the horsemen separate to accompany their respective
favorites.  If the season is dry, the dust made by loping horses is blinding;
but the racers continue, apparently as unmindful of the mud-coating that accu-
mulates on their almost nude, perspiring bodies as if they were within but a few
steps of victory.

On they go from the point of starting over the southern hills, thence eastward
to Thunder Mountain, along the western base of which they proceed to the
basaltic rocks through which the Zuñi river runs.  Keeping close to the mesas
that form the northern boundary of the valley, the racers cross the river on
their return at a point about 2 miles west of the pueblo, whence they continue
to the western end of the southern hills first crossed.  These having been
skirted, they pass over the low, sandy corn-fields to the goal, followed by the
yelling horsemen, who wave yards of brilliant calico as they dash forward with

the final spurt of the racers. When the goal is reached, the first racer of the winning side takes the stick into his hands for the first time since starting. With renewed energy the individual members of the successful party put forth every remaining effort to be the first to arrive at the central plaza of the pueblo. He who gains it first is considered the superior racer of all, and his honor is indeed well earned. Running as rapidly as possible once around the heap of stores, at the same time breathing from his hand the "breath of life," the victor, stick in hand, continues at a running pace to his home.

Curiosity prompted me to note the time occupied in performing this feat, which was found to be exactly two hours.

Like almost every undertaking of the Zuñi, the foot-race has more or less of a religious significance, as will be seen from the initiatory ceremonies. The opposing racers who await the signal to give the stick its first toss place turquoises or shell beads beneath the stick that they may be sacrificed at the first lifting of the foot. In the belief of the Zuñi the stick has a tendency to draw the racers on, and as long as it can be kept in advance their success is, of course, assured. The cause thus follows the effect in the same manner as it does when in Zuñiland the summer comes because the butterflies appear, and it departs because the birds take their flight.

Training for a Zuñi foot-race begins at childhood. At almost any time a naked youngster of four or five years may be seen playing at kicking-the-stick outside the door of his home, or, if a year or two older, coming from the cornfield—where he has been dutifully engaged in frightening off the crows—tossing the stick as far as his little feet will allow him.

•Mr John G. Owens [a] wrote the following account of the same game:

Ti-kwa-we, or Game of the Kicked Stick.[b]—This is the great national game of Zuñi. Among Zuñi sports it ranks as baseball does among our own. It is indulged in by almost the whole male population, from boys of 5 or 6 to men of 40. Any evening of the summer one can see crowds of twenty or thirty boys skirting the southern hills and kicking the stick. Practiced thus during eight months of the year, they have an especial occasion when they contest for the championship, and this is one of the great jubilees of the tribe. Although the women do not take part, yet they show equal interest with the men and become as much excited.

The time of holding this contest is usually in the spring, between the planting of the wheat and the corn. The Priest of the Bow makes six prayer-plumes and six race-sticks. The prayer-plumes consist of small sticks with the white feathers from the tail of a certain species of hawk tied to one side; the race-sticks are about the size of the middle finger. The priest then takes these sticks and places them on the trail toward the south, and for four days they remain there untouched. At the end of this time he, and any others who wish to join in the race, will run out to where the sticks have been placed, and as they arrive they breathe on their hands and then kick the sticks home, making a circle of 2 or 3 miles.

Four days later a representative of each clan, each with a picture of his clan painted on his back, will run out in much the same manner. By this time most of the people have returned from their wheat-planting and the ti-kwa-we is in order. At present there are six estufas in Zuñi—Ha-e-que, Ha-cher-per-que,

[a] Some Games of the Zuñi. Popular Science Monthly, v. 39, p. 42, New York, 1891.
[b] This game was described by Mr F. W. Hodge in The Anthropologist for July, 1890. I have thought well to repeat it here in connection with the other games, and also to make some corrections and to add several points not mentioned in that article.

Choo-per-que, Moo-ha-que, O-ha-que, and Uts-ann-que. The contest lies between the members of these different estufas, and not between the members of the different clans or parts of the pueblo, as has been stated by some writers.

Whatever estufas wish to contest select their men. When the men have been selected it is announced in the evening from the house-tops. This generally takes place three or four days prior to the race. This race is generally held at Zuñi, but may be held at one of the farming pueblos, as Pescado, Ojo Caliente, or Nutria; in any case it is estufa against estufa. On the evening of the day before the race each side sends for a Priest of the Bow. Upon arrival he puts into the mouth of each one a piece of glass about 1 inch long; and with some sacred meal, taken from his pouch, he paints a mask on each one's face, then blesses them, and they repair to the hills 3 or 4 miles distant. They depart in absolute silence. Not a word may they speak unless they hear or frighten some wild animal in front of them. If the sound comes from behind, it is considered an ill omen. Having reached the hills, they dig a hole about the length of the arm and deposit in it some sacred meal, native tobacco, hewe, shells, and other things held valuable by the Zuñis, and then retire a short distance and do not speak above a whisper. In a little while one will start for the pueblo, saying nothing, and the rest follow in single file. As they return, any manifestation of power, as thunder or lightning, is considered a good omen, as it will make them strong.

The priest who blessed them before they started awaits their return and accompanies them to the house of one of the racers or that of any member of the same estufa. As they reach the door of the house, those within say, "Have you come?" "We have," they reply. "Come in and sit down." The priest then blesses them, and a single cigarette is made of native tobacco and passed among the number. Then they retire for the night. Next morning everything is alive in Zuñi. Indeed, for several days past the whole population has been somewhat excited over the coming event. Everyone takes sides, from the gray-haired old warrior, who believes the ti-kwa-we to be the greatest game ever held, to the blushing maiden, whose lover is one of the contestants. Excitement runs high, and the gambling disposition of the Indian has its fullest encouragement. The small boy meets his playmate and stakes all his possessions. The veteran gambler once more tries the turn of fortune, and to counteract his heavier betting he makes a long prayer to Ah-ai-u-ta or plants an additional plume. The contestants themselves engage in betting, and every conceivable thing of value to an Indian is either carried to the plaza, south of the old Spanish church, where it is put up against something of equal value held by an opponent, or is hurried off to the trader's store and turned into money. Ponies, sheep, goats, money, beads, bracelets, all are wagered. Sometimes also they sell the race. This is not generally admitted by the Zuñis, but I have it on good authority that it has been done.

The day for the race has arrived; the runners have been up since early morning, and have taken a spin over part of the course. During the morning nearly all the members of the estufa drop in to tell them how much they have wagered on their success and to encourage them. About an hour before the time to start they eat a little hewe, or paper bread, soaked in water. Hewe is one of the chief breadstuffs of the Zuñis, and a good hewe-maker is in reputation throughout the tribe as a good pastry cook is among us. Hewe is made from corn batter spread with the hand on a large flat stone over a slow fire. It takes but a moment to bake it, is almost as thin as paper, very crisp, and will vary in color according to the color of the corn used. This repast of hewe is accompanied by a piece of humming-bird, as the flight of that bird is so very swift.

The runners then bathe in a solution made from a root called que-me-way. The time for the contest is at hand. The every-day attire is exchanged for the simple breech-clout. The hair is done up in a neat knot on the top of the head, and the priest pronounces a blessing as he fastens in it an arrow-point, the emblem of fleetness. He then places a pinch of ashes in front of each racer, and, standing before him, holding an eagle-wing in each hand, he first touches the ashes with the tips of the wings and then brushes the racer from head to foot. Then turning to the north, he touches the wings together and says a prayer, the same to the west, south, east, the earth, and sky. I suppose the idea of the Zuñi in this to be, that as he has sent a prayer to the four points of the compass, the earth, and sky, he has cut off every possible source of misfortune and danger.

Everything being now ready, the priest leads his favorites to the course across the river. Excitement in the pueblo has reached its height; the most venturesome are offering big odds in the plaza, and now all assemble to see the start.

Should a side be at all doubtful of its success in the race, an old woman is procured to sit and pray during the entire race. She sits in the middle of the room. The racers sweep the floor around her and then pile up everything that is used about the fire, such as pokers, ladles, stirring-sticks, and even the stones used to support the pots during cooking: these are to make their opponents warm; also the mullers with which they grind the corn, and the brooms: these will make them tired. A woman is chosen rather than a man, because she is not so fleet of foot. . . .

As each side is brought to the course the priest gives a parting blessing, and the runners take their positions opposite their opponents in single file along the course. The tik-wa, or stick to be kicked, is about the size of the middle finger. That belonging to one side has its ends painted red and that of the other side, its center painted red, so that they may be easily distinguished. The rear man of each file places the tik-wa across the base of his toes and sprinkles a little sacred meal upon it. Surrounding the racers will be three or four hundred mounted Indians dressed in the gayest colors. All is now ready; each rider has his eye on his favorite side, an old priest rides in advance and sprinkles sacred meal over the course, the starters kick the sticks, and the wildest excitement prevails. As each racer left his home he put into his mouth two shell beads— the one he drops as a sacrifice as he starts, the other when he has covered about one-half the course. The stick is tossed rather than kicked, and a good racer will toss it from 80 to 100 feet. Over the heads of the runners it goes and falls beyond the first man. He simply points to where it lights, and runs on. The next man tries to kick it, but should he fail to get under it he goes on, and the next man takes it. The race is not to the swift alone, although this has much to do with it. The stick can in no case be touched with anything but the foot, and should it fall into a cactus bush, a prairie-dog hole, or an arroyo much valuable time is lost in getting it out. Not infrequently it happens that one side will be several miles in advance of the other when the stick falls into some unnoticed hole. The wild and frenzied yelling which takes place as those who were behind come up and pass can only be imagined and not described. So skill in tossing it plays a prominent part. On, on they go to the southern hills, east to Ta-ai-yal-lo-ne, north to the mesas, follow these west for miles, then to the southern hills, and back again to the starting-point. The distance traversed is nearly 25 miles, and they pass over it in about two hours. Racing is indulged in by the excited horsemen as they approach the goal, and it is not unusual to see a pony drop over dead from exhaustion as they near the village. The successful runner crosses the river and runs around the heap of wagered goods near the church, then, taking up the tik-wa in his hands for the first time, he inhales, as he thinks, the spirit of the tik-wa, and thanks it for being so good to him. He then runs to his home, and, if he finds a woman awaiting him, hands the stick to her, who breathes on it twice, and he then does the same. Returning it to the woman, she places it in a basket which she has ready for it; and the next day one of the racers wraps it up with some sacred meal in a corn-husk and deposits it about 6 inches below the surface of the ground in an arroyo, where it will be washed away by the rains. Meanwhile the winners have claimed their stakes, and, should another estufa have a set of men to put up, the winners of the first race must compete with them until all have had a chance, and the great Zuñi races are over for that year.

Mrs Matilda Coxe Stevenson [a] says:

There are but two exclusively religious games of tíkwawe played annually. In one, members of the kíwi⁺siwe (chambers dedicated to anthropomorphic worship) play, and in the other the clans take part. Both of these races are for rains to water the earth that the crops may grow. They take place some days previous to corn planting, which usually occurs from the 10th to the 15th day of May.

Other games of tíkwawe may occur at any time when not forbidden by the retreat of the Ah'shiwanni for rain.

Tíkwanĕ race of the Kíwi⁺siwe: The Ah'pí⁺'läshíwanni (Bow priesthood), or warriors, convene at the full moon of April and remain in session throughout the night. On the following morning they prepare télikyináwe (prayer-plumes). These offerings to the Gods of War are deposited at noon the same day at a shrine north of the village. This shrine is on the ground supposed to have been occupied as the home of the Gods of War during their stay at Ítiwanna (the site of the present Zuñi). The other prayer-plumes are made into five ⁺káĕtchiwe (singular, ⁺káĕtchinĕ) or groups of télikyináwe bound together at the base. The sticks of four groups are colored black, and are offerings to the deceased members of the Ah'pí⁺'läshíwanni. The ⁺káĕtchiwe are deposited at midnight on the four sides of the village by such members of the Ah'pí⁺'läshí-wanni as may be designated by the elder brother Bow-priest, or director of the organization, in excavations carefully concealed by stone ledges, set in plaster, which extend along the exterior of houses, furnishing seats for those who like to sit out in the balmy afternoon of a New Mexican winter or to enjoy the cool breezes after sunset in summer time. These ledges are identical with those before many other Zuñi dwellings. The depositors of the plumes know just which slab to remove in order to have access to the depository. The fifth group consists of two télikyináwe, one of which is dotted with the various colors for the zenith, the other is black to represent the nadir. These are offerings to the Sä'lämobia, certain warrior gods of the zenith and the nadir. This group is planted in an excavation, also concealed by a slab seat, on the west side of Síaátéwita, or sacred dance plaza. After the placing of the télikyináwe the Ah'pí⁺'läshíwanni continue their songs and ceremonies in the ceremonial chamber until sunrise, and soon afterward the elder brother Bow-priest announces from a house-top that the people of the kíwi⁺siwe will run in four days.

The director of each kíwi⁺sina (plural kíwi⁺siwe) gives formal notice to his people,[b] and the young men who wish to take part in the race appear at the

---

[a] Zuñi Games. American Anthropologist, n. s., v. 5, p. 469, 1903.

[b] Every male receives involuntary and voluntary initiation into the Kótikili, a fraternity associated with anthropomorphic worship, becoming allied with one of the six kíwi⁺siwe.

appointed time. Those from the Héiwa (north), Hé'kapawa (nadir), and Chú-
pawa (south) kíwi'siwe represent the side of the elder God of War, while those
from the Múhe'wa (west), Óhe'wa (east), and Úp'sänáwa (zenith) kíwi'siwe
represent the side of the younger God of War. After an early breakfast (the
runners having exercised before the meal) nothing more is eaten during the
day but crushed héwe (wafer-like bread) in water.

In the afternoon the first body of Ah'shiwanni [a] (the elder brother Bow-priest
being also Rain-priest of the nadir) proceed about a mile south of the village,
over the road leading to the present home of the Gods of War, and here the elder
brother Bow-priest lays upon the ground a láshowanĕ (one or more plumes tied
together), composed of two upper wing-feathers of a bird called shó'kapiso,[b]
and the younger brother Bow-priest places a similar láshowanĕ on the ground
and west of the other, the distance between the two láshowanĕ being the
length of the extended arms from finger tip to finger tip. The Ah'shiwanni
group west and the Ah'pi'·läshíwanni east of the plumes; the elder brother Bow-

Fᴵɢ. 911. Kicking billets of the Bow-priests (the plumes are attached only when the tíkwawe
    are made as offerings to the Gods of War); Zuñi Indians, Zuñi, New Mexico; from Mrs Ste-
    venson.

priest standing with his fellows of the Ah'pi'·läshíwanni, a line is made south
of the plumes by drawing, or rather pushing, the foot over the earth from west
to east.

Six members of the Ah'pi'·läshíwanni selected by the elder brother Bow-
priest have each a tíkwanĕ (figure 911), made by himself. Three of the tíkwawe are colored black at either end and midway, indicating the sticks of the
elder God of War; and three are painted black midway only for those of the
younger God of War.

The six warriors, clad only in breechcloths, stand by the line, the one at the
east end having the tíkwanĕ of the elder God of War, the man at the right
having that of the younger God of War, and so they alternate down the line.

---

[a] Mrs Stevenson designates the Ah'shiwanni of the six regions, whose prototypes are
the members of the Council of the Gods, as the first body of Ah'shiwanni. There are a
number of other Ah'shiwanni in Zuñi.

[b] A bird, as the Zuñi say, which flies but never tires. Mrs Stevenson failed to obtain
a specimen, but she is almost sure it is a species of hawk.

Each warrior places his right foot on the line and the stick across the foot near the toes; he then sprinkles meal upon the stick and prays for rain and for success in the race. The Ah'shiwanni also sprinkle meal and pray for rain. In the meantime the runners gather at the base, which is south of the pueblo and just across the river which flows by the village.

The racers (the number is not limited) wear only kilts, and the long hair is drawn back and tucked into the handkerchief, or banda, at the back, the hair being brought over the band and tucked in from the top. A member of the Bow-priesthood marks off the line on the earth, similar to the one described, upon which the runners take position, facing south. The warrior who stands some feet beyond the line carries a bow and arrows in his left hand and an arrow in his right. He directs the runners in the course they are to take, and, facing east, prays and sprinkles meal eastward. The meal is thrown four times, the fourth being the signal for the start. No word is spoken. The course is south to the group of Ah'shiwanni and Ah'pi⁀ᵗläshíwanni—a course that must never be deviated from in these races, as this is the road of the Gods of War. On reaching the body awaiting them, each runner passes between the two láshowawe previously described. Bending and extending his hands toward the plumes, he brings his hands to his mouth and draws in a breath from the plumes, that he may run like the shóᵗkapiso, which flies but never tires. The runners do not halt, but pass right on. Each Pi⁀ᵗläshíwanni in the line calls out the name of the kíwiᵗsina he represents as he kicks the tíkwaně into the air. The runners of each kíwiᵗsina at once look to their appropriate sticks. They are followed by the first body of Ah'shiwanni and Ah'pi⁀ᵗläshíwanni, except the elder and younger brother Bow-priests. The Ah'shiwanni and Ah'pi⁀ᵗläshíwanni, however, do not attempt to keep pace with the runners, who move in a circuit, but return instead to the láshowawe, which are guarded by the elder and younger brother Bow-priests, passing between the latter and on to the village.

The tíkwawe are kicked into the river, to go to Kóᵗhluwaláwa (abiding place of the Council of the Gods), and the runners hasten to their homes. The ceremony of washing the hair of the runners occurs before the race and also on the morning after the race.

The younger brother Bow-priest makes an excavation the depth of his arm, and the two láshowawe are deposited therein, with prayers by the elder and younger brother Bow-priests to the úwannami (rain makers) for rains. These two now proceed to the base, where the large crowd gathered to greet the returning runners still remains.

At this point the elder brother Bow-priest cries out that the ä'notiwe (clans) will run in four days.

The race of the ä'notiwe may occur simultaneously at one or more of the farming districts, where most of the Zuñi at this season are gathered. It also takes place in Zuñi, provided a Pí⁀ᵗläshíwanni is present to start the racers. The observances previous to the race of the ä'notiwe are much the same as those for the race of the kíwiᵗsiwe. A member of each clan makes the tíkwaně to be used by the racers of his clan, and he is free to select that of either one of the Gods of War. The runners dress as on the previous occasion, and their hair is done up in the same manner. The clan symbol is painted on the breast of each runner, and that of the paternal clan is painted on the back. Those of Píchikwe (*Cornus stolonifera*) clan have a conventional design of the dogwood, including the roots, on the breast, and below a macaw or raven with the head pointing to the left, according to the division of the clan to which the man belongs.

The Pí⁀ᵗläshíwanni makes a line near the river bank, south of the village, by drawing or pushing his foot over the earth, as has been described, and the runners stand upon the line, facing south, each clan being together, the runner at the west end of the line placing the tíkwanĕ across his foot, as before noted. The Pí"tläshíwanni stands in advance of the runners, and, facing east, prays and throws the meal four times eastward, the fourth time, as before, being the signal for starting. The same course is followed as that pursued by the people cf the kíwi"siwe. Each of these races covers only about 4 miles.

No thought of betting is in the Zuñi mind when these races for rains occur. While deep interest is exhibited by the women, as well as by the men, in these purely religious races, the real enthusiasm occurs at the time of the betting races, when about 25 miles are covered.

The betting race is not confined to the kíwi"siwe, nor to any section of the village, although statements to the contrary have been made. A man approaches another with his plan for a race, and if it be acceptable to the other a race is arranged for. It is heralded from the housetop by a civil officer of the village, who shouts, " To-morrow there will be a race! " Those to be associated with the race gather at the houses of the two managers. The swiftest runners are sure to be present. After some discussion the originator of the race visits the house of the other manager and learns from him how many runners he will have in the contest. He then returns to his house and selects the same number for his side. The number varies from three to six on a side, one side representing the elder, the other the younger, God of War.

Each manager calls at the house of one of the first body of Ah'shiwanni— those of the north and the zenith excepted—and announces, " My boys will run to-morrow. You will come to my house to-night." The friends of each party gather at the two houses, the runners being on one side of the room, the friends on the opposite side. When the Shíwanni (sing. for Ah'shiwanni) bearing a basket tray of broken héwe arrives, he takes his seat on his wadded blanket, the manager sitting opposite to him. The Shíwanni places the basket upon the floor and asks for corn-husks. Preparing as many husks as there are runners for the side, he sprinkles prayer-meal into each husk, and, after adding bits of white shell and turkis beads, folds it and lays it on the héwe in the tray. Raising the tray with both hands to his face, he prays for success, and, drawing four breaths from the contents of the tray, says, " Si " (Ready). The runners approach, the Shíwanni deposits a handful of broken héwe from the tray into the blanket supported by the left arm of each runner, and hands a corn-husk package to each. The body of runners who represent the elder God of War goes to a point north of the village ; and the other goes south. An excavation the depth of an arm is made by an ancient corn-planter at each point, when each runner opens his husk package, deposits the contents in the excavation, and drops in the héwe as offerings to the Gods of War and the ancestors. The one who prepares the earth to receive the offerings covers the opening, leaving no trace of the excavation.

All now sit perfectly still and listen for sounds from the departed. When they hear any noise which they suppose comes from the dead, they are gratified, and say, " Éllakwa, nána " "(Thanks, grandfather)."

After walking a short distance they halt and wait again for some manifestation. Should they hear a few notes from the mocking bird, they know the race will be in favor first of one side and then of the other—uncertain until the end. If the bird sings much, they will meet with failure. If they hear an owl hoot, the race will be theirs.

The runners return to the houses which they left and retire for the remainder of the night in a large room, the family having withdrawn to another apartment. Sometimes a runner goes to an arroyo and deposits offerings of precious beads to the Gods of War, or to a locality where some renowned runner of the past was killed by an enemy, and, after offering food to the Gods of War, with a prayer for success in the race, he sits and eagerly listens for some sound from the deceased. After a time he moves a short distance and listens again. He then moves a third time and listens, and if he hears anything from the dead he is quite sure of success. If he hears the whistling of the wind he is also likely to meet with success, and if he hears an owl hoot his success is assured. In this event he imitates the owl during the race, which annoys the opposite side, for they know the reason for the owl-like cries.

At sunrise each runner carries a corn-husk containing bits of precious beads and meal a distance from the village and sprinkles the offering to the úwannam pí'ᵗläshíwanni (deceased members of the Bow-priesthood) of the six regions, for success.

It is the custom for the runners to exercise for the race in the early morning, returning to the houses of the managers, where they eat a hearty breakfast; but they must not drink coffee, as this draught distends the stomach. After this early meal nothing is partaken except a small quantity of wafer-bread and water. They remain at the managers' houses until the hour for the race.

By afternoon the betting and excitement have increased until every available object of the bettors is placed in Téwita ᵗhlánna (the large plaza). Crowds gather around the managers, who are busy looking after the stakes. Everything is wagered, from a silver button to a fine blanket. Yards of calico are brought out, silver belts and precious beads; in fact, all the possessions of many are staked, especially those of the old gamblers, who, having lost heavily in the gambling den, hope to regain their fortunes.

The objects are stacked in two heaps in Téwita ᵗhlánna, the two managers having charge of arranging the articles. A blanket from one heap finds its counterpart in the other, and the two are placed together, forming the base of a third pile. Drawing in this way from the two piles is continued until they are consolidated into one great heap. Much of the forepart of the afternoon is consumed in this work. When the managers return to their houses and announce to the runners that the task of arranging the stakes is completed, the latter remove their clothing and, after donning a kilt of white cotton or some other light material, take medicine of the Shúmakwe fraternity into their mouths, eject it into their hands, and rub their entire bodies, that they may not be made tired from running. A piece of humming-bird medicine, consisting of a root, is passed around; each runner takes a bite, and, after chewing it, ejects it into his hands and rubs his body, that he may be swift like the bird.

The hair is brought forward and a Pí'ᵗläshíwanni forms a long knob by folding the hair over and over and wrapping it with yarn. He then places an arrow point in the knot to insure fleetness; and lifting ashes with two eagle wing plumes, he passes them down either side of the body of each racer and sprinkles ashes to the six regions. This is for physical purification.

Medicine is sometimes put into the paint used on the tíkwanĕ, which for the betting races is painted red instead of black; and a bit of this paint is slipped under the nail of the index finger of the right hand. If a runner is observed to keep his thumb pressed to his finger, it is known that he has medicine under the nail, and those making the discovery are apt to bet high on that side, for they believe that the medicine will bring success. Failure in such cases is attributed to the bad heart of the runner.

The wives of the two Ah'shiwanni who were present on the previous night go each to the house visited by the husband and remain while the runners are absent. Several parcels, including two blankets, are removed from the heap in the plaza and carried to each house and deposited beside the woman for good luck to the runner.

The runners are accompanied to their base by their managers and Ah'pĭ‘‘läsh-ĭwanni. Crowds gather. Every man who can obtain a horse is mounted. All is excitement, the women's enthusiasm being almost equal to that of the men, for each wife is interested in the side her husband has chosen, and every maiden is interested in the side of her favorite admirer. While the men gather about the runners as they prepare for the race, and follow them, the women must content themselves in the village. The two tíkwawe designating the sides of the elder and the younger God of War are made by the Pĭ‘‘läshíwanni of the side of the second manager, and are carried by a runner of this party to the base, where he holds the sticks out to the opposite side, one of the party taking the tíkwanĕ of his choice. The racers do not form in regular line. Each leader places the stick across his foot near the toes and sprinkles it with meal; then they cry out, " Si! " "(Ready!)." The stick must not be touched with the hand after it is placed on the foot. It is often thrown a long distance, and no matter where it may rest it must be managed with the foot. There is nothing more exciting to the Zuñi, except the scalp dance, than this game of tíkwanĕ. The equestrians urge their ponies onward to keep pace with the racers, who run southward over the road of the Gods of War for a distance, then around to the east, crossing the river. On they go, keeping to the foot-hills.[a] Recrossing the river several miles west of Zuñi, they bend around to the east, and return by the southern road to the base, when the members of the successful party vie with one another in reaching the great plaza, for he who is first to pass around the heap of wagered articles is the hero of the hour. As they run around this pool they extend their hands toward it and, bringing them to their mouths, draw in a breath, and pass on to the house of the manager whence they started, where the victor deposits the tíkwanĕ of his side in a basket of prayer-meal, while all present make offerings of bits of precious beads in a basket.

The wife of the Shíwanni takes the hand of the victor and, standing, brings her clasped hands four times before his mouth. Each time he draws a breath. The waving of the hands four times is repeated before each runner, who draws as many breaths.

After the prayers the victor empties the contents of the basket, which includes the meal and bead offerings and the tíkwanĕ, into a corn-husk and carries it to his home. After each runner returns to his home he drinks a quantity of warm water as an emetic, and when relieved he retires for the night. It is not uncommon for a runner to be so affected by the race that the manipulations of a masseuse (the Zuñi are experts in this practice) are necessary to restore him. The following morning the head of each runner is washed in yucca suds, and he bathes. After the morning meal the tíkwanĕ of the Elder God of War is deposited, with the contents of the corn-husk carried by the runner from his manager's house, at a shrine on Úhana-yäl'lannĕ (Wool mountain), while the tíkwanĕ of the younger God of War and the other offerings are deposited on Tówa-yäl'lannĕ (Corn mountain).

The most prominent religious positions do not debar men from taking part in

---

[a] There are six stone heaps which direct the runners in their course. These monuments, which are some 4 feet high, are supposed to have been made by direction of the Gods of War, and are distinct from those made by men and women who whirl a stone or bit of wood around the head in the left hand, from left to right, four times, and throw it over the shoulder onto the heap, that the fatigue that would otherwise come to the body may be cast into the stone or chip. The words expressed are " ‘Hlon yútet-tchi hánasima tínatu " (" This place tired, unlucky, be settled "). These mounds are supposed to have been begun by the Gods of War. Vases containing medicine of these gods are believed to be buried beneath the mounds, though these objects are too sacred to be commonly referred to.

these betting races. One of the fleetest as well as most enthusiastic runners of the present time is the kómosona (director-general) of the kíwiᵗsiwe.

There are many informal games of tíkwaně in which young men hurriedly gather for sport, and sometimes a considerable stake is raised. One race observed by the writer, in which great enthusiasm was exhibited, began at 5 o'clock in the afternoon, the parties returning after 7. There were three racers on a side, the kómosona being one, but he lost on this occasion.

While there is much betting and considerable interest is manifested in these informal races, there is no ceremony associated with them. Each runner bets on his side. Outside parties bet one with another, one holding the stakes; or more frequently, a third party has charge of the stakes, which are heaped in the large plaza. Sometimes the articles are afterward carried to the kíwiᵗsina to which the successful party belongs, while again they pass to the winner in the plaza, he, in turn, dividing the profits among the runners of his side. While much interest prevails at the informal races, and great enjoyment is derived from them, the excitement is as nothing compared with that of the more formal affairs.

It is interesting to see the very young boys in their foot races and to observe how closely they follow their elders in the rules governing the stakes. Wagers are always made, as the races would be of little interest to the younger boys without the element of chance associated with them.

Beginning at so early an age, there is no wonder that these people develop into the swiftest of runners. The writer has never known the Zuñi to lose a foot-race with other Indians, nor with the champion runners of the troops at Fort Wingate, who sometimes enter into races with them. It is quite common for the Zuñi and Navaho to race. Though these races are always informal, the stakes are often large, and the Navaho leave their precious beads, silver belts, bridles, and valuable blankets behind them when they depart for the pueblo. Their love for gambling prevents them from learning lessons from sad experiences.

ZUÑI. Zuñi, New Mexico. (Cat. no. 4994, Brooklyn Institute Museum.)

Fifteen sticks (figure 912), 4½ inches in length, pieces of sapling with the bark on, this being cut with distinguishing marks. Collected by the writer in 1904.

These are special kicking sticks used in the clan races in the spring. At the sacred foot races at this season the estufas first compete, and four days afterward the clans. Each clan has its own stick, tikwawe, which is cut with a mark to distinguish it. Each clan is represented in this race by as many men as possible.

——— Zuñi, New Mexico. (Brooklyn Institute Museum.)

Cat. no. 3056. Water-worn pebble (figure 913), 3½ inches in length, which has been used as a pestle in a paint mortar.

It was collected in 1903 by the writer, to whom it was described as a kicking stone, atikwannai, originally used in racing, like the kicking stick.

Cat. no. 3064. Ring of twig (figure 914), wrapped with white cotton cord, 3 inches in diameter; and slender wooden rod (figure 915), 27½ inches in length, with a kind of knob at the end.

Collected by the writer in 1903. The following description was given: The game of tsi-koi ti-kwa-wai, or ring ti-kwa-wai, is played by women and Kayemashi at the Rain dance. They start in the

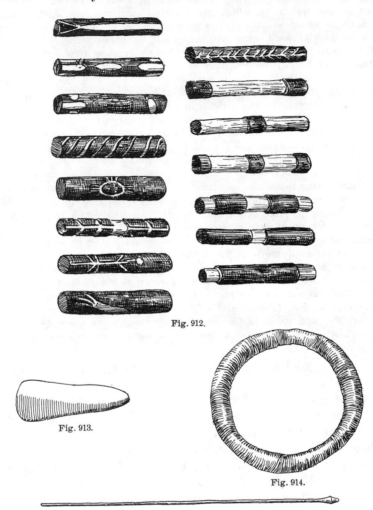

Fig. 912.

Fig. 913.

Fig. 914.

Fig. 915.

FIG. 912.   Kicking billets used in clan races; length, 4½ inches; Zuñi Indians, Zuñi, New Mexico; cat. no. 4994, Brooklyn Institute Museum.

FIG. 913.   Kicking stone; length, 3½ inches; Zuñi Indians, Zuñi, New Mexico; cat. no. 3056, Brooklyn Institute Museum.

FIG. 914.   Tossing ring for race game; diameter, 3 inches; Zuñi Indians, Zuñi, New Mexico; cat. no. 3064, Brooklyn Institute Museum.

FIG. 915.   Tossing rod for race game; length, 27½ inches; Zuñi Indians, Zuñi, New Mexico; cat. no. 3064, Brooklyn Institute Museum.

middle plaza and run some three hundred or four hundred yards in a small circuit down to the Middle of the Earth and back to the plaza. The clowns use a regular kicking stick, only one, and the women use one ring. Each woman has a stick, tslam-mai. They play the game maybe once or twice during a summer. Its object is to cause rain. The game usually follows a dance, but if the cacique orders it, the women play the game without reference to the dance. It is sometimes played by men alone, and sometimes for money. Dick gave the name of this game as ya-mu-nai tsi-ko-nai or ya-mu-nai ti-kwa-wai.

Additional particulars concerning this game are furnished by Mrs Matilda Coxe Stevenson in her paper on Zuñi Games,[a] where she describes it under the name of 'síkon-yä'muně tíkwaně.

Implements.—Slender sticks [figure 916], the length of an arrow shaft, zigzagged in black, symbolic of lightning; a ring, about 2½ inches in diameter, composed of yucca ribbons, and a tíkwaně, or racing stick. . . .

This is a foot race run only by order of the Ah'wan tä'-chu (Great Father) Kóyemshi, and is exclusively for rains. A chosen number of women, each supplied with a stick, stand in line to the left of a number of men. The latter are provided with a tíkwaně, which they kick; and the women who play against the men use a yucca ring, tossing it with their sticks. Though the distance covered is short the latter seldom win.

Mr John T. Owens [b] described the following game:

A-we-wō-po-pa-ne.[c]—This is played by only two persons, but each usually has several backers, and considerable betting is done. One place is designated as the stone-home. One hundred stones are placed in a row a certain distance apart. Each stone must be picked up and carried separately and placed, not thrown, in the stone-home. Another point, several miles distant, is taken, and the game is for one to run to the distant spot and return, while the other gathers up the stones. As it is a contest of speed and judgment, not chance, it becomes very exciting.

Fig. 916. Ring, tossing rod, and kicking billet for race game; Zuñi Indians, Zuñi, New Mexico; from Mrs Stevenson.

## FOOTBALL

Information concerning the game of football is extremely meager and unsatisfactory. The specimens commonly designated as footballs by collectors are, as a matter of fact, intended mostly for the game of hand-and-football or the ball race.

Football is mentioned as occurring among four Algonquian tribes (Massachuset, Micmac, Narraganset, Powhatan), but particulars are given only for the Micmac. It is spoken of also among the

[a] American Anthropologist, n. s., v. 5, p. 493, 1903.
[b] Some Games of the Zuñi. Popular Science Monthly, v. 39, p. 40, New York, 1891.
[c] There is a slight resemblance in this contest to our sport, the potato race.

Wyandot, Catawba (with uncertainty), Eskimo, Chukchansi, Topinagugim, Achomawi, Nishinam, Skokomish, Mono, Paiute, and Washo. The game was played by men (Micmac, Paiute); by men and women opposed (Topinagugim), and by men, women, and children (Eskimo). The balls were of buckskin (Micmac, Eskimo, Topinagugim, Achomawi, Nishinam, Mono, Paiute), or of stone (Chukchansi), and the goals were two sticks, erect (Paiute, Topinagugim, Nishinam, Mono) or placed slantingly (Micmac), or lines drawn at the ends of the course (Eskimo, Chukchansi).

In a California game (Topinagugim, Mono) the ball is kicked by successive players who are lined up along the course, corresponding with a game in which the ball is similarly tossed along the course with curved or spoon-shaped sticks (Mono). In one game (Topinagugim) men and women are opposed, the men kicking the ball and the women tossing it with flail-shaped baskets. The game appears to be most popular among the Eskimo, with whom in one instance it is complicated by the ball being whipped as well as kicked.

ALGONQUIAN STOCK

MASSACHUSET.   Massachusetts.

William Wood [a] wrote:

For their sports of activity they have commonly but three or four, as football, shooting, running, and swimming: when they play county against county there are rich goals, all behung with wompompeage, mowhackies, beaver skins and black otter skins. It would exceed the belief of many to relate the worth of one goal, wherefore it shall be nameless. Their goals be a mile long, placed on the sands, which are even as a board; their ball is no bigger than a handball, which sometimes they mount in the air with their naked feet, sometimes it is swayed by the multitude, sometimes also it is two days before they get a goal; then they mark the ground they win and begin there the next day. Before they come to this sport they. paint themselves, even as when they go to war, in policy to prevent mischief, because no man should know him that moved his patience, or accidentally hurt his person, taking away the occasion of studying revenge. Before they begin their arms be disordered and hung upon some neighboring tree, after which they make a long scroll on the sand, over which they shake loving hands and with laughing hearts scuffle for victory. While the men play, the boys pipe, and the women dance and sing trophies of their husbands conquests; all being done, a feast summons their departure. It is most delightful to see them play in smaller companies, when men may view their swift footmanship, their curious tossings of their ball, their flouncing into the water, their lubber-like wrestling, having no cunning at all in that kind, one English being able to beat ten Indians at football.

MICMAC.   Nova Scotia.

Mr Stansbury Hagar [b] says:

The only other Micmac game [than the bowl game] of which I have learned is tooădijik or football. The goals were of two sticks placed slantingly across

---

[a] New England's Prospect, p. 73, London, 1634.

[b] Micmac Customs and Traditions. The American Anthropologist, v. 8, p. 35, 1895.

each other like the poles of the traditional wigwam. About a score of players, divided into two parties, faced each other at equal distances from the center of the field. The ball was then rolled in by the umpire, and the object of the game was to kick it between the goal posts. In more recent times a player may catch his opponent by the neck and thus hold him back until he can obtain the ball himself, but scalping was anciently employed as a means of disposing of an opponent.

NARRAGANSET. Rhode Island.

Roger Williams [a] gives pasuckquakohowauog, they meet to football, and says:

They have great meetings of foot-ball playing, only in summer, town against town, upon some broad sandy shore, free from stones, or upon some soft heathie plot, because of their naked feet, at which they have great stakings, but seldom quarrel.

POWHATAN. Virginia.

William Strachey [b] says:

Likewise they have the exercise of football, in which they only forcibly encounter with the foot to carry the ball the one from the other, and spurned it to the goal with a kind of dexterity and swift footmanship, which is the honour of it; but they never strike up one another's heels, as we do, not accompting that praiseworthy to purchase a goal by such an advantage.

In his vocabulary he gives: "A ball, aitowh."

FIG. 917. Footballs; diameters, 2¼ and 3¼ inches; Labrador Eskimo, Ungava; cat. no. 90031, 90032, United States National Museum.

ESKIMAUAN STOCK

ESKIMO (LABRADOR). Ungava. (Cat. no. 90031, 90032, United States National Museum.)

Buckskin-covered balls, one nearly spherical, 2¼ inches in diameter, and the other rather flattened, 3¼ inches in diameter, both covered with a single piece of buckskin, with a draw string, as shown in figure 917; contained in a net bag, made of knotted thongs, with a thong draw-string at the mouth.

---

[a] Key into the Language of America, London, 1643.
[b] The History of Travaile into Virginia Britannia, p. 77. Printed for the Hakluyt Society, London, 1849.

Collected by Mr Lucien M. Turner,[a] who describes them as footballs. He says:

Football calls out everybody, from the aged and bent mother of a numerous family to the toddling youngster scarcely able to do more than waddle under the burden of his heavy deerskin clothes.

ESKIMO (KOKSOAGMIUT).    Fort Chimo, Labrador.    (Cat. no. 90285, United States National Museum.)

Buckskin ball, with median seam, 1½ inches in diameter, and whip, consisting of four loops of buckskin, tied in the middle with a single thong, attached to a short wooden handle (figure 918).

Collected by Mr Lucien M. Turner,[b] who says:

FIG. 918.   Football and driver; diameter of ball, 1½ inches; Koksoagmiut Eskimo, Fort Chimo, Labrador; from Turner.

Figure 918 represents the football . . . and the whip for driving it.   The Eskimo are very fond of this game.   All the people of every age, from the toddling infant to the aged female with bended back, love to urge the aí uk toúk, as the ball is termed.   The size of the ball varies from 3 to 7 inches in diameter. They have not yet arrived at perfection in making a spherical form for the ball, but it is often an apple shape.   It is made by taking a piece of buckskin or sealskin and cutting it into a circular form, then gathering the edges and stuffing the cavity with dry moss or feathers.   A circular piece of skin is then inserted to fill the space which is left by the incomplete gatherings.   This ball is very light and is driven either by a blow from the foot or else by a whip of peculiar construction.   This whip consists of a handle of wood 8 to 12 inches in length.   To prevent it from slipping out of the hand when the blow is struck, a stout thong of sealskin is made into the form of a long loop which is passed over the hand and tightens around the wrist.   To the farther end of the whip handle are attached a number of stout thongs of heavy sealskin. These thongs have their ends tied around the handle and thus form a number of loops of 12 to 20 inches in length.   These are then tied together at the

    [a] Ethnology of the Ungava District, Hudson Bay Territory.   Eleventh Annual Report of the Bureau of Ethnology, p. 255, 1894.
    [b] Ibid., p. 256.

bottom in order to give them greater weight when the ball is struck by them. A lusty Eskimo will often send the ball over a hundred yards through the air with such force as to knock a person down.

At Fort Chimo the game is played during the late winter afternoons when the temperature is 30° to 40° below zero. It is exciting and vigorous play where a large crowd joins in the game.

Sometimes the ball is in the form of two irregular hemispheres joined together, making a sphere which can be rolled only in a certain direction. It is very awkward and produces much confusion by its erratic course.

ESKIMO (CENTRAL). Cumberland sound, Baffin land, Franklin.
Dr Franz Boas [a] says:

Another game of ball I have seen played by men only. A leather ball filled with hard clay is propelled with a whip, the lash of which is tied up in a coil. Every man has his whip, and is to hit the ball and so prevent his fellow-players from getting at it.

ESKIMO (ITA). Smith sound, Greenland.
Dr A. L. Kroeber [b] says:

Among amusements is ball-playing. The ball is of sealskin, and is stuffed with scraps of skin, so as to be hard.

ESKIMO (WESTERN). St Michael, Alaska.
Edward William Nelson [c] describes the game:

Football (i-tĭg'-ŭ-mi-u'-hlu-tĭn).

The ball (ŭñ'kak) used in this game is made of leather, stuffed with deer hair or moss, and varies in size, but rarely exceeds 5 or 6 inches in diameter. The game is played by young men and children. The usual season for it is at the end of winter or in spring. I saw it played in various places from Bering strait to the mouth of the Kuskokwim; at Cape Darby it was played by children on the hard, drifted snow; it is also a popular game on the lower Yukon.

Two of the participants act as leaders, one on each side choosing a player alternately from among those gathered until they are equally divided. At a given distance apart two conspicuous marks are made on the snow or ground which serve as goals; the players stand each by their goal and the ball is tossed upon the ground midway between them; a rush is then made, each side striving to drive the ball across its adversaries' line.

Another football game is begun by the men standing in two close, parallel lines midway between the goals, their legs and bodies forming two walls. The ball is then thrown between them and driven back and forth by kicks and blows until it passes through one of the lines; as soon as this occurs all rush to drive it to one or the other of the goals.

The northern lights (aurora) of winter are said by these people to be boys playing this game; others say it is a game being played by shades using walrus skulls as balls.

[a] The Central Eskimo. Sixth Annual Report of the Bureau of Ethnology, p. 570, 1888.
[b] Bulletin of the American Museum of Natural History, v. 12, p. 300, New York, 1900.
[c] The Eskimo about Bering Strait. Eighteenth Annual Report of the Bureau of American Ethnology, pt. 1, p. 335, 1899.

IROQUOIAN STOCK

WYANDOT.   Kansas.

Mr William E. Connelley writes the author as follows:

They played a game of ball which they say was much like our modern football, but I never could get enough information about it to warrant me in describing it as in any way different from the well-known game of Indian ball.

MARIPOSAN STOCK

CHUKCHANSI.   Table mountain, Fresno county, California.

Dr J. W. Hudson describes the following game under the name of eye:[a]

Two or more men play on a side, using a stone ball, she'-lĕl o'-lol ("stone ball"). At a signal each captain kicks (foot casts) his respective ball forward to his partners, who forward it in the same manner to a goal line, wĕx, 400 yards distant. The one whose ball is first over the line wins.

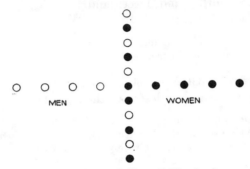

FIG. 919.  Plan of ball field; Topinagugim Indians, California; from a sketch by Dr J. W. Hudson.

MOQUELUMNAN STOCK

TOPINAGUGIM.   Big creek, 2 miles north of Groveland, California. (Field Columbian Museum.)

Cat. no. 70224.  Buckskin-covered ball, filled with deer hair, with median seam, 4½ inches in diameter.

Cat. no. 70225.  Buckskin-covered ball, filled with moss, with median seam, 7 inches in diameter.

These were collected by Dr J. W. Hudson, who describes them as footballs.

He also describes the following game under the name of puskaw, football:

The ball is an oblate spheroid, 13 inches long by 8 inches in its shorter diameter, and consists of buckskin filled with deer hair. A straight, level course of about 500 yards is laid out, at one end of which the two balls are placed about 12 feet apart. The two opposing starters, pa-chu'-pĕ, stand about 50

[a] Ey-ĕ' is name for manzanita tree, and it is probable the ball was once made from this dense, heavy timber.—J. W. H.

feet behind their respective balls, and, at the signal, "Wisaetch!" the two opponents rush forward and kick their balls to their respective partners stationed next to them on the course, also running after the ball to assist, if necessary. No interference or handling of the ball is allowed. The penalty is usually the confiscation of the stakes. The number of players regulates the length of the course. Often fifty play.

Dr J. W. Hudson describes also the following ball game, played between men and women under the name umta:

The ball, pûs'-pûtch-ki, consists of an oblate spheroid 4 by 7 inches in diameter, covered with buckskin and stuffed with deer hair.

The goals are two sets of poles, 3 feet apart and 8 feet high, bent at the top to form an arch, and 600 yards apart. The men are stationed in a line on one side and the women on the other [figure 919]. The starters, five men and five women, arranged alternately, stand in a line in the center of the field, at right angles to the goal course. At a word, a man casts down the ball and each side tries to secure it. The women must advance the ball with their hands, or with a handled basket, a-ma-ta, while the men can kick only, and must not throw or touch the ball with their hands, nor can they interfere with their hands. The women are very expert and throw the ball long distances.

PUJUNAN STOCK

Nishinam. Mokelumne river, 12 miles south of Placerville, California.

Dr J. W. Hudson describes the following game:

Pâs'-ko, football.[a]—The ball, pâs-kö, is oblong, 12 inches in longest diameter, covered with buckskin and stuffed with deer hair. There are eight players to a side. One ball is used. The goals consist of pairs of poles, 3 feet apart, at the ends of a 1,000-foot course. Rough play is the rule, as a player is allowed to run with the ball in his hands, and interference is permissible.

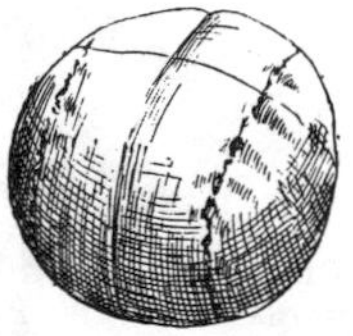

SALISHAN STOCK

Skokomish. British Columbia.

Mr Charles Hill-Tout [b] refers to a kind of football under the name of tcquila.

SHASTAN STOCK

Fig. 920. Football; diameter, 4 inches; Achomawi Indians, Hat creek, California; cat. no. $\frac{50}{4119}$, American Museum of Natural History.

Achomawi. Hat creek, California. (Cat. no. $\frac{50}{4119}$, American Museum of Natural History.)

Ball covered with buckskin (figure 920), 4 inches in diameter. Collected in 1903 by Dr Roland B. Dixon, who describes it as a football, pwatoqwaiwi.

---

[a] The name of this game, as also probably the game, was of Miwok introduction.— J. W. H.

[b] Notes on the Sk·qo'mic of British Columbia. Report of the Seventieth Meeting of the British Association for the Advancement of Science, p. 488, London, 1900.

SHOSHONEAN STOCK

MONO. Hooker cove, Madera county, California. (Cat. no. 71440, Field Columbian Museum.)

Ball covered with buckskin filled with hair, 4½ inches in diameter.

Collected by Dr J. W. Hudson, who describes it as used in a football game called tanasukwitokoin.

The above ball is not the right shape. It should be oblong, 8 by 6½ inches. It is called o-no-wi, and is filled with deer hair.

Two balls are laid on the starting line, a-na-wi'-a-nu-a-we', 20 feet apart, and at a signal each captain kicks his ball to his partners, who forward it to the goal, a-nă-nă-ko'-i-nă, a hole between a pair of stakes, 350 yards distant. No interference whatever is permitted.

Another football game with the same name, ta-na-sü-kwi-to'-ko-in, is played with one ball, 7 inches in diameter, which is dropped in the center of the field and kicked or carried in almost the same manner as modern football. The goals are pairs of upright poles, 5 feet between and 400 yards apart.

PAIUTE. Pyramid lake, Nevada. (Cat. no. 37155, Free Museum of Science and Art, University of Pennsylvania.)

Buckskin-covered ball (figure 921), 3 inches in diameter. It was collected by the writer in 1901 through Miss Marian Taylor.

Called wut-si-mo and used in a football game by men, say, four on a side. The object is to kick the ball between two goals, tu-bi, made of willow sticks, and some 8 or 10 feet high. The goals are about 50 yards apart, the players starting in the center. They wear only a loin cloth.

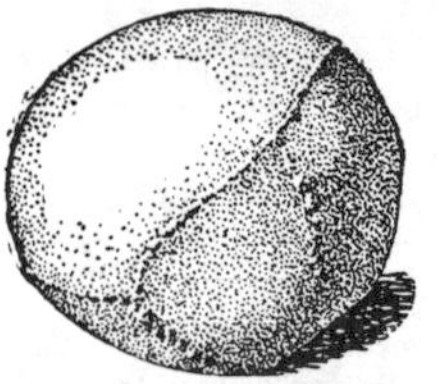

SIOUAN STOCK

CATAWBA. South Carolina.

Mrs R. E. Dunlap,[a] of Leslie, York county, South Carolina, writes the author that the Catawba formerly played a game of football which they called wachippu.

FIG. 921. Football; diameter, 3 inches; Paiute Indians, Nevada; cat. no. 37155, Free Museum of Science and Art, University of Pennsylvania.

WASHOAN STOCK

WASHO. Carson valley and Lake Tahoe, Nevada.

Dr J. W. Hudson describes this tribe using a football, kawmal, 6 inches in diameter, and filled with the inner bark of the sagebrush.

The goals, maw'-tap, consist of two sets of poles, 10 feet high and about 4 feet apart, at either end of the field, which is about 300 feet long. The game is like our football. There are three players to a side, and the ball is cast up in the center of the field by a captain. The game is called pă-lăw'-ya-păw.

## HAND-AND-FOOT BALL

I have classified under the name of hand-and-foot ball a woman's game played with a large ball, which is struck down with the hand

---

[a] In a letter, September 1, 1901.

and kicked back with the foot. The ball is covered either with buckskin (Cheyenne, Eskimo, Mandan) or with bladder netted with sinew (Grosventres, Crows).

It is commonly played by one woman at a time, but among the Eskimo two or four play. The Cheyenne count the game with sticks, and their ball has a thong attached.

The game has been found among two Algonquian tribes (Cheyenne, Grosventres), among the Eskimo, and among four Siouan tribes (Assiniboin, Crows, Mandan, Winnebago). Included in this division is a ball with a thong, from the Arapaho, which is struck only with the hand.

ALGONQUIAN STOCK

ARAPAHO.   Wind River reservation, Wyoming.   (Cat. no. 36977, Free
      Museum of Science and Art, University of Pennsylvania.)
Buckskin ball (figure 922), with median seam, $2\frac{1}{2}$ inches in diameter, one face marked with a cross in colored quill work, attached to a thong 19 inches in length.

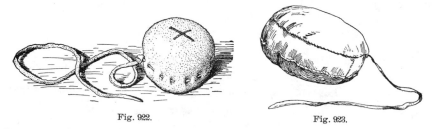

Fig. 922.                              Fig. 923.

FIG. 922.  Ball with thong; diameter, $2\frac{1}{2}$ inches; Arapaho Indians, Wyoming; cat. no. 36977, Free Museum of Science and Art, University of Pennsylvania.
FIG. 923.  Hand-and-foot ball; diameter, $9\frac{1}{4}$ inches; Cheyenne Indians, Montana; cat. no. 69978, Field Columbian Museum.

The end of the thong is held in the hand, and the ball is thrown up and caught.

Collected by the writer in 1900. The name is kowwha; it is used in a girl's game.

CHEYENNE.   Cheyenne reservation, Montana.   (Field Columbian
      Museum.)
Cat. no. 69978.  Kicking football (figure 923), covered with buckskin, irregularly elliptical, with two faces, consisting of disks of buckskin sewed to a middle band 2 inches wide and painted red, to which is attached a buckskin thong 24 inches in length; diameter, $9\frac{1}{4}$ inches.

Collected by Mr S. C. Simms in 1901. The thong is held in the hand and the ball kicked repeatedly. It is used in a woman's game.

24 ETH—05 M——45

Cat. no. 68977. Buckskin ball flattened (figure 924), with median seam, painted red, 7½ inches in diameter; accompanied by twenty counting sticks, willow twigs, painted red, 8½ inches in length.

These were collected in 1901 by Mr S. C. Simms, who says the ball is kicked in the air and caught on the foot, the operation being repeated until the player misses. A stick is given for each successful stroke. This is a woman's game.

CHEYENNE. Oklahoma.

Mr Louis L. Meeker writes that girls kick a little ball in the air, counting the number of times it is done without letting ball or foot touch the ground.

———— Colorado.

Prof. F. V. Hayden [a] gives under ball: e-hu-a-si-wa-to, to play ball with the foot.

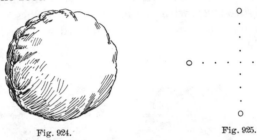

Fig. 924.                    Fig. 925.

FIG. 924. Hand-and-foot ball; diameter, 7¼ inches; Cheyenne Indians, Montana; cat. no. 68977, Field Columbian Museum.

FIG. 925. Position of players in women's football game; Western Eskimo, Alaska; from Nelson.

GROSVENTRES. Fort Belknap, Montana. (Cat. no. $\frac{50}{1896}$, American Museum of Natural History.)

Ball, covered with a bladder and twined with a network of sinew; diameter, 6 inches. Described by the collector, Dr A. L. Kroeber, as a football.

ESKIMAUAN STOCK

ESKIMO (WESTERN). St Michael, Alaska.

Mr E. W. Nelson [b] describes the following game:

Women's football (ûñ-käl'-û-g'it). . . . This game is played by women usually during the fall and winter. The ball used is generally considerably larger than the one used in the men's game. The four players stand opposite each other [figure 925].

Each pair has a ball, which is thrown or driven back and forth across the square. The ball is thrown upon the ground midway between the players, so that it shall bound toward the opposite one. She strikes the ball down and back toward her partner with the palm of her open hand. Sometimes the ball

[a] Contributions to the Ethnography and Philology of the Indian Tribes of the Missouri Valley, p. 295, Philadelphia, 1862.

[b] The Eskimo about Bering Strait. Eighteenth Annual Report of the Bureau of American Ethnology, pt. 1, p. 336, 1899.

is caught on the toe or hand and tossed up and struck or kicked back toward the other side. The person who misses least or has fewer "dead" balls on her side wins. At times this game is played only by two women.

SIOUAN STOCK

ASSINIBOIN. Fort Union, Montana.

Mr Edwin T. Denig [a] says:

The women play hand and foot ball.

CROWS. Crow agency, Montana. (Cat. no. 154335, United States National Museum.)

Football (figure 926), covered with bladder and twined with sinew; diameter, 6 inches. Collected by Dr W. J. Hoffman, who gives the name as buh tse.

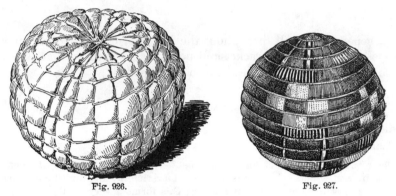

Fig. 926.                              Fig. 927.

FIG. 926. Hand-and-foot ball; diameter, 6 inches; Crow Indians, Montana; cat. no. 154335, United States National Museum.

FIG. 927. Hand-and-foot ball; Mandan Indians, North Dakota; from Maximilian, Prince of Wied.

———— Crow reservation, Montana. (Field Columbian Museum.)

Cat. no. 69646. Bladder filled with antelope hair, inclosed in a network of sinew; diameter, 6¾ inches.

Cat. no. 69645. Football, similar to the preceding, 8½ inches in diameter.

Cat. no. 69647. Football, similar to the preceding, 7 inches in diameter.

These specimens were collected in 1901 by Mr S. C. Simms, who describes them as juggling footballs, boop tcje, used in a woman's game. The object is to keep the ball in the air the longest time by kicking it or by the greatest number of kicks without a miss.

MANDAN. Fort Clark, North Dakota.

Maximilian, Prince of Wied,[b] says:

The women are expert in playing with a large leathern ball [figure 927], which they let fall alternately on their foot and knee, again throwing it up and

[a] Unpublished manuscript in the library of the Bureau of American Ethnology.
[b] Travels in the Interior of North America, translated by H. Evans Lloyd, p. 358, London, 1843.

catching it, and thus keeping it in motion for a length of time without letting it fall to the ground.  Prizes are given, and they often play high.  The ball is often very neat and curiously covered with dyed porcupine quills.

WINNEBAGO.  Wisconsin.

Mr Louis L. Meeker communicates the following description of a game played by the Winnebago girls and some others:

They take a light soft ball, such as a stuffed stocking foot, place it on the toe, and standing on one foot, kick it up a few inches.  Then as it falls they kick it back again, so as to send it up as often as possible without letting it fall to the ground, keeping count of the number of times.  When it falls to the ground or when the foot is placed on the ground the ball is passed to another player. The first to count 100, or any number agreed upon, wins.


TOSSED BALL


In general, the ball throughout the North American continent was propelled with a bat or racket and not touched with the hands.  The following exceptional games have been recorded:


ALGONQUIAN STOCK

ABNAKI.  Quebec.

Lafitau [a] says:

Their ball is nothing but an inflated bladder, which must always be kept up in the air and which in reality is upheld a long time by the multitude of hands tossing it back and forth without ceasing; this forms a very pretty sight.

MIAMI.  St Joseph river, Michigan.

Charlevoix [b] says, after describing lacrosse:

The second game is very like this one, but not so dangerous.  Two boundaries are marked out, as in the first game, and the players take up all the ground which is between them.  The one who begins throws a ball up into the air as perpendicularly as possible, so that he may easily catch it again and throw it towards the goal.  All the others have their arms raised, and the one who seizes the ball either goes through the same maneuver or throws it to one of his party whom he considers more alert or more skillful than himself, for in order to win the ball must never fall into the hands of the adversaries.  Women play this game also, but rarely.  They have four or five on a side, and the one who lets the ball fall loses.

MONTAGNAIS.  Camp islands, Labrador.

George Cartwright [c] says:

At sunset the Indians amused themselves with playing at ball.  This amusement consisted only in tossing the ball at pleasure from one to another, each striving who should get it; but I soon perceived they were very bad catchers.

[a] Moeurs des Sauvages Ameriquains, v. 4, p. 76, Paris, 1724.

[b] Journal d'un Voyage dans l'Amérique Septentrionnale, v. 3, p. 319, Paris, 1744.

[c] A Journal of Transactions and Events during a Residence of nearly Sixteen Years on the Coast of Labrador, v. 1, p. 237, Newark, 1792.

CHIMMESYAN STOCK

NISKA.  Nass river, British Columbia.
Dr Franz Boas [a] describes a game:

Tlēt!: a ball game.—Four men stand in a square: each pair, standing in opposite corners, throw the ball one to the other, striking it with their hands. Those who continue longest have won.

ESKIMAUAN STOCK

ESKIMO (CENTRAL).  Cumberland sound, Baffin land, Franklin.
Dr Franz Boas [b] says:

The ball [figure 928] is most frequently used in summer. It is made of sealskin stuffed with moss and neatly trimmed with skin straps. One man throws the ball among the players, whose object it is to keep it always in motion without allowing it to touch the ground.

KOLUSCHAN STOCK

TLINGIT.  Alaska.
Dr Aurel Krause [c] says:

Ball is played by children as well as adults. The young people of the village often passed the time in a game in which two sides placed themselves opposite each other and threw a thick leather ball back and forth, whereby they exerted themselves never to let it come to the earth.

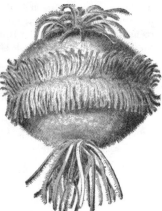

FIG. 928.  Ball; Central Eskimo, Cumberland sound, Baffin land, Franklin; cat. no. IV A 6822, Berlin Museum für Völkerkunde; from Boas.

MUSKHOGEAN STOCK

CHOCTAW.  Mississippi.
Capt. Bernard Romans [d] says:

The women also have a game where they take a small stick, or something else off the ground after having thrown up a small ball which they are to catch again, having picked up the other; they are fond of it, but ashamed to be seen at it. I believe it is this propensity to gaming which has given these savages an idea of a meum and tuum above all other nations of America.

Captain Romans [e] describes also a game played with a large ball of woolen rags, which he says the men and women play promiscuously with the hand only.

[a] Fifth Report on the Indians of British Columbia. Report of the Sixty-fifth Meeting of the British Association for the Advancement of Science, p. 583, London, 1895.
[b] The Central Eskimo. Sixth Annual Report of the Bureau of Ethnology, p. 570, 1888.
[c] Die Tlinkit-Indianer, p. 164, Jena, 1885.
[d] A Concise Natural History of East and West Florida, v. 1, p. 81, New York, 1775.
[e] Ibid., p. 79.

NATCHESAN STOCK

NATCHEZ.   Louisiana.

Le Page du Pratz [a] wrote:

The young people, especially the girls, have hardly any kind of diversion but that of the ball: this consists in tossing a ball from one to the other with the palm of the hand, which they perform with tolerable address.

PUJUNAN STOCK

NISHINAM.   California.

Mr Stephen Powers [b] describes the following game:

The pos'-kâ huk'-um-toh kom-peh' (tossing the ball) is a boys' game. They employ a round wooden ball, a buckeye, or something, standing at three bases or corners, and toss it around from one to the other. If two of them start to exchange corners, and the third "crosses out" or hits either of them, he scores one, and they count up to a certain number, which completes the game.

SALISHAN STOCK

THOMPSON INDIANS (NTLAKYAPAMUK).   British Columbia.

Mr James Teit [c] says:

The Lower Thompson had a ball game in which the ball was thrown up by one player. The player who caught it ran with it until overtaken by another player, who in his turn ran with it until a certain goal was reached.

SIOUAN STOCK

ASSINIBOIN.   Fort Union, Montana.

Mr Edwin T. Denig [d] says:

The women play hand and foot ball.

HIDATSA.   Fort Clark, North Dakota.

Maximilian, Prince of Wied,[e] referring to a visit of this tribe at Fort Clark, on November 27, 1833, speaks of some of the women "playing with a leathern ball, which they flung upon the ice, caught it, and then threw it into the air, catching it as it fell."

ZUÑIAN STOCK

ZUÑI.   Zuñi, New Mexico.   (Cat. no. 5000, Brooklyn Institute Museum.)

Cotton cloth-covered ball (figure 929), ovate, with median seam, 6 inches in diameter.

[a] Histoire de la Louisiane, v. 3, p. 5, Paris, 1768.

[b] Tribes of California. Contributions to North American Ethnology, v. 3, p. 331, Washington, 1877.

[c] The Thompson Indians of British Columbia. Memoirs of the American Museum of Natural History, v. 2, p. 278, New York, 1900.

[d] Unpublished manuscript in the library of the Bureau of American Ethnology.

[e] Travels in the Interior of North America, translated by H. Evans Lloyd, p. 422, London, 1843.

This was made for the writer by Nick Graham, as a copy of a ball used by the clowns, or Koyemshi, in a game in the plaza at Zuñi, May 27, 1904, which he described as follows:

The clowns produced a large, soft ball, and one of them made a mark with his foot across the middle of the plaza from north to south. Sides were chosen, half the clowns ranging themselves on one side and half on the other. One side had the ball, and one of the players on that side would run forward with it to the line and try to strike a player on the other. If he hit him, the latter went to the striker's side, but if he missed, the other side threw the ball.

Mrs Matilda Coxe Stevenson [a] says under popone (wool-bag or ball):

This game is also played by the Kóyemshi and the Néwekwe fraternity during the intermission of the dances.

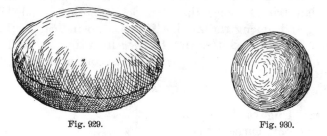

Fig. 929.                     Fig. 930.

FIG. 929.   Ball; diameter, 6 inches; Zuñi Indians, Zuñi, New Mexico; cat. no. 5000, Brooklyn Institute Museum.
FIG. 930.   Stone foot-casting ball; diameter, 4 inches; Chukchansi Indians, Madera county, California; cat. no. 70894, Field Columbian Museum.

Two sides are formed in line, and a man runs out from one side and turns his back to his opponents, one of whom advances and throws a small bag filled with wool. If he succeeds in striking the one who has his back turned, the latter must join the side of the one who strikes; but should the one endeavoring to strike be hit from the other side before he returns to his ranks, he must pass to his opponent's side.

FOOT-CAST BALL

A game of casting a heavy stone ball with the top of the foot, the object being to see who can throw it farthest; observed only in California by Doctor Hudson among the tribes of two stocks (Mariposan and Moquelumnan).

MARIPOSAN STOCK

CHUKCHANSI. Madera county, California. (Cat. no. 70894, Field Columbian Museum.)
Stone ball (figure 930), 4 inches in diameter. Collected by Dr J. W. Hudson, who describes it as used in the foot-putting game.

---

[a] Zuñi Games. American Anthropologist, n. s., v. 5, p. 495, 1903.

MOQUELUMNAN STOCK

APLACHE.  Big creek, north of Groveland, Tuolumne county, California.

Doctor Hudson describes the following game under the name of sawa puchuma (sawa, stone; puchuma, to lift or cast with the top of the foot):

A pecked stone ball, about 3 inches in diameter, is cast with the top of the right foot. The left foot must not get out of position. The one who can throw it farthest wins.

## BALL JUGGLING

The sport or game of throwing two or more balls into the air at the same time has been observed among the Eskimo and an adjacent Algonquian tribe, among the Bannock, Shoshoni and Ute (Shoshonean), and among the Zuñi. There is no indication that it was borrowed from the whites, and further investigation will doubtless result in its discovery in other parts of the continent.

ALGONQUIAN STOCK

NASCAPEE.  Ungava, Labrador.

Mr Lucien M. Turner [a] says:

While walking out the girls generally toss stones or chips in the air and strive to keep at least two of them up at once. The Eskimo often practice this also, and, as it appears to be a general source of amusement among the Innuit, I suspect that the Indian borrowed it from them.

ESKIMAUAN STOCK

ESKIMO (CENTRAL).  Cumberland sound, Baffin land, Franklin.

Dr Franz Boas [b] says:

A third game of ball, called igdlukitaqtung, is played with small balls tossed up alternately from the right to the left, one always being in the air.

ESKIMO (ITA).  Smith sound, Greenland.

Dr A. L. Kroeber [c] says:

The Adlet among them also juggle, some with as many as five pebbles at once.

SHASTAN STOCK

ACHOMAWI.  Pit river, California.

Dr J. W. Hudson describes these Indians as casting up lenticularly-shaped stones over and over, juggling.

---

[a] Ethnology of the Ungava District, Hudson Bay Territory.  Eleventh Annual Report of the Bureau of Ethnology, p. 321, 1894.

[b] The Central Eskimo.  Sixth Annual Report of the Bureau of Ethnology, p. 570, 1888.

[c] Bulletin of the American Museum of Natural History, v. 12, p. 300, New York, 1900.

SHOSHONEAN STOCK

BANNOCK. Fort Hall reservation, Idaho. (Cat. no. 37066, Free Museum of Science and Art, University of Pennsylvania.)

Two perforated marbles collected by the writer in 1900. They are called marapai and are said to be used in juggling.

SHOSHONI. Wind River reservation, Wyoming. (Cat. no. 36882, Free Museum of Science and Art, University of Pennsylvania.)

Set of three gypsum balls (figure 931), name tapa, 2 inches in diameter.

Collected by the writer in 1900. They are used by women in a juggling game, described by Dr George A. Dorsey [a] as follows:

Occasionally rounded, water-worn stones are used. The Shoshoni name for the game is nă-wá-tă-pi ta-na-wa-ta-pi, meaning to throw with the hand. The usual number of balls used is three, although two or four may be used. The object is to keep one or more of the balls, according to the number used, in the air by passing them upward from one hand to the other, and vice versa, after the fashion of our well-known jugglers. The balls are about an inch in diameter,

Fig. 931.                              Fig. 932.

FIG. 931. Juggling balls; diameter, 2 inches; Shoshoni Indians, Wyoming; cat. no. 36882, Free Museum of Science and Art, University of Pennsylvania.
FIG. 932. Juggling balls; diameter, 1¼ inches; Uinta Ute Indians, White Rocks, Utah; cat. no. 37121, Free Museum of Science and Art, University of Pennsylvania.

and are painted according to the fancy of the owner, one of the sets collected having been painted blue, another red, while a third set was white. Contests of skill with these balls are occasions of considerable betting among the women, stakes of importance often being wagered. The usual play of the game is when two or more women agree upon some objective point, such as a tree or tipi, to which they direct their steps, juggling the balls as they go. The individual who first arrives at the goal without having dropped one of the balls, or without having a mishap of any sort, is the winner of the contest. . . . All Shoshoni who were interrogated on this point declared that the art of juggling had long been known by the women, and that before the advent of the whites into Wyoming contests for stakes among the women was one of their commonest forms of gambling. This game was also observed among the Bannocks, the Utes and the Paiutes. . . .

UINTA UTE. White Rocks, Utah. (Cat. no. 37121, Free Museum of Science and Art, University of Pennsylvania.)

Set of three red clay balls (figure 932), 1½ inches in diameter. Used by women in a juggling game. Collected by the writer in 1901.

[a] Journal of American Folk-Lore, v. 14, p. 24, Boston, 1901.

## ZUÑIAN STOCK

ZUÑI.  Zuñi, New Mexico.  (Cat. no. 3085, Brooklyn Institute Museum.)

Four red clay balls (figure 933), 2 inches in diameter.

Collected in 1903 by the writer, to whom they were described as follows:

Women make balls of red clay as big as hens' eggs for the boys to gamble with. They use two, throwing them up and keeping one in the air. They keep count, and the one who scores highest wins.  The game is called ha it-zu-lu-lu-na-wai; the ball, hai-muk-kia-ma-wai.

## HOT BALL

Dr J. W. Hudson describes the following game as one for training young men:

An old man goes out at night and takes a stone ball which he puts in the fire and heats very hot.  He then removes the ball from the fire and throws it as far as he can with wisps of straw.  A number of youths are lined up, on the

Fig. 933.                    Fig. 934.

FIG. 933.  Juggling balls; diameter, 2 inches; Zuñi Indians, Zuñi, New Mexico; cat. no. 3085, Brooklyn Institute Museum.

FIG. 934.  Hot ball; diameter, 2¼ inches; Mono Indians, Madera county, California; cat. no. 71439, Field Columbian Museum.

alert, heads down, to locate where the ball strikes, and at the moment it falls they run and try to get it.  He who finds it first gets the first honor, but he who brings it to the camp gets the stakes.

## MARIPOSAN STOCK

CHUKCHANSI.  Fresno county, California.  (Cat. no. 70893, Field Columbian Museum.)

Two stone balls, 2 inches in diameter.

Collected by Dr J. W. Hudson, who describes them as probably used in the game of hot ball.

## SHOSHONEAN STOCK

MONO.  Hooker cove, Madera county, California.  (Cat. no. 71439, Field Columbian Museum.)

Four stone balls (figure 934), 2¼ to 2¾ inches in diameter.  Collected by Dr J. W. Hudson, who describes them as used in the game of hot ball.

# MINOR AMUSEMENTS

From the recorded accounts, meager as they are, it appears that the Indians of North America had the same kinds of minor amusements and children's plays as occur in other parts of the world and survive in our own civilization. Thus, for example, Mr Nelson [a] gives descriptions of twenty-two [b] such amusements in addition to those of which accounts have been extracted for the present work.

Rev. J. Owen Dorsey [c] in the same way describes forty-one such plays, beside those mentioned in this volume, as existing among the Teton Dakota. Of these, thirty-one are readily classified as imitative and dramatic, twelve [d] of these referring to war and combat, six [e] to hunting, four [f] to religion, and nine [g] to social customs and domestic employments; three [h] are ring games, similar to those of civilization, four [i] are simple contests of action, and three [j] may be classified as miscellaneous.

According to Mr Dorsey, each of these games, and of the other children's games which he enumerates, has its own special season or seasons and is played at no other time of the year. Children of one

---

[a] The Eskimo about Bering Strait. Eighteenth Annual Report of the Bureau of American Ethnology, pt. 1, p. 337, 1899.

[b] Rope jumping; blind man's buff; hide and seek; tag; twin tag; ring around; tossing on walrus skin; tug of war; arm pulling; pole pulling; stick raising; finger pulling; foot pulling; neck pulling; head pushing; battering ram; wrestling; knee walking; high jumping; horizontal jumping; hurdle jumping; kaiak racing.

[c] Games of Teton Dakota Children. American Anthropologist, v. 4, p. 329, 1891. For further information about Dakota children's games, see Ogalala Games, by Louis L. Meeker, in Bulletin of Free Museum of Science and Art, v. 3, p. 23, Philadelphia, 1901.

[d] Running toward one another; taking captives from one another; how they are brought up (follow my leader); hide and seek; throwing stones at one another; they hit one another with earth; use mud with one another; throwing fire at one another; throwing chewed leaves into the eyes; they wound one another with a grass which has a long sharp beard, míchapécha; wrestling; they kick at one another.

[e] Hunting for young birds; egg hunting; trampling on the beaver; deer game; grizzly-bear game; goose and her children.

[f] Ghost game; mystery game; pretending to die; playing doctor.

[g] Courting the women; going to make a grass lodge; playing with small things; playing with large objects; they make one another carry packs; sitting on wooden horses; old woman and her dog; causing them to scramble for gifts; flutes.

[h] Howf! howf!; snatching places from one another; they do not touch one another.

[i] Who shall get there first; hopping; jumping from a high object; they play neck out of joint (tumbling, somersaults).

[j] Hoop that is made to roll by the wind; sport with mud horses; ball of mud made to float is thrown at.

sex seldom play with those of the other.  In accordance with the original plan I shall dismiss with this mere mention the games played without special implements.  There is much, however, in them, as well as in the Indian toys and playthings, that would repay comparative study, although our information about them is scanty.

Mr Dorsey says the Teton use sleds of different kinds.  Among the Oglala the boys coast down hill on a piece of wood or bark like a barrel stave, with a rein tied to one end, which they hold, standing erect, with one foot advanced and the rein drawn tight for support.[a]

Yankton boys have a kind of sled, huhu kazunta, made of rib bones lashed together with rags (figure 935).

FIG. 935.  Bone sled; length, 14 inches; Yankton Dakota Indians, Fort Peck, Montana; cat. no. 37613, Free Museum of Science and Art, University of Pennsylvania.

I have classified the following amusements, all of which may be regarded as games of dexterity, under thirteen different heads, having here restricted myself to those of which more than one mention occurs. It is difficult to decide from present data whether certain of them may not have been borrowed from the whites.  Though the Indians generally are a conservative people, they have, at the same time, high powers of mimicry and imitation.  Of this gift the anecdotes of the Hopi clowns related by Mr A. M. Stephen in his unpublished manuscript afford many interesting illustrations.

Mr Dorsey describes the skill with which Teton children make playthings of clay, copying animal forms with amazing fidelity.  Indian children in general are given to making pictures, often painting or cutting them high up on the rocks.  Among other amusements one has been noted where they laid pebbles on the ground to form outline pictures of various objects.

---

[a] Louis L. Meeker, Ogalala Games.  Bulletin of the Free Museum of Science and Art, v. 3, p. 35, Philadelphia, 1901.

## SHUTTLECOCK

A game of shuttlecock, played with a wooden battledoor, is common among the tribes on the Northwest coast. The Zuñi play with corn-husk shuttlecocks, stuck with feathers, batted with the hand, and a similar object was found in a cliff-dwelling in the Canyon de Chelly. Only the two forms occur, and no other distribution has been observed.

### PIMAN STOCK

PIMA.   Arizona.

The late Dr Frank Russell [a] described the following game:

Kwaïtusïwïkŭt.—The children sometimes amuse themselves by tossing into the air corncobs in which from one to three feathers have been stuck. They do not shoot arrows at them.

### SALISHAN STOCK

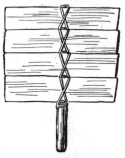

FIG. 936. Battledoor; length, 12¼ inches; Bellacoola Indians, British Columbia; cat. no. IV A 6772, Berlin Museum für Völkerkunde.

BELLACOOLA.   Dean inlet, British Columbia. (Cat. no. $\frac{16}{1541}$, $\frac{16}{1542}$, American Museum of Natural History.)

Battledoor, made of thin, unpainted boards, 11½ by 13½ inches, and shuttlecock, consisting of a small piece of twig, stuck with three feathers.

These specimens were collected by Mr George Hunt and Dr Franz Boas, who gave the names as laetsta and koamal.

——— British Columbia.   (Cat. no. IV A 6772, Berlin Museum für Völkerkunde.)

Wooden battledoor (figure 936), made of four wooden slats lashed to a handle; length, 12½ inches. Collected by Capt. Samuel Jacobsen.

CLALLAM.   Washington.

A Clallam boy, John Raub, described this tribe as playing the wooden battledoor game like the Makah. The name of the battledoor, he said, was acquiaten; of the shuttlecock, sacquiah.

SKOKOMISH.   British Columbia.

Mr Charles Hill-Tout [b] describes a game called tckwie:

This was a kind of shuttlecock and battledore, and a favourite pastime of the girls.

[a] In a memoir to be published by the Bureau of American Ethnology.

[b] Notes on the Sk.qō'mic of British Columbia. Report of the Seventieth Meeting of the British Association for the Advancement of Science, p. 488, London, 1900.

WAKASHAN STOCK

HESQUIAHT. Vancouver island, British Columbia. (Cat. no. IV
  A 1489, Berlin Museum für Völkerkunde.)
Battledoor (figure 937), wooden plaque, with a handle of the same
  piece, 14 inches in length; and shuttlecock (figure 938), a twig
  tied with three feathers. Collected by Capt. Samuel Jacobsen.
KWAKIUTL. Nawiti, British Columbia.

Dr C. F. Newcombe gives the name of the battledoor of slats as
quemal and of the shuttlecock as quemlaiu. The game is quumla.
Two or more play. If there are many players, they stand in a ring.
They throw always to the right and in front of the body. The one
who lasts longest wins.

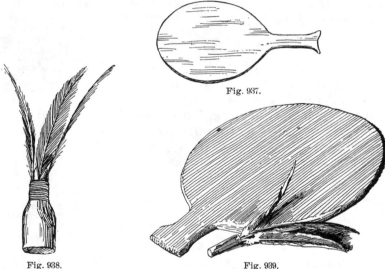

Fig. 937.

Fig. 938.        Fig. 939.

FIG. 937. Battledoor; length, 14 inches; Hesquiaht Indians, Vancouver island, British Columbia;
  cat. no. IV A 1489, Berlin Museum für Völkerkunde.
FIG. 938. Shuttlecock; length, 3 inches; Hesquiaht Indians, Vancouver island, British Columbia;
  cat. no. IV A 1489, Berlin Museum für Völkerkunde.
FIG. 939. Battledoor and shuttlecock; diameter of battledoor, 9 inches; Makah Indians, Washington; cat. no. 37389, Free Museum of Science and Art, University of Pennsylvania.

MAKAH. Neah bay, Washington. (Cat. no. 37389, Free Museum of
  Science and Art, University of Pennsylvania.)
Battledoor (figure 939), consisting of a thin circular board of cedar
  wood, 9 inches in diameter, with a wooden handle; and shuttlecock, consisting of a branch of salmon-berry wood having surf-
  duck feathers inserted.

These objects were collected by the writer in 1900. The name of
the bat was given as klahaiac; that of the shuttlecock as kokoei;
to play the game, klahatla.

Dr George A. Dorsey [a] describes the game as played equally by boys and girls under the name of thahatla; the bat he gives as tlahayak.

NIMKISH. Nimkish river, British Columbia. (Cat. no. $\frac{16}{81261}$, American Museum of Natural History.)

Battledoor (figure 940), consisting of eight strips of cedar wood lashed with cedar bark to two sticks on either side to form a rectangle $9\frac{1}{2}$ by $10\frac{1}{2}$ inches, with a cedar-wood handle in the center, 17 inches long. Collected by Dr Franz Boas in 1900.

OPITCHESAHT. Vancouver island, British Columbia. (Cat. no. IV A 7119, Berlin Museum für Völkerkunde.)

Wooden battledoor (figure 941), a round plaque of wood with a handle of the same piece, 12 inches in length.

The collector, Capt. Samuel Jacobsen, gives the name as eidzatsek, that of the shuttlecock as tklapaek.

Fig. 940.                             Fig. 941.

FIG. 940. Battledoor; length, 17 inches; Nimkish Indians, British Columbia; cat. no. $\frac{16}{81261}$, American Museum of Natural History.

FIG. 941. Battledoor; length, 12 inches; Opitchesaht Indians, Vancouver island, British Columbia; cat. no. IV A 7119, Berlin Museum für Völkerkunde.

## ZUÑIAN STOCK

ZUÑI. Zuñi, New Mexico. (Cat. no. 16306, Free Museum of Science and Art, University of Pennsylvania.)

Shuttlecocks (figure 942), square thick bundles of corn husk, tied around at the top, and having four feathers inserted; height, from 5 to 7 inches. Made by Mr Cushing in 1893.

[a] Games of the Makah Indians of Neah Bay. The American Antiquarian, v. 23, p. 71, 1901.

Mr John G. Owens [a] describes the game as follows:

Pō-kē-an.—This game is somewhat similar to our popular game called battle-door and shuttlecock.  Green corn-husks are wrapped into a flat mass about 2 inches square, and on one side are placed two feathers, upright; then, using this as a shuttlecock and the hand for a battledoor, they try how many times they can knock it into the air.  Some become very skillful in this, and as they return the shuttlecock to the air they count aloud in their own language—Tō-pa, quil-ē, hī, ă-wē-ta, ap-ti, etc.  The striking resemblance to our European game suggests a common origin, and it may easily have been introduced through contact with the Spaniards.  This, however, is doubtful, and I am inclined to think that we must give the Indian the credit of inventing this game rather than borrowing it, as similarity of product by no means proves identity of origin.

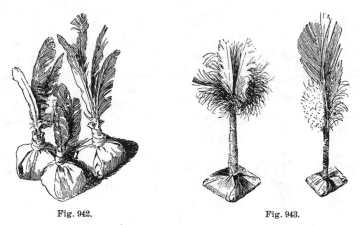

Fig. 942.                    Fig. 943.

FIG. 942.  Shuttlecocks; height, 5 to 7 inches; Zuñi Indians, Zuñi, New Mexico; cat. no. 16306, Free Museum of Science and Art, University of Pennsylvania.
FIG. 943.  Shuttlecocks; height, 8 inches; Zuñi Indians, Zuñi, New Mexico; cat. no. 3087, 3088, Brooklyn Institute Museum.

ZUÑI     Zuñi, New Mexico.    (Cat. no. 3087, 3088, Brooklyn Institute Museum.)

Two delicate packets of woven corn husk (figure 943) stuck with down feathers, 8 inches in height.

Collected by the writer in 1903.  The name was given to him as pokianawai.

Mrs Matilda Coxe Stevenson describes this game under the name of poᵗkinanane (plural, poᵗkiannawe), the implements being made of corn husks neatly interlaced, forming a square of about an inch and a half, with two delicate feathers projecting from the center.  She says: [b]

So named because the sound produced by the shuttlecock coming in contact with the palm of the hand is similar to the noise of the tread of a jack rabbit upon frozen snow.  The game is played as frequently by the younger boys as by their elders, and always for stakes.

[a] Some Games of the Zuñi.  Popular Science Monthly, v. 39, p. 39, New York, 1901.
[b] Zuñi Games.  American Anthropologist, n. s., v. 5, p. 492, 1903.

One bets that he can toss the shuttlecock a given number of times. While ten is the number specially associated with the game, the wagers are often made for twenty, fifty, and sometimes a hundred throws. In case of failure the other player tries his skill, each party alternating in the game until one or the other tosses the shuttlecock (only one hand being used) the given number of times, which entitles him to the game.

The Zuñi claim that this game originated with them.

## TIPCAT

The game of tipcat, played with a small billet, usually pointed, which is struck with a club, appears to be known in America, at least to certain tribes. Hennepin's account seems to refer to it, and the cat made by Mr Cushing is similar to those used by boys in our streets. The Zuñi game is peculiar in the ball tied to a stick which is used to hit the billet.

### IROQUOIAN STOCK

HURON. Ontario.

Father Louis Hennepin [a] says:

The children play with bows and with two sticks, one large and one small. They hold the little one in the left and the larger one in the right hand; then with the larger they make the smaller one fly up in the air, and another runs after it and throws it at the one who sprung it. This game resembles that of children in Europe.

### SIOUAN STOCK

DAKOTA (TETON). South Dakota.

Rev. J. Owen Dorsey [b] describes the game under the name ichapsil echunpi, making the wood jump by hitting it:

When the boys play this game an imaginary stream is marked off on the ground, and the players stand on imaginary ice near the shore. They take turns at knocking at a piece of wood, in order to send it up into the air. He who fails to send up the piece of wood loses his stakes, and he who succeeds wins the stakes.

### ZUÑIAN STOCK

ZUÑI. Zuñi, New Mexico. (Cat. no. 16309, Free Museum of Science and Art, University of Pennsylvania.)

Small double-pointed billet (figure 944), 2¾ inches in length, with a bat, consisting of a small bag-shaped buckskin ball (figure 945), attached to the end of a handle made of a small twig, 19 inches in length—a model made by Mr Cushing, who describes it as known in Zuñi as the jumping-toad game.

---

[a] A Description of Louisiana, p. 303, New York, 1880.
[b] Games of Teton Dakota Children. The American Anthropologist, v. 4, p. 341, 1891.

QUOITS

The following games are akin to our game of quoits, but they do not appear to have anything in common with it apart from a general resemblance. At the same time it is not unlikely that the game played with stones by the Tarahumare, Mohave, and Zuñi may have been borrowed from the Spaniards. The last-named play with iron disks, rayuelas. The Zuñi regard their game as Mexican. I have here incorporated a Navaho game like ring-toss, which may have had likewise a foreign origin.

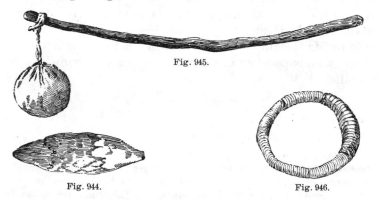

Fig. 945.

Fig. 944.                                Fig. 946.

FIG. 944.  Tipcat (model); length, 2¼ inches; Zuñi Indians, Zuñi, New Mexico; cat. no. 16309, Free Museum of Science and Art, University of Pennsylvania.
FIG. 945.  Bat for tipcat (model); length, 19 inches; Zuñi Indians, Zuñi, New Mexico; cat. no. 16309, Free Museum of Science and Art, University of Pennsylvania.
FIG. 946.  Ring for game; diameter, 4½ inches; Navaho Indians, Arizona; cat. no. 3632, Brooklyn Institute Museum.

ALGONQUIAN STOCK

MICMAC.  Nova Scotia.
  Dr A. S. Gatschet writes: [a]

  They have also the quoit game, and play it as Americans do; subale'wit, he plays the quoit game; nin subale'wi, I play at quoits; subale'-udi, the disk-shaped stone quoit.

ATHAPASCAN STOCK

NAVAHO.  Chin Lee, Arizona.  (Cat. no. 3632, Brooklyn Institute Museum.)
Yucca-wrapped ring (figure 946), 4½ inches in diameter, half its diameter painted white.
  Collected by the writer in 1903. Two common sticks, about a foot high, are set up as pegs about as far apart as one can pitch, and if the ring falls so that its green edge touches the peg it counts twice as much as the white. When it falls on the peg the game is won. The ring is called bas, ring.

---

[a] From Baddeck, Nova Scotia, August 28, 1899.

ESKIMAUAN STOCK

ESKIMO (WESTERN).   Liesnoi island, Alaska.   (Cat. no. 90436, United States National Museum.)

Eleven flat polished ivory disks (figure 947), 1⅜ inches in diameter and one-fourth of an inch thick.   Five have a single comma-shaped hole in the middle, and five three holes in a line across the piece.   The eleventh piece appears to belong to another set.   Collected by W. J. Fisher, Coast and Geodetic Survey.

This appears to be the game observed by Mr Ivan Petroff[a] among the Kaviagmiut:

The Kaniags were inveterate gamblers.   They frequently lost all their possessions in a game they called "kaganagah," which was played as follows: Two seal-skins were spread out at a distance of 8 or 10 feet from each other, and a flat, round piece of bone, about the size of a silver eagle was deposited upon each, the edge of the disk being marked with four black dots.   The players, whose number was never more than four, but generally two, divided into two

FIG. 947.  Ivory gaming disks; diameter, 1⅜ inches; Western Eskimo, Alaska; cat. no. 90436, United States National Museum.

parties, and each put up some article of value.   Each gambler had five wooden disks, and these he threw from the edge of one skin to the other, trying to cover the bone disk.   When all the disks had been thrown, the players examined their relative positions.   If the bone disk had been covered, the lucky thrower received from his opponent three bone sticks, or marks; but if he had covered only one of the black dots of the disk he received two marks, and the wooden disk which had fallen nearest to the bone procured for the thrower one mark, and the marks were subsequently redeemed with valuables.

———— Kodiak island, Alaska.

Capt. Uriy Lissiansky[b] says:

The Cadiack men are so fond of gaming that they often lose everything they possess at play.   They have a very favorite game called kroogeki.   Four or more men play at it; that is, two against two, or three against three.   Two skins are spread on the ground, at the distance of about 12 feet from each other.   On each skin is placed a round flat mark made of bone, about 4½ inches in circumference, with a black circle and center marked on it.   Every player has five wooden pieces, like what are called men in the game of draughts or backgammon, and distinguished in the same manner by color.   The players kneel, and, stretching themselves forward, lean on the left hand, throwing the

[a] Tenth Census.   Report on the Population, Industries, and Resources of Alaska, p. 143, Washington, 1884.

[b] A Voyage round the World, p. 210, London, 1814.

draughts with the right, one after another, adversary against adversary, aiming at the round mark. If a man hits the mark, his antagonist endeavors to dislodge the draught by placing his own there. When all the draughts are expended on both sides, it is examined how they lie, and they are counted accordingly: for every draught touching the mark, 1; for that which lodges on it, 2; for that which cuts the black circle, 3, etc. In this manner the game continues till the number 112, which is the point of the game, is gained. The numbers are counted by small sticks made for the purpose.

### KERESAN STOCK

KERES. Cochiti, New Mexico.

A Keres boy at St Michael, Arizona, named Francisco Chaves (Kogit), described the following game to the writer in 1904:

Waiso.—A tin can is set up, on which stakes—money, buttons, or matches— are placed. Several boys throw flat stones at the can, and the one who knocks the can down, or comes nearest to it, wins. The stones, waiso, are smooth flat pebbles about 4 inches in diameter, picked up for the occasion.

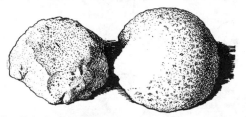

FIG. 948. Stone quoits; diameters, 3¼ and 3 inches; Tarahumare Indians, Chihuahua, Mexico; cat. no. 16343, Free Museum of Science and Art, University of Pennsylvania.

### PIMAN STOCK

PIMA. Arizona.

The late Dr Frank Russell [a] described the following game:

Haeyo.—This game affords considerable amusement for the spectators as well as the participants. Four men provide themselves with moderately large stones, hayakŭt, which they throw between two holes set about 50 feet apart. All stand at one hole and try successively to throw into the other. If but one succeeds in throwing into the hole, he and his partner are carried on the backs of their opponents across to the opposite goal. If both partners throw into the hole they are carried across and then return to the first hole, the "horses" who carry them attempting to imitate the gallop of the horse.

TARAHUMARE. Chihuahua, Mexico. (Cat. no. 16343, Free Museum of Science and Art, University of Pennsylvania.)

Hemispheric disk of quartzite (figure 948), 3½ inches in diameter, and another of lavalike stone, 3 inches in diameter.

Collected by Dr Carl Lumholtz, who describes them [b] as used in a game called cuatro, four, which resembles our game of quoits:

It is called rixiwátali (rixíwala=disk), and two and two play against each other. First one stone is moistened with spittle on one side to make it

---

[a] In a memoir to be published by the Bureau of American Ethnology.
[b] Unknown Mexico, v. 1, p. 277, New York, 1902.

" heads or tails " and tossed up. The player who wins the toss plays first. Each has three stones, which are thrown toward a hole in the ground, perhaps 20 yards off. One of each party throws first, then goes to the hole and looks at it, while the other players make their throws. The stone falling nearest to the hole counts 1 point; if it falls into the hole, it counts 4; if the stone of the second player falls on top of the first stone in the hole, it " kills " the first stone. The game is out at 12. To measure distances, they break off small sticks. Lookers-on may stand around and bet which of the players will win.

### SKITTAGETAN STOCK

HAIDA (KAIGANI).    Prince of Wales island, Alaska.
Dr C. F. Newcombe describes the following game:

A narrow stone about a foot in length is erected at some 20 feet from a base, and any number of players, from two to six, try to knock it down, each with a round ball-like stone. He who first scores ten knockdowns wins. This game is called q'ŭsqEdE'ldŭñ.

FIG. 949.   Stones for lükia; lengths, 4¼ and 5 inches; Kwakiutl Indians, Vancouver island, British Columbia; cat. no. 37906, Free Museum of Science and Art, University of Pennsylvania.

### WAKASHAN STOCK

KWAKIUTL.   Nawiti, Vancouver island, British Columbia. (Cat. no. 37906, Free Museum of Science and Art, University of Pennsylvania.)

Two ovate pieces of worked lava, 4½ and 5 inches in length (figure 949).

They were collected by Dr C. F. Newcombe, who describes them as used in the game of lükia, played by boys:

Played with oblong stones having one end slightly thin, so as to remain where they fall when thrown, and two mark sticks or goals. The players, from two to twelve, equally divided on two sides, each have one stone, except the last, who has two. Each side begins in turn and plays alternately. The object is to get nearest the mark, and it is allowable to drive an opponent's stone by striking it with one's own. That side wins which first scores 10 nearest.

YUMAN STOCK

MOHAVE. Colorado river, Arizona.
  Capt. John G. Bourke[a] says:

The day was passed in looking in upon the Mojave living close to the fort, and noting what was of most interest. They were nearly all engaged in playing "shinny" or "quoits." The quoits were two round, flat stones, 4 inches diameter; the side which could first throw them both into the hole, 20 paces away, won the game.

ZUÑIAN STOCK

ZUÑI. Zuñi, New Mexico. (Cat. no. 16344, 16345, Free Museum of Science and Art, University of Pennsylvania.)
Thin disks of sandstone, from 2¼ to 5 inches in diameter; a piece of corncob; and two silver buttons (figure 950); implements for a game like quoits, reproduced by Mr Frank Hamilton Cushing in 1893.

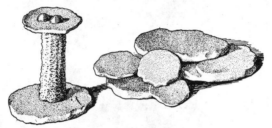

FIG. 950. Standing-cob game; Zuñi Indians, Zuñi, New Mexico; cat. no. 16344, 16345, Free Museum of Science and Art, University of Pennsylvania.

The corncob is set on a sandstone disk with a smaller disk on top of it, the silver buttons, which are used as stakes, being put on the upper disk. The players throw at this target with other disks of sandstone. The game was described by Mr Cushing under the name of the standing-cob game.
  Mr John G. Owens[b] describes this game as follows:

Than-kā-lā-wā.—This game is usually played in the spring, and resembles somewhat our game of quoits. In place of the ordinary quoit they use flat stones. Any number may take part. A small stone or even a corn-cob is set up, and on this each places his stake. To determine which shall pitch first they all throw for some distant point. He who comes nearest to the mark chosen pitches first, and each one follows according to his throw; then the game begins. The distance pitched is nearly 100 feet. The object is to knock over the stake or pool. If the pool is knocked over, and the stone pitched goes beyond it, it counts nothing; if just even with it, the one who pitched has another chance; if it remains behind, he takes everything, and all put up again. They count it great sport, and some become very skillful in pitching.

---

[a] Notes on the Cosmogony and Theogony of the Mojave Indians. Journal of American Folk-Lore, v. 2, p. 171, 1889.
  [b] Some Games of the Zuñi. Popular Science Monthly, v. 39, p. 40, New York, 1891.

ZUÑI.   Zuñi, New Mexico.   (Brooklyn Institute Museum.)

Cat. no. 3096.   Two stone disks, 4½ and 5 inches in diameter, one a broken upper stone for the metate (figure 951).

Cat. no. 3097.   Flat stone disk, 4 inches in diameter; one side flat, the opposite side convex and marked with incised lines, as shown in figure 952.

Fig. 951.                                                    Fig. 952.

FIG. 951.  Stone quoits; diameters, 4½ and 5 inches; Zuñi Indians, Zuñi, New Mexico; cat. no. 3096, Brooklyn Institute Museum.

FIG. 952.  Stone quoit; diameter, 4 inches; Zuñi Indians, Zuñi, New Mexico; cat. no. 3097, Brooklyn Institute Museum.

The specimens just described were collected by the writer in 1903.

The stones are called tankalanai.   It is a winter game for men and boys.   Each one has a quoit.   They set a corncob up on the ground and put the stakes—turquoises, silver beads or buttons, or money—on top of the cob and throw at it in turn.   The first player throws his stone from the cob at some distant mark, about as far as he can.   The players then stand at this point and throw at the cob until one of them knocks it down.   Then the one whose quoit fell nearest to the stakes (not the cob) wins all.   After a player throws he draws a ring around his stone to mark where it fell when he takes it up to throw again.   A stone, a chip, or any convenient object is put on the cob to lay the stakes on.

Cat. no. 3098.   Sandstone disk (figure 953), 3½ inches in diameter, with a cross incised on one face and on the other the face of the sun.

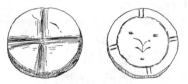

FIG. 953.  Sun quoit; diameter, 3½ inches; Zuñi Indians, Zuñi, New Mexico; cat. no. 3098, Brooklyn Institute Museum.

It was presented to the writer by Zuñi Dick in 1903.   He gave the name as tankalana yettokia, and said it was anciently used on Corn mountain by the Sun priest.

Mrs Matilda Coxe Stevenson, in her paper on Zuñi Games,[a] states that the Zuñi assert that this game came from Mexico.

---

[a] American Anthropologist, n. s., v. 5, p. 496, 1903.

## STONE-THROWING

A game of throwing stones at a mark is reported from two tribes.

### SHOSHONEAN STOCK

BANNOCK. Rossfork, Idaho. (Cat. no. 37065, Free Museum of Science and Art, University of Pennsylvania.)

FIG. 954. Stone ball used to throw at a mark; diameter, 2¼ inches; Bannock Indians, Rossfork, Idaho; cat. no. 37065, Free Museum of Science and Art, University of Pennsylvania.

Stone ball (figure 954) pitted with a hammer stone and perfectly spherical; diameter, 2⅞ inches.

Collected by the writer in 1900.

The name given was tin-bin ter-ow-a-ko, and it was described as used in a game of throwing at a mark, the players betting which would come nearest.

### TANOAN STOCK

TEWA. Santa Clara, New Mexico.

Mr T. S. Dozier [a] writes:

The old Tewa game of kou-wa-di has almost passed into disuse. Only two or three times have I seen it played. It consisted in throwing a kou-e (stone) at a target, with about the same rules as are observed in the arrow game. It was played just after that game, the game of marbles and that of tops taking its place now.

## SHUFFLEBOARD

A game played on the ice by women, like shuffleboard, has been observed among the Dakota. Four accounts are recorded.

### SIOUAN STOCK

ASSINIBOIN. Fort Union, Montana.

Mr Edwin T. Denig [b] says that the women play billiards with flat stones on the ice.

DAKOTA (TETON). Pine Ridge reservation, South Dakota.

Dr J. R. Walker [c] describes the game of woskate icaslohe, played by women on the ice with a stone ball, tapaiyan, and wooden cylinder, cannúbi, calling it the game of bowls.

DAKOTA (YANKTON). Fort Peck, Montana. (Cat. no. 37611, Free Museum of Science and Art, University of Pennsylvania.)

Two small wooden cylinders (figure 955), 1¼ inches in diameter and 1½ inches in length; and a flat oval stone about 3 inches in diameter.

---

[a] Some Tewa Games. Unpublished manuscript in the Bureau of American Ethnology.
[b] Unpublished manuscript in the library of the Bureau of American Ethnology.
[c] Journal of American Folk-Lore, v. 19, p. 29, 1905.

The latter is marked on one side in ink with eyes and mouth simulating a human face. An iron ball, about three-fourths of an inch in diameter, accompanies these specimens.

These objects were collected by the writer in 1900. They were made by Black Chicken. The game, umpapi, is played on the ice exclusively by women. The cylinders are set up and struck with the stone, ihe, or with the bullet, which is shoved with the hand.

FIG. 955. Implements for umpapi; length of cylinders, 1¼ inches; Yankton Dakota Indians, Fort Peck, Montana; cat. no. 37611, Free Museum of Science and Art, University of Pennsylvania.

HIDATSA. Fort Atkinson, North Dakota.

Henry A. Boller [a] says:

The mania for gambling was by no means confined to the men. The women and young girls were equally imbued with it; and, sitting down on a smooth place on the ice, they would roll a pebble from one to the other for hours together. Young infants were often kept on the ice all the while, their mothers, or those who had them in charge, being too much engrossed with their play to pay them any attention.

## JACKSTRAWS

The game of jackstraws would seem a natural and logical development from the game of stick-counting. The only intimations the writer has had of it in America are among the Eskimo and the Haida. The first of the two games described by Mr Nelson is somewhat like our game of jackstones; the second is identical with our jackstraws.

### ESKIMAUAN STOCK

ESKIMO (WESTERN). St Michael, Alaska. (Cat. no. 178970, United States National Museum.)

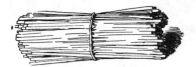

FIG. 956. Jackstraws; length, 4½ inches; Western Eskimo, St Michael, Alaska; cat. no. 178970, United States National Museum.

Bundle of 109 small squared pine splints (figure 956), 4½ inches in length.

Collected by Mr E. W. Nelson, who describes the game played with them as follows: [b]

A bundle of from 50 to 75 small, squared, wooden splints, about 4 inches long and a little larger than a match, are placed in a small pile crosswise on the back of the player's outstretched right hand. The player then removes his hand quickly and tries to grasp the falling sticks between his thumb and fingers, still keeping

[a] Among the Indians: Eight years in the Far West, 1858–1866, p. 197, Philadelphia, 1868.
[b] The Eskimo about Bering Strait. Eighteenth Annual Report of the Bureau of American Ethnology, pt. 1, p. 332, 1899.

the palm downward. If one or more of the sticks fall to the ground it is a miss and the next player tries. Every time a player succeeds in catching all of the falling sticks, he lays aside one of them as a counter until all are gone, when each player counts up, and the one holding the greatest number is the winner. These squared splints are similar to those used as markers in the first game described [a game of dart throwing, see page 387]. Small stakes are sometimes played for in this game, as in the first.

The bunch of slender splints already described are also used to play a game exactly like jackstraws. The player grasps the bunch of sticks between the thumb and forefinger of the right hand, resting one end upon the floor; then he suddenly releases them and they fall in a small heap. The players have a small wooden hook, and each in succession removes as many of the sticks as he can without moving any but the one taken. Each player keeps those he succeeds in removing, and the one holding the largest number at the end is the winner. Both men and women play this game, but usually not together.

## SKITTAGETAN STOCK

HAIDA. Prince of Wales island, Alaska.

Dr C. F. Newcombe says these Indians have the cheese-straw game (jackstraws) which they call hlketosgan, and play precisely like the European game.

## SWING

Only four notices of the swing occur, one of which appears to refer to a late and civilized form.

### ALGONQUIAN STOCK

ARAPAHO. Wyoming.

Dr A. L. Kroeber [a] relates a flood myth in which Crow-woman, the wife of a man, urges a girl named River-woman, whom her husband has taken as a new wife, to go with her to a swing which she had hung on a tree that leaned over a pool in the river. After refusing three times, the girl went and swung, when the rope broke and she fell into the pool and was drowned.

### CADDOAN STOCK

PAWNEE (SKIDI). Oklahoma.

In the story of " Coyote Rescues a Maiden," Dr George A. Dorsey [b] refers to the girl who had the power of attracting buffalo through being swung by her brothers.[c]

WICHITA. Oklahoma.

Dr Albert S. Gatschet communicated to me the following name for the swing of children: neeniku'yassash.

---

[a] Traditions of the Arapaho, p. 11, Chicago, 1903.
[b] Traditions of the Skidi Pawnee, p. 254, Boston and New York, 1904.
[c] The same story is found among the Caddo. Traditions of the Caddo, p. 51, Washington, 1905.

SIOUAN STOCK

DAKOTA (TETON).   South Dakota.

Rev. J. Owen Dorsey [a] describes the following game, as played by girls and boys:

Hóhotéla, Swinging, is an autumnal game.  The swing is attached to a lean-ing tree after the leaves have fallen.  When four ropes are used, a blanket is laid on them, and several children sit on the blanket and are pushed forward. Those who push say "Hohote, hohote!  Hohotela, hohotela!" as long as they push them.  When two ropes are used, only one child at a time sits in the swing.

STILTS

Our information about the use of stilts is extremely meager, the name from the Wichita and two recent specimens, boys' playthings, from Shoshonean tribes, being practically all.  They are mentioned as existing among the Maya by Bishop Landa,[b] who refers to a dance on high stilts in honor of the bird deity Yaccocahmut.

This description was suggested to me by Dr Ed-uard Seler to explain the picture of a figure on what appears to be stilts, that occurs in plate xxi of the Troano Codex (figure 957).

A clue to the origin of these implements may be found in the employment of planting sticks as stilts by boys in Zuñi.

CADDOAN STOCK

WICHITA.   Oklahoma.

Dr Albert S. Gatschet communicated to me the fol-lowing name for stilts among terms for outdoor games from the Wichita language collected in 1892: Hāk i'arits, stilts, walking wood.

FIG. 957. Stilt-walk-ing (?); Maya In-dians, Yucatan; from pl. XXI, Co-dex Troano.

SHOSHONEAN STOCK

HOPI.   Oraibi, Arizona.   (Cat. no. 38703, Free Museum of Science and Art, University of Pennsylvania.)

Pair of stilts (figure 958), hokia, two cottonwood poles, 54½ inches in length, with a crotch wrapped with colored rags.

Collected by the writer in 1901.   They are used by boys.

[a] Games of Teton Dakota Children.   The American Anthropologist, v. 4, p. 329, 1891.
[b] Relation des Choses de Yucatan, p. 223, Paris, 1864.

SHOSHONI. Wind River reservation, Wyoming. (Cat. no. 36886, Free Museum of Science and Art, University of Pennsylvania.)

Pair of stilts (figure 959), made of saplings, with a forked crotch, the lower part of which is bound with willow bark; length, $42\frac{1}{2}$ inches.

.Collected by the writer in 1900.

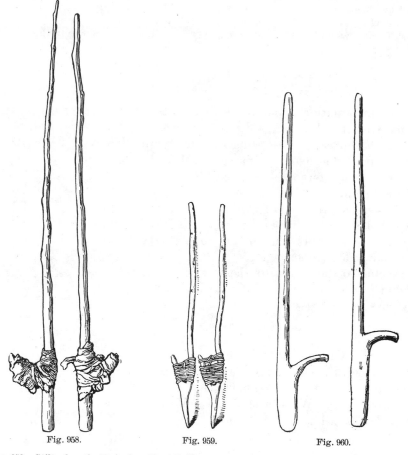

Fig. 958.          Fig. 959.          Fig. 960.

FIG. 958.  Stilts; length, $54\frac{1}{4}$ inches; Hopi Indians, Oraibi, Arizona; cat. no. 38703, Free Museum of Science and Art, University of Pennsylvania.

FIG. 959.  Stilts; length, $42\frac{1}{4}$ inches; Shoshoni Indians, Wyoming; cat. no. 36886, Free Museum of Science and Art, University of Pennsylvania.

FIG. 960.  Digging sticks (used as stilts); length, 30 inches; Zuñi Indians, Zuñi, New Mexico; cat. no. 3188, 3189, Brooklyn Institute Museum.

## ZUÑIAN STOCK

ZUÑI.  Zuñi, New Mexico.

The writer was informed in Zuñi that boys frequently employ a pair of digging sticks (figure 960); tasakwiwai, to walk on in the manner of stilts.

## TOPS

The top is one of the most widely diffused of Indian children's playthings. The assertion has been made that it is of recent introduction, but its general use, taken in connection with its existence in prehistoric times in Peru, would seem to point to its having been known before the period of contact with the whites.

The most usual form is the whip top, made of wood, horn, stone, or clay, and sometimes painted in colors. Spinning tops is a winter game and is commonly played on the ice. Tops consisting of disks of wood, bone, or ivory, with wooden or bone spindles, also occur. On the Northwest coast a pierced slat is sometimes used to hold the top while the string is being unwound. The strings are of sinew or bark cord.

Top spinning occurs as a game among the Eskimo, the player endeavoring to run round the house while his top is spinning. The Niska try to see who can keep his top spinning longest. Among the Oglala the player tries to whip and hold his top in a square. Some of the wooden peg tops of the Pueblos have a hole in the side to make them hum when they spin. Of all forms, these peg tops seem most likely to be of European introduction. The spindle and cord tops seem to be related in form and mechanism to the spindle employed in weaving, and the whip top appears to be analogous to the whipped ball, but this remains mere conjecture.

Fig. 961. Whip top; height, 3½ inches; Arapaho Indians, Wind River reservation, Wyoming; cat. no. 36980, Free Museum of Science and Art, University of Pennsylvania.

### ALGONQUIAN STOCK

ARAPAHO. Wind River reservation, Wyoming. (Cat. no. 36980, Free Museum of Science and Art, University of Pennsylvania.)

Wooden whip top (figure 961); height, 3½ inches. Collected by the writer in 1900.

——— Cheyenne and Arapaho reservation, Oklahoma.

Mr James Mooney [a] says:

Tops are used by all Indian boys, and are made of wood or bone. They are not thrown or spun with a string, but are kept in motion by whipping with a small quirt or whip of buckskin. In winter they are spun upon the ice. The younger children make tops to twirl with the fingers by running a stick through a small seed berry.

---

[a] The Ghost-dance Religion. Fourteenth Annual Report of the Bureau of Ethnology, pt. 2, p. 1006, 1896.

BLACKFEET. Montana. (Cat. no. 16190, Field Columbian Museum.)
Two pieces of wood resembling whip tops (figure 962). Collected
by J. M. McLean.

CHEYENNE. Oklahoma.

Mr Louis L. Meeker [a] writes:

They have also whip tops (ne'-do-hi-yon"-hsist, or whirling game). They
are played in winter. When the ice breaks up in the spring, they are thrown
into the water as it rises, with the imple-
ments for the other winter games, and carried away. Playing winter games in summer is popularly supposed to make hairs
grow on the body where tweezers will be
required to remove them—a nursery tale.

CHIPPEWA. Apostle islands, Wisconsin.

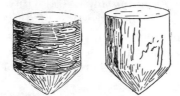

FIG. 962. Whip tops; heights 2 and 2¼
inches; Blackfoot Indians, Montana;
cat. no. 16190, Field Columbian Museum.

J. G. Kohl [b] says:

The Indian boys manage to make tops
out of acorns and nuts as cleverly as our
boys do. They also collect the oval stones which are found on the banks of
the rivers and lakes and use them on the ice in winter. Barefooted and active,
they run over the ice, and drive the stones against each other with whips and
sticks. The stone that upsets the other is the victor.

——— Michigan.

Baraga [c] gives the following definitions:

Top (boy's plaything), towéigan; I play with a top, nin towéige.

CREE. Edmonton, Alberta. (Cat. no. 15070, Field Columbian Museum.)

Wooden whip top and whip (figure 963). Collected by Isaac Cowie.

FIG. 963. Whip top and whip; height of top, 2¼ inches; length of whip, 22¼ inches; Cree Indians,
Alberta; cat. no. 15070, Field Columbian Museum.

GROSVENTRES. Fort Belknap, Montana. (American Museum of
Natural History.)

Cat. no. $\frac{50}{1811}$. Top of solid black horn (figure 964), 2¾ inches in
length, accompanied by a whip with four buckskin lashes, and
a wooden handle painted red, 13 inches in length.

[a] Notes on Cheyenne Indian Games communicated to the Bureau of American Ethnology.
[b] Kitchi-Gami, Wanderings round Lake Superior, p. 84, London, 1860.
[c] A Dictionary of the Otchipwe Language, Cincinnati, 1853.

Cat. no. $\frac{50}{1878}$.  Top, a disk of wood (figure 965), 4 inches in diameter, painted red, with wooden spindle 7 inches in length.

Both of the above were collected by Dr A. L. Kroeber in 1901.

NORRIDGEWOCK.  Norridgewock, Maine.

Rasles [a] gives the following definitions:

Pébésk8mañgan, toupie sur la glace, &c.; sur la terre, arip8dangan.

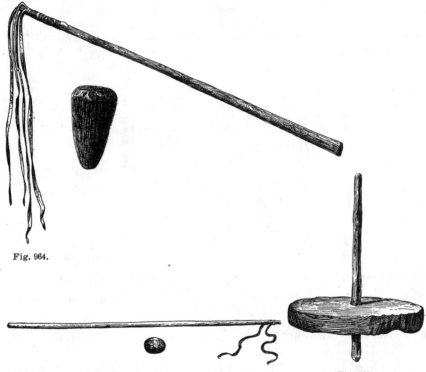

Fig. 964.

Fig. 966.　　　　　　　　Fig. 965.

FIG. 964.  Whip top and whip; height of top, 2¾ inches; Grosventre Indians, Montana; cat. no. $\frac{50}{1811}$, American Museum of Natural History.

FIG. 965.  Top; diameter, 4 inches; Grosventre Indians, Montana; cat. no. $\frac{50}{1878}$, American Museum of Natural History.

FIG. 966.  Whip top and whip; diameter of top, 1¼ inches; Sauk and Fox Indians, Iowa; cat. no. $\frac{50}{3518}$, American Museum of Natural History.

SAUK AND FOXES.  Iowa.  (Cat. no. $\frac{50}{3519}$, American Museum of Natural History.)

Ovate ball of stone (figure 966), 1¾ inches in diameter, with a whip made of a peeled stick, 21 inches long, having two leather lashes.

Collected by Dr William Jones, who describes them as whip top and whip, played on the ice.  The top is called nimitcihi, dancer.

[a] A Dictionary of the Abnaki Language in North America.  Memoirs of the American Academy of Science and Arts, n. s., v. 1, Cambridge, 1833.

CHIMMESYAN STOCK

NISKA.  Nass river, British Columbia.

Dr Franz Boas [a] describes a top as follows:

Halha'l: spinning top, made of the top of a hemlock tree.  A cylinder, 3¼″ in diameter and 3″ high, is cut; a slit is made on one side and it is hollowed out.  A pin, 2½″ long and ¼″ thick, is inserted in the center of the top.  A small board with a wide hole, through which a string of skin or of bear-guts passes, is used for winding up the top.  It is spun on the ice of the river.  The board is held in the left hand, and stemmed against the foot.  Then the string is pulled through the hole with the right.  Several men begin spinning at a signal.  The one whose top spins the longest wins.

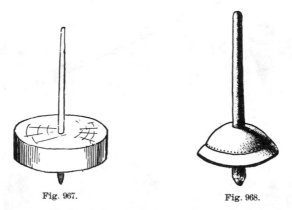

Fig. 967.                                    Fig. 968.

FIG. 967.  Top; diameter, 3 inches; Tsimshian Indians, Hazelton, British Columbia; cat. no. 53115, Field Columbian Museum.
FIG. 968.  Top; height, 3¼ inches; Central Eskimo, Cumberland sound, Baffin land, Franklin; cat. no. ₃₄₆₆⁶⁰, American Museum of Natural History.

TSIMSHIAN.  Hazelton, British Columbia.  (Cat. no. 53115, Field
      Columbian Museum.)

Top (figure 967), consisting of a disk of wood 3 inches in diameter,
      with a wooden spindle 6 inches in length.  Collected by Dr
      George A. Dorsey, who describes it as a child's toy.

ESKIMAUAN STOCK

ESKIMO (CENTRAL).  Cumberland sound, Baffin land, Franklin.  (Cat.
      no. ₃₄₆₆⁶⁰, American Museum of Natural History.)

Wooden top (figure 968), with a wooden whirl and a spindle, 3½
      inches in length.

   Collected by Capt. James S. Mutch, and figured by Doctor Boas,[b]
who says it was probably spun on the ice.

---

[a] Fifth Report on the Indians of British Columbia.  Report of the Sixty-fifth Meeting of the British Association for the Advancement of Science, p. 583, London, 1895.
[b] Eskimo of Baffin Land and Hudson Bay.  Bulletin of the American Museum of Natural History, v. 15, p. 53, New York, 1901.

ESKIMO (CENTRAL: AIVILIRMIUT and KĬNIPETU). West coast of Hudson bay, Keewatin.

Dr Franz Boas [a] describes the following game:

A large cake of ice is formed in the shape of a top (kipekutuk) with a flat surface and a dull point which fits into a shallow hole. One man sits down on the piece of ice, while two others spin it around by means of sticks. This game is often indulged in at the floe edge, when waiting for the pack-ice to come in with the tide. Generally a man who is the butt of all the others is induced to sit on this top, and is spun around until he is made sick.

ESKIMO (LABRADOR). Ungava bay. (United States National Museum.)

Cat. no. 90281. Wooden top (figure 969), conical, with band of red paint around the top; height, 2 inches.

Fig. 969.      Fig. 970.        Fig. 971.           Fig. 972.            Fig. 973.

FIG. 969. Top; height, 2 inches; Labrador Eskimo, Ungava bay; cat. no. 90281, United States National Museum.

FIG. 970. Top; height, 4¼ inches; Labrador Eskimo, Ungava bay; cat. no. 90282, United States National Museum.

FIG. 971. Top; height, 3¼ inches; Labrador Eskimo, Ungava bay; cat. no. 90283, United States National Museum.

FIG. 972. Top; height, 2¼ inches; Labrador Eskimo, Ungava bay; cat. no. 90284, United States National Museum.

FIG. 973. Wooden top; height, 4¼ inches; Western Eskimo, Bristol bay, Alaska; cat. no. 56045, United States National Museum.

Cat. no. 90282. Wooden top (figure 970), with two bands of red paint, and spindle of the same piece at the top; height, 4½ inches.

Cat. no. 90283. Wooden top (figure 971), a flat disk, 3¼ inches in diameter, with a spindle 3¾ inches in length.

Cat. no. 90284. Wooden top (figure 972), a disk, with a spindle below; the top concave and painted on the upper side with circle of red paint at the edge.

All these specimens were collected by Mr Lucien M. Turner.

ESKIMO (WESTERN). Bristol bay, Alaska. (United States National Museum.)

Cat. no. 56045. Wooden top (figure 973), 4¾ inches in height.

[a] Eskimo of Baffin Land and Hudson Bay. Bulletin of the American Museum of Natural History. v. 15, p. 110, New York, 1901.

Cat. no. 56045*a*. Wooden top (figure 974), 4½ inches in height, the lower part painted blue with red ring on top and blue above.

Cat. no. 56046. Ivory disk (figure 975), 2¼ inches in diameter, the top decorated with incised lines, and ivory pin, 3⅞ inches in length.

Cat. no. 56047. Wooden top (figure 976), a disk of wood, 4½ inches in diameter, with the top convex and ornamented with incised circles painted red and black, having a wooden spindle, 4½ inches in length.

Cat. no. 56048. Bone disk (figure 977), 1⅛ inches in diameter, with the bottom ornamented with nine black spots, and bone pin, 1¾ inches in length.

All the foregoing specimens were collected by Mr Charles L. McKay.

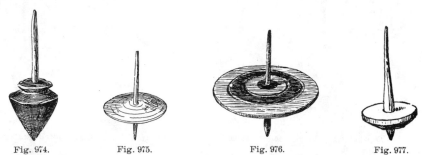

Fig. 974.          Fig. 975.          Fig. 976.          Fig. 977.

FIG. 974. Wooden top; height, 4½ inches; Western Eskimo, Bristol bay, Alaska; cat. no. 56045*a*, United States National Museum.

FIG. 975. Ivory top; height, 3⅞ inches; Western Eskimo, Bristol bay, Alaska; cat. no. 56046, United States National Museum.

FIG. 976. Wooden top; diameter, 4¼ inches; Western Eskimo, Bristol bay, Alaska; cat. no. 56047, United States National Museum.

FIG. 977. Bone top; height, 1¼ inches; Western Eskimo, Bristol bay, Alaska; cat. no. 56048, United States National Museum.

ESKIMO (WESTERN). Point Barrow, Alaska. (Cat. no. 56491, United States National Museum.)

Top,[a] consisting of a shaft of pine and a disk of spruce (figure 978), 4¼ inches in diameter, ornamented with blacklead marks, forming a border about one-fourth of an inch broad; height, 5¼ inches. It is called kaipsa.

Collected in 1882 by Lieut. P. H. Ray, U. S. Army.

——— Lower Yukon, Alaska.

Mr Edward William Nelson [b] gives, under top spinning (uiwuk), the following description:

In winter, along the lower Yukon and adjacent region to the south, the children of both sexes gather in the kashim, and each child in succession spins

[a] The Point Barrow Eskimo. Ninth Annual Report of the Bureau of Ethnology, p. 376, 1892.

[b] The Eskimo about Bering Strait. Eighteenth Annual Report of the Bureau of American Ethnology, pt. 1, p. 333, 1899.

its top. The moment the top is spun the owner runs out through the entrance passage and attempts to make a complete circuit of the house and enter again before the top stops spinning. A score is made every time this is done successfully.

Continuing, Mr Nelson [a] says:

.From Kuskokwim river to Cape Prince of Wales, on both the mainland and the islands, children of both sexes were found using tops. These are commonly of disk shape, thin at the edge, and perforated in the center for a peg. One from Cape Prince of Wales [figure 979] is of walrus ivory; it is 2½ inches in diameter and has a hole an inch wide in the middle, which is closed by a neatly-fitted wooden plug of the same thickness as the top, through which passes a spindle-shaped peg 4 inches long. This is the general style of top used in the region mentioned, but another kind is made to be spun ·with a guiding stick and cord; these are often used by men as well as boys.

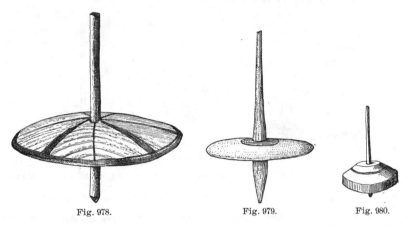

Fig. 978.                    Fig. 979.                    Fig. 980.

FIG. 978. Top; height, 5¼ inches; Western Eskimo, Point Barrow, Alaska; cat. no. 56491, United States National Museum.

FIG. 979. Top; height, 4 inches; Western Eskimo, Cape Prince of Wales, Alaska; cat. no. 45478, United States National Museum.

FIG. 980. Ivory top; height, 3 inches; Western Eskimo, Kotzebue sound, Alaska; cat. no. 127908, United States National Museum.

Referring to the tops spun by children on the lower Yukon, he says:

These toys are spun between the two hands, the upper part of the spindle being held upright between the palms.

ESKIMO (WESTERN). Kotzebue sound, Alaska. (Cat. no. 127908, United States National Museum.)

Disk of ivory (figure 980), 2⅝ inches in diameter, the top convex and marked with an incised line painted red, with a wooden spindle 3 inches in length. Collected by Lieut. George M. Stoney, U. S. Navy.

_____

[a] The Eskimo about Bering Strait. Eighteenth Annual Report of the Bureau of American Ethnology, pt. 1, p. 341, 1899.

KERESAN STOCK

KERES.  Sia, New Mexico.  (Cat. no. 134362, United States National Museum.)

Wooden top (figure 981) with conical base and flat top, having a hole leading into a small cavity near the top of the base and a nail point; height, 2⅞ inches.  Collected by Col. James Stevenson.

KIOWAN STOCK

KIOWA.  Oklahoma.  (Cat. no. 152905, United States National Museum.)

Wooden top (figure 982), 2⅛ inches in height, with a bone pin. Collected by Mr James Mooney.

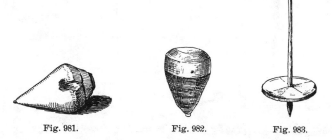

Fig. 981.          Fig. 982.          Fig. 983.

FIG. 981.  Top; height, 2⅞ inches; Keres Indians, Sia, New Mexico; cat. no. 134362, United States National Museum.

FIG. 982.  Top; height, 2⅛ inches; Kiowa Indians, Oklahoma; cat. no. 152905, United States National Museum.

FIG. 983.  Ivory top; height, 3¼ inches; Yakutat Indians, Port Mulgrave, Alaska; cat. no. 16298, United States National Museum.

KOLUSCHAN STOCK

YAKUTAT.  Port Mulgrave, Alaska.  (Cat. no. 16298, United States National Museum.)

Ivory disk (figure 983), 3⅞ inches in diameter, with a wooden spindle 3¾ inches in length.  Collected by Dr W. H. Dall.

LUTUAMIAN STOCK

KLAMATH.  Upper Klamath lake, Oregon.  (Cat. no. 61729, Field Columbian Museum.)

Disk of white-pine bark (figure 984), 2½ inches in diameter, through which is thrust a 4-inch stick, sharpened at each end.  A second specimen (61728) is similar to the first except that the disk is of cedar bark and instead of being beveled at the edge is cut off square.

These specimens were collected in 1900 by Dr George A. Dorsey and described by him under the name of heshtalxeash.[a]

MARIPOSAN STOCK

YOKUTS. Tule River reservation, Tulare county, California. (Cat. no. 70506, Field Columbian Museum.)

Two wooden hand tops (figure 985); lengths, $4\frac{1}{4}$ and $2\frac{1}{4}$ inches. Collected by Dr J. W. Hudson, who describes them as toys for hand spinning.

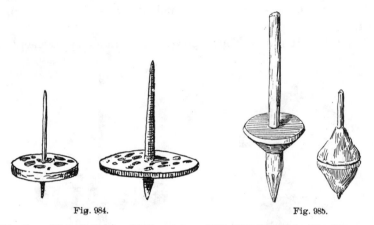

Fig. 984.

Fig. 985.

FIG. 984. Tops; Klamath Indians, Oregon; cat. no. 61728, 61729, Field Columbian Museum.
FIG. 985. Hand tops; lengths, $4\frac{1}{4}$ and $2\frac{1}{4}$ inches; Yokuts Indians, Tule River reservation, Tulare county, California; cat. no. 70506, Field Columbian Museum.

MAYAN STOCK

MAYA. Yucatan.

Dr Alfred Tozzer writes:

A top game is called in Maya polkirich. The tops are made of wood in the common shape and spun in a circle marked on the ground in the center of which is the object to be won or lost. Certain rules govern this.

SALISHAN STOCK

CLALLAM. Washington.

A Clallam boy, John Raub, informed the writer that the boys of this tribe play with tops like those used by the Makah (figures 1002–1004), which they call tsuchichaiootklen.

---

[a] Certain Gambling Games of the Klamath Indians. American Anthropologist, n. s., v. 3, p. 20, 1901.

THOMPSON INDIANS (NTLAKYAPAMUK). British Columbia. (American Museum of Natural History.)

Cat. no. $\frac{16}{8609}$. Fir-wood top (figure 986), with iron pegs at top and
bottom and twisted bark cord; height, 3¾ inches.

Collected by Mr James Teit, who says:

Formerly the pins of tops were made of bone instead of iron. Most tops
had buckskin thongs instead of bark strings, as they were considered superior
for making them spin. Tops were generally spun on smooth ice, and the amusement was indulged in occasionally by adults. Sometimes boys tried to split
one another's tops by trying to spin one on top of the other.

Cat. no. $\frac{16}{8644}$. Disk of yellow pine bark (figure 987), 3 inches in
diameter and five-eighths of an inch thick, with wooden spindle
5 inches in length.

Collected by Mr James Teit, who gives the name as salelaepten.

Fig. 986.                    Fig. 987.

FIG. 986. Top; height, 3¾ inches; Thompson Indians (Ntlakyapamuk), British Columbia; cat.
no. $\frac{16}{8609}$, American Museum of Natural History.
FIG. 987. Top; diameter, 3 inches; Thompson Indians (Ntlakyapamuk), British Columbia; cat.
no. $\frac{16}{8644}$, American Museum of Natural History.

Mr Teit [a] further says:

Tops or whirligigs were used. These were generally made of a thin circular
piece of wood, or more frequently a piece of yellow-pine bark, through the center
of which was inserted a pin a fourth to half an inch in diameter and about 5
or 6 inches long, the circular piece of wood being allowed to remain about the
middle of the pin. The one who made his top spin the longest won.

### SHOSHONEAN STOCK

BANNOCK. Fort Hall reservation, Idaho. (Cat. no. 37067, Free
Museum of Science and Art, University of Pennsylvania.)
Finger top, or teetotum (figure 988), made of the end of a cotton
spool, with a peg for twirling; height, 1½ inches.

---

[a] The Thompson Indians of British Columbia. Memoirs of the American Museum of
Natural History, whole series, v. 2, p. 281, New York, 1900.

This was collected by the writer in 1900. The name was given as temeinigakin.

HOPI. Oraibi, Arizona. (Cat. no. 51978, 55308, 67011, 67060, Field Columbian Museum.)

Four tops, made of wood.

These were collected by Rev. H. R. Voth, who furnished the following information:

> Top spinning is often indulged in among the Hopi boys. The tops are of different sizes and forms, and are spun with a little whip, which consists of a stick from 10 to 15 inches long, to which any kind of a string is tied. The top is taken between the thumb and forefinger, or sometimes the middle finger, and sent with a twirl spinning over the ground, after which it is kept in motion by quickly striking its lower point with the whip. Sometimes it is started by winding the string of the whip around the point and withdrawing it with a quick motion, being much the same as when a white boy starts his top with a string.

—————— Arizona. (United States National Museum.)

Cat. no. 22512. Wooden top (figure 989), made from a billet, the body cylindrical, painted red, the base conical, with traces of green paint, a boss at the top; height, $4\frac{3}{4}$ inches. Collected by Maj. J. W. Powell.

Cat. no. 68834. Wooden top (figure 990), a flat disk, painted with concentric rings of black, white, blue, and yellow on top, having a wooden spindle $9\frac{1}{2}$ inches in length. Collected by Col. James Stevenson.

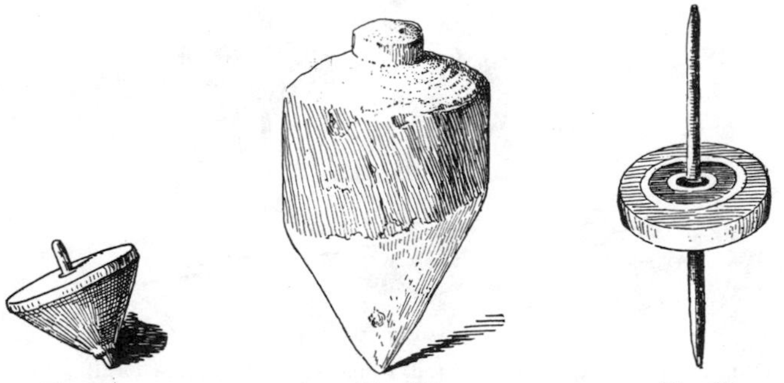

Fig. 988.                    Fig. 989.                    Fig. 990.

FIG. 988. Finger top; height, $1\frac{1}{4}$ inches; Bannock Indians, Idaho; cat. no. 37067, Free Museum of Science and Art, University of Pennsylvania.

FIG. 989. Whip top; height, $4\frac{1}{4}$ inches; Hopi Indians, Arizona; cat. no. 22512, United States National Museum.

FIG. 990. Top; height, $9\frac{1}{4}$ inches; Hopi Indians, Arizona; cat. no. 68834, United States National Museum.

—————— Oraibi, Arizona. (Cat. no. 38624, Free Museum of Science and Art, University of Pennsylvania.)

Wooden tops, conical (figure 991), painted blue, white, and red, with black bands between, and the top painted with concentric circles of blue, white, black, and red; height, 4 inches; accompanied by whips consisting of sticks with long single buckskin lashes.

The foregoing were collected by the writer in 1901.   The top is
called riyanpi; the whips, wowahpi.

PAIUTE.  Southern Utah.   (Cat. no. 9436, Peabody Museum of
          American Archæology and Ethnology.)
Two tops (figure 992), with clay whirls 1½ and 1¾ inches in diame-
      ter, cemented with gum, having wooden pins, 5 inches in length.
      Collected by Dr Edward Palmer.

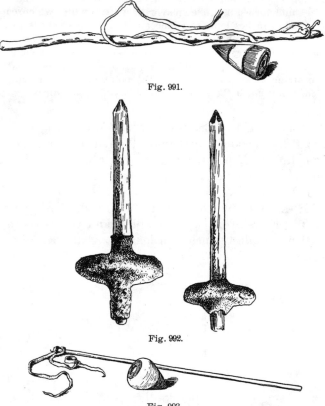

Fig. 991.

Fig. 992.

Fig. 993.

FIG. 991.  Whip top and whip; height of top, 4 inches; Hopi Indians, Oraibi, Arizona; cat. no.
38624, Free Museum of Science and Art, University of Pennsylvania.
FIG. 992.  Tops; length, 5 inches; Paiute Indians, southern Utah; cat. no. 9436, Peabody Museum
of American Archæology and Ethnology.
FIG. 993.  Whip top and whip; height of top, 3¼ inches; Shoshoni Indians, Wyoming; cat. no.
36885, Free Museum of Science and Art, University of Pennsylvania.

SHOSHONI.  Wind River reservation, Wyoming.   (Cat. no. 36885,
          Free Museum of Science and Art, University of Pennsyl-
          vania.)
Whip top (figure 993), nara pugi, and whip, temaki.   The top made
      of wood, 3½ inches in length, painted yellow and blue; the whip,
      a stick, 24 inches in length, with leather thong.   Collected by the
      writer in 1900.

SIOUAN STOCK

CROWS.  Crow reservation, Montana.  (Field Columbian Museum.)

Cat. no. 69660.  Conical wooden top (figure 994*a*), with rounded base and flat top, painted red; height, 3 inches; with whip, a twig with three buckskin lashes.

Cat. no. 69662.  Cylindrical wooden top (figure 994*b*), with hemispheric base and flat top, painted black; height, 3 inches; with whip.

Cat. no. 69663.  Wooden top, cylindrical billet, pointed alike at both ends; painted red; height, 3 inches.

Cat. no. 69664.  Cylindrical wooden top, with conical base, having an iron nail-head in the center; unpainted; height, 4 inches.

Cat. no. 69665.  Top, similar to the preceding; height, 2½ inches; with whip.

Cat. no. 69666.  Top, similar to no. 69660; unpainted; height, 3¼ inches.

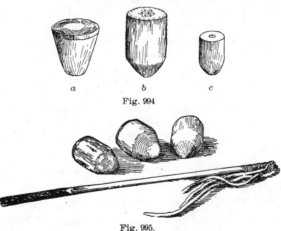

*a*          *b*          *c*

Fig. 994

Fig. 995.

FIG. 994 *a*, *b*, *c*.  Whip tops; heights, 3, 3, and 1⅜ inches; Crow Indians, Montana; cat. no. 69660, 69662, 69667, Field Columbian Museum.

FIG. 995.  Whip tops and whip; Oglala Dakota Indians, Pine Ridge reservation, South Dakota; cat. no. 22125 *a*, *b*, *c*, *d*, Free Museum of Science and Art, University of Pennsylvania.

Cat. no. 69677.  Catlinite top (figure 994*c*), bullet-shaped, with a wooden plug extending from top to point; height, 1⅝ inches. The plug takes up the shock when the top is thrown.

These specimens were collected in 1901 by Mr S. C. Simms, who gives the name memashscha.

DAKOTA (OGLALA).  Pine Ridge reservation, South Dakota.  (Cat. no. 22125 *a*, *b*, *c*, *d*, Free Museum of Science and Art, University of Pennsylvania.)

Two wooden tops (figure 995), rudely cut from a sapling, 1¾ inches in diameter at top and 2⅝ and 3 inches in length.  One is painted yellow, with red center on top and beveled edge, blue at the top, the lower pointed end painted red and yellow. The other is painted blue on top, with red beveled edge and the pointed end yellow and red. A third top is similar, but unpainted. A whip consists of a stick, 17 inches in length, with a lash made of hide, cut in three thongs, attached with sinew.

These specimens were collected by Mr Louis L. Meeker,[a] who gives the name as can wakiyapi, and says:

Players contend for position in a square marked on the ground or on ice. The game is to whip the top into the square and keep it there. On ice a square is marked and each player starts his top outside the square, trying to whip his top inside. When one succeeds, he holds the square while he keeps his top there. Should the top fall or run outside the ring, the others press in. The tops are rudely shaped from hard-wood sticks.

DAKOTA (TETON). South Dakota.

Rev. J. Owen Dorsey[b] gives the following account:

Chan káwachípi, Spinning tops.—Tops are made of ash, cedar, buffalo horn, red catlinite, or of stone. They put a scalp lock on the upper surface, ornamenting the latter with several colors of paint. They make the top spin by twirling it with the fingers, or by whipping. When they make it spin steadily by whipping they redden the scalp lock, and as it revolves very rapidly it seems to be driven into the ground. This game is played on the ice or snow; sometimes on ground which has been made firm and smooth by trampling. For a whip each player takes a tender switch, to the small end of which he fastens a lash of deer hide. He braids one-half of the lash, allowing the rest to hang loosely. They place the tops in a row, after putting up stakes, and say: "Let us see who can make his top spin the longest distance."

Dr J. R. Walker[c] describes the game of tops among the Teton as played by making a square about 5 feet across. The players spin their tops outside of the square, and drive them into the open side of the square with their whips while they are spinning.

DAKOTA (YANKTON). Fort Peck, Montana. (Free Museum of Science and Art, University of Pennsylvania.)

Cat. no. 37614. Two whip tops, rudely carved, peg-shaped, with the top edge beveled; one with the top painted red and beveled edge blue, the other blue, with a red edge; the whip a peeled twig, 15 inches in length, with hide lash.

Cat. no. 37615. Whip top of wood (figure 996), 4 inches in height. It shows much use.

Cat. no. 37616. Whip top of horn (figure 997), a tip of horn, hollowed, 2½ inches in length.

These tops were collected by the writer in 1900. A top is called kawacipi; a wooden top, cankawacipi; the whip, icapsinte.

---

[a] Ogalala Games. Bulletin of the Free Museum of Science and Art, v. 3, p. 33, Philadelphia, 1901.

[b] Games of Teton Dakota Children. The American Anthropologist, v. 4, p. 338, 1891.

[c] Sioux Games. Journal of American Folk-Lore, v. 19, p. 33, 1906.

HIDATSA. Fort Berthold, North Dakota. (Cat. no. 178969, United States National Museum.)

Wooden top, 2¾ inches in height, with a bone pin (figure 998). Collected by Dr Washington Matthews, U. S. Army, who describes it as an ice top.

OMAHA. Nebraska.

Mr Francis La Flesche described to the writer a game like whip top, played with stone balls on the ice. Clay balls and river pebbles are also used. The name, moodedeska, is an old word and not descriptive. This game is played also by the Dakota and the Ponca.

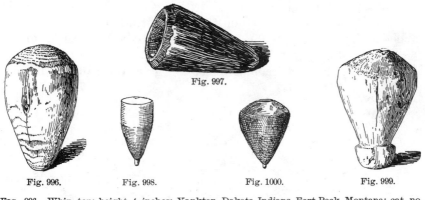

Fig. 997.

Fig. 996.  Fig. 998.  Fig. 1000.  Fig. 999.

FIG. 996. Whip top; height, 4 inches; Yankton Dakota Indians, Fort Peck, Montana; cat. no. 37615, Free Museum of Science and Art, University of Pennsylvania.

FIG. 997. Horn top; height, 2¼ inches; Yankton Dakota Indians, Fort Peck, Montana; cat. no. 37616, Free Museum of Science and Art, University of Pennsylvania.

FIG. 998. Top; height, 2¼ inches; Hidatsa Indians, Fort Berthold, North Dakota; cat. no. 178969, United States National Museum.

FIG. 999. Top; height, 3¼ inches; Tewa Indians, Santa Clara, New Mexico; cat. no. 46828, United States National Museum.

FIG. 1000. Top; height, 2¼ inches; Tewa Indians, Santa Clara, New Mexico; cat. no. 151956, United States National Museum.

SKITTAGETAN STOCK

HAIDA. Queen Charlotte islands, British Columbia.

Dr C. F. Newcombe informed the writer that he had seen this tribe make little tops, which they spun with the fingers.

TANOAN STOCK

TEWA. Santa Clara, New Mexico. (United States National Museum.)

Cat. no. 46828. Wooden top (figure 999), roughly worked, the base terminating in a hemispheric knob; height, 3¾ inches. Collected by Col. James Stevenson.

Cat. no. 151956. Wooden top (figure 1000) with iron point; height, 2¾ inches. Collected by Capt. John G. Bourke, U. S. Army.

Mr T. S. Dozier says:

The Tewa of Santa Clara call a top pfet-e-ne; playing a top, i-vi-pfet-e-ne-o-a-rai-mai. This no doubt is of modern date, but the small boys are the most expert top spinners I ever saw. It is played without gain, but in the old way, where the other fellow may have his top ruined by being knocked out of the ring.

TIGUA. Isleta, New Mexico.

An Isleta boy named J. Crecencio Lucero described the boys of this pueblo as playing with tops, napiri, which they spin with a string.

### WAKASHAN STOCK

HESQUIAHT. Vancouver island, British Columbia. (Cat. no. IV A 1490, Berlin Museum für Völkerkunde.)

Wooden top (figure 1001), with handle to hold when spinning; height of top, 2¾ inches; length of handle, 3⅞ inches.

The collector, Capt. Samuel Jacobsen, gives the name as jäh-jäh-jakei.

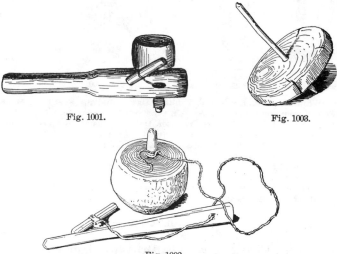

Fig. 1001.                          Fig. 1003.

Fig. 1002.

FIG. 1001. Top, with handle; length of handle, 3⅞ inches; Hesquiaht Indians, Vancouver island, British Columbia; cat. no. IV A 1490, Berlin Museum für Völkerkunde.

FIG. 1002. Top; diameter, 2⅜ inches; Makah Indians, Neah bay, Washington; cat. no. 37390, Free Museum of Science and Art, University of Pennsylvania.

FIG. 1003. Top; diameter, 3¼ inches; Makah Indians, Neah bay, Washington; cat. no. 37391, Free Museum of Science and Art, University of Pennsylvania.

MAKAH. Neah bay, Washington. (Free Museum of Science and Art, University of Pennsylvania.)

Cat. no. 37390. Hemispheric wooden top (figure 1002), with spindle at the top in one piece; diameter, 2⅜ inches; accompanied by sinew cord and perforated stick, with which the top is held and through which the cord is drawn.

Cat. no. 37391. Perforated wooden disk (figure 1003), 3¼ inches in diameter, with spindle; accompanied by sinew cord.

Cat. no. 37392.   Peg top of hard wood with wooden peg in one piece
   (figure 1004) ; height, 3¼ inches.

These tops were collected by the writer in 1900 and are called
bo-bus-ca-die.

Charlie Williams described another form of top to the writer, a
kind of teetotum, made of alder bark, perforated, and played with
the fingers.

Dr George A. Dorsey[a] states that the three varieties of tops,
ba-buthl-ka-di, were described to him by Charlie Williams as in use
among the Makah before the advent of the whites, but he thought
that they had been derived from northern Indians.

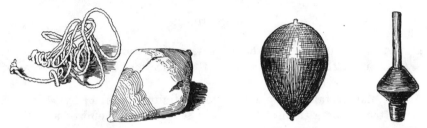

Fig. 1004.                    Fig. 1005.          Fig. 1006.

FIG. 1004.  Top; height, 3¼ inches; Makah Indians, Neah bay, Washington; cat. no. 37392, Free
   Museum of Science and Art, University of Pennsylvania.
FIG. 1005.  Top; height, 2⅛ inches; Nootka Indians, Vancouver island, British Columbia; cat.
   no. IV A 1485, Berlin Museum für Völkerkunde.
FIG. 1006.  Top; height, 2¼ inches; Nootka Indians, Vancouver island, British Columbia; cat.
   no. IV A 1484, Berlin Museum für Völkerkunde.

NOOTKA.  Vancouver island, British Columbia.  (Berlin Museum
   für Völkerkunde.)
Cat. no. IV A 1485.  Wooden top (figure 1005), 2⅛ inches in
   height.
Cat. no. IV A 1484.  Top with bone whirl and
   wooden pin (figure 1006), 2¼ inches in height.
   The collector, Capt. Samuel Jacobsen, gives the
name as jäh-jäh-jakei.

### ZUÑIAN STOCK

ZUÑI.  Zuñi, New Mexico.  (Cat. no. 127698,
   United States National Museum.)
   Wooden top (figure 1007) with conical base and
   rounded top, having a hole leading into a small
   cavity at the top of the base, and a nail point;
   height, 4 inches.  Collected by Col. James
   Stevenson.

FIG. 1007. Top;height,
4 inches; Zuñi In-
dians, Zuñi, New
Mexico; cat. no.
127698, United
States National
Museum.

Two others (cat. no. 69146 and 129070) are similar to the preceding, and another (cat. no. 69413) is somewhat smaller, 3 inches

[a] Games of the Makah Indians.  The American Antiquarian, v. 23, p. 73, 1901.

in length. Still another similar top, collected by the writer in 1902, is in the Free Museum of Science and Art of the University of Pennsylvania (cat. no. 22603). The tops are spun with a cord. The name was given to the writer as moktatonai.

### BULL-ROARER

The bull-roarer, or whizzer, used ceremonially by the Hopi, Zuñi, Navaho, Apache, and other tribes, is employed in the same form as a child's toy, the latter being presumably borrowed from the implement used in religious rites. A few examples will suffice.

### SIOUAN STOCK

DAKOTA (OGLALA). Pine Ridge reservation, South Dakota. (Cat. no. 22127, Free Museum of Science and Art, University of Pennsylvania.)

A thin, flat, rectangular piece of wood (figure 1008), 1¼ by 5¾ inches, attached by a thong 36 inches in length, to the end of a stick 31 inches long.

This is described by the collector, Mr Louis L. Meeker,[a] as a boy's plaything, under the name of tateka yuhmunpi.

FIG. 1008. Bull-roarer; length of stick, 31 inches; Oglala Dakota Indians, Pine Ridge reservation, South Dakota; cat. no. 22127, Free Museum of Science and Art, University of Pennsylvania.

DAKOTA (TETON). South Dakota.

Dr J. Owen Dorsey [b] describes the instrument as follows:

Chan' kaóbletuntun'pi, Wood having edges, . . . : A straight piece of wood is prepared, with four sides or edges, and is fastened by a strip of hide to another piece of wood which is used as a handle. The boy grasps the handle, whirls it around his head, making the four-cornered piece move rapidly with a whizzing noise.

OMAHA. Nebraska.

Mr Francis La Flesche described the bull-roarer, as used by Omaha boys as a plaything, under the name of gahoota. It is made of a stick, 6 inches long, with a notch cut at one end, and fastened to the end of a whip. Mr La Flesche did not know the meaning of the name.

---

[a] Ogalala Games. Bulletin of the Free Museum of Science and Art, v. 3, p. 34, Philadelphia, 1901.

[b] Games of the Teton Dakota Children. The American Anthropologist, v. 4, p. 343, 1901.

## Buzz

A whirling toy made of a flat piece of bone, pottery, or gourd shell, or of a heavy bone, with one or two cords on each side, is a common toy among Indian children. The Plains tribes use a knuckle bone tied with a piece of sinew. A remarkable form, in which a conical piece of wood is made to revolve on a wooden spindle, is found among the Eskimo. Evidence as to the antiquity of the disk-shaped buzz is afforded by a clay-stone disk (figure 1009) with two perforations, from the cliff-ruins in the Canyon de Chelly, in the Museum of the Brooklyn Institute.

Fig. 1009.                                    Fig. 1010.

FIG. 1009.  Stone buzz; diameter, 1¼ inches; cliff-ruins in Canyon de Chelly, Arizona; cat. no. 10679, Brooklyn Institute Museum.

FIG. 1010.  Bone buzz; Atsina (Grosventre) Indians, Fort Belknap, Montana; cat. no. $\frac{50}{1819}$, American Museum of Natural History.

### ALGONQUIAN STOCK

ARAPAHO. Oklahoma.  (Cat. no. 165819, United States National Museum.)

Toe bone of cow or ox, painted red and tied with sinew strings, having wooden handles at the ends; length, 20 inches.  Collected by Rev. H. R. Voth.

GROSVENTRES.  Fort Belknap, Montana.  (Cat. no. $\frac{50}{1819}$, American Museum of Natural History.)

Toe bone of cow or ox (figure 1010), tied with sinew, having wooden pegs inserted at the ends of the cord.  Collected by Dr A. L. Kroeber.

### ESKIMAUAN STOCK

ESKIMO (CENTRAL).  Cumberland sound, Baffin land, Franklin. (Cat. no. $\frac{60}{3469}$, American Museum of Natural History.)

Buzz (figure 1011), made of a disk of skin, 2⅜ inches in diameter, with serrated edges, having two perforations for the string.

The specimen here described was collected by Capt. James S. Mutch and is figured by Doctor Boas.[a]

---

[a] Eskimo of Baffin Land and Hudson Bay.  Bulletin of the American Museum of Natural History, v. 15, p. 53, New York, 1901.

Eskimo (Central: Aivilirmiut and Kinipetu).   West coast of
    Hudson bay, Keewatin.   (Cat. no. $\frac{60}{2531}a$, $\frac{60}{2734}b$, American
    Museum of Natural History.)

Disk of sandstone (figure 1012), 1½ inches in diameter, and another
    of bone, each with two perforations, through which pass strings
    made of sinew.   Collected by Capt. George Comer.

Dr Franz Boas [a] figures these objects.

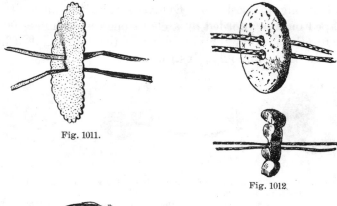

Fig. 1011.

Fig. 1012.

Fig. 1013.

Fig. 1011.   Buzz; diameter, 2⅜ inches; Central Eskimo, Cumberland sound, Baffin land, Frank-
    lin; cat. no. $\frac{60}{3465}$, American Museum of Natural History.
Fig. 1012.   Buzzes; diameter, 1½ inches; Central Eskimo (Aivilirmiut and Kinipetu), west coast
    of Hudson bay, Keewatin; cat. no. $\frac{60}{2531}a$, $\frac{60}{2734}b$, American Museum of Natural History.
Fig. 1013.   Buzz; length, 3⅛ inches; Ita Eskimo, Cape York, Greenland; cat. no. 18391, Free Mu-
    seum of Science and Art, University of Pennsylvania.

Eskimo (Ita).   Cape York, Greenland.   (Cat. no. 18391, Free Mu-
    seum of Science and Art, University of Pennsylvania.)

Hourglass-shaped piece of ivory (figure 1013), 3⅛ inches in length,
    perforated by two holes, through which an endless sinew string
    is passed.   Collected by Mr Henry G. Bryant.

---

[a] Eskimo of Baffin Land and Hudson Bay.   Bulletin of the American Museum of Natural History, v. 15, p. 112, New York, 1901.

ESKIMO (ITA).  Smith sound, Greenland.  (Cat. no. $\frac{60}{44}$, American Museum of Natural History.)

A flat bone in the shape of an hourglass or figure 8, with a looped string passing through two holes in its middle, described by Dr A. L. Kroeber under the name of hieqtaq, or bull-roarer.

ESKIMO (WESTERN).  Wainwright inlet, Utkiavi, Alaska.  (Cat. no. 89722, United States National Museum.)

Board of pine wood ( figure 1014), $3\frac{1}{2}$ inches long and $2\frac{1}{2}$ inches wide, with two round holes in the middle, through which is passed a piece of stout sinew braid, the ends of which are knotted together.

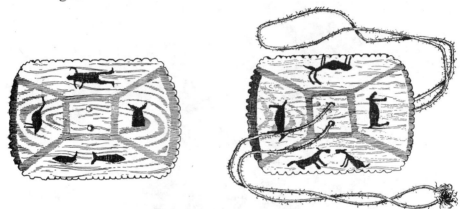

FIG. 1014.  Buzz; length, $3\frac{1}{4}$ inches; Western Eskimo, Wainwright inlet, Alaska; cat. no. 89722, United States National Museum.

Collected by Mr John Murdoch,[a] who describes it as follows:

When the board is placed in the middle of the string it can be made to spin around and whiz by alternately pulling and relaxing the ends of the string. The board is rather elaborately painted.  One end has a border of black lead on both faces, the other a similar border of red paint, which appears to be red lead.  Broad red bands form a square 1 inch across around the holes, with lines radiating from each corner to the corners of the board, on both faces. On the space between these lines are figures rudely drawn with black lead.  On one face, in the first space, is a goose; in the second, a man with a staff; in the third, the conventional figure of a whale's tail; and in the fourth, a whale, with line and float attached to him, pursued by a whaling umiak.  On the other side, the first space contains a dog or wolf walking; the second, two of these animals, sitting on their haunches, facing each other; the third, another walking; and the fourth, a reindeer in the same attitude.

a The Point Barrow Eskimo.  Ninth Annual Report of the Bureau of Ethnology, p. 378, 1892.

Eskimo (Western). Nuwuk, Alaska. (Cat. no. 89806, United States National Museum.)

Block of spruce (figure 1015$a$), fitted with a shaft of narwhal ivory.

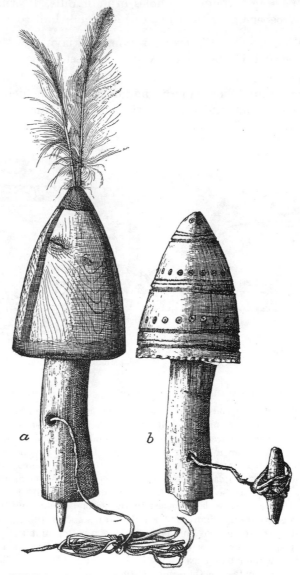

Fig. 1015 $a$, $b$.  Whirligigs; lengths, 10¼ and 9 inches; Western Eskimo, Nuwuk, Alaska; cat. no. 89806, 89807, United States National Museum; from Murdoch.

This fits loosely into a tubular handle, which is a section of the branch of an antler with the soft inside tissue cut out.  A string of seal thong passes through a hole in the middle of the handle and is fastened to the shaft. This string is about 8 feet long, and about half of it is tied up into the hank to make a handle. The specimen was collected by Mr John Murdoch,[a] who describes it as follows:

It works very much like a civilized child's whirligig. The string is wound around the shaft and a smart pull on the handle unwinds it, making the block spin round rapidly. The reaction, spinning it in the opposite direction, winds up the string again. A couple of loose hawk's feathers are stuck into the tip of the block, which is painted with red ocher for about an inch. Four equidistant stripes of the same color run down the sides to a border of the same width round the base. This was made for sale and appears to be an unusual toy. I do not recollect ever seeing the children play with such a toy. It is called kai'psa (Gr. kâvsâk, "a whirligig or similar toy").

Another specimen (cat. no. 89807, United States National Museum) is made of a solid tip of a mountain sheep's horn (figure 1015*b*), and is elaborately ornamented with a conventional pattern of lines and of circles and dots, incised and colored red with ocher. The shaft is of hard bone, and the line has a little wooden handle at the end. The block is so heavy it will hardly spin. A similar object, collected by Mr E. A. McIlhenny at Point Barrow, Alaska (cat. no. 42369, Free Museum of Science and Art, University of Pennsylvania), is described by him as a whirligig, kaipsak. It differs from the specimens described in being made entirely of wood, and is quite new and unused.

### SHOSHONEAN STOCK

Hopi. Oraibi, Arizona. (Cat. no. 128488, United States National Museum.)

Five disks of clay stone (figure 1016), from 1⅜ to 2½ inches in diameter, each perforated with two holes, having a cord of woolen yarn passing through them with its ends tied to form a loop on each side.

FIG. 1016. Buzzes; diameters, 1¼ and 2¼ inches; Hopi Indians, Oraibi, Arizona; cat. no. 128488, United States National Museum.

Two of the specimens which are figured are painted in red, white, and black, with star or flower-shaped designs on both sides. The others are plain. These were collected by Col. James Stevenson and were designated as child's toys. Two other specimens in the United

[a] Ethnological Results of the Point Barrow Expedition. Ninth Annual Report of the Bureau of Ethnology, p. 376, 1892.

States National Museum (cat. no. 68803 and 128918), both collected by Colonel Stevenson, are similar to those above described.

MONO.    Hooker cove, Madera county, California.    (Cat. no. 71454, Field Columbian Museum.)

Small bone, pivosy (figure 1017), of a metatarsal bone of a deer, with loops at each end, described by the collector, Dr J. W. Hudson, as a bone whirligig.

FIG. 1017.  Bone whirligig; Mono Indians, Madera county, California; cat. no. 71454, Field Columbian Museum.

————Hooker cove, Madera county, California.    (Cat. no. 71442, Field Columbian Museum.)

Pottery disk (figure 1018), 2 inches in diameter, decorated with four spots of red paint, with cotton cord.  Collected by Dr J. W. Hudson, who describes it as a whirligig.

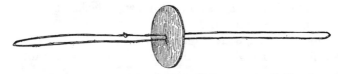

FIG. 1018.  Buzz; diameter, 2 inches; Mono Indians, Madera county, California; cat. no. 71442, Field Columbian Museum.

### SIOUAN STOCK

CROWS.    Crow reservation, Montana.    (Cat. no. 69668, Field Columbian Museum.)

Whirling toy, made of a joint bone of an ox, painted red, tied around with a sinew string, extending 8 inches on each side, and having hand grips, made of twigs, at the ends.

Collected by Mr S. C. Simms, who gives the name as ewahpoa-rooahcooah.

FIG. 1019.  Bone buzz; length, 11¼ inches; Oglala Dakota Indians, Pine Ridge reservation, South Dakota; cat. no. 22126, Free Museum of Science and Art, University of Pennsylvania.

DAKOTA (OGLALA).    Pine Ridge reservation, South Dakota.    (Cat. no. 22126, Free Museum of Science and Art, University of Pennsylvania.)

Toe bone of a cow or ox (figure 1019), tied with sinew, with two small sticks inserted at the end of the cord.

This specimen was collected by Mr Louis L. Meeker,[a] who describes it as a boy's toy under the name of hohouh yuhmunpi.

DAKOTA (TETON). South Dakota.

Rev. J. Owen Dorsey [b] thus describes the implement:

Hohú yukhmun'pi, Making the bone hum by twisting the cord.—Bone is not the only material used, for the toy is sometimes made of stone or of a circular piece of wood. The toy is made thus: Some deer or buffalo sinews are twisted together; parts of a deer's foot are cooked till soft, and are strung together on the sinew. To the ends of the sinew are fastened two sticks which serve as handles, one stick at each end, each being at right angles to the sinew. The sinew is twisted, and when pulled taut the toy makes a humming sound.

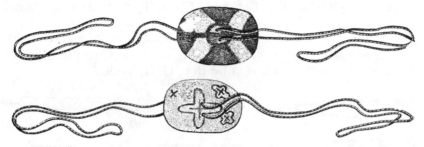

FIG. 1020. Buzz; diameter, 2¾ inches; Maricopa Indians, Arizona; cat. no. 2927, Brooklyn Institute Museum.

YUMAN STOCK

MARICOPA. Arizona. (Cat. no. 2927, Brooklyn Institute Museum.) Wooden disk (figure 1020), 2¾ inches in diameter, perforated with two holes, through which a cord passes. Collected by Mr Louis L. Meeker in 1904.

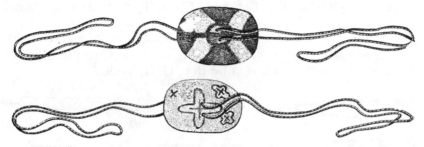

FIG. 1021. Buzz; diameter, 3 inches; Zuñi Indians, Zuñi, New Mexico; cat. no. 3069, Brooklyn Institute Museum.

ZUÑIAN STOCK

ZUÑI. Zuñi, New Mexico. (Cat. no. 3069, Brooklyn Institute Museum.)

Disk of dried gourd shell (figure 1021), 3 inches in diameter, pierced with two holes, through which a string passes.

Collected by the writer in 1903. The name was given as huwa-wananai.

---

[a] Ogalala Games. Bulletin of the Free Museum of Science and Art, v. 3, p. 34, Philadelphia, 1901.

[b] Games of Teton Dakota Children. The American Anthropologist, v. 4, p. 343, 1891.

## POPGUN

The writer has a record of the popgun from seven tribes, of which three are Siouan. The evidence is not sufficient to establish proof of its existence before the time of native contact with the whites. At the same time the two finely finished popguns (figure 1022) excavated by Dr George A. Dorsey at Ancon, Peru, now in the Field Columbian Museum, bring its aboriginal character in North America within the bounds of probability.

ALGONQUIAN STOCK

CHEYENNE. Oklahoma. (Cat. no. 165964, United States National
　　Museum.)
Popgun (figure 1023), consisting of a wooden tube, marked with
　　burned designs, 10 inches in length, and a stick, or plunger, 16¾
　　inches in length. Collected by Rev. H. R. Voth.

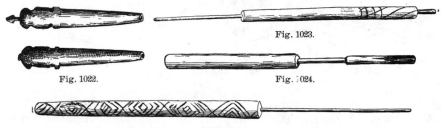

Fig. 1023.

Fig. 1022.　　　　Fig. 1024.

Fig. 1025.

FIG. 1022. Wooden popguns; length, 5 inches; Ancon, Peru; cat. no. 5309, Field Columbian
　　Museum.
FIG. 1023. Popgun; length, 10 inches; Cheyenne Indians, Oklahoma; cat. no. 165964, United
　　States National Museum.
FIG. 1024. Popgun; length, 12¼ inches; Sauk and Fox Indians, Iowa; cat. no. $\frac{50}{3508}$, American
　　Museum of Natural History.
FIG. 1025. Popgun; length, 12⅝ inches; Arikara Indians, Fort Berthold, North Dakota; cat. no.
　　8424, United States National Museum.

SAUK AND FOXES. Iowa. (Cat. no. $\frac{50}{3508}$, American Museum of
　　Natural History.)
Popgun of elder wood (figure 1024), 12½ inches in length.
　This was collected by Dr William Jones, who gives the name as
paskesi gani, fighting thing, and says that it was used by boys with a
bow and a belt of blue-joint arrows in playing war.

CADDOAN STOCK

ARIKARA. Fort Berthold, North Dakota. (Cat. no. 8424, United
　　States National Museum.)
Wooden popgun (figure 1025), a tube, 12⅝ inches in length, marked
　　with burned designs, and a wooden plunger. Collected by Dr
　　C. C. Gray and Dr Washington Matthews, U. S. Army.

### MARIPOSAN STOCK

YOKUTS.  Tule River reservation, Tulare county, California.  (Cat.
   no. 70505, Field Columbian Museum.)
Popgun of elder (figure 1026), with maple piston, for shooting wads;
   length, 14½ inches.  Collected by Dr J. W. Hudson.

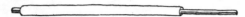

FIG. 1026.  Popgun; length, 14¼ inches; Yokuts Indians, Tule River reservation, Tulare county,
California; cat. no. 70505, Field Columbian Museum.

### SIOUAN STOCK

DAKOTA (OGLALA).  Pine Ridge reservation, South Dakota.  (Cat.
   no. 22131, Free Museum of Science and Art, University of
   Pennsylvania.)
Popgun, epahoton (figure 1027), a piece of sapling, three-fourths
   of an inch in diameter and 6½ inches in length, with a hole
   burned through the center, the outside being ornamented with
   burned lines, as shown in the figure.
   Collected by Mr Louis L. Meeker, who states that popguns are used
by Oglala boys to shoot wads of elm bark.[a]

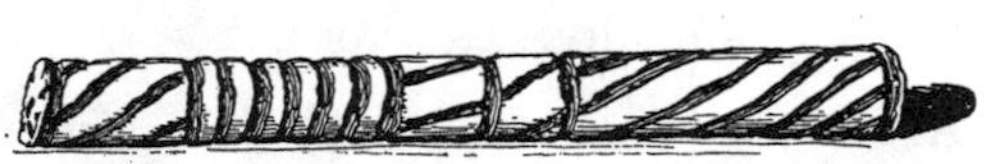

FIG. 1027.  Popgun; length, 6¼ inches; Oglala Dakota Indians, Pine Ridge reservation, South
Dakota; cat. no. 22131, Free Museum of Science and Art, University of Pennsylvania.

DAKOTA (TETON).  South Dakota.
   Rev. J. Owen Dorsey [b] says:

I'pahotun'pi un'pi, Pop-gun game.—In the fall, when the wind blows down
the leaves, the boys make pop-guns of ash wood.  They load them with bark
which they have chewed, or else with wild sage (Artemesia), and they shoot at
one another.  The one hit suffers much pain.

   Dr J. R. Walker [c] describes the popgun under the name of ipaho-
tonpi, and gives the names of the parts as tancan, body; wibopan,
ramrod; and iyopuhdi, the wadding.  The latter, he says, is made by
chewing the inner bark of the elm, and using it while wet.

FIG. 1028.  Popgun; Omaha Indians, Nebraska; from drawing by Mr Francis La Flesche.

OMAHA.  Nebraska.
   Mr Francis La Flesche told the writer in 1893 that Omaha boys
made popguns (figure 1028), batushi (to push, to crack), of elder,
which they stop with two wads of nettle fiber.  These Indians were

[a] Bulletin of the Free Museum of Science and Art, v. 3, p. 35, Philadelphia, 1901.
[b] Games of Teton Dakota Children.  The American Anthropologist, v. 4, p. 337, 1891.
[c] Journal of American Folk-Lore, v. 19, p. 35, 1905.

probably acquainted with the popgun before white contact. They made them through the winter, and in the summer threw them away. The following, he said, is the òrder of the boys' games: Shinny (tabegathe, ball to strike) in spring; throwing sticks and target shooting in summer; shinny in the fall; tops, bone sliders, and popguns in winter. The plum-stone dice game is played at all seasons.

### BEAN SHOOTER

The implement to which for convenience the name of bean shooter has been given is a mechanical contrivance not unlikely to have been borrowed from the whites, found thus far only in the Southwest and on the Northwest coast.

FIG. 1099. Bean shooter; length, 12¼ inches; Hopi Indians, Oraibi, Arizona; cat. no. 38626, Free Museum of Science and Art, University of Pennsylvania.

#### SHOSHONEAN STOCK

Hopi. Oraibi, Arizona. (Cat. no. 38626, Free Museum of Science and Art, University of Pennsylvania.)

Bean shooter (figure 1029), made of a piece of cane, 12¾ inches in length, with a spring, consisting of a bent strip of wood, the ends of which are secured in holes cut in the cane. Collected by the writer in 1901.

Mono. Hooker cove, Madera county, California. (Cat. no. 71445, Field Columbian Museum.)

Wooden splint (figure 1030), 10 inches in length, used as a toy for flipping mud balls. Collected by Dr J. W. Hudson.

FIG. 1030. Stone flipper; length, 10 inches; Mono Indians, Madera county, California; cat. no. 71445, Field Columbian Museum.

#### WAKASHAN STOCK

Kwakiutl. Alert bay, Vancouver island, British Columbia.

Dr C. F. Newcombe writes as follows, describing what he calls the figure 4 dart shooter:

Among the Kwakiutl, of the Nimpkish tribe, this is called HEndlEm. In use a small stick is placed across the top of the pliant side pieces and is shot to some little distance by pressing on the trigger piece which is horizontal to the figure 4. The figure is held in front of the body with both hands with the short end of the trigger downwards, and the perpendicular stem of the 4 horizontally. It is frequently used when children are sick and small sticks are shot in different directions to chase away the spirit supposed to be causing the sickness. It was used as lately as two years ago at Alert bay. Sets of four of this instrument are employed by grown-up people—relatives of the sick. The sticks are left lying about after the performance, but the guns are burned when done with. This goes on for four nights in succession. The noise of the two flexible sides coming together when the stick is ejected is supposed to aid the good work. At night the four shooters are left loaded near the sick child to scare the ghost or spirit. They are also used as a game by children.

MAKAH. Neah bay, Washington. (Free Museum of Science and Art, University of Pennsylvania.)

Two stone flippers, made of curved pieces of whalebone, one single and the other double, recurved. Collected by the writer in 1900.

OPITCHESAHT. Vancouver island, British Columbia. (Cat. no. IV A 7117, 7118, Berlin Museum für Völkerkunde.)

Curved splint of whalebone (figure 1031), 4 inches in length.

The collector, Capt. Samuel Jacobsen, gives the name as tklamayek.

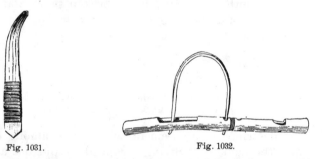

Fig. 1031.                                    Fig. 1032.

FIG. 1031. Stone flipper; length, 4 inches; Opitchesaht Indians, Vancouver island, British Columbia; cat. no. IV A 7117, 7118, Berlin Museum für Völkerkunde.
FIG. 1032. Bean shooter; length, 10 inches; Zuñi Indians, Zuñi, New Mexico; cat. no. 3066, Brooklyn Institute Museum.

ZUÑIAN STOCK

ZUÑI. Zuñi, New Mexico. (Cat. no. 3066, Brooklyn Institute Museum.)

Bean shooter (figure 1032), consisting of a tube of wood, with a wooden spring; length, 10 inches.

Collected by the writer in 1903. The name was given as keto ananai.

## CAT'S CRADLE

Cat's cradle is known to all the tribes of whom direct inquiry has been made. The Zuñi explain it as the netted shield of the War Gods, and as taught to the latter by their grandmother, the Spider. The idea seems to underlie the tradition among the Navaho also that the play was taught them by the Spider people. In addition to cat's cradle the Indians have a variety of tricks and amusements with string.[a] Charlie Williams, at Neah bay, Washington, described the following as a common amusement among the Makah:

A string is tied about the neck with a false knot. It is pulled tight and comes off. This is called tu-a-oss. The string is sometimes tied about the toe.

The writer saw this trick performed with many grimaces by an old Shoshoni woman at Fort Washakie, Wyoming.

Dr Alfred Tozzer described the trick of splicing a cut rope in the mouth, as seen by him among the Maya at Chichen Itza, Yucatan. The rope is arranged as shown in figure 1033, the point *a* being concealed from the audience, who consider the ring an unbroken piece of rope, circled twice. The rope is then cut at *b* and four ends shown, *a* still being concealed from the audience. The two ends below *b* are placed in the mouth, but, the string having been cut at *b*, a small piece only is left around the longer loop at *a*, which the tongue easily frees from the loop of the main string; the string when taken from the mouth thus shows an unbroken surface at *b*, as the small piece cut at *b* and running from *b* to *a* and back to *b* is still concealed in the mouth.

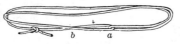

FIG. 1033. Cord arranged for trick of splicing in the mouth; Maya Indians, Chichen Itza, Yucatan; cat. no. 2815, Brooklyn Institute Museum.

Mr Dorsey describes an amusement with string among the Teton Dakota under the name of " String wrapped in and out among the fingers," etc.

ALGONQUIAN STOCK

SAUK AND FOXES. Tama, Iowa.

These Indians described the game of cat's cradle to the writer under the name of sah-sah-nah-ki-á-ti-wi, parcel.

ATHAPASCAN STOCK

APACHE (WHITE MOUNTAIN). Arizona. (Cat. no. 3001, Brooklyn Institute Museum.)

The cat's cradle (figure 1034) figure was collected by the writer from a White Mountain Apache girl at Albuquerque. She called it ikinasthlani.

---

[a] Consult String Figures and Tricks, by Prof. Alfred C. Haddon. American Anthropologist, n. s., v. 5, p. 218, 1903.

HUPA.   California.

Mr Pliny Earle Goddard [a] says:

The Hupa make several varieties of cat's cradle.

NAVAHO.   St Michael, Arizona.   (Free Museum of Science and Art, University of Pennsylvania.)

The following games of cat's cradle were collected by the writer. The figures were made by a single individual, who used his lips and teeth when necessary.   The intermediary stages were not considered or exhibited.

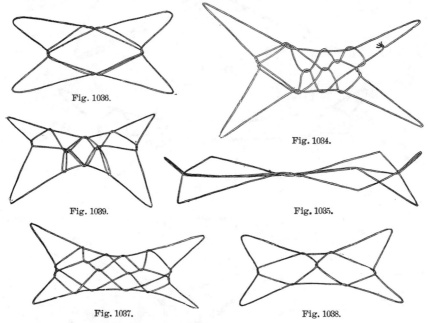

Fig. 1036.

Fig. 1034.

Fig. 1039.

Fig. 1035.

Fig. 1037.

Fig. 1038.

FIG. 1034.   Cat's cradle, i-ki-nas-thla'-ni; White Mountain Apache Indians, Arizona; cat. no. 3001, Brooklyn Institute Museum.

FIG. 1035.   Cat's cradle, atsinlt'lish, lightning; Navaho Indians, St Michael, Arizona; cat. no. 22712, Free Museum of Science and Art, University of Pennsylvania.

FIG. 1036.   Cat's cradle, sûtso, big star; Navaho Indians, St Michael, Arizona; cat. no. 22713, Free Museum of Science and Art, University of Pennsylvania.

FIG. 1037.   Cat's cradle, sô' lani, many (group of) stars; Navaho Indians, St Michael, Arizona; cat. no. 22714, Free Museum of Science and Art, University of Pennsylvania.

FIG. 1038.   Cat's cradle, sô ahóts'ii, twin stars; Navaho Indians, St Michael, Arizona; cat. no. 22715, Free Museum of Science and Art, University of Pennsylvania.

FIG. 1039.   Cat's cradle, sô bidē' huloni, horned stars; Navaho Indians, St Michael, Arizona; cat. no. 22716, Free Museum of Science and Art, University of Pennsylvania.

Cat. no. 22712: atsinlt'lish, lightning, figure 1035.
Cat. no. 22713: sûtso, big star, figure 1036.
Cat. no. 22714: sô' lani, many (group of) stars, figure 1037.
Cat. no. 22715: sô ahóts'ii, twin stars, figure 1038.
Cat. no. 22716: sô bidē' huloni, horned stars, figure 1039.

[a] Life and Culture of the Hupa, p. 61, Berkeley, 1903.

Cat. no. 22717: dilyehe, Pleiades, figure 1040.

Cat. no. 22718: mâ'i aɬts' âyilaghuɬi, coyotes running apart, figure 1041.

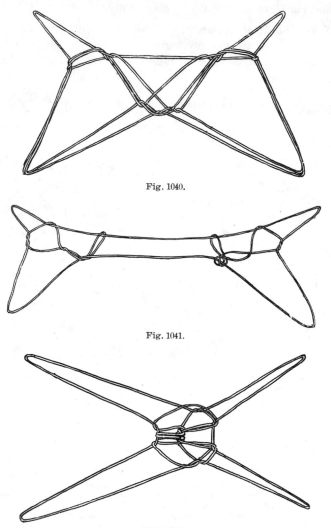

Fig. 1040.

Fig. 1041.

Fig. 1042.

FIG. 1040.   Cat's cradle, dilyehe, Pleiades, Navaho Indians, St Michael, Arizona; cat. no. 22717, Free Museum of Science and Art, University of Pennsylvania.

FIG. 1041.   Cat's cradle, mâ'i aɬts' âyilaghuɬi, coyotes running apart; Navaho Indians, St Michael, Arizona; cat. no. 22718, Free Museum of Science and Art, University of Pennsylvania.

FIG. 1042.   Cat's cradle, nashja, owl; Navaho Indians, St Michael, Arizona; cat. no. 22719, Free Museum of Science and Art, University of Pennsylvania.

Cat. no. 22719: nashja, owl, figure 1042.

Cat. no. 22720: t'lish, snake, figure 1043.

Cat. no. 22721: nashúi dich'izhi, horned toad, figure 1044.

Cat. no. 22722: łesis, poncho, figure 1045.

Cat. no. 22723: hoghan (hogan), figure 1046.

Cat. no. 22724: chizh joyełi, packing (carrying) wood, figure 1047.

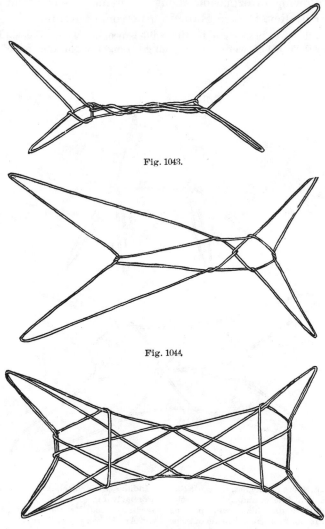

Fig. 1043.

Fig. 1044.

Fig. 1045.

FIG. 1043.  Cat's cradle, t'lish, snake; Navaho Indians, St Michael, Arizona; cat. no. 22720, Free Museum of Science and Art, University of Pennsylvania.

FIG. 1044.  Cat's cradle, nashúi dich' izhi, horned toad; Navaho Indians, St Michael, Arizona; cat. no. 22721, Free Museum of Science and Art, University of Pennsylvania.

FIG. 1045.  Cat's cradle, łesis, poncho; Navaho Indians, St Michael, Arizona; cat. no. 22722, Free Museum of Science and Art, University of Pennsylvania.

Of the specimens just mentioned, cat. no. 22712, lightning, was found by the writer in Isleta (figure 1064) under the same name, and cat. no. 22714, many (group of) stars, at the same place, but the name there was not obtained; cat. no. 22715, twin stars, occurs in Zuñi as lightning (figure 1069), and cat. no. 22724, packing (carrying) wood, also in Zuñi (figure 1068).

The following information about the game was communicated to the writer by Rev. Berard Haile in a personal letter:

Cat's cradle owes its origin to the Spider people. They, the spiders, who in the Navaho's belief were human beings, taught them the game for their

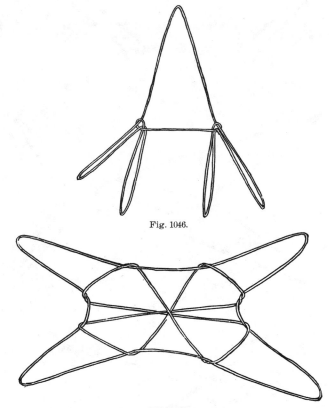

Fig. 1046.

Fig. 1047.

FIG. 1046. Cat's cradle, hoghan (hogan); Navaho Indians, St Michael, Arizona; cat. no. 22723, Free Museum of Science and Art, University of Pennsylvania.
FIG. 1047. Cat's cradle, chizh joyeli, packing (carrying) wood; Navaho Indians, St Michael, Arizona; cat. no. 22724, Free Museum of Science and Art, University of Pennsylvania.

amusement. The holy spiders taught the Navaho to play and how to make the various figures of stars, snakes, bears, coyotes, etc., but on one condition—they were to be played only in winter, because at that season spiders, snakes, etc., sleep and do not see them. To play the cat's cradle at any other time of the year would be folly, for certain death by lightning, falling from a horse, or some other mishap were sure to reach the offender. Otherwise no religious meaning is said to attach to the game. Even the above information was only extracted with much patience and scheming. I may add that one Navaho claimed that the cat's cradle is a sort of schooling by which the children are taught the position of the stars, etc. Though this might be a satisfactory explanation, it was not approved by the medicine man from whom I obtained the above. Na' atlo, it is twisted, is the term for cat's cradle.

NAVAHO.   Chaco canyon, New Mexico.

Cat's cradle (figure 1048), called carrying wood, chizh joyełi.   Figure made for the writer by Dr Alfred Tozzer, who collected the specimen, with others, among the Navaho in 1901.

In addition to the above figure, Dr Tozzer furnished Prof. Alfred C. Haddon [a] with the following list of cat's cradles, which he collected among the Navaho:

Man, dĕnnĕ; sternum with ribs, ai-yĭt; woman's belt, sĭs; bow, at¹-ti; arrow, ka; two hogans, naki-hogan or at¹-sa-hogan; sand-painting figure, ᵏos-shis-chĭ; coyote, ma-ĭ; bird's nest, a-to; horned toad, na-a-sho-ĭ-di-chĭzi; butterfly, ga-hĭkĭ; star, so-a-hinat¹san-ⁿtĭ-ĭ.

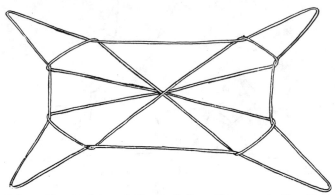

FIG. 1048.   Cat's cradle, carrying wood; Navaho Indians, Chaco canyon, New Mexico; cat. no. 22738, Free Museum of Science and Art, University of Pennsylvania.

The general name for these figures is na-ash-klo, according to Mr Tozzer. The term na signifies a "continuous movement;" ash is "I," and klo is the root word of "weaving." Perhaps "continuous weaving" would be a fair translation of the Navaho word.

Professor Haddon gives directions for making the hogan, two hogans, and carrying wood, many (group of) stars, owl, and lightning, and illustrates the perfected figure of each.

TSETSAUT.   Portland, British Columbia.

Dr Franz Boas [b] mentions their playing the game of cat's cradle.

### ESKIMAUAN STOCK

ESKIMO (CENTRAL).   Frobisher bay, Baffin land, Franklin.

Capt. Charles F. Hall [c] says:

The Innuit social life is simple and cheerful. They have a variety of games of their own. In one of these they use a number of bits of ivory, made in the

---

[a] String Figures and Tricks. American Anthropologist, n. s., v. 5, p. 220, 1903.

[b] Report of the Sixty-fifth Meeting of the British Association for the Advancement of Science, p. 568, London, 1895.

[c] Arctic Researches, p. 570, New York, 1860.

form of ducks, etc., such as Sampson's wife gàve me, as just mentioned.  In another, a simple string is used in a variety of intricate ways, now representing a tuktoo, now a whale, now a walrus, now a seal, being arranged upon the fingers in a way bearing a general resemblance to the game known to us as "cat's cradle."  The people were very quick in learning of me to play chess, checkers, and dominoes.

## Eskimo (Central).   Cumberland sound, Baffin land, Franklin.

### Dr Franz Boas [a] says:

The women are particularly fond of making figures out of a loop, a game similar to our cat's cradle (ajarorpoq).  They are, however, much more clever than we in handling the thong, and have a great variety of forms, some of which are

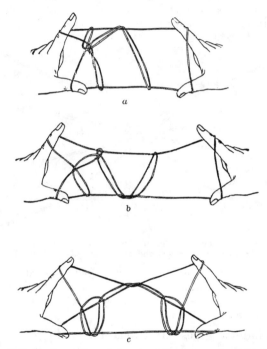

Fig. 1049 *a*, *b*, *c*.  Cat's cradle; *a*, deer; *b*, hare; *c*, hills and ponds; Central Eskimo, Cumberland sound, Baffin land, Franklin; from Boas.

represented in figure 1049.  For example, I shall describe the method of making the device representing a deer [figure 1049*a*].  Wind the loop over both hands, passing it over the backs of the thumbs inside the palms and outside the fourth fingers.  Take the string from the palm of the right hand with the first finger of the left, and vice versa.  The first finger of the right hand moves over all the parts of the thong lying on the first and fourth fingers of the right hand and passes through the loop formed by thongs on the thumb of the right hand; then it moves back over the foremost thong and takes it up, while the thumb lets go the loop.  The first finger moves downward before the thongs lying on the fourth finger and comes up in front of all the thongs.  The thumb is placed into the loops hanging on the first finger and the loop hanging on the first finger of the left hand is drawn through both and hung again over the same finger.

---

[a] The Central Eskimo.  Sixth Annual Report of the Bureau of Ethnology, p. 569, 1888.

The thumb and first finger of the right and the thumb of the left hand let go their loops. The whole is then drawn tight.

In addition to the above, Doctor Boas[a] illustrates two other cat's cradles from this locality, one called amaroqdjung, wolf (figure 1050a), and the other ussuqdjung (figure 1050b), and he describes the manner in which all are made.

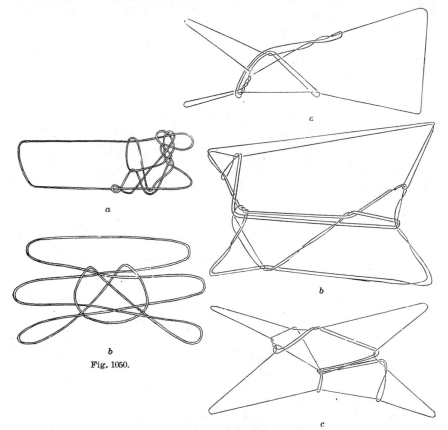

Fig. 1050.

Fig. 1051.

FIG. 1050 a, b. Cat's cradle; a, amaroqdjung, wolf; b, ussuqdjung; Central Eskimo, Cumberland sound, Baffin land, Franklin; from Boas.

FIG. 1051 a, b, c. Cat's cradle; fox, raven, polar béar; Ita Eskimo, Smith sound, Greenland; cat. no. $\frac{60}{212}$, $\frac{60}{210}$, $\frac{60}{209}$, American Museum of Natural History; from Kroeber.

## ESKIMO (ITA). Smith sound, Greenland.

Dr A. L. Kroeber[b] figures the following cat's cradles: Fox (figure 1051a), raven (figure 1051b), polar bear (figure 1051c), narwhal (figure 1052a), hare (figure 1052b), and walrus head (figure 1052c).

[a] Internationales Archiv für Ethnographie, v. 1, p. 233, Leiden, 1888.
[b] Bulletin of the American Museum of Natural History, v. 12, p. 298–300, New York, 1800.

KERES. Acoma, New Mexico.

An Acoma Indian at Zuñi named James H. Miller gave the name of cat's cradle as napainet.

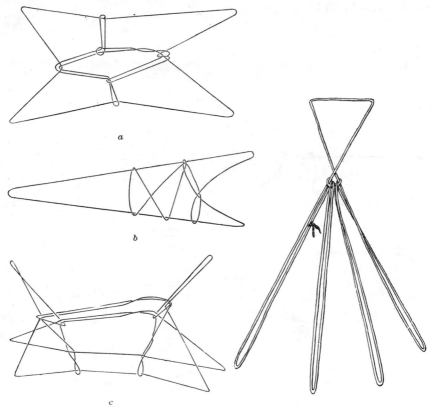

Fig. 1052.                                    Fig. 1053.

FIG. 1052 *a, b, c.* Cat's cradle; narwhal, hare, walrus head; Ita Eskimo, Smith sound, Greenland; cat. no. $\frac{60}{913}$, $\frac{60}{911}$, $\frac{60}{914}$, American Museum of Natural History; from Kroeber.
FIG. 1053. Cat's cradle, chicken foot; Keres Indians, Cochiti, New Mexico; cat. no. 4979, Brooklyn Institute Museum.

——— Cochiti, New Mexico. (Brooklyn Institute Museum.)

The following cat's cradles were collected by the writer in 1904 from Francisco Chaves (Kogit), a Keres boy from Cochiti, at St Michael, Arizona:

Cat. no. 4979: spinakaiyaka, chicken foot, figure 1053.

Cat. no. 4980: polaka, butterfly, figure 1054.

Cat. no. 4981: wisdyakka, bow, figure 1055.

Cat. no. 4982: sjonanakka, bat, figure 1056.

He gave the name as kokominnaoowishiyan, string playing; kokomin, string.

KULANAPAN STOCK

POMO. Ukiah, California. (Cat. no. 3000, Brooklyn Institute Museum.)

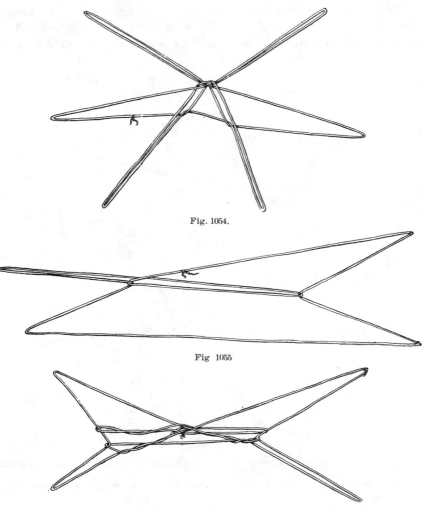

Fig. 1054.

Fig 1055

Fig. 1056.

FIG. 1054. Cat's cradle, butterfly; Keres Indians, Cochiti, New Mexico; cat. no. 4980, Brooklyn Institute Museum.

FIG. 1055. Cat's cradle, bow; Keres Indians, Cochiti, New Mexico; cat. no. 4981, Brooklyn Institute Museum.

FIG. 1056. Cat's cradle, bat; Keres Indians, Cochiti, New Mexico; cat. no. 4982, Brooklyn Institute Museum.

This cat's cradle (figure 1057) was collected by the writer from a Pomo Indian man at Albuquerque. He gave the general name of the amusement as datidatu, tangled up, and of this figure as tsudium, humming bird.

MAYAN STOCK

MAYA. Chichen Itza, Yucatan. (Cat. no. 2813, 2814, Brooklyn Institute Museum.)

Dr Alfred Tozzer has furnished the writer two cat's cradles from this tribe. One (figure 1058) is called a chicken's foot. A is held on the little finger, B on the middle finger, and C on the thumb.

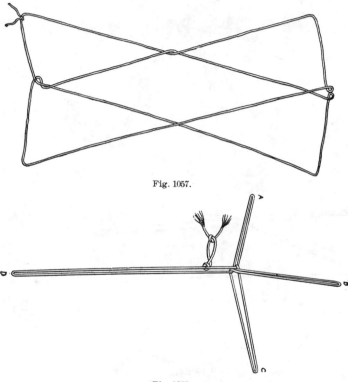

Fig. 1057.

Fig. 1058.

FIG. 1057. Cat's cradle, tsudium, humming bird; Pomo Indians, Ukiah, California; cat. no. 3000, Brooklyn Institute Museum.
FIG. 1058. Cat's cradle, chicken's foot; Maya Indians, Yucatan; cat. no. 2813, Brooklyn Institute Museum.

In another (figure 1059) A is held in the mouth of the operator and D in the hand of an assisting person. B and C, held in each hand by the operator, are pulled outward from the center as D approaches the center. The operation is called sawing wood.

SALISHAN STOCK

CLALLAM. Washington.

A Clallam boy, John Raub, described this tribe as playing cat's cradle, which they call tskusli skutsisen.

SHUSWAP.   Kamloops, British Columbia.

Dr Franz Boas [a] says:

Children and women play cat's cradle.

SKOKOMISH.   British Columbia.

Mr Charles Hill-Tout [b] says these Indians were acquainted with qauwilts, or the cat's cradle game.

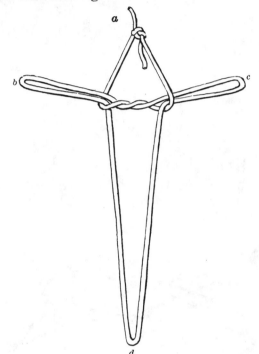

FIG. 1059.   Cat's cradle, sawing wood; Maya Indians, Yucatan; cat. no. 2814, Brooklyn Institute Museum.

SONGISH.   British Columbia.

Dr Franz Boas [c] says:

Hqwauā'latcis, the game of cat's cradle.—A great variety of figures are made. Only one person is required to make these figures.   Sometimes the teeth must help in making them.

THOMPSON INDIANS (Ntlakyapamuk).   British Columbia.

Mr James Teit [d] says:

Many children's games were played by the smaller boys and girls.   "Cat's cradle" was one of these [figure 1060].   Strings were fixed on the fingers in

[a] Second General Report on the Indians of British Columbia.   Report of the Sixtieth Meeting of the British Association for the Advancement of Science, p. 641, London, 1891.

[b] Notes on the Sk'qō'mic of British Columbia.   Report of the Seventieth Meeting of the British Association for the Advancement of Science, p. 488, London, 1900.

[c] Second General Report on the Indians of British Columbia.   Report of the Sixtieth Meeting of the British Association for the Advancement of Science, p. 571, London, 1891.

[d] The Thompson Indians of British Columbia.   Memoirs of the American Museum of Natural History, whole series, v. 2, p. 281, New York, 1900.

different ways, so as to present many forms, such as the "beaver," the "deer," the "buckskin," the "conical lodge," the "women's house," the "man stealing wood," etc.

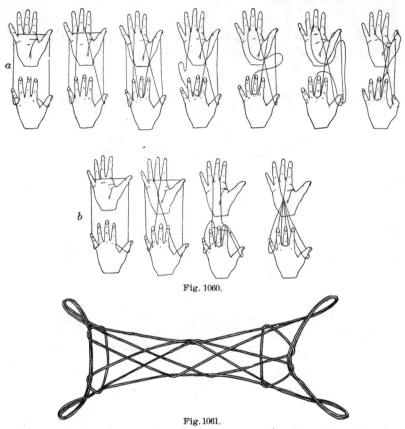

Fig. 1060.

Fig. 1061.

FIG. 1060.  Cat's cradle; a, dressing a skin; b, pitching a tent; Thompson Indians, British Columbia; from sketches by Harlan I. Smith.

FIG. 1061.  Cat's cradle; Tigua Indians, Isleta, New Mexico; cat. no. 22729, Free Museum of Science and Art, University of Pennsylvania.

The figure called pitching a tent is found in Zuñi, under the name of brush house (figure 1070).

### SHOSHONEAN STOCK

Hopi.  Walpi, Arizona.

The Indians at the First Hopi mesa informed the writer, in 1905, that they knew a number of cat's cradles and called them all ma-mal-lac-bi.

### TANOAN STOCK

Tewa.  Hano, Arizona.  (Brooklyn Institute Museum.)

The following cat's cradles were collected by the writer in 1905:

Cat. no. 7129, bo-tāñ-la.

Cat. no. 7130, a-gai-yo-sin-i.

TIGUA.  Isleta, New Mexico.  (Free Museum of Science and Art, University of Pennsylvania.)

The following cat's cradles were collected by the writer at Isleta in 1902:

Cat. no. 22729, figure 1061.

Cat. no. 22730, pakula, star, figure 1062.

Cat. no. 22731, figure 1063.

Cat. no. 22732, vopiridai, lightning, figure 1064.

The only name my informant could give for the amusement was thlu, string.  He did not know names for all the figures he was able to make.

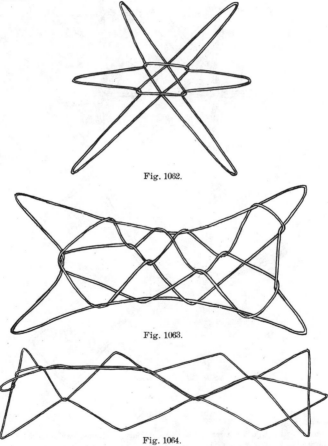

Fig. 1062.

Fig. 1063.

Fig. 1064.

FIG. 1062.  Cat's cradle, pakula, star; Tigua Indians, Isleta, New Mexico; cat. no. 22730, Free Museum of Science and Art, University of Pennsylvania.

FIG. 1063.  Cat's cradle; Tigua Indians, Isleta, New Mexico; cat. no. 22731, Free Museum of Science and Art, University of Pennsylvania.

FIG. 1064.  Cat's cradle, vopiridai, lightning; Tigua Indians, Isleta, New Mexico; cat. no. 22732, Free Museum of Science and Art, University of Pennsylvania.

Cat. no. 22731 occurs among the Navaho as many (group of) stars (figure 1037), and cat. no. 22732 as lightning (figure 1035).

WAKASHAN STOCK

MAKAH.   Neah bay, Washington.

Charlie Williams described the Makah as playing cat's cradle under the name of howwutsoksh.

The figures corresponded with those of our common child's play. The first he called bow, bistati; the second, devilfish, tiththupe. Another figure was the frog, wachit.   Girls and boys play.

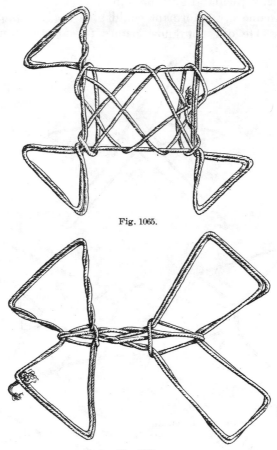

Fig. 1065.

Fig. 1066.

FIG. 1065.   Cat's cradle, hpaish, mealing stone; Maricopa Indians, Arizona; cat. no. 2921, Brooklyn Institute Museum.
FIG. 1066.   Cat's cradle, kpaitch, turtle; Maricopa Indians, Arizona; cat. no. 2922, Brooklyn Institute Museum.

YUMAN STOCK

MARICOPA.   Arizona.   (Brooklyn Institute Museum.)

The following cat's cradles were collected for the writer by Mr Louis L. Meeker:

Cat. no. 2921: hpaish, mealing stone (figure 1065).
Cat. no. 2922: kpaitch, turtle (figure 1066).

ZUÑIAN STOCK

ZUÑI.  Zuñi, New Mexico.  (Free Museum of Science and Art, University of Pennsylvania.)

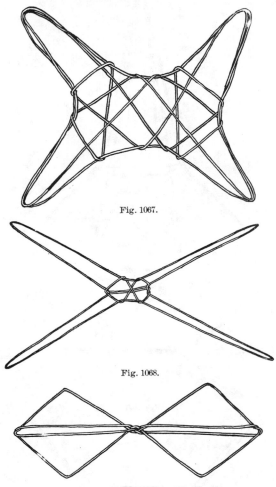

Fig. 1067.

Fig. 1068.

Fig. 1069.

FIG. 1067.  Cat's cradle, pichowainai, netted shield; Zuñi Indians, Zuñi, New Mexico; cat. no. 22604, Free Museum of Science and Art, University of Pennsylvania.

FIG. 1068.  Cat's cradle, pishkappoa pichowainai, netted shield; Zuñi Indians, Zuñi, New Mexico; cat. no. 22605, Free Museum of Science and Art, University of Pennsylvania.

FIG. 1069.  Cat's cradle, pichowai wailolo, lightning; Zuñi Indians, Zuñi, New Mexico; cat. no. 22606, Free Museum of Science and Art, University of Pennsylvania.

The following cat's cradles were collected by the writer in Zuñi in 1902:

Cat. no. 22604: pichowainai, netted shield (figure 1067).

Cat. no. 22605: pishkappoa pichowainai, netted shield (figure 1068).

Cat. no. 22606: pichowai wailolo, lightning (figure 1069).

Cat. no. 22607: pichowai hampunnai, brush house (figure 1070).

Cat. no. 22608: pichowai hampunnai, brush house (figure 1071).

Cat. no. 22609: tslempistonai pichowainai, top crossbeam of ladder (figure 1072).

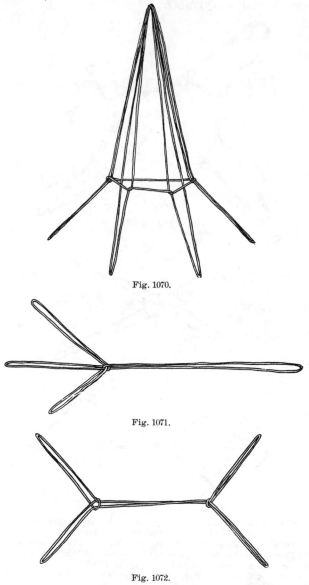

Fig. 1070.

Fig. 1071.

Fig. 1072.

FIG. 1070.   Cat's cradle, pichowai hampunnai, brush house; Zuñi Indians, Zuñi, New Mexico; cat. no. 22607, Free Museum of Science and Art, University of Pennsylvania.

FIG. 1071.   Cat's cradle, pichowai hampunnai, brush house; Zuñi Indians, Zuñi, New Mexico; cat. no. 22608, Free Museum of Science and Art, University of Pennsylvania.

FIG. 1072.   Cat's cradle, tslempistonai pichowainai, top crossbeam of ladder; Zuñi Indians, Zuñi, New Mexico; cat. no. 22609, Free Museum of Science and Art, University of Pennsylvania.

Cat. no. 22610: pichowai atslonononai, sling (figure 1073).

Cat. no. 22605 occurs among the Navaho as packing (carrying) wood (figure 1047), and cat. no. 22606 as twin stars (figure 1038).

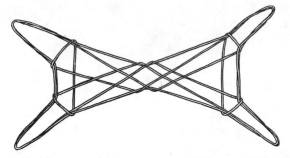

FIG. 1073.   Cat's cradle, pichowai atslonononai, sling; Zuñi Indians, Zuñi, New Mexico; cat. no. 22610, Free Museum of Science and Art, University of Pennsylvania.

My informant in Zuñi stated that the cat's cradle was called pichowainai or pishkappoa, the netted shield, figures 1067 and 1068, actually representing this shield, which was supposed to have been carried by the War God. The idea is borrowed from the spider web, and cat's cradle was taught to the little boys, the twin War Gods, by their mother, the Spider Woman, for their amusement.

# UNCLASSIFIED GAMES

Into this category of unclassified games, arranged by stocks, have been put the miscellaneous games of which but a single record exists, and which, with the information now at hand, can not be assigned to a place in any of the preceding series, nor yet regarded as of foreign origin. It will be seen that these games are few in number and of little apparent significance. One, the Clatsop game described by Lewis and Clark, may be the guessing game played with wooden disks, imperfectly described.

## ALGONQUIAN STOCK

ILLINOIS. Illinois.

Joutel says:[a]

A good number of presents still remaining, they divide themselves into several lots, and play at a game, called of the stick, to give them to the winner. That game is played, taking a stout stick, very smooth and greased, that it may be harder to hold it fast. One of the elders throws the stick as far as he can; the young men run after it, snatch it from each other, and at last he who remains possessed of it has the first lot. The stick is then thrown again; he who keeps it then has the second lot, and so on to the end. The women whose husbands have been slain in war often perform the same ceremony and treat the singers and dancers whom they have before invited.

## ATHAPASCAN STOCK

NAVAHO. St Michael, Arizona.

Rev. Berard Haile describes the following game in a letter:

Tsin beedził, the great game of the Earth-winner. The Earth-winner, Ni'-nahuiłbi'i, plays with the gambler, who lays a wager that he can outdo the Earth-winner in strength. A test is made by placing a pole 6 inches in diameter in the ground about 2 feet deep. The pole is about 8 feet in height, and the gambler pushes it over on a run. The Earth-winner thus loses the game. In consequence of this event, the Navaho, out of respect for their great teacher of games, who, they say, came from Mexico, do not play this game.

TAKULLI. Stuart lake, British Columbia.

The Reverend Father A. G. Morice [b] says:

Tə'ko· is another pastime which is somewhat childish in character. In most cases it is played by the fireside in the camp lodge during the long winter evenings. Its necessary accompaniments [figure 1074] are a blunt-headed stick and two small, thin, and springy boards firmly driven in the ground, one close by each

[a] Historical Journal of Monsieur La Salle's Last Voyage to Discover the River Mississippi. French's Historical Collections of Louisiana, v. 1, p. 186, New York, 1846.

[b] Notes on the Western Dénés. Transactions of the Canadian Institute, v. 4, p. 112, Toronto, 1895.

player. The two opposite parties sit facing each other and throw the tə'ko·
against the little board on the other side, upon hitting which it rebounds to the
knees of the successful player, who is then entitled to recommence and continue
as long as luck favors him. Failing to get at the mark, the tə'ko· is handed to
the other partner. The number of points obtained indicates the winner. The
old men profess to be ignorant of that game, which is probably adventitious
among our Indians.

### CHINOOKAN STOCK

CLATSOP. Mouth of Columbia river, Oregon.

Lewis and Clark [a] describe the following game:

Two pins are placed on the floor, about the distance of a foot from each other,
and a small hole is made between them. The players then go about 10 feet
from the hole, into which they try to roll a small piece resembling the men used
in draughts; if they succeed in putting it into the hole, they win the stake; if
the piece rolls between the pins, but does not go into the hole, nothing is won or
lost; but the wager is wholly lost if the checker rolls outside the pins.

FIG. 1074. Implements for tə'ko·; Takulli Indians, British Columbia; from Morice.

### ESKIMAUAN STOCK

ESKIMO (CENTRAL). Cumberland sound, Baffin land, Franklin.

Dr Franz Boas [b] says:

The säketän resembles a roulette. A leather cup with a rounded bottom and
a nozzle is placed on a board and turned round. When it stops the nozzle points
to the winner. At present a tin cup fastened with a nail to a board is used for
the same purpose [figure 1075].

Their way of managing the gain and loss is very curious. The first winner
in the game must go to his hut and fetch anything he likes as a stake for the
next winner, who, in turn receives it, but has to bring a new stake, in place of
this, from his hut. Thus the only one who loses anything is the first winner of
the game, while the only one who wins anything is the last winner.

Again, of the Eskimo of the west coast of Hudson bay, Doctor
Boas [c] says:

Women gamble with a musk-ox dipper, which is turned swiftly around. The
person away from whom the handle points wins the stake, and has to place a
stake in her turn.

---

[a] History of the Expedition under the Command of Lewis and Clark, v. 2, p. 784, New
York, 1893.
[b] The Central Eskimo. Sixth Annual Report of the Bureau of Ethnology, p. 568, 1888.
[c] Eskimo of Baffin Land and Hudson Bay. Bulletin of the American Museum of Natural History, v. 15, p. 110, New York, 1901.

This game corresponds in general principle with roulette, or rather with the spinning arrow.

ESKIMO (CENTRAL: AIVILIRMIUT and KINIPETU). West coast of Hudson bay, Keewatin. (Cat. no. $\frac{9}{2735}b$, American Museum of Natural History.)

Dr Franz Boas [a] says:

Small hoops of whalebone (terkutuk) are joined crosswise [figure 1076]. Then they are placed on the ice or hard snow when the wind is blowing. The young men run to catch them.

A similar game is mentioned by Rev. J. Owen Dorsey among the Teton Dakota (see p. 715).

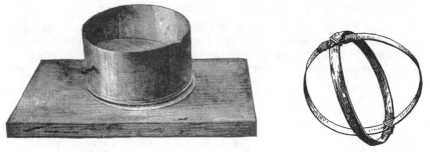

Fig. 1075.                                        Fig. 1076.

FIG. 1075. Säketän, or roulette; Central Eskimo, Cumberland sound, Baffin land, Franklin; cat. no. IV A 6854, Berlin Museum für Völkerkunde; from Boas.
FIG. 1076. Whalebone hoops; diameter, 3¼ inches; Central Eskimo (Aivilirmiut and Kinipetu), west coast of Hudson bay, Keewatin; cat. no. $\frac{9}{2735}b$, American Museum of Natural History.

———— West coast of Hudson bay, Keewatin. (Cat. no. $\frac{60}{2731}b$, American Museum of Natural History.)

Dr Franz Boas [a] says:

Boys play hunting seals [figure 1077]. Each of them has a small harpoon and a number of pieces of seal-skin with many holes. Each piece of skin represents a seal. Each of the boys also has a hip-bone of a seal. Then one boy moves a piece of skin which represents a seal under the hole in the hip-bone, which latter represents the blowing-hole in the ice. While moving the piece of skin about under the bone, the boys blow like seals. Whoever catches with the little harpoon the piece of skin in one of the holes retains it, and the boy who catches the last of the pieces of skin goes on in turn with his seals. The little harpoons are made by the fathers of the boys, the pieces of skin are prepared by their mothers.

MAYAN STOCK

MAYA. Yucatan.

Dr Alfred Tozzer [b] describes the following game:

Wăk pel pul, to throw six, is played with six sticks [figure 1078] made of any kind of wood, which has branches directly opposite each other. They each rest

———————

[a] Eskimo of Baffin Land and Hudson Bay. Bulletin of the American Museum of Natural History, v. 15, p. 111, New York, 1901.
[b] In a letter to the writer, November 7, 1903.

on the large end, and each has marks on the upper part, running from 1 to 6, which show the count. The one with six notches is placed in the middle, and the others in a circle around it. Rocks, cocoa beans, or money are then thrown in an endeavor to knock down as many as possible.

SKITTAGETAN STOCK

HAIDA (KAIGANI). Prince of Wales island, Alaska.

Dr C. F. Newcombe describes the following game under the name of kwai indao:

A set of 40 or 50 sticks, representing ten different numbers, are placed in a row. The players alternately try to repeat from memory, blindfold, the order in which these ten numbers run.

The same collector describes also the following game:

Twenty or forty small sticks, 6 inches long, are taken in the palm, thrown up in the air, and caught on back of hand. They are then thrown up again, if any are caught, and if possible an odd number caught in the palm. If an odd number—one, three, five, or seven—be so caught, one stick is kept by the player, who

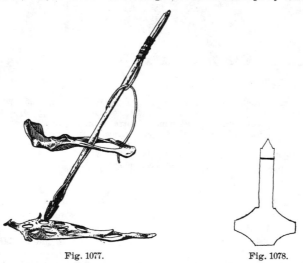

Fig. 1077.                    Fig. 1078.

FIG. 1077. Game of sealing; length of harpoon, 12¼ inches; Central Eskimo, west coast of Hudson bay, Keewatin; cat. no. ₂⁶₃₈₁ b, American Museum of Natural History.
FIG. 1078. Stick for wăk pel pul; Maya Indians, Yucatan; from sketch by Dr Alfred Tozzer.

tries again. If none or an even number be caught, the opposite player takes his turn. He who takes the last stick wins all his opponent's sticks and takes them all up and goes on as before. Boys or girls play. The game is called hăl hai' jao, "turn around game."

WAKASHAN STOCK

KWAKIUTL. Nawiti, British Columbia. (Cat. no. 85850, Field Columbian Museum.)

Two flat slats (figure 1079), 1½ inches wide at top, and 15½ and 21 inches long, the lower ends sharpened to a point. Two flat slats, 1½ inches wide at top and 13 inches long, with transverse white lines across the flat sides at top, and lower part cut round to form a handle.

Two wooden darts, with blunt heads, 35 and 38 inches in length, one with a rattle in the handle end.

Collected in 1904 by Dr C. F. Newcombe, who describes the game as follows:

The flat piece is set firmly in the ground at an inclination from the player to form a kind of springboard. The players stand at about 10 feet from the board and throw the darts at it. The game is to catch the dart on the rebound as many times as possible, and he who first catches it ten times, not necessarily without an intervening miss, is the winner. No counters are used. This game is only played in the fall, when drying salmon. The game is k'lemgua, the dart k'lemgwa·iu, and the spring klemgwa·yas.

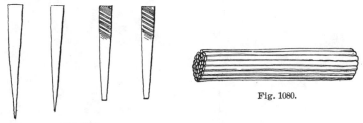

Fig. 1080.

Fig. 1079.

FIG. 1079. Slats for k'lemgua; lengths of slats, 15¼ and 21 inches; Kwakiutl Indians, British Columbia ; cat. no. 85850, Field Columbian Museum.

FIG. 1080. Sticks for mena (stopping-breath game); length, 6¼ inches; Kwakiutl Indians, British Columbia; cat. no. 85857, Field Columbian Museum.

KWAKIUTL. Nawiti, British Columbia. (Cat. no. 85857, Field Columbian Museum.)

Bundle of forty sticks (figure 1080), 6½ inches in length. These were collected in 1904 by Dr C. F. Newcombe, who describes them as used in a game called menă.

The sticks are laid in two parallel rows of twenty each, and one player tries to pick up as many sticks as possible and make two other similar rows while the other player stops his breath by holding his nose and mouth. It is played by men and boys, by two or more players in turns. The counters are called menasu.

——— Nawiti, British Columbia. (Cat. no. 85856, Field Columbian Museum.)

Bundle of forty sticks, 6 inches in length.

These were collected in 1904 by Dr C. F. Newcombe, who describes them as follows:

These sticks—the same as used in menă, are also employed in a counting game. The bundle of forty is arranged in bunches of from one to five, placed in any order in one or two lines. One player tries to commit to memory the number of sticks in each bunch in their order from left to right, and then turns around, and with his back to the sticks calls the number after the watcher says gĭnīts? or " how many?" If correct, each bunch correctly named is put in one place, but if wrong, in another. The sticks are the unit for scoring. He who gets the greatest number of sticks wins. The game is called gĭnīts, and the sticks gĭnītsa·iu.

KWAKIUTL. Nawiti, British Columbia. (Cat. no. 85355, Field
    Columbian Museum.)
Ring of whalebone (figure 1081), $2\frac{1}{2}$ inches in diameter, supported
    on a stick in a horizontal position, and twenty-four unpainted
    sticks, $8\frac{3}{4}$ inches in length.
Collected in 1904 by Dr C. F. Newcombe, who describes them as
used in a game called quaquatsewa·iu.

The players drop the sticks held in one hand through the ring, to see who
can get the highest number through. This is done with the eyes open, blindfolded, and blindfolded after turning round.

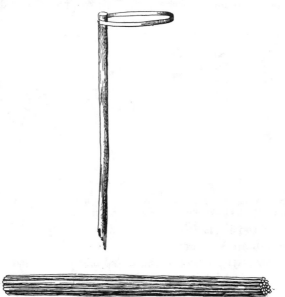

FIG. 1081.  Stick-dropping game; length of sticks, $8\frac{3}{4}$ inches; diameter of ring, $2\frac{1}{4}$ inches; Kwakiutl
    Indians, British Columbia; cat. no. 85355, Field Columbian Museum.

———— Vancouver island, British Columbia.
Dr Franz Boas[a] describes a game like the first in this series:

Tl'ᴇ'mkoāyu.—A stick, about 3 feet long, with a knob at its end, is thrown
against an elastic board which is placed upright at some distance. If the stick
rebounds and is caught, the player gains 4 points. If it rebounds to more than
half the distance from the player to the board, he gains 1 point. If it falls
down nearer the board than one-half the distance, or when the board is missed,
the player does not gain any point. The two players throw alternately. Each
has 10 counters. When one of them gains all the counters, he is the winner of the
stake. When the stick falls down so that the end opposite the knob rests on the
board, the throw counts 10 points.

Another game he mentions as follows:[b]

T'ē'nk·oayu, or carrying a heavy stone on the shoulder to test the strength of
those who participate in the game.

---

[a] Sixth Report on the Indians of British Columbia.  Report of the Sixty-sixth Meeting
of the British Association for the Advancement of Science, p. 578, London, 1896.
    [b] Ibid.

ZUÑIAN STOCK

ZUÑI.  Zuñi, New Mexico.  (Cat. no. 3063, Brooklyn Institute Museum.)

Two rings (figure 1082), made of twig, one 3½ inches in diameter, wrapped with green and blue yarn in alternate quarters, and the other, 2¾ inches in diameter, wrapped with plain white cord. Collected by the writer in 1903.

Boys play.  The large ring is thrown down, and the object of the game is to toss the small ring so that it will fall within the large one. The rings are called tsi-ko-nai.

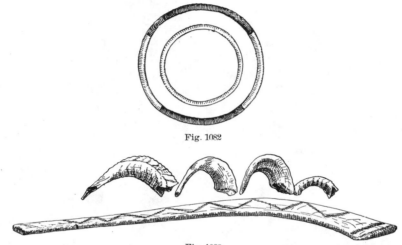

Fig. 1082.

Fig. 1083.

FIG. 1082.  Ring game; diameter of large ring, 3½ inches; Zuñi Indians, Zuñi, New Mexico; cat. no. 3063, Brooklyn Institute Museum.
FIG. 1083.  Implements for "horns kill," or "killing the rabbit;" Zuñi Indians, Zuñi, New Mexico; from Mrs Stevenson.

——— Zuñi, New Mexico.

Mrs Matilda Coxe Stevenson[a] describes a game called saithlätawe, horns kill, or killing the rabbit:

Six goat-horns [figure 1083] are placed in line on the ground an equal distance apart, and the players stand some rods away.  The game is begun by a player starting to run and throwing a rabbit-stick toward the horns.  He is entitled to as many horns as he strikes, and may continue to throw the stick as long as he is successful in striking a horn; but when he fails to strike one, another plays.  The one who strikes the largest number of horns wins the game.

[a] Zuñi Games.  American Anthropologist, n. s., v. 5, p. 489, 1903.

# GAMES DERIVED FROM EUROPEANS

It is obvious that there has been steady modification of old Indian customs under the influence of the whites, and that the Indians have absorbed European ideas, many of which have in time become difficult of recognition as foreign in origin. These facts are true to a certain extent of their games. An excellent example of incorporation is found in the Navaho game of baseball. In spite of tribal traditions, it appears that the Navaho learned the game from the whites when they were imprisoned at the Bosque Redondo after 1863. The following account of the game was furnished the writer by Rev. Berard Haile, of St Michael, Arizona:

Aqejólyedi, Run around ball.—This game is not played at present in its original form, but was quite frequently played fifteen or twenty years ago. The ball, joł, was made, before rag time, of the bark of a shrub called azhi' (bark) or awe ts'ăl, baby's cradle, which owes its name to the fact that it was used for bedding in cradles. This bark was covered with the hide of deer, goat, horse, or any animal which can be eaten by the Navaho with impunity. Therefore bear, coyote, or dog hides would not be allowed as a covering for the ball. There were two halves to the cover, which were sewed together in the center with the sinews of deer or buckskin strips. The ball is the sign of the evil-spirit wind, and therefore must disappear as soon as vegetation begins and until after the harvest. The stick, or bat, bĕ-akăli, something to strike with, was an oak stick of this shape: J. Oak is hard and has great resisting power, and is used in nearly all the Navaho religious ceremonies. Though I have no authority for it, I am inclined to believe it is used to signify the power of Godhead. The curvature of one end of the bat is made by placing the stick in hot ashes, and then bending in the forks of another twig. In shinny the reversed stick Γ is used. In this game the batter takes hold of the curved end and strikes the ball with the thin end, which is about of the thickness of the middle finger. In shinny, however, he holds the thin end and strikes the ball with the knotty end of the stick.

The terms of the game and the points to be scored by the winning side having been agreed upon, the players line up in about the position of the subjoined diagram [figure 1084].

I have given the four bases the names of east, south, etc., although they are not thus called by the Navaho. They have a name for east, meaning the first place to run to, and for north, na"ilyed, run is finished.

The pitchers are called ałch'i'náalni', he throws toward him; for the other players there are no names. The pitcher may throw high or low, and the batter may strike at the ball from either direction; there may also be two or three batters at the bat at one time, and a batter may be allowed to retire after two or three strikes and take up the bat at another more opportune time. The fourth strike compels the batter to run for first base, as also when he hits the ball, fair or foul, fly or grounder. Once on the base he is safe until he leaves it, though he may lead off, or until another batsman hits the, ball.  The runner and his side (one out is sufficient) are retired if the runner is touched or hit with the ball by the enemy, either before reaching first base or while he is making for any of the other points.  The chase thus becomes interesting.  Anything and everything is allowed to the runner to evade being touched by the ball; he may describe a circle, dodge, jump, or knock the ball out of his enemy's hand to reach his base.  Making the circuit scores one point, and whichever side scores most runs, or the number of runs agreed upon, is the winner.

This is another of the Great Earth-winner's games.  Being challenged by his Indian followers or companions, they gradually learned the games from him; they staked him for his wife, cheated him, and he lost; whereupon the Indians dispersed and played his games in their newly acquired countries.

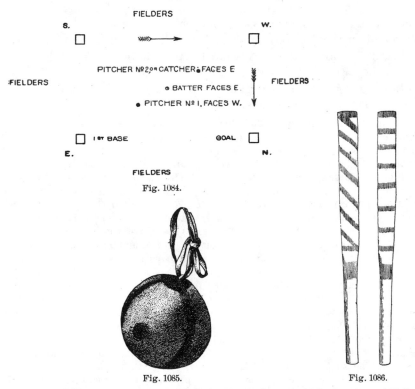

Fig. 1084.

Fig. 1085.                                     Fig. 1086.

FIG. 1084.  Ball field; Navaho Indians, St Michael, Arizona; from sketch by Rev. Berard Haile.
FIG. 1085.  Ball; diameter, 2⅜ inches; Thompson Indians, British Columbia; cat. no. ₁₆₈₅₅, American Museum of Natural History; from Teit.
FIG. 1086.  Bat; length, 24¼ inches; Thompson Indians, British Columbia; cat. no. ₁₆₈₅₅, American Museum of Natural History; from Teit.

In the same category I would place the similar ball game of the Thompson Indians of British Columbia, described by Mr James Teit,[a] who says:

Formerly a favorite pastime was playing ball.  The ball used was a kind of knot found on fir-trees.  The knot is nicely rounded off, and sometimes covered

---

[a] The Thompson Indians of British Columbia.  Memoirs of the American Museum ′ Natural History, whole series, v. 2, p. 277, New York, 1900.

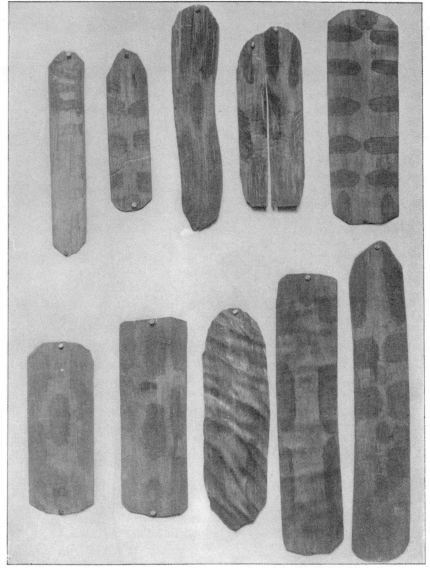

BARK PLAYING CARDS; LENGTHS, 5 TO 10 INCHES; UINKARET INDIANS,
ARIZONA; CAT. NO. 11217, UNITED STATES NATIONAL MUSEUM

with buckskin.  Other balls were of stone, or of deerskin stuffed with vegetable material [figure 1085].  There were two ways of playing it.

One way was quite similar to that of " rounders."  The bat used in this game was a short straight stick, about 4 inches wide at one end [figure 1086].  Each side took turns in batting.  Four stones were placed about 20 yards apart, in the form of a square.  These were called " houses."  The man who held the bat was bowled to by a man of the opposite party, who stood about in the center of the ring. .If the batter missed the ball, his place was immediately taken by the next man of his party.  If he struck the ball with his bat, he immediately dropped the latter, and ran to the first house, or the second if he could manage it.  The object of the opposite party was to catch the ball as quickly as possible, and strike the man with it while he was running from one house to the other, thereby knocking him out of the game.  If the man managed to get back to his starting-point, he was allowed another chance to bat.  The game is still frequently played by the young men.

I have made no mention of playing cards, which are widely used, games being played either with cards purchased from the traders, or with native copies more or less closely resembling them.  The ten flat pieces of cedar bark (plate xxi, cat. no. 11217, United States National Museum) collected by Maj. J. W. Powell from the Uinkaret in northern Arizona, which were figured as dice in the writer's paper on Chess and Playing Cards, proved on comparison to be copies of playing cards.  The games played by the Indian with cards are easily recognizable as common Spanish and American games.

The remaining games which I am able to identify as of European origin may be included in a single class—games played on boards or diagrams, like merils.  They may be regarded as games of skill and calculation, a kind of game which otherwise appears to be entirely lacking.

### ALGONQUIAN STOCK

CREE and CHIPPEWA.  Muskowpetung reserve, Qu'appelle, Assiniboia.  (Cat. no. 61994, Field Columbian Museum.)
Board and men (figure 1087), the board 9 inches square, with cross diagram with holes in which the men—small green painted pegs, with one larger one—are inserted.

They were collected by Mr J. A. Mitchell, who describes the game under the name of musiṇaykahwhanmetowaywin:

This game is played by two persons, one playing the king piece or oke-mow, against his opponent's thirteen pawns.  Moves can be made in any direction by any of the pieces, provided the lines of the diagram are followed.

The king has the power to take the opposing pieces and can take as many pieces in one move as are left unprotected, but only following the lines of the board.  The pawns have no power to take the king, but endeavor so to press it as finally to checkmate.  The king is technically known as musinay-kah-whan.

The game is one which has been long known to the Indians and is much admired by them.  Many skillful players have been developed, some being more particularly skilled in manipulating the king piece, while others make the pawn their special play.  The play is invariably for stakes of some kind.

MICMAC.  Nova Scotia.

Dr A. S. Gatschet [a] writes:

The majority of the games they play now are borrowed from the whites. Their checker game is the same as ours and played on a checkerboard. A checker stone is called adena'gan (plural, adena'gank), while the checkerboard is adenagenei'. The checkers are either disk-shaped and smooth (mimusχa-witchink adena'gank) or square (esgigeniχi'tchik adena'gank).

The game is called after the moving of the stones from square to square; nin adnai', it is my move; kit adnāt, it is your move.

PASSAMAQUODDY.  Maine.

Mrs W. W. Brown [b] describes the following game:

Ko-ko-nag'n has a resemblance to the game of checkers, but, although nearly all are more or less proficient at the latter game, there are only a few who understand ko-ko-na-g'n. This, unlike any other game, may be played by male and female opponents. It is the least noisy, the skillful play requiring delibera-tion and undivided attention. A smooth surface is marked off into different-sized spaces, and pieces of wood, round and square, marked to qualify value, are generally used, though sometimes carved bone is substituted.

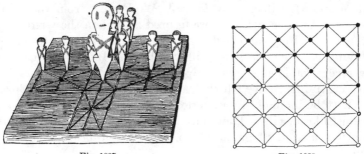

Fig. 1087.                    Fig. 1088.

FIG. 1087. Board game and men; dimensions of board, 9 inches square; Cree and Chippewa Indians, Assiniboia; cat. no. 61994, Field Columbian Museum.
FIG. 1088. Board game; Keres Indians, Acoma, New Mexico.

This may be the game referred to by Rasle among the Norridge-wock Indians, where he says:

Un autre jeu où l'on place des grains sur des espèce de lozanges entrelassées, di'r (dicitur), mañmadöañgñ.

KERESAN STOCK

KERES.  Acoma, New Mexico.

An Acoma Indian named James H. Miller, employed at Zuñi, de-scribed to the writer under the name of aiyawatstani, chuck away grains, the game illustrated in figure 1088. Twenty-two white and twenty-two black pieces are used on each side. He explained that they learned the game in the olden time when they first came out of the ship-pap (si-pa-pu) away in the north. Iyatiko, the mother, made all the games.

---

[a] From Baddeck, Nova Scotia, August 28, 1899.

[b] Some Indoor and Outdoor Games of the Wabanaki Indians. Transactions of the Royal Society of Canada, v. 6, sec. 2, p. 43, Montreal, 1889.

KERES. Cochiti, New Mexico.

A Keres boy at St Michael, Arizona, named Francisco Chaves (Kogit), described the Indians at Cochiti as playing the game of paitariya on a board represented by the diagram here given:

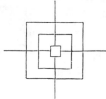

KOLUSCHAN STOCK

YAKUTAT. Port Mulgrave, Alaska. (Cat. no. 16300, United States National Museum.)

Twenty-two carved wooden chessmen (figure 1089), from $1\frac{7}{8}$ to $3\frac{3}{8}$ inches in height. Collected by Dr W. H. Dall.

FIG. 1089. Chessmen; height, $1\frac{7}{8}$ to $3\frac{3}{8}$ inches; Yakutat Indians, Port Mulgrave, Alaska; cat. no. 16300, United States National Museum.

MARIPOSAN STOCK

YOKUTS. Tule River reservation, Tulare county, California. (Cat. no. 70377, Field Columbian Museum.)

Flat stone, 13 by $10\frac{1}{4}$ inches, with top etched as shown in figure 1090, and twenty-four pieces of clay, conoid in shape, twelve black with two small holes in the top, and twelve red. Collected by Dr J. W. Hudson.

PIMAN STOCK

PAPAGO.  Mission of San Xavier del Bac, Pima county, Arizona.

Mr S. C. Simms informs me that he saw the game of coyote and chickens, pon chochotl (figure 1091), played by this tribe on a diagram traced on the smooth ground.

A red bean was used for the coyote and twelve grains of corn for the chickens.  Another form of the game was played with twelve chickens on each side.  This latter was played for money, the first game being regarded as too easy to bet on.  Both Papago and Mexicans play, mostly men.

———— Pima county, Arizona.

Mr S. C. Simms described the Papago as playing a game (figure 1092) on a star-shaped diagram which they called ohohla (Spanish, jeoda).[a]

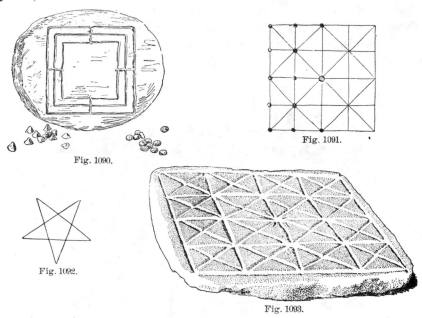

Fig. 1090.

Fig. 1091.

Fig. 1092.

Fig. 1093.

FIG. 1090.  Stone game board and men; dimensions, 13 by 10¼ inches; Yokuts Indians, Tule River reservation, Tulare county, California; cat. no. 70377, Field Columbian Museum.
FIG. 1091.  Game of coyote and chickens; Papago Indians, Arizona; from sketch by Mr S. C. Simms.
FIG. 1092.  Star game; Papago Indians, Arizona; from drawing by Mr S. C. Simms.
FIG. 1093.  Stone game board for tuknanavuhpi; length, 9 inches; Hopi Indians, Oraibi, Arizona; cat. no. 38613, Free Museum of Science and Art, University of Pennsylvania.

SHOSHONEAN STOCK

HOPI.  Oraibi, Arizona.  (Cat. no. 38613, Free Museum of Science and Art, University of Pennsylvania.)

Stone board (figure 1093), 7 by 9½ inches, inscribed with three equidistant cross lines in both directions, dividing the surface into

———————————————————————————————
[a] Probably geoda, geode.

sixteen rectangles, each of which is crossed by diagonal lines. The central point is marked with a star.

Collected by the writer in 1901.

Two men play, using white and black stones, which are arranged as shown in figure 1094. The game, called tuknanavuhpi, is like fox and geese. White leads. The object is to jump over and take an opponent's piece, which is continued until one or the other loses all. A player may jump in any direction. When a line across one end of the board becomes empty, it is not used again, so the players' field becomes more and more contracted.

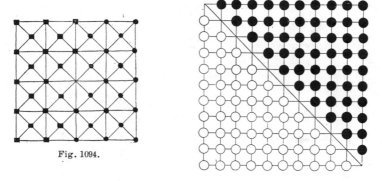

Fig. 1094.

Fig. 1095.

FIG. 1094. Arrangement of men in game of tuknanavuhpi; Hopi Indians, Oraibi, Arizona.
FIG. 1095. The game of totolospi; Hopi Indians, Walpi, Arizona; after drawing by Dr J. Walter Fewkes.

HOPI. Oraibi, Arizona. (Cat. no. 55356, Field Columbian Museum.)

Stone slab inscribed with a diagram similar to the preceding.

This is described by the collector, Rev. H. R. Voth, in 1899, as a gaming board, tûkvnanawöpi.

This game is generally played by either two or four persons, each side having twenty pokmoita, animals, which consist of corn, pieces of corncob, charcoal, etc., and are placed on the board in tiers. First one side moves into the center, this piece being, of course, jumped, and then the moves are made alternately by the two sides. Moves and jumps may be made in any direction, and the latter over as many pieces as may be found with a vacant place right behind them. As soon as a tier of squares is vacant it is abandoned, so that finally the pieces are crowded into three or two squares, and even into one square. The inclosed spaces outside the squares are called houses. In these the killed animals are placed.

—— Walpi, Arizona.

Dr J. Walter Fewkes [a] describes the game of totolospi as follows:

To-to-lós-pi resembles somewhat the game of checkers, and can be played by two persons or by two parties. In playing the game a rectangular figure [figure 1905], divided into large number of squares, is drawn upon the rock, either

[a] Journal of American Ethnology and Archæology, v. 2, p. 159, Boston, 1892.

by scratching or by using a different colored stone as a crayon. A diagonal line, tûh-kí-o-ta, is drawn across the rectangle from northwest to southeast, and the players station themselves at each end of this line. When two parties play, a single person acts as player, and the other members of the party act as advisers. The first play is won by tossing up a leaf or corn husk with one side blackened. The pieces which are used are bean or corn kernels, stones and wood, or small fragments of any substance of marked color. The players are stationed at each end of the diagonal line, tûh-kí-o-ta. They move their pieces upon this line, but never across it. (On this line the game is fought.) The moves which are made are intricate, and the player may move one or more pieces successively. Certain positions entitle him to this privilege. He may capture or, as he terms it, kill one or more of his opponent's pieces at one play. In this respect the game is not unlike checkers, and to capture the pieces of the opponent seems to be the main object of the game. The checkers, however, must be concentrated and always moved towards the southeast corner.[a]

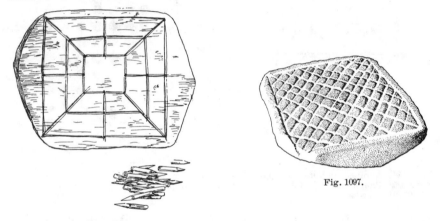

Fig. 1097.

Fig. 1096.

FIG. 1096.   Game board and men; length of board, 9 inches; Mono Indians, Madera county, California; cat. no. 71519, Field Columbian Museum.
FIG. 1097.   Stone game board for totolospi; length, 4½ inches; Tewa Indians, Hano, Arizona; cat. no. 38612, Free Museum of Science and Art, University of Pennsylvania.

This game is now rarely played on the East Mesa, but is still used at Oraibi. It is said to have been played in ancient times by the sun and moon, or by other mythical personages. Figures of this game formerly existed on the rocks near the village of Walpi, and may be the same referred to by Bourke.

Mr A. M. Stephen, in his unpublished manuscript, gives this definition: Totolospi, a primitive sort of checkers.

MONO.   Hooker cove and vicinity, Madera county, California. (Cat. no. 71519, Field Columbian Museum.)
Board, 9 inches in length, with inscribed design (figure 1096), and holes for pegs at the intersection of lines; accompanied by pegs of two sizes.
Collected by Dr J. W. Hudson, who designates it as yakamaido, square game, or Indian checkers.

---

[a] It would appear from Doctor Fewkes's sketch of the board that only one player moved toward the southeast and that his opponent went in the opposite direction.

Omaha. Nebraska.

Mr Francis La Flesche told the writer in 1893 that the Omaha learned the game of checkers from the whites about twenty years before and that they called it wakanpamungthae, gambling bowed head, or bowed-head game.

Tewa. Hano, Arizona. (Cat. no. 38612, Free Museum of Science and Art, University of Pennsylvania.)

Stone board (figure 1097), 4¾ inches square, inscribed with diagonal lines, ten in one direction and fifteen across. Collected in 1901 by the writer, to whom it was described as used in a game like fox and geese, totolospi,[a] and played with little broken sticks, black and white, which are arranged as shown in figure 1098.

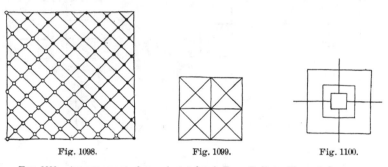

|  Fig. 1098. | Fig. 1099. | Fig. 1100. |

FIG. 1098.  Arrangement of men in totolospi; Tewa Indians, Hano, Arizona.
FIG. 1099.  Game of picaria (pedreria); Tigua Indians, Isleta, New Mexico.
FIG. 1100.  Game of picaria (pedreria); Tigua Indians, Isleta, New Mexico.

———— Santa Clara, New Mexico.

Mr T. S. Dozier [b] describes a game of pitarilla (pedreria), said to be of Pueblo origin, but doubtless of Spanish introduction:

In this game the crosses are marked by each player in turn where the men are placed, the object being to get three men in a row, always in a straight line; then one of the opposing player's pieces, the latter being grains of corn or pebbles, may be moved to the center. When all of the men of any player are moved by this process to the center, the other has won them. There are two figures used, the first [figure 1101] being a little more complicated than the other [figure 1102], though the same rule obtains in both.

A boy from Santa Clara at Mother Catherine's school at St Michael, Arizona, described the preceding game (figures 1101, 1102) under the name of bidaria (pedreria), as played at Santa Clara, and, in

[a] See note, p. 160.
[b] Some Tewa Games.  Unpublished MS. in Bureau of American Ethnology, May 8, 1896.

addition, the game of kuang, or jack rabbit, played with twelve stones, ku, on a board (figure 1103). Another board game (figure 1104) he described under the name of akuyo, star.

TIGUA. Isleta, New Mexico.

A boy from Isleta, named J. Crecencio Lucero, described the people of this pueblo as playing a board game which they call picaria (Spanish, pedreria), little stone. They use diagrams of two kinds, represented in figures 1099 and 1100.

———— Taos, New Mexico.

Dr T. P. Martin, of Taos, describes the following game, the name of which translated into English is Indian and jack rabbits:

Two play. A diagram of sixteen squares is marked on the sand, as shown in figure [1105]. Twelve small stones are arranged at points where the lines

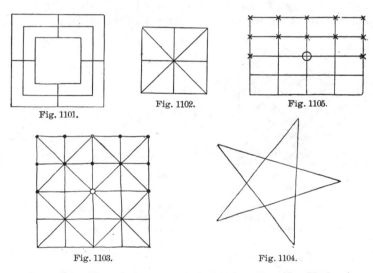

Fig. 1101.

Fig. 1102.

Fig. 1105.

Fig. 1103.

Fig. 1104.

FIG. 1101. Game of pitarilla (pedreria); Tewa Indians, Santa Clara, New Mexico; from sketch by Mr T. S. Dozier.
FIG. 1102. Game of pitarilla (pedreria); Tewa Indians, Santa Clara, New Mexico; from sketch by Mr T. S. Dozier.
FIG. 1103. Game of k'uâng, jack rabbit; Tewa Indians, Santa Clara, New Mexico.
FIG. 1104. Star game (akuyo); Tewa Indians, Santa Clara, New Mexico.
FIG. 1105. Game of Indian and jack rabbits; Tigua Indians, Taos, New Mexico; from drawing by Dr T. P. Martin.

intersect, on one side, as in the figure. The opposing player, occupying the one in the center at the beginning of the game, holds a stick, with which he points at the squares. The small stones are moved one at a time, and the object is to move them square by square without losing any until they occupy corresponding positions on the opposite side of the diagram. The player with the stick, who moves in turn, endeavors to catch the stones by jumping, as in draughts. Vocabulary: Name of the game, ko-app-paw-na, Spanish fuego de la liebre; board, or diagram, whee-e-na, Spanish reyes; pieces, kō-na, Spanish liebre; stick, tu-na-mah; to take a piece, con-con-we-la (the rabbit gets out from the man); some of the old men, however, shout au-gala, eat up.

ZUÑIAN STOCK

ZUÑI. Zuñi, New Mexico. (Cat. no. 16550, 17861, Free Museum of
Science and Art, University of Pennsylvania.)
Cardboard, inscribed with diagram (figure 1106), for the game of
awithlaknakwe, or stone warriors, and twenty-six pieces, or men
(figure 1107), consisting of disks made from shards of pottery,
used in the game.

The disks are in two sets, twelve plain and twelve perforated,
with a hole in the center, both 1⅛ inches in diameter. In addition,
there are two pieces, one plain and one perforated, somewhat larger
than the others.

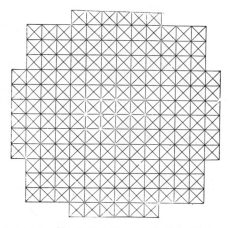

FIG. 1106. Game of stone warriors; Zuñi Indians, Zuñi, New Mexico; cat. no. 17861, Free
Museum of Science and Art, University of Pennsylvania.

These implements were made in 1893 by Mr Frank Hamilton
Cushing, who furnished the following account of the game:

Played by two or four persons upon a square board divided into one hundred
and forty-four squares, each intersected by diagonal lines. At the opening of
the game each player places six men in the center of the six squares at his
side of the board. The latter usually consists of a slab of stone pecked with the
diagram [figure 1106]. The men consist of disks of pottery about 1 inch in
diameter [figure 1107], made from broken vessels, those upon one side being
distinguished by being perforated with a small hole, while those on the other
side are plain. The object of the game is to cross over and take the opponent's
place, capturing as many men as possible by the way. The moves are made one
square at a time along the diagonal lines, the pieces being placed at the points
of intersection. When a player gets one of his opponent's pieces between two of
his own, it may be taken, and the first piece thus captured may be replaced by a
seventh man, called the Priest of the Bow, which may move both on the diagonal
lines and on those at right angles. A piece may not be moved backward.
When four persons play, those on the north and west play against those on the
south and east.

Vocabulary: Board, a-te-a-lan-e, stone plain; straight lines, a-kwi-we, canyons or arroyos; diagonal lines, o-na-we, trails; ordinary men, a-wi-thlak-na-kwe; seventh piece, pi-thlan shi-wani (mósona), Priest of the Bow.

The latter piece by power of magic is enabled to cross the canyons. The game is commonly played upon house tops, which are often found marked with the diagram.

The resemblance of the disks employed in this game to the prehistoric pottery disks which are found in the ruins in the southwestern United States and Mexico suggests that the latter may have been employed similarly in games. There is no evidence, however, that the board game existed before the coming of the whites. It was probably introduced by them and does not furnish an explanation of the prehistoric disks.

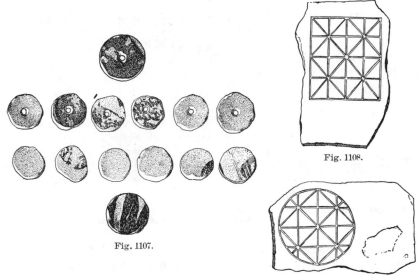

Fig. 1108.

Fig. 1107.

Fig. 1109.

FIG. 1107. Pottery men for game of stone warriors; diameters, 1¼ and 1⅜ inches; Zuñi Indians, Zuñi, New Mexico; cat. no. 16550, Free Museum of Science and Art, University of Pennsylvania.

FIG. 1108. Stone game board; Zuñi Indians, Zuñi, New Mexico; cat. no. 3099, Brooklyn Institute Museum.

FIG. 1109. Stone game board; Zuñi Indians, Zuñi, New Mexico; cat. no. 3099, Brooklyn Institute Museum.

ZUÑI. Zuñi, New Mexico. (Cat. no. 3099, 3100, Brooklyn Institute Museum.)

Two flat stones inscribed with diagrams, as shown in figures 1108, 1109, and 1110.

Collected by the writer in 1903. The name was given as awithlaknanai. Nick Graham stated that this is a Mexican game. The third form (figure 1110), he said, was introduced into Zuñi the year before by an Indian from Santa Ana, a Keresan pueblo near the Rio Grande.

Zuñi.  Zuñi, New Mexico.  (Cat. no. 5049, Brooklyn Institute Museum.)

Long stone slab, inscribed with the diagram shown in figure 1111.

This was found by the writer on a house top in Zuñi, and was explained by the natives as used in a game with white and black pieces, played like the preceding.  The positions of the pieces at the beginning of the game are indicated by black and white circles.  The name of the game was given as kolowis awithlaknannai, the kolowisi being a mythic serpent.  Another form of the same game (figure 1112) was made for the writer by Zuñi Nick (Nick Graham), who described it under the name of awithlaknan mosona, the original awithlaknannai.

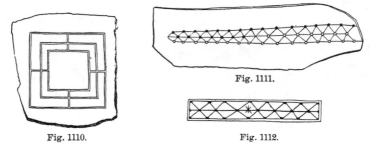

Fig. 1111.

Fig. 1110.                           Fig. 1112.

FIG. 1110.  Stone game board; Zuñi Indians, Zuñi, New Mexico; cat. no. 3100, Brooklyn Institute Museum.

FIG. 1111.  Kolowis awithlaknannai; length of diagram, 33 inches; Zuñi Indians, Zuñi, New Mexico; cat. no. 5049, Brooklyn Institute Museum.

FIG. 1112.  Awithlaknan mosona; Zuñi Indians, Zuñi, New Mexico.

Mrs Matilda Coxe Stevenson [a] describes the game of awe ʰhlacnawe, stones kill, as follows:

Implements.—A number of small stones (a different color for each side), and geometrical markings on a stone slab or on the ground.

There is no specified size for the " board," it being larger or smaller according to the number of angles.  The stones are placed on all the intersections of the geometrical drawing except the central one.  The first player moves to the center, where his " man " is jumped by his opponent.  The stones may be moved in any direction so long as the lines are followed.

In a note Mrs Stevenson says:

Some of the older men of the Zuñi declare that this game, when it came originally to Zuñi from Mexico, was played with one set of stones and a stick for the opposite side, and that the use of the double set of stones is an innovation of their own.

---

[a] Zuñi Games.  American Anthropologist, n. s., v. 5, p. 496, 1903.

# APPENDIX

## RUNNING RACES

For purposes of comparison with the kicked-stick or ball race, and in order not to lose sight of the fact that the ball race is not the only form of race game practised by the Indian, the writer has inserted the following collection of data in this appendix, confining the body of the text exclusively to games in which implements are employed.

### ALGONQUIAN STOCK

Missisauga. New Credit, Ontario.
  Rev. Peter Jones [a] says:

Foot races, in which they show much swiftness, are common among them.

────── Rice lake, Ontario.
  G. Copway [b] says:

Foot racing is much practised, mostly, however, by the young people. Thus in early life they acquire an elasticity of limb as well as health of body which are of priceless value to them in subsequent years.

### ATHAPASCAN STOCK

Apache (Mescalero). Fort Sumner, New Mexico.
  Maj. John C. Cremony [c] says:

Racing on foot is another diversion frequently resorted to by the active, restless Indians, and the women generally manage to carry off the palm, provided the distance is not too great. The officers at the post offered a number of prizes to be competed for, the fastest runner to take the prize apportioned to the distance for which it was offered. The longest race was half a mile, the next a quarter, the third 300 yards, and the fourth 100. It was open for men under 40 years of age and over 15, and for girls from 15 up to 25. About a hundred Apaches and Navajoes entered for the prizes, and practiced every day for a week. At the appointed time everybody in camp assembled to witness the contest. Among the competitors was the Apache girl, Ish-kay-nay, a clean-limbed, handsome girl of 17, who had always refused marriage, and she was the favorite among the whites. Each runner was tightly girded with a broad belt, and

---

[a] History of the Ojebway Indians, p. 134, London, 1861.
[b] The Traditional History and Characteristic Sketches of the Ojibway Nation, p. 58, Boston, 1851.
[c] Life Among the Apaches, p. 304, San Francisco, 1868.

looked like a race horse. Ten entered for the halfmile stake, which was a gaudy piece of calico for a dress or shirt, as the case might be. At the word they went off like rockets, Nah-kah-yen leading handsomely, and Ish-kay-nay bringing up the rear, but running as clean and easy as a greyhound. Within 400 yards of the goal she closed the gap, went by like a steam engine, and got in an easy winner, 6 yards ahead of all competitors. For the quarter-mile race she again entered, but was ruled out by the other Indians, and their objections were allowed, it being decided that the victor in either race should not enter for another.

NAVAHO. New Mexico.

Dr Washington Matthews[a] describes Hastseltsi, or Hastseiltsi, as a Navaho god of racing. His personator takes no part in the dance or in any act of succor.

His function is to get up foot races; hence a good runner is selected to enact this character. He goes around among the assembled crowd challenging others, who are known to be good racers, to run with him. He does not speak. He approaches the person whom he wishes to challenge, dancing meanwhile, gives his peculiar squeaking call, which may be spelt " ooh ooh ooh'—ooh ooh'," beckons to him, and makes the sign for racing, which is to place the two extended fingers together and project them rapidly forward. If he wins in the race, he whips his competitor across the back with his yucca scourges; if he loses, his competitor may do nothing to him. If the losing competitor asks him to whip gently, he whips violently, and vice versa; but the flagellation is never severe, for the scourges of yucca leaves are light weapons. He races thus some six or seven times or until he is tired; then he disappears. Each race is only about 200 yards. The people fear him, yet a man when challenged may refuse to race with him. He often resorts to jockeying tricks with his opponent, such as making a false start. He may enter a medicine-lodge to get up a race, but for no other purpose. Hastséltsi is a very particular god and likes not to touch anything unclean.

CADDOAN STOCK

WICHITA. Oklahoma.

In The Story of Child-of-a-Dog, as related by Dr George A. Dorsey,[b] the hero is challenged to run a foot race with four brothers, his brothers-in-law. The starting place is a pole stuck in the ground. He wins the race by the aid of magic objects given him by two women, his wives.

Again, in the story of The Swift-Hawks and Shadow-of-the-Sun,[c] there is a description of a foot race between the people of the east and the west sides of a village. The chief of the east side has a dark complexion, is called Shadow-of-the-Sun, and kills those whom he overcomes in the race. He is finally beaten by the last of four brothers.

As in other stories, his body is burned by the victor and his many victims come out alive from the fire.

[a] The Night Chant, a Navaho Ceremony. Memoirs of the American Museum of Natural History, whole series, v. 6, p. 25, New York, 1902.
[b] The Mythology of the Wichita, p. 133, Washington, 1904.
[c] Ibid., p. 207.

There is also an account in The Coyote Who Lost his Powers [a] of a foot race between the coyote and a strange man, a Shooting Star, in which the coyote has the choice of running on top of the ground or under the ground. He chooses to run on top of the ground, while his opponent runs under the ground. The coyote wins and kills the other, and then restores the latter's victims to life by gathering their bones and putting them into the fire.

In The Coyote, Prairie Turtle, and the Squirrel [b] the coyote and the prairie turtle run a foot race, which the latter loses.

### ESKIMAUAN STOCK

ESKIMO (WESTERN). St Michael, Alaska.

Mr E. W. Nelson [c] says:

Foot racing, ûk-whaun'. This is a favorite sport among the Eskimo, and is practiced usually in autumn, when the new ice is formed. The race extends from one to several miles, the course usually lying to and around some natural object, such as an island or a point of rocks, then back to the starting point.

### IROQUOIAN STOCK

SENECA. New York.

Morgan [d] states:

Foot races furnished another pastime for the Iroquois. They were often made a part of the entertainment with which civil and mourning councils were concluded. In this athletic game the Indian excelled. The exigencies, both of war and peace, rendered it necessary for the Iroquois to have among them practiced and trained runners. A spirit of emulation often sprang up among them, which resulted in regular contests for the palm of victory. In these races the four tribes put forward their best runners against those of the other four, and left the question of superiority to be determined by the event of the contest. Before the time appointed for the races they prepared themselves for the occasion by a process of training. It is not necessary to describe them. They dressed in the same manner for the race as for the game of ball. Leaping, wrestling, and the other gymnastic exercises appear to have furnished no part of the public amusement of our primitive inhabitants.

### MUSKHOGEAN STOCK

MUSKOGEE. Georgia.

Réné Laudonnière [e] wrote:

They exercise their young men to runne well, and they make a game among themselves, which he winneth that has the longest breath. They also exercise themselves much in shooting.

---

[a] The Mythology of the Wichita, p. 253, Washington, 1904.

[b] Ibid., p. 273.

[c] The Eskimo about Bering Strait. Eighteenth Annual Report of the Bureau of American Ethnology, p. 340, 1899.

[d] League of the Iroquois, p. 307, Rochester, 1851.

[e] Hakluyt's Voyages, v. 13, p. 413, Edinburgh, 1889.

PIMA.   Arizona.

The late Dr Frank Russell [a] wrote as follows of relay races:

At various points in Arizona I have found what appear to have been ancient race tracks situated near the ruins of buildings.  One of these was seen on the south bank of the Babacomari, 3 miles above the site of old Fort Wallen.  It is 5 meters wide and 275 meters long.  It is leveled by cutting down in places, and the rather numerous bowlders of the mesa are cleared away.  In the Sonoita valley, 2 miles east of Patagonia, there is a small ruin with what may have been a race track.  It is 6 meters wide and 180 meters long.  At the northern end stands a square stone 37 centimeters above the surface.  These will serve as examples of the tracks used by the Sobaipuris, a tribe belonging to the Piman stock.  The dimensions are about the same as those of the tracks that I have seen the Jicarilla Apaches using in New Mexico.  The tracks prepared by the Pimas opposite Sacaton Flats and at Casa Blanca are much longer.

The relay races of the Pimas did not differ materially from those among the Pueblo tribes of the Rio Grande or the Apaches and others of the Southwest. When a village wished to race with a neighboring one, they sent a messenger to convey the information that in four or five days, according to the decision of their council, they wished to test their fortunes in a relay race, and that in the meantime they were singing the bluebird (or, as the case might be, the hummingbird) songs and dances in preparation.  Both had the same time to practice, and the time was short.  In this preparation the young men ran in groups of four or five.  There were forty or fifty runners in each village, and he who proved to be the swiftest was recognized as the leader who should run first in the final contest.  It was not necessary that each village should enter the same number of men in the race; a man might run any number of times that his endurance permitted.  When the final race began each village stationed half its runners at each end of the track, then a crier called three times for the leaders, and as the last call (which was long drawn out) closed the starter shouted "Tâ'wai!" and they were off on the first relay.  Markers stood at the side of the track and held willow sticks with rags attached as marks of the position of the opposing sides.  Sometimes a race was ended by one party admitting that it was tired out, but it usually was decided when the winners were so far ahead that their runner met the other at the center, where the markers also met.  The women encouraged their friends with shouts in concert, which were emitted from the throat and ended in a trill from the tongue.  At the close of the race the winning village shouted continuously for some time, after which the visitors would go home, as there was no accompanying feast.

THOMPSON INDIANS (Ntlakyapamuk).   British Columbia.

Mr James Teit [b] says:

Foot races were frequently run, and bets made on the result.  The best runners traveled long distances to meet each other.  Sometimes celebrated Okanagan, Shushwap, and Thompson runners competed with one another.  The

---

[a] In a memoir to be published by the Bureau of American Ethnology.
[b] The Thompson Indians of British Columbia.  Memoirs of the American Museum of Natural History, whole series, v. 2, p. 280, New York, 1900.

largest bets were made on races between champions. It is said that when the Indians were numerous, and almost all the men in constant training, there were some excellent long and short distance runners among them. Two men of the Spences Bridge band were said to be the fastest runners in the surrounding tribes. One of them raced against horses and against canoes paddled downstream.

SHOSHONEAN STOCK.

HOPI. Walpi, Arizona.

Mr A. M. Stephen, in his unpublished manuscript, gives the following vocabulary of racing among the Hopi:

Wa'-zrik-yu'-wü-ta, running; wa-wa'-si-ya, a short-distance race; yüh'-tü, a long-distance race; tcüle'-yüh-tü, race on the eighth morning of the Snake dance; tcu'-tcüb-ti añ'-am-yüh-tü, race on the ninth morning of the Snake dance; le'-len-ti yüh-tü, race on the ninth morning of the Flute ceremony; la-kon'-yüh-tü, race at sunset by women on the eighth day of the Lalakonti; la'-la-kon-ti añ'-am-yüh-tü, race at early sunrise by men on the ninth day of the Lalakonti; ti'-yot-wa'-zri, a race between two youths; ta'-kat-wa'-zri, a race between two men; to'-tim-yüh-tü, a race between many men; ta'-tak-yüh-tü, a race between several men; Ho'-pi ta'-cab-wüt a'-müm wa-zri, a race between a Hopi and a Navaho; Ho'-pi ta'-cab-müi a'-mum-yüh-tü, a race between several of each people (Hopi and Navaho); ka-wai'-yo ak-wa-zri, a race between two horsemen; ka-wai-yo-mü-i ak yüh-tü, a race between several horsemen.

SIOUAN STOCK

CROWS. Upper Missouri river, North Dakota.

In a report to Isaac I. Stevens, governor of Washington Territory, on the Indian tribes of the upper Missouri, by Mr Edwin T. Denig, a manuscript in the library of the Bureau of American Ethnology, there occurs the following:

Foot racing is often practiced by the Mandan and Crows. The former nation before they were so much reduced by smallpox had a regular race course 3 miles in length, in which any and all who chose could try their speed, which they did by running three times around this space, betting very high on either side. They still practice the amusement, but not so much as formerly. Foot races among the Crow Indians are usually contested by two persons at a time, a bet being taken by those concerned, and many more by the friends and spectators on either side, consisting of blankets, buffalo robes, or some other article of clothing. They mostly run about 300 yards, and in starting endeavor to take every advantage of each other, a dozen starts being often made before the race begins. These Indians also run horse races, betting one horse against the other. The same trickery and worse is displayed in their horse as in their foot races, and often the loser will not pay.

The Sioux also have foot races, in which anyone may join, provided he bets, which, if they have anything to stake, they are sure to do. The name of being a fast and long runner is highly prized among them all; indeed after that of being a warrior and hunter that of being a good runner is next to be desired, but the principal aim in all these amusements appears to be the winning of each other's property. They, of course, occupy and enable them to pass agreeably some of the long summer days, but we never see these things introduced without the bets or prospects of gain, and from this fact, together with the earnestness exhibited in betting and in the contest, we conclude it to be no more than another mode of gambling, to which they are all so much addicted.

## MANDAN. North Dakota.

Prof. F. V. Hayden[a] describes the Mandan foot race as Olympic in character:

A race-course of 3 miles on the level prairie was laid off, cleared of every obstruction, and kept in order for the express purpose. Posts were planted to mark the initial and terminating points, and over the track the young men tested the elasticity of their limbs during the fine summer and autumn months, to prepare themselves for the hardship of their winter hunts. On the occasion when races were determined on by the chiefs, the young men were informed by the public crier, and every one who had confidence in his prowess was admitted to the lists. Each of the runners brought the amount of his wager, consisting of blankets, guns, and other property, and sometimes several judges or elderly men were appointed by the chief of the village, whose duty it was to arrange the bets, regulate the starting, and determine the results of the race. As the wagers are handed in, each is tied to or matched with one of equal value, laid aside, and when all have entered, the judges separate, some remaining with the property staked at the beginning of the race-course, and others taking their station at its terminus. Six pairs of runners whose bets have been matched now start to run the 3-mile course, which is to be repeated three times before it can be decided. The ground is laid out in the form of an arc, describing two-thirds of a circle, the starting point and goal being but a few hundred yards distant from each other, the intermediate space being filled up by the young and old of the whole village. The runners are entirely naked, except their moccasins, and their bodies are painted in various ways from head to foot. The first set having accomplished about half the first course, as many more are started, and this is continued as long as any competitors remain, until the entire track is covered with runners, at distances corresponding with their different times of starting, and the judges award the victory to those who come out, by handing each a feather painted red, the first six winning the prize. These, on presenting the feathers to the judges at the starting-point, are handed the property staked against their own. The first and second heats are seldom strongly contested, but on the third, every nerve is strained, and great is the excitement of the spectators, who with yells and gestures, encourage their several friends and relations. The whole scene is highly interesting, and often continued for two or three days in succession, to give everyone an opportunity to display his abilities. Those who have shown great fleetness and powers of endurance, receive additional reward, in the form of praise by the public crier, who harangues their names through the village for many days afterwards. This is a fine national amusement, and tends much to develop the great muscular strength for which they are remarkable. They also immediately on finishing the race, in a profuse state of perspiration, throw themselves into the Missouri, and no instance is known where this apparent rashness resulted in any illness.

---

[a] Contributions to the Ethnography and Philology of the Indian Tribes of the Missouri Valley, p. 430, Philadelphia, 1862.

WINNEBAGO.  Prairie du Chien, Wisconsin.

Caleb Atwater [a] says:

Athletic games are not uncommon among them, and foot races afford great diversion to the spectators.  The women and children are present at these races and occupy prominent situations, from which they can behold everything that passes, without rising from the ground where they are seated. Considerable bets are frequently made on the success of those who run.

YUMAN STOCK

MARICOPA.  Arizona.

Mr Louis L. Meeker describes the foot race in this tribe as follows:

A whole company run, side against side, from opposite goals, a flagman marking where each two pass.  Each side runs in order.  The final position of the flag marks victory.

## SUMMARY OF CONCLUSIONS

(1) That the games of the North American Indians may be classified in a small number of related groups.

(2) That morphologically they are practically identical and universal among all the tribes.

(3) That as they now exist, they are either instruments of rites or have descended from ceremonial observances of a religious character.

(4) That their identity and unity are shared by the myth or myths with which they are associated.

(5) That while their common and secular object appears to be purely a manifestation of the desire for amusement or gain, they are performed also as religious ceremonies, as rites pleasing to the gods to secure their favor, or as processes of sympathetic magic, to drive away sickness, avert other evil, or produce rain and the fertilization and reproduction of plants and animals, or other beneficial results.

(6) That in part they agree in general and in particular with certain widespread ceremonial observances found on the other continents, which observances, in what appear to be their oldest and most primitive manifestations, are almost exclusively divinatory.

---

[a] Remarks made on a Tour to Prairie du Chien, p. 117, Columbus, 1831

# INDEX

(A Tabular Index to Tribes and Games will be found on pages 36–43.)

O